STORIED STADIUMS

OTHER BOOKS BY CURT SMITH

America's Dizzy Dean

Long Time Gone

Voices of the Game

A Fine Sense of the Ridiculous

The Storytellers

Windows on the White House

Of Mikes and Men

Our House

STORIED STADIUMS

BASEBALL'S HISTORY
THROUGH ITS BALLPARKS

CURT SMITH

FOREWORD BY BOB COSTAS

CARROLL & GRAF PUBLISHERS
NEW YORK

FOR
OLIVIA AND TRAVIS

STORIED STADIUMS
BASEBALL'S HISTORY THROUGH ITS BALLPARKS

Copyright © 2001 by Curt Smith

Carroll & Graf Publishers
A Division of Avalon Publishing Group Incorporated
161 William St., 16th floor
New York, NY 10038

First Carroll & Graf edtion 2001

Designed by Kathleen Lake, Neuwirth and Associates, Inc.

Library of Congress Cataloging-in-Publication Data is available.

ISBN 0-7867-0948-0

9 8 7 6 5 4 3 2 1

Printed in the United States of America
Distributed by Publishers Group West

ACKNOWLEDGMENTS

"**O**ur house is a very, very, very fine house." Crosby, Stills, Nash, and Young are tied to music, not baseball. Some of the game's houses are very fine—others, cold and banal. All are peculiar to America's greatest and oldest sport.

I wish to thank people—sadly, some long deceased—for bringing this book alive. A number of writers were helpful: Les Biederman, Furman Bisher, Bob Broeg, Bob Burnes, David Chase, David Condon, Joseph Durso, Leo Egan, Joe Falls, Charlie Feeney, Til Ferdenzi, Peter Gammons, Michael Gershman, Ray Gillespie, Jerome Holtzman, Bill Koenig, Leonard Koppett, Allen Lewis, Jim Mandelaro, Jim Murray, Phil Mushnick, Ross Newhan, Marty Nolan, Scott Pitoniak, Shirley Povich, Rob Rains, Lowell Reidenbaugh, Prentis Rogers, Harold Rosenthal, Russell Schneider, Bill Schulz, Morris Siegel, Ken Smith, John Steadman, Bob Stevens, Larry Stewart, George Vecsey, Tim Wendel, Paul White, George Will, and Dick Young.

Many broadcasters contributed facts and recollections. Bob Costas has written a lyric Foreword. I also want to thank Nat Allbright, Mel Allen, Joe Angel, Harold Arlin, Richie Ashburn, Bud Blattner, Marty Brennaman, Jack Brickhouse, Jack Buck, Harry Caray, Skip Caray, Joe Castiglione, Tom Cheek, Jerry Coleman, Ken Coleman, Dan Daniels, Jerry Doggett, Jimmy Dudley, Gene Elston, Lanny Frattare, Earl Gillespie, Curt Gowdy, Milo Hamilton, Merle Harmon, Ernie Harwell, Mark Holtz, Waite Hoyt, Pat Hughes, Ernie Johnson, Charlie Jones, Harry Kalas, Ralph Kiner, Larry King, Tim McCarver, Sean McDonough, Ned Martin, Al Michaels, Jon Miller, Monte Moore, Bob Murphy, Lindsey Nelson, Dave Niehaus, Joe Nuxhall, Bob Prince, Byrum

Saam, Vin Scully, Lon Simmons, Ken Singleton, Dick Stockton, Chuck Thompson, Bob Uecker, Dave Van Horne, Warner Wolf, Bob Wolff, and Jim Woods.

I am grateful to baseball players: George Brett, George Kell, Harmon Killebrew, Stan Musial, Pee Wee Reese, Phil Rizzuto, Bobby Richardson, Brooks Robinson, and Carl Yastrzemski. Major- and minor-league officials, architects, and coaches were helpful: Lee Allen, Michael Allen, Dick Bresciani, Joe L. Brown, A. Bartlett Giamatti, Glenn Geffner, Warren Giles, Jim Healey, Bowie Kuhn, Larry Lucchino, Gabe Paul, Laurel Prieb, Wendy Selig-Prieb, Jack Redding, Jimmie Reese, Earl Santee, Bud Selig, Brent Shyer, Stu Smith, Joseph Spear, and Bill Veeck. I also want to thank President George W. Bush, Phil Hochberg, and Tip O'Neill.

A Hall of Fame exhibit blares "Famous Ballparks." Its staff was crucial: Jim Gates, Librarian; Jeff Idelson, Vice-President, Communications and Education; Bruce Markusen, Manager of Program Presentations; Patricia Kelly, Director of the Photograph Collection; Dale Petroskey, President, a Michigander who loved Tiger Stadium; and Ted Spencer, Curator. Bill Francis, Senior Researcher, and Scott Mondore, Manager, Museum Programs, were especially helpful.

My literary agent, Bobbe Siegel, helped create this book. My wife, Sarah, endured hundreds of hours of research, writing, and editing. Our children, Olivia and Travis, will soon discover Fenway Park and Wrigley Field. Philip Turner and Keith Wallman edited the manuscript with insight and care. Nicholas Wyatt, a student at the University of Rochester, supplied research. The facts and opinions herein, of course, are mine.

Finally, I wish to thank my friend, Bill Goff, and artists William Feldman, Joseph Golinkin, Andy Jurinko, Thomas Kolendra, Bob Novak, and Bill Purdom for this book's splendid fine art lithographs. The author Willa Cather wrote, "A book is made with one's own flesh and blood of years. It is cremated youth." The above were generous with their time re: baseball's houses—and I cannot help but be generous in my gratitude toward them.

—May 25, 2001, Rochester, New York

CONTENTS

Foreword by Bob Costas   xi

1. Anticipation   1
2. Pastures of Plenty   4

BEGINNINGS (1862–1908)

3. Fine and Dandy   13
4. Please Come to Boston   29

CLASSIC PARKS (1909–'61)

5. You Wear It Well   55
6. Down on the Farm   64
7. Just the Way You Are   101
8. My Kind of Town   126
9. The Hungry Years   144
10. Old Cape Cod   175
11. Happy Talk   203
12. Where You Lead   230
13. The Wonder Years   262

THE COOKIE-CUTTERS (1962–'91)

14. Up on the Roof   301
15. Down on My Knees   327

16. Where's That Rainbow? 351

17. The Impossible Dream 391

18. Look What You've Done 415

19. Show Me 445

BACK TO THE FUTURE (1992–2000)

20. Been to Canaan 465

21. Rocky Mountain High 499

THE ROAD NOW TAKEN (2001–)

22. Yesterday Once More 523

23. Postlogue 535

Sources 541

Bibliography 543

Appendix 545

Index 578

FOREWORD

BOB COSTAS

Players, managers, broadcasters, memories. All are essential to baseball, and as *Storied Stadiums* shows, so too are distinctive ballparks. Why do people still talk about the Polo Grounds and Crosley Field? Why do they go to Wrigley, even when the Cubs don't contend? Which is to say almost always. Why do the Red Sox sell out, first place or last? Fans like the ambience—the baseball feel.

I think of a photo from Don Larsen's 1956 World Series perfect game. It shows Mickey Mantle making a running, backhanded catch of a long fly ball. You see the bleachers, the auxiliary scoreboard, the shadows in the outfield—that look of October in the Bronx. Could this be any place but Yankee Stadium?

My first trip to the place Red Barber always referred to as the Big Ballpark came in 1959. I sat with my dad and a cousin in the left-field bleachers behind the 457-foot sign. We had our gloves, and each inning we would move a row or two closer to the field. You have to respect our reasoning: 490 feet, no chance, but 457? We were a cinch to catch a homer. Somehow that didn't happen, but something just as memorable did.

In those days you could leave the ballpark by way of the warning tracks, walking all the way around the great baseball cathedral before exiting through the bullpen gates that abutted the street and the elevated subway. The Yankees' Hank Bauer then patrolled right field: I stood at the low wall in front of the 344 sign and mimicked him robbing homers. Then came the bleacher wall in right-center, and an early brush with harsh reality. The 407 sign that looked so sparkling white on TV was, upon closer inspection, filled with graffiti. Dim-witted desecraters had scrawled stuff like "Sam loves Sally" and other more salacious items. I was seven, and I hated Sam and Sally. I didn't care what they did on their own time, but I couldn't grasp why they would desecrate a shrine. Come to think of it, I still detest them.

Anyway, soon enough, walking with my father, we reached the flagpole and monuments in dead center: 461 feet from home plate, and with the pitcher's mound rising, a little kid couldn't even see the batter's box. In the '70s, Yankee Stadium was remodeled, outfield shrunk, and monuments put behind the fence. Not in 1959: They were right there on the field, just three of them then—Babe Ruth, Lou Gehrig, Miller Huggins. I looked at them and had the only possible sane reaction for a seven-year-old. I burst into tears. My dad asked why. "Whaddaya mean why? Because the Bambino, the Iron Horse, and the Little Skipper are buried right here beneath this hallowed ground. That's why." And then this inescapable thought: someday Joe DiMaggio and Mickey Mantle would lie there, too. It was all too magnificent, too sad, too dramatic to bear. My dad's explanations to the contrary fell on deaf ears. So he did the next best thing. He picked me up and held me over his head to get me laughing, then put me on his shoulders for the rest of the walk around the track. He was wearing a yellow polo shirt. He smelled like *Old Spice*. I liked him a lot that day. That was my first visit to Yankee Stadium.

No such awe or sense of landscape was generated by the multisport, artificial turf clones that blighted baseball's landscape in the 1960s and '70s. They were impersonal and nondescript; soulless, with no suggestion of history, no sense of place. Baseball's best move of the past decade has been to spurn them by building new "old" ballparks—a Camden Yards, a Pac Bell Park, a Coors Field. Of course, they can't carry the history of an Ebbets or Forbes Field, and in some cases I wouldn't want to defend the way they were financed, but at least they pay tribute to the game while providing a good baseball atmosphere.

Storied Stadiums talks about all that, and more. As you make your way through Curt Smith's fine book, consider this: At least some of the keys to baseball's future lie in its past.

Grant me paradise in this world;
I'm not sure I'll reach it in the next.

—the sixteenth-century Venetian painter
Tintoretto, presaging Wrigley Field

1

ANTICIPATION

In 1988, A. Bartlett Giamatti first saw a model of the Baltimore Orioles' proposed new park. He knew instantly that it could take baseball back to the future. "When this park is complete," he said, "*every team is going to want one.*" Its quirks, odd angles, and dark green intimacy hinted baseball paradise—the game as it once was, and could be again.

In time, the model corkscrewed into Oriole Park at Camden Yards. Giamatti's view now writes baseball's *lingua franca*—its coin half-prayer and half-command. Increasingly, the pastime boasts stadiums heavy with individuality. Camden Yards—born April 6, 1992—shows that "if you build it [right], they will come."

They came in 1994–'95 to heirs in Cleveland, Denver, and Arlington, Texas; 1997–'98, Atlanta and Phoenix; 1999–2001, Detroit, Houston, Milwaukee, Pittsburgh, San Francisco, and Seattle; and by way of hope, future parks in Cincinnati, Philadelphia, San Diego, and perhaps Boston, Miami, Minneapolis, Montreal, and New York. Each daubs sites that once spun baseball's web—Crosley Field, the playful furnace of Sportsman's Park, Shibe Park's surf of sounds, the green boxed fortress at Michigan and Trumbull.

For the half-century after 1908, baseball worshiped Xanadus of personality—jewels, not yet dowagers, siring "an infinite feeling for the spirit of the past," wrote Ellen Glasgow, "and the lingering poetry of time and place." In its 10 major-league cities—the 16 fields where its ballclubs merged—for the one team (Cleveland) with two parks and the city (St. Louis) where two teams shared one—and moreover, farms, burgs, and villages—the Golden Age of parks knocked boredom down.

Recall the ivy at Wrigley Field, monuments at Yankee Stadium, the steep-walled rectangle of Comiskey Park, or a stretch of Forbes Field acreage grown sated with base hits. All joined other early twentieth-century sites—League Park, Fenway Park, Braves Field, the Polo Grounds—with their rich, imposing names. "They created a common experience," says television's Larry King, who grew up near another temple, Brooklyn's Ebbets Field. "Across America, entire cities revolved around the park."

A visitor did not expect to see mascots, glitz, or exploding scoreboards. *Baseball* owned his sensibility. "You *cared* about the players because you *knew* them. The fans were down close," said Cooperstown Class of '93 Harmon Killebrew. "They could see guys sweat, hear 'em curse. They felt like actors in a field of play."

Through the 1950s, stadiums rivaled family around the dinner table. Then Suburban-Ho: Baseball threw sanity a curve. Like the '60s, it left the city for more sterile climes. Cities lost the game's buzz of conversation. Baseball lost cathedrals of the outdoors. Replacing them: multisport ovals from Anaheim to Queens. "The last twenty years have given us cookie-cutters built more for bull fights than baseball," said another Hall of Famer, Carl Yastrzemski '89. "You don't know whether you're in Atlanta or Mongolia."

Harmon Killebrew is a gentle man. Mention "cookie-cutters," and he spits contempt. He recalls when shopkeepers hailed players near the park, even bad seats seemed close enough to touch the field, and noise ferried past eateries, gas stations, and gentle backyards. "That's some trade," poet John Updike said of what came later. Baseball traded orbs of poetry for slabs of prose.

Classic parks forged a Mayberry of puppies and emerald turf and picket fences and small-town marms—frozen in amber, but fixed and sure. There they were, a city's El Dorado, yet mythy and sweetly rural. Green Acres was the place to be—especially when the home team won.

Can we retrieve a past where baseball is again all-meaning? Perhaps not. At its best the game seems too—what?—Rockwellian for some. Redemptive are urban, personal, and unorthodox parks where embracing baseball is as natural as a smile.

2

PASTURES OF PLENTY

Classic parks have become baseball's ex post facto Holy Land—the kindly light that led. Their crusade began in 1909 (opening, Forbes Field and Shibe Park), ended in 1923 (Yankee Stadium), and begot Comiskey Park, League Park, Griffith Stadium, the Polo Grounds, Fenway Park, Crosley Field, Navin Field, Ebbets Field, Wrigley Field, Braves Field, and Sportsman's Park. Looking back, the effect turned heads.

At the time, these urban, mainly structural steel, reinforced concrete parks spun a globe of big-league hue. Yet birth was indigent, not immaculate. "The most ignored parks in history come *before* the Wrigleys and Ebbets Fields," said the late Hall of Fame historian Lee Allen. "If we don't *love* them it's because we don't *know* them." Like, say, the first Comiskey Park, they had a deep and honest identity. Unlike Fenway, they leave little to the imagination—lacking reputation, frame of reference, and fixed sense of place.

Pre-classic parks—roughly between the Civil War and William Howard Taft—bespoke a kind of baseball arcadia. The Greeks are said to have invented the first major grandstand for a sporting event. (Their name for a footrace watched by spectators evolved into *stadium*.) The start of organized big-league ball—May 4, 1871, Hamilton Field, Ft. Wayne, Indiana, before 200 fans on the Jailhouse Flats: host Kekiongas 2, Forest City of Cleveland 0—flaunted parks, grounds, and bowls. Their Olympus was intimacy; you were right on the field.

Jailhouse Flats and Pittsburgh's Union Park and Philadelphia's Jefferson Street Grounds linked insects, cow dung, potholed infields, a single deck, small wooden bleachers, and vast outfield terrain. Like admission fees, fences later mixed necessity and afterthought.

"Typically the parks were built in stages—patchwork, spartan," said Allen, "but also by locals, from scratch, without government aid, but unbounded confidence." He paused. "Looking back, they were symbolic of the age."

Each less Yankee Stadium than Prairie Home Companion park buoyed baseball's rise from periphery to center. The game as we know it took root then, and there.

It is possible, if picaresque, to trace major-league teams from birth to the present. Take the Orioles. (Sadly, owner Peter Angelos already has.) Their roots grew from Milwaukee's Lloyd Street Grounds (1900–'01) by way of Sportsman's Park in St. Louis (1902–'53) to Baltimore's Memorial Stadium (1954–'91) and Camden Yards (1992–). Put your Redlegs on. Their genealogy ties Cincinnati's Avenue Grounds (1876–'77), Bank Street Grounds (1880 and '82–'83), League Park (1884–1901), Redland Field (1902–'11), Crosley Field (1912–'70), and Cinergy Field, née Riverfront Stadium (1970–). "How do you get there from here?" actress Shirley MacLaine asked in her biography. You get the idea. Continuum counts.

Baseball today has thirty big-league arenas. Retreat to polo turf and fairgrounds and garbage dumps. Were we a thousand miles from radio, a car for Everyman, and color photography?—to George Eastman, "a mirror with a memory." Neither were they around the bend. More than half a century divided the Phillies' Recreation Park and Shibe Park (1883–'86 and 1938–'70, respectively). What fused them was *hospitality*. Each treated you like a guest, made other sports something to take or leave.

The *New York Times*' William Safire once likened Richard Nixon to a layer cake: To know him, you must imbibe each layer. Ballparks, too, can be perfectly clear. The newest layer is baseball's "new old" homes— born, 1992. Already flaking: the oval or circular multipurpose layer— *circa* early '60s–'90s—that began, say, with D.C. and Shea Stadiums. (Theoretically, its stadiums would feed many sports; in fact, they well fed none). By contrast, the delicious '09–'23 steel and concrete layer still dominates current memory. Only three of 14 sites remain: Fenway Park, Wrigley Field, and remodeled Yankee Stadium.

Even older are open fields and enclosed wooden plots. To know a ballpark, you must sample their layer.

Nineteen-forties children heard a whopper: On his deathbed, Lincoln implored Abner Doubleday, "General, save baseball. Protect it for the future." Myth, and pipe dream: Doubleday did not invent the sport. The man who did, Alexander Cartwright, formed the first town team of amateur gentlemen—the Knickerbockers of New York.

In 1845, his new set of rules forged the geometry of the diamond. "Cartwright was an engineer and draftsman," said historian and longtime *St. Louis Post-Dispatch* columnist Bob Broeg. "He invented nine players to a team, nine innings to a game, three outs a side, and set the batting order. For the first time all bases were ninety feet away." By the early '50s, most cities along the eastern seaboard had at least one organized club. To many, baseball became a link with the outside world.

In 1862, Lee invaded Maryland, Richard Gatling perfected his machine gun, and Congress passed the Homestead Act. To the northeast, teams mixed throw, slide, and the first enclosed field, designed by William Cammeyer, in Brooklyn's Williamsburg section. Union Grounds, former site of a skating club at Lee Avenue and Rutledge Street, was horseshoed, had oak seats, and housed a large-for-its-age 1,500 spectators. It forecast Brooklyn as a franchise, well, more byzantine than most. Outfield distances were 500 feet. The exception: a one-story building, 350 feet from home plate, in play *inside* the right-field fence.

Before Ft. Sumter, few teams imported players from outside their area. After Appomattox, the rush to commerce rivaled a river shedding ice. In 1866, the national champion Philadelphia Athletics were said to pay three players. The '69 Cincinnati Red Stockings became the first solely professional team. "If you had pros, you had to pay them," said Allen. "That meant luring people to watch them. That meant building wooden parks."

In 1871, many housed the new National Association of Professional Baseball Players. Go figure/it figures. One team, Cammeyer's New York Mutuals, played home games in Brooklyn.

"I started at the bottom in this business," said actor Art Carney, "and worked my way right into the sewer." Ibid, the NA, dissolving in 1876 into the National League—the distinction counts—of Professional Base Ball *Clubs*. The NL named managers, hired players by contract, and gave owners the upper hand. Slowly, it sacked contenders—the 1882–'91 American Association, '84 Union Association, and 1890 Players League—which, folding, left a ministry of parks. The post-1891 Nationals absorbed AA teams, expanded to 12 clubs, then axed '99's Baltimore, Cleveland, Louisville, and Washington. Those tatters spun a new major league.

In 1900, the minor Western League blared Detroit, Milwaukee, Minneapolis, and St. Paul. President Ban Johnson renamed it (American League), put a team in Chicago (White Sox), and moved Grand Rapids to Cleveland's once-NL League Park. A decade earlier, Rutherford B. Hayes exclaimed, "If a Napoleon ever became president, he could make the executive almost what he wished to make it." William McKinley was now president, X-rays were discovered, and what the American wanted was to dent the older National.

In 1901–'02, the AL swiped ex-National parks in Baltimore and St. Louis. It also began fleecing past and current NL clubs of scrubs and stars. In 1903, the two leagues agreed to a truce. Said Broeg, "The NL had enough of a players' war." It baptized what became, if not a Beulahland, exactly, a folk-passion symbol of the American Century: the World Series. From a distance, can we divine a fact present at creation? We can. To survive, the Americans needed to build only four new parks: Boston, Chicago, Philadelphia, and Washington.

"They made it easy for us," Johnson later noted of extinct NL and minor-league teams. "Building parks usually cost a hell of a lot of money. We got 'em by default—just like a lot of players." It was a road, once crossed, few would double back upon till Curt Flood and Marvin Miller.

Forget hacks, flacks, and spinners. Baseball has never been as lithe as Lassie, winsome as a Wythe, or pervasive as Lucille Ball. It *is* America's richest dowry—older than Broadway; simpler than Faulkner; less regional than the Grand Ole Opry; more populist than the Grand Walt Disney. True/yet: Boxing and horse racing were hits before Cartwright unsheathed his stick. Buoying baseball was the enclosed park—and how the park changed its game.

Change one was strategic. Early fields had no outfield bleachers. Fences flanked each lot's remotest edge—six hundred feet or even farther from the plate. Offense passed go only when outfield stands arose. "Don't get me wrong," chirped Bill Veeck. "Clubs didn't do it to increase home runs, but seating—*profit!*" Ironically, greed became a fan's sock-happy friend. Bleachers cut power distances. Baseball swapped defense-first for a kind of long-ball carousel.

Change two was commercial. Early gentleman investors owned most parks. Renting them, they charged clubs admission and kept the pot. Enclosed plots crossed the Rubicon; finally, teams got a percent of the profit. All grasped how peripheral cash (scorecards, or concession sales) might augment a stadium's core (ticket sales, then and now).

"The last change was demographic," Veeck observed. "The first fields were what we now call suburban. As more people moved into the cities, enclosed parks moved the game downtown." Increasingly, baseball tied immigrants' foreign language to the U.S. English-speaking tongue.

By 1876, America had turned from wilderness to settlement, agrarian to manufacturing, states' rights to United States. In a century, the number of states had leapt from 13 to 38; population, 2.5 million to 46 million; area, 889,000 square miles to 3 million. Nearly 8 in 10 lived on farms or in towns that relied on agriculture. Almost one in five people was foreign-born. By 1900, the tide of immigrants presaged Eric Goldman's "MetroAmerican." Cities exploded in the industrial postwar boom. In one part of lower Manhattan, nearly 1,000 persons an acre filled tenements. One block squeezed and elbowed 2,781.

Self-interest led baseball to where the action was. "Its challenge was to build on a plot close enough to the city to attract spectators, but large enough to fit a park," noted the History Channel's *Ballparks*. Public transit helped. Brooklyn's two main districts reached Union Grounds on the Flushing, Division Avenue, and Greenpoint horse cars. Too, shoe-horning: Adjacent streets forged parks' stencil. To be in the money meant no place was too bizarre. Cammeyer built on the site of the old Union Skating Club. In Chicago, White Stockings owner Charles Comiskey's first park replaced a cricket grounds.

Slums, lumberyards, swamps, and vacant lots—all tumbled in baseball's craze for cash. *Caveat emptor*. Allen laughed. "It was a lesson that would reappear."

Historian Allen Nevins called *The Deerslayer* a "story [of] ... an America now so far lost in time and change that it is hard to believe it ever existed. But it did exist." So, pre-classic parks.

Their end was inevitable. One reason, size: Most housed less than 15,000 fans. Another, a cheapskate gloss: Most lacked dugouts. Players sat on uncovered field benches. Few had even bare-bones frills. An exception: Chicago's West Side Park at Loomis and Congress Streets, hailed for its "neatly furnished toilet-room with a private entrance for the ladies." The horseshoed grandstand and bleachers, respectively, held 2,500 and 3,500 patrons. Redolent of the 1990s were 1890s suites. A dozen rooftop boxes had individual chairs.

A writer was asked what he would take if his house were on fire and he could remove one thing. He replied: "I would take the *fire*." At least 21 parks caught fire in the 1890s. Most began accidentally by discarded cigars or matches; in one year, twenty people died. Flames strafed or wrecked Baltimore, Boston, Chicago, and Philadelphia. Owner Barney Dreyfuss skipped Louisville without a blink. Games shifted to other cities; the league then moved its team; and Dreyfuss rafted the Ohio to the Allegheny and Monongahela—his companion, Honus Wagner—where, on June 30, 1909, amid the pine cover and postcard feel of the Oakland section of Pittsburgh, he opened baseball's second "fireproof" concrete park—Forbes Field.

In 1911, the Polo Grounds swapped sparks with Washington's

National Park. The bigs' *final* wooden park—St. Louis' Robison Field—lasted till 1920. By then, doyens peopled concrete kirks like jukebox Ebbets Field, that shooting gallery of an edifice, and Griffith Stadium, with its canyon of an outfield, or Crosley Field, hard by a home run–dented laundry, and Braves Field, by the tracks of the Boston and Maine. We would inhale—in reminiscence, still are—League Park, Navin Field, Shibe Park, the Big Ballpark in the Bronx.

They can wait: It is enough to note how they helped baseball matter. For now, batter-up for their predecessors. They, too, gave baseball a chary tenderness, middlebrow and middle-class.

Beginnings

1862–1908

3

FINE AND DANDY

It is said that with the exception of the Equator, everything starts somewhere. Baseball started as an organized game in New York. Its Knickerbockers knit historic firsts: organized team (1845), outfits (high collars and long pants, *circa* '49), and dynasty. (An anomaly: June 19, 1846. New York Nine 23, Knicks 1—the same score as a 1963 Mets–Chicago game. You know who won.)

The Knicks began at 26th Street and Madison Avenue, then moved across the Hudson River to Elysian Fields in Hoboken, New Jersey. Elysian means paradise in Greek. In 1852, paradise meant Brooklyn, forging its first organized team. In '58, the two cities hatched an all-star series. Venue: New York's Fashion Race Course. Cost: about 1,500 paid up to 50 cents. Site: a few hundred yards from Shea Stadium. Perhaps the miracle of pay-for-play foretold the Miracle Mets.

"Maybe God did have a plan," laughed Dick Young, former *New York Daily News* columnist. "Baseball and New York joined at the hip." From Jamaica via the Bowery through the East Side to Staten Island, the "New York" mode of play became town ball's El Dorado. "There were two opposing styles of field," said Jack Redding, 1968–'82 Hall of Fame librarian. "New York's diamond reflected Cartwright's rules. Massachusetts' was rectangular, like cricket."

Hallo Bucky Dent. Boston's style waned v. New York's.

New York and Brooklyn teams won amateur titles in 1858–'59 and '68 and 1861–'65 and '70, respectively. "Thirteen years of organized baseball, and nine times the city wins it all," said Redding, a New York native. "No wonder lots of people elsewhere were glad to see the amateur era end—and the professional's begin."

New York's began with the '71 National Association. Doctors Mishap and Malady quickly paid house calls on its ward. In 1875, the New York Mutuals folded with the league. A year later, joining the NL, they vanished in eight months. Lindsey Nelson cheerily conspired with memory. "How bad was this!" said the Mets 1962–'78 broadcaster. "Even *we* weren't kicked out of the league! The Nation's biggest city loved baseball, but now it didn't have a team."

Like *that,* New York's prepotency had ended with a thud. "Amateur champs, pro chumps," sniffed Redding. "The late 1870s were low"— until *New York Herald* publisher James Gordon Bennett, building the original Polo Grounds to house polo clubs, opened it to baseball on September 29, 1880. Soon tenants graced 111th to 112th Streets between Fifth and Sixth Avenues. "One was [owner John Day's] NL Giants [then Gothams]. The other was the American Association Metropolitans," Nelson said, simply, and then, "the Mets—amazing. People think they were born in 1962. They were bonkers a hundred years before!"

At Polo Grounds I and II, a 10-foot canvas fence divided adjacent diamonds. "I was in the lot's southwest corner," said Redding, "and II the southeast. Trouble came when two games occurred at once." Fielders would crawl under the fence, crash the AA outfield, and return the ball to the NL park. "Add to this fans standing in the outfield, there being no bleachers, and brushing against the fielders," Redding mused. "You can see why people said, 'If it doesn't happen at the Polo Grounds, it doesn't happen, period.' "

On May 12, 1883, the Mets played their first game at the Polo Grounds. Year Two linked an ex-city dump (Metropolitan Park, a.k.a.

the Dump), dungy air (factory smoke crossed the East River), an AA flag (New York's first), and first sanctioned World Series. (The NL Providence Grays' Charlie [Old Hoss] Radbourn beat the Mets thrice.) The verdict girded Day's *Weltanschauung.* "He'd always thought the AA was inferior to the National," said Young. "The Series confirmed it." Straightaway he sold ten regulars and, ultimately, the Mets.

They moved to watery St. George Grounds. Outfielders wore rubber shoes. Ground sloped downhill from third base to the left-field pole. Gentle-rowed stands, on the other hand, became Staten Island's funhouse of precocious peals. "A play, *The Fall of Babylon,* was staged here," Lee Allen noted, "and a platform put in right field. You had a new ground rule—a hit into Babylon was a single. Once, actors dressed like soldiers held polished shields to reflect sun into the eyes of [Baltimore] hitters. Another day elephants ended batting practice by crashing the outfield on their way to the zoo."

In June 1885, the Statue of Liberty arrived a pop fly away: Onlookers could scale the grandstop, peer toward Manhattan, and see the Lady riveted. By 1887 they saw a different view: Folding, the Mets floated up the Hudson River. In 1962, the Metropolitan Baseball Club of New York would re-emerge to fill the city's need for a grand and unleavened eloquence. That, as they say, was in another country.

The National League's (also, Giants') first game in New York (May 1, 1883) hosted a former president (Ulysses S. Grant) and its then-largest baseball crowd (15,000). Both augured a smugness in the Apple's behavior to outsiders and to itself. "President Grant sat in the rear of the main [Polo Grounds] grandstand," a journal read, "and often joined in the applause accorded players Roger Connor, Mickey Welch, and John Montgomery Ward." Grant enjoyed the day more than Gotham's John Troy, booting five balls at shortstop. At 3:25 and 3:40 P.M., gongs ordered Boston and New York, respectively, to the field for a fifteen-minute drill. At 3:55, captains Jack Burdock (Boston) and Buck Ewing (New York) tossed a bat to decide the batting order. (Burdock won, and made New York hit first. Beaneaters: 5–3.)

Baseball is subjective: What seems vanilla to you may appear chocolate to me. By any taste, the Polo Grounds enticed. In 1884, it flaunted two-league doubleheaders. On May 31, 1886, New York drew baseball's first crowd of more than 20,000 (20,709 *v.* Detroit). In 1888, novelty rolled a 7: Winning the flag, the Giants lost their home.

Harold Rosenthal shook his head. "Talk about ingratitude," said the ex–*New York Herald Tribune* reporter. "The Giants take the '88 flag, and learn in early '89 the city's going to tear down the Polo Grounds to complete Frederick Douglass Circle at 110th and Fifth." The Giants tried charity ($10,000) and bribery (of city officials). Neither worked. The *New York Clipper* wrote: "The Polo Grounds seems . . . part of the club, and to deprive the club of its grounds is like depriving it of part of its honor."

In February, the city told the Giants they were "free to leave." Briefly they detoured to the Mets' St. George Grounds. (It blared a restaurant, ice cream parlor, tennis courts, lacrosse fields, water fireworks and geysers, and picnic area by the field.) Less grand *was* the field. Bullets from Buffalo Bill's *Wild West Show* ringed power alleys. A 1888 production of *Nero, The Fall of Rome* crumpled grass to mud. Young laughed. "Play scaffolding became a ground rule."

On June 14, the Giants traded Rome for the uptown at 155th Street and Eighth Avenue former Manhattan Field. Like the Eternal City, it soon seemed a dinosaur.

"**J**ust try to keep all the Polo Grounds straight!" Redding urged by way of wonder. "This one had horse stables under the stands and a tiny center field [360 feet]" and a right- and center-field incline. Polo Grounds III (first game, July 8, 1889) was large (5,500-seat stand, plus bleachers) and bathtub-shaped (a half-circle with straight sides) and flanked Brotherhood Park (home of the 1890 Players League Giants).

Like PG I and II, blasts from one den spiked the other: Mike Tiernan whacked an inside-the-*parks* home run. The '89 Giants won the pennant—apparently, exhausting providence. Their next flag flecked 1904. "By then," added Rosenthal, "the PL was over. The Brotherhoods folded, and since their park was larger Day bought it"—debuting on April 22, 1891 (17,335 saw Boston win, 4–3), renaming it (what else?) the Polo Grounds (IV), and hiring John McGraw in 1902.

For two decades, the Giants found oddity, sanctuary, and—at last—stability beneath Coogan's Bluff. They also made a millionaire of an immigrant bookseller and lay minister. In 1886, two Columbus, Ohio, firms asked Harry M. Stevens to sell scorecards at a game. Stevens dickered for rights, moved to New York, and added ice cream to his venue—and more.

"One day it was too cold for ice cream," said Ted Spencer, Hall of Fame curator, "so he sent one of his boys around the corner to a market to buy what they called at the time 'dachshund' sausage. Up he sent his people into the stands, yelling, 'Get your red hots!' " Soon a patron could also sample corned beef hash, corned beef and cabbage, chicken à la king, soup, Virginia ham and spinach, and Irish stew. "Harry Stevens gave us two baseball traditions—programs and ballpark cuisine."

Between bites, McGraw spawned the hit and run, answered to "Little Napoleon," and won his first of 10 pennants. Five and 11 times, respectively, Joe "Iron Man" McGinnity pitched both ends of a doubleheader and Tim Keefe and Amos Rusie won 30-something games. Roger Bresnahan minted firsts: shin guards, a batting helmet, catcher to bat leadoff.

Above all, a Polo Grounder hailed a Factoryville, Maryland–born industry on the mound.

Baseball wells with single-season art: 1934, Dizzy Dean's 30–7; '59, Elroy Face's 18 successive triumphs; 1968, Bob Gibson's 1.12 earned run average; '99, Pedro Martinez's 23–4 and 2.40 ERA. All were child's play v. Christy Mathewson. In 1905, he blanked the A's thrice to win the National League's first World Series. In 1908, the "Big Six" won a modern league–best 37 games, completed 34, and had 12 shutouts and a 1.43 ERA. His instinct and fadeaway forged 83 shutouts and a NL-tying 373 victories. "There were great pitchers," said Lee Allen, "and there was Matty."

A visitor watched by climbing trees. Others spied from beyond left field in buildings set on stilts. In center, the full-of-Irish bleachers, dubbed Burkeville, eyed horseshoe lengths (left and right, 277 and 258 feet: center, 500) and swaying heights (left, 4 feet high; center, a 3-foot string between posts; power alleys, 15 sloping to 4; and bullpens, 25 to 15) and a house of mirrors wrinkle. (A ball into the seats could be a homer. Another past the same spot might stay in play.)

"You ask, 'How was that possible?' I will tell you," Allen mused. "In left field, the stands came into fair territory about 10 feet. A couple feet behind the seats were the bullpens, in play. It was the only park in base-ball with two left-field foul poles." The pens later moved to the alleys. Stands also grew. "First, bleachers were built to left- and right-center. Next came center bleachers [to the left and right of the future clubhouse wall]. Later [1908–'09], another stage: The double deck goes to the foul poles and bleachers around the outfield."

The building ended rites worthy of recall. Pre-1909, you could rent a carriage, park it on the track between the bleachers and rope fence, and freebie as a celebrant in Manhattan's post-gilded cabaret.

In the evaluating and rubbing together of the American Century, Fred Merkle merged bad luck, fumbling, and ghosts, deflations, and pratfalls of the past—"until Bobby Thomson's [1951 'Shot Heard 'Round the World'] homer," said Young, "probably the Polo Grounds' most remem-bered play."

On September 23, 1908, the Giants' Harry McCormick scored from third base on Al Bridwell's ninth-inning, game-winning single to beat the Cubs—or did he? Merkle, on first base, failed to touch second; where-upon Chicago infielder Johnny Evers stabbed the base for the forceout; at which point umpire Hank O'Day bellowed "Outtt!" The Cubs argued that the run shouldn't count. Agreeing, O'Day was upheld by NL presi-dent Harry Pulliam. The game, and season, ended in a tie.

Stairway to Heaven, or Eve of Destruction? On October 8, the tunes clashed by the Harlem River. Two hundred and fifty thousand people stormed the Polo Grounds to see New York and Chicago replay their game: "at stake," said Young, "the pennant." Fewer than one in six had tickets. Others might (and did) beat gates, scale the wall, break and try to burn the outfield fence, and watch from trees or telephone poles. Fire-men used high-pressure hoses. Police used clubs "to carry them [rioters] away," read the *Chicago Record-Herald,* "stark raving mad." Onlook-ers toppled: one from the stand to break his leg; another, to his death from a subway platform. Skip nicety: The tone was beery, working-class, and slightly *déclassé.* Cubs Win! 4–2, then struggled to the clubhouse.

The dictionary defines *fan,* derived from *fanatic,* as "a person whose extreme zeal, piety, etc., goes beyond what is reasonable." Like riot, fire was unreasonable: On Friday morning, April 14, 1911, it wrecked the stand. Giants president John Brush vowed quickly to rebuild: Polo Grounds V would transport baseball to a steel and concrete age. Till then, Oh irony! The Giants needed shelter at The Rockpile/Highlanders Park/The Hilltop/a.k.a. Hilltop Park.

"For years, the Giants thought they owned New York," chuckled Rosenthal. "Then, in 1903, two bartenders [Frank Farrell and Big Bill Devery] bought the [AL Baltimore] Orioles [for $18,000] and moved them to Manhattan." Hilltop was built between 165th and 168th Streets. The 15,000-seat hearth opened on April 30: New York 6, Washington 2.

The renamed Highlanders flowed from place (Hilltop's elevation) and name (President Joseph Gordon evoked the British army's famed Gordon Highlanders). McGraw didn't care. "By 1911," said Rosenthal, "all he worried about was that the Giants own New York—and yet because of fire have to bow for six weeks to a league they detest in a park they hate" that was also redolent of the age.

"Hilltop's clubhouse was in center field [like the Polo Grounds]," Young recalled. "The outfield fence had a 'Bull Durham' sign [like many parks, shaped like a bull]. If you wanted, you left through a gate in the outfield [like Forbes Field and Yankee Stadium]." Hilltop fused pitching (center field topped 540 feet) and beauty (seats faced the Hudson and New Jersey Palisades) and vagary. (Al Orth, Joe Lake, and Russell Ford '07-'08-'12 lost 21 games. By contrast, Jack Chesboro won 41 in 1904.) Ironically, '04's finale inverted Bob Stanley and Mookie Wilson in 1986: Chesboro wild-pitched Boston's Lou Criger home with the flag-losing run.

By late 1911, the 'Landers needed a larger house. "One plan [Farrell Park, at 225th Street] fell through," said Rosenthal. "Another was fifty years ahead of its time. [A floating park, on the Allegheny River, intrigued the '60s Pittsburgh Pirates.]" Spurning animus, Farrell and Devery accepted the Giants' offer to come on down.

"Brush was so grateful for the Highlanders' letting him use Hilltop," marveled Allen, "that he invited them to share the Polo Grounds!" On October 5, 1912, Hal Chase's homer beat Washington, 8–6, in Hilltop's final game. Its plot now houses Columbia Presbyterian Church. "All they did," said a writer of New York City's last wooden shrine, "was swap one church for another."

"There were three million people in Brooklyn," broadcaster Red Barber said of post–World War II baseball, "and if every one of them wasn't rooting for the Dodgers, every one seemed to be." At the time, their teams were exquisite and second-guessable. Looking back, Flatbush stirs an alchemy of look, sound, and feel.

We shall address those Dodgers later. Note merely how offspring spurred the pastime's throb. Brooklyn baseball began a century before proving that even in the fifty-second World Series—Game Seven, October 4, 1955, Brooklyn 2, Yankees 0, after losing seven straight Series, five to New York—a franchise could run into luck.

In time, Brooklyn meant seeking the best, expecting the worst, its open veins bleeding, and courting history's baggage. Not in *1855*. For amateur teams like the Atlantics and Excelsior, tomorrow lay out ahead like a day behind the rain. "People say Cooperstown is really the birthplace of baseball," said *The Boys of Summer* author Roger Kahn. "Maybe, maybe not. One can make a case for Brooklyn. Think of the first amateur park and teams"—Union Grounds, whose Eckfords and Atlantics won the national title in 1862–'63 and 1864–'65 and '70, respectively. Baseball was already the future borough's link with the outside.

Each decade has games that KO boredom: 1960, Maz v. the Yankees; '75, Match Six of the Reds–Red Sox Series; 1988, Kirk Gibson and his dreamstuff fall; '96, Jim Leyritz saving the Bronx Bombers in Oktoberfest Game Four. The best 1870s baseball often graced Union's rival. Capitoline Grounds was built in Brownsville by Reuben Decker and Hamilton Weed, opened in the early '60s, and each winter became a skating rink. A brick outhouse moored right field: Homers over the shed won the batter a bottle of champagne.

In 1869, more than 15,000 filled Capitoline to see the Philadelphia A's and Atlantics. Jackie Gleason said, "Some people drink to find religion. Some drink to get sociable. *Me?* I drink to get bagged." On June 14, 1870, the Atlantics beat the Red Stockings, 8–7, in 11 innings. Hundreds beat a path to the local restaurant/bar, Mike Henry's, to tout the end of Cincinnati's win streak—79 games.

"Brooklyn and baseball meant each other," said former *New York Daily Mirror* writer Ken Smith. "As crowds grew, clubs began leaving open lots." Enclosed parks soon greased the city's postwar awakening.

In 1871, Union welcomed the Mutuals. "Leave it to Flatbush!" Smith mused. "*New York* didn't have a park, so it played home games in *Brooklyn*"—as perverse as a paper that, in the dialect of its borough, screamed an injury to Waite Hoyt: "Hert Hoite." In '72, Candy Cummings won 34 games, lost 19, and invented the curveball. Alaska hailed its first major gold strike. The Sioux War blared Sitting Bull and Crazy Horse. The Desert Land Act buoyed irrigation. Limits seemed, well, so un-American. "People here are far less raw and provincial than their fathers," said *The Nation* of America at age 100. "They have . . . mixed more with people of other nationalities, thought more and had to think more . . . spent more for ideas and given more away." The NL was born in 1876. A year later, it gave away the *Mutuals*.

Brooklyn had four papers, two baseball palaces, then–490,000 people, and no team. Miffed, Charles Byrne formed a minor-league Interstate club. On May 12, 1883, before 6,000 Brooklynites and the 23rd Regiment Band, he opened the 2,600-seat, double-decked Washington Park. Its namesake: General George Washington, whose Revolutionary War Battle of Long Island quarters spiked the same block. "Even that first year," said Smith, "the team drew well." Like most parks, a fan could stand in the outfield beyond a temporary rope barrier.

By 1884, Byrne coaxed the AA into awarding a team—the Bridegrooms. Opening Day forebode Babe Herman and Casey Stengel and two runners sharing third: Brooklyn 11, Washington 3, on 10 D.C. errors. In 1889, fire destroyed the park. Brooks soon embraced a larger (3,000 capacity), longer (by 48 feet), and wiser park: *Sans* support poles, Washington Park II blazed a truss style of beams, struts, and girders.

Segue to 1957: Brooklyn's forte was *portability*. Truss framework would let Byrne and club secretary Charles Ebbets uproot the stand if they ever chose to move.

The 1886–'89 Bridegrooms played on Sunday at Ridgewood Park— a.k.a. Wallace's Grounds, Horse Market, or Meyerrose's Park. Then in Queens, on the Brooklyn line, the patch is now Brooklyn's through redistricting. "[1950–'79 owner Walter] O'Malley used to say that the Dodgers wouldn't be the *Brooklyn* Dodgers if they played in Queens,"

Young mused. "He didn't know that had happened seventy years before."

In 1889, Brooklyn drew 353,690 people (including 95,395 in eight games v. St. Louis, more than the Browns would in 1933). The Montagues then met the Capulets in postseason war. "This was a sports rivalry unlike any that ever was or probably ever will be," Steve Jacobson wrote of Brooklyn and New York. "The fans rode the subway from their homes to the turf of the other team and cheered their raving hearts out. Each meeting was an angry collision. And sometimes it was close to hatred." The '89 Bridegrooms hated the post-season, losing to New York. Its upside was more abiding: Byrne saw that the rivalry was good.

"He wanted to maximize Brooklyn's games with the Giants," said Rosenthal. Ditching the AA, Byrne sought: 1) the NL's more prestigious niche; and 2) lodging at Manhattan's Eastern Park. The Players League beat him there. "Worse, the AA hated him for dumping it, so they put a *new* team at Ridgewood Park. The Bridegrooms were trapped." Trudging to Washington Park II, they caught fly balls, not bouquets.

"**I**f youth is a defect," wrote poet Robert Lowell, "it is one we outgrow too soon." In 1891, Carnegie Hall opened, Ibsen completed *Hedda Gabler,* and Brooklyn outgrew the folding PL and AA. It joined the NL, usurped Eastern Park, and was renamed the Trolley Dodgers (for doing that). By '98, Byrne died, Ebbets became president, and the Dodgers moved to Washington Park III. In an extempore pronouncement, they soon signed a 15-year pact at a lot on Third Street between Fourth and Fifth Avenues.

Brooklyn's last pre–steel and concrete plant bound yo-yo fences (42 feet high in right; 12 in left and center), distances (at one time or another, 300–376, 444–500, 400–445, and 215–295 feet from left to right), shrimpy foul turf (15 feet to the backstop), and large-for-its time capacity (18,000). Factories and the Gowanus Canal fouled the air. Breezes from Jamaica Bay made pop flys a puzzle. A 220-foot flagpole dwarfed the center-field scoreboard. Ads covered right's board, which rested on supporting legs. Fielders retrieved balls by crawling below it in the mud.

Rosenthal formed a smile. "From the start things were incongruous in

Brooklyn, USA." The 1889–'90 Dodgers won the pennant. Brooklyn lured only 189,200 in 1901. On July 6, 1907, W.P. III bulged with 23,876 patrons. Increasingly, talk fixed on a larger, better-paying place. Ignore reminiscence: Tomorrow had a date at Ebbets Field.

A Giants victory had opened Washington Park II. On October 5, 1912, they closed its successor with a 1–0 shutout. Later, Shannon's Regimental Band played a dirge. California, here we come.

Like Brooklyn, Chicago became a surpassing personality of early baseball in the flesh. Ironically, its stronghold of enthusiasm sprang from the late 1860s hardly-as-regal burg of Rockford, Illinois. Said ex-*Chicago Tribune* writer David Condon: "The Rockfords were skilled and sturdy" and had genes that seemed to bloom.

In 1871, the Rockfords bred Chicago's National Association White Stockings. Their Union Grounds presaged the Cubs' 1969 catalepsy: "It topped a *dumping* ground," said Condon, "on the shore of Lake Michigan." Pitchers liked the deep foul lines (375 feet)—hitters, low walls (6 feet)—bankers, size (7,000, with special sections for ladies and politicians). No one liked the Great Chicago Fire that gutted the park.

Rockford alumnus William Hulbert then forged another NA team—its grounds: 23rd Street, near old Union Field—and set about crashing the National. "He had an in," Condon mused, "since he was already league president." First NL game: May 10, 1876. Stockings 6, Cincinnati 0. First year: a title (52–14). Best pitcher: Albert Spalding (47–13). Best hitter: batting champion Roscoe Barnes (.429). On May 2, the getting that was good got even better. Barnes clubbed the NL's first homer off the Reds' William (Cherokee) Fisher.

Hold this dawn against a high noon of America. A land boom hit the Dakotas. George Westinghouse built an empire based on generators. Edison patented the phonograph, and invented the first practical incandescent bulb. Main Street's stage of faith, myth, and industry sired a swelling-in-the-heart-Grant Wood sort of cavalry to the rescue.

Heraclitus said a man cannot stand in the same river twice. By 1878,

America thought it could ford any stream. The Stockings opened Lakefront Park, south of Randolph Street and the Illinois Central railroad tracks. To blewey with wading: Player/manager Adrian (Cap) Anson won '80-'81-'82 flags and whacked 383 of his 2,995 hits. Even the infield had a home-field edge of ashes, boulders, broken bottles, and glass. "On one hand, the club built an adjacent bridge so that you could see from outside the park," gibed Condon. "On the other, they start building fences so that fans had to pay to see. Schizophrenia!"

Pitchers paid when the renamed '83 Colts turned Lakefront I into II. The new site held 10,000 (grandstand, 2,000; bleacher, 6,000; rest, standing room) and foretold private suites (18 rows of boxes with armchairs and curtains). Like many parks, it cut outfield turf by abutting nearby streets. Center field was 300 feet from home plate. Right and left field—196 and 180, respectively: baseball's smallest—hit you in the face.

Bill Veeck's laugh mixed nicotine and beer. "You like offense, you loved Lakefront," he said. "It was so small that early homers counted as doubles. Not surprisingly, the [1879–'83] Stockings topped the league." In '84, home runs again became dingers. "Anson, Ned Williamson, and [Philadelphia's] Jack Manning hit three in a game." Williamson's 27, all but two at home, led the NL through 1921.

On Opening Day 1998—Good Friday—alcohol was banned from Fenway Park for the first time since Prohibition. Tongue-in-cheek, Red Sox manager Jimy Williams mused, "I make it a point never to drink in the dugout." At Lakefront II, pitchers drank less for joy than longevity. Said Veeck: "Maybe it helped Chicago outlive the other seven NL charter teams."

In June 1885, the Colts left their built-for-a grandstand pagoda, used by the First Cavalry Band, for West Side Park at Congress and Throop Streets. The plot daubed color: arriving carriages, two-spired grandstand with 16-foot-wide stairway, fine woodwork, bathtub shape, and bicycle track around the field. John Clarkson '85 hatched the "drop" ball, won 53 games, and pitched 623 innings. Elsewhere, West Side's 216-foot foul lines, like Lakefront II, gave batters a deep and enduring leverage.

Jack Brickhouse sighed. "Hitters had a field day," said the popular former Cubs announcer. "So did moving vans." In 1885–'86, '91, and '93, respectively, Chicago won pennants, trooped to South Side Park, and was evicted by the Columbia Exhibition to find, if not Nirvana, a spitspot of ballast: 16,000-seat West Side Grounds, Chicago's first double-decked ark, sailing a ship's log of luxury (boxes covered the grandstand) and room (foul lines: 340 and 316 to left and right, and 560 to center). "This was the first park where many called the team the Cubs," said Brickhouse. "The reason was they had so many kids." Fans stood near them in the outfield; "Keystone" cops patrolled.

Take in a breath. Resolve not to bellow *walker*. The Cubs were antipodal to today's hero of every dog that is under. Tinker-to-Evers-to-Chance became a sonnet worth living by. As a boy, Mordecai "Three Fingers" Brown lost parts of two fingers in a feed cutter. It later helped his curve and keyed a 239–130 record. Chicago won flags in '06-'07-'08 and '10 and took a global tour to the Pyramids. Frank Chance managed the '06ers to a modern mark for wins (116).

Two clouds dimmed the idyll. The first was baseball's. "In August 1894," said Veeck, "somebody tossed a lit cigar in the rubbish in a game with Cincinnati. All of a sudden, fire!" The second cloud knifed monopoly: At last the once-Colts had a rival.

"In the late nineteenth and early twentieth century, leagues came up and died each year," said Brickhouse. "PL, NA, AA, the [1914–'15] Federal League. Only the National stuck around." Thus, in 1900, the NL agreed to let the minor American League put a franchise in Chicago. "They thought no problem," he continued. "The AL was bush. Who'll see them?" Further, the new "White Sox" chose the hardscrabble South Side ex-Chicago Cricket Club at 39th Street and Princeton Avenue. The NL roared: That (owner Charles) Comiskey, picking grounds as shabby as the team!

On April 24, 1901, Chicago beat Cleveland, 8–2, in the Sox'—also, AL's—big-league ingress. One writer called South Side Park II "unfit to play." Fit: players who won the pennant and often packed the steep-rowed stands. Ban Johnson now dropped *minor league*. "It was a term," he conceded, "to make the Cubs complacent enough to let us in." Declaring war, Ban's intuitions were in tune. By 1903, AL-NL peace spun a yearly postseason "[Chicago] City Series." A guest could ride the elevated subway from West Side Grounds to the Sox cabash of 15,000 seats and overhanging roof and jigsaw of an outfield fence: The swankiest piece skirted the J. F. Kidwell Greenhouse building in right-center. "It almost fell down," Veeck laughed, "when the [last-in-the-AL .230 batting average 'Hitless Wonders'] Sox won the '06 Series [v. the Cubs, four games to two]." Blared the *Tribune:* "Sox Win Pennant by Great Pluck. Facing Seemingly Impassable Barriers, They Gamely Fight to Top."

In 1907, Doc White won 27 games. "He was an evangelist, song-writer, and dentist," mused Condon. "A year later he must have felt like drilling." Ed Walsh won 40 sets, completed 42, and had 12 shutouts and 464 innings. His killjoy was the final day: Chicago lost the pennant. Twenty losses spoiled Walsh's 1910 league-low 1.27 ERA. That June 27, the Sox waved a cock-a-whoop welcome to steel and concrete Comiskey Park. "Score one for the Pale Hose," said Veeck, their lead short-lived.

Six years later, the Cubs assumed the plat that made their ageless, peerless, (since 1945) World Seriesless munchkin of a (cable TV-vended) franchise America's (Most Irresistible) Team.

To the south and east, factories hugged a river, bratwurst rested on the tongue, and the term *Ace* was born (for 1860's Asa Brainard, pitching *each* game for the amateur unbeaten Red Stockings). "Southern Ohio's a cornball place," said Lee Allen, a Cincinnati native. "From the start, baseball fit in"—was born here. Baseball's Bethlehem gripped the juncture of the Ohio.

In 1868, a Cincinnati lawyer/businessman bought the Red Stockings. Aaron Champion built Lincoln Park Grounds, a.k.a. Union Grounds, next to Union Terrace, and named Harry Wright center fielder/manager of baseball's first professional team. Wright, in turn, coined hitting and fielding practice and standard uniforms—jockey-style cap, half-sleeved blouse with soft collar, flannel knicker, and bright red stocking. Both treated thrift like lepers at a bazaar.

"To Champion," Allen said, "cash batted cleanup." Quickly, it bought/brought stars: Brainard of Brooklyn's Excelsiors; the Washington Nationals' Wright; shortstop/younger brother George Wright of the Unions of Morrisania (now Bronx); Mutuals third baseman Fred Waterman; right fielder Cal McVey from the Indianapolis Actives; and second baseman Charlie Sweasy and left fielder Andy Leonard from the Irvingtons of Irvington, New Jersey. George Wright got the highest salary—$1,400. Night jobs paid the bulldog: piano maker, bookkeeper, hatter, insurance seller, marble cutter, jeweler, and engraver.

Cassandras knocked the spending. How could amateur ball survive? Bill Murray says of life in the film *The Razor's Edge:* "There is no payback. Not now." Union Grounds' began May 4, 1869. The Red Stockings traveled over 11,000 miles, played before more than 200,000 patrons, and finished 57–0. The '70ers won another 22 straight games. "People said Champion thought he could buy a [National Association] pennant." Writer Bob Broeg smiled. "They were right. So was he."

The NA died in late 1875. Soon the Nationals made Cincinnati a '76 charter team. At one end, the Stockings pioneered concession stands (ham sandwiches and hard-boiled eggs), lemon peel and water drinks (10 cents a glass), and first big-league Ladies Day. The other: They lodged at Avenue Grounds, on Spring Grove Avenue near Arlington Street, and the union of Bank Street and Western Avenue. Neither worked: Tradition stung its subject.

"Cincinnati left the NL [in 1880] partly due to quarrels over selling beer on Sunday," Allen said. "But a bigger problem was '69. Its memory overwhelmed everything that came later." Picture baseball without Cincinnati. You can't. The dots don't connect. They did in the early '80s. Exiled to the 1882–'83 American Association, the future NL Reds found that one bad turn deserved another. In '83, the Union Association *Outlaw* Reds evicted the AA from their Bank Street grounds. Its park sat off Duck Street, which is what both leagues soon did.

Only retrospect can take a fractured time and somehow make it whole. The Outlaw Reds inherited a beat-up playing field. "The Stockings scorched it," said the ex-announcer Waite Hoyt, "even stole home plate." Moving to League Park I—built that winter at a brickyard on Western Avenue at Findlay; the Reds played there through 1970—they found trouble of their own.

One died and six were hurt when stands collapsed. Rebuilt, League Park II aped Chicago's Lakefront II: Homers to right became doubles. "The Reds' response was to lengthen the distance," said Allen. "It was the harbinger of change." In 1890, Cincinnati again crashed the NL. Most franchises try to turn a *team* around. The '94 Reds turned around their *field*. The first-base line had paralleled Western Avenue; facing Western, L.P. II flanked right and center field. Was its number up? A first: The Reds put theirs on a uniform.

George Bush called Ronald Reagan "that rarity in Washington—a politician who was funny on purpose." Reagan aired '30s Cubs games over WHO, Des Moines, giving baseball a full course of aside. By contrast, William McKinley treated it as a side dish he forgot to order. The Ohio governor skipped League Park II's first game. In 1897, as president, he greeted the Washington Senators in the Oval Office. "Talk about angering Reds fans," Allen laughed. "Salute baseball in Washington, but ignore it here!" Late coming to baseball's grip, McKinley missed another first: LP II painted center field's wall black to help batters see the pitch.

"We have been here before," wrote British poet/painter Dante Gabriel Rossetti. "But when or how I cannot tell." In 1901, Cincinnati could: Fire ruined League Park II. Its colonnade-style sloping boomerang of a successor fronted pillars and columns from Chicago's 1893 Columbian Exhibition. "Palace of the Fans" mixed a 450-foot right field, "rooter's row" (box seats down both foul lines), and belated sale of beer (twelve mugs for a buck). Filled, you were unfulfilled: The '02 Reds finished fourth and barely challenged for a decade.

In 1911, Garry Herrmann became club president. Fire soon wrecked the *Palace*'s wooden stands. William Bendix as TV's Chester A. Riley canted, "What a revoltin' development *this* is." Rhinelanders vowed that their park would never burn again. The offshoot was a parlor redolent of Ebbets Field and the Polo Grounds and other summer alcazars. At Crosley (née Redland) Field, home talk buzzed like cicadas upon its lush and humming earth.

4

PLEASE COME TO BOSTON

At the Hall of Fame, a small plaque laurels a second-floor wall. "Boston," it reads, "is the only major league city to field a professional team every year since professional baseball's [1871] start." Often that team has been a quirky, motley lot.

Name a better outfield than the 1950s' Ted Williams, Jim Piersall, and Jackie Jensen? ("Can't," agreed the shoe salesman in Nashua, New Hampshire, "but as usual, it's not enough.") Was this the year Tom Brewer and Frank Sullivan untangled the Bosox pitching staff? ("Maybe," cried the Cape Cod vacationer, swizzling his Narragansett. "But who's Pumpsie Green, and how do we unload him?") Could skipper Pinky Higgins (or Billy Jurges or Billy Herman) inspire the regulars—or starters challenge the hated Yanks? Would Don Buddin, fielding a ball at shortstop, *ever* manage not to heave it in the box seats beyond first base?

Why did Felix Mantilla greet grounders like root canal? Could Dick Stuart, jibed the adage, even pick up a hot dog wrapper without dropping it? Amid grinding teeth, other queries took a cut. When would the Red Sox steal a base? When would the bullpen not self-immolate? Was this the biblical year when Williams, Jensen, and Frank Malzone got even a shroud of a supporting cast? ("Sure," said Berkshires residents, "the same year Vermont goes Democratic.") In Calvinist New England, did the Red Sox disprove "life after death," or invert it?

Imagine two strangers marooned on a South Sea isle from Providence, Rhode Island, and Presque Isle, Maine. They differ in age, race, job, and religion. Their common link is New England's parish team. For good or ill, the Sox have bound generations from Long Island Sound via northern New Hampshire to the eastern tip of New Brunswick. Gentle reader, recall the ungentle age pre–Galen Cisco and Dom DiMaggio and even Smoky Joe Wood. It was not always so.

Boston baseball began three decades pre–Red Sox—to be exact, the 1871 NA charter Red Stockings. Yearly, the Sox test loyalty. Harry Wright's '72–'75 Red Stockings rewarded it with pennants. As we have seen, the NA then segued into the National League of Professional Baseball Clubs. South End Grounds—a.k.a. Boston Baseball, Union Baseball, or Walpole Street Grounds—found a new tenant in the NL Red Caps.

On April 29, 1876, the Caps uncorked their first game: Hartford 3, Boston 2. Next year Arthur Soden bought them. "Common sense," he said, "tells me that baseball is played primarily to make a profit." Later, Red Sox fans knew sportsman/owner Thomas A. Yawkey. Even from afar, he was a friend of ours. Arthur Soden was no Tom Yawkey.

Soden owned the future Beaneaters and Braves through 1906. (Boston owned them until '53, one of two NL charter teams continuously active.) The Red Caps won pennants in 1877, '78, and '83. A half-century later, politicos chimed, "Prosperity is just around the corner." Soden's led him to expand the site on Tremont Street—his first of six renovations. Williams often scored "the knights of the keyboard." He would have liked how Soden tore out the press box to increase capacity, making writers something to take or leave.

Like Williams, early Hubball mixed the good, bad, and ugly. *Good:* In 1894, Hugh Duffy hit an all-time .438. "[Jimmy Collins] reinvented third base," mused Jack Redding, "becoming first to play away from the bag." The 'Eaters won titles in '91–'92–'93–'97–'98. Charles (Kid) Nichols won 297 games in 1900–'09. Outfielder Tommy McCarthy flaunted attitude—then a noun, not adjective. "What a pioneer. He'd drop flys on purpose to force runners," said Redding. "Out of that"— the infield fly.

South End Grounds II bound a twin-spiraled roof, 6,800-seat grand-stand, and six spires above the double deck. "It was a breakthrough," observed TV's *Ballparks* special. "For the first time attention was paid to architecture. Witches peaks passed for decoration. It looked like a place where armored knights, not players, fought." Sullivan Tower, a free-loader's Eden, loomed beyond right. "Unlike Soden, they didn't worry about profit." Redding chuckled. "They dared, 'You raise the wall, and we'll raise the tower.' " Pause. "Soden did, and so did they."

Bad: At Fenway Park, marijuana mars the bleachers. On May 15, 1894, fire did. Fans scoffed "Play ball!" as seats began to burn. Recant-ing, some fled through a hole in the center-field fence. The area was less immune. Lost: 13 brick and 164 wooden buildings, nearly $1 million in damage, and 1,000 families homeless. Wrecked: The Braves' tiara of a park. Revealed: Valued at more than $75,000, South End Grounds II was insured for barely half. "To be born a Boston fan," columnist Mark Shields would muse, "is to learn early that life is not going to work out."

Ugly: For two months the '94 Beaneaters played at Dartmouth, or Congress Street, Grounds. (On May 30, Bobby Lowe whacked a big-league-first four homers in a game.) They returned to rebuilt South End Grounds III on July 20, and found it downsized with insurance money. "What irony!" said ex–*Boston Herald* writer Leo Egan of the one deck, puny foul lines, right-field incline, cigar factory beyond the bank, and sheep meadow of a center field. Small and cramped, it bellowed limits. By contrast, infinite were the "Miracle Braves." On September 7, 1914, they moved to larger Fenway Park, won the pennant, and played the World Series in the Red Sox' since-1912 home.

The charter '01 AL Pilgrims won five of baseball's first 15 World Series. Ironically, Ban Johnson had opposed a Boston franchise. He changed his mind on learning that the NL wanted to revive the American Associa-tion, make *it* a second major league, and put a team in the Hub. "They wanted to keep the AL out of here," said Lee Allen. "It's amazing what competition will do."

The future Red Sox (or Puritans, Americans, Plymouth Rocks, Somersets, or reviewing the century, the massively ironic Speed Boys), debuted at a 9,000-seat grounds on Huntington Avenue owned by the New Haven Railroad that had a toolshed in play, popgun right field (280 feet from home plate), other un-Fenway distances (left-center and center field, 440 and 635[!] feet away), and whose highway paved a Cyclone, Gray Eagle, and first-ever Oktoberfest. Pilgrims progress bared cleavage. Boston brooked '05-'06-'07-'11's second division. From 1901-'04, on the other hand, Denton True Young—Cyclone, in deference to his fastball—won 119 games. On May 8, 1901, he started Huntington's inaugural (Pilgrims 10, A's 4). "Young was thought," wrote Grantland Rice of the Sox all-time leader in complete games, win, and losses, "the greatest of all pitchers."

In 1903, Young won 28 games, the Sox took their first pennant, and a best five-of-nine game series decided baseball's first champion. "We can beat Pittsburgh no matter how good [Honus] Wagner is," shilled patrons at Boston's McGreevey's saloon. "Enough said [translated into 'Nuff ced']," McGreevey added, lifting his arms in certainty. Boston lost three of the first four games; then, in stunning role reversal, turned tomorrow on its head. Before Match Five, Pittsburghers gave McGreevey an umbrella: "You'll need this to ward off our base hits." He replied, "We may make a few of our own, don't you know," and danced on the Boston dugout. The 11–2 Young victory whipsawed the Classic. The Pilgrims won, five games to three.

"**T**hat was just in baseball," Soxaphile and U.S. Speaker of the House of Representatives Tip O'Neill recalled eight decades later. "Think outside the lines." In 1903–'04, the Lumiere brothers produced the first photographic plates. The Wright brothers flew successfully. The first transpacific cable was completed. Secured: Panama's independence, portending the canal. Published: Jack London's *Call of the Wild*. Elected: Theodore Roosevelt, as president, hailing "the strenuous life." TR trust-busted, strike-mediated, and could not abide being pygmy in any way.

Such writhings intrigued the Hub. In 1904, *Boston Globe* owner Charles Taylor bought the Pilgrims for son John. *That* transfixed. A Patriots Day doubleheader packed 36,034 into Huntington Avenue; the Beaneaters drew 5,667. The Pilgrims soon went forth to another Series: "No chance," huffed NL champion Giants manager John McGraw, voiding the Classic. "The other league's a joke. We don't play bush leaguers." The *Sporting News* pronounced the Pilgrims "world champions by default." Where was "Baseball's Bible" in 1946–'67–'75–'86?

In 1907, Tris Speaker, 19, arrived in Boston from Hubbard, Texas, to strut impatience with confines of any kind. Among his untrivia: best-ever 793 doubles; still-AL-high 35 assists in 1909 and '12; and .345 lifetime average. Even Tris was not infallible. In 1911, Ed Karger threw a pitch that the A's Stuffy McInnis lined to right. Thinking it a warm-up toss, Speaker failed to run. McGinnis completed an inside-the-park home run.

"For years, the Braves owned Boston," recalled 1966–'74 and 1979–'89 Sox broadcaster Ken Coleman, born eight miles from Fenway Park. "Once the Red Sox started winning, the Braves struggled as distant number two." How could they best Grounds which hosted Bill Cody's Wild West Show? Sniffed "Nuff Ced" McGreevey: "Who's going to play second base, Sitting Bull?"

The '03–'13 Braves trolled the second division. Six times, they lost 100 or more games. Disparity grew on October 7, 1911: The Sox left Huntington for Fenway Park. The NL's riposte: its *own* steel and concrete site, at Commonwealth Avenue, on the future site of the Allston Golf Club. On August 18, 1915, Boston edged St. Louis, 4–3, in Braves Field's first game.

Today, the Red Sox' ex-site houses the indoor athletic facility of Northeastern University. A World Series Exhibit Room, in the Cabot Cage, hails the '01–'11 AL age. Nearby, Tufts Medical College shrouds the former third base. Presaging Jim Lonborg's knee, Jose Santiago's arm, and Butch Hobson's elbow, leave it to the Towne Team to arrange emergency care.

Sacking myth, W. C. Fields was never banned in Boston. He *did* hate baseball, which seems becoming. The early bigs couldn't decide if they would rather be in Philadelphia.

The 1866–'68 Athletics took the national title. On October 31, 1871, they won the NA's first pennant. Teams named Philadelphia and the Centennials joined it in '73–'75. A year later, the NL made the A's a charter member. On April 22, 1876, they hosted Boston in the first game at Jefferson Street Grounds at 29th Street and Jefferson Avenue. There is no puzzle to '76's Coronado: George Hall's five dingers led the league.

Philadelphia Inquirer reporter Allen Lewis covered baseball from 1949 to 1979. "I'd hear about these popgun lines," he said, "and swimming pool behind the right-field fence." Few filled it post-1876: The A's drowned in bills. Baseball was playless in Philadelphia till: a) Oakdale Park welcomed the '82 charter A.A. Athletics; and b) sporting goods dealer Albert J. Reach bought the last-place Worcester, Massachusetts, club, moved it to Center City, and baptized a new team—the Phillies.

The A's moved to Forepaugh Park at 35th and Dauphin. The Phils took up at Recreation Park on Ridge Avenue between 24th and 25th Streets, then settled at the Philadelphia Baseball Grounds, at North Broad and West Huntingdon, a blur of fashion (five turrets flanked the pavilion) and tilt (right and left field were 310 and 500 feet, respectively, from home plate) and fumbling. Jack Redding sighed. "[1887] Opening ceremonies delayed the game. It was worth the wait. The first nine Phils hit safely [winning, 19–10]." Elsewhere, luck trembled between farce and fellow suffering.

"You could see the early trends," said ex-Phillies voice Bill Dyer. The infield teemed with ruts. A 15-foot-wide bicycle track carved an outfield incline near the fence. Catcher Jack Clements wore a glove on his wrong hand—or no glove at all. Manager George Stallings bore baseball's first player revolt. On August 6, 1894, a plumber's stove started a fire that "cost something like $80,000 to the club," Dyer added. "But what [Phillies owner] Bill Baker got back [after a week at the University of Pennsylvania Athletic Field] was so much better"—an expanded arabesque of 18,000 capacity and 4,000 standing room.

Phils manager Danny Ozark forged a bevy of 1970s malapropisms. He dismissed a losing streak: "Even Napoleon had his *Watergate*." Of an infielder, Danny said, "His limitations are limitless." He praised Phillies players. "We have a wonderful *repertoire*." Rapport, or repertoire: To Philadelphia, Baker Bowl eclipsed the Taj Mahal, the Hermitage, and the Czar's Winter Palace.

The Phillies' 1895–1938 lodge blared baseball's first cantilevered stand. (*Webster's:* "A large bracket or block projecting from a wall to support a balcony, cornice, etc.") Baker Bowl's wooden seats tied center field to the left-field line. Distances to left (335 to 341 feet, depending on the year) and center (408) seemed more or less commonplace. Antithetic were right-center (300) and right field (272), where convention hit the dirt.

"At the center-field clubhouse wall," said Lewis, "the bleacher angled and bisected a 30-feet-high right-center-field wall." Self-interest had its fling: A huge sign touted A. J. Reach Sporting Goods. Ibid., wall height array: left, as short as four feet; clubhouse to right-center, high as 12 (a 12-foot screen crowned it); right, high as 60 (a 20-foot screen topped tin over brick).

"How tough are Phillies fans?" announcer Bob Uecker asks as Everyman. "They go to the airport to boo bad landings." The Hump, a hillock under which a Philadelphia and Reading Railroad tunnel rent center field, could be more benign. Righty Ed Delahanty thrice batted over .400, twice went six-for-six, and whacked four inside-the-parkers on July 13, 1896. He hit one ball so hard it split in two. Another broke a second baseman's leg. Lefties owned/signs draped the right-field wall: Elmer Flick '00, hitting .378, and "Coca Cola" and "Lifebuoy Health Soap Stops B.O." All liked how anonymity took a hike. "It might be an exaggeration to say the outfield wall cast a shadow across the infield," wrote Red Smith. "But if the right fielder had eaten onions for lunch the second baseman knew it."

A visitor might see lightning split the flagpole, swimming pool fill the clubhouse basement, and circus horse dive off a platform into a pond near third base. "They had it all," Bill Dyer said: crusades, midget auto racing, donkey basketball, roller and ice skating, and police and fire department parades. Sadly, on August 8, 1903, 500 people jammed a railing atop the third-base stands to watch a fight on 15th Street. The stands collapsed, killing 12 and injuring 200.

Baker Bowl closed, no longer vaguely Messianic. The Phillies sued.

Soon Bill Baker put hat in hand, donned a renter's pose, and visited A's president and owner Cornelius McGillicuddy—Connie Mack.

In 1901, the American League placed charter stakes in Baltimore, Boston, Chicago, Cleveland, Detroit, Milwaukee, Washington—and Philadelphia, where Mack moved his new team to single-deck Columbia Park, at 29th Street and Columbia Avenue, with a modest size (9,500) and covered stand (from first to third base) and open bleachers (most seats cost a quarter and flanked each line) and Brewerytown section of hops and hits. All helped him break the bank.

Napoleon Lajoie hit a league-record .422. At age 19, second baseman Eddie Collins began the first of a record 25 years at one position. The 1902 A's won the pennant and drew 442,473, quadrupling the Phils' attendance. The '05ers waved another flag. Completing 35 games, Eddie Plank won 24. Rube Waddell sang a larger-than-life psalm: 27 victories, 1.48 ERA, and .200 opposing average. "I still remember," Mack later said, "Rube making his outfield sit down while fanning the side."

In September, Waddell tried to pluck a hat off roommate Andy Coakley's head. Byplay ended play. Said Dyer: "Rube tripped over a suitcase, fell hard on his pitching shoulder, and was finished for the year. Some antic." New York's Christy Mathewson blanked the A's thrice in the Series. Chief Bender won the Americans' only game, 3–0. Mack brightened at the bottom line. On September 30, a record 25,187 had packed Columbia with more standing than seating room.

"A dummy could see they needed more room," laughed Redding. "And Mack was no dummy."

In 1904, Bethlehem Steel was formed, *Madame Butterfly* premiered, and the Phillies returned to Baker Bowl. Its centaur arrived in 1911 to forge years of 28–13, 19–17, 22–8, 27–15, 31–10, 33–12, and 30–13. Grover Cleveland Alexander threw four 1915 no-hitters, had a league-best 90 shutouts (including '16's record 16), and won an NL-tying 373 games (with Christy Mathewson). "He led the NL in strikeouts four straight years," said then-Phils manager Pat Moran, "in ERA three times, and winning percentage"—with a 272-foot fence. No wonder that Alex went back to drinking.

In 1915, Baker Bowl hosted its only World Series. On October 15, Alex beat Boston for Philly's sole pre-'80 Classic victory. "The other highlight came the next day," Lewis noted. "Woodrow Wilson became the first president to throw out the first ball at a Series." (Wife Edith, the real fan, kept score.) By 1918, most teams had traded wood for steel and concrete. In a revealing nihilism, the Phillies traded Alex to the Cubs. They then proceeded to become the wretched of the earth.

The 1919–'38 Quakers won 1,129 games, lost 1,889, and finished an otherworldly 713½ out of first. Exception: Cy Williams won three home run titles, and Gavvy Cravath a fifth. Frank O'Doul '29 turned 254 hits into a .398 average. Rule: Erskine Mayer '14 yielded Honus Wagner's 3,000th hit. In 1933, Philly drew 156,421 mourners—2,031 per date. Managers came and went: Jack Coombs, Cravath, Bill Donovan, Kaiser Wilhelm, Art Fletcher, Stuffy McInnis, Burt Shotton, Jimmy Wilson, and Hans Lobert. Luck changed more slowly than fall in Alabama.

By default, trivia trumped triumph. In 1930, Chuck Klein batted .386 with 40 homers, 170 RBI, and 250 hits: None led the league. The former steelworker won the MVP Award and Triple Crown, respectively, in 1932–'33. "I guess the law of averages caught up." Three sheep and a ram mowed his outfield between games. From left to right, policemen sat on milk cartons every five to 10 feet. Blank boards covered Prohibition-age liquor ads. The right-field wall bore a sign "Sale or Rent." No ball cleared the clubhouse wall, but Rogers Hornsby whacked one through its window. "Ball Hawk George"—Philly's Hilda Chester—caught fouls behind the plate and graced Fox Movietone Newsreels, theater's web site of the time.

"A lot of guys liked to explore the town at night," Lee Allen began. "This made for fun the next day. Once Hack Wilson lay down in the outfield to catch his breath as Brooklyn changed pitchers. Suddenly he looks up to see a baseball ricocheting off the wall. Hack jumps up, gets the ball, and fired perfectly to second base to get the runner. Out! Right? Wrong." The ball had been thrown by starter Walter Beck, incensed at a pitching change. "The Phils liked small pleasures, not knowing any other kind."

On April 12, 1909, Mack fled Columbia Park for new digs at 21st Street and Lehigh Avenue. "Once Shibe Park opened," recalled Dyer, "it was only a matter of time until the Phillies became a tenant." Baseball's first concrete and steel park made Baker Bowl look more Jurassic than it was. In 1927, ten right-field bleacher rows collapsed and hurled two hundred people onto Huntingdon Street. One man was trampled to death; 41, hospitalized. Opening Day '38 shouted *quid* to Brooklyn's *quo:* Ernie Koy and Emmett Mueller homered, in the first inning, in their first big-league at-bats.

Accident, and precedent. "Time to mourn," said Lewis, "time to go." On June 30, 1938, baseball's last wooden park took a final strike three.

At Pennsylvania's other end, towns like Edinboro, Oil City, and Titusville formed the core of the Pirates (née Alleghenies) flock. The road to Pittsburgh, over hills heavy with farmland mixed with small towns shot by Ansel Adams, was long and hard. In 1876, it began at the city's first enclosed ballpark—Union Park—in the International Association.

The IA died in 1880. In '82, Pittsburgh joined a stable league (AA) and built Exposition Park at the juncture of the Allegheny and Monongahela (1970–2000 site of Three Rivers Stadium). A year later floods rafted the future Bucs to Exposition Park II Upper Field. By 1887, the first AA-turned-NL team moved to Recreation Park, originally built for the '84 Union Association, on a plot bounded by Allegheny, Grant, and Pennsylvania Avenues, and the Ft. Wayne Railroad Yards.

"Give baseball its due," urged Pirates owner Barney Dreyfuss. "It's stupid, exciting, dishonest—anything but dull, and all at the same time." *Exempli gratia.* The Players League debuted/died in 1890. Brooklyn PL second baseman Louis Bierbauer had been a '86–'89 NL Athletic. "All players were chattel," noted 1936–'55 Pirates voice Rosey Rowswell. "Bierbauer was expected to rejoin the A's."

Instead, the 'Ghenies heisted him—thus, "Pirates." Neither name helped in 1887–1900. Eleven times the Bucs placed sixth, seventh, or eighth in a mostly eight-team league. Plumbing abysmality, "They tried anything," said Rowswell, "to divert attention." One year catcher Fred Carroll carried a pet monkey at home and on the road. "Dying, the pet was buried in a pre-game ceremony beneath home plate."

In 1891, the Pirates turned Exposition Park II into a 16,000-seat roofed frigate. Its twin-spired hull soothsayed Forbes Field's vast outer garden (lines, 400 feet; center, 450). Warring elements made each sail a guess. In 1900–'01, wind sheared the roof. On July 4, 1902, more than a foot of water from the Allegheny drenched the outfield and changed the rules: Any hit became a single. The Pirates swept a doubleheader from Brooklyn: Suddenly, sunlight danced off the waves.

Jupiter aligned with Mars when Louisville folded in late 1899 and Dreyfuss moved to Pittsburgh and stocked it with ex-Colonels. In his 1955 essay, "The Game for all America," Ernie Harwell wrote, "There's a man in Mobile who remembers a triple he saw Honus Wagner hit in Pittsburgh 46 years ago." Some recollect still. The Flying Dutchman's 1897–1917 bric-a-brac: eight batting, six slugging percentage, and three RBI titles, 3,430 hits, 252 triples, .329 career average, 17 straight years over .300, 720 steals, and Hall of Fame 1936. Said Paul Waner: "Keep your Marions and Rizzutos and Reeses and Applings. At shortstop, Honus Wagner was the bow-legged best."

Fred Clarke hit .406 for '97 Louisville. The player/manager and Wagner led the Bucs to the 1901–'02–'03 pennant. Jack Chesboro '02 won 28 sets. Vic Willis took 69 games in '06–'08. Weaned on famine, Pittsburgh found its riches almost unbelievable. Then, in 1909, Dreyfuss left for the arcadia of Forbes Field. On June 29, a bugler played taps and nearly 6,000 stood at Exposition as the flag fell for the final time.

A 1910s broadside dubbed Washington, D.C. "First in War, First in Peace, and Last in the American League." By the 1870s, it was no trick to call the capitol "First in Teams Begun and Lost—and Last in the Bottom Line."

D.C's sadness followed false euphoria, like the South before Pickett's Charge. As early as 1859, the Nationals and Olympics played at the White Lott, or Ellipse, site of the National Christmas Tree, between the White House and Washington Monument. Later, Abraham Lincoln often left his office to watch several innings. Legend touts him playing town ball as an 1860 gaggle arrived to crown Abe the GOP nominee. "I am glad to hear of their coming," he told the bigwigs. "But they will have to wait a few minutes to have another turn at bat."

Town ball amused the ordinary and towering, self-assured and unself-confident, devious and trustworthy person who was the 16th President of the United States. It obsessed his successor, Andrew Johnson, "so caught up with the prospect of a two-inter-city match [baseball's first *ménage à trois*] between the Washington Nationals, Philadelphia Athletics, and Brooklyn Atlantics that he gave government clerks and employees time off to watch," wrote I. Kirk Sale of *Sport* Magazine.

"Johnson set the whole White House entourage up on plush straight-back chairs along the first-base line and that day became the first President to watch inter-city baseball teams." Inviting them to the White House, he hailed the churnings of provinciality. "Baseball was still regional," mused former *Washington Post* sports editor Shirley Povich. "D.C. teams played by Washington game rules—no outfield fences, and a batter could *recircle* the bases. A ball eludes the fielder, and you might get two home runs on a single hit."

In 1866, Washington beat Richmond, 102–87: Like pitching, attendance seemed MIA—or was baseball SOS? Soon sports promoter and pool-room overseer Michael Scanlon built D.C.'s first enclosed park near 17th and S Streets, N.W. Olympic Grounds sat 500, and tickets cost a quarter. Johnson waved from the club balcony. It didn't help: Most seats went unsold. In 1871–'73–'75, the NA Olympics, Nationals, and Washingtons folded. Povich smiled. "One team ['72's Nats] lasted five weeks at 16th and R Streets' National Grounds."

Mock it, if you will: Babylon kept bobbing on the Potomac. In 1876, D.C. wooed the National League. The '84 AA Washingtons rented Athletic Park, a 450-by-490-foot plot at S and 9th Streets. More tony was Washington's first major wooden park—6,000-seat/peewee right field/long left field/built opposite the Capital Buildings/home of the Union Association National Unions/now, site of the U.S. Senate underground parking garage—Capitol Grounds. Nothing worked: For decades, Washington would swarm unobserved in catatonia and disarray.

In 1884, expiring, the Washingtons and Unions must have felt like Harry Truman. "If you want a friend," he said, famously, "get a dog."

"**P**eople are here from all over the country," the ex-*Washington Star* columnist Morris Siegel noted. "You'd think clubs would draw—but

they didn't. Maybe too little home-town loyalty. Maybe too great a fixa-
tion with politics."

In 1885, D.C. joined the Eastern League and won a pennant. Next
year the Nationals gained a new name (Statesmen) and league
(National). Finally, a big-league nook!—or was it? The '88 Statesmen
became the Senators. The NL by and by impeached them. Then, in 1891,
the AA Nats opened National, a.k.a. Boundary, Park (cap., 6,000, at The
Boundary at Seventh Street and Florida Avenue) by cutting 125 oak trees
and stuffing stump holes in the infield. Some trees still lolled over the
outfield fence. "They stopped would-be homers and knocked balls back
into play," said Povich. Pause. "Actually, it helped. Few balls were hit by
Washington."

The AA folded in 1892. Eight decades earlier, the British had taken
Washington. The NL now did. On April 16, the new Senators, losing to
the Giants, 6–5, began an eight-year run as sport's 98-pound weakling.
Like Johnson, their reign blurred Church (of baseball) and State (the
presidency). On June 6, Benjamin Harrison became the first president to
see a major-league game: Cincinnati 7, Senators 4. In July he saw them
lose again, 9–2. "So much for the Bully Pulpit," said Siegel. "Hail to the
Chief" put few fannies in the seats.

In 1899, Buck Freeman's 25 taters led the league. "Some gratitude,"
Povich hooted. That fall the NL kicked four teams out of office—and
put the Senators out of misery. "Again, no ball. Then, one day that
'other league' paid Washington a call."

On Opening Day 1901, 9,772, including Admiral Dewey, hero of
Manila Bay in '98's Spanish-American War, packed American League
Park at 14th Street and Bladensburg, N.E. Umpires of the time
announced starting lineups—"until today!" mused Povich. E. Lawrence
Phillips took a megaphone, stood behind home plate, and bellowed
starters to the crowd. Two years later the Senators moved to Seventh and
Florida, renamed the site AL Park II, fixed the second division, and more
or less stayed there through 1961.

"These identical coliseums—screw them, blow 'em up!" said Siegel,
and he began to laugh. "They should take a page from American League
Park [II]." Grounds help stored the flag between games in a doghouse

near the outfield flagpole. One day, removing it, the keeper forgot to close the door. "That afternoon a Senator batter hits a liner over the head of the A's center fielder [Socks Seybold]." The ball rolled inside the house. "The outfielder sticks his head and shoulders inside and what happened? He got stuck. When his teammates rescued him, the batter had completed the only inside-the-dog house homer."

At such moments it seemed possible that D.C. might shed its sackcloth of past ruin. Even 1901–'09 president Theodore Roosevelt—said daughter Alice Roosevelt Longworth, "Father and all of us regarded baseball as a mollycoddle game. Violence . . . appealed to us. Father wouldn't watch it, not even at Harvard"—spurned strike three. In 1907, a paper wrote: "The President said he regards the game of baseball as the typical American outdoor sport."

Wooing one foil, baseball yielded to another. On March 17, 1911, American League Park II's stands caught fire from a plumber's blow lamp and burned to the ground. Bureaucrats abstained from what came next: efficiency born of time.

In 18 days, a single-deck stand rose from first base to third. Opening Day was April 12. On schedule, the Senators unveiled D.C. baseball's remembered mosque. "My house, my house, though thou art small," George Herbert might have said about Griffith Stadium, "thou art to me the Escurial."

The 1962 New York Mets were so pathetic—40–120—that they turned and became an enduring fashion in the ephemera capital of the world. Their metaphor of initials—Marvin Eugene Throneberry—mimed Alfonse at the plate and Gaston in the field. "[Marv] looked like Mickey Mantle hitting," mate Richie Ashburn recalled, "but he didn't get the same results." Lacking gravitas, Marvelous Marv turned self-effacing. "Hey!" he flogged a Mets fielder who dropped a fly. "What you trying to do? Steal my fans?"

Once Marv tripled, but was called out by umpire Dusty Boggess for missing second base. Coach Cookie Lavagetto intercepted an angry Mets manager. "Don't bother arguing," he told Casey Stengel. "He missed first base, too."

Throneberry's riposte hailed common sense. "What does everybody want me to do? I hit the ball a long way. I just had a little trouble because I haven't been to third in a while." Such a man deserved a coda, and found it in 1963. "Marv was upset the other day because the writers gave me a birthday cake," said Stengel. "He asked how come they didn't give him one. I told him, 'They would have, but they were afraid you'd drop it.'"

Imagine Johnny Carson hosting *The Tonight Show*. Ed McMahon answers, "Cleveland's 1899 National League baseball team." Carson, as Carnac, replies, "Who made the '62 Mets look like Murderers Row?" The '99 Spiders brooked losing streaks of 14, 16, and a still-record 24 games, and finished 20–134, or .149, the NL's worst-ever percentage. Straightaway it dropped them like a wrong note in *South Pacific*.

Cleveland's plight heaped connotation upon irony: Improbably, the Spiders had once moored the league. "What highlights," blared ex-*Cleveland Plain Dealer* columnist Russell Schneider. "Take Jess Burkett [forging 1895–'96 batting titles at .423 and .410]. Or Cy Young, with a 35–10 record in 1895 [winning at least 21 games in eight straight years]. The entirety of early baseball here wasn't that one long, lousy year."

The Spiders' 1879–'84 National League Park had a tree-specked outfield. Hung: pitcher Jim McCormick, 20–40 in '79. Cleveland then left the NL, joined/fled the AA, and resurfaced in 1887's antipodean National League Park II. "Pitchers loved *this* ['87–'88 AA and '89 NL] place," Schneider said of its 410-feet foul lines. In 1890, lightning, not batters, wrecked it.

Cleveland's next stop threw subtlety to the breeze. Ask your nearest seven-year-old what baseball nicety he likes. He will spurn the pitchout, hit-and-run, and vagaries of the slider. He likes the long ball, the soul-crushing poke, the prodigious deed—the homer. League Park's 290 feet to right field made children of us all.

Frank D. Robison bought the team in 1889. A decade later he and brother M. Stanley added the Browns, transferred Young, Burkett, and other Spiders, and mimed the fox taken as a naïf who winds up taking the taker. "As owners, the Robisons' goals were to help St. Louis—and destroy Cleveland's baseball future," said 1963–'72 and 1978–'84 Indians president Gabe Paul. Respectively, they thrived and failed.

The '89–'98 Spiders spun a 718–628 meshwork. In 1901, they became the AL Indians. Nap Lajoie averaged .338, took the 1903–'04 batting title, and entered Cooperstown '37. Addie Joss (1902–'10) won 160 games (including four years of at least twenty), had a 1.89 ERA (second-best-ever to Ed Walsh), but died at 31 (of tubercular meningitis).

By 1908, the Tribe finished second behind Detroit. "The future was again great for Cleveland," said Schneider, "but bad for wooden parks." On April 21, 1910, League Park II became the bigs' fourth steel and concrete grandstand. Suddenly, Cleveland didn't reek of Metsomania after all.

After the Civil War, an American might focus on his city's order of priorities. In Cleveland, that meant commerce; Atlanta, food and shelter; Houston, Westward-Ho!; St. Louis, pitch and hit.

Even now, something remains, if but a vague recollection, of baseball's birth at Veto Park, near today's Fairgrounds Park, on St. Louis' then-Grand Avenue Grounds. Early games were amateur. In 1875, they turned professional in the one-year NA. The Red and Brown Stockings knit at Red Stocking and Grand Avenue Park, respectively. On May 5, 1876, the Brown Stockings darned their first NL game: St. Louis 1, Cubs 0.

The next-year Nationals tossed St. Louis in the trash. "Some cities created interest from the top down," said Bob Broeg. "After the NL dumped us, we did it locally, lots of neighborhood games, from the bottom up." In 1882, the local Park and Club Association's Chris Von der Ahe forged the AA Browns. "A lot of other teams already were professional," said Broeg. "At last we caught up"—or was it passed?

Von der Ahe owned a tavern. His charter Browns occupied a twin-spired site (Sportsman's Park I) of short right field (285 feet), vast center (460), and 6,000 (later, 12,000) person capacity at Grand Avenue and Dodier Street. Foul turf was teeny. Beer, on the other hand, flowed as freely as foul balls. In 1881, Von der Ahe turned Augustus Solari's two-story house into a beer garden. Broeg laughed. "It was wacky enough for Brooklyn!" The garden lay *inside* the field of play.

"According to rules then," he said, "fielders could go into the seats to get a ball and throw it to the pitcher's box, after which the ball could be used to put out a runner. At Sportsman's Park, this meant a right fielder could charge into the beer garden, interrupt people eating and drinking at their tables, and retrieve the ball." Behind it the clubhouse abutted a Japanese cannon of bamboo wrapped with steel wire.

Von der Ahe dressed players in silk uniforms, put them in regal carriages, and carted gate receipts in a wheelbarrow. Many flowed from third baseman Arnie Latham, a.k.a. the Fleetest Man on Earth. Latham '87 stole 129 bases. (In 1909, the Giants coach, then 49, became the oldest big-leaguer to swipe a base. "Forget Brock or Wills," added former *Post-Dispatch* writer Ray Gillespie. "Latham was Dorian Gray.")

In 1884 and '86, respectively, the UA and NL Maroons folded after playing at Union Grounds Park. "This left the Browns," said Broeg, "until in '91 *they* hit the street." The AA's death again led St. Louis to the National. Von der Ahe made Sportsman's Park a baseball field/racetrack, left Grand Avenue for the Maroons' old den, renamed it League Park, and (re) rebuilt six times.

"Fire," Broeg explained. "As a last hurrah, Von der Ahe built what he called 'tall, majestic' columns behind the stands—supposedly, to help fans' vision."

Even 10/200 sight couldn't miss the contretemps ahead.

St. Louis survived the cut when the '99 Nationals shrank from 12 to eight teams. "Credit the new owners," Broeg said. "God knows it wasn't their record. The Browns hadn't won a pennant in a decade. The Robisons were so annoyed that they took all the brown uniform stuff off and put red on it."

"Redbirds," I said.

"Bingo. One day a woman watching the game was overheard by reporter Willie McHale of the *St. Louis Republic*. She said, 'Oh, what a lovely shade of Cardinal!' The Cardinals they became."

League Park became Robison Field. Right and right-center goosed offense (290 and 330 feet). Other fields hyped pitching: left 470 feet, center 500, left-center 520, and left-field pole 625 feet, or nearly one-eighth of a mile. In 1902, some hitters caught a break: The AL moved its

Milwaukee team. Suddenly, Sportsman's housed the renamed Browns, who lived there 'till '53.

The old/new Browns grappled. Often, *neither* gripped the upper hand. Said Broeg: "You never knew what the two teams would do, except that it wouldn't work." Each finished last five times from 1901–'18. By 1909, Robison and Sportsman's held 21,000 and 18,000 seats, respectively: One year they drew only 233,315 *combined*. Christy Mathewson faced the Cardinals 25 times and had 24 victories and one no-decision. Aberrant was Slim Sallee, becoming the only Redbirds pitcher to steal home.

In 1916, Frank Robison's daughter bought the Cardinals. Local investors soon bought her out. "So much for baseball's first female owner," said Gillespie. "Which brings us to the old-boy network" of a lawyer, former player, and now Browns vice-president. "Branch Rickey had once managed the Browns. The Cardinals steal him to run the team and Rickey goes to the Browns and gets them to let the Cardinals play at Sportsman's Park."

On June 6, 1920, the Cards cut the Cubs, 5–2, in St. Louis' last wooden game. New president Sam Breadon sold Robison Field, took the money, and invested in Rickey's cause (farm system) and effect (profit). Eight decades later *Baseball Weekly* held a poll to choose "Baseball City USA." Von der Ahe would have bought a round of drinks: St. Louis triumphed in a walk.

On April 15, 1954, a city 845 miles to the east returned to a kind of major-league euphoria. Acquiring the Browns, more than three hundred thousand baseball and—it soon become apparent—victory-starved fans lined the route along Howard, Charles, and Baltimore Streets to cheer a mélange of floats, bands, Baltimore Orioles officials, cheerleaders, Vice-President Nixon, native Baltimorean Mrs. John McGraw, and last/least, former Browns. "One of the greatest thrills I've ever had," long-time *Baltimore News American* columnist John Steadman said, understandably. When Baltimore last played the bigs, planes seemed futuristic, cars were playthings for the wealthy, and Uneeda's boy downed a slicker for Nabisco crackers.

In 1882, owner Harry Von der Horst built Oriole Park I, on 25th Street, then Huntingdon Avenue, near Greenmount Avenue, for $5,000.

The double-decked nest had twin bleachers, chairs from Forepaugh's Theatre in the grandstand, and room for 6,000 warblers. Like the Braves, A's, and Giants, the '88 Orioles built a screen over center field to fix rooftoppers in their sight. "When they blocked their view," said Steadman, "people protested. They thought poaching their proprietary right."

In 1891, Oriole Park expanded, the American Association folded, and the Birds' aviary became the National's. It barracked dining, dancing, 25 cent postgame band concerts, a next-door amusement park, 11,000–person capacity, and Who's Who of glamor boys. The new birdhouse blazed pitcher Bill Hoffer, 78–24 in 1895–'97, and two future Brooklyn managers. Ned Hanlon won 1894–'95–'96 pennants. Wilbert Robinson once got seven hits in seven at-bats. Wee Willie Keeler hit 'em where they ain't. Joe Kelley batted over .300 for 12 straight years. Third baseman John McGraw revealed warts and all. "Life," murmured once-Orioles announcer Bailey Goss. "It's what the O's had, and what they took out of others."

"Say the 1920s, and you think Yankees. The 1890s meant the Orioles," Jack Redding hailed their footnotes and fancy dans. "The park was as memorable as the team." Separate bicycle racks on Barclay Street served ladies and gentlemen. Right field sloped downhill to the fence. Beneath it, Brady's Run leaked to make defense alien. In 1894, fire nearly destroyed the park. Greed soon led Hanlon to nearly destroy the team.

Brooklyn owner Charles Byrne died in 1897. Soon Hanlon became O's president and Dodgers manager. "[Brooklyn secretary] Charlie Ebbets and I got to thinking," he said. "We could make more money in Brooklyn, so we sent 'em our best." Birds flew north and east. The Brooks won the '99 pennant. The Orioles, shorn of tuft, fluttered from the NL. "It's nice that they then joined the new league [American, as a charter member]," said Redding. "It's too bad that they never had a chance."

The AL O's debuted April 26, 1901. Ban Johnson threw out the first ball, Iron Man McGinnity dueled Win Kellum, and 10,371 chirped happily: Baltimore 10, Boston 6. At Oriole Park IV, ornithology wed peculiarity: A right-center-field flagpole and large tree behind the fence extended into play. McGraw became manager, then left for New York (NL Polo Grounds). Johnson topped him by moving the American's *franchise* there. "He wanted to have a team in the big city," Redding said of Little Napoleon. "It was part of the big-league war."

On September 29, 1902, Boston won the Orioles' final game, 9–5. Baltimore joined the International League and brooked the 1914–'15 Federal League Terrapins. The FL died in 1916. The Birds thrived in now-14,000-seat Oriole Park. "For a long time," Steadman said, "Baltimore was content with the minors." For surcease it often followed another blue-collar, albeit big-league, city. Detroit was hard hat, lunch bucket, and umbilically tied to baseball. Such combinations are hard to find.

J oe Falls has covered the Tigers since the 1950s. "Detroit [is] one of the great baseball towns," he wrote in 1975. "This is a town of three million managers—all of them right. And a town of beer drinkers—all of them thirsty. This is a town that in seventy-five years has developed a true passion for a boy's game and a love-hate relationship for the men who play it."

Like the O's, White Sox, and Indians, Detroit evolved from the "other" league. In 1880, the NL chose the Detroit Wolverines a.k.a. Detroits or Creams to play at Recreation Park. *Hits:* Detroit won the '87 flag and 10 of 15 games *v.* the AA Browns in a cross-country "World Series." *Runs:* Dennis (Big Dan) Brouthers won '89–'90–'91 batting titles. The 1886 Wolves finished 87–36, or .707. *Errors:* The '86ers didn't win the pennant. (90–34 Chicago did.)

A man stuck in the mud with his car was once asked by a wayfarer whether he was really stuck. "Well, you could say I was," said the man, "if I was going anywhere." By 1901, Detroit was going from the National to American League. For two years it played Sunday at Burns—a.k.a. West End—Park. Monday–Saturday had dibs on Bennett Park, built atop an old haymarket's cobblestones, at the corner of Michigan and Trumbull Avenues. "Imagine!" said Arthur Brooks, whose grandfather owned a lumberyard, Brooks Lumber, still in business beyond right field. "Baseball, in the exact same place, for an entire century [through 1999] and more."

Bennett Park (a.k.a. Navin Field, 1912; Briggs Stadium, '38; and Tiger

Stadium, '61) opened April 28, 1896. Detroit beat Columbus, 17–2, as George Stallings hit to center, a fan tripped outfielder Frank (Gold Brick) Butler, and Stallings rounded the bases for the park's first homer. The site honored ex-Wolves catcher Charlie Bennett, who lost both legs in a 1894 train accident. Archetype Hughie Jennings doubled as 1891–1918 short-stop and 1907–'20 manager.

In 1955, Connie Mack named Jennings baseball's best—save McGraw and Casey Stengel—manager. Turn-of-the-century skippers ragged play-ers. Hughie caressed. "Never waste your time and energy scolding a man in anger," he said. "Angry, your reasoning is not sound." "Ee-yah!" Jen-nings whooped from the coaching box upon '07–'08–'09 pennants. "The city was blowing its top," Ty Cobb wrote later. "Extra newspaper editions heralded every game. Everyone in town seemed to own a tin whistle, using them to imitate Jennings' piercing sound effects."

Detroit lost the '07–'08 and '09 Series to Chicago and Pittsburgh, respectively. Small matter. People of a certain age gather yet in Hope and Holland to recall Cobb and Sam Crawford and Germany Schaefer and Charley O'Leary and a region's lore. "The first you remember," said Tigers 1960–voice Ernie Harwell, smiling. "Players—and especially the park."

Bennett Park welded 10-foot fences, a wooden grandstand, 8,500 (1901) or 14,000 ('10) capacity, and home plate in a pitcher-friendly spot. "Most games then were played in the afternoon," said Harwell. Batters stared directly at the setting sun. Its placement helped George Mullin start 44 games, complete 42, and toss 382 innings in 1904. Despite it, Crawford won the AL home run and RBI title, respectively, in 1908 and '10.

"Unfair!" Cobb stormed. "With that plate it's a miracle we survived!" Ralph Waldo Emerson wrote of Napoleon, "He was no saint—to use his word, 'no Capuchin,' and he is no hero in the high sense." Cobb three times topped .400, won 12 batting titles, took the '09 Triple Crown, was named 1911 MVP, and stole a then-best 892 bases. He retired with a .367 average, pre-Rose Everest 4,191 hits, and Somerset of grudge.

Some spurned the Tigers' churlish deity. Others panted to see him play. "I saw Ty Cobb when I was a kid," brayed Brooks. "My grandfather had a deal with the Tigers: Whenever it snowed he would hitch up the horses and plow our lumberyard, then he would plow all around the stadium. The Tigers gave him four tickets to every game for that."

To watch, many built "wild cat" bleachers on National and Cherry Streets. The Tigers solved that puzzler by hanging three-feet-wide by 40-feet-high canvas strips behind the outfield seats. Moochers then beat a path to kegs on adjacent roofs.

"That's what baseball does to people in Detroit," Falls would write. Boy's game. Man's thirst. "Ee-yah!" indeed.

The cant of baseball's early age touched even future *non*-big-league sites. A visitor hailed *sluggers* (an *eagle-eye*) with their *foot in the bucket* who *hit the dirt* and earned the *horse collar* or shook a *slump* and (after clubbing a *long strike*) *laid it down* or *teed off* in their *groove,* and of batted balls that became a *blooper, bleeder, banjo hit* or *Baltimore chop, clothesline,* or *Texas Leaguer,* and fielders who made a *boner* or *boot* or *circus catch* or *shoestring catch* or were *handcuffed* at the *hot corner* or *keystone bag* or (who, behind the plate) donned the *tools of ignorance* or (whose talent) voided the *squeeze play* or (whose charity) sired the cry of *butterfingers,* and of pitchers (a *chucker* or, if left-handed, *southpaw* or, if inept, a *scatter-arm* or, adept, *Houdini*) who *winged* the *apple* or *beanball* or *rabbit ball* or *gopher ball* or *cripple* (if behind the batter) or *free ticket/Annie Oakley* (if he walked the hitter) or *high, hard one* to *fan* or *whiff* or *strike out* or, in a *shutout, whitewash* the hitters so that, bespectacled (a *Cyclops*) or not, he could avoid a *Mexican standoff* and, not *crabbing,* become a *meal ticket,* not *grandstander.*

"Think of the age as a work in progress," said longtime *Sporting News* columnist Lowell Reidenbaugh. "Today's an arrival. Their's was an adventure." In Keokuk, Iowa, Perry Park hosted the 1875 Westerns. Two outfield lakes formed a dragnet; players submerged while chasing flies. In Indianapolis, the 1884 AA Blues and '87 NL Hoosiers played in a cornfield (Seventh Street Parks I and II) before moving home plate to the southwest, not southeast, part. (*Un*changed: a 10-foot left-field net.) In Providence, the 1878–'85 NL Grays built the first screen behind home plate to save onlookers from foul balls. "Otherwise, they could make a mess of your suit or dress," said former *New York Journal-American* reporter Til Ferdenzi. Their park's name: the Messer Street Grounds.

A tiny 450-square-foot plot housed the AA's '84 Columbus Senators. The mire of Syracuse's '90 AA ers was the calendar, not size. Each Sunday the Stars played at Three Rivers Park, 12 miles north of town. "Many citizens," read a paper, "demanded that 'blue laws' be enforced." On August 3, Syracuse left for nearby Iron Pier amusement park, and police vowed to stop the game. "Fearing the gendarmes, Louisville did not appear [ultimately, forfeiting]. However, the umpires and Syracuse did." Wilmington, Delaware's, Union Street Park proved equally second-guessable. On September 15, 1884, the 2–15 UA Quicksteps received 16–63 Kansas City. No fans appeared. "Who says that players don't notice the size of a crowd?" wrote a columnist. Forfeiting, Joe Simmons waved his Quicksteps off the field.

On September 25, 1882, the Grays and Brown Stockings tendered the first true doubleheader at the Agricultural County Fair Grounds in Worcester, Massachusetts. In Rockford, Illinois, even one game could tickle. Trees bordered foul lines and loomed behind the catcher. Baseball's first warning track abutted the outfield fence; "its name," said Ferdenzi, "taken from the adjacent race track's drainage gutter." Third base was on a hill, and home plate in a depression to rival the 1930s. Runners ran downhill in their zest to score.

"Forget *national* pastime," Lee Allen noted. "Baseball was regional." The NL Troy (NY) Trojans' Mickey Welch completed his first 105 starts. AA Worcester's Harry Stovey hit 14 homers in 1884 to set a single-year record. In Providence, "Old Hoss" Radbourn pitched '84's last 27 games. In Buffalo, Jim (Pud) Galvin '83–'84 won 92. Reidenbaugh shook his head. "Only Cy Young completed more games [631] or pitched more innings [5,959]."

Buffalo's 1879–'83 cabin mixed 210-feet foul lines and Evel Knievel alleys. On May 21, 1881, a dinger left the Express Grounds toward Lizzie Bluett's cottage, at 599 West Avenue, bordering the Bisons' park. It broke her collarbone as she drank coffee and read a newspaper.

Dramatist/humorist George Ade once returned from a trip to England. "The time to enjoy a European tour," he sniffed, "is about three weeks after you unpack." Pre-1900 teams could stuff home cooking in the drawer. The Trojans trekked to Albany, New York (Riverside Park, 1880–'82); NL '90 Pittsburgh Innocents, Canton, Ohio's Mahaffey Park (1,125 feet above sea level, baseball's highest pre-Denver site); FL Newark Peppers (Harrison Park, New Jersey, 1915, 21,000 capacity); and NL Pirates, Wheeling (Island Grounds, 1890). Mike Tiernan was high on grass. It buried his hit for an inside-the-park homer.

In 1882, Ft. Wayne, Indiana, hosted the final postseason playoff game—Grays v. White Stockings. The '85 Bisons trod Elmira's Maple Avenue Driving Park. The '98 Exiles played in Charlotte, New York, in what is now Rochester, on the Genesee River near Lake Ontario. Neutrality even flagged September 6, 1903: The AL Pilgrims landed at Warwick, Rhode Island's Rocky Point Park. "Home runs hit the ocean," gibed Redding, "and made pitchers take a bath."

Return with us to TV's Carnac. The answer is "Louisville Baseball Park"—the NL Grays' '76–'77 household. Carnac replies, "What is the only ex-ballpark site [Victorian homes now stud it] on the National Register for Historic Preservation?"

Answer: "The Hole"—Kansas City's Association Park. Question: "What 1886 NL field was excavated to create a roadbed for Independence Avenue?" The former site of Ranson's Pond lay 25 feet below field level.

A: "Please don't shoot the umpire. He is doing the best he can." Q: Which Association Park outfield sign conjured the age's wooden pre-classic parks?

CLASSIC PARKS

1909–'61

5

YOU WEAR IT WELL

Picture an American football field. Each is 100 yards from one goal line to another and 53½ yards wide. Fix your favorite pro basketball court: 94 feet by 50 feet, its basket 10 feet high. A tennis court is 78 feet long by 36 feet wide. Even height net and serving box size are identical. Variety takes a dive.

Custom decrees 90 feet between bases and 60 feet, 6 inches from home plate to the pitcher's mound. Elsewhere, look backward, angel. "Thanks to [Alexander] Cartwright," said former commissioner Bowie Kuhn, "the distance to the outfield, height of fence around the field, or territory between seats and foul lines" sheds the uniformity of ball and chain.

In 1908, vaudevillian Jack Norworth wrote "Take Me Out to the Ball Game" and the American Tobacco Company printed the first four-color, made-to-be-swapped, Mother, don't throw out these baseball cards. The bigs' first steel and concrete site, Shibe Park, opened in '09 Philadelphia. Through 1914, 11 classic fields were forged from the grid of city streets. "Each fit on an urban parcel, which made for some unique angles," said author Michael Gershman in 1998. "Ballparks assumed a symmetrical form as they took on the lines of their property."

Fenway Park resembled a pinball emporium. Forbes Field became a pitcher's friend. At Crosley Field, an uphill berm flanked the outfield wall. The Polo Grounds clubhouse towered above stairs in deep center field. Even outsides varied. Ebbets Field seemed an apartment building. Shibe's Beaux Arts tower and churchlike dome behind the plate mimed the French Renaissance. Each aped an extended kin, vivid and benign.

"Your uncle Sid and your aunt Thelma that you love and that you see two or three times a year, well, you see John Franco eighty times a year, or Bernie Williams, or Mark McGwire," mused Gershman. "You know more about them than you know about your family. In a sense, they *are* your family." The classic park was the street where they lived.

Bob Costas recalls first spying Yankee Stadium's triple-tiered enormity. "Seeing your first major-league game in a classic park is like what James Fenimore Cooper wrote of in his novels," he said. "It's a rite of passage"—like Dorothy spying the Emerald City.

From its opener—April 18, 1923: Yankees 4, Boston 1—"The House That Ruth Built" canonized its maker. Years later, Jack Webb as Sergeant Joe Friday wore badge No. "714"—Ruth's home-run record—on TV's *Dragnet*. Babe deified the long ball, fulfilled his appetites, and spawned a near-messianic baseball age.

Like Ruth, the Big Ballpark in the Bronx bred bipolarity. Millions thought it Mecca. Others, miming Irving Howe, claimed, "We know the nightmare is ours." The Stadium shaped the game played within. A long out to left-center or center field—Death Valley—would be a home run in Tiger (née) Briggs Stadium. A homer off its foul pole—only 296 and 301 feet to right and left field—might have hit Fenway's 37-foot-high wall for a single. It made a difference.

In football, players must advance ten yards in four tries. Wrote George Vecsey: "It can exist anywhere a hundred yards of flat round rests." By contrast, a man who at 23 saw his first big-league game learned "that in all the old parks *where* the game is played could decide *how* the game came out." Richard Nixon recalled little about it "except that the day was July 4 [1936], the Washington Senators lost a double-header at Griffith Stadium, and a rookie named DiMaggio put one in the seats."

Griffith sat one mile from the White House and had baseball's second-smallest capacity (27,410). It took a trolley ride of 402 feet to reach left field. Home runs and victory rarely pricked the Senators' god-awfulness. "Those Damn Yankees, why can't we beat 'em?" cursed Joe Hardy in the 1958 movie. The Nats seldom did.

No Senator of sanity cried, "Let's play two." To the west and north, the eldest son of professor Frederic Will recalled Ernie Banks—"Mr. Cub"—who *did*. Smacking nonchalance, both shared the friendly environs of Chicago's Wrigley Field.

George Will liked its bleachers, grass, hand-operated scoreboard, and nearby L tracks. "I was amazed," he said, "that there wasn't a bad view in the house—or [from] next-door rooftop seats." The North Side cabash tied twin bills (a tightwad's dream: two for one), grandstand flanking foul terrain, and flag with a white "W" (on blue background) or blue "L" (against white) atop the scoreboard to semaphore the verdict for those outside the park. Isolated in attention were ivy on the brick outfield wall (outfielder Lou Novikoff called it poison ivy; others thought him wall-shy) and gales off Lake Michigan. Blowing out, they led pitchers to schizophrenia. "Cub fans," laughed Will, "trekked across the street to a bar."

The Cubs' fiercest 1876–1966 rivalry entailed a trip by rail to St. Louis' Grand Avenue and Dodier Street. A high screen covered the right-field pavilion. Left and center field yawned 355 and 430 feet, respectively, from home plate. Until 1958, the Cardinals were baseball's southern- and westernmost team. Sportsman's Park linked draught beer, steep-rowed stands, and raucous pilgrims. Said Bob Broeg: "The spiritual following was enormous." To Middle America, going to St. Louis meant a sort of coming home.

As we have seen, the bathhouse had two tenants. The 1902–'53 Browns played Anna, a salaried governess, to the Cardinals' Royal Palace of

Siam. Its King was as great a Falstaff as any player who ever lived. In 1931, then–general manager Branch Rickey said of his chatterbox pitcher, "I'm a man of some intelligence. I've had some education, passed the bar, practiced law. I've been a teacher, and I deal with men of substance, statesmen, business leaders, the clergy. Then *why*"—he demanded, mumbling to himself—"do I spend my time arguing with Dizzy Dean?"

Ol' Diz won 18 games in 1932. He won or topped twenty the next four years. In 1947, Dean became a Browns announcer. They needed him, once drawing 80,922 for a *year*. "These peanut guys are going through the stands," Diz said one day of a vendor. "They is not doing so good because there is more of them than there is of customers."

The Browns were of, but preceded, Lake Woebegone. On August 19, 1951, their poem of bleakness lifted when 20,299 trooped into the grandstand to celebrate the AL's silver anniversary. Between games of a doubleheader Eddie Gaedel, 26, a three-foot-six-inch midget wielding a miniature bat, sprang from a three-tiered paper-mâché birthday cake and marched toward the plate.

The uniform number ⅛ graced the vaudeville actor's back. "It was all [owner Bill] Veeck's idea," the Browns Ned Garver said. "He'd inked Gaedel to a contract, and when the midget got to the plate, he showed it to the umpire. The crowd was going bananas, and all Gaedel did at Veeck's orders was stand up there, motionless, in a deep crouch, and take four balls."

None came nearer the plate than the Browns did to first place.

Another classic hearth was Brooklyn's shooting gallery of a parlor. The Dodgers fled Ebbets Field in 1957. Enduring is a Flatbush of the mind.

"Just being in Brooklyn was amazing," said longtime Dodgers shortstop Pee Wee Reese. "It was like entering a bar and saying, 'Hi ya, Ben,' or 'How you doing, Joe?' The damn stands were right on top of you."

At Ebbets Field you got a good view from almost all its 32,111 seats— if you weren't behind a post. It tied housewife Hilda Chester (with cow bell) and pygmy size (the left-center field lured balls like flypaper) and combination cement wall/scoreboard/wire mesh screen in right. One ad penned a Dodger parable—"Watch for Danny Kaye in *The Secret Life of Walter Mitty*." Another hailed clothier Abe Stark at the scoreboard base—"Hit Sign, Win Suit."

Both joined other goings-on of memory. Umpire George Magerkurth, knocked out by a Giants fan. The bird that flew out of Casey Stengel's hat. Leo Durocher, lancing Van Lingle Mungo: "He talked like Edgar Bergen doing Mertimer Snerd from the bottom of a well. And he drank a bit. A bit of everything."

In Brooklyn, baseball *was* the fans.

One legatee lay 150 miles to the north and east. A visit blurred blue caps and red hose and low-cut stirrups and ageless RED SOX across heaving woolies; vendors and police and skim of smoke across the field; sunlight of early summer or darkness of early fall; fielder crouched, batter cocked, and pitcher draped against the grandstand—above all, the surety that there is no place that you would rather be.

"All folks know is how Tom Yawkey fixed it after buying it [in 1933]. Before then it was a joke," write Til Ferdenzi said of Fenway Park. "I grew up here, and remember how lots of chairs didn't have bottom parts. There were bird turds on seats. And if you wanted a long nap—boy, this was the place to go."

Bart Giamatti was 10 when his father, hand-in-hand, first took him to Fenway—by then (1948), a bandbox bijou. "We went through the tunnel," he said, "and saw emerald grass and bases whiter than I'd ever seen"—also, sharp angles, low fences, asymmetrical alleys, scarce foul terrain, and left-field wall topped by a 23-foot screen. Fenway sent baseball's ribbon of news to Kittery, Maine, and Mystic, Connecticut, and Montpelier, Vermont. All inhaled the high deeds and low comedy of New England's team.

In 1999, the Yawkeys vowed to build a new park that would seat 44,130, have luxury boxes, and rise as the Sox played at their '12 arcade. "And now Boston knows," wrote Ed Linn of Ted Williams' 1960 retirement, "how England felt when it lost India." Pray that Gibraltar tumbles and, yes, the Rockies crumble before we lose Fenway Park.

It seemed impossible for baseball in this age to snatch defeat from the jaws of victory. "Anywhere you went—the fans would be calling up to you," announcer Red Barber said. "Anything could happen at Ebbets Field." The Redhead smiled. "Yes-sir," he said, finally, "and usually did." Ibid., other outposts of baseball's classic trace.

Forbes Field brandished "the loveliest setting of any major-league field, with tree-filled Schenley Park and University of Pittsburgh's towering Cathedral of Learning out beyond 12-foot-high left-field wall," wrote *Sports Illustrated*. "Box seats directly behind home plate have limited vision because of flat-floor construction. Best spots are first-floor boxes behind first or third base, and also reserved seats beyond fourth row in same general area."

At Crosley Field, seats filled a "Sun Deck" pavilion (a.k.a. "Moon" at night). Cincinnati led the league in smallest size (27,603) and turf (387 to center) and most lemonade sales and brown-bagging out-of-towners. They saw the bigs' night inaugural (May 24, 1935), first pitcher to toss two straight no-hitters (Johnny Vander Meer '38), and player to row over an outfield fence (when the Ohio River flooded). Dingers dented cars at an adjacent laundry. Fielders turned luckless on a left-field terrace. "The Reds taught you how to go up the incline," said converted catcher Ernie Lombardi upon falling. "They just didn't teach you how to come down."

Careers toppled elsewhere. At Baker Bowl, a fan amended right field's Lifebuoy Soap sign: "The Phillies use Lifebuoy and they *still* stink." In 1938, the Quakers joined the A's at Shibe Park. Sight was intimate (two decks encased three-fourths of the field), outfield, large (center took a 468-foot belt), and fans, boo-birds who knew baseball more than breeding. Twelve times the 1938–'49 A's and Phillies placed eighth in an eight-team league.

For forty years, Chicago's South Side hailed like calamity. The 1919 Black Sox took a pennant at white-cubed Comiskey Park. In 1959, Nellie Fox and Luis Aparicio helped "Go-go" win again. Comiskey seemed closer than 15 blocks from the stockyards when wind blew from the west. By contrast, air brightened ninety miles away: The first big–league team to change cities in half a century—the Braves of Boston since 1876—fled anonymity to briefly bathe in Milwaukee's love.

The '50s Braves forded a river of handclapping through Wisconsin, upper Michigan, and parts of Minnesota, Illinois, and Iowa. Burghers waved cowbells, bore rain and snow, and ate bratwurst on rye. County Stadium became, a writer said, "an insane asylum with bases." The Indians crazed *their* public at tiny League Park (22,000 capacity, and 290 feet down the right field line) and a too-large goliath. Municipal Stadium sat on Cleveland's north rim, ¼ mile from downtown, and opened in 1932. Giant (74,208-seat) size reaped peewee luck.

The 1934–'46 Indians played weekday and Saturday at League Park. In 1947, they deserted it for the huge lakefront bowl. At first, Nirvana: The '48 Tribe won the Series. Then, *memento mori*. Luke Easter hit Municipal's longest homer. One day Vic Power stole home twice. Len Barker threw a perfect game. Nothing helped Cleveland crush a vengeful Deity.

To a goodly portion of Ohio, statistics rang like chimes. Last pre-1995 title, '54; last pennant race, 1959; once in the first division since '63. When the '49 Tribe was eliminated, now-owner Veeck buried the 1948 flag beyond the center-field fence. For success, you motored to Tiger (née Briggs) Stadium (neé Navin Field)—three hours and a world away.

Even as a boy I loved Tiger Stadium. Its center-field flagpole lay 440 feet from home plate. An upper-deck right-field overhang turned routine flies into two-run homers. The empyrean housed more than 54,000, yet reeked of intimacy. Said my sister on entering it:"I feel like I'm back in Lassie League!"

In 1975, Joe Falls wrote: "The Boston writers, the Chicago writers, even the New York writers, the most provincial of all, tell you they like watching games in Detroit's ballpark. They have been to the other cities and they have seen the gleaming new stadiums. They have seen the massive steel and concrete ovals and have dined in the plush stadium clubs." Detroit was different. It gave you the game. "The people turn out in sport shirts, T-shirts, undershirts, and sometimes no shirts at all," Falls mused. "For a buck and a half, the bleachers are the best buy in town. You can get a sunbath and get on the other center fielder's nerves and maybe even get a girl."

By the 1990s Baltimore's Camden Yards bred heirs from Cleveland to Seattle. Each had private suites, vaunted hip cuisine, and spurned pedestrian look and feel. Suddenly, Tiger Stadium's core brooked a catch-up gloss. The team said that rebuilding it would be quixotic. Too expensive. Little parking. Corporate boxes couldn't fit in a Wilsonian drawer. In 1999, the cabaret closed where Goslin dazzled, McLain cavorted, and Kaline played ball. It still seems as real as any relative.

"When you walk into Detroit's ballpark, you know you are no place else in the world," Falls had written. A wonder of classic parks is that Tiger Stadium was not alone.

In 1955, the Athletics fled Philadelphia for a sturdy mirror of Middle America. Their playpen—Kansas City's 30,611-seat Municipal Stadium— had turquoise seats, a pitcher's feel, and children's zoo in foul territory. A mechanical rabbit popped out of the ground behind the plate with balls for the umpire. A mule—Charlie O., named for owner Charles O. Finley—grazed beyond the right-field fence. People knew the jackass. Two years later, apostasy: Baseball dealt Ebbets Field for a site built for track and field. Los Angeles Memorial Coliseum braved a 251-feet left-field pole, center-field stands nearly 700 feet from home plate, and 93,000-seat capacity. ("It's the only place," began a *mot*, "that can hold almost a hundred thousand people and two outfielders.")

Surrealism crowned the New World Dodgers—Wally Moon's wrong-field drives ("Moon Shots") falling, like chips, over the forty-feet-high left-field screen; record hordes, advent of the trumpet blare, "CHA-A-A-R-G-E!," sport's ongoing call to arms, and a distant fan who said of baseball-watching in this freakish yard, "It was like a game in pantomime. My seat was in another time zone."

In 1962, the ex-Brooks found Coronado in the five levels, surpassing beauty, and flowering lawn of Dodger Stadium. New York's other expatriate found fool's rush, not gold. The 1958–'59 Giants played at San Francisco's 22,900-seat Seals Stadium. Many bought transistor radios. A visitor thought them hearing aids: thus, "the City of the Deaf." The '60 Giants moved to larger Candlestick Park. Advantage, weather: freezing nights, peanut shells that hindered fielders, and sudden sandstorms that hampered play.

Built on a point, Candlestick became a testament to wind. Stu Miller was blown off the mound in the '61 All-Star Game. "There were years," Willie Mays said, "I figure the wind cost me an easy fifteen homers."

Mays' heart still abided in New York—specifically, the oblong café at 157th and 159th Streets and Eighth Avenue. Each classic park had personality. None was more gloriously absurd than the park across the Harlem River from Yankee Stadium, flowing gently to the sea.

"Memory," wrote Alexander Chase, "is the thing you forget with." Not at the Polo Grounds. It had a burlesque scope (left and right field were 279 and 257 feet away. Mays owned its Sahara [483 feet away] of a center), patchwork quilt of girders, pigeon stoops, and roofed bullpen shacks, and emerald turf that shrouded the horizon. Remembering: John McGraw's ten flags, 1921 Giants–Yankees' first all-New York Series, and Carl Hubbell buoying Heywood Broun. "During the reign of Hubbell," the writer mused, "first base itself was a marathon route."

In 1951, Bobby Thomson hit his Home Run Heard 'Round the World to write "The Miracle of Coogan's Bluff." Giants manager Leo Durocher later said, "Show me a good loser and I'll show you an idiot." One day in 1957, bony-kneed Bob Prince won a bet by waltzing five hundred feet from the clubhouse in center field to home plate carrying a briefcase and clad in stockings, pumps, a fluorescent jacket, bow tie, and red bermuda shorts.

"That's how it was in every park," said the Pirates voice. "Wild, different memories." At Ebbets Field, Gladys Goodding played the organ. In Pittsburgh, live bands were—ouch—instrumental. At Milwaukee, the denizens sang with gusto equal to their beer. Before ballparks turned generic, even the National Anthem carved a Grand Canyon of a divide.

6

DOWN ON THE FARM

Red Orsmby once made a horrid call behind the plate. A woman screamed, "If you were my husband, I'd give you poison." The umpire struck back: "Lady, if you were my wife, I'd take it." Philadelphia's plat at West Lehigh Avenue and North 21st Street poisoned fans weaned on ad-hoc wooden parks.

Shibe Park marked a dividing line that, once crossed, few would double back upon. The 1909–'70 cabash touted the first baseball ramps, umpire and visiting team rooms, terra-cotta trim above each archway and window, and the cupola—the age's sky box. It was the first double-decked arena, built by modern material and design. "For the first time," said Joseph Spear, chief architect, the Kansas City firm of Helmuth, Obata and Kassabaum (HOK Sport), "the top half of a deep single deck could be cut off, lifted, and pushed forward." Upshot: people closer to, if higher from, the field.

After Shibe, supports linked most ballpark upper and lower levels. Said Spear: "They brought fans nearer the diamond than was ever possible in the wooden-seat age." Pro: Parks were fashioned to fit the game.

Con: Sad sacks behind the posts brooked partial view. Looking back, the trade helped make "players . . . identifiable as recognizable human beings," wrote *Sports Illustrated* columnist Ron Fimrite, "not, as in the newer parks, dimly seen as remote and faceless figurines."

HOK Sport designed most of baseball's 1990s "new old" theaters. Each gained from early 1900s technology and concrete and structural steel. "That did it," Spear observed. "It revolutionized ballpark design and construction." Concrete and steel let planners round facade angles behind the plate, extend stands down each foul line, and spawn the double deck.

Spear smiled. "In 1909," he said, "Pennsylvania was the heart of our booming steel industry." Check the grid. Connect the lines. The Keystone State fired baseball's first two steel-and-concrete kilns.

"**B**aseball parks," photographer Jim Dow has written, "are the contemporary equivalent of cathedrals. They're the outgrowth of that medieval ideal. They show the aspirations of their community." Shibe inveigled with its green wall and intruding fans and seamless web of angled blocks and planes and triangles. Its playhouse staged the perfect meritocracy—fans sunning; hand-painted signs on the outfield fence; players sweating in close-up shots; the main gate column that became Shibe's prosopopoeia.

By 1942, Baker Bowl hosted the Alpine Musical Bar. Said '38–75 announcer Byrum Saam: "Talk started about building an indoor sports arena." Instead, Baker fell in '50: Today's site melds a car wash, parking lot, gas station, and bus garage. Seven blocks away Shibe housed the 1909–'54 A's and 1938–'70 Phillies. The 5,100-seat Deliverance Evangelistic Church now vaults brick and concrete, stands 108 feet tall at the tip of the cross, and includes a gym, day-care center, chapel, and sanctuary. Take the pulpit, near first base: Reverie links Dick Sisler (homering to win a flag) and Dick Stuart (treating grounders like Kryptonite) and Jimmie Foxx (hitting balls over tall buildings in a single bound). "Think religion has ghosts?" Saam wondered. "Try baseball in Philadelphia."

In 1901, Ban Johnson asked Cornelius McGillicuddy to manage Philly's AL charter A's. Both tapped minority stockholder Ben Shibe. "He was a baseball manufacturer," said once–voice Bill Dyer. "He also shared Mack's wish to build a temple to the game." Their sanctum rose, in under a year, on 5¾ acres of North Philadelphia farmland, on the former site of a brickyard and city pound. Sod arrived from Columbia Park. Hitters did a double take.

"Buildings didn't abut the park," said Saam, "so distances weren't limited." Left and right field measured 360 feet in early '09. They rose/fell by August to 378 and 340. Alleys and center were 393 and 515, respectively. An eight-foot wall ringed the outfield. Bleachers flanked the lines: Each covered a garage, which held 200 cars.

Baker's largest pre–'09 crowd, 23,377, watched the Phils and Pirates in August 1908. Shibe's debut—April 12, 1909—combined 30,162 payees, 5,000 guests or gatecrashers, and others on nearby roofs. Mayor John E. Reyburn threw out the first ball. Ten thousand packed a slope behind the outfield. Cincinnati 1860s shortstop George Wright yapped: "It's the greatest sight I've ever seen." Cheerily offhand, baseball loves ritual. The ticket window opened at 12:15 P.M. At 7 A.M., first-in-line George McFadden mimicked Charlemagne again nearing Spain.

Absent were later stages of Philly angst—a creased forehead, the weary face, pursed lips, the plaintive sigh. A's win! 8–1, over Boston behind Eddie Plank.

Growing up, how does a body learn baseball? Falling in love with a team. To me, the Senators meant the cellar; Red Sox, Dead Sox; Pirates, line drives to the alley. From faraway parks came simian sounds and static-lapped voices. The Mets existed only when the Yanks were rained out.

Baseball teems with dynasties less robotic than methodical. Ruth and Gehrig. Boys of Summer. M&M Boys. Big Red Machine. The 1910–'14 Philadelphia Athletics won four flags, three World Series, and more games than any club. Forget the '64 Phils. Shibe became a pastiche of hits and runs and fancy. Most players regarded academe like Sunday school in Hades. By contrast, Mack hired college men—Jack Barry (Holy Cross), Chief Bender (Carlisle), Eddie Collins (Columbia), Jack Coombs (Colby), and Plank (Gettysburg). Inverting, say, Buddy Rosar, the Taft/Wilson A's threw mellowspeak a curve.

Picture McGillicuddy, tall and gaunt, in suit and tie, a scorecard in one hand, signaling to fielders from the dugout, his name trimmed to fit a box score. Mack liked piety and privacy, using a) a weathervane to signal hitters, and b) opera glasses to steal signs from a building beyond right-center. "That's Connie," laughed Saam. "Whatever it took to win."

In 1910, it took Coombs (31–9) and Bender (23–5) and Cy Morgan (18–12). Mack's "$100,000 infield" (first to third, Barry, Collins, Stuffy McInnis, and Frank [Home Run] Baker) put the Athletics in the money—their first Series since '05. Coombs beat the Chicago Cubs thrice. The A's won, four games to one. At age 10, they seemed the very practitioner of baseball's quality and code.

The 1905 Giants beat Mack to win the NL's first Oktoberfest. In '11, the teams met again. "In '05 John McGraw put the Giants in special uniforms," said Jack Redding, "black except for white stripes and socks. Now out they came once more." Christy Mathewson edged Bender, 2–1. Baker's Game Two homer beat Rube Marquard, 3–1. Home Run then touched Big Six for a Game Three tying, nickname-making blast (A's, 3–2.) "In those days," said New York's Fred Snodgrass, "hitting two homers in two days was extraordinary." Bender took Sets Four and Six. Mack had another title.

"I still think my 1912 team was my best of that era," he later said, "but Joe Wood kept winning those games [34–5 for Boston]." Mack took his third World Series in 1913. By now, victory grew around Shibe Park like vines on a trellis.

In 1900, eight thousand automobiles saw the USA. By 1914, more than four million did—up nearly 50,000 percent. Ford and Chevrolet ads flanked Quaker Wheat Berries. The former head of Princeton University brayed a reformer's zeal. "We are not put unto this world to sit still and know," said Woodrow Wilson before becoming president. "We are put into it to act."

The '14ers won Philly's fifth pennant in 10 years. Collins hit .344. Bender, Plank, and Bob Shawkey won 47 games. Clearly they augured gold. "Sure, the [Miracle] Braves had come on," said Lee Allen. Last on July 18, they won 68 of their final 87 games. "Still, the A's would beat 'em, right? The Braves didn't even have a home-field presence"—moving Series games to larger Fenway Park, upwardly mobile before its time.

A Series first and last: Mack and Boston manager George Stallings wore street garb. By October 13—Boston .243 catcher Hank Gowdy batted .545, including three doubles, triple, and homer; the Braves won each game—a Philadelphian had his choice: dry cleaning, or fumigation.

The nineteenth-century British statesman Benjamin Disraeli muttered, "It was worse than a crime—it was a blunder." To many, Mack now committed both: Needing cash, he stripped A's from baseball's alphabet.

"Where to begin?" asks the mosquito in the nudist camp. With Plank, 305–181. In 1915, he left for St. Louis of the Federal League. Bender thrice led the AL in winning percentage. Herb Pennock '12–'34 was 241–162. Four times Shawkey won 20 or more games. Coombs took 158. All moved to FL Baltimore, the Red Sox, Yankees, and Ebbets Field.

One bad turn deserved another. Barry went to Fenway. Collins tumbled to Chicago. Baker led the 1911–'12–'13–'14 AL in dingers. "Connie needed money," said Saam, "so he cut Baker's pay." In turn, Baker retired, returned, and was peddled to the Yankees. "His wife died in 1920. So he sat out another year. When he came back, the dead ball was gone." In '21, Babe Ruth bopped 59 homers. Baker seemed an oddity.

Ruth had less subtlety than a Jack Dempsey jab. The gentler Mack's farewell launched a KO to Philly's head. Germany unveiled poison gas. The U.S. Coast Guard surfaced. The 1915 A's won 43 games. Seven straight years they finished last. Some fixed 1911–'14 to the '20s detriment. Others shunned them like a locked room in a deserted house. "What a contrast," said Allen. "Once the A's couldn't miss a break." On May 15, 1912, Ty Cobb attacked a heckler. Ban Johnson suspended him. Incensed, the Tigers staged a sympathy strike. On May 18, Detroit fielded sandlotters at Shibe. The A's raked Allan Travers, 24–2. He later became a Jesuit priest. The A's began to rebuild their church.

In 1913, Mack added left-field seats and covered the pavilion. "Envision the park," a journal read. "Stands reach to the center-field flagpole." In 1925, more reworking: A second tier tied third and first base, respectively, to center and right's corner. "Seventy percent of the park was now double-decked," Lewis noted. "Shibe stayed there for the rest of its life." Oddments merged: Left field traded 380 (1921) via 344 ('22) for 312 ('26). Left-center rose from 387 to 405. Right '21–'26 dumped 380 for 307. Center dwindled from 502 to '22's 468. "Notice the trend starting here," said Allen, "clubs moving fences in, then out, trying for the home-field advantage"—baseball's millennium in the morn. Mack's mound was 20 inches—the bigs' highest. Mezzanine seats upped capacity to 33,000. Nothing ushered profit to the door.

Shibe Park became a reverse Midas September 8, 1916. Eighteen paid to watch the once-dynasty duel New York.

In 1928, Jimmie Foxx joined the A's. One day he hit against the Yankees. Pitcher Lefty Gomez kept spurning his catcher's signs.

Bill Dickey finally bearded the reluctant warrior. "How the hell do you want to pitch to Foxx?"

"To tell the truth," Gomez said. "I'd rather not pitch to him at all."

Think of Ken Griffey, Jr., baseball's Strong-arm Kid, or Mark McGwire, swinging like Big Klu by way of the Bambino. Ralph Kramden in TV's *The Honeymooners* vowed to send wife Alice "to the moon." Some say that's where Foxx's pokes landed. Double X hit 302 of his 534 homers with the 1925–'35 Athletics. In 1932, he whacked 58—and lost two more to rain. Said Bob Feller: "Jimmie Foxx could hit a home run over most walls with half a swing." The righty hitter loved Shibe's left-field wall.

Foxx's cast was abiding to a Philadelphian. Born in Milwaukee, Aloys Syzmanski led Mack to long, "Oh, how I wish I had more players named Al Simmons." In 1926, he got 253 hits; '27, averaged .393; '30–'31, won batting titles. Mickey Cochrane '29–'31 hit from .331 to .359. George Earnshaw won 67 games. As a boy, Lefty Grove taught himself pitching by throwing rocks. The man went 31–4 in 1931. Eight times he won 20 or more games. ERA titles bound '30–'33. Poised and spiky, he was even better than his record. "He lived for pressure," said Simmons, "the crucial game."

Recalling Mack's 1915–'16 purge, the A's roster made you pinch yourself. It was '10–'14 again. The '29ers won the pennant. Mack teased reporters the day before the Series: Who would pitch against the Cubs? Earnshaw or Grove. His choice seemed burlesque: Red Sox retread Howard Ehmke, 35, to start a game where only the nerveless need apply.

"Ehmke hadn't pitched much," Simmons noted, "so Connie thought he'd surprise. He had him spend the last month following the Cubs around." The A's won, 3–1: Ehmke fanned 13, a Series high. A day later Earnshaw beat Chicago, 9–3. At Shibe, the Cubs took Game Three (3–1) and led Four (8–0, in the seventh). "Simmons comes up, hits one out," said former writer Ken Smith. "Five of the next six guys single. Then Hack Wilson loses [Mule] Haas' fly in the sun, and it turns into a three-run inside the park homer." The 10-run frame set a Series record, whip-sawed the Classic, and beat the Cubs, 10–8. Baseball hailed a sensational, spectacular, unanswerable game.

Chicago led Match Five, 2–0. "Comes the ninth inning," Mack recalled, "and Haas homers and Simmons and Bing Miller double." The necropsy: A's, 3–2. Ehmke never won another big-league game.

"[In 1930] most teams could have used me," Ehmke mused. The NL batted .303. Each Cardinals regular hit more than .300. Foxx smashed 37 homers and 156 RBIs. Mack won his eighth flag with seven future Hall of Famers. They played against a backdrop of avenging, command-ing names.

To wit: the Rajah, the Fordham Flash, the Iron Horse, the Lip, Marse Joe, the Wild Horse of the Osage, the Mechanical Man. Respectively: Rogers Hornsby; Frankie Frisch, buskined and urbane; Henry Louis Gehrig, the Pride of the Yankees, a quiet man, a hero; Leo Durocher; Joseph Vincent McCarthy, Philadelphian by birth and Victorian by bent; Pepper Martin, termed by Durocher "a hellion in cleats"; Charlie Gehringer, of whom a teammate said, "He'd say hello at the start of spring training and good-bye at the end of the season, and the rest of the time he let his bat and glove do all the talking for him." Another name— Mickey Cochrane, a.k.a. Black Mike—tweaked baseball's stagey, white-maned prosecutor/judge.

"He got his job," tweaked Will Rogers of Kenesaw Mountain Landis, not through the *New York Times*. "Somebody said, 'Get that old boy who sits behind first. He's out there every day anyhow.' So they offered him a season pass and he jumped at it." A team's play can be unprint-able; '29 Series language was. After Game Four, Landis called managers Mack and McCarthy to his room. "If these vulgarities continue, I'll fine the culprits a full Series share." Mack warned his players. In turn, Cochrane mocked the Cubs: "After the game we'll serve tea in the clubhouse." Mack winced: Landis might impose a fine. Instead, he shook Cochrane's hand after Earnshaw's Game Five–winning, Series-clinching win. Said the Judge: "Where's the tea?"

The 1930s A's won a second straight title. Then, in 1931, the Cardinals' Martin formed a bridge between unlikelihood and myth. "We're disappointed [over St. Louis' Series victory]," said Iron Mike, "but with our team we'll be back." Again Mack began hari-kari—the act, not announcer. Like 1910–'14's, the team broke up: In 1933–'35, Mack sold Cochrane to Detroit, peddled Simmons and Dykes to Comiskey, sent Foxx to Boston. Cochrane won two more pennants. Double X hit a Red Sox record 50 homers in '38. Slowly, Shibe restocked its what-might-have-been reserve.

FORBES FIELD

Rivalry links geography and memory. Cubs–Cardinals. Red Sox–Yankees. Giants–Dodgers—baseball's Athens and Sparta. Bill Terry sniped, "Is Brooklyn still in the league?" Juan Marichal clubbed John Roseboro. Willie McCovey owned Don Drysdale. All dispelled the notion that baseball is a noncontact sport.

The Phillies' main rival played 305 miles to the west in a neighborhood of Pittsburgh that conjured the uptown soda fountain, matronly librarian, and streets of leaves, stick dams, and unlocked homes. "You had the smell of grass, could park six blocks away, take a walk through the neighborhood," ex-Pirates mikeman Bob Prince etched their '09–'70 abode. "The House of Thrills it was, and in memory still is."

Forbes Field evolved from envy: That Ben Shibe's green and tended yard! In fall 1908, Pirates owner Barney Dreyfuss began a search for the idyll—James Fenimore Cooper wrote a novel, *Satanstoe,* about such a site—that "will make them forget [Shibe Park]," he told friend and baron Andrew Carnegie. Dreyfuss's tract in the future Oakland-Schenley section sat three miles from the business district. "There was nothing there but a livery stable and a hot house, with a few cows grazing over the countryside. A ravine ran through the property [ultimately, right field]. I knew the first thing necessary to make it suitable for baseball was to level off the entire field."

Critics panned downtown's snub. Oakland Orchard! Dreyfuss Folly! Barney smiled. His park would be expandable, accessible by trolley car, and far from the smog of mills. Ultimately, Forbes billed pine cover, a gaping lawn, ivied left-field wall, double-decked right-field pavilion, and sun-baked infield where players (see Tony Kubek, 1960 Series) despaired of their lives. In '09, the ravine was filled, ground leveled, and building begun on the suburban cabin.

"We shape our buildings," Churchill said. "Thereafter, they shape us." Racetrack architect Charles Leavitt had designed New York's Belmont Park. He now shaped a park named chiefly to atone. Dreyfuss had fled Germany at 17 to escape military training. [John] Forbes Field hailed the French and Indian War general who bivouacked troops in Oakland, captured Fort Duquesne in a decisive battle, and in 1758 renamed it Fort Pitt.

Many parks are functional. Some sport vision. Others dab a past almost rhapsodically square. Forbes' '09 all-of-the-above yoked the junction of Bigelow Boulevard, Joncaire Street, the Cathedral of Learning, and another French and Indian name—(General Henry) Bouquet (sic Boquet) Street after the Swiss soldier who aided the Brits at Fort Duquesne. In the early 1900s a fractured melting pot—Slavs, Poles, Italians, Germans—trooped to southwest Pennsylvania. Some proceeded to the flatlands of the Middle West. Thousands stayed among the hills and rivers that split the forest like aorta through the heart.

The Roman Quintilian wrote, "It is feeling . . . that makes us eloquent." In an urban, harsh, and sterile world—even then—Pittsburgh's feeling linked rock and stand and floral glens. Forbes became both pleasance and pioneer.

Men worked double shifts to open it on schedule. Forbes rose in 122 days. On June 30, 1909, 30,338 swamped the 25,000-seat park. Thousands stood behind a rope barrier. Johnny Evers hit the first pitch for a single. The Cubs won, 3–2.

Dreyfuss hymned I told you so. "One friend bet me a $150 suit we would never fill the park, and we filled it five times the first two weeks." The Bucs yawl aired two decks from beyond first to the left-field line.

Right abutted Schenley Park. Left and center seats rimmed a 12-foot wooden fence. Behind the plate, player and umpire clubhouses propped the grandstand. Beyond it, yawning turf (left to right, 360, 442, and 376 feet. Deepest: left-center's 462 flagpole) put the kibosh on homers.

In 1910, the Reach *Baseball Guide* wrote: "The formal opening of Forbes Field . . . was an historic event, the full significance of which could be better felt than described. Words must fail to picture in the mind's eye adequately the splendors of the magnificent pile President Dreyfuss erected as a tribute to the national game, a beneficence to Pittsburgh and an enduring monument to himself. For architectural beauty, imposing size, solid construction, and public comfort and convenience, it has not its superior in the world"—ibid., Forbes' first-year Bucs.

The '09ers had a 2.07 ERA, won 110 games, and drew a league third-best 534,950. The Series began, serving youth: Rookie Babe Adams beat Detroit, 4–1, before 29,264 at Forbes. Game Two changed umpiring more than Richie Phillips. In the first inning Dots Miller drove to right. "The ball's going toward the bleachers," plate umpire Billy Evans said, "and fans sitting on the field in front of the barrier stand up. This messes my vision and that of [partner Bill] Klem's."

Helpless, Evans asked where the ball landed. "It was a home run," a fan said, pointing to the turf, "the ball landed there." In baseball's bible, only God eclipses the men in blue. "If it landed there before bouncing into the stands," Evans said, "it's a ground-rule double." Next day he urged baseball's governing body, the National Commission, to plant backup umpires on each line. "Up to now, you've made them sit in a box seat," Evans told it. "Why not help them save us from embarrassment?"

The Series resumed in the city of Lions and Tigers and (by train) even Bears. Detroiters gaped as the first Pirate batted. Four umpires graced the field.

On October 16, Adams hurled his third complete-game victory to win the Series. Forbes drew 81,885 acolytes—"more in three games," said former *Pittsburgh Press* writer Les Biederman, "than the entire Series of '07 or '8." The Bucs galley presaged the atypical. One day two Pirates led off base. "[Christy] Mathewson was pitching. There's so little light he has to approach the catcher to see his signs." The batter lined to right-center. Suddenly, lightning lit the ball like a scene from *The Natural*. "Amazin'," marveled Red Murray. "It helped me make a barehand catch." DeMille could not have staged it better.

No one threw a no-hitter in Forbes' 4,728 matches. Unassisted triple plays, on the other hand, seemed more common than the cold. In 1925, Pirates shortstop Glenn Wright caught Jim Bottomley's liner, stepped on second to double Jimmy Cooney, and tagged Rogers Hornsby before the Rajah could retouch first. Two years later, the now-Cub restaged his craft: Paul Waner lined out, Wright touched second, and *sans* clue Clue Barnhart ran into the waiting ball.

"To see the unusual, go to Forbes," a saying went. "The impossible, go twice." On September 1, 1890, Exposition Park hosted Brooklyn in baseball's first triple-header. Thirty years later, Forbes reprised its last three-for-the-price-of-one. "Three teams in each league got money from the Series pool," Biederman said. In 1920, the Bucs and Reds met to decide the third-place club. Cincinnati won, 13–4 and 7–3. The writer laughed. "The Bucs then won the meaningless third game [6–0]. The age was a stickler for rules." Chief Wilson '12 hit 36 triples—a still-bigs record. Al Mamaux '15 and Adams '20 hurled eight shutouts. Some parks stir taters. Forbes spurred the bunt, hit and run, speed, and defense.

In 1925, Dreyfuss grooved a lollipop to lefties: Two decks shrank right field from 376 to 300 feet. Pitching countered in '32: A 14½-foot in-play screen topped right's 9½-foot concrete wall. Left waxed from 360 to 365. Center field and the flagpole waned to 435 and 457. "Forbes was huge," said Kiki Cuyler '21–'27, who hit .312 lifetime and four times led the NL in steals. "Just one of the things that made it so special."

Forbes' oddities befit your uncle Fred. Cars and trucks were repainted and sold under the left-field seats. A small scoreboard draped center field. The backstop was baseball's farthest from home plate—110 feet. The batting cage was moved in 1923 to left-center from behind the plate. Both places were in play: too, the flagpole bottom and light tower cages in left-center, center, and right-center field.

Emotion warps reason. Reflection bronzes it. Biederman observed that "Forbes was big on eccentricity." He was not slighting history.

As Jack Paar would say, "I kid you not." The Pirates were the first to: use a tarpaulin (1906); put padding on the outfield wall ('30s); host an evening All-Star Game (1944); wear knit uniforms (1970); berth a night Series match (1971); and have a player go 7-for-7 in a nine-inning game (Rennie Stennett '75 at Wrigley Field). Forbes launched radio baseball on August 5, 1921. Station: KDKA, Pittsburgh. Announcer: Harold Arlin, 26. Score: Pirates 8, Phillies 5. Time of game: one hour and 57 minutes. Arlin used a telephone as microphone, sat behind the screen, and chatted as around a pot-bellied stove.

Westinghouse-owned KDKA debuted Election Night 1920: Harding over Cox, 404 electoral votes to 127. "We were looking for programming," Arlin said, "and baseball seemed a natural. I went out to Forbes Field and set up shop."

"Did everything work?" a reporter said.

Arlin formed a smile. "Sometimes the transmitter didn't work. Often the crowd noise would drown us out. We didn't know whether we'd talk into a total vacuum or whether somebody would hear us."

Like a centerfold, TV leaves little to fantasy. Radio leaves all. It is hard now to conceive retail stores mounting sidewalk speakers, or streets filled with play-by-play, like shopping malls with Musak. Harder: Arlin pinch-speaking for the Sultan of Swat.

Ruth arrived at Pittsburgh's William Penn Hotel to find a speech for KDKA delivery. "He was going on my show," Arlin said. "How could Babe flub words right in front of him? I introduce him and this big, garrulous guy—he can't say a word."

"Babe Ruth froze," the reporter said.

"Mute," he jabbed. "I grab the speech and now *I'm* Ruth. I read the script and Babe tries to compose himself, smoking and leaning against the wall. You know something? We pulled it off. I sign off and Babe Ruth hasn't made a sound."

Retrieve a time before fiber optics. The sound Forbes heard in the 1920s was the uncorking of champagne.

As Arlin canted, a free Nation neared in Ireland. In Baltimore, H. L. Mencken rebuked the "booboise." In Indiana, the Ku Klux Klan boasted nearly 500,000 members. Bookstores hawked Sherwood Anderson's *Winesburg, Ohio.* Sacco and Vanzetti forged a *cause célèbre.* Alcohol's "reign of terror is over," vowed ex–big leaguer and revivalist Billy Sunday. It yielded to Prohibition—and the hammerlock of organized crime.

The early '20s yoked speakeasies and raccoon coats and Clara Bow and Rudolph Valentino. Jack Dempsey became the Frank Merriwell of boxing. Pie Traynor threw ennui in the pit. "He'd scoop everything off the field—grass, dust, and gravel," a rival said, "and fling it over to first base with the ball. It was like a sandstorm—only worse." Honus Wagner retired in 1917. Traynor '20–'37 succeeded, but not supplanted, him: 2,416 hits, .320, and a palatine at third base. Said a writer: "So and so doubled down the left-field line, and Traynor threw him out."

Quietly, like a rivulet, the Bucs flowed with stars. Ten times Max Carey led the league in stolen bases. In 1924, Glenn Wright and Clyde Barnhart had 235 RBI. Find a greater year than Kiki Cuyler's '25: 220 hits, 144 runs, 26 triples, and .357. Vic Aldridge had a .682 winning percentage. Forbes now held 41,000 seats: Dreyfuss would need them for the Series v. Washington.

It opened October 7 before 41,723: D.C. 4, Bucs 1, the steady, fundamental way. "Pitching!" mourned manager Bill McKechnie. "Walter Johnson had it." The Senators soon fronted, three games to one. Aldridge won Match Five. Back at Forbes, Pittsburgh tied the Series: 43,810 crooned revival. "Indeed," said Voltaire, "history is nothing more than a tableau of crimes and misfortunes." The final game shouted Johnson's. The Big Train yielded 15 hits. "He might have survived even that," noted Traynor, "if his defense hadn't cracked."

Roger Peckinpaugh's eighth-inning homer gave the Nats a 7–6 lead. More recall the AL MVP's two late-inning muffs—his Series' seventh and eighth!—sowing four unearned runs. "I can still see Cuyler now," McKechnie said in 1955. "The errors had tied the score. Eighth, two out, bases full, Kiki fouling off pitch after pitch, then doubling to right to score the two final runs."

The Bucs won, 9–7, their first title since 1909 and last till '60. "It's been a long time coming," sang Crosby, Stills, Nash, and Young. Bill Mazeroski would be a long time gone.

It is doubtful that the Bucs knew this at the time. In 1927, exhausting providence seemed a universe away. The French soldier Marshal Ferdinand Foch once visited the Grand Canyon. "What a marvelous place," he observed, "to drop one's mother-in-law." Forbes was a great place to drop Cooperstown's sole brothers. Lloyd Waner—5'8½" "Little Poison"—hit .355 and ripped a still-rookie best 223 hits. "Big Poison"—brother Paul—staged a Musial '48/Mantle '56/ Yastrzemski '67 year: NL-high in average (.380), RBI (131), and four other categories.

That September, the Waner brothers hit "bounce home runs" at Redland Field. (Fair balls bouncing into seats were pre-'31 dingers). On October 1, Pittsburgh beat Cincy, 9–6, to win the flag. The rightness of things seized you—the Bucs in the Series!—except their foil was as great a team as ever lived.

"Keep in mind what was going on," said Lee Allen. "Lindbergh had just soloed the Atlantic. *The Jazz Singer* was going on [a talking movie]." Who was Helen Cane? The Boop-boop-be-doop Girl. "All America wanted to focus on was the Yankees." The pinstripes hit .307, clinched on Labor Day, and outhomered Pittsburgh, 158–54.

The Classic began October 5. After a 10 A.M. workout, "Traynor and the Waner brothers and other Pirates went into the stands to look us over," said Miller Huggins. "I thought I'd give them something to see." The Yankees manager told practice pitcher Waite Hoyt to hurl hard but down the middle. Earle Combs and Bob Meusel sprayed hits to Forbes' power alleys. Ruth and Gehrig tattooed Schenley Park. Yogi Berra said, "It ain't over till it's over." This Series was already. The Bombers swept. "There are teams," a writer said, "and there are the Yanks." It was easy to discern between the two.

Leaders are said to make a difference because they will, not wish, it. Lloyd Waner hit a lifetime .316. Paul Waner won three batting titles. Shortstop Arky Vaughn '32 topped the league at .385. Ted Williams was said to have had better than perfect vision. Vaughn's approached the Kid's: 937 walks and 276 Ks in 6,622 ups. The *Pittsburgh Press* styled the '30s Bucs: "L. Waner, P. Waner, Vaughn, and Traynor." Archetypal fan "Screech Owl" McAllister found each worth screaming by.

In 1932, Forbes tendered a rare two-league doubleheader: Pirates–Phils and Negro East-West League Homestead Grays—Philadelphia Hilldales.

The Grays' Josh Gibson treated Forbes like putt-putt golf. On May 25, 1935, Ruth hit the last three homers of the then-NLer's career. "I didn't think it would come down," said Guy Bush, yielding No. 714. "Leave it to Babe to [be first to] clear the [86-foot-high right-field] roof." Only 16 balls vaulted it: Willie Stargell hit five. Chuck Klein hit four homers in one 10-inning match. Pittsburgh gashed the Braves, 14–2, in Forbes' '40 nightlifter. Traded to Boston, P. Waner got hit 3,000 in 1942 off the Pirates' Rip Sewell.

In 1938, Pittsburgh finished two games behind the Cubs. "Dreyfuss had died in 1932," said Biederman. "His son-in-law, Bill Benswanger, was sure they were going to make the Series. So he ordered a new deck of seats [Crow's Nest] built on the grandstand roof [also, a press box with baseball's first elevator]." A visitor could leave through an exit gate in right-center field. On June 30, 1934, the Bucs lodged a Dreyfuss monument of bronze and granite to its left.

It seemed heartfelt, even natural, for what a writer dubbed "the Hialeah of ballparks." Recalling 1927, the Pirates were tired of win-place-show.

COMISKEY PARK

Former Texas governor John Connally once mused of the Vietnam/student protest/sexual revolution early 1970s, "Everything about it was big!" Everything was big about Comiskey Park 1910–'90 a.k.a. White Sox Park, Charles A. Comiskey's Baseball Palace, or Baseball Palace of the World. "Comiskey had visited both Forbes Field and Shibe Park," official baseball historian Jerome Holtzman said. He liked, and envied, them. In late 1909, the Sox president decided to move his team from South Side Park to a new address. In the argot of the day, he headed "upstairs," not uptown.

Comiskey hired Chicago architect Zachary Taylor Davis to build a shrine at the hub of West 34th and 35th Streets, Portland Avenue (now, South Shields Avenue), and South Wentworth Avenue (Dan Ryan Expressway). He broke ground on February 15, 1910. For luck, the Sox laid the green cornerstone on St, Patrick's Day. Later it became an article of faith that Comiskey Park was an accident waiting to occur. Not Opening Day, July 1: 32,000 overflowed the 28,000-seat park. Gaping, they found it grand.

"Hundreds of automobiles," the *Chicago Tribune* said, "carted spectators to the game." Four bands played. A military unit marched. The new park rose in five months for $750,000. (Forbes had cost $2 million.) Mixing myth, truth, and thunderclap, Reach hailed "a gala day in Chicago, and a red-letter day in the eventful life of the white-haired chief [Comiskey] of the Chicago American League club. The afternoon witnessed the formal opening and dedication of the White Sox's new ball park and the evening was devoted to . . . the historical event by a great banquet at which a host of notables, including most of the grandees of the baseball world, were the guests of Comiskey. A record-breaking crowd witnessed the opening game . . . at what may be without hesitation . . . declared to be the finest ball park in the United States." Sox rookie Lena Blackburne singled for Comiskey's first hit. Missing: runs. The Browns' Barney Pelty bested Ed Walsh, 2–0.

Return with us to their South Side of Chicago—blue collar, working class, Catholic, Irish, and Eastern European. They have an ardor for the underdog, work in stockyards and slaughterhouses, and abide the hardscrabble life. Their steel and concrete home wraps double-decked to the bases from home plate. A single tier trims the left and right-field wall. Comiskey is named the Old Roman. "He wanted an ornate facade," mused writer David Condon, "to fit his moniker." Funds lapse and a brick facing replaces it. Arch windows stud a classical look.

Its roots are less august; the park had been a truck garden and garbage dump. No buildings intrude to dent a fence. Comiskey can stretch distances, and has. Bill Veeck laughed, "He even had a committee visit other fields and then design the park. [Ed] Walsh was a member." The expanse—363 down the lines; 382 power alleys; 420 to center—trenches batters in belligerence.

In 1911–'12, Walsh twice pitched a complete-game twin bill. In late '13, Chicago began a tour of Australia, China, Japan, the Philippines, and Egypt. "They tie the Giants [3-all] in Cairo. The next day they make a triple play in the shadow of the Pyramids," said Veeck. "The good news that is they played a command performance [before King George] in London. The bad is that they sailed back on the [British luxury liner] *Lusitania*," torpedoed on May 3, 1915.

Eddie Collins arrived that spring to air a choke grip and *bonhomie*. One day pitcher Red Faber forbode Luis Aparicio. "We're ahead [4–2]," he said, "and Mack tries to delay the game hoping it'll rain. They hit me intentionally with a pitch. I figure I'll speed it up—so I start stealing hoping to get thrown out." The A's refused: Faber stole second, third, and home. The '15–'16 Sox finished third and second. You could hear the Old Roman's horselaugh. "Big" was around the bend.

Grab a pen, find paper, and begin. Q: When did the Cubs, Red Sox, and Indians last win a Series? Answer: 1906–'18–'48, respectively, recited like the Rosary. Name the White Sox' save-'19 last title. Hoseaphiles would like you to know.

"It's natural," said Condon, and he began to laugh. "The garish [1919] eclipses the good." The Black Sox caused baseball's quiet desperation. The '17ers preceded it. On May 5–6, Chicago was no-hit twice. The Sox then crooned the Fanfare of the (Un) Common Man. Happy Felsch had 102 RBI. Eddie Cicotte dwarfed Early Wynn's '59: 28–12 and 1.53 ERA. In June, Americans began arriving at Saint-Nazaire, a major World War I point of entry. On October 6 the Giants arrived for the Sox' first post-'06 Series. The Comiskeys soon made up for lost time.

Cicotte and Faber won, 2–1 and 7–2. The Classic moved to the Polo Grounds, where a turn of scenery unhosed the Sox, 2–0 and 5–2. Returning to Comiskey, the Giants led, 5–2, on six Sox errors. The ALers rallied: Faber, relieving, won again, 8–5. The Series reverted to Coogan's Bluff: Red v. Rube Benton. "Why not?" manager Pants Rowland said of Faber's fourth game/second start. "He throws the knuckleball. Pitching arms don't tire"—but fielders' arms can err.

Collins led off the fourth by grounding to Heinie Zimmerman. The third baseman threw wildly; Dave Robertson dropped a fly, Collins taking third; and Felsch grounded to Benton, who threw to Zimmerman. "Here's where the fun began," said Rowland. Heinie began chasing Collins toward home. Eddie eluded catcher Bill Rariden. Zim was last seen pursuing him across the plate. "*Goat?*" he bellowed. "Who the hell was I supposed to throw the ball to? Klem?" Chick Gandil singled for two runs. Sox win, 3–0! their second/last title.

Collins hit .409. Shortstop Buck Weaver batted .333. Catcher Ray Schalk snubbed a soupçon of doubt. "This is it," he roared. "This is what we're here for." The memory jarred during the long free fall ahead.

The 1920–'58 World Series spurned Comiskey Park. In 1918, it visited *sans* Sox. "The Cubs won the pennant, and Comiskey was bigger than Wrigley Field," said Condon, "so they moved three games there." A year later Chicago won the pennant by 3½ games: its Classic hump, Cincinnati. "I knew at the time that some finagling was going on," said the Reds Edd Rousch. "Rumors were flying all over the place."

Not flying: Comiskey's money. "Cheap!" cried pitcher Dickie Kerr. "Players hated it. But they played for him"—for a while. In 1919, Joe Jackson hit .351. Lefty Williams pitched 27 complete games. Cicotte's 29–7 became an orb of Sox hauteur. In Game One, he plunked the first batter. "It sent a pre-arranged sign to gamblers," Holtzman said. Cincinnati won, 9–1: The fix was on. Williams had walked only 58 for the year. He passed six in Match Two: Reds, 4–2. Back at Comiskey, Kerr won, 3–0. The '19 Hose batted .287. The next two days they got six hits and no runs: Cicotte and Williams lost again. How easy it was going to be—except that Chicago had won one of the first five games.

"Remember," Veeck noted, "the Series was then best-of-nine." Desperate, Comiskey hoped for a return to form. His players hoped to receive payola. Eight—Cicotte, Jackson, Felsch, Weaver, Charles (Swede) Risberg, Fred McMullin, Williams, and Gandil—had conspired to throw the Classic. "They'd done their part," said author Richard Lindberg. "Now they expected [gambler] Arnold Rothstein to do his." Dawdling, he irked them. Chicago won Games Six and Seven. October 9 ended the ignominy: Reds, 10–5; Williams retired one batter. Talk crested: Was the Series on the level?

Gandil and Cicotte, respectively, got $30,000 and $10,000. Jackson took $5,000, but hit a Sox-high .375. A year later Faber, Williams, Kerr, and Cicotte won 87 games. Said Condon: "You'd never know '19 was crooked." On September 28, 1920, a Chicago grand jury struck. "Eight Indicted! Query Goes On!" the *Tribune* blared. Comiskey suspended the now-Black Sox. A small boy outside the court presaged *Eight Men Out*: "Say it ain't so, Joe." Cicotte said it was. "I've lost everything," he said, "job, reputation, everything." The jury cleaved. "Not Guilty!" brayed the August 21, 1921 *Trib*. Jurors and defendants trekked to a restaurant. Commissioner Landis didn't care, banning the eight for life. The blow became a White Sox death sentence: Soon, they hoped merely to avoid miming Atlantis in the American League.

Kerr '21 quit baseball: "Damned if I'll take what that cheapskate bid." Faber's 25–15 filled the breach. Collins got his 3,000th hit. Schalk caught four no-hitters and made a putout at each base. In 1925, the Sox and Giants toured Europe. The French Baseball Federation gave Comiskey a silver medal. Queen Marie of Romania threw out a first ball. Cowboy Tom Mix lent Comiskey horse chips and his routine.

Chicago missed the first division from 1921–'35. Eight managers came and fled. The 1920 South Siders drew 833,492. In '32, 233,198 watched the Pale Hose shrink. "By now," said a writer, " '19 seemed another century."

The '27 Sox ditched Comiskey's wooden pavilion. Replacing it: a $1 million, twin-tiered outfield stand. "Nearly the entire park was roofed and double-decked. Only center ['s bleachers] were open," said Condon. "It was very intimate." Capacity rose to 52,000. Distances tottered. Foul lines: 365 (1927), 362, 342 ('34), 353, 340, and 352 (1937). Power alleys: 375 ('27), 370, and 382 ('42). Center: 455 ('27), 450, 436 ('34), 422, and 440 ('37). In 1934, the Sox got Al Simmons and moved the plate 14 feet toward the outfield. He flopped. It U-turned.

Frank Thomas became Chicago's '90s "Big Hurt." For 21 years Luke Appling hurt in another way—hence, "Old Aches and Pains." His forte was costly: Luke endlessly fouled balls. Comiskey died in 1931. "For a while," Veeck said, "he was tempted to make Luke pay for fouls hit to customers." Instead, OAAP hit .310 lifetime, won '36–'43 batting titles, and set a then-shortstop mark for chances, assists, putouts, and games. He also grasped the Pleasure Palace's old-timey feel.

"Appling was chasing a grounder," said Barnum Bill, "when he caught his cleats on a coffee pot in the ground from when Comiskey was a dump." It seemed *nouveau* on July 6, 1933. "That year Chicago had the Century of Progress world exhibition," Condon mused, "and [*Tribune* sports editor] Arch Ward wanted a sports event to complement it"—i.e., the All-Star Game, before 47,595, to raise money for a players' charity. Mack and McGraw managed. Said the latter: "We have a sell-out, a big crowd, a fine day, and I hope the best team wins." Ruth hit the first All-Star homer, off Wild Bill Hallahan.

The poet Goethe wrote, "I am the spirit that always denies." The pre-midcentury Sox seldom denied malaise. Comiskey hosted the first Negro Baseball All-Star Game: West 10, East 7. Its first night game lit '39: Sox 5, Browns 2. Give Ted Lyons a 260–230 record and A for symmetry: In 1942, his 20th year, he started 20, completed 20, and had an AL-best 2.10 ERA. "Hey-Hey!" boomed Jack Brickhouse on Chicago's first telecast—April 16, 1948, in an exhibition at Wrigley Field: Sox 4, Cubs 1. In a moment rich with feeling, the large man with a larger voice buoyed both sides of the Second City. None kept the Hose from a full-cycle bath.

In 1934, Jimmie Foxx hit the first ball into Comiskey Park's center-field bleachers. (Later: Hank Greenberg '38, Alex Johnson '70, Dick Allen '72, Richie Zisk '77, Tony Armas '84, and George Bell '85.) In 1938, pitcher Monte Stratton went hunting. An accident cost his leg. Bob Feller '40 blazed the AL's first opening-day no-hitter. "Don't look back," jabbed preternatural Satchel Paige. "Somebody might be gaining on you." Not the White Sox. On August 13, 1948, Paige pitched before 51,013 at Comiskey: Tribe, 5–0.

Rare 16-millimeter 1949 film shows Zeke Bonura sliding, Bobby Doerr covering second base, and a blur of type on the scoreboard. "Chicago Cardinals. Comiskey Park," read the script. "Pittsburgh Steelers, Washington Redskins, Los Angeles Rams, Philadelphia Eagles." The next year hardship spread. Ted Williams crashed into the left-field wall and broke his elbow in the All-Star Game. The Nationals won, 4–3, in 14 innings. "Some leagues are zero for a game," a Sox pitcher said. "Our team is zero for a decade."

The 1941–'50 Hose once made the first division. General manager Frank Lane arrived in '49 to rebuild—the field. An inner "homer fence" cut right and left to 332. Power alleys fell 20 feet to 362. A five-foot canvas wall shrank center from 440 to 420, then 415. (Pens moved from left and right foul ground to behind the fence.) The diminution helped—if you were a visitor.

"What a joke!" Lane later laughed. "We start on April 22. Eight games later, we've homered eight times, and the other guys 15!" The Good Neighbor Policy applies to state, not baseball: Lane vowed to kick the inner fence out of town. On June 5, he removed it before dawn: The Yankees opened at Comiskey that night. "Talk about luck!" he said. "I take it down. That night two of our guys hit drives that would a' been homers if I'd kept it up!"

The Sox hadn't made a World Series in thirty years. The more things change . . .

CROSLEY FIELD

In 1999, Mike Schmidt was named to baseball's All-Century Team. His rearview mirror kept Pollyanna from gripping the upper hand. "I loved Philly," the third baseman said, "but when I played, things were more subdued. You had those flying saucer–type stadiums. There was no atmosphere. You go to a game [today], and it's like a big party. I would have given anything to play in that atmosphere."

New old parks spring from the Real McCoy: a Forbes Field, Comiskey Park, the boomerang at Western and Findlay. The latter site— a.k.a. the Cincinnati Base Ball Grounds—housed the 1884–'89 American Association Reds. It was rebuilt for the NL, renamed League Park, burned, and reopened, then columned, expanded, and renamed Palace of the Fans. Light my fire: The *Palace* burned in 1911. Redland Field opened April 11, 1912: Reds 10, Cubs 6. "Eighty-six years [through 1970] in one place," said Ohioan Lee Allen, "the history of baseball's cradle."

Politics, or ball: Some want polarity to stop at the water's edge. Reds 1902–'27 president Garry Herrmann hated it even lapping at the shore. Example meant bipartisanship: Goodwill begot goodwill. On Dedication Day (May 18, 1912), Herrmann extended his hand to Ban Johnson (ex–Cincinnati sportswriter) and Charles Comiskey (1890s Reds manager). "That's baseball there," said Allen. "Its roots linked both leagues." Add to Cincinnati's *sangfroid* a fine feeling for the individual.

"And that's the wonder of this country," said Willy Loman in *Death of a Salesman*, "that a man can end [up] with diamonds here on the basis of being liked." It was easy to like the Reds' chalet. The backstop was 38 feet from home plate—baseball's shortest. Wedged into a grid, the patch favored pitchers: left to right, 360-420-360. A hillock sloping to the fence replaced the warning track. In early '27, the field was turned, plate moved toward center, length shrunk (339, 395, and 337), and size upped (30,000). It wed right-field seats, two outfield line pavilions, and double decks between the bases.

"Redland," said Herrmann, "attracts the wholesome and ordinary person." It evoked an America of fishing holes and Masonic Lodges and strawberry socials. "Perfect," he added, "for our town."

In 1788, settlers pushed south and west to a juncture of the Ohio. Stopping at flatlands—"the Basin," locals said—they founded what Longfellow called the "Queen City of the West." It was named for the Society of the Cincinnati, a group of Revolutionary War officers, founded by George Washington. (The society honored Cincinnatus, a Roman patriot who returned to the farm after serving his city in battle.) A visitor noted civility, beauty, and history: Mark Twain vowed to come there for the apocalypse because it was always 20 years behind the time. "Given all that," Lee Allen said, "what's amazing is how it looked ahead."

Somewhere in its core baseball eclipsed what John Gunther called Cincinnati's "certain stately and also sleepy quality." The Reds fused firsts: professional team (1869); charter member of first NL and AA year ('76 and '82, respectively); twin nine-inning no-hitter (May '17, the Reds Fred Toney and Cubs Jim Vaughn); big-league park leased to the Negro League ('20s Cuban Stars); daily radio coverage ('29); and night game ('35). Another blared hospitality: a clubhouse for home and visiting players. "In most cities, visiting players rode trolleys or buses to get to the game," said Allen. "They'd be heckled, taunted. In Cincinnati they dressed at the park"—and often ducked a dressing-down.

Heinie Groh '17 used a bottle bat to lead in hits and doubles. Manager Christy Mathewson resigned to take a commission in the Army. The Reds hired Pat Moran, drew a record 532,501, and hailed their first NL flag (clinching September 16, 1919) and World Series (or did the Black Sox lose?) "That is the triumph of enduring notoriety over fleeting fame," the *Washington Post* wrote in 1986. "The Red Sox always lose in the end [that year to New York], but in ways that are so imaginative and heart-rending as to be more memorable than victory."

The Reds had wanted in the worst way to amount to something, and did; but not quite in the way they had expected, or hoped. They are still the *other* team in the Black Sox Series. Don't look a gift horse: Post-'19 Cincinnati would struggle to beat *any* team. Gunther's "sleepy quality" seldom seemed as real.

Redland was built for $225,000. The team began renting it in 1920 for dance and film. The *Cincinnati Enquirer* scored "immoral dancing" and "vulgar conduct between boys and girls in unlighted parts of the grand-stand." More vulgar was Reds play. The '27-'37ers dredged the second division. Cincy '31-'34 placed last.

The Greek playwright Sophocles was said to see the world "steadily," and "[see] it whole." Hope chirped episodically. Twice Edd Rousch hit in 27 straight games. Eppa Rixey skipped the minors to win a Reds-high 179 games. Curt Walker tripled twice in an inning for the first time since 1900—and last until the '46 Browns' Al Zarilla. "For a lousy team," said manager Jack Hendricks, "our people were amazing."

In 1929, Harry Hartman found a chair behind the backstop, stripped to his underwear, and as radio and public address voice gave you two for the price of one: verbal arrows marked *socko* and *belto* and *whammo* and *bammo*. "Cincinnati's old-fashioned," said Lee Allen. "Harry fit in"—at 5-6 and 320 pounds, a showman and adventurer.

By 1933, Sid Weil lost the Reds to bankruptcy. The bank hired Leland Stanford MacPhail. MacPhail sold radio, refrigerator, and auto manu-facturer Powel Crosley a majority percentage. Crosley named him gen-eral manager, renamed Redland Field for himself, and hired a distant relative of writer Sidney Lanier. "He was like nothing they'd ever heard before," MacPhail said of Red Barber, wowing listeners over then-500,000 watt WLW.

In 1935, Barber's born-for-radio voice called Ernie Lombardi's four doubles in as many innings. The catcher hit .300 ten times, averaged .306 lifetime, and won the 1938 batting title (.342)—but how? "Forget infield hits," teammate Frank McCormick chuckled. "He'd hold his hands low, that interlocking golf grip, and smack the ball around the field." Memory links his crouch position, barehand catching, sidearm release, and '38 MVP. That year McCormick had 209 hits and Ival Goodman, 30 homers. Neither buoyed the Reds above fourth place: '19 seemed long ago.

In 1909, George Cahill built five steel towers for the Palace of the Fans. He then strung lights for a local set: Elks Lodges of Cincinnati *v.* Newport, Kentucky. "Night baseball has come to stay," enthused Garry Herrmann. "It needs further development, but proper lighting conditions will make the sport immensely popular." Hopscotch to 1931. The Reds shared portable lighting equipment with the touring House of David for a night exhibition. By 1935, more than one in four Americans was out of work. Most were employed 9 to 5. MacPhail swayed owners to try night ball. "I saw it happen at Columbus [AA, as general manager]. You make it easier to get to games."

On May 24, 1935, Franklin Roosevelt threw a switch in the White House that lit Crosley Field: 20,422 saw the bigs' first night game—Reds 2, Phillies 1. "In July, another first," said Allen. Baseball's southern and westernmost team visited for its next-to-last night game of the year. Like Cincinnati, St. Louis moved the unhip and unboutique. "The place was packed with people who came by train from Kentucky and Tennessee. People spilled onto the field." Ropes kept them from fielders. Nothing kept the first woman from a big–league batter's box. "Kitty Burke was a publicity hound entertainer," said MacPhail successor Warren Giles, "and rushed on the field, grabs Babe Herman's bat, and tells Paul Dean to pitch." Like many Reds, she grounded out.

Precedents flew. In 1935, the Braves' Babe Ruth fell on the berm, walked off, and never played again. Crosley hosted the first Ladies Night game: July 15, 1936. Lasting to a historian was January '37's Mill Creek flood. Twenty-one feet of water covered ex-Redland: Pitcher Lee Grissom and traveling secretary John McDonald rowed a boat over center field. The rooftop press box overlooked a new size (33,000, from box and foul-line seats), line on the center-field wall (high '37 flood tide), and revised stretch (left: 320 [1921], 352, 339, and 328 [1938]; center, 417 [1926], 395, 393, 407, 393, 407, and 387; right, 382 [1921], 400, 383, 377, and 366). "Those numbers [328, 387, 366] lasted till Crosley's [1970] end," said Allen. Left to right: Walls stood 18, 13½ feet, and 7½ feet (4½ wire feet above 3 concrete).

The '38ers housed the All-Star Game; 27,607 saw a 4–1 NL win. In June, anything worth pitching was worth pitching twice. Johnny Vander Meer no-hit Boston, 3–0. Four days later the Reds shared Brooklyn's night debut. Vandy, from New Jersey, was scheduled to pitch. "They even gave me a night," he said. "That's the jinx. You don't get past the third." MacPhail, now Dodgers president, couldn't get past selling tickets. "Lines stretched around the block. Meanwhile, I'm warming up, sit down, warm up, sit down, do it again."

Play started 78 minutes late. Vander Meer Kd seven, walked eight, and cobbled his second straight no-hitter. Play-Doh, Formica, and floating soap were invented in Cincinnati. Dr. Albert Sabin ripened his oral polio vaccine, and Dr. Henry Heimlich began his lifesaving maneuver. At that moment a Rhinelander—Germans comprised a quarter of the city's population—would have traded them for a Vandy handshake and a ball.

"Sometimes baseball seems on a different planet," MacPhail would muse. In 1939, it seemed of, if not from, the larger world. Neville Chamberlain chose appeasement. The Third Reich swallowed Czechoslovakia. Jack Benny and Fred Allen dueled on NBC Radio. On September 1, German tanks crossed the Polish frontier. "Welcome," said an NBC report, "to hell." The Reds reached, if not heaven, John Winthrop's "Shining city on a hill." Frank McCormick led the '39 NL in RBI (128). Bucky Walters finished 27–11. Paul Derringer used five different curveballs to go 25–7. Bill McKechnie became the first to manage three different NL titleists (also, Pittsburgh '25 and St. Louis '28). Cincy then went forth against the Yanks.

Wright Morris wrote of Norman Rockwell, "His special triumph is in the conviction his countrymen share that the mythical world he evokes exists." Mythical, or invincible? New York vaulted to a 3–0 game Series lead. Game Four filled 3,000 new second-deck seats built beyond first and third. The score was tied at 4 in the tenth. "What happened next," said Vander Meer, "was never explained. On an error, Charlie Keller dazed Lombardi in a collision at the plate. "The ball came up [on a throw home] and hit Ernie in the cup. Folks think he was sleeping. He was paralyzed, the ball rolled 14 feet away, and Walters hadn't backed up the play." Joe DiMaggio scored the final run, 7–4.

The next year a fan had a brainstorm. "Have him sell coffee," he said of Lombardi. "He's a walking advertisement for caffeine."

In 1940, the new census wagged, "131, 669, 275." For McKechnie, a springtime of possibility bred an autumn of content. Each Opening Day temporary seats graced the left-field gradient. The event occasioned a yearly pregame parade. "Floats, clowns, jugglers, the Reds," said Allen. Cincinnati normally oozed Mayberry's modesty and self-deprecation. Today reserve wore not a stitch: Goodman's homer beat the Cubs.

McCormick became MVP. A canvas shield stirred a rhubarb. "Crosley built it behind center field to protect batters' eyes from street light glare," Allen explained. "During day games it was taken down. One day the Reds accidentally left the canvas up and Harry Craft hit it in the ninth. For thirty minutes McKechnie fumed it should have been a game-winning homer. The umps called it a double—since it was Cincinnati's mistake." The Brooks won in 11. The Reds won another flag.

The Series opened in Cincinnati: Detroit's Bobo Newsom over Derringer, 7–2. Walters won, 5–3. The Tigers took two of three games at home. Down, 3–2, the Reds returned to baseball's HO-scale den. Walters spliced five hits, 4–0. Game Seven hovered over the next 21 years. "Newsom had won two," McKechnie later said. "Win the third, and he's a legend." Bobo fronted, 1–0, as Cincy hit in the seventh. McCormick and Jimmy Ripple doubled. Ripple advanced on a bunt and scored on Billy Myers' fly. Derringer retired the last six Tigers: Reds win, 2–1, their last title for 35 years. The story would soon wend like frames in flag-waving/cracker barrel/Capra celluloid.

Later, a writer mused, "Partly because of [Crosley's] size, there are really no bad seats; only sun area is in Sun Deck bleachers [called Moon Deck for night games]. Ticket prices are below average and ushers are efficient and polite. Expect only moderate tip. Refreshment stands are adequate, prices reasonable, food good," including bratwurst, fried shrimp, and 16-ounce lemonade. Among those inhaling was Harry Thove. Giles laughed. "Our most famous [1940s] fan! He had a white suit with red stripes, one red and one white shoe, a straw hat with red band, a red and white parasol," danced an unfailing jig, and flashed 12 gold teeth.

The '42 Reds built Giles Garden—a.k.a. Giles Chicken Run or Picnic Grounds—beyond an inner 342-foot right-field fence. Batters dented parked cars between the left-field wall and laundry. "Hit This Sign and Win a Spiedler Suit!" read the Superior Towel and Linen Service. Lombardi went *truly* long: Landing in a truck, his dinger traveled for thirty miles. In 1943, 38,017 jammed Crosley for the Cubs. A Pirates '47 twin bill lured a paid record 36,961, many trooping from Union Terminal. The right-field screen went down (1950) and up again ('53). Crosley '57 was repainted, better lights installed, and "a colossal new scoreboard," said *Sports Illustrated*, placed in left-center field. "The new board will be 55 feet high and 65 feet wide and is designed so that it will be visible from any seat in [the] park.

"One feature will be the flashing of a player's batting average [another first] as of that morning each time he goes to bat." Another became a conundrum wrapped in hard-to-get-a-handle-on: Balls often rolled under the scoreboard. Lodged, it was a double; bounding back, it kept in play.

"**W**e few, we happy few," wrote Shakespeare, "we band of brothers." A few conspired to help the post-'40 Reds survive. Vander Meer '41–'42–'43 led the league in Ks. In 1944, Joe Nuxhall was a 15-year-old pitcher from Hamilton, Ohio. "Holy smoke! I'm in trouble now!" said the youngest player to make the bigs. "I pitch two-thirds of an inning and get bombed [five walks, a wild pitch, two hits, and five earned runs]."

Later Nuxie became a starter/reliever. He was shorter (three inches) and heavier (49 pounds) than Cincy's whip-armed stopper/coming-by-third-base/6-foot-6 and 170-pound Ichabod Crane. "I knew that when we found that [Ewell] Blackwell would pitch," said Braves infielder Gene Mauch, "Sibby Sisti, our regular shortstop, would come down sick. He'd pull a muscle, something so that he wouldn't have to play. I would have to play!"—especially in 1947. The Whip led the NL in Ks (193), complete games (23), and wins (22), including 16 straight. For one year, rival benches resembled a hospital tent at Shiloh.

Postwar life fused peace and prosperity. Tell '45–'55 Cincinnati. Attendance shrank to 548,086. Seven managers conjured Winston Churchill: "An empty cab drove up and Clement Attlee got out." Solace was where you found it. Grady Hatton's '46 fly robbed John Sain of a perfect game. Crosley hosted the 1953 All-Star Game: Enos Slaughter's catch off Harvey Kuenn helped the NL win, 4–1. Nihilism pierced even a visitor. In '45, the Giants Danny Gardella left a suicide note for teammate Nat Reyes. "Reyes looks up," said writer Dan Daniel, "and he sees the window of the Cincinnati hotel room open. Then he looked out the window" and rubbed his eyes.

Giggling, Gardella hung from the ledge.

LEAGUE PARK

Joe Engel was '40s owner and president of the Chattanooga Lookouts. One day a holdout player wired him, "Double my salary or count me out." Joe answered by telegram: "1–2–3–4–5–6–7–8–9–10." *Capacity* was counted out north and east of Crosley Field. "Tiny, you bet," said writer Russell Schneider of Cleveland's League Park. "Except when it came to the bizarre."

Baseball's fourth steel and concrete park opened April 21, 1910. That year Freud published *Psychoanalysis*. "Contrary to myth," said a writer, "it didn't explain why people like the Indians." League's first game was not, as Wes Westrum malapropped, a "cliff-dweller": Tigers, 5–0, at East 70th Street, Linwood Avenue, Lexington Avenue Northeast, and Dunham (now, East 66th) Street. It did flaunt the AL's smallest size (21,000) but highest percent of box and grandstand seats (60). Right field loomed 290 feet from the plate. Center, right-center, left, and left-center, respectively, rose 420, 400, 385, and 415. Left of center a 505 corner hinted of Indiana. "Except for right," observed Bob Feller, "a pitcher's heaven—and hitter's hell."

Rapid Robert rubbed his hands. "Distances," he said, "were screwy." Juxtaposed was site: urban, and accessible. In 1998, Michael Gershman wrote of Camden Yards: "Fortunately, they didn't build at the intersection of two Interstates. It was built in the city. The city was part of the park. The park was part of the city." Likewise, Cleveland's lodge.

Self-interest forged its cast. A bartender and two homeowners refused to sell property. Thus, League snaked around it. Twin-tiered stands ringed around the plate, segued to covered pavilions behind the bases, and ended in the left-field seats. Boxes beyond the dugouts clutched each line. A 20-foot concrete wall tied right's pole to center. Pens pricked each foul corner. "Tradition," said Schneider. "[By late '09] this had been League's shape for years."

In 1910, Tribe president Ernest Barnard swapped wood for steel and concrete. Detroit's Sam Crawford pointed to right field. "So that's Barney's dream," he said. "I'll show him"—and, homering, did. One day Washington stole eight first-inning bases. Ray Caldwell's '19 debut nixed thunder (beating the A's, 2–1) for lightning (a bolt knocked him to the ground). Caldwell laughed: "In the '10s, these were our exceptions, not rule."

In '10, Cy Young won his 500th game. Joe Jackson '11 batted .408. Nap Lajoie '14 got his 3,000th hit. You can't tell the players: Post-'16, you could. "First time," said outfielder Jack Graney, "a team [his] wore numbers on their sleeves that matched the scorecard." Marty Kavanagh hit the first AL pinch-hit grand slam: a grounder that rolled through a left-center wall hole. Tris Speaker arrived from Boston to make four unassisted double plays—a record for an outfielder. In 1919, he became player/manager. Cleveland could see Speaker as Father Christmas and not be deceived. Noel occurred on Columbus Day 1920: The Indians won their first World Series. They got there *en famille*.

In 1920, Speaker rapped a bigs record 11 straight hits. Jim Bagby went 31–12. The Indians hit .303 and drew a record 912,832. Sally Rand was her time's *primo* fan dancer. Joe Sewell '20–'30 fanned only 114 times in 7,132 at-bats. Stan Coveleski learned control by hurling rocks at tin cans. The Tribe "learned me a spitter." It, and guile, evolved into Hall of Fame '69. Five times he won 20 games.

Renamed Dunn Park's largest crowd—29,266; paid 28,676—greeted the Yanks. (It reverted to League on owner James Dunn's 1927 death). In August, new seats forged greater size (22,000) and shorter length (376 and 450, left and center). Dunn topped right's wall with a 28-foot wire screen—"let's make homers a little harder." *Un*changed: the trolley service of ex-President Frank D. Robison and overflow behind a right-field rope. "When they packed, like, a World Series," said Speaker, "the foul line read 240, not 290."

The best-of-nine began at Ebbets Field. Coveleski beat Rube Marquard, 3–1. Brooklyn riposted, 3–0 and 2–1. Stan tied the Classic, 5–1, before 25,734 at League. Sam Cook sang, "Don't know much about history." On October 10, Cleveland made it on Elmer Smith's first-ever Series slam. It soon turned small potatoes. The Indians led, 7–0. Shortstop Bill Wambsganss mourned—and hoped. A Cleveland scout watching Wambsganss in the Central Association was once asked, "What's he got?" The scout said, "Well, he has the funniest damn name I ever heard"—German for a kind of overcoat. The '14 Tribe promoted him. The shortstop shifted to second. Said incumbent Ray Chapman: "Bill, you're the only second baseman I'll ever play next to." In 1920, Ray died after being hit in the head by Yankees submariner Carl Mays. "More history," said Schneider. "The first big leaguer's death caused by a thrown pitch."

Depressed, Wambsganss hit .154 and made two errors in the first four Series games. A newsman consoled him: "Stay with it. This could be your day." Brooklyn's Pete Kilduff and Otto Miller led off the fifth safely. Clarence Mitchell then lined Bagby's pitch to Wambsganss (out one), who touched second (two) and tagged Miller (trifecta)—the Series' first/only unassisted triple play.

Tribe '09 shortstop Neal Ball nabbed three for the price of one. In 1968, the Nats' Ron Hansen tripled his pleasure at Municipal Stadium. Said then-Tribe voice Herb Score: "What *is* it with the Indians?" Wrote Ring Lardner: "It was the only time in World Serious history that a man named Wambsganss had ever made a triple play assisted by consonants only."

Afterword: "Old-timers feared we'd go back to the days before 1900," said outfielder Charlie Jamieson. Instead, Cleveland mocked them. Once it scored in each inning to whack Boston, 27–3. Emil Levsen '26 beat the

Red Sox, 6–1 and 5–1—the last big to throw two complete games in a day. In 1928, Johnny Hodapp became the first ALer to get two hits in an inning—twice. Wes Ferrell '32 no-hit the Browns. That August he became the first 20th-Century pitcher to win 20 games his first four years.

League came to have a strange witching power. "It was so damn small!" said Sewell. "Fans practically fell on the field." The '32 White Sox blew their top when Earl Averill's ninth-inning triple won, 12–11. "George Moriarty was the home plate umpire," added left fielder Joe Vosmik. "His ball and strike calls had enraged them [Chicago] all day." Leaving the field, Moriarty fought Sox players in the runway. Spiking him, they broke his hand. AL president Will Harridge unfurled a hair-shirt: Hose manager Lew Fonseca and three players were fined $1,350. Pitcher Milt Gaston was suspended. (Moriarty got a reprimand.) Shelved, they could probe a park *too* damn small.

"Look at left and center," Averill began. League was baseball's sole two-flagpole park. One topped the bleachers. The other flanked the board players crawled under to retrieve a ball. "But right," and Earl began to laugh, "was the trademark"—Wrigley's ivy, Fenway's wall. Twenty-four vertical steel girders tied the pole to right-center. Wire covered the bottom 20 feet. Supports hung above it. "If a ball went between supports, it was like a field goal"—here, homer. Striking one, it stayed in play: Drives might glance into the *left*-field corner.

By 1932, Comiskey Park housed 52,000. Even D.C.'s Griffith Stadium had 34 percent more seats. "There was no way we could compete," said Schneider, presaging baseball's '90s Darwinism. The Tribe soon found a larger hearth: As we shall see, vast Municipal Stadium turned proportion on its ear. League's grandstand was razed in 1950. Ticket booths and left-field seats now form the League Park Community Center. Visiting, you recall Bill Veeck in '46 after 14 years meandering between two homes—by turn, too small and large. "We can't seem to get it [the park] right."

Bizarrely, Washington would.

GRIFFITH STADIUM

The late critic William A. Henry III wrote of America's "purple mountain majesties, amber waves of grain, Norman Rockwell Thanksgiv-

ings, the flag-raising at Iwo Jima, the World Series, and astronauts landing on the moon." All seemed "interlocked because they, in turn, have
evoked a swelling sense of personal participation in national pride and
purpose." Too, Opening Day's presidential bandstand of nostalgia, faith,
and myth.

In 1909, when William Howard Taft watched his first big-league
game, "the game was interrupted by the cheering," read the *Washington
Post,* "which spread . . . from the grandstand to the bleachers as the
crowd recognized the President." (At 300 pounds, the ex-amateur
pitcher was hard to miss.) A year later he became the first president to
throw out the "first ball" in the nation's capital. "President Taft, in spite
of a big bay window," wrote Morris A. Bealle, "threw the ball with the
finesse and grace of an accomplished player."

Griffith Stadium burned in early 1911. Rebuilt, it opened April 12:
Senators 8, Boston 5. Taft trooped to their 27,410-seat fort at Larch
(later, Fifth) Street, W Street (later, Howard University), Georgia a.k.a.
Seventh Street (now, J. Frank Kelley Lumber and Mill Works), and
Spruce (now, U) Street. "Some concrete was unpoured," an account
read. "The only box seats installed were for the Presidential party." In
1912, the *Titanic* struck an iceberg and sank four days before Opening
Day: 1,595 died, including Taft's military aide Archie Butt. "Taft was
heartsick," said *Post* columnist Shirley Povich, "and thought it unseemly
to attend the game."

That spring Clark Griffith became Senators a.k.a. Nationals manager.
"He'd been a turn-of-the-century pitching star," added writer Morris
Siegel, "and he was a great showman determined to create a ritual of
presidents. So he scheduled a *second* Opening Day." Taft corkscrewed
out of his seat to uncork a belated first ball. The Senators had won 16
straight games. Scalpers got $50 for a box seat. "In time, Clark con-
vinced Ban Johnson to let him open each year at home," Siegel noted,
"because of the visibility it gave the game."

In 1920, Griffith mortgaged his ranch to buy the team. He later
claimed to have hatched the first ball/Hail to the Chief/Eureka rite. "I
inaugurated the custom back in 1912," he boasted in a *This Week* article. The title mocked self-effacement: "Presidents Who Have Pitched for
Me." A famed epigram etched the Senators' faint sense of possibility.
"First in War, First in Peace, and Last in the American League."

It was not easy to reach Griffith Stadium. "A driver will need radar," a writer mused, "what with confusions of Washington traffic patterns." Arriving, you found that the Nats made normalcy take a hike. "Before the game resumes," the P.A. mikemen said, "spectators in front-row boxes must remove their garments." The crowd tittered. "Coats," he said, "must be removed from the railings."

The park was a work in progress. A 1915 cab ride from the White House cost 25 cents. Siegel laughed. "A homer cost more." Dimensions gaped. Left: 407 feet (1911) via 424 and 358 ('26) to 407 and 402 ('36)—baseball's longest. Left-center: 391. Center: 421. Right: 326 (1911) through 328 and 320 ('26 and '61, respectively). The visitor's pen dotted the left-field corner. A 12-foot "long bleacher" wall reached left-center field (383). To its right five houses and a giant tree stood beyond center: The wall jutted in, then back around them at a right angle to 457. Further right a four-foot home bullpen wall—423 feet: later, 441 (1930), 394 ('51), and 426 ('61)—met the right-field fence. A loudspeaker horn peered from center. The first-base line drooped from home to first. "It tilted downhill," added Povich. "They thought it would help the Senators' slow batters and boost attendance." Pause. "Oh for two."

Two tiers circled the plate from first to third base. In 1920, Griffith stretched the decks to each pole—with a kicker. "For some reason, the roof of the new stands was higher than the old," Povich moaned. "It looked like some damn carpenter worked with a bottle—not a saw!" The addition foresaw a theme. Fences rose, and shrank. Capacity veered from 32,000 (1921) through 25,048 ('48) and 35,000 ('52) to 27,550 ('61). Only one club topped a million—'46's 1,027,216. "Piecemeal!" exclaimed a U.S. senator. Like Congress, Griffith would try anything. If it didn't fly, he tried something else.

In 1912, America elected as president an ex–Davidson College baseball player. Six times he opened the Nats season. The first: April 10, 1913, 2–1, over New York. Unlike Woodrow Wilson, many trained to Union Station, then rode the trolley to Georgia and Spruce. A ten-cent bleacher seat offered the best view of Walter Johnson leaving the bullpen for the mound. William Shakespeare portended the Big Train: "Why, man, he doth bestride the narrow world like a colossus." Something about him lured warmth and adulation, capable of kindness, and adored by much of the working press.

In 1906, Johnson was plucked from Idaho's Snake River Valley League to get a $100 bonus, $350 monthly salary, and train fare to D.C.—"plus enough return money if I didn't make it." Johnson '07 won his first of 416 games. A year later he blanked New York three times in four days. "They didn't play on Sunday," said manager Joe Cantillon. "It's the only thing that broke the streak." Nineteen ten *made* him: The Train one-hit Philly, 3–0, his first of seven Opening Day shutouts. Thirty-eight complete games, 25 wins, and 313 Ks also *changed* him. Boys named Walter began studding the area. A Bethesda, Maryland, high school bears his name.

One cause was skill. Johnson sidearmed 3,508 Ks, had a record 110 shutouts, and 10 times won 20 or more games—for teams that broke a pitcher's heart. In 1913, he fused 36–7, 55⅔ straight scoreless innings, and MVP. Another: Walter's nice-guy manner. Once a year Jimmy Dudley came to Griffith from Charlottesville, Virginia. "It'd be a Sunday," said the future Indians voice. "My father used him as a standard if I got out of hand. 'Walter Johnson would never do a thing like that.' "

The Train blurred black and white. "A little black boy named Snowball used to hang around the clubhouse," said Dudley, "doing any jobs to be around his heroes." Once a policeman primed to yank him from the park. Johnson shoved the cop against the wall. "Don't ever lay hands on this boy again! Dadgum your soul, I mean it!"

Reminiscence forged a smile. "Remember that Washington was segregated," said Dudley, "and that 'dadgum' was the strongest language anyone heard Johnson use."

Wilson's successor treated language as swearword, not strength. "Sometimes [Warren Harding's] meandering words would actually capture a struggling thought," jeered William Gibbs McAdoo, "and bear it triumphantly, a prisoner in their midst, until it died of servitude and overwork." *Harding* died in 1923. His replacement restored the office's moral rubric. An April 15, 1924, picture shows photographers standing on the Nats dugout as Calvin Coolidge prepares to throw.

Deliverance had avoided D.C. since 1901. In 1924, it crashed through the door. Goose Goslin led the AL with 129 RBI. Johnson again was MVP. On August 29, the Nats beat New York, 11–6, to take first place for good. They clinched their first flag September 29, returned from Boston, and paraded before 100,000 on Pennsylvania Avenue to the Ellipse. Coolidge vowed to attend the Series. Wife Grace was the real fanatic. "Where did you learn that?" Griffith asked of her perfect score-card. "At college," said Mrs. Coolidge. "I was the official scorer of the baseball team."

On October 4, diplomats, a military band, and the cabinet trekked to Griffith. Coolidge became the first president at a Series opener. He smoked a cigar, which expired with the Senators: The Giants beat Johnson, 4–3, in 12. "Greed was Clark's enemy," said Siegel. "He put in temporary seats in front of the bleachers," swelling attendance to 35,760. "The seats turned two routine pops into homers." D.C.'s Tom Zachary won Game Two. New York then won two of three at the Polo Grounds. Down, 3–2, the Griffiths returned home. Grace and Silent Cal again watched Zachary triumph. At this point Johnson had lost his first two games.

"Keep in mind," Siegel said, "This was Johnson's first Series—and the last [John] McGraw managed." New York led Game Seven, 3–1, as player-manager Bucky Harris, 27, hit in the eighth: bases full, two out. "The Boy Wonder" grounded to 18-year-old third baseman Fred Lindstrom. The ball hit a pebble, bounced over his head, and tied the score. Harris then summoned Johnson from the pen. "That's pretty far gone," Walter said of his age, 36, "to be walking into the last game of the Series." The sky turned gray. Washington's heart found its stomach. Said the *Post*: "Time and again as tense moments tumbled after each other in the thrilling battle President Coolidge fell into the spirit which held the throng."

Inning followed inning. In the 12th, D.C.'s Muddy Ruel popped behind the plate. Hank Gowdy tripped on his mask. Griffith mused: "It just up and bit him." Reprieved, Muddy doubled. Johnson reached on an error. With one out, Earl McNeely again bounced to Lindstrom. The ball again hit a stone. Ruel scored: Nats, 4–3. "I guess the Good Lord didn't want us to win that game. That's all there was to it," said the Giants Heinie Groh. "Nice work," Coolidge told Johnson. "Glad you won."

Washington was now First in Baseball. History's flash greased the Senators' pan.

In 1928, Coolidge said, "I do not choose to run." Herbert Hoover, who did, was endorsed by Charles Lindbergh for president. A song on the wireless replied with praise-by-association:

> You remember Hoover, back in the war.
> Saved us from the Kaiser, now he'll give us something more.
> He'll serve as the President of the land of the free.
> If he's good enough for Lindy, he's good enough for me.

For a long time Hoover seemed good enough for America. Few found malice in a Quaker whose modesty and propriety, not newly formed, were neither bogus nor offensive. "Baseball," the then–commerce secretary said in 1925, "is the greatest of all sports." He cheered Sam Rice (.350) and Goslin (116 RBI). MVP Peckinpaugh hit .294. The Nats again made the Series. Game Three packed Griffith's largest-ever crowd—38,701. D.C. led in the eighth, 4–3. Pittsburgh's Earl Smith then drove to right-center. "Rice dove into the temporary [17 rows of] seats," said Povich, "and 15 seconds later comes out with the ball." Umpire Cy Rigler called Smith out. The Bucs claimed that a hometowner gave Rice the ball. Pittsburghers drank a fifth. Rice *took* it. He died in 1974. "At no time," a letter by Sam read, "did I lose possession of the ball."

At 41, Johnson '26 tossed his last Opening Day shutout. Goslin's .379 led '28 ALers. Rice retired with 2,987 hits. Heinie Manush batted .350, .307, and .342 in 1930–'32. He also buoyed a popular film of the day. An actor was trying to sleep in an upper berth. His trick was intoning, "Heinie Manush, Heinie Manush" to the rhythm of the train. The uptake was predictable: on road trips, players chanted whenever Heinie neared his berth. "I never got much sleep on the train after that." The Nats slept through 1926–'32. Like Hoover, their luck ran out too soon. Rusted cars became Great Depression tents ("Hoover hovels") where at night jackrabbits ("Hoover dog") flanked men asleep in parks. The paper cloaking them was a "Hoover blanket." Alone in the dock, Hoover beseeched a jury that deemed him unfit to serve. A crowd taunted him by chanting "Beer! Beer! Beer!" at a 1931 Series game. Few recalled how in '29 the former Stanford shortstop brought his entire Cabinet to Opening Day.

In 1960, Hoover and Indian prime minister Jawaharlal Nehru were introduced at another Series at Yankee Stadium. The next day Joe Garagiola said, "You amaze me, Yog. You've now become such a world figure that you draw more applause than either a prime minster or former president. Can you explain it?"

"Certainly," Yogi Berra said. "I'm a better hitter." When Hoover died in 1964, a memorial postage stamp carried the epitaph, "Engineer, President, Humanitarian." In baseball, unlike politics, two out of three ain't bad.

7

JUST THE WAY YOU ARE

"The lamps are going out all over Europe; we shall not see them lit again in our lifetime," British foreign minister Sir Edward Grey mused at the dawn of World War I. The lights went out over Brooklyn in 1957. For many, they have never reappeared. "Baseball in Brooklyn was like another planet," said native Larry King. Ernie Harwell was a 1948–'49 Dodgers announcer. "Fanatically loyal," he said. "It's the only place I've known where people made a *vocation* of being a fan."

Until 1898, Brooklyn was an independent city. Incorporated into New York City, it still felt like a Nation-State. Its capital was Ebbets Field—to author Roger Kahn, "a narrow cockpit of iron and concrete along a steep cobblestone slope"—in the Crown Heights district of Flatbush. In 1902, the Dodgers had nearly left Brooklyn for Baltimore. They now pined for a larger field. "[Charles] Ebbets needed more seats," said Lee Allen of Washington Park. He searched till finding a site used as a garbage dump—"Pigtown," for swine not exactly a gourmet.

The 4½-acre plat linked Bedford Avenue, Sullivan Place, Franklin

Avenue (later, Cedar/McKeever Place), and Montgomery Street. On one hand, it lay a pop fly from the Brooklyn Rapid Transit Company. On the other, 40 people owned parcels of ground. Allen laughed. "Charley had to convince each to sell." In time, a single lot remained. Its owner was out of town. Unfazed, Ebbets sent agents to California, Berlin, Paris, and finally Montclair, New Jersey. Would the last holdout sell? "Would five hundred dollars be too much?" replied the owner. Ebbets sighed. In Brooklyn, spunk was *already* the Peepul's Choice.

Ground broke March 14, 1912. A reporter asked, "What are you gonna' call your park?" Ebbets paused. "I hadn't even through about it." The writer persisted: "Why don't you call it Ebbets Field?" He nodded. "All right. That's what we'll call it." Herbert Hoover said, "If a man has not made a million dollars by the time he is 40, he is not worth much." Ebbets, 53, had not made a million. Businessmen Steve and Ed McKeever had. He sold them half-interest for $100,000. They soon found that their park might be, uh, a tad more unusual than most.

Ebbets Field opened April 5, 1913. "The Yankees [née Highlanders] had just been renamed," Dick Young noted, "so they came for an exhibition game." The superintendent lost the key to the park. Designers forgot to build a press box: Scribes sat in the lower deck. Ultimately, pols and players trudged to the flagpole in center field. Ebbets turned to an aide. "The flag, please," he said. The aide, shall we say, reddened. "Sorry, Charley. We forgot the flag." A year earlier Casey Stengel joined the Bums. His inside-the-parker now baptized the park: Nap Rucker beat New York, 3–2.

"Charley had enormous power," said Allen. "[On April 9], he got the NL to let him open the season day before everyone else." The day broke cold; only 12,000 showed. Later Ebbets seemed as small as a school you revisit years after reading Shakespeare. In 1913, it made Caesar look like Tom Thumb: left field, 419 feet; center, 450; right-center corner, 500. By contrast, right held pitching accidental: 301. A 20-foot barrier linked left to center field. A nine-foot concave concrete wall, sloped toward home, stretched to right's line. Bedford Avenue flanked it from the pole to center. A boy could watch the Dodgers through a gap under the metal gate. A double deck linked right field around the plate to beyond third base. Single-deck concrete bleachers reached the left-field wall.

Later, film used Brooklyn to rouse laughter. "Baseball Bill Bendix!" Young yawped of TV's future Chester A. Riley. "He'd say 'Brooklyn' in a movie, and the theater'd erupt." Early Ebbets was strictly business. Roman arches graced a brick facade. Turnstiles and gilded ticket windows spurned shabby-genteel. Surpassing: the rotunda at the main entrance—an 80-foot circle enclosed in Italian marble. Baseball stiches tiled its floor. The chandelier vaunted baseball-bat arms holding base-ball-shaped gloves. The domed ceiling stood 28 feet high.

Wilbert Robinson—Uncle Robbie—managed from 1914 to '31. Honus Wagner, 41, became the oldest this century to grand-slam (inside-the-park, v. Jeff Pfeffer). In 1916, the Dodgers drew 447,747, more than tripling '14's 122,671. A visitor paid more than the average fan. "Ebbets was cheap," barbed Allen. "He had fewer 25 cent seats than any team [3,000, v. Boston's 10,000], and wanted the league to put a limit of 2,000. The owners said no." Brooklyn won the flag—its first—but lost the '16 Series to Boston. (Ebbets' catchpenny greed raised grandstand seats from $3 to $5.) Curious is how Wilbert got a $5,000 bonus. "Only in Brooklyn," Young gaped. "Robinson *lost*."

Like Ebbets, Wilbert found his park chockablock with quirk. "It'll drive you crazy if you let it," he said. Phillies outfielder Gavvy Cravath did. Brooklyn's George Cutshaw grounded benignly to right. The ball hit the wall, bounced up its shelf, and left Cravath empty-handed—and Ebbets for a homer. The '18 Dodgers, a.k.a. Robins, traded Stengel for headhunter Burleigh Grimes. One day Charlie Grimm lay down in the batter's box. "What you doing?" said umpire Bill Klem. Grimm shook his head. "Grimes is going to throw at me anyway, so I thought I'd duck early."

Five years Grimes won more than 20 games. Zack Wheat's .335 led '18's NL. The 1909–'26 outfielder hit .317 and owned Christy Mathewson. "Anything can happen at Ebbets Field," went the cliché, except that it was no cliché, "and usually does." Jack Daubert won an out-of-court suit for salary lost when the '18 season ended early. Ebbets then shipped the two-time batting king to Cincinnati. In 1919, an ex-Robin returned to Ebbets Field. The crowd rose. Stengel bowed and doffed his cap. A sparrow flew away.

Later, a reporter asked where he found the bird. "When I went to right field in the last of the first, I saw it stumbling along the base of the wall and I guess it wasn't looking a great deal where it was flying and hit the wall and was stunned. Well, don't you know I picked it up, figuring I would take it into the dugout and give it some water or something or other and I didn't know what to do with it, so you'll forgive me or maybe someone else because I put it in my hat. Then I forgot about it when I was coming in because I was first up to the plate. Honest, I was as surprised as anyone when it flew off my head."

Paid by the word, Stengel would have owned the borough.

"Brooklyn's funny," said Uncle Robbie. "They get a silver lining, and keep looking for the cloud." On May 1–3, he tied and lost twice in 26, 13, and 19 innings, respectively. "Fifty-eight innings, and no win. It had to get better," and briefly did. Grimes went 23–11. Attendance reached 808,722. Brooklyn took a second flag and 2–1 game Series lead. The Indians then won the still-best-of-nine event. Street vendors pawned hot dogs and lemonade. The Dodgers hit into Bill Wambsganss' unassisted triple play. The cry "Wait Till Next Year" linked borough precincts. Next year waited till 1941.

"It was often easy," said a writer, "to focus on players, not the team." The '21–'29ers once cracked the first division. Dazzy Vance, 31, reached the bigs after six years in the minors. He led the '22–'28 NL in Ks, threw a no-hitter, and won 197 games. In 1924, Vance won 15 straight games. On September 6, Brooklyn briefly took the lead. A day later Ebbets swelled: More than 7,000 used a telephone pole to ram its left-field exit gate. Their ire bespoke '25. Charles Ebbets died on its April 18 opener. Successor Ed McKeever caught a cold-turned-pneumonia and died May 27. Robinson replaced him. The Dodgers fell to seventh.

Flaunting cool and humor, Flatbush left you guessing. Bleachers shrank left field to 383 feet. Right coursed from 301 through 285 (1921) via 292 ('22) and 301 ('26). Its fence rose from 9 to 38 feet. "The lower 19 [bottom 9 sloped; top 10 rose vertically] were concrete," said Young. "Atop that, another 19 feet of wire screen." On August 15, Floyd Caves (Babe) Herman hit with Hank DeBerry, Vance, and Chick Fewster on base. Fact and muse merge. Herman lined off the screen. DeBerry scored.

Dazzy neared third and turned the bag. The right fielder threw home. Retreating, Vance met Fewster, sliding into third. The undiscerning Babe charged there head-down. Three Dodgers now shared the base. Thinking himself out, Fewster left and was tagged. Herman retired toward second and was put out by the second baseman. "The Dodgers have three on base." Punch line: "Yeah, which base?" Later, cartoonist Willard Mullin spawned the Brooklyn Bum. "Where else but Brooklyn," wondered Robinson, "could you double into a double play?"

On September 12, 1930, Al Lopez hit the NL's last "bounce" homer. "The rule then changed," said Lee Allen. "Balls bounced in the stands became a double." The '31–'38 Dodgers placed seventh twice and sixth thrice. Lefty O'Doul's .365 won the '32 batting title. Johnny Frederick '32 pinch-hit a record six dingers. Uncle Robbie died. Dizzy and Daffy (Paul) Dean blanked Brooklyn in a two-for-the-price-of-one. On May 30, 1934, its largest crowd, 41,209, filled Ebbets. Babe Ruth briefly became a coach.

The Bums built a press box, put a second deck from left to center field, and bought a right-field scoreboard. Capacity became 35,000. Center's wall began at 15 feet, became 19, and shrunk to 13 at the screen. The board protruded five feet at a 45-degree angle. Acreage changed: 384 (1931) via 356 ('34) to 365 ('40); left-center, 365; deep center at a wall angle, 407; center, 466 (1930) to 400 ('39); right-center, 415; right field, 297 ('38). "In right, the scoreboard and wall had 29 different angles," said Leo Durocher. Pinball was the effect. Ebbets' caliope was the park.

POLO GROUNDS

Thomas Wolfe called presidents between Lincoln and Theodore Roosevelt "The Lost Americans: their gravely vacant and bewildered faces mixed, melt, swam together. Which had the whiskers, which the burnsides, which was which?" Like madams in the night, it was difficult to tell. John Garfield became president in 1881. Two years later the American Association New York baseball club acquired a bewildering name. "My big boys, my giants," manager Jim Mutrie called his fourth-place clique. (Later, the then-National League Gothams inherited their name.)

The King of England granted a 17th-century plot in upper Manhattan to John Lion Gardiner. A Gardiner heir married Borough President James J. Coogan. By 1890, his estate housed the Players League in the 16,000-seat wooden Polo Grounds. The NL later usurped the park. "It was in a strange place," said Ken Smith, "a hollow, 115 feet below Coogan's Bluff," at the future juncture of the Harlem River, Harlem River Drive, West 157th and 159th Streets, the Harlem River Speedway, IRT rail yards, and Croton Aqueduct.

The Polo Grounds blared irony: Polo was never played there. "They had football, track," said Smith, "boxing, tennis, midget auto racing, soccer, and [1891–1957 and 1962–'63] baseball." In April 1911, it had fire, too. The damage led owner John Brush, a victim of locomotor ataxia, to rebuild. Brush sat in his wheelchair, gazed at the pyre, and according to author Joseph Durso, turned to his wife, a former actress, and said, "I want to build a concrete stadium, the finest that can be constructed. It will mean economy for a time. Are you willing to stand by me?" She was.

For two months the Giants played at the AL Highlanders' Hilltop Park. On June 28, they returned to a double-decked horseshoe shaped by the hollow in which it sat. "It was better fit for football," Allen said. "You could hit a pop homer [down the lines]." Flower beds graced the chasmal center field. Foul turf formed a vast semicircle from the plate to each line. The park grew in fits: temporary seats '11; concrete infield stands '12; outfield concrete double deck '22. "By then a second tier extended to either side of center's two new bleacher sections." Capacity traded 16,000 for 34,000 (October '11) and 55,000 (1926).

Left field dealt 277 for 287/280 (1921–'23). An upper-deck overhang leaned 21 feet over the field. Bullpens moored left-center and right-center. Left-center, left of pen: 447. Left-center, right of pen: 455. A 60-foot high and wide clubhouse stood between/beyond the bleachers. Center scrapped 433 (1911) for 483 ('23), 485 ('27), 505 ('30), and 430 (1931). Bleacher corners: 475. Right-center, left of pen: 449. Right-center, right of pen: 440. Right inched from 256 (1921) to 258 ('31). "Those dimensions!" Smith roared. "Weirdest in the world."

Ibid., it seemed, of fences. Right field's tilted from 11 feet high (pole) to 12 (bleachers). Center's 20-foot tarp draped the 10-foot right-center fence. A 19-foot 1911–'22 concrete wall tied left to center field. After

1922, left began at 17, became 18 in left-center, fell to 16, 14, and finally to 12. "Between these fences a low wall fronted the bleachers," said Allen. A 16½-foot high hitter's backdrop flanked the clubhouse runway. "Its steps began at 460 feet. To the rear wall it was about 505. You thought you were in New Jersey."

On May 30, 1921, John McGraw dedicated a five-foot memorial near its base for an ex-Giant killed in World War I: "In Memory of/ Capt. Edward Leslie Grant/ 307th Infantry-77th Division/ A.E.F./ Soldier-Scholar-Athlete/ Killed in action/ Argonne Forest/ October 5, 1918/ Philadelphia Nationals/ 1907–1908–1909–1910/ Cincinnati Reds/ 1911–1912–1913/ New York Giants/ 1913–1914–1915/ Erected by friends in Baseball, Journalism, and the Service."

By then, McGraw had managed the Giants since 1902: "[He fit] the historic pattern of the American success story," Lloyd Lewis wrote, "the legend of the boy who, on native wit and vitality, crashes through up to the top." McGraw crashed to flags in 1904–'05–'11–'12–'13–'17 (later '21–'22–'23–'24). His flaws, shills branded virtue. His virtue, foes dubbed sin. Little Napoleon riled umpires, signed boozers, profaned players, bent rules, and bred strategy: the Baltimore chop, hit and run, pitchers covering first and third, and grounds help stacking the field. The Giants became baseball's most hated club. McGraw didn't care. "The team that loses gracefully loses easily."

His '11 titleists drew a league-high 675,000. Christy Mathewson went 26–7. Larry Doyle had 25 triples. The Classic began as '05's ended: Matty, 2–1, over the A's, before 38, 281. "People were standing in the outfield, in the aisles," said Allen of the Polo Grounds. "They couldn't wait for what came next"—or could they? Philly won three straight. "We're still alive," McGraw barbed when the Giants took Game Five. Next day the A's spelled his evil eye: 13–2 on 13 hits. Matty hailed victory 300. Rube Marquard won his 21st straight game. New York took another flag, then outhit the Red Sox, .270–220, outscored them, 31–25, had a 1.71 ERA, and lost the Series, 4–3–1.

People speak of "tripping the light fantastic." McGraw's had a bitter gloss: The Giants made 17 muffs.

A Politburo member crows over the Kremlin's latest five-year plan. "How is it working?" asks a comrade. The bureaucrat replies: "Ask me in the thirteenth year." The 1913 Yankees visited the Polo Grounds for one year. They left in late '22. McGraw managed his 1,000th game. The Giants signed Jim Thorpe, who batted .143, and won their third straight pennant. "The Yanks were lousy through the '10s," said Harold Rosenthal. "The Giants weren't [first/second eight times 1911–'20]. The Yankees outdrew them only once ['18]. McGraw's primacy was a given"—before October.

On October 12, 1913, he and coach Wilbert Robinson went drinking. "Damn it," said Little Nap, "you're making too many coaching mistakes [in the Series v. Philadelphia]." Robbie exploded, "The hell I am. You're making more." McGraw fired him. Uncle Robbie doused McGraw with beer. Six days later the Dodgers hired him to manage. "In New York baseball," Allen said, "you could be in Brooklyn today, Yankee Stadium tomorrow"—or second, like the '14 Giants. The '16ers won a record 26 straight games—and finished fourth. On September 4, Mathewson pitched and won his last Giants game. "Seems Like Old Times," Carmen Lombardo wrote in 1946. McGraw's scent more of elegy than melody.

On October 15, 1917, White Sox manager Pants Rowland sought to console Nap after another Series swoon. "Get away from me, mister," snapped McGraw. His tenant's whammy was worse. Yankees half-owner Jacob Ruppert wanted Miller Huggins to manage. Partner Tillinghast Huston liked Robinson. Huggins signed October 26. "Ultimately," said Allen, "that led to Ruppert taking charge, buying Huston out," and building Yankee Stadium.

Now-Yankee Home Run Baker made a 1918 game-ending triple play. The '19 Giants hailed their future in the making. McGraw, Charles A. Stoneham, and Tammany pol Francis X. McQuade bought the Brush estate's controlling interest. On May 4, the Nationals played their first Sunday game at the Polo Grounds. In September, they beat Philadelphia, 6–1. Time of game: a record 51 minutes. "They wanted their season over with," a writer said of the second-placers. Soon they would want a key to a Ruthian can of worms.

In 1915, Babe Ruth hit his first homer, at the Polo Grounds, off the Yankees' Jack Warhop. On January 5, 1920, New York bought him from Boston. "He was a burst of dazzle and jingle," Jimmy Cannon wrote, "Santa Claus drinking his whiskey straight and groaning with a bellyache caused by gluttony."

Ruth '20 hit 29 dingers. (No pre-'19 big had over 24.) A year later he led the AL in six categories, including homers (54, topping any team). Even nicknames screamed carnival—the Bambino (also, Big Bambino). Behemoth of Biff. Caliph of Clout. Colossus of Club. Goliath of the Grand Slam. King of Clout. Prince of Powders. Sultan of Swat. Wizard of Whack. "He was the first national superstar," noted George Will, "the man who gave us that category." By any name, Ruth miffed McGraw. Be careful about what you wish for. "The Giants wanted the Yankees as a tenant," laughed Smith. "Now they were a pygmy in their park." The 1920 pinstripes became first to draw a million—1,289,422—v. the Giants' 929,609.

Ruth '21 topped the league: 170 RBI, 177 runs, 144 walks, .512 on-base, .846 slugging, and 59 homers. The Yanks won their first pennant. Four AL teams batted over .300. Brooklyn's Zack Wheat reached the seats, circled the first-base bag, and fell. "All of a sudden I felt this cramp," he said. Wheat rose, dusted his pants, and finally completed a trek around the bases. "The 'longest home run,' " said Rosenthal, "ever hit."

Stengel arrived to help McGraw win the flag. On October 5, 1921, in the first-since-'06 one-city fall festival, Pittsburgh's KDKA aired radio's first Classic game. "[New York Herald Tribune columnist] Grantland Rice called it [ALers, 3–0]," said Allen. The Giants took the Series. Babe batted .313, but fanned 8 times in 16 ups.

"Don't blame Ruth. Can happen to anyone," McGraw said after his first title since 1905. Victory, not '11–'12–'13–'17 defeat, sired grace, refusal to gloat, and reluctance to offend.

"I like my team," Nap said in early '22. It was easy to see why. Frank Frisch hit over .300 for 11 straight years. George "High Pockets" Kelly "made more important hits for me," said McGraw, "than any player I ever had." The Bombers' Joe Bush went 26–7. Their shortstop, Everett Scott, was nearing 1,000 straight games. "I'm riding a train that gets wrecked. The team's playing in Chicago. So I spend $40 for a cab to get to the park on time." The Giants and Yankees clinched again. The Series returned to best-of-seven. Game Two tied, 3–3. The Stonehams won the other four, then kicked the Yanks off Manhattan Isle. "They'll have to move to Long Island, or the Bronx," puffed McGraw, "and nobody'll ever hear from them again." The car is not for Everyman. Dewey defeats Truman. TV is just a fad.

Gloria Swanson starred in *Prodigal Daughter*. W. B. Yeats won the '23 Nobel Prize for Literature. The Giants synthesized McGraw's Gaelic mix of hope and portent. Frisch led the league in hits (223). Irish Meusel fronted in RBI (125). Ross Youngs—to McGraw, "the greatest outfielder I ever saw"—seven times topped .300. Kelly homered in three straight innings v. Chicago. "No wonder," said Nap, "we were the first to hold first place each day of the season."

By October, radio linked Washington, D.C., via New York to Massachusetts. The network's baritone, a singer and piano player, called the first Series in its entirety. Graham McNamee filled a ground-level chair at the Polo Grounds and Yankee Stadium and used a carbon microphone, scorebook, and his throaty, bursting voice. He etched record Series attendance (301,430) and Ruth (crashing three dingers) and Stengel (batting .417 and wafting an inside-the-park Game One–winning [5–4] home run). Scrawled Damon Runyon: "This is the way old Casey Stengel ran running his home run home when two were out in the ninth inning and the score was tied, and the ball still bounding inside the Yankee yard. This is the way—his mouth wide open. His warped old legs bending beneath him at every stride. His arms flying back and forth like those of a man swimming with a crawl stroke. His flanks heaving, his breath whistling, his head far back. . . . The warped old legs, twisted and bent by many a year of baseball campaigning, just barely held out under Casey until he reached the plate, running his home run home. Then they collapsed."

Anticlimax followed, like Vic Damone succeeding Crosby. The Yanks won Game Two, 4–2. Twice Ruth went deep. The McGraws took a 2–1 game lead; again, Stengel homered. The Bombers then won three straight and first of 26 titles. Ruth hit .368. Stengel batted .417. Twenty-six years later, legs still warped, old Casey became their manager.

Charles Stoneham smiled. "If you were a Giants fan," he said of the Jazz Age, "sometimes Cooperstown came to you." The '24 'Jints blared a Hall of Fame infield. First to third: Bill Terry, debuting in 1923; Frisch, scoring 121 runs; captain Travis (Stonewall) Jackson, six times batting .300; and rookie Fred Lindstrom. Kelly homered in a record six straight games. On September 27, McGraw took his 10th and final pennant.

Quid: Pitcher Art Nehf got three hits in the October 4 game at Washington. "The next Series pitcher," said Allen, "would be Orel Hershiser ['88]." Quo: McGraw lost his sixth in nine Series. That winter the Giants and White Sox toured France. The French Baseball Federation gave McGraw a silver medal for "promoting the game." A friend lauded him. "Hell," he said, "I'd have traded it for a couple runs last October."

Four straight flags were more than any NL team had won, or would win again. "We're almost there [winning a last Series]," McGraw said. The Giants dealt Frisch to St. Louis for Hornsby. Mel Ott, 18, hit the first of 511 homers—his sole inside-the-park. Lindstorm '28 got a record nine hits in a double-header. A battery tied pitcher Garland "Bob" Buckeye, 260-pound NFL lineman, and 250-pound catcher Frank "Shanty" Hogan. Bigger was Carl Hubbell, 25, landing from the Texas League. One day runner Andy Reese jolted Gabby Hartnett. The Cubs catcher grabbed him to keep from falling near home plate. "Never saw anything like it," said Terry. "As Hartnett holds him, Reese gets tagged out by the [Cubs] third baseman."

Giants lose, 3–2. McGraw's protest is denied. He finishes second for the second straight year. Almost will last till 1933.

Sometime in the late '20s celebrity turned and stung its subject. "Before Ruth, McGraw was the game's greatest figure," Allen recalled. "But he hadn't won many Series, and now couldn't win that last pennant." In 1929, Hubbell no-hit the Bucs. Ott had 11 straight games of at least one ribbie. The Polo Grounds became first to use a public address system. Said Stoneham: "Let's see if we can wire the umpires for sound and connect 'em to the P.A." It flopped. (In 1931, he put speakers above the Grant Memorial.) The Giants fell to third.

Freddie Fitzsimmons '30 won 19 games. Mused McGraw: "With our club, who couldn't?" New York hit .319—a twentieth-century high. Terry forearmed .401—the last NLer with four hits each 10 at-bats. He also passed 100 RBI six times. Lindstrom hit .379. Ott added .349. The Giants ERA was 4.61. "Part of it was our short lines," said Hubbell. "Part our pitching stunk."

Depression deepened. Contagion roiled the 16 million unemployed. Terry, Ott, and Terry led the '31 league in runs, walks, and triples. Almost: the Giants finished second. A year later attendance crashed to a worst-since-'18 484,868. On June 3, McGraw resigned. Kudos skipped the last eight years. "There will never be another like him," a writer said of Cooperstown '37. Stoneham hoped that of the '32ers. They finished a non-almost last.

FENWAY PARK

The Red Sox won five of baseball's first 15 World Series—but none since 1918—the year that the Twenty-sixth Division entered France. (Its moniker was the Yankee Division: Who says the military lacks humor?) Extremes link the Olde Towne Team. Ted Williams and Roman Mejias. Carl Yastrzemski and Don Giles. Years that peal—1946, 1948–'49, 1967, 1977–'78, 1986.

In 1988, I visited Bart Giamatti at his New York office. Admitting to a state of Red Sox fan, I asked if that bespoke masochism or loyalty. Giamatti roared his teddy bear of a laugh. "No question," said the longtime Soxaphile. "Clearly, it speaks of both." If the Sox 'r' us, Fenway Park is the Sox. Take Texas. Its spiritual core is—what?—Houston or the Alamo. In New England, such doubt would be as unlikely as Dick Stuart snaring a ground ball. Later, Hubball came to mean sadness, memory, and evenings in the rain. Fenway's *entrée* differed.

The '12 Sox moved Huntington Avenue's grass one mile to the north and west and hailed a steel-and-concrete park. You can look it up: Fenway opened the week that the Titanic sank. First game: April 20. Pitcher/batter: Boston's Buck O'Brien and New York's Guy Zinn. Score: Sox 7, Highlanders 6. Star: Tris Speaker, driving in the winning run. A crowd of 27,000 filled the grandstand and wings flanking foul lines beyond the infield.

The Sox now demand a larger park to brook today's luxury suite/ corporate-boxed/Golconda of an age. Fenway has bronzed Babe Ruth through Joe Cronin via Billy Rohr to Yaz. Call it passé, or sacrosanct. Above all, call it ours.

"I went there as a kid," observed Tip O'Neill of the union of Jersey and Lansdowne Streets. "You never knew what would happen—pop-fly homers down the lines, a ball off the Wall. A guy could miss an inside-the-park homer. Nothing was uniform. Let me tell ya', that was the miracle of the place."

Fenway bagged straightaway hitters. Center field stood 488 feet from home plate, then fell to 468 and 389, respectively, in 1930–'34. Right-center began at 380, rising to 383 in '55. Further right required a deeper indrawing of breath—405 feet—until '40's 380 built-for-Williams bullpen. Baseball's deepest center corner—a.k.a. the Triangle—measured 550, 593, and 420 in 1922–'31–'34. By contrast, right and left—initially, 314 and 324 feet; now, 302 and 310—knocked pitching down.

Wall heights were just as antipodal. Center and right-center read 18 and 9 feet; the right-field pole, 3. The pre-'34 left-field wall was 25 feet high. A parallel 10-foot incline—Duffy's Cliff, for '10–'17 outfielder Duffy Lewis—ended near dead center field. By 1936, new owner Thomas Yawkey cut the berm, painted the wall green, raised it to 37 feet, built a 23-foot net to protect windows on Lansdowne Street, and put tin over a framework of 2-by-4 foot wooden railroad ties. A ball hitting the ties might bounce toward second base. Finding tin, it dropped at a fielder's feet.

The plot linked scarce foul ground, a tier of grandstand, right-to-center bleachers, and red brick facade. "From the outside it looked like part of the neighborhood," Williams said. Leaving its belly, you elbowed your way into a large-for-the age 35,000–person capacity. (Current, 33,871. Seats: roof, 2,168; boxes, 13,121; reserved grandstand, 12,075; and bleachers, 6,507.)

Bowie Kuhn connived with memory. "In my job, you're supposed to be objective," baseball's 1969–'84 commissioner said. "I loved, though, how Fenway made you a participant, not spectator." By 1918, the Red Sox nearly tripled the crosstown Braves' gate. Forget some future curse. Fenway housed a team near the solstice of its prime.

For those who recall Rudy York, it is improbable but true: The early Sox won with pitching, defense, and speed. Joe Wood '12 went 34–5. His Gettysburg was September's clash with Walter Johnson. "Remember Dempsey and Tunney," mate Larry Gardner later mused. "Newspapers ran comparison charts—height, weight, chest size, reach." Thousands sat on grass behind poles or ropes. Speaker doubled in the sixth. Lewis then lofted down the right-field line. Outfielder Doug Moeller couldn't reach it. Speaker scored: Sox, 1–0. A reporter asked Johnson if he threw faster than Wood. "Mister," Walter said, "isn't nobody does that."

What the Royal Rooters did was endue the '12 Oktoberfest with a neoteric character. "They were our loyalest [sic] fans," said Gardner. "They loved baseball and booze." Before the Polo Grounds opener the Rooters marched singing around Times Square. (Later the New Haven Railroad's "The John Barleycorn Excursion" decamped for Boston.) The Sox won and tied Games One-Two, then split the next four. Behind, 3–2–1, the Giants took Game Seven, 11–4. Worse, Fenway was oversold. Refusing to leave, the Rooters fought police. "To hell with Queen Victoria!" one screamed while breaking the outfield fence.

"How you do top *this*?" a writer said. Easily, as it happened. Wood, relieving/winning his third game, yielded the final match/10th-inning/2–1 lead run. Its bottom spawned a denouement foreign to Boston's niche as heartbreak kids. Leading off, Clyde Engle popped to Fred Snodgrass. The center fielder saw, but missed, the ball. Engle reached second. Harry Hooper lined to Snodgrass and Steve Yerkes got a walk. In 1908, Fred Merkle's gaffe cost McGraw a pennant. Now Speaker gift-horsed a pop between first baseman Merkle, Zelig-like at first base, and catcher Chief Meyers. Both looked it in the mouth.

Reprieved, Tris singled, tying the game. Gardner's fly to right scored Yerkes, concluding it. The ex-Pilgrims had again found Canaan: Red Sox 3, Giants 2, winning the Series, 4–3–1.

Was God a Sox fan? In a reverse twist of fate, another break presaged the last eighty years. In 1913, Wood fell on his throwing hand and broke a thumb. Today, with surgery, he might miss a month. Instead, Joe was told to exercise it. The thumb got worse. He later quit. Succeeding him: 20-game winners Ray Collins (20 in 1914), Babe Ruth (23 and 24, '16–'17), and Carl Mays (22 and 21, '17–'18). "Want a comparison?" ex–Sox announcer Ken Coleman said. "You're talking pitchers like [the '60s] Koufax and Drysdale."

In 1915, even *fifth* starter Wood had a league-best 1.49 ERA. The Series split hairs: each match, decided by a run. The Sox and A's paired Games One-Two. Three and Four left Fenway for larger Braves Field: Twice Lewis hijacked Gavvy Gravath to save a 2–1 win. In 149 regular-season games, Hooper homered twice. Ibid., Game Five: Sox win (the game, 5–4, and Series, 4–1). Recall Arnold Early, Ike Delock, and other Sox tatters. None pitched in the '16 Classic. Ernie Shore, Dutch Leonard, and Ruth, beating Brooklyn, did. What hitting there was, was done by Gardner: two dingers, including one that he didn't see: "Brooklyn's Jack Coombs was pitching and I was angry because I wasn't hitting. He throws, I close my eyes, and swing from the heels."

Coleman formed a smile. "Back then, even bad turned out good." On June 23, 1917, Ruth walked the first batter and was ejected for arguing. Shore, relieving, retired the next 27 Nats. That winter manager Bill Carrigan retired. Successor Jack Barry asked, "Babe, how'd you like to play left field?"—and pitch. Ruth hit a league-tying 11 homers. Play ended early in '18 to trudge troops to war. Boston won the Series *v.* Chicago. Its Everest: Babe's then-record of 29⅔ straight scoreless innings. "They were the gambler who breaks the bank and then can't buy a break," said the late *Herald Traveler* writer Al Hirshberg. "In a decade the Sox used up their luck."

Boston had beaten the Yanks 18 straight times—in *New York*. In 1927, Carrigan returned to manage an outfield of Skinny Shaner, Ira Flagshead, and John Tobin. "Same uniform," he said. "Different world."

A native of Peoria, Harry Frazee once played in Boston. The Broadway financier and ex-bellhop bought the Sox after the 1916 Series. Frazee was said to have offered $60,000 for Walter Johnson. Oh, say, he could even see—the first to play "The Star-Spangled Banner" before a game (September 9, 1918). Harry's real anthem, alas, was greed. In January 1920, needing cash, he sold Ruth to New York for $125,000 and a $300,000 loan. Among Frazee's would-be hits was *My Lady Friends*. A critic noted the billboard: "They're the only friends the SOB has."

Babe's exile spun a sign on Boston Common and Faneuil Hall—"For Sale." Tip O'Neill stoked a cigar. "Superfluous," he said. "Frazee didn't need any ideas." Each New Year's Eve Guy Lombardo and his Royal Canadians played, "The Music Goes 'Round and 'Round." Frazee's kept winding up at 42nd and Broadway. To New York streamed Wally Schang, Mike McNally, Everett Scott, Waite Hoyt, "Bull Joe" Bush, "Sad Sam" Jones, George Pipgras, and Herb Pennock. Of the Yanks' '23 players, 11 had been Red Sox.

"You're going to ruin the Sox in Boston for a long time," their then-manager told Frazee on learning of Ruth's sale. Dub Ed Barrow Nostradamus. They won a single pennant in the next 47 years.

Ruth knew that Tiparillos don't feed the bulldog. "Fifteen thousand fans show up for [September '19's] Babe Ruth Day, and all I got was a cigar." Boston got less: Its American League Baseball Company draped the second division through 1933. The '32ers lured 182, 150—2,365 per date. A year later the Sox greeted a patrician patriarch. "As much as he saw himself as the man who owned the team," Bart Giamatti said of Tom Yawkey, "to most he *was* the team."

Team offices open onto Yawkey Way [pre-'77 Jersey Street]. Next door medal/mettle links two pioneers. One plaque hails Sox '33–'47 general manager Eddie Collins. The other: "Thomas Austin Yawkey 1903–76. In Memory. From Those Who Knew Him Best—the Red Sox employees." In 1933, the AL went looking to save the Sox. Yawkey's uncle had owned the Tigers. Detroit's current boss knew his family. "They've got money," Walter Briggs told peers. "I don't think the league should be a bank." (The Sox owed it $150,000.) Collins was an ex–prep schoolmate. "You love the game," he told Yawkey. "I know [owner Bob] Quinn will sell it to the right man." He did, for $1.5 million, and Yawkey, 30, was.

The new owner began reworking Fenway. In 1934, a four-alarm blaze ruined construction. Digging deep, Yawkey continued to build. The left-field wall was still too near for some. Lefty Gomez mused: "If you were a right-handed pitcher and threw sidearm, your knuckles would scrape it." Up went a quilt of wall advertisements. One scrawled, "Be wise. Clear heads choose Calvert [whiskey]." You recall a fan: "The only thing worse than watching the Red Sox drunk"—pause—"is watching them sober."

A third plaque reads: "New Fenway Park. Built—1912. Reconstructed—1934. Boston American League Baseball Company. Thomas A. Yawkey, President." That August, 46,766 jammed Fenway for a doubleheader. In September 1935, a record 47,627 saw another two-for-the-price-of-one. "Those never-to-be equaled marks," said 1951–'65 Sox voice Curt Gowdy, "came from lax fire laws and league rules tightened after World War II."

The 1934 Sox more than doubled '33's attendance. Five years later a man trooped to Fenway who became the Townies' core.

BRIGGS STADIUM

"**I** have to be careful about [Vin] Scully," Red Barber wrote of his protégé. "He's my boy." I have to be careful about the Tigers' steep-walled rectangle. In 1999, the *Wall Street Journal*'s Bryan Gruley visited Michigan and Trumbull. "In an instant that never fails to surprise me, there it is, a vast and majestic cavern of blue and orange and shimmering green. Standing there, I know I will miss this frozen moment more than anything. It's like seeing someone you love whom you haven't seen in a while: she's the same, but she makes you catch your breath a little." Tiger (neé Briggs) Stadium closed in the final fall of the American Century. Ernie Harwell has broadcast in Brooklyn, the Polo Grounds, Baltimore, and Detroit. "This was really," he said, "the best park of them all."

The Tigers 1912–'99 pleasance tied asymmetrical lines, a yawning center field, and 125-foot flagpole—baseball's highest in-play curio. A right-field overhang turned pop flies into homers. Steep-pitched stands placed you high above the field. The ghosts of Greenberg and McLain and Goslin graced the green and shadowed turf. Look at third base: Cobb's spikes cut a hapless fielder. See the plate: Bill Freehan is blocking Lou Brock. In right, Kirk Gibson has just bombed Goose Gossage. By rote, tableaus reemerge.

Aromas blur: hops and mustard and hot pretzels and grease. Stores sell baseball cards and autographed balls and beanbags and bobbing dolls. Kids wear baseball gloves and Tigers shirts and pants and wristwatches. Infidels don a Yankees cap. Fathers take a hand, find the ticket, and approach the park. Slowly, by twos and threes, you near the lush and humming earth. "It's so generational," said Harwell. "A grandfather brought his son, who brought his son, who brought his son."

Let a Soxaphile proclaim it: I loved the Tigers' den.

America 1912 sowed a Flanders Field of possibility. New Mexico and Arizona became states. Color photography bloomed. Once a plaything for the wealthy, cars buoyed Detroit. In 1900, 8,000 saw the USA. Now more than 3 million did—up nearly 40,000 percent.

In 1911, Ty Cobb had broke the bank: .420, 147 runs, and league-best 40-game hitting streak. Cobb '12 batted. .409. On April 20 he and Sam Crawford forged two double steals. George Mullin's eleventh-inning single beat Cleveland, 6–5. "Welcome to Detroit's first concrete game," Joe Falls wrote of its single-deck cabash. The Tigers had played here since 1896.

"[Frank] Navin was the owner, and he'd built the park incrementally," Falls observed. "Now he decided to tear down its wood and build from scratch." His makeover housed 20,000, cost $500,000, and renamed Bennett Park Navin Field. We're in the money: In 1977, a new press box cost $600,000. Opening Day '12 made money: 24,384 ministered to baseball's newest park.

Later, Tiger Stadium became a hitter's paradise. Paradise lost went first. Navin's initial homer bounced through a left-center-field scoreboard door. The outfield made offense a fall guy: 370, 467, and 345 right to left. The Tigers pined for an edge. "When slugging teams came,"

Ty wrote, "we'd put in temporary stands, turning triples and inside-the-parkers into ground-rule doubles. It balanced out." *Talent* outs.

Cobb led the AL in 1913–'14–'15–'17–'18–'19 (.390–.368–.369–.383–.382–.384). In 1922, his .401 trailed George Sisler's .420. Crawford '14 led in triples (26). Bobby Veach '19 topped in hits. Even Ty pitched two innings in 1918. The '12–'22ers' ERA veered between fourth and eighth. Slowly, the pattern formed. "Pitching!" said Cobb. "We never had enough!"

The 1915 Tigers won 100 games. On September 16, Carl Mays faced Detroit. Cobb missed his first pitch and shouted, "There's something wrong with that ball!" The umpire discarded it. Ty missed the next pitch. "He's doctoring the ball—that pitch sailed 18 inches." The ump tossed it out of play. Mays threw. The ball mixed yin and yang. Cobb missed and flung his bat. "You cheater!" he screamed. "No one can make a ball sail like that unless he's doctoring it. I'll run ya' out of this league." Instead, the Tigers ran punch-drunk to riddance.

Once Boston came to town: two out, ninth inning, Sox, 3–2. George Moriarty streaked from third for home. Out! called the umpire. Sox catcher/manager Bill Carrigan spit tobacco juice in Moriarty's face. Moriarty ripped off his mask. Soon they were gouging legs, jaws, and arms. "Finally, Carrigan ran into the clubhouse," said Moriarty. "The crowd ran after him. They've got clubs, rocks." Navin asked them to stop. They refused, awaiting Carrigan. Years later Rough Bill formed a smile. "To the rescue comes this kindly groundskeeper who gives me an old hat, rubber boots, and crummy coat, smears my face with mud, and sticks a rake in my hand." Carrigan fooled the mob. "By the time they find I'm gone, I'm on a club car toward Chicago."

Photos show Cobb, spikes high, slashing catchers. Most avoided him. Carrigan *courted* him. Once Bill slugged Ty in the face with the hand that held the ball. Cobb was out—and out cold, removed on a stretcher. Ty '15 led the league in runs, hits, total bases, and steals—a record 96. On June 18, he swiped home twice v. Washington. Harry Coveleski and Hooks Dauss went 46–26. Boston still finished 2½ games ahead.

"Great timing," said Navin of Detroit's alpha. "No team had ever won as many games as we did and *not* won the pennant." A Depression, world war, four presidents, and 19 years passed before its omega came again.

Motown's poet and essayist, lay preacher and family man laughed softly. "Something about Tiger Stadium eclipsed how the team was doing," said Harwell. "If they lost, you could look at the ballpark or our guys or the opposition. It felt right"—a Boswell of baseball's charm.

In 1923, Navin built a second deck from first base to third. "The capacity now will be 29,000," he said: 40,884 gathered for the Yanks. Austerity ebbed: The Tigers added a rooftop press box and elevator. Distance zagged: left, 341 (1926) via 339 to 367 ('31) to 339 ('34); center, 455 to 469 ('31); right, '30's 372. Cobb didn't care. On May 5, 1925, the Peach picked 6-for-6. Johnny Neun '27 turned an unassisted triple play. For Harry Heilmann '16–'32, four titles draped uneven years: .394–.403–.395–.398 in 1921–'23–'25–'27. "Mr. Navin would give me a two-year contract," he said, "and I'd take it easy the second year." Even *easy* wowed: 1922–'24–'26–'28, .356–.346–.367-.328. "Consistency," said Cobb. "It rivaled the noon-day whistle." Too, the Sultan of Swat.

The 1939–'64 Voice of the Yankees had relatives in Detroit. "As a kid, I'd take a train up from Alabama," Mel Allen said. One day he saw Ruth catch an eighth-inning fly. Babe then sat in the *Tigers* dugout for the top of the ninth.

"Where were the umpires?" a writer said.

"Babe Ruth could do anything he liked. Anyway, the Tigers were way ahead. The Yankees then start a rally and bat around." Ruth left the dugout, plucked a bat from the Yankees bench, and smashed a three-run homer. "Yankees win. The crowd couldn't believe it," Allen said, his head bobbing like Louis Armstrong's. "But then, neither could I."

Ruth and Cobb jousted like Romans and Macabees. In 1924, Ty taunted him: "Something around here really stinks. Like a polecat." Later they fought at home plate for half an hour: Detroit forfeited the game. Once Babe whacked a ball that landed two blocks beyond center field—800 feet away. "Maybe the sign above the door was for him," Navin huffed—"Visitors Clubhouse—No Visitors Allowed." On July

13, 1934, Ruth banged homer No. 700. "I want that ball back!" he bellowed rounding second. Lennie Bieleski must have heard him. He traded it for a better seat, $20, and autographed ball.

A quarter-century earlier Detroit had won the pennant. Skill relit its glow. In 1929, Charlie Gehringer hailed his Day at Navin by singling thrice, homering, and handling 10 chances. The Mechanical Man batted over .300 in 13 of 16 full years. He also mimed the strong, silent type. One breakfast roommate Chief Hogsett asked Charlie to pass the salt. Gehringer ignored him. Finally, Chief said, "Did I say anything wrong, Charlie?" He sniffed: "You could have pointed."

Hank Greenberg pointed to the '34 All-Star Game. Said Mickey Cochrane: "He had 103 RBI at the break and didn't make the team." Mickey, who did, fused .320, 76 ribbies, and MVP for the year. The Tigers gripped reporters. Gehringer became "Mr. Tiger." Greenberg evolved into "Hancus Pancus." Lynwood Rowe turned "Schoolhouse/ Schoolboy/Schoolie." In August, the rookie beat Washington, 4–2, for an AL-tying 16th straight victory. The 1933 Tigers ended 25 games behind Washington. On September 24, 1934, they won their first flag in 25 years.

"Hell, yes, we can win a Series," Cochrane cried by way of mocking 1907–'08–'09. His team didn't listen: St. Louis won, four games to three. Detroit *still* had not won an Oktoberfest. "It could be worse," jibed Greenberg. "Forget their fluke year [1914]. We could be stuck in Boston."

BRAVES FIELD

No Boston Brave matched the panache of the Tigers' part-Gibraltar and part-child. A *team,* however, did. Many will concede in trying to recapture the year 1914 that they were lucky through accident of birth. The Miracle Braves! They gilded myth, and cast the legend—its plot as recalled as last rites, or first love.

Patsy Donovan had managed the '10–'11 Red Sox. "Tish, tish," he told players, or "Tut, tut, boys, please don't say those [obscene] words." Braves manager George Stallings, on the other hand, grasped 1998– Sox manager Jimy Williams: "Baseball knows two languages— English and profanity." Said former player Jimmy Austin: "He cursed something awful." Stallings readied for a year that long ago settled in New England's bones.

Only Joe Connolly hit over .300. Ex-Cub second baseman Johnny Evers won the last Chalmers MVP car. Save center field, shortstop is baseball's high-hat position. "It gives you the stage," wrote Boston columnist Dave Egan, "but you need range, speed, arm"—a Wagner, an Ozzie Smith. Such combinations are hard to find. Rabbit Maranville played for 1912–'20 and '29–'35 Boston. His *vitae* tied 2,670 games, 5-foot-5 and 155 pounds, and the first basket catch. "He is a midget," Tom Meany added, "with the arms and shoulders of a weight lifter."

Maranville '14 batted .246. Lacking pop, Braves pitching turned supernatural. "Seattle Bill" James, Dick Rudolph, and George "Lefty" Tyler finished 68–30. On July 19, the Braves trailed by 14½ games. In September, they took, lost, and retook the lead. The once-Beaneaters and Giants moved a morning/afternoon Labor Day doubleheader to Fenway: 74,163 spied the glass. Boston won by 10½ games. "They did it *slow*," Stengel said of the '69 Mets, "but *fast*."

In the movie *The Way We Were*, Robert Redford and a friend are lounging in a boat—sun alight, water clear—as they stage a game. Best month? Redford asks. Best song? Best year? The Braves' best Classic was '14's sweep of the 1910–'11–'13 champion A's. Rudolph beat Chief Bender, 7–1. James blanked Eddie Plank, 1–0. Game Three took 12 frames: Boston's Hank Gowdy smacked the Series' sole homer. (In 1917, he became the first player to enlist in World War I.)

"Wonder what they're doing?" Stallings mused before the final. "Packing or puking?" Evers singled for the 3–1 clincher. The Braves held Philly to a .172 average. "Who can explain it?" Ezio Pinza warbled in *South Pacific*. "Who can tell you why? Fools give you reasons. Wise men never try."

By 1900, the National League had juggled 31 franchises in a quarter-century, including Buffalo, Syracuse, and Troy, New York, Baltimore, Cleveland, Detroit, Indianapolis, Kansas City, Louisville, Washington,

D.C., and New England's Hartford, Providence, and Worcester. Boston's '76 charter team also traded nicknames. Beaneaters became Doves (for owner John Dovey) and later Rustlers (William Hepburn Russell). In 1912, James Gaffney bought them. "He was Tammany Hall," nodded Tip O'Neill, "and was called a Brave," which he named the club. It morphed into Bees (1936), was renamed Braves ('40), and called Braves Field the Bee Hive ('36–'41). In 1953, it swapped another name—Boston for Milwaukee.

The NLers first played at South End Grounds III on Walpole Street. "For years the Braves owned Boston," said 1940–'52 Braves announcer Jim Britt. "Then comes Fenway, and they're distant number two." Gaffney panted for his own steel (750 ton) and concrete (8 million pound) home: In 1914, he bought the Allston Golf Course (on Commonwealth Avenue), left South End Grounds (last game: August 11, 0–0, called by darkness, *v.* Cincinnati), and spent '15 at Fenway. Expenses soared: Braves Field cost more than $1 million. *Terra firma* crumbled: A dozen horses and mules were buried in an infield cave-in. The August 18, 1915, first game augured better things for Boston's diaspora: Braves 4, St. Louis 3. The plot housed 40,000. Thousands were turned away.

Each classic park had a distinctive character. The Braves' bound tall grass (mowed high, to aid pitching), ten-foot wall around the park, uncovered pavilion down each line, small right-field bleacher area ("Jury Box," as in twelve men), and single-deck covered grandstand behind home plate and along the lines. Trolley cars on the Commonwealth line ushered a visitor to the park. A large stucco building had ticket arches, housed the business office, and abutted the field. A ground-level scoreboard crowned left's fence. One day New York's Johnny Rawlings and Bill Rariden hit through-the-wall homers—"gaps," Britt explained, "kept open by a lazy scoreboard boy."

Fenway hailed the dinger. At Braves, the dead ball lived. "Forget Murderers Row," said the Hall of Fame's Jack Redding. "Gaffney loved triples, speed, and pitching." Foul lines mimed a taxi ride—402 feet. Center flanked the lot's farthest edge—550 feet. Ty Cobb '15 did a double take. "Nobody will ever hit a baseball out of *this* park." It took two years for a batter—the Cardinals' Walt Cruise—to clear the wall. The Boston and Albany Railroad rimmed the outfield. In 1925, Bernie Neis *literally* went yard off St. Louis' Art Reinhart.

As we have seen, the Red Sox rented Braves Field for the 1915–16 Series. Boston '16 edged Brooklyn, 2–1, in 14 innings. Joe Oeschger and Brooklyn's Leon Cadore pitched 26 in 1920: Darkness called the game, 1–1. Offense woke with '28's inner fence. "They didn't build it to increase seating," said Redding, "but help homers." Left, left-center, center, and right field fell to 320, 330, 387, and 364, respectively. An eight-foot wall linked left to right-center. New bleachers sat 6,000 more behind. "Great idea," Britt added. "Too bad it flopped."

On June 2, 1928, Les Bell hit three homers in the stands—and barely missed another. By mid-month, 47 once in play had gone deep. "The problem was *who* was hitting them!" wowed Lee Allen. It is no trick to observe that rivals had the edge.

Like hope, the new seats vanished. "Each week, they took more down," Egan wrote of late 1928. "The club put up string [to designate ground-rule doubles]." The scoreboard moved from left-center to above the Jury Box. (A larger board replaced it.) Ads dotted the left and right-center fence. Center's added a batter-friendly green. Capacity dropped to '48's 37,106. The inner wall—"fence within a fence"—kept moving. "A long-time theme is clubs moving fences to help themselves," said Allen. "Few parks changed their dimensions as much as Braves Field." Would it be a bandbox like Fenway? A canyon like Griffith? The Braves couldn't make up their mind.

Left field wore 340 (1930), 354, 359, 368, 350 (1940), 334, and 1944's 337. Left-center fled 330 via 359 for '42's 365. Center caught its breath: 395, 387, 426 (1936), 407, 385, 401 (1942), 375, 390, 380, and—whew—'46's 370. Right-center field bookended 362 and 355 ('42–43). Right followed the red ball from 297 (1929) and 364 ('33) via 297 and 376 and 378 ('38) through 350, 340, 320 (late '43), 340 (early '44), 340, 320, 318, 320, and '48's 319. "They should have made the inner fence portable," said Redding. "It'd have saved a lot of work."

In 1936, home plate moved toward the backstop. Gaffney later cut a notch in the right-field seats. "You can still see it in Nickerson Field [bought by Boston University, coverted to football, and now flanked by the Myles Standish dorms]," said Braves '50–'58 pitcher Ernie Johnson. In 1946, the field shifted to the right. Heights joined the wandering:

right, 10 (6 screen above 4 wood); left at the scoreboard, 64 (1949); right-center, 20, 25, and 19 ('46–'48–'53)—the NL's Green Monster.

The worst environment is to be cold, hungry, and unemployed. The '40s Braves planted trees behind center to hide railroad smoke. Elsewhere, curiosa coursed through the Charles. In 1932, 51,331 paid to see the Phils. The '35 Braves preferred salary to commission: 95 watched July 28. A '38 hurricane ripped New England. A Redbird hit to center— and Al Lopez caught it behind the plate. In 1945, Lou Perini, Guido Rugo, and Joe Maney—The Three Steam Shovels—bought the team and installed sky boxes and lights. (The first night game: May 11, 1946.) Owning, as opposing to chiding them, became a chore.

Perini OKd $500,000 to fix plumbing, brace supports, and paint seats. Work continued Opening Day: It was soon plain in one section that the paint was wet. "Their clothing was damaged," Curt Gowdy said. "So the Braves apologized and told fans to take it to the dry cleaners." A "Paint Account" opened at the local bank. Team lawyers took to accepting claims. More than 18,000 arrived. The Braves paid about $6,000. How was it possible?—but it was.

"After Yawkey arrived, the Red Sox became a rock," said Egan. "The Braves seemed like a circus." Exceptions read like credits. A 1930 rookie bopped 38 homers. Three years later Wally Berger pinch-hit a last-day grand slam for Boston's first post-'20 first division. In 1935, he led the NL in taters (34) and RBI (130)—and Babe Ruth ended his career as a Braves scrub and vice president. "He was coming home," said Jim Britt. On Opening Day, Babe jolted Carl Hubbell for a single and home run.

Six times the '25–'38 Nationals placed seventh or last. In 1935, they drew barely 3,000 per date. Scorn spurred a boozer's bent. "There is much less drinking now than there was in 1927," Maranville said in 1929. "I know because I quit drinking on May 24, 1927." Watching, you rushed to start.

8

MY KIND OF TOWN

Emile Lazarus' "Whoever wants to know the heart and mind of America had better learn baseball" has been reviewed more than Hitler's nap on D-Day. Whoever wants to know baseball had better learn a riot of ivy, brick, bluegrass, wind off Lake Michigan, drop-dead closeness, and animal-cracker size. "In this day of computerized scoreboards and electronic message boards," said former voice Jimmy Dudley, "Wrigley Field is still as refreshing as a pretty girl in a flimsy dress on a windy day."

Take a car, bus (25 minutes from the Loop), or El (10) to Chicago's North Side. Emerging, you near a shrine once peopled by a seminary. Scalpers and groupies mix. Calypso players bang inverted detergent drums. Charters import pilgrims from the far outposts of Wrigleyville. "It's heaven on earth," said a Bleacher Bum. "Wrigley is the best place," Swingin' Sammy chimed. "I never want to leave." Senor Sosa needn't worry. The Cubs prize its quirks, odd angles, and a hand-operated scoreboard. You pass a bevy of two-story brownstones. Ahead: the junction of West Addison and North Clark.

A fire station lies a block away. Wooden souvenir stands dot the sidewalk. Passersby dart into the Cubby Bear and Murphy's Bleachers. The park is painted white and trimmed in blue. A five-piece band plays near the ticket windows. Request "Easter Parade," for the hell of it. "We Are the Champions" is seldom heard. Ballhawks flock behind the left-field wall. From Sheffield Avenue the upper deck opens, putting geography in relief. Play cards while awaiting batting practice. Enter through a tunnel, up a walkway, and toward the field. Then it hits you: tended, painted, and not a bad seat in the house.

Ivy cloaks the red brick outfield wall. Lower seating links one foul pole to another. The upper deck hangs above it: Vertigo and communion vie. Bleachers rise from the corners to form a deep V in center field. Atop it the board gives line scores, lineups, and other goings-on. After the game a banner etches W(in) or L(oss). Yardarms fly flags of league cities, states they represent, the province of Quebec, and standings of NL teams, arranged by division, and falling or rising to reflect the day. Two foul pole flags hail No. 14 and 26—Ernie Banks and Billy Williams. Rooftoppers pad unofficial attendance. Even dead, Harry Caray still means "Take Me Out to the Ball Game."

"Walking through the crowds into that great small old stadium, and there they were in the flesh," wrote the poet Donald Hall. "I can see them now in their baggy old pants, the players that I had heard about, of whom I'd seen photographs, but there they were, really walking around, live people, and the absolute enchantment, the enthrallment, the tension of starting the game, 'Play ball.' "

Richard Nixon began his *Memoirs:* "I was born in the house my father built." Wrigley outlived the league for which its house was built. In 1914–'15, three big leagues strutted: the AL, NL, and Federal League. The eight-team FL linked Indianapolis ('14 only), Newark ('15), Baltimore, Brooklyn, Buffalo, Kansas City, Pittsburgh, St. Louis, and the Chicago Whales. In 1914, leasing a lot at Addison and Clark, Whales owner Charles Weeghman tapped Zachary Taylor Davis to design a park. Davis had planned Comiskey Park. He now charted a simple 14,000-seat home. Whales a.k.a. North Side Ball Park or Weeghman Park tied a V-shaped brick and concrete grandstand, wooden bleachers, and ample length: left, 319, 335, and finally 327; power alleys, 364; center, 440; right, 356 to 345.

"I thought it'd house the Whales for years," Weeghman chortled in March '14. The FL died on December 22, 1915. Weeghman then bought and moved the Cubs from West Side Grounds to renamed Cubs Park. "Early on," he said, "you saw what kind of park this would be. First game: April 20, 1916. Score: Cubs, 7–6, in 11 innings. Pitcher: Claude Hendrix. Batter: Cincinnati's Red Killefer. Homer: Reds' Johnny Beall. Watching: mascot Joa the Cubbie Bear. (In July, he was placed in an Addison Street cage.) A visitor did a double take: Weeghman was the first owner to let you keep a foul ball.

In 1918, Hippo Vaughn led the league in ERA, shutouts, and victories. Bill Veeck, Jr., was son of the Cubs' 1919–'33 president. "You'll recognize the '18 Series," he laughed. "The Cubs lost, and greed won." Home games moved to larger Comiskey Park. Players vowed to strike unless each winner and loser got $2,500 and $1,000, respectively. U.S. soldiers were dying in Europe. Would-be strikers were thought depraved. "We didn't get a cent," said a Cubs pitcher, "not even a medallion." Briefer, better: Games took from one hour and 42 minutes to 1:57.

The 1906–'07–'08–'10 Cubs won pennants. Post-'18ers went a decade *sans* flag. "Now hast thou but one bare hour to live," wrote an English dramatist, "and then thou must be damn'd perpetually!" The Cubs seemed damned annually. On one hand, seven managers climbed the down staircase. On the other, Grover Cleveland Alexander led the '20 NL in five categories. On August 25, 1922, wind from the west whipped balls toward the wall: Cubs 26, Phillies 23, 51 hits, 23 walks, 10 errors, 25 left on base, and game time—3:01!

"Start with the breeze," said *Daily News* reporter-turned-mikeman Hal Totten, 23. On April 23, 1924, he called Chicago's first game on radio: Cubs 12, Cards 1. "Wind from the east or northeast [off Lake Michigan] helps a pitcher. From the west, good-bye. Then there's altitude [more than 600 feet above sea level] and heat. The weather changes the game more than any park." Renamed Wrigley Field changed the Cubs.

In 1918, Weeghman sold Cubs Park to William Wrigley. The gum squire lowered the field, put a scoreboard in left, and double-decked the grandstand. Capacity rose to 20,000 (1923), 38,396 ('27), and 40,000 ('28). Wrigley said: "People called it Dorr's House." Groundskeeper Bobby

Dorr's six-room apartment abutted the left-field corner gate. Left to right read 364, 436, and 321 feet. "For the first time," noted Veeck, "Wrigley's shell resembled today's." The '25 Cubs did, too, placing last. Chicago began training on Catalina Island, off Los Angeles, near Wrigley's villa. "Hell, it was great," said 5-foot-6, 195-pound left fielder Hack Wilson. Warren Brown later wrote: "He was a high-ball hitter on the field, and off it."

Wilson became the first to exhale a ball off the scoreboard. Pop paid the piper: the '27ers were Chicago's first team to draw a million. Arm: Charlie Root won 26 games. Glove: Shortstop Jimmy Cooney forged an unassisted triple play. Bat: Wilson led the league in 1926–'27–'28 dingers. In 1929, Rogers Hornsby topped in runs, total bases, and slugging. The Cubs hit .303, drew 1,485,166, and won the pennant. One day Cincy's Evar Swanson lost Norm McMillan's inside-the-parker. "Later their relief pitcher [Dutch Kemner] goes to pick up his jacket in the bullpen, and the ball pops out," said Hornsby. "Talk about luck." It had lodged in a sleeve.

"I don't care who wins," 1944–'55 voice Bert Wilson would jaw, "as long as it's the Cubs." They added temporary seats for the '29 World Series (capacity, 50,740). Wilson cared. Philadelphia won, four games to one.

"**T**he Cubs are [Ronald] Reagan's kind of team," columnist David Broder wrote in 1984. "They prefer not to work at night. They believe that three hours of labor in the afternoon are enough for any job. They know the old ways are best. God intended baseball to be played on grass and under the sun, so they play it that way. They appreciate beautiful surroundings. There is no more gracious ball park than Wrigley Field."

For a hitter, there was no more gracious year than 1930. The Phillies' Chuck Klein had 429 total bases and a .687 slugging percentage. Wilson bound a then-NL and still-baseball-high 56 taters and 191 (née 190) ribbies. "There are great years," said manager Joe McCarthy, "and there was Hack's." Riggs Stephenson is Chicago's all-time hitter (.336). Kiki Cuyler averaged over .300 five of his seven Cubs years. In 1930, they had 134 and 110 RBI, respectively. Said Veeck: "Baseball's only all-100 RBI outfield [since Boston 1884]."

In June, 51,556 overlapped the North Side park. "Forget fire regulations," said Veeck of Wrigley's largest-ever crowd. Charlie Grimm—

sunny Jolly Cholly—evolved into its ambassador *sans* résumé. The 1918–'36 NLer later became a scout, coach, manager, and announcer. "When a Cubs regular homered," James Enright wrote, "Charlie whistled all of the bench warmers out of the dugout, each with a bat in hand, and lined them up in two rows with bats upraised to form an arch for the homer hitter to pass underneath as he returned to the dugout, accompanied by Grimm in a suitably majestic manner." In 1961, Grimm joined the original eight-member College of Coaches. "The Cubs have been playing without players for years," a critic patronized. "Now, they're going to try it without a manager."

On January 26, 1932, William Wrigley died. Son Philip inherited the club. In July, shortstop Billy Jurges was shot twice in a hotel room by Violet Popovich Valli. "He'd spurned her," wrote David Condon, "but he didn't prosecute." Silk's purse, sow's ear: Valli signed a singing contract with local clubs and theaters. "Violet (What I Did For Love) Valli," read ad material, "the Most Talked-About Girl in Chicago." The Grimm of memory soon entered the dugout. Chicago won 37 of its last 57 games. Jolly became the first manager hired after midseason to finish first. "Keep 'em happy!" he cried. Kiki Cuyler's flag-clinching triple did.

The 1930 Yankees had dealt Mark Koenig to Detroit. Acquiring him, the '32 Cubs withheld a full Series share. "In charity, there is no excess," wrote Francis Bacon: To ex-mates, excess flaunted greed. The Yanks won Games One-Two. In No. 3, Ruth bats at Wrigley. He eyes the home dugout. Root throws a strike, then ball. The Yankees bellow "cheapskates." The Cubs yell "flatfoot" and toss liniment. Root throws ball two. A fan flings a lemon. Babe chucks it toward the Cubs. He raises two fingers: the count, 2–2. Debate stirs: Did Ruth point to center? "Hell, he never called it," Root vowed. "If he had, next time up I'd have stuck the pitch right in his rear." The next pitch struck the seats. Later, a writer asked about prophesying his blast. A light went on. Teammate Frank Crosetti said that Ruth harangued each Yank: "If anybody asks the greatest day in the Babe's life, it's today when I pointed where I'd homer."

Check *Webster's* under "consolation": Cuyler, Gabby Hartnett, and Frank Demaree homered. New York swept: 12–6, Red Ruffing over Root; 5–2, Lon Warneke v. Lefty Gomez; 7–5 and 13–6. "The Cubs lance at windmills," said Brown of baseball's Don Quixote. The Yanks lanced the game.

SPORTSMAN'S PARK

Grimm's America worshiped the geometry of the diamond. Bylines blurred Damon Runyon, the Salieri of the short story, and Grantland Rice—"Grannie," the courser of the press box—and Ring Lardner, *le père grand* of "Alibi Ike." Special issues hailed "our national game." Inning-by-inning digests draped telegraph office windows. "When they referred to the Giants, it was the New York Giants," said HBO Television's 1991 documentary, *When It Was a Game.* "The Dodgers were a Brooklyn institution—seemingly forever. There was an American League team in St. Louis"—and a National.

The 1902 AL Browns left Baltimore for St. Louis' Sportsman's Park. In 1920, the Cardinals left Robison Field to join them at Sullivan Avenue, North Spring Avenue, Dodier Street, and North Grand Avenue (now, North Grand Boulevard). They found an ad-lib job.

"In 1909, Browns owner Robert Lee Hedges put a second deck between the bases," wrote Bob Broeg. "He turned around the field, so the stands behind the plate became left-field seats." The stands were razed in '12. A pavilion replaced them behind an 11-foot-6-inch outfield wall. Center field was 430 feet from the plate. Left and right measured 368 and 335 ('21, 340 and 315). "Steel and concrete!" Hedges boasted of the now-25,000-seat empyrean. He was less proud of his team.

The '18 Browns hoisted bats as rifles on Opening Day to salute soldiers who trudged to war. George Sisler aped a platoon. In 1920, he had a record 257 hits. Sisler '22 batted .420—and safely in a league-high 41 straight games. "He's the nearest thing," chimed Cobb, "to a perfect ballplayer"—save eyesight. In 1923, flu inflamed his sinuses, causing double vision. Sisler still retired with a .340 average.

Urban Shocker '21–'22–'23 went 71–41. In 1922, Ken Williams became the first ALer to homer thrice in a game and go 30–30 (39 dingers and 37 steals). "More like him," said ex–*Globe Democrat* writer

Bob Burnes, "and they'd still be there." Instead, the '20–'34 Americans nine times scraped the second division. Eight skippers sought vainly to rally the reserves.

In 1928, Heinie Manush detrained from Detroit to bat one point lower than Goose Goslin's .379. Coach Jimmie Austin, 46, stole home. Another, Charley O'Leary, 52, scored a run. Broeg laughed: "They were the oldest players ever to do this. So much for youth shall be served." Beggars can't be choosers: Stanford football fullback Ernie Nevers beat the A's, 3–1.

Pratfall was contagious. Attendance plunged from 712,918 (1922) to 88,113 ('33). A pop bottle struck the Yanks' Whitey Witt on the head. Earl Combs hit the left-field wall, braved a fractured skull, shoulder, and knee, and almost died. On August 23, 1931, the A's Lefty Grove sought an AL record 17th-straight win. "It was 0–0 into the third," said Browns skipper Bill Killefer. "Then Jimmy Moore [replacing Al Simmons, visiting a doctor in Milwaukee] missed an easy ball to let Fred Schulte score the only run." Grove later wrecked furniture and lockers. "One wasn't there," he raged of Simmons. "The other [mates] couldn't score a run." Increasingly, they resembled the Browns.

In 1925, Browns owner Phil Ball built tiers to each pole—and a roof over the right-field pavilion. The $500,000 makeover upped size by 9,000 (to 34,000) and distance (left/right field, 355/320. Bleachers cut center to 426). On July 2–3–4, 1929, the Tigers cracked eight homers to right. The next day Ball built a 156-foot-long screen to the line. Leave it to the Brownies: A day later Manush clanged three balls off the wire. Former *Sporting News* publisher J. G. Taylor Spink dubbed it "the only outfield place with seating where you couldn't catch a homer." Four of Babe Ruth's 60 homers would have hit the barrier in 1927. In '32, Jimmie Foxx had 58—and as a *visitor* 12 times struck the screen.

Browns offices filled 2911 North Grand Avenue. Cardinals digs around the corner moored 3623 Dodier Street. "Two quarters, two identities," said Branch Rickey. The Redbirds' flowed from Sam Breadon: In 1920, he sold Robison Field, bought the Fort Smith, Arkansas, Western Association team, and launched Rickey's brainchild—the farm system. Jim Bottomley helped: on September 16, 1924, knocking in a record 12 runs. "Rogers Hornsby was a picture athlete, and acted like one," said ex-Yankee Jerry Coleman. "Never smoking, drinking, or reading fine print or attending a movie for fear it would hurt his batting eye." He was a natural, and knew it: MVP 1925-'29; NL high, '22-'25 homers (42 and 39); seven batting titles, including '24's .424; and league-best .358 career average.

In 1922, Hornsby hit safely in 33 straight games. The Rajah replaced Rickey as manager in '25. "What a trade," said Broeg. "Rickey stayed as general manager. Hornsby became the only player-manager to win a Triple Crown ['25]!" Flint Rhem and Bottomley led with 20 wins and 120 RBI, respectively, in 1926. Jesse Haines went 13-9. "He'd come over in 1920," said Rickey. "That's how good our farm system was. He's the last guy we bought for more than 25 years."

In June, Grover Cleveland Alexander, 39, arrived from Chicago. The Cardinals clinched their first flag September 24. The '26 Series opened at Yankee Stadium: New York, 2-1, and St. Louis, 6-2, behind Alexander. Haines spliced four hits, 4-0. Next, Ruth thrice went long: New York, 10-5. "One blast [off Rhem] cleared the right-center pavilion," Hornsby said, "landed on Grand Avenue, and smashed a show window of the Wells Chevrolet Company." Ruth later posed for pictures in its doorway. Herb Pennock won Game Five, 3-2, before 39,552 at Sportsman's. Said Bottomley: "Our backs are at the wall"—or were they up?

Alexander won, 10-2, at the Stadium: The Series again was tied. Next day gilded muse and fact. Cardinals lead, 3-2; three on, two out, and Tony Lazzeri up; alcoholic and epileptic Alex trudges from the pen; swing and miss! The seventh-frame rally dies. "Then you top it," said Haines. "Last of the ninth, Ruth on first, two out, tries to steal, we nab him."

Disbelieve it, if you would. Cardinals (finally) win! The (bigs) South(ern and westernmost team) would rise again.

"In 1928," said Bob Broeg, "I went to my first game." He saw much about which to reminisce. The Redbirds drew 778,147 customers, more than they ever had, and won the pennant. Bottomley led the league in doubles, triples, RBI, and total bases. Hornsby batted a league-high .387—for Boston via New York.

"That's where he'd gone in [December 1926]," said Broeg, "traded to the Giants for Frankie Frisch." Frisch '27 hit .337. In '28, he made his fifth World Series. The Yanks swept, 4–1, 9–3, and 7–3 twice. "Nothing went right," said Frisch. "Before Ruth's second [Game Four] homer, [Willie] Sherdel thought he'd struck him out. But Cy Pfirman, behind the plate, charged quick pitch. Ruth homered, and then went deep again."

Season in a series: In 1929, Chick Hafey forged an NL-record 10 straight hits. The Cards had three skippers (Bill McKechnie, Billy Southworth, and Gabby Street). "If Gabby was known for anything," said Burnes, "it was for catching a ball dropped [by Walter Johnson] from the top of the Washington Monument." Street now made a prophecy. "I think he's going to be a great pitcher," he told St. Louis Mayor Victor Miller of Jay Hanna Jercome (Dizzy) Dean, "but I'm afraid we'll never know from one minute to the next what he's going to say or do."

Born in a shack to Arkansas sharecroppers, Dean was the son of a migratory cotton picker. His formal education ended in the second grade—"and I wasn't so good in first grade, either." At 18, ignoring curfew, Dean bumped into the president of the Texas League at 4 A.M. "Good morning, Mr. President," he said. "So the old boy is out prowling by hisself, he? Well, sir, I'm not one to squawk. Us stars and presidents must have our fun."

Diz won his first game on '30's final day. The Cardinals won their third flag in five years. The Series turned on the A's' Jimmie Foxx's Game Five/ninth-inning/scoreless-breaking/bleacher-finding blast off Burleigh Grimes. Soon St. Louis turned to a man who pawed the earth and slid headfirst and wore no underwear.

For seven years John Leonard Roosevelt (Pepper) Martin stoked anonymity in the Cardinals' minor-league assembly factory. He became foreman in 1931. "Pepper loved auto racing before auto racing was cool," Burnes said. He carried spare parts in a wardrobe trunk. Grease covered his hair, face, and hands.

"Swarming up from the Texas wheat fields, the Georgia cotton lands, the West Virginia coal mines, the Oklahoma cow ranges, [Pepper's Cardinals a.k.a. St. Louis Swifties, Runnin' Redbirds, or indelibly, the Gas House Gang] redramatized for the public that old traditional story about the talent of common men," drama critic Lloyd Lewis wrote. They believed in work, zest, fondness for the familiar, and reverence for everything American.

The Gang baited rivals, dirtied umpires, dropped water bags from windows, and disrupted lobbies with workmen's tools on road trips. Their band—the Mississippi Mudcats—used fiddles and harmonicas, washboards and guitars that played "Rock Island Line" and "The Wreck of the Old '97" on train rides to Cincinnati and points east. Said Frisch: "I am possibly the only manager that carried an orchestra. We traveled with more instruments than we did shirts or anything else."

Gas House rose from cartoonist Willard Mullin's 1930s sketch of gas tanks on the shabby side of railroad tracks. He painted several players with clubs, not bats, on their shoulders entering the good part of town. First baseman Rip Collins said: "I'll wager that no ball club ever had more fun playing ball than we did. It wasn't that we broke training. It was merely anything for a laugh." In 1930–'31 and 1934 they won three flags and two Series. They were raucous, defiant, and sleek.

"Hold that success against the tone of the country," said Broeg. "In the '30s states around St. Louis were on their knees, and you wouldn't draw flies. Then came Sunday and the habitual double-header. By 9 A.M., when gates opened, the park instantly filled with folks from the Ozarks and beyond. They were almost sure to see Dizzy Dean pitch—the Cardinals staggered it that way. It pulled them in from the hinterlands."

He paused. "Until the Dodgers and Giants went to California, St. Louis had more than half of the *country* to itself." Then, slowly. "Bob Feller grew up in Iowa and Mickey Mantle Oklahoma, and they both told me that the big event of their lives was when their dads mustered a couple dollars to come to a Cardinal game. This was the focal point for an entire part of America."

In 1931, Hafey's .3488 average edged Bill Terry (.3486) and Bottomley (.3481). Frisch hit .313. On July 12, 45,770 mocked Sportsman's 34,000 capacity. "Forget fire rules," said Lee Allen. "Fans packed the field. A record was set for doubles [32, including 21 in Game Two, for a Cubs twin-bill] that'll never be passed." The Cards won the flag by 13 games. Martin hit .300.

"Young man, I'd rather trade places with you than any other man in the country," Commissioner Landis told him after St. Louis won the Series, four games to three. "Well, that'll do fine, Judge," Pepper said, "if we can trade salaries"—$4,500 for Landis's $60,000. Martin had 12 hits, a .500 average, and five steals. "That son of a bitch," A's catcher Mickey Cochrane said. "I was so worried about him I forgot how to hit [.160 average]."

In 1933, Frisch became player/manager. "A man is up to bat four times a day as a rule," he said. "Why can't he hustle?" Joe Medwick agreed: 18 triples and 110 runs. Collins had 35 dingers. Martin had 35 steals—and the key to Frisch's sanity. "Frank," he upturned a team meeting, "I can't decide whether to paint my midget auto yellow or red. What do you think?" Once Stan Musial lost a fly that conked him on the head. Retrieving it, Pepper inquired of his friend. "I'm OK," Stan said. "Then," said Martin, "you won't mind if I laugh."

Diz '32–'33 went 38–33. In 1934, he vowed that "Me 'n' [brother] Paul will win 45 games this year." They won 49. One day Dean strewed three hits in a twin-bill opener. Paul then no-hit the Dodgers. "Dawgonnit," Diz protested. "If I'd a' knowed Paul was gonna throw a no-hitter, I'd a' throwed one, too." Hearing, you believed.

Captain Leo Durocher recalled: "I don't say we were the best club in 1934. But we *thought* we were the best." On August 10, the Cards trailed New York by 7½ games. They won 20 of the last 25 to clinch on the final day. The Series followed. Headlines screamed: "Dean: 'Me 'n' Paul'll Win Four' [*v*. Detroit]." Ol' Diz won Game One, 8–3, at Navin Field. The Tigers replied, 3–2.

Games Three–Five reverted to St. Louis. Respectively: Paul Dean, 4–1; Tigers, 10–5; and Tommy Bridges over Diz, 3–1. A Game Four image swells of Dean, a pinch-runner, racing toward second. "Martin had hit a grounder, Diz went in head first," Frisch said, "and [shortstop Billy] Rogell hit him in the head." Papers had a field day: "X-Rays of Dean's Head Show Nothing."

Paul took Game Six, 8–3. The final turned on St. Louis' seven-run third frame. In the seventh, Medwick tripled, slid into third baseman Marv Owen, and declined to blink. He faced apples, oranges, grapefruit, bottles, and cans on returning to left field. Finally, Landis called Owen, Medwick, Frisch, Bill Klem, and Tigers manager Mickey Cochrane to his box.

"Did Owen do anything to you as you slid into the base?" the Judge asked.

Medwick: "It was one of those things that is likely to happen any time a player slides."

Landis turned to Frisch: "Get him out for his own protection."

Diz won, 11–0. From the yawning deep you recall Marty Marion circa '42: "When you put those birds on your uniform [Cardinals atop a baseball bat] you feel like you have the winning way."

YANKEE STADIUM

The Cardinals have won nine World Series. The Big Ballpark in the Bronx boasts 26. Its first lit the year the *New York Tribune* posted advertisements for Macy's Department Store of topcoats from $28.25 to $57.50. "Take along plenty of smokers," 1923 text advised New York's baseball cognoscenti. "And may we also suggest the following items to contribute to your enjoyment of the National Game: Italian briar pipes (42 cents apiece); three Castle cigarettes, packed in airtight tins of fifty each (at $2.05); or Tampa blunts ($2.63 for a can of 50)." Many enjoyed them on City Plot 2106, Lot 100, across the Harlem River from Manhattan, bordered by 161st Street and River Avenue in the Bronx, once owned by John Lion Gardiner, and bought in 1921 by Jacob Ruppert and Till Huston from William Waldorf Astor for $600,000.

"This is the story—briefly told—of the construction of the largest baseball stadium in America," Joseph Durso wrote in *Yankee Stadium* about the role of the White Construction Company. "It is about the building in twelve months of a three-deck, reinforced-concrete and structural steel grandstand and over 40,000 square feet of wooden bleachers for the American League Base Ball Club of New York, Inc., more familiarly known as the Yankees." Construction began in May 1922. The first baseball field termed *stadium* rose in 185 working days.

Quickly, it evolved into sport's then-58,000-seat Basilica. Arch-shaped windows, 36 ticket booths, and 40 turnstiles graced the outside. Steel girded three decks. A Roman facade trimmed the upper tier. The grandstand wrapped home plate beyond the bases. (Five hundred workers turned 45,000 cement barrels into 35,000 yards of concrete). Wooden bleachers flanked the outfield fence. (Nearly a million board feet of

Pacific Coast fir arrived by boat through the Panama Canal.) A glimpse hatched self-congratulation: Talk fixed *The* Yankee Stadium.

"It dwarfed anything in sport," said a writer. In *Literary Digest*, F. C. Lane called it "the last word in ball parks. But not the least of its merits is advantage of position. From the plain of the Harlem River it looks up like the Great Pyramid . . . from the sands of Egypt." George Herman Ruth's take was more bourgeois: "Some park," he said—built by, and *for*.

Ruth knew that baseball was more intuitive than intellectual. He fused instinct, empathy, and a raw feel for life. "In truth, as the years pass, [he] does not seem so much mortal as part of our native mythology," Ron Fimrite would write. "Like rock and roll and the model T, Ruth was a seminal American invention." Dead for half a century, Babe still seems umbilically tied to glut. He drank before and after games. Breakfast might include two steaks, a dozen eggs, three pots of coffee, and a slab of ham. Ruth smoked cigars by the thousand, wooed youth by the million, and made love to women by the hundred. He could play harder, hit longer, and curse better than any player of his time. "Boy," mate Joe Dugan marveled, "when he hit one, you could hear it all over the park. The sound when he'd get a hold of one—it was just different, that's all."

Twelve times Ruth led the AL in dingers. Double your fun: He went deep twice a record 72 games. In 1920, Babe's 54 topped his own mark by 25. "To equal that kind of jump," *Sports Illustrated* wrote, "[Mark] McGwire would have to hit 130 this year ['99]." Ruth hit .342 lifetime. He was big—6–2 and 215—and a big-gamer: in 10 Series, .326, 15 taters, and 33 RBI. Records slant a hyperbolic/larger is better/Ruthian sort of way: suspension (five, 1922), fine ($5,000, '25, for insubordination), salary ($80,000, 1930), and slugging (.690, career).

Stories still make his coffin rise. In 1925, Babe ate a dozen or two dozen hot dogs and brooked "the stomachache [i.e., gonorrhea] heard 'round the world." Ruth didn't homer once for several weeks. He was superstitious. "So he stuffed me into a locker with orders to stay there," said '30–'31 roommate Jimmie Reese, "and he homered twice. For four days, I had to stand in that hot box until the streak ran out." One day they collided on a fly. Reese lay bleeding as players tended Babe. "I was praying," he said. "If the big ape doesn't get up, I'm thrown out of New

York." In August 1948, Waite Hoyt was a sweltering pallbearer of Ruth's cancer-wracked body. "Lord," Dugan moaned, "I'd give my right arm for a beer." Waite murmured, "So would the Babe."

What remains is the sunny-dark star, a full-sized Everyman, with whopping power—and The House That He Built.

"**B**abe's drawing power helped Ruppert erect the park," crowed Durso. "The Colonel, in turn, tailor-made it for his pokes" down the right-field line. Bullpens between the grandstand and bleachers lay perpendicular to the field: left- and right-center field, 395 ('28, 402) and 350 feet, respectively, from the plate. Center—490—and right-center (429) hurt power. Left-center a.k.a. Death Valley flummoxed it—500. Said the *New York Sun:* "The flag pole seems almost beyond the range of a siege gun as it rears its height in distant center field." On the other hand, left shadowed home—280 feet ('28, 301). Right howled Bambino: 295. Height also payed to pull: foul lines, 4 feet; near the bullpens, 8; right-center, 14½ Wrote Ken Smith: "Ruth couldn't have built an easier park."

It opened April 18, 1923. John Wrok Philip Sousa and the Seventh Regiment trekked to the flagpole. Manager Miller Huggins raised the '22 pennant. Al Smith tossed the first ball to catcher Wally Schang; 74,217 cheered the surpassing personality of the big city in the flesh. "People spilled onto the street," an account read. "[An estimated 20] thousands were turned away." Firsts: pitch, Bob Shawkey; batter, Chick Fewster; hit, Boston's George Burns; homer, who else? "A [three-run, game-winning 4–1] white streak [homer] left Ruth's 52-ounce bludgeon," Grantland Rice wrote in the *New York Herald Tribune.* "On a low line it sailed, like a silver flame, through the gray, bleak April shadows, and into the right-field bleachers. And as the crash sounded, and the white flash followed, fans rose en masse in the greatest vocal cataclysm baseball has ever known."

Money is sport's mother's milk. On May 21, Ruppert bought Huston out with a final $1.5 million. Ten days later he and the Yanks came clean. "Jake bought two sets of uniforms so his players' wouldn't be dirty," Lee Allen said. "Unprecedented." Too, Ruth's MVP '23: franchise-high .393 and league-best in runs (151), homers (41), RBI (131), walks (170), on-base (.545), slugging (.764), and total bases (399). The Yanks won the Series, then moved home plate 13 feet toward the fence.

"Before then there had been a place called 'Bloody Angle,' " said Harold Rosenthal. "In left-center, it suddenly jumped out from the grandstand to bleachers. All sorts of crazy bounces." Left-center dropped from 500 to 490. New bounces didn't help. The '25ers plopped to seventh.

Shortstop Everett Scott ended his 1,307 consecutive-game streak. *Another* began. In 1923, Lou Gehrig, 19, played for Columbia v. Rutgers. Superscout Paul Krichell hurried back to Yankee Stadium. "I think," he told general manager Ed Barrow, "I saw another Ruth today." Lou pinch-hit on June 1, 1925. Next day Wally Pipp braved a headache. Huggins put Gehrig at first. For 13 straight years the Iron Horse scored and drove in 100 or more runs. Five times he topped 40 dingers and 150 RBI. Gehrig buoyed seven Series (10 homers and 35 RBI), set an AL ribbies mark (184, '31), and had 15 steals of home. "Every day—any day," said Bill Dickey, "he just goes out and does his job."

On August 29, 1925, Ruth missed batting practice. Huggins suspended him, fined Babe $5,000, and hailed a playbill of new talent: Earle Combs, Mark Koenig, and Tony Lazzeri. In 1926, Ruth lashed a 626-foot homer in Detroit. "By the time it finished bouncing," said Lazzeri, "it was two blocks from the park." The Yankees lost the Series to St. Louis: Only 38,093 saw Game Seven at the Stadium.

Barrow's 1921–'45 pinstripes won 14 pennants and 10 World Series. "Tough loss," he said of '26, and then, "Somehow we forgot it in the year ahead."

Ahead was Murderers Row—depending on stripe and view, baseball's Rashomon of a team. Huggins liked its arms. In 1927, Herb Pennock and Wilcy Moore went 38–15. Hoyt—"the aristocrat of baseball," chimed writer Will Wedge—led the AL at 22–7. New York won 110 games, slugged an all-time .489, and hit 102 more homers than the *runner-up* A's. Combs batted .356. Gehrig whelped 47 homers, hit .373, added 175 RBI, and became MVP. The '27ers drew a Stadium-high 1,161,015. Most came to see the fast-lane Centaur of the Bronx.

"Keep in mind the time," said Smith. "No TV. Not a lot of radios. Papers and newsreels were it. And Ruth was everywhere." He homered in exhibition games in St. Paul, Indianapolis, and Dayton. In Buffalo, Babe wrestled kids in the field. Pinstripes played and watched at Sing Sing

Prison. Games began at 3 P.M.—thus, 5 o'clock Lightning. "We'd beat you in the late innings," puffed Huggins, "if not before." On July 4, New York slit the second-place Senators, 12–1 and 21–1. Ruth later cleared Comiskey Park's new grandstand roof. He whacked No. 60, off the Nats' Tom Zachary, the last day of September '27. "Between him and Gehrig," marveled Barrow, "107 homers—almost twice any other *team*." The Classic was just as cockeyed: New York, 5–4, 8–1, 6–2, and 8–3.

Baseball's fuel is hope. A generation's already ran on the Yanks'. Lindsey Nelson, eight, was attending class in Columbia, Tennessee. The Series game wafted from a radio in a nearby room. Said Nelson: "I found that by paying attention I could hear the broadcast as I sat in class." A teacher was talking about Julius Caesar. Nelson was more intent on hearing Gehrig double. Referring to Caesar, the teacher asked, "Lindsey, who was that?" Lindsey jabbed, "Gehrig—doubled to right!" Like the Bombers, his priority was ball.

"Think of it," Rosenthal would write. "[From '21 to '64] the Yankees never waited more than four years for a title." They became the Team of the Century: 37 pennants, 20 MVP awards, a *nonpareil* 14 retired numbers and 37 Hall of Famers. Said Barrow, simply and accurately: "The Yankees mean baseball in every corner of the land."

In 1928, America did not yet mean Depression. Calvin Coolidge said, "I do not choose to run." Herbert Hoover, who did, became the Republican Party nominee—rural, Prohibition, and Protestant. Ruth backed Tammany Hall, broken speech, anti-Prohibition, and Catholic Al Smith. "We must protect for the world," Hoover said of civic Zion, "this Gibraltar of western civilization." Smith even lost New York. *In* New York, Ruppert yanked left-field boxes, built concrete bleachers, and pushed the top decks beyond each line. Oddments merged: Right-field seats were dubbed "Ruthville" or "Gehrigville." Beneath second base a 15-foot-deep brick-lined vault stored electrical/telephone boxing tackle. Jack Dempsey whipped Jack Sharkey to win the heavyweight title. Knute Rockne told Notre Dame v. Army "to win one for the Gipper." The '28 pinstripes won another for themselves.

"Imagine you're the Giants or Dodgers." Huggins laughed, "How can you compete for news?" One day Ruth batted righty, missed two pitches, turned left-handed, and knocked in two runs. The Series was another walk: St. Louis fell in four. "Series sweeps back to back," Barrow said. "No one's done it before." Precedent, not River Avenue, seemed the Stadium's crib.

The '29ers became first to regularly put numbers on their uniforms. "They're based on the batting order," Ruppert said. (Ruth wore No. 3; Gehrig, cleanup, 4.) Babe wed actress Claire Hodgson at 5 A.M. "Only time we can miss crowds," she said. A day later Ruth homered, touched second, and tipped his cap to Claire. Marriage did not, well, tame him. Pitcher Tom Sheehan rode a taxi to the Bronx from mid-Manhattan. Babe told the cabbie to stop. "I gotta' girl waiting for me in this apartment," he said. "Tom, you stay here in the cab. I'll be back." He was, in 15 minutes.

Writers chose discretion. Their blackout draped *other* Yanks. Hoyt drank so heavily that he entered a hospital to dry out. Papers explained the stay by dubbing him amnesiac. Ruth sent Waite a telegram: "Read about your case of amnesia. Must be a new brand."

The Yanks bought Lefty Gomez from PCL San Francisco. Ruth signed a '30–'31 pact for $160,000. Famous last words: "No one," said Barrow, "will ever be paid more than Ruth." On May 21, 1930, he hit three straight homers against the A's. September retraced old times. Ruth pitched at Fenway, winning, 9–3. New York finished third but drew a most-since-'21 1,169,230. On August 21, 1931, Babe smacked No. 600. Gehrig then went deep, too. "It was one of 19 times they homered in the same inning," said Lee Allen. "They did it in a game 72 times." Together they scored 312 runs—*half* of the Red Sox' 625.

Limits seemed heretical. "New York's three teams had a round-robin playoff to raise money for the unemployed," said Allen. "Field events were held between games. Ruth hit right-handed and *still* won the fungo contest." Gomez won 21 games and bared his secret of success: "It's simple—clean living and a fast outfield." All three befriended Jimmie Reese.

One night the rookie and Gehrig played bridge against Babe and Harry Rice on a train. "We were up $1.25 when Lou chose to go to bed," said Reese. "Lou was a conditioning stickler. If he was playing marbles, he wanted to be ready. About 12 o'clock we're ahead a buck and a quarter and Lou says, 'I quit. I'm going to bed. We've got a game tomorrow.' Exhibition game was all."

Ruth told Gehrig to forget it. "You quit, I'm going to tear the [score] sheet up.' Lou looked at me and said, 'What do you think, Jimmie?' I said, 'Anything you want.' So Lou says, 'All right, we'll play one more game.' It so happened we beat them again. So now Babe owes us two dollars and a half."

Again Ruth vowed to tear the sheet. Gehrig called his bluff. (Reese died in July 1994. Ruth hadn't paid.) A year later Joe McCarthy became skipper, succeeding Bob Shawkey, who replaced the dying Huggins in 1929. His stripes won 10 pennants and seven World Series—including four straight in '36–'39. The dynasty was retributive: Some called McCarthy push-button. Others hailed perhaps the best manager of all time.

Once Ruth and Reese arrived shortly before a game. Marse Joe ripped Babe's friend. "Where the hell you been?" Ruth urged Reese to tell McCarthy to go to hell. "That's all right for you," Jimmie replied, "but I'm keeping my mouth shut.' " It shocked few when the '32 Yankees shut the American League's.

Winston Churchill once said of former British prime minister Herbert Asquith, "His children are his best memorial." On May 30, 1932, the Yankees put a memorial to Huggins just to the left of deep center field. Gehrig hit four dingers in a game. Gomez went 24–7. New York won its first Series since 1928. Crowed McCarthy: "Nothing can stop us." One man *topped* them. Josh Gibson '34 is said to have cleared the Stadium, inside the left-field flagpole, in a Negro League doubleheader.

The old order passeth. Ruth took a $17,000 cut to $35,000, hit homer 700, and was released. On July 5, Gehrig hit a record 17th inside-the-parker. Braving lumbago, he was later helped off the field. Next day McCarthy placed Lou at shortstop. "He led off the game, singled, and left," said Lee Allen. "Joe never meant to put him in the field. Anything to save the streak." Gehrig won the Triple Crown (49 homers, 165 RBI, and .363). Gomez tied a league-best 6 shutouts, 2.33 ERA, and 26–5 record.

On June 1, 1935, New York hit a record six solo dingers—Dickey (two), Frank Crosetti, Ben Chapman, George Selkirk, and Red Rolfe. The team had only 104 homers: worse, placing second for the third straight year. "That's OK for most teams," growled McCarthy. "Not for us." Murderers Row seemed far away.

9

THE HUNGRY YEARS

Forget politesse. Municipal a.k.a. Lakefront or Cleveland Public Municipal Stadium may be baseball's worst-ever outdoor/classic/steel and concrete fort. It should not, however, be dismissed.

Municipal's bare-boned bent—to architects, "Stripped classicism"—prophesied Milwaukee and Baltimore 1950s stadiums. It was also the first built with taxpayer funds: "Important," said Bill Veeck, "because it had to be designed for other sports." Paying bonds requires daily use. If this is Tuesday, it must be soccer; Thursday, rodeo, Sunday, the NFL. Baseball thrives in a lopsided shoebox. Football likes a bowl. Public parks voided the overhang, short porch, in-play board, and sprawling alley. "Forget Fenway's [37-foot] Monster," said Tribe president Gabe Paul, "or Ebbets' different wall heights." Worst was distance. You were a county fair from the field.

"Mistake on the Lake" flowed from The Law of Unintended Consequences. Cleveland wanted the 1932 Summer Olympics. Ergo, public money built a shrine. The horseshoe sat 78,000, rose in 370 days, and cost $2,844,000. Ironically, *L.A.* got the Games. At that point the white elephant kicked Cleveland in the head. "Be careful about what you wish for," said Paul. "The Olympics get away, and the park is a leviathan." How to fill it? The Indians had a thought.

League Park was large enough for weekday games, but not weekends and holidays: A bigger plot would earn more cash; more cash, better players; better players, another year like '20. The Mistake opened July 3, 1931: boxing's Max Schmeling v. Young Stribling. The bigs debuted July 31, 1932: Philly's Lefty Grove beat Mel Harder, 1–0. A week later Cleveland's Johnny Burnett hit Municipal's first homer. Stephen Spender's "I Think Continually of Those" ends: "Born of the sun they travelled a short while towards the sun." Drives here traveled a long while toward the seats. Foul lines were genial: 322–320 feet in '32–'33. A double deck ended at yawning alleys (435). An incline preceded center (470). Fences were low (5 feet, 3 inch concrete) but foul turf large (grounds help stored tools). "People like hitting," said Earl Averill. "No wonder the Indians returned to League."

The 1934–'46 Tribe played 77, 77, 76, 63, 58, 46, 33, 45, 34, 29, 34, 31, and 36 home games at League Park, respectively. Municipal housed the rest: August 2, 1936; May 30–September 1937 and April 1938–June 1939 Sunday and holiday; June 27, 1939–September 1946 Sunday, holiday, and night; and April 15, 1947–September 26, 1993. It linked railroad tracks, a shoreway, East Ninth Street, West Third Street, and Donald Gray Lakefront Gardens Port Authority Dock 28. At night the temperature might plummet. The wind blew mostly out. High stands ricocheted currents around the park. "In Boston, you say, 'Let's go to Fenway,' " said Veeck. "Nobody said, 'Hey, let's go to Cleveland Stadium.' It was never a star." The 1935 All-Star Game drew 69,831. Next March Dick Bartell mocked a future All-Star pitcher. "We've got faster guys in our league than [Bob] Feller. Why, he's not as fast as Van Lingle Mungo."

The Giants shortstop changed his mind: Feller Kd him 13 of 18 ups. On August 23, 1936, the son of Van Meter, Iowa, fanned 15 Browns in his first big-league start. "I think," manager Steve O'Neill mused, "this kid is going to be around for a while." Feller's 17 strikeouts soon tied Dizzy Dean's record. On October 2, 1938, the prodigy, 19, whiffed 18 Tigers. Feller won 266 games (76 from '39–'41), seven times led the AL in Ks (career 2,581), and threw a record 12 one-hitters (including June 27, 1939, Municipal's night debut).

"When night ball started there," Averill said, "League's end was a given." Hal Trosky bashed 77 dingers in 1934–'35. Pitcher Wes Ferrell homered twice in a game. The Tribe had this thing about triple plays. Boston loaded the bases with none out and Joe Cronin up. His liner glanced off Odell Hale's head and caromed to Billy Knickerbocker. The shortstop tossed to Roy Hughes at second. Hughes then threw to first. The 1934–'39 Tribe placed third four times. "Fun, no pennant," noted Lee Allen. The natives were getting restless.

In 1940, the Tigers arrived at Municipal two games up, with three left. Manager Ossie Vitt threw Feller in the opener. Detroit's Del Baker threw in the towel. "He figures they can't beat Feller," said Paul, "so they save Hal Newhouser and Fred Hutchinson and pitch Floyd Giebell." Fruit and produce from the stands struck Hank Greenberg as he readied to catch a fly. "Ladies Day," he said afterward. "Some ladies." Later, an upper-deck ice peddler dropped bottles off Birdie Tebbetts in the pen. Tigers win the game, 2–0, and pennant. (In 1941, Giebell retired with a 3–1 mark).

Lou Boudreau '40 bloomed: .295 and 101 RBI. Rud Rennie later wrote: "Boudreau can't run and his arm's no good, but he's the best shortstop in the league." On May 15, 1941, Joe DiMaggio singled at Comiskey Park. He proceeded to bat safely in the next 55 games. On July 17, the bigs' then-largest night crowd, 67,468, packed Municipal. DiMag walked once, was twice robbed by Ken Keltner, and smacked Jim Bagby's 1–1 eighth-inning pitch to Boudreau, who began a game-saving/streak-ending double play.

Five months later, Nazi tanks drove to forty miles from Moscow. By turn: A Soviet counterassault stunned the Wehrmacht. The Japanese wrote a "day that will live in infamy." Franklin Roosevelt asked Congress to declare war on Japan. Soon players dotted places like Burma and Bataan. Boudreau, 24, became the century's youngest big-league manager. Feller spent nearly four years in the Navy. On August 24, 1945, 46,477 saw him K twelve, yield four hits, and beat Newhouser, 4–2. Boudreau laughed. "He got nine starts the rest of the year and won five, including a one-hitter." The warrior was back.

America neared "the blessed hush of victory." You read of Yalta and Okinawa and Iwo Jima and Remagen. At the Elbe, American and Soviet troops toasted one another with captured German champagne. The

Highlanders at Hilltop, *William Feldman.* In 1903, the New York Highlanders moved uptown, and upstairs, to the leading pre-classic stadium, Upper West Side Hilltop Park. In 1913, they changed their home (to Polo Grounds) and name (to Yankees).

Shibe Park Forever, *Andy Jurinko.* The first classic park tied steel, two-tiered stands, and 468-foot center field, and was forged from the grid of Philadelphia's streets. From 1909-70 and 1938-54, respectively, the Phillies and A's played at 21st and Lehigh.

Forbes Field Forever, *William Feldman.* The Pirates' '09-71 hull was perhaps baseball's loveliest: ivied wall, pi̇̈
cover, yawning acreage, Longines scoreboard, in-play batting cage, Maz's 1960 homer *v.* the Yanks — above a
Roberto Clemente.

In Another League, *William Feldman.* July 16, 1941: Joe DiMaggio hits in his 56th straight game. From 1910-4
the Indians played in tiny League Park — right field, 290 feet; capacity, 22,000. Balls off right's wall ofte̊
caromed to the left-field corner.

niskey Park Diptych, Andy Jurinko. The White Sox' 1910-1990 steep-walled rectangle was symmetrical, double-
ked, and a pitcher's Eden. This scene etches 1988. Years that truly resonate: 1919 (Black Sox scandal) and '59 (Go-
pennant).

nd Old Griffith, Andy Jurinko. The Senators 1911-61 home fused Gulliver turf (457, center; 402, left), Lilliputian
e (27,401), and outfield quirk (a giant tree decreed the right-center wall). Here D.C.'s Mickey Vernon bats in 1953.

lo Grounds Matinee, Andy Jurinko. Polo was never played here. 1891-1957 and 1962-63 baseball was. The bizarre
tied tiny lines, Sahara of a center field, and *nonpareil* N.L. history from Christy Mathewson via Bill Terry to John
Graw's 10 flags.

Amazing Polo Catch, *Bill Purdom.* September 29, 1954: Baseball's *primus inter pares* grab. Willie Mays robs Vic Wertz to save Game One of the World Series. Note the Eddie Grant memorial, 483-foot sign, clubhouses, and team offices near the Chesterfield sign.

Fenway Park Gold, *Andy Jurinko.* Ted Williams bats *v.* Cleveland's "Boudreau Shift," 1946, in the Red Sox 1912- cabash. Fenway's stars: The Wall, Triangle, Williamsburg, and Pesky's Pole. A year later the Sox yanked left-field ads — hence, *Green* Monster.

Fenway Park Triptych, *Andy Jurinko.* July 19, 1987 — Sunday in the Fens. Wade Boggs hits *v.* Oakland amid a 37-foot left-field wall, hand-operated scoreboard, Citgo sign, sparse foul turf, and SRO crowd. Fenway is baseball's smallest park.

Tiger Stadium Panorama, *Andy Jurinko.* The flagpole lay 440 feet from the plate. An overhang turned routine flies into homers. The empyrean sat 52,416, yet blared intimacy. From 1912-99 Cobb, Gehringer, and Kaline played at the corner of Michigan and Trumbull.

Crosley Field Revisited, *Bill Purdom.* 1964, Frank Robinson bats. Cincinnati baseball long meant the boomerang at Western and Findlay. It had the National League's smallest size and turf, highest lemonade sales, a sun pavilion, and steep left-field incline.

Above Ebbets Field, *Andy Jurinko.* Cathedral of the Underdog, Brooklyn USA. The Dodgers' 1913-57 arcade tied Hilda Chester, the Symphonie, "Hit Sign — Win Suit," bird under Casey Stengel's hat, and two men on third. Anything could happen here, and did.

Ebbets Field Matinee, *Andy Jurinko.* Brooklyn lost seven World Series. The exception: 1955. Here, Gil Hodges touches Whitey Ford for a '56 Game One blast. Note the cement scoreboard, wire screen mesh, inviting left-center, and two-tiered bleachers.

Outside Wrigley Field, *Thomas Kolendra.* "Let's play two!" cried Ernie Banks. Cubs Nation would settle for winning one World Series (their last, 1908). Pilgrims gather in '45 at Addison and Clark. Said Jack Brickhouse: "Anyone can have a bad century."

Wrigley Field Triptych, *Andy Jurinko.* Of Kate Smith, FDR said, "This *is* America." The Friendly Confines *are* baseball. A 1988 etching shows the scoreboard, flags, breeze blowing out, and not a seat to be had. The ivy, unlike the Cubs, has bloomed.

Braves Field Panorama, *Andy Jurinko.* Boston's 1915-52 N.L. home tied tall grass, an inner wall, ground-level scoreboard, and right-field bleachers — "jury box," as in 12 men. The Braves kept moving fences in and out. In 1953, they moved to Milwaukee.

Splendid Sportsman's Park, *Bill Purdom.* The 1902-53 and 1920-66 Cardinals played at Grand Avenue and Dodier Street. Dizzy Dean led the '34 Gas House Gang. Midget Eddie Gaedel batted in '51. Here Ted Williams hits *v.* the Redbirds in the 1946 Series.

Tribe had not won since nearly the *last* war ended. Ahead: the Church of Baseball's reward for flaunting the patience of Job.

The '46 Indians were sixth, but drew a record 1,057,289. On April 30, Rapid Robert no-hit the Yankees. Like baseball, he was glad to be home. Feller went 26–15, Kd a record 348, and had the most complete games (38) since '16's Grover Cleveland Alexander. On June 22, Veeck bought the Tribe and began posting NL scores at Municipal and League. "A small change, but telling," he said. "Till now one league shunned the other." On September 21, Bill closed League—Detroit, 5–3. "It was crumbling"—and too small for what Veeck had in mind.

In 1937, the son of 1919–'33 Cubs president William Veeck planted ivy at Wrigley Field. He now primed to unstuff shirts and "then get out of the way so that their hot air doesn't hurt you." Veeck '47 moved spring training from Florida to Phoenix—"more tolerant," he later said. In April, Jackie Robinson cracked baseball's color line. "One afternoon when [our] team trots on the field," added Barnum Bill, "a Negro will be out there with them. I want to sign him quickly so that there won't be much pressure." Larry Doby belonged to the Negro League's Newark Eagles. Veeck bought him July 5 for $10,000. Three hours later he pinch-hit at Comiskey Park.

The Tribe put teepees in center field, then swapped them for an inner fence. Lengths became 321 (foul line), 362 (cross of fence and wall), 365 (alleys, from 435), and 410 (center, *v.* '39's 450). "Here's all you need to know," Veeck said later. "No one ever hit a ball into the center-field bleachers." Hitting baseball ought not to be a chore. It was July 10, 1947: Don Black no-hit the A's, 3–0. In September he collapsed of a cerebral hemorrhage. What Veeck wanted to topple was baseball's attendance carousel.

GRIFFITH STADIUM

On March 4, 1933, Roosevelt took the oath of office—for some, the president *still*. Unemployment topped 13 million. A banking crisis shrouded FDR's inauguration. Rud Rennie left Florida training camp to travel north with the Yankees. "We passed through southern cities which looked as though they had been ravaged by an invisible enemy," he wrote. "People seemed to be in hiding. They even would not come out to see Babe Ruth and Lou Gehrig. Birmingham, a once-thriving, bright metropolis, looked as if it had been swept by a plague."

In Wisconsin, farmers dumped milk on roads to lift prices. In Iowa, auctions halted because of bloody protests against foreclosure. Every state had closed its banks or reduced their capacity to act. America seemed a cross of Dogpatch and Hades. "First of all," Roosevelt countered in his inaugural address, "let me reassert my firm belief that the only thing we have to fear is fear itself—nameless, unreasoning, unjustified terror." The seas didn't part. Curtains, however, spread.

Slowly, fitfully, America began to heal. The nation's shaman ministered—jaunty and effervescent, laughing, always *leading*—"all grin and gusto," wrote Arthur Schlesinger, "but terribly hard inside . . . who had been close enough to death to understand the frailty of human striving, but who remained loyal enough to life to do his best in the sight of God."

Even now, he elicits father of the New Deal, scourge of Nazi Germany, and man who hailed "my little dog Fala" and whom Adolf Hitler feared. "One remembers Roosevelt as a kind of smiling bus driver," Samuel Grafton said, "with cigarette holder pointed upward, listening to the uproar from behind as he took the sharp turns. They used to tell him that he had not loaded his vehicle right for all eternity. But he knew he had it stacked well enough to round the next corner and he knew when the yells were false and when they were real, and he loved the passengers."

Once, ceding a salary larger than Herbert Hoover's, Babe Ruth said: "But I had a better year than he did!" A Washingtonian would tell you: Few years were better at Griffith Stadium.

An exception was 1933. Player/manager Joe Cronin drove in 118 runs. Alvin Crowder and Earl Whitehill went 46–23. The Senators won a team-high 99 games. Like '24, the Series traveled the D.C.–New York axis. The Giants won twice at the Polo Grounds. Rain held Game Three's crowd to 25,727. FDR watched Whitehill blank the ex-McGraws. The last two games made a hash of Nats revival. Carl

Hubbell won, 2–1, in 11 innings. Game Five began the 10th tied at 3. Mel Ott won the Classic by homering off Fred Schulte's glove.

Cronin batted a Series .318. Three years earlier his good works eased Depression: .346, 126 RBI, and MVP. He hit a lifetime .301, twice led the league in doubles and once in triples, and was, even more than Luke Appling and Arky Vaughn, the best shortstop of the '30s. "He even won a pennant his first year as manager!" mused Morris Siegel. How could the Senators dump such a star? Boston owner Tom Yawkey had a way. In early 1935, he approached Clark Griffith and asked, "What will you take for Cronin?"

"Why," the Senators owner said, "he's just married Mildred [Griffith's niece]."

Yawkey asked what matrimony had to do with shortstop. Griffith dodged: "Oh, I couldn't sell Joe." The meeting began thirty minutes later. Griffith whispered, "I'd want too much money for him anyway."

Yawkey said, "Put your figure down on the back of the envelope." Griffith did, and wrote, "Of course, I won't have anybody to play short-stop, so you'll have to throw in Lyn Lary."

The figure was $250,000. A postage stamp then cost three cents, scotch $2.50 a quart, rooms $3 nightly at a Washington luxury hotel. Yawkey said, "That's it." For the Senators, it was.

A year earlier (1934) broadcaster Arch McDonald trudged to Griffith from Class-A Chattanooga. The Senators berthed the second division 24 of the next 27 years. Harry Truman said of politicians, "If you can't convince 'em, confuse 'em." In baseball, if you can't win, distract 'em. McDonald wooed his audience with "right down Broadway" (called strikes) or "ducks on the pond" (Nats runners) or upon a rare D.C. homer, "There she goes, Mrs. Murphy." When a hometown drive found the bleachers, "our boys" banked a 6–4–3, or a reliever left the bullpen to record a save, Washington, brace thyself: "Well," Arch would say, quoting from a hillbilly ballad, " 'They Cut Down the Old Pine Tree.' "

Driftless is the lot of a baseball man. He boards a plane, flies to a city, hops the team bus, and finds the hotel. He checks in, gets his room, and suffers walls more cookie-cutter than Three Rivers Stadium. At the park, he knots dugout talk, the game, and gnawing night.

"The road'll make a bum of the best of 'em," writer Dan Daniel cried of baseball's itinerance. "And, kid," he told a colleague, "you ain't the best." Players try movies, museums, books, and other treats—anything to dent boredom. A contrast is the home front's pressure of family, friends, and public speaking—making up for lost time.

Some visit pals in every city. Many never meet a bar they don't like. All reminisce outside the lines. Louis Norman Newsom left one team for another *sixteen* times. Four times he was [re] acquired by Washington. "Clark Griffith," a writer said, "just loves to play pinochle with him." On Opening Day 1936, Newsom started against the Yanks. A batter bunted toward third. Bobo neared the ball, stopped for Ossie Bluege, and was hit in the head by the shortstop's throw. Siegel laughed. "The showboat goes to the bench and a doctor applies a cold towel. Is he hurt? The season lost?" He returned, winning, 1–0.

FDR smiled, having tossed the first ball with his unorthodox, over-handed lob. He loved hitting—"I get the biggest kick out of the biggest score"—e.g., Griffith's July 7, 1937, All-Star Game. Watching the AL's 8–3 rout was a pitcher who towered in retirement. Later, McDonald asked Walter Johnson, "Is [Bob] Feller as fast as you are?" Johnson was modest, honest, and possessed of a can-do certitude. "I think I threw a little faster."

On Flag Day 1937, the self-hyped "largest flag in the world" covered the outfield. The '41 Griffiths installed a 41-foot right-center scoreboard. Three-dimensional 15-foot National Bohemiam bottles topped it post-'45. Next door was an out-of-play right-field clock. "Variety!" began writer Shirley Povich. "Hits to center could hit an angle and bound around. In right, the clock was out of play. *In* play was the area between it and the board." The ball might drop into the fielder's hands—or, stick-ing, become a homer. Memory merged. May 28, 1941: first night game (Yankees, 6–5). August 15: Rain pelted the eighth inning. The Nats led Boston, 6–3, but forfeited when grounds help pokily covered the field. 1946: Detroit's George Kell hits. The hurler wends his 2–2 pitch. "Sud-denly the lights go out," said then-manager Bluege. "When they come on again, Kell, the ump, catcher, infielders, and outfielders are lying on the ground." Only the pitcher, standing, knew he had kept the ball.

The Nats kept theirs in the park. George Case six times led the league in steals. Cecil Travis hit as high as .359. Rick Ferrell caught D.C.'s four knucklers—Dutch Leonard (20–8 '39), Sid Hudson (17–16 '40), Newsom (15–14 '46–'47), and Early Wynn (17–15 '47)—and 1,884 games, behind only Carlton Fisk. "Pitching, speed, and average," said Griffith. "One year ['45] we hit one homer [Joe Kuhel's inside-the-park] in 77 home games."

Babe Ruth reached the tree beyond center. The Senators could have used the Negro League's Bambino. "He was the son of a steel worker," said Griffith of Josh Gibson, "and his shots showed it." The 1937–'48 Homestead Grays scheduled home games at Griffith Stadium. Thrice Gibson cleared a wall behind the left-field seats. Hank Greenberg's 1945 final-day grand slam beat St. Louis, 6–3, helping Detroit nip the Nats. "They finished 1 and ½ games behind," said Povich. "Josh could have made that up in one day's double-header."

POLO GROUNDS

Ethel Merman was asked if Broadway had been good to her. "Yes," she said, "but I've been good to Broadway." Scrap Broadway for Coogan's Bluff and Merm, King Carl. Carl Hubbell 1933–'37 went 115–50, tied a bigs mark for longest 1–0 victory (18 innings), and became '33 MVP. Hal Schumacher that year won 19 games. Bill Terry hit .322. "We'll turn it [the Giants' 3–6 Classic history] around," vowed Terry of the Series v. Washington. New York won, four games to three. Hubbell had a 2–0 record and 0.00 ERA.

The '34 Giants hosted the second All-Star Game. "Baseball's been with us more than 125 years," said Jimmy Dudley, attending. "It's still always asking, 'What's next?' " Hubbell put the first two ALers on base. Next: 48,363, fretting, and catcher Gabby Hartnett, asking time. "Settle down," he told Hubbell, "throw the thing"—Hubbell's screwball. He did. Ruth and Gehrig fanned. "Up came Jimmie Foxx," said Dudley, "who always regarded left-handers like a fox looks at lamb chops." Hubbell took the taker. Foxx K d. The Bluff rivaled Jericho.

Al Simmons and Joe Cronin whiffed to start the second inning. "Five of the best hitters ever came to bat against King Carl," said Dudley, "and only Foxx got a foul." Bill Dickey singled. Hubbell struck out pitcher Lefty Gomez. "That's how Lefty likes to remember it—six Ks in seven batters—makes him feel like a hitter." A real hitter wed a league-best 35 homers and 135 RBI. "You can see him [Ott] now," said Terry, "not very big [5–9, 170 pounds], his right foot lifted before contact."

On September 16, Dizzy and Daffy Dean beat New York twice before 62,573, the league's largest-ever crowd. In 1935, 63,943 saw a sweep of Brooklyn. "The Giants were the actors' team going back to McGraw," mused Ken Smith. "He knew many as friends. Hubbell, Ott, Terry, as many big names as the Yanks. The Polo Grounds was the place to be." In September 1936, 64,417 (57,900 paid) overfilled the bathtub for a set-to with the Cards.

From midtown, a visitor found the Grounds by cab (FDR Drive), private car (Eighth Avenue), or subway (Independent Line's D train to the 155th Street Station). The Brush Stairway tied the bluff and Speedway and ticket booths behind home plate. Harry M. Stevens, Inc. patrolled concessions. Ushers petitioned tips. Your best view was "from lower deck behind first or third upper deck along foul lines," *Sports Illustrated* later wrote. "In lower stands, protective screen in back of home plate can be visual nuisance. Field boxes along foul lines distort view of diamond." Sun lapped left-center's upper deck where stands turned toward the field.

"Center-field bleachers," wrote *SI*, "are binocular territory." Foul lines neared a phone booth: left, 279 (1930) via 280 ('43) to 279 ('55). Right: 258 to 259, earning the snarl "Polo Grounds home run." Center mimed the beasty deep: 480 (1934), 430, 505, 490, back to 505 ('44), 448, 490, 484, and 505 ('49), 483, 480, 483, 480, 475, and 483 (1962–'63). No batter hit the clubhouse wall. "Even the markers were nuts," said Lee Allen. "For some reason the lines were never marked. Others were." Left field was deeper than right: An overhang made it *closer*. "The overhang was 21 feet, so you'd think it was 258 to the left-field upper deck," Allen noted. "Actually, because of the trajectory of the ball, you only had to hit it *250*."

Curiosa merged. A nine-feet second-deck photographers' perch tied the pole to right-center. Drainage reeked: The water table lay only 2–6 feet behind the surface. The pasture sloped: A left fielder at the wall stood eight feet below second. *MIA*: NL coats of arms, removed in the

1920s from the grandstand facade. *SOS:* By outfielders, losing balls in the corner beyond boxes that almost touched each line. "If the old-style parks meant personality," said Harold Rosenthal long after the Polo Grounds died, was razed, and became an apartment complex, "this park was the person of its time."

The actor Robert Young later said, "I feel myself being drawn to television like a man in a canoe." Hubbell felt drawn to a Falstaffian sort of skill. Said Terry: "In 1936 he wins 16 in a row. Next year he took eight more"—a record 24. Ott led the '36 NL in homers (33) and slugging (.588). The Giants won their 11th flag. Horace Stoneham succeeded his father as Giants president. In Spain, enter Civil War; China, the Japanese; the Polo Ground, the first all-New York Series in 13 years.

It began September 30: a Hubbell win, 6–1. Lefty Gomez then bested five pitchers, 18–4. The Series shifted to the Bronx. Freddie Fitzsimmons and Hubbell lost, 2–1 and 5–2. "No reason," said Terry, "we can't win three straight." Six reasons hit more than .300. The Giants took Game Five, 5–4. A day later the Yankees battered four hurlers around the Bluff. Joe DiMaggio batted .346. By reputation, the rookie already aired a graceful front when under pressure. He caught Game Two's final out, neared the clubhouse, and kept running up its steps.

The rookie phenom—a Joe Hardy, a Joe D.—is especial to baseball. Cliff Melton '37 Kd 13 in his first bigs game. In May, 61,756 watched Brooklyn end Hubbell's streak. A month later he faced Dizzy Dean for the final time: Carl finished 8–3 *v.* sport's Will Rogers. What the Giants couldn't finish was a Series, again bowing to the stripes, four games to one.

Hubbell hurt his elbow. The '39ers fell to fifth. The June 6 Giants hit seven homers—five in inning four. On July 15, shortstop Billy Jurges and umpire George Magerkurth swapped spit on a disputed call down the left-field line. NL president Ford Frick suspended each 10 days, fined both $150, and decreed two-foot screens inside each pole. "The first modern foul pole," said Red Barber. "No longer would umps have to guess."

On August 13, the Giants again whacked seven taters. Terry suspended second baseman Burgess Whitehead. "The next day he shows up in full uniform at Yankee Stadium," Bill said, "and asks to work out."

Joe McCarthy refused; whereupon Whitehead rejoined the Giants; at which point he jumped the team. Terry suspended him again.

By spring 1940, Nazi dominoes littered Europe. The Giants littered the second division. Their first night game drew 22,260. In 1941, Ott forged homer 400 and ribbie 1,500. That December he became player-manager, replacing Terry. The Polo Grounds housed the '42 All-Star Game—its second. Rain held the crowd to 33,694. On September 26, the Giants forfeited to Pittsburgh. "Kids were admitted free if they brought scrap metal to aid the war," wrote Dick Young. "In the eighth the Giants led when the kids got antsy and rushed the field."

For the last time Ott led in homers. John Mize, late of St. Louis, topped in RBI. One day the Giants and Phillies stranded a record 30 runners. On August 18, 1943, Hubbell won his 253rd and final game. King Carl retired in December. His team retired earlier—last for the first time since World War I. Ott smacked dinger 511, hurt his knee, and retired—New York's last title link to '33–'36–'37. The Giants again placed last. Attendance hit a record 1,219,873.

"After the war years," Stoneham recalled, "fans were ready." You could be forgiven for wondering about the team.

SPORTSMAN'S PARK

A '30's St. Louisian seldom asked about the Swifties. Joe Medwick '36 tied one record and set another: 10 straight hits and 64 doubles, respectively. By 1937, Dizzy Dean was 121–65. "He threw so smoothly and efficiently," said Bob Broeg, "that my guess is if he'd stayed healthy, he'd have pitched in the bigs into the '50s." Instead, "the stunning comic heroic," wrote Lloyd Lewis, "most famous of all living pitchers" ran out of luck at the All-Star Game.

Lou Gehrig homered. Irate, Diz then threw a fastball to Cleveland outfielder Earl Averill, whose drive struck a glancing blow off Dean's left toe.

"Your big toe is fractured," a doctor told Jay Hanna.

"No, it ain't," he said. "It's broke."

A doctor put Dean's broken toe in a splint. Medwick waxed: e.g., the

'37 MVP/Triple Crown/league-high in 12 categories. Frisch waned: benching himself when Terry Moore nearly passed him on the bases. "Any time they can run down the Flash," he rued, "it's time to quit." Prematurely, Dean returned to the rotation, hurt his arm, lost his fastball, and was traded to the Cubs in 1938.

"Podnuh," barked Diz, "I ain't just a'woofin' ": On off–days or before games a goat policed Sportsman's outfield. "He was chewing grass," added Frisch, sacked in '38—or was Mize chewing pitchers? Big Jawn '39 hit a league-best .349. In 1940, he led it in ribbies, slugging, and homers. The '30–'41 second-division Browns were less immune to hemorrhage: Attendance fell off the cliff. Night ball began May 24, 1940, before 25,562. A week later the Cardinals went after dark.

On July 9, both housed the All-Star Game: NL, 4–0. Broeg sighed: "Except for '44 [and Ol' Diz], it was about the last experience the clubs shared."

By 1941, the Browns seemed allergic to life support. AL owners set a meeting for December 8. Thy Brother's Keeper was not something to take or leave. "They were going to let the Browns relocate in Los Angeles," said Broeg of the day after Pearl Harbor. "Then war travel restrictions killed the idea." Marooned, the Browns sulked. Their tenant again was getting good.

Enos (Country) Slaughter was baseball's pre–Charlie Hustle. Terry Moore tended center field like a shepherd. Shortstop Marty Marion debuted in 1940—to Red Barber, "easy as a bank of fog." A year later Whitey Kurowski arrived at third. "I've always said that Musial hit 1,200.00 that year," he allowed of another rookie. "Stan played at Springfield and hit .400, then went up to Rochester and hit .400, then came up to St. Louis and hit .400." Branch Rickey played a worldly note: "You could make a study of Musial's life, and learn how to be a decent human being."

In 1942, you studied the first team (Brooklyn) to win over 100 games (104) and *not* win a pennant. The Dodgers led by 10½ games in August. St. Louis went 43–8 to take 106. "That '42 team," Slaughter said of his 22-year suzerainty, "was the best I ever saw." The Redbirds averaged only 26 years of age. A record nine Yanks graced the AL All-Star team. Their Fall Classic began on cue: stripes, 7–4, at Sportsman's Park. St.

Louis replied, 4–3, then moseyed east. Kurowski's Game-Five last-inning blast beat Red Ruffing, 4–2, to cap a Series-ending thunderclap. (Games Three and Four: 2–0 and 9–6).

Wrote Frank Graham: "The Yankees have finally found a team they can't frighten half to death just by walking out onto the field, and taking a few swings in batting practice."

The 1926–'46 Redbirds won six World Series. The Browns conjured '45 one-armed outfielder Pete Gray. "He didn't belong in the majors," said manager Luke Sewell, "and knew he was being exploited." Sportsman's bridged the teams. Center field shrunk to 422. Left and right read 426 and 422. Right field surged, then ebbed: '38–'39's 332 and 310. The backstop remained 75 feet from the plate.

"It was homey, like a friend," said Broeg. The site pooled a twin-tiered stand, right-field pavilion, and left-field bleachers. "Great variety," said Bob Burnes. "Hit it down the [right] line, it's gone. Straightaway, you're dead." A *Globe Democrat* ad blared a "Star of the Day." Screechin' Mary Ott presided from her box behind a dugout. Later, St. Louis' archetype fan might visit the Club Boulevard bar at Sullivan and North Grand. "She never missed a game. Always there, always loud," said Broeg. "It was part of the park, like the bowling alley at Fenway"—or Diz.

Dean retired on May 14, 1941, to become a Cardinals and Browns broadcaster. "I hope I'm as good as I was a pitcher," he said. "Now I know how a prisoner feels walking to his death." Concern seems baffling now. In 1942, the *Sporting News* called Dean "baseball's announcer with the worst diction." By '44, it named him "announcer of the Year." Runners "slud," Dean's personal past tense. Batters "swang." Pitchers "throwed" the ball with great "spart." ("Spart," he confided, "is like gumption or fight. Like the Spart of St. Louis, that plane Lindbergh flowed to Europe.") Faking a double steal, players "are now returning to their respectable bases." That hitter, Dean said, "is standing confidentially" at the plate.

The St. Louis Board of Education tried to yank Diz from the air. He replied: "I'm just tryin' to learn 'em English." He became a blend of Ma Kettle, Tennessee Ernie Ford, and a John Huston western—ultimately, leaving for the prestigious household of CBS. "They got to be my words," said Diz, " 'cause no one else would have 'em."

In 1943, Howie Pollet, Max Lanier, and Mort Cooper ranked 1–2–3 in ERA. The Cards took the flag, but lost October to the Yanks. St. Louis '44 topped 100 wins for the third straight year. Marion batted .267, had only 6 homers, but was MVP. "One belongs to New York instantly," wrote Thomas Wolfe. "One belongs to it as much in five minutes as in five years." The Subway Series belonged to New York 13 times from 1921 to '56. By contrast, St. Louis' first was also its last.

"Hell, no," Cardinals manager Billy Southworth huffed in early '44, "we don't take wins for granted." Sportsman's first/sole AL title took most by surprise. Nels Potter went 19–7. Vern Stephens added 20 homers and 109 RBI. The Browns' first sellout in 20 years—37, 816—cheered a last-day clinching. Tradition took a bath: The Browns outdrew the Swifties, 508,644 to 461,968. "Could those upstarts win the Series?" Jack Kramer recalled. An inquiring city wanted to know.

Denny Galehouse won the opener, 2–1, over the NLers' Cooper. Four Browns errors tripped Game Two, 3–2. Kramer then won, 6–2, for a 2–1 game lead. The Redbirds rallied: 5–1, 2–0, and 3–1. Browns hurlers should have sued for non-support. "Look at our ERA," bellowed Galehouse—1.49 v. the Cards' 1.96. The Browns hailed the last World Series where both teams shared a common site by making 10 errors to the Cardinals' one. "We should have known better," a writer said. "It was too good to last."

By 1946, Preacher Roe had found how to retire Musial: "I'd throw him four wide ones, then try to pick him off." That spring Joe Garagiola joined his hometown team. His job included washing mates' sanitary hose. " 'Stan, you were a good hitter but we used to always put on your socks 'TGIF'—Toes Go In First,' " Joe G. kidded. "Anything to help the Man." In turn, the Man helped the '46ers a) erase a 6½ game Dodgers lead; b) take baseball's first best-of-three playoff, 4–2 and 8–4, v. Brooklyn; and c) do what five other NL teams had not—beat the Red Sox.

Musial led the league in average (.365) and six other categories. Slaughter scored an NL-high 130 runs. Kurowski and Red Schoendienst batted .301 and .281. Pollet, Harry (the Cat) Brecheen, and Murry Dickson went 51–31. Unmoved, oddsmakers made the Redbirds a 7-to-20 underdog. "We want to keep our edge [during the NL playoff]," Red

Sox manage Joe Cronin said, slating exhibitions with AL players. On October 1, Mickey Haefner hit Ted Williams on the elbow. St. Louis lost Game One, 3–2. Next day, reality: Ted didn't hit out of the infield. Boston fell, 3–0, to Brecheen.

Cronin wasn't worried: "We'll handle this thing at Boston," he said before Game Three. "We don't want to come back to St. Louis." Boo Ferriss won Fenway's first Series game since September 1918. Game Four seemed as long to Boston: 12–3, Cards. Slaughter, Kurowski, and Garagiola each had four of a record-tying 20 hits. In 1946, Autumn Occasion box and bleacher seats cost $7.20 and $1.20, respectively. Game Five made the price worthwhile. Leon Culberson, portending, homered. Joe Dobson beat St. Louis. The downside was Ted: He still wasn't hitting. "I'm sure due to hit one," T. Ballgame said. He would, in '47.

The Series returned to Sportman's: Brecheen again winning, 4–1. A day off preceded Boston's first Game Seven since 1903. The Sox scored a first-inning run: Moore, robbing Williams, saved another. St. Louis scored thrice. Boston then tied, 3-all. Slaughter singled to start the eighth. With two out, Harry Walker came to bat. What happened next is still dogma reduced to cliché. Manager Eddie Dyer ordered the hit-and run. Walker hit to left-center, weak-armed Culberson fielded the ball, and Slaughter spied third. Leon relayed to shortstop Johnny Pesky, who—at this point, accounts cleave—turned toward the plate and a) was or was not startled to see Enos running and b) did or not hesitate before throwing up the third-base line. Country scored the tie-breaking (4–3) run.

The Sox would not be the Sox without a final, anguished, Lucy-took-the-football tease. The tying run reached third with one out in the ninth. "Time to bear down," said Brecheen, and did: the first pitcher since '20 to win a Series triad. "Holding" the ball hovered like a Northeasterly over Pesky's life. "Culberson lobbed the ball to me," he often said. "I would have needed a rifle to nail Slaughter."

Pesky was/was not a goat. Garogiola batted an un–Joe G. 316. Later, entraining at Union Station, Williams locked his compartment, began to weep, and failed to draw the blinds. Hundreds intruded on private grief—as public as Ted's .200 Series average, or Slaughter's mad dash for home.

On July 7, 1989, President Bush hailed Little League Baseball's 50th anniversary. Leaving the White House, three recent big-leaguers snubbed kids by hailing their limousine. Stan Musial, 68, on the other hand, braved 97-degree heat for an hour to sign each autograph. "Doesn't surprise me," said Cardinals 1945–'69 voice Harry Caray. "I could wear you out with stories about Stan the Man."

In 1940, Musial hurt his arm. The Class C pitcher-turned-outfielder shaped .331, 475 homers, and pre-Rose NL record 3,630 hits into Cooperstown Class of '69. Stan was nicknamed at Ebbets Field. Mourned a diehard: "Here comes that man again!" Musial became the apotheosis of St. Louis 1942–'63: 1943–'46–'48–'50–'51–'52–'57 batting crowns (.357, .365, .376, .346, .355, .336, and .351). Three MVP Awards—'43–'46–'48. Two RBI titles—1941–'56 (131 and 109). Career top ten: doubles, extra base hits, RBI, runs, and walks. "Toss in steals, and Musial routs Williams in total bases [7,811–6,927]," said Bob Broeg. Self-made, he was not self-absorbed. "The key to hitting," Stan mused, "is to relax, concentrate—and don't hit a fly to center field."

Musial's Hermitage was 1948: .376, 135 runs, 230 hits, 39 homers, and 131 RBI. "One more homer," Dyer said, "and he tied for the Triple Crown." The Cardinals finished second. (Ibid., '47. On September 22, Musial got five hits off five straight pitches by five different men.) Next year they won 98 games, one less than Brooklyn, and drew 1,430,676, more than they ever had or would at Sportsman's Park.

The Cardinals had won nine pennants in 21 years. Their next occurred after an 18-year hiatus. Default briefly fixed you on St. Louis' *other* team. Huffed Broeg: "Some consolation prize."

The '47 Browns pitched Dean, 37, on Closing Day. He singled, spaced three hits in four innings, and pulled a muscle. "He's come out of retirement," said manager Muddy Ruel, "now he'll go back in." The game drew 3,174. The '50 seventh-placers lured just 247,131. On June 8, St. Louis lost, 29–4, to Boston. Willing to try anything, they also hired a sports psychologist.

Dr. David Tracy used hypnosis to spur confidence. "There's no proof that his pep-talks won more games," said then–Browns voice Bud Blattner, "but the Browns did seem more confident while losing." Once Tracy tried to hypnotize a Senators postgame TV audience into buying RCA sets. Viewers, he said, would flock to their nearest appliance store.

Bob Wolff was the Senators TV voice. Next morning he got a call from the Federal Communications Commission. "You can't do this," an official told him. "Why not?" Wolff said. "It shouldn't be done." Bob: "Is there a rule against it?" The official said, "No, but I believe there will be." Wolff: "Did it have any effect on the viewers?" Official: "We got a lot of phone calls from people saying it put them to sleep." The Browns evoked forty winks with a Tooth Fairy kind of surety.

In 1951, Bill Veeck bought the team. He promptly began a rescue mission. "Bill was establishment but wooed the common man by shunning ties," Blattner said. He liked to drink, seem a regular fellow, and tub-thump the Browns. One night Veeck returned from a speech at Herron, Illinois. "Ya' know," he told his driver, "wouldn't it be nice to just once get our leadoff man on base in the first?" Blattner nodded. Barnum renewed his utopia. "Getting a man on in the first would be some event."

By and by Bill called Bud to his office. "Meet our new leadoff man, Eddie Gaedel." The 3-foot-6 midget barely reached the desk. "Bet I could hit anybody that they pitch." Veeck snapped, "If you make one move with that bat at home plate it'll be your *last*." On August 19, a huge-by-Browns-rule 20,299 graced a twin-bill. Veeck vowed a Golconda for the AL's semicentenary, and delivered: jugglers, acrobats, aerial bombs, and recently signed Satchel Paige on drums. Gaedel sprung from a papier-mâché cake. "Bill set them up," said Blattner of the pre–Game Two pastiche. "People thought *that* was the celebration."

The P.A. announcer promptly turned a switch: "Leading off, batting for Frank Saucier, No. ⅛, 3-foot-9, 62 pounds, 26-year-old Eddie Gaedel." The umpire called time. Browns manager Zack Taylor produced a contract. Tigers pitcher Bob Cain fumed. Gaedel doffed his cap, crouched, and put bat on shoulder. "Try pitching to a six-inch strike zone," Cain recalled. Gaedel took four straight balls. AL president Will Harridge told Veeck to send the midget packing. Bill lanced the needle: "Please advise the minimum height of players in the American League."

A week later Taylor sat in a rocking chair on the field. "Fans got plac-ards. 'Hit away' or 'bunt,' " said Blattner. "Zack did as they voted." The Browns would not be a Reverse Midas for long.

"In '47, [Cardinals owner] Sam Breadon had sold out to Fred Saigh and Bob Hannegan, and by the early fifties, they were in bad shape financially," said Veeck. "They tried things like opening at night [April 18, 1950, before 20,871.] Rumors started that the Cardinals would leave. Gussie [August A.] Busch bought 'em to save the club—and drive me out of town."

In 1953, Veeck sold Sportsman's to the Anheuser-Busch brewery for $800,000 and leased it back for $175,000 a year. Busch wanted to rename it Budweiser Stadium. The league jumped down his throat. Gussie settled for Busch. He built new boxes, reworked the clubhouse, and put a cock-a-hoop neon Budweiser eagle under the left-field score-board. "When a Cardinal homered," said Veeck, "the eagle flapped his wings and flew from one end to another." Before 1954 the flagpole anchored center field. Busch stuck it behind the fence, added bleachers, and built an outfield warning track. St. Louis was becoming his.

That spring announcer Milo Hamilton joined the Browns. "I wasn't ready for the big leagues. Course, neither were the Browns." In May they hosted Philadelphia on a cold, wet night. Manager Rogers Hornsby despised Bobo Holloman, but needed him to start. "Rogers figures, 'Bobo'll get shelled, and I'll ditch him in the minors,' " laughed Blattner. Instead, Bobo got his first big-league start, win, and no-hit game. The '53ers drew 297,238. Veeck wanted out of St. Louis. AL owners wanted him out of baseball. "I tried to move to L.A. but they wouldn't let me," Bill wrote in his 1961 memoir, Veeck—As In Wreck. Broke, he sold. The Browns became the Baltimore Baseball Club Inc.

Schoendienst became the first Card to outhit Musial since 1942. (He retired with 2,449 hits, .289 average, and only 346 Ks in 8,479 ups.) On May 2, 1954, Stan had five homers and 11 RBI in a Sportsman's double-header. Nate Colbert hit five dingers in a '72 twinner to tie Musial's record. Such a day deserved a coda, and got it the next morning. Col-bert, a St. Louisian, admitted to sharing Stan's paradise. "I was in the right-field pavilion," said the then-Knotholer. Play word-association. *Eerie* wins.

The '54 Cards hit 35 balls off the right-field screen. "Without it, Musial would have had 10 more homers," said Broeg. General manager Dick Meyer scrapped the barrier. It didn't help. Frank Lane, replacing Meyer, restored the screen. Said Frantic Frankie: "Keeping the ball in play is a condition, I believe, desired by fans." What they really desired was to clone the Man.

Briggs Stadium

Detroit hoped to copy 1935. Charlie Gehringer fanned only 16 times in 610 ups. MVP Hank Greenberg had 170 RBI. The Tigers broke their all-time attendance record—1,034,929. Sadly, paranoia curdled Motown's *sangfroid*. "We'd lost four Series in a row," said Gehringer. "Who wonders why we worried?"

Schoolboy Rowe lost the opener, 3–0, to Chicago. Detroit braced for what lay ahead. Instead, it won three staight. Rowe then lost to Lon Warneke. "We go back to our park," Detroit's Goose Goslin recalled. "We're ahead [three games to two], but is it going to happen again?" The ninth inning began 3-all. The Cubs' Stan Hack tripled: Tommy Bridges stranded him. Mickey Cochrane then singled and took second on Gehringer's out. Goslin faced Larry French. "If they pitch this ball over the plate," he told umpire Ernie Quigley, "you can take that monkey suit off." They/he did. Goose singled. Wrote Grantland Rice of Detroit's first title: "The leaning tower can now crumble and find its level with the Pisan plain. After waiting for forty-eight years, the Detroit Tigers at last are champions of the world."

Business lives by supply and demand. In 1935, owner Frank Navin double-decked the right-field pavilion. Its upper deck was 10 feet wider than the lower—thus, overhung. Capacity became 36,000. Right and center field shrank to 325 and 459 (formerly, 372 and 469). That winter Navin died of a fall from a horse. Successor Walter Briggs unhorsed the status quo. A second tier welded left and center. Distances fell to 340 and 440. Size leapt again: 58,000. "The city council will provide space," Briggs said, "by closing off a street behind the outfield."

By 1938, a roof extended to left-center and right-center field. (Bleachers lay between.) Briggs put a scoreboard in center, and renamed Navin Briggs Stadium. Posts blocked about 10,000 seats, but put the top deck within a whisper of the turf. The backstop nearly hugged home plate. Regular Patsy O'Toole yelled "Keep Cool with O'Toole." Tropical were deflecting balls (off the angular 5-foot concrete fence) and '35–'40 wire outfield screen heights (left, 20 via 30 to 10 and 12; center, 9; right, 8). Left of the 440 mark stood a 125-foot-tall flagpole: baseball's highest-ever in-play bar.

The Tigers now began a period so various as to make their lair a keeper of baseball faith. "Frank Lary killed the Yankees here," *Baseball Weekly*'s Bill Koenig wrote. "Reggie Jackson hit a roof-top light tower here. Fred Lynn drove in 10 runs in a game here. Mark 'The Bird' Fidrych manicured the mound and talked to the ball here."

You reached it by bus, cab, or foot on Michigan Avenue. Most drove to two blocks east of the John Lodge Expressway. A band stalked the stands. Frozen custard led sales. Ushers rarely growled. Green shaded seats and walls. "Owners claim Briggs Stadium is the best park in baseball," wrote *Sports Illustrated.* "Contented Detroit fans admit it probably is." In 1937, they saw Detroit's third MVP (Gehringer) in four years hit a league-high .371. Cochrane was beaned, KOing his career. Lou Gehrig's 2,130 straight games streak ended in 1939. Frank Price was an usher. "I was standing behind the Yankee dugout. He came out to take infield practice. Someone tossed him a glove and he bobbled it. He picked up his glove and started to walk back to the dugout. He didn't say a word, but he waved at me. That was the last time he stepped on a field as a player."

Detroit's player was Greenberg. In 1938, Hank knocked in 183 runs. In 1940, he led the AL in homers and RBI. Bobo Newsom '40 won 21 games. Four regulars hit more than .300. In September, Detroit clinched its third flag in seven years. The Classic ricocheted: Again Detroit led, three games to two. Rowe and Newsom then lost at Crosley Field. Manager Del Baker mused: "The Series used to be best-of-nine. Too bad it's not best-of-five."

Briggs hosted '41's best-of-one All-Star Game. "What people recall," said Greenberg, "is Ted [Williams' three-run, ninth-inning 7–5 winning blast *v.* the Nationals]. There he was around the bases"—joyous, loping, alight. Lucent in '44: Detroit's Dizzy Trout, 27–14, and MVP Hal Newhouser, 29–9. Next year Prince Hal became the only pitcher to win that award back-to-back. In July, Greenberg homered in his first game out of khaki. Hank's last-day slam clinched the Tigers' sixth flag.

The 1945 Series matched comic shortstops Roy Hughes (Chicago) and Skeeter Webb (Detroit). It was long (seven games) and dreary (the winning Tigers hit .223). "What you remember," wrote Warren Brown, "is how [Chicago] tavern owner 'Billy Goat' Sianis bought a box seat for his goat." Sianis was kicked out of Wrigley Field. He then cast a "goat curse" on the Cubs. For a long time you wondered if Detroit was haunted, too.

Much of 1946–'50 was spent hoping that '45 was not an accident. Briggs' largest-ever crowd, 58,480, watched the '46 Red Sox. (Its smallest, 404, flecked September 24, 1928). A year later 58,369 paid to see New York. On June 15, 1948, Detroit became the last AL club to install lights, v. the A's, before 54,580. Gates opened at 6 P.M. "The game didn't start till 9:30," laughed Vic Wertz, "because we didn't think lights would take effect till then." George Kell's .343 led '49ers. On June 23, 1950, the Tigers and Yankees whacked 11 homers. Detroit finished only three games out of first. Attendance soared to 1,951,474. "Enormous interest," mused Ernie Harwell. "It was a miracle, given the decade ahead."

Detroit 1951–'60 never placed above fourth or drew fewer than 884,658. Bob Feller '51 no-hit the Bengals. "That year the All-Star Game was moved from Philly to Detroit to celebrate our 250th birthday," said Wertz. Harry Heilmann died on its eve. A day later the AL did, 8–3. In 1953, Detroit lost to Boston, 23–3. Mickey Mantle '56 hit the roof. The next day the *Detroit Times* printed a mock photo of Al Kaline standing there: "Mantle Shift." Tigers general manager John McHale called the paper to whine about Al's safety. "Don't take him up there again."

Joe Falls laughed. "No humor—but we didn't have cause." Virgil Trucks threw two no-hitters. Newhouser won his 200th game. Harvey Kuenn four times led the league in hits. Kaline '55 and Kuenn '59 won batting titles (.340 and .353). Frank Lary's 21 wins topped '56 Americans. Detroit later made a 13-player deal with the even lowlier A's. Charlie Maxwell began homering on Sunday. In 1960, Detroit traded Kuenn and manager Jimmy Dykes for Tribe outfielder Rocky Colavito and skipper Joe Gordon. The Tigers still limped 26 games behind.

"A decade like this, and most cities don't survive," said Harwell. The wonder is that people made a beeline for their dowager, talked baseball at the assembly plant, and heard the Bengals turn toothless on the air.

WRIGLEY FIELD

In 1990, Ronald Reagan wrote *An American Life*. In Depression Iowa, he was already an American original. Four Des Moines stations, including Reagan's WHO, broadcast the Cubs. "Some actually called games from Wrigley," said the Dutchman. "I was hundreds of miles away doing them by re-creation." A Western Union operator sent Morse Code to the studio. The operator gave the paper to Reagan, who etched play he never saw. One day the wire stopped. Reagan considered returning to the station. "Then I thought, no, if we put music on people will turn to another station doing it in person." What to do? Make a big *to*-do.

"Foul balls don't make the box score," he said, "so for seven minutes I set a record." Bill Jurges was at bat. Reagan had him hit fouls to each corner of the park. Pitcher Dizzy Dean used the resin bag, mopped his brow, tied a shoe. A fight started. Kids dueled for bric-a-brac. "None of this happened," said Reagan, "but at home it seemed real." Finally, the game resumed. The operator handed Reagan the paper. He began to laugh. "It said, 'Jurges popped out on first ball pitched.' "

In 1935, Billy Herman lined balls for a .341 average. Catcher Gabby Hartnett became MVP. On September 27, Bill Lee beat Dean, 6–2, to clinch the flag. "In the first two [Series] games," Commissioner Landis later wrote, "Cub bench jockeys were swearing at the Tigers and at [plate umpire and ex–Detroit manager] George Moriarity." The commissioner winced. "I have always prided myself on . . . lurid expressions," he told both teams before Game Three. "I must confess that I learned from these young fellows some variations of the language even I didn't know existed." He ordered them to stop cursing. The Cubs stopped winning. "Maybe we should skip October," said manager Charlie Grimm. Add '35 to '32 and '29.

Bill Veeck reworked Wrigley. First, he yanked the left-field scoreboard. Replacing it: a 27-foot-high by 75-foot-wide hand-operated scoreboard behind and atop the center-field stands. "It had line scores inning by inning," said Jimmy Dudley. "Sometimes guys running it brought a 6-pack. Then, they might miss a couple innings. One night they must have inhaled some hard stuff—the numbers started appearing upside down." In 1937, he built concrete bleachers: Dimensions dealt 364, 436, and 321 for 355, 400, and 353. Veeck planted ivy on the new outfield wall: Unlike the Cubs, it flowered.

The wall featured six red gates (in 1981–'85, painted blue and green, respectively). Veeck '38 widened box and grandstand seats, cutting size to 38,396. Dedicated: the William Wrigley, Jr., Water Fountain, near the Frank Chance plaque. "It was sealed by a handshake between the previously quarreling [Joe] Tinkers and [Johnny] Evers," said mikeman Jack Brickhouse. If only the Cubs could now choke-hold the Yanks.

"If this ballpark came to life, it would be a grandfather with a throaty laugh," wrote the Knight Ridder Company. "Perhaps he would be called Pop-Pop Ralph. His bush hair and eyebrows would be luminous silver, and he would belie his age. He would smoke a pipe and tell riveting stories of the past. He would offer a sturdy knee, and he would cry only during the happy times. His soul would be pure. Then, again, Wrigley Field has always been more than just a stadium. It is not a place merely to watch but to experience and embrace something beyond baseball."

In 1938, the Cubs experienced their last three-year itch. "Every kid knew the Cubs had to win the pennant every three years," Brickhouse chorused. "Like clockwork. It was providential." They did not win in 1941—nor, well, you know the rest. The '38 Cubs scored 12 runs in an inning. Hartnett replaced Charlie Grimm as manager. Pittsburgh fronted for most of the year. On September 27, it visited Wrigley for a three-set series. The Cubs trailed by 1½ games. Dean won the first match, 2–1. Next day inning nine began 5-all.

"It was gray and cold," Hartnett said, "and Wrigley had no lights. The ump told our teams one more inning." The game would end if neither scored. The Bucs and first two Cubs went meekly. Mace Brown threw, Gabby swung, and the ball cleared left field. "A lot of people have told me they didn't know the ball was in the bleachers," Hartnett would say. "Maybe I was the only one who did." A day later Lee won,

1–0. The Cubs clinched October 1. Again, the Yankees loomed. Lee lost, 3–1. Diz led Game Two, 3–2, until Frank Crosetti homered in the eighth.

"You never would have done that if I'd had my fastball!" Dean screamed as Crosetti rounded second.

Replied the Yanks shortstop: "Damned if you ain't right." Final: 6–3. The Cubs entrained for New York for the inevitable: 5–2 and 8–3, Chicago's fourth straight Series dud. Herbert Hoover once proclaimed a view of America-in-bloom. "We are nearer the final triumph over poverty than ever before in the history of any land." The Cubs' would take a long and winding road.

Post-'38 Cholly broadcast, managed AA Milwaukee, and awaited the Cubs' next cry for help. In 1941, Philip Wrigley became the first owner to install an organ. "He also bought equipment to put in light towers," said announcer Bob Elson. On December 7 the Japanese attacked Pearl Harbor. The Cubs gave towers, lights, and cables to the government. In '42, Lennie Merullo tied a bigs record four errors in an inning. The shortstop named his son, born that day, Boots. Chicago '44 lost 13 of its first 14 sets. The call went forth: *Get Grimm!* Bill Nicholson led the NL in runs (116), homers (33), RBI (122) and total bases (317). Said Brickhouse: "Marty Marion beat him by a point for MVP."

John F. Kennedy called a group of Nobel Prize laureates "the most extraordinary collection of talent . . . that has ever been gathered in the White House—with the possible exception of when Thomas Jefferson dined alone." The wartime '45ers topped an ordinary league. Andy Pafko had 110 ribbies. Batting champion Phil Cavarretta (.355) became Chicago's fourth MVP (Frank Schulte '11, Hornsby '29, and Hartnett '35). The Cubs passed one million for the first time since '31. "At the team victory party," James Enright wrote, "Grimm had a pair of shears. Everybody who had a necktie on contributed. He had a quilt made. It's . . . the oddest pennant souvenir in the history of the game."

History is said to repeat itself. A corollary, said British prime minister Arch Balfour, is that "historians repeat each other." The Tigers had played the Cubs in 1907–'08–'35. Chicago tied the Series with a Game Six 8–7/28-hit/38-player/3-hour-and-28 minute burlesque. "It was just a tease," a writer mused. "You knew we'd lose Game Seven." A fan would tell you: The Cubs never got anything for free.

Grimm was unusual: a Cub who was funny on purpose. One day a Wrigley led off first and Lou Novikoff—"The Mad Russian"—hit to right-center field. The runner rounded third, held up, and retreated. Head down, Novikoff passed second and slid into third. Coaching, Charlie raced to the bag. "Where the hell are ya' going?" Lou rose and said, "Back to second if I can make it."

The Wrigleys gripped reverse after '45 Grimm's Fairy Tale—598–786 through 1955. A generation matured never knowing the first division. "What do you do?" asked Veeck. "Light a candle, not curse the dark." A midwesterner lit Stan Hack (.301 career) and Claude Passeau (Cubs 125–94) and Hank Sauer a.k.a. "the Mayor of Wrigley Field" ('52 MVP) and '47 All-Star Game (before 41,123). Chicago's eternal flame was a quick-wristed infielder plucked for $20,000 from the Kansas City Monarchs.

In time, Ernie Banks embodied the Chicago National League Baseball Club: shortstop/first baseman captain/inspiration two-time MVP/Good Humor Man/Mr. Cub. He homered for the first time September 20, 1953. Once Vernon Law hit Banks in the nose. He was removed on a stretcher. Sauer, whose proboscis bulged, jibed, "Ernie, how can you be so dumb as to get hit in the nose?" "Hank," Banks replied, "if that ball hits you in the nose it carries for a homer." He canonized "Let's Play Two!" and loved Wrigley's short alleys and whipping wind: The park hosted 290 of Ernie's 512 home runs.

Banks '55 socked a record five slams. In 1958, he led in dingers (47), ribbies (129), and slugging (.614). Said manager Bob Scheffing: "You're talking MVP"—again in '59. Ernie passed 40 homers and 100 RBI five times in six years. He offset celebrity by seeming a regular fellow. "Baseball is a fascinating game," Banks said gently. "There's so much to it. And records don't mean much at all."

As Cavarretta '54 was fired ("We're lousy," Wrigley said, scoring his "defeatist attitude"), the '58ers made Dale Long a backstop (baseball's first post-'06 lefty catcher), and Stan Musial got his 3,000th hit (May 13,

1958, off Moe Drabowsky), records meant all. Said Brickhouse: "A Cubs fan is born so that he can suffer."

Who hit Wrigley's center-field scoreboard? Golfer Sam Snead '51, tee-ing from home plate. (Barely missing to the right and left: Bill Nicholson and Roberto Clemente, respectively.) In 1952, Ronald Reagan called two innings on St. Louis radio to promote his movie, "The Winning Team." "Harry [Caray], I've had so much fun. Thanks for putting me on," said Dutch, leaving. "I have another appointment." In 1988, now president, Reagan did a half-inning on WGN-TV. "Harry, it's been so much fun, but I have another appointment." Caray shook his head: "What goes around, comes around"—e.g. manager Grimm.

In 1949, Wrigley again axed him. A decade later Charlie began stint three. On May 6, 1960, the Cubs occupied the cellar. "Phil called me in," said Brickhouse, "and said, 'I want to make a trade. You take care of it.' I said, 'Who's involved?' He looked at me and said, 'I want to trade [Cubs radio analyst Lou] Boudreau for Grimm.' "

"Boudreau for Grimm?" Brickhouse repeated.

"Yes," Wrigley answered. "Charlie's worrying himself sick over the team. He's out walking the streets when he should be resting. If the Cubs don't kill him first his sore feet will."

Grimm moved to radio. Boudreau replaced him on the field. "A man-ager for a broadcaster," said Brickhouse. Only with the Cubs. In November 1983, at 85, the unsinkable and recyclable Jolly Cholly finally sank, ashes scattered over Wrigley Field. Said Banks: "His career was a creature of [baseball's] habit," as renewable as the sun.

FENWAY PARK

Each age wears symbols of its special place and time. World War II had the Andrews Sisters. The 1990s blazed Madonna. Other names span generations. Reagan, scripted from radio to the presidency. Johnny Car-son, lauded for hale, light commentary. John Wayne in baseball woolies—the greatest hitter who ever lived.

Ted Williams was long-limbed like a pelican, elegant as a stallion, and jittery like a colt. Ty Cobb flaunted average (.367 lifetime). Chuck Klein crushed balls that left one zip code for another. Tommy Henrich panted for pressure—thus, "Old Reliable." Teddy Ballgame did all of the above. Bobby Doerr approached him in '39 spring training. "Wait 'till you see Foxx hit," Doerr said. Boomed the rookie: "Wait 'till Foxx sees me hit!" No hitter who lived surpassed the Seasons of the Kid.

Statistics are said to lie. Tell that to pitchers. Six batting titles—1941–'42–'47–'48–'57–'58 (.406, .356, .343, .369. .388, and .328). Four home run and RBI titles—1941–'42–'47–'49 (37, 36, 32, and 43) and '39–'42–'47–'49 (145, 137, 114, and 159, with Vern Stephens). Two MVP awards (1946–'49) and Triple Crowns ('42–'47). Team-high 521 homers and .344 average. Last man to bat .400. Hall of Fame '69. Williams' laundry list would surfeit dry cleaners from Kennebunk to Holyoke.

For Curt Gowdy, remembrance was neither faint nor selective. "All this despite missing five years in military [World War II and Korea]. Take away that and there'd be no place in the record books for anyone but Ted." Time to second-guess: Statistics *may* lie. "I wanted people," he said, "to say, 'There goes the greatest hitter whoever lived.' " By any reckoning, they do.

Williams buoyed a team formed largely from without. Lefty Grove forged Fenway's best percentage (.764) for a Red Sox left-handed pitcher. Jimmie Foxx's '38 tied 50 home runs and 175 RBI. Said infielder Bobby Doerr: "Mr. Yawkey kept trying to buy a pennant." Failing, he would build from within.

Four farmers—the Kid, Doerr, Dom DiMaggio, and Johnny Pesky—formed the Sox' '40s core. Doerr thrice hit more than .300. Pesky pulled eight of seventeen career homers off the right-field—hence, Pesky's—Pole. Enduring to a cultist was bespectacled DiMaggio's moniker—"The Little Professor." Ted hit .428 at '41 Fenway. "He loved its tiny foul ground [would-be outs hit seats], center backdrop [no fence ads]," said Gowdy, "and how seats above it weren't sold [white balls leaving white shirts]." Bullpens—"Williamsburg"—moved to right-center from foul turf beyond the dugouts. In 1946, Ted returned from war to find New Englanders waiting like parishioners hoping to meet the Pope.

The '46ers drew 1,416,944 v. '42's prior high (730,340). Boston won 104 games and played 60–17 at home. Dave (Bo[o]) Ferriss knew pitching (AL-best 25–6) and hitting (.250 lifetime). Pesky hit .335. Williams whacked Fenway's longest-ever blast—502 feet, to right—off the straw hat of Joseph A. Boucher, 56, a construction engineer from Albany. "The sun was right in our eyes," he said. "They said it bounced a dozen rows higher, but after it hit my head, I wasn't interested." The seat is now painted red—21, bleacher section 42, row 37.

In July, Williams homered twice, one off Rip Sewell's blooper, or "eephus," pitch in the All-Star Game at Fenway. On September 13, he poked the only inside-the-parker of his career to clinch the flag, 1–0. It seems alien to say it: Boston had never lost a World Series. Pulling, T. Ballgame treated left field like a constitutional offense. He rent Cleveland in the opener of one doubleheader. Tribe manager Lou Boudreau then shifted all but his left fielder to the right-field side of second: *Now*, hit one through. Ty Cobb urged Ted to go to the other field. The Kid refused.

Cardinals manager Eddie Dyer made a note. In the Series he left only one player on the left side of the diamond—the Williams Shift. The Splinter bunted. As Enos Slaughter tore around the bases, George Vecsey wrote, he "was like a steam engine racing his way across the country, telling people: 'Look—look—the men are back—the war is over—baseball has survived!' " Its effect on Boston was more abiding—a belief in Murphy's Law (if something can go wrong, it will) over the Law of Averages (life is fair; things even out).

The Sox had expected to win. Losing bred doubt. Green paint replaced ads on the left-field wall. If you can't beat em: In 1948, Boston hired ex–Yanks manager Joe McCarthy. Marse Joe had made the stripes wear suits and ties. Williams hated them. At spring training, McCarthy ate breakfast in a bright open-necked sports shirt. "Anyone who can't get along with a .400 hitter," he said, "is crazy." Later, Ted called McCarthy "the best manager I played for. He installed a more businesslike attitude in 25 guys than any man I ever saw."

Efficient, or robotic? On July 4, the Sox trailed by 11 games. By Closing Day, Cleveland led by one. Detroit crushed Bob Feller. Meanwhile,

Boston ripped New York. Fenway primped for the AL's first playoff—its last till Bucky Dent. "They counted us out!" McCarthy whooped. A reporter told the Kid that Bob Lemon would pitch the playoff. "I don't care if he's beaten us 20 times this year," cried Williams. "We'll knock his brains out tomorrow."

Boudreau picked Gene Bearden, not Lemon. Marse Joe made that surprise look smaller than a buoy on Nantucket Sound. Rumor expected him to tap Ellis Kinder or Mel Parnell. "Maybe I'll get the word tonight in a dream," McCarthy told reporters. Or better still, just find some nice little man and rub his curly head." Perhaps he did, starting journeyman Denny Galehouse.

Jimmy Dudley was a rookie Indians announcer. "Going into Fenway," he said, "was like throwing the Christians to the lions. Lord, the Sox were so good at home!" Boudreau wrecked a '48 all-Boston Series by blasting two home runs. Final score: 8–3. Maybe the Christians had a better pitcher.

"I think Cleveland would have beaten anybody," said Pesky. The point is: It beat Boston. The Sox have lost the pennant or Series on the next to last or last day of 1946–'48–'49–'67–'72–'75–'78–'86. The pre–'86 worst was '49. The infield yoked Billy Goodman (.298), Doerr (.309), Vern Stephens (.290), and Pesky (.306). Parnell won 25 games—a Sox lefty high. Kinder added 23. Said a mate: "Ellie could drink more bourbon and pitch more clutch baseball than anyone I knew." Boston even had McCarthy.

In Ernest Hemingway's *The Old Man and the Sea,* Santiago, the older man, says to Manolin, "Have faith in the Yankees, my son. Think of the great DiMaggio." A painful heel spur had shelved Joe all year. On June 28, a Fenway night record 36,228 gathered for his return. DiMag crashed a third-inning home run: Yankees, 5–4. Next day DiMag torched two more: 9–7. Pesky still remembers. "One of them went over the wall, the screen, and everything: It might have gone to the Hotel Kenmore, for all I know." A day later DiMag's three-run belt hit the left-field tower. The noise was insupportable. The Yankees swept the series. A small plane trailed a banner: THE GREAT DIMAGGIO.

"It's one of those great American events, like the coming of snow or

the end of school," said Bart Giamatti of the Sox' fiercest rivalry.
Williams was more prosaic: "Christ, I wanted to beat the Yankees!"—
especially '49's. Boston fell 12 games behind. Then, as in '48, it jelled to
within a game and a half of New York by Labor Day—before, as psy-
chologists say of human beings, reverting to form. The final week Boston
took a one-game lead. Ahead: at Yankee Stadium, its last two. They were
austere, riveting: Bombers, 5–4 and 5–3. Williams sought isolation;
McCarthy, a flask. Ted later managed the Senators and Rangers: "I'd go
up in the room and start worrying and just start eating. I called up
McCarthy and he said, 'You're better than I am. I used to do the same
but I'd start drinking.' "

Kinder, who never stopped, thought far less of his old manager.
McCarthy yanked him in the final. "If he leaves me in, I stop the Yankees
and we win [the pennant]." On the train back to Boston he tried to
punch Joe in the mouth.

"**W**e were never mad that we lost the Series and then barely missed
two straight pennants," Parnell mused. "We were just disappointed."
How could it *happen*?—so needlessly, and heedlessly. In June 1950,
Boston tied a league record for most runs, 29–4, v. St. Louis. McCarthy
soon resigned. Some were glad to see him go. Others sought a time when
perspective was in season.

Gallup says Americans would rather relive the 1950s than any decade.
Not Boston: Only the '55ers vied past Labor Day. By now, Fenway's core
tied history and strategy. A net-finder might be an out at Comiskey Park.
The initials of Yawkey and wife Jean R. (TAY and JRY) in Morse Code
graced two vertical scoreboard stripes. The home plate screen, built to
protect a visitor, was the bigs' first of its kind. To a child, the park's mass,
shadows, and gentle sweep of stands pricked even Sox repose.

In 1957, a writer found Fenway good: "Oddly shaped but most
attractive, this is great park in which to view game. It is hard to find
really bad seat in the rambling one-level stands. Sit in section along the
left-field line and listen to the more pungent comments. Special 'skyline'
boxes swing out from either side of rooftop press box. Ushers are plenti-
ful, courteous. The 18 refreshment stands are easily accessible from most
seats for a quick snack. Subway from nearby Kenmore Square station

connects with all parts of Greater Boston, as well as to all New England via railroad, bus, or airplane. It's easy to drive to Fenway and there's supposed to be parking space for 8,500 cars in vicinity, but don't rely on it. Leaving park area after game can be difficult. Taxis are comparatively few, and if it is day game, downtown working crowd heading for home invariably clogs way."

Nothing clogged rebuff or hope. Check: The '53 Sox scored 17 runs in an inning. Checkmate: Herb Score later blanked Boston, 19–0, after a black plastic cat, failing as a lucky rabbit's foot, was buried below a bullpen headstone. Jackie Jensen's MVP year was 1958. Jimmy Piersall's life is doubtless known: manic depression, prognosis, shock, and resilience, if not recovery. In 1957, sport's Lawrence Welk, 40, shunned Geritol to win a fifth batting title (.388). Preparing to *leave* baseball, the Splinter had corkscrewed *into* baseball.

On September 28, 1960, the Sox retired No. 9. Ted walked, flied to center, and hit to the right-field fence. "If that one didn't go out," Ted told Vic Wertz, "none of them will today." In the eighth, Williams batted against Jack Fisher, 21. The lights were on. The ball wasn't carrying. Fisher threw. Williams lofted to right, exiting like a deity—a home run, No. 521, in his final time at bat.

Ten thousand, four hundred and fifty-four Fenway (dis)believers had tonsils redder than T. Ballgame's hose. At home plate, Ted declined to tip his cap. "I just couldn't do it," he said. "It just would not have been me." John Updike offered an angelic gloss: "God does not answer letters."

In 1958, a writer noted: "Williams is the greatest hitter since Ruth, and last year was . . . his finest. Because of him, Boston finished third. Without him, it is hard to say how far they could sink." The Athens of America was about to find out.

10

OLD CAPE COD

It is always darkest before—the night. The '36 Braves hosted their first All-Star Game. Bungling intruded, an unwelcome guest. Read the *Boston Globe*: "The team said that all *reserved* seats had been sold out, which led many to assume the game was sold out"—creating 12,000 empty seats. In 1929, owner Judge Emil Fuchs became manager: two for the price of one. "A manager must no longer chew tobacco and talk out of the side of his mouth," he ordained. "The club can't do any worse with me as manager than it had done the last few years." Case denied: The Braves placed eighth for the first time since '24.

One day, Boston loaded the bases with none out. Fuchs turned to his players. "What shall we try for now, boys?"

"How about a squeeze play?" said one.

The Judge's face turned red. "No," he said, "let's score in an honorable way."

Later, Fuchs told an ex-Yankees third baseman to play shortstop. "What's shortstop?" Joe Dugan snapped. Fuchs was less street-smart

175

than old school. "Show Mr. Dugan where the clubhouse is and how to take off his uniform."

Fuchs yielded to Bill McKechnie, who left for Cincinnati in 1938. Replacing him was a clown and semigrammarian who later told a U.S. Senate Committee, "I became the manager of several big-league teams and was discharged. We call it discharged because there was no question I had to leave." In 1943, a Boston taxi hit Casey Stengel and put him in the hospital. A columnist named the cabbie Hub "Man of the Year." Once Max West returned to Boston's dugout after fanning. He spotted a passed ball, thought it a foul tip, and tossed to the Phils catcher, who tagged out a Braves runner trying to score. Stengel stewed: Should he fine and/or suspend West? At that moment Max stopped at the water cooler—where a foul ball broke two teeth. Casey's '39–'42 Braves finished last. By 1943, there was "no question": Discharged, Casey "had to leave."

In 1942, Jim Tobin homered thrice in a game—the bigs' first pitcher to do so since 1886. On April 27, 1944, the righty no-hit Brooklyn, 2–0. Wallace Stevens wrote: "He that of repetition is most master." Tobin mastered a rain-shortened five-frame June 22 no-hitter *v.* Philadelphia. By '46 he was out of baseball. Boston's both sides now: In 1902, Beaneater Charles (Togie, or Horse Race) Pittinger won 27 games. A year later Horse rode the NL in six *wretched* categories: losses, runs, earned runs, home runs, walks, and hits.

"It was a first," said Lee Allen. The Braves lived nearer last.

Food for thought. People consume 26,000 hot dogs and sausages, 38,000 cups of soda and beer, and two tons of pretzels, popcorn, and peanuts at an average big-league game. (They also frequent more than 50 bathrooms, which use 40,000 gallons of water. The median park holds more than 10,000 feet of plumbing and 2,100 60-foot pilings.) It is not known how many fried clams—baseball's best—were inhaled daily at Braves Field.

In 1945, Tommy Holmes hit .352 and safely in a then-NL record 37 straight games. Boston '46 cracked its first first division since 1934. For the first time the '47ers drew a million—1,277,361. "As opposed to later," said Allen, "the Braves had about matched Red Sox attendance [1,427,315]." Boston's Bob Elliott batted .317, had 113 RBI, and became MVP. Some teams evoke a name. Say Pittsburgh, and you think

Clemente. Cincinnati, Pete Rose. St. Louis, the Man (Stan) whom Ford Frick, dedicating a statue, called "Baseball's perfect warrior, baseball's perfect knight." Shortstop at Wrigley means Ernie Banks; second base in Brooklyn Jackie Robinson; center field anywhere, the "Say-Hey Kid." Pitching at Braves Field meant Warren Spahn and Johnny Sain.

Spahn '47 led the league in blankings (7) and ERA (2.13). A *mot* began: "Spahn and Sain and two days of rain." Sain '48 went 24–15. Spahn added 15 of his 356 victories for the Boston-turned-Milwaukee Braves. Holmes hit .325. Alvin Dark batted .322 and was a Gibraltar at short. Second baseman Eddie Stanky blazed "the intangibles," said Leo Durocher. "He can't run, he can't hit, he can't throw, all he can is beat you." The Braves clinched their first-since-'14 flag over New York, 3–2, drawing 1,455,439, more than they ever had, or would again. The Troubadours—a.k.a. The Three Earaches—prowled the grandstand, blurring vaudeville and melody.

The '48 Braves led in pitching (3.37 ERA) and hitting (.275). The latter fled the Series v. Cleveland. The opener packed 40,135 into Braves Field. It turned in inning eight: a) The Indians' Bob Feller picked Phil Masi off second base; b) Bill Stewart called Masi safe, refuted by photos; and c) Holmes singled for the only run. Feller allowed two hits. "Guess," he jowled, "that was two too many." Next day Bob Lemon beat Spahn, 4–1. The Tribe won Games Three-Four, 2–0 and 2–1, at Cleveland. Mused a Brave: "My mother-in-law would have a higher average."

Early Wynn said he would knock down his grandmother to win. In Game Five, the Braves finally made Tribe pitching cry uncle. Boston torched five hurlers, 11–5, Spahn beating Feller, before a record 86,288. Game Six returned to the Hub. The Braves trailed, 4–1, scored two eighth-inning runs, and put the ninth-frame equalizer on base. The elegiac Sibby Sisti then bunted into a double play: Braves lose, 4–3. "Take away one game [five]," said Braves skipper Billy Southworth, "and we scored six runs all Series."

Years later Southworth still bewailed the Series. Nodding, pitcher Ernie Johnson added humor and regret.

"Two little ladies entered the park about the fifth inning and sat down behind a priest," Ernie said. " 'What's the score, Father?' they said. The priest said, 'Nothing-nothing.' One lady told the other, 'Oh, good, we haven't missed anything.'

"In the eighth inning a pinch-hitter batted for the local team. He makes the sign of the cross before stepping into the box. The little old lady leaned over and said, 'Father, father, will that help?' The priest turned around and said, 'Not if he can't hit.' "

Peroration. In 1951, attendance fell to 487,475. Holmes replaced Southworth. The '52ers placed seventh. Rookie Eddie Mathews hit 25 homers. Charlie Grimm replaced Holmes. "We were playing to the grounds help," mused Jolly Cholly. The Braves played their last home game September 22: 8,222 watched Brooklyn clinch a tie for the flag. "The Braves kept trying to hang on," said Southworth. "What's sad is that in a couple years they had Mathews, Hank Aaron, Spahn, Burdette, Joe Adcock. They'd have drawn anywhere. It's the Sox who might have moved." Instead, the Braves drew 281,278, a National's postwar low. A loyalist grasped hope like rafts in Boston Harbor.

The Braves dispersed to homes in Charlotte and Marion, Wisconsin, and Oil City, Pennsylvania. Next spring they trekked blankly to spring training. "We were in Bradenton," said Johnson, "when we got the news." On March 18, 1953, the Braves of Boston, since 1876, decamped for Wisconsin's largest city. Thousands packed bars and churches and bowling alleys to kill their new club with love. At Braves Field, tickets dropped from windows into waiting trucks on Gaffney Street. The park was sold to Boston University, which peddled seats to a Rhode Island softball stadium.

Today a visitor finds a sense of time standing still, but moorings ripped away. Grass transplanted from South End Grounds is gone. AstroTurf blares the handiwork of our antiseptic time. Left are fixtures and photographs—the first-base grandstand, right and center outer wall, Gaffney Street ticket entrance, a plaque dedicated in 1988—memory less honor than mirror of the heart.

In 1950, the Braves visited Fenway for the annual City Series. Ted Williams faced Johnson, who curved the outside corner. "Great decision," Johnson joked. "In seconds it's rolling to the Hotel Kenmore. Afterward we're walking through the clubhouse. Southworth put his arm around me, and said, 'Don't worry, he's hit them off better pitchers than you.' "

Two years later, veteran Vern Bickford faced Ted in Bradenton. In the first inning he got Williams out. Vern later told teammates, "Ted's up this inning. I'm gonna' see how far that big donkey can hit one."

Johnson asked, "What are you gonna' do?"

Bickford said, "Lay it in there about ¾ speed and see what happens."

Knowledge can birth pressure. "Sometimes, in batting practice," said Johnson, "if a batter sees a lollypop coming he'll get antsy, hit it on the ground or otherwise screw it up." Williams hit the light tower in right-center field. "We're roaring as the inning ends. Bickford comes back, shakes his head, and says, 'Well, I got my answer.' "

We all did in March 1953.

EBBETS FIELD

The late 1930s shook with uproar. In Brooklyn, they shook with Larry MacPhail. In 1938, the NL hired him to keep the Dodgers from going under: title, executive vice-president; control, "full and complete . . . over the operation of the club"; dessert, unlimited expense account. He prized his niche as a baseball Balboa, severe and tart and visionary.

"There is no history," wrote Churchill, "only biography." MacPhail's changed Brooklyn. He obtained Hugh Casey, Dolph Camilli, Pete Reiser, and Pee Wee Reese. On June 15, 1938, the second (Johnny Vander Meer's straight no-hitter) shall be first (Ebbets night game). Catcher Ernie Koy beat Olympic champion Jesse Owens in a 100-yard dash. "It helps," he said of the pregame event, "to have a 10-yard start." MacPhail augured Charlie Finley by dyeing official balls: John Mize hit the first "yellow homer." Leo Durocher became player/manager. The '39ers drew 955,668. The NL moved a September doubleheader from Philly to Brooklyn. "They hoped Brooklyn could get a million," said Lee Allen, "so for the first time games were transferred from one park to another."

The patient healed. "MacPhail took over," Red Barber wrote, "in the last year of a five-year radio ban" signed by New York's three clubs in 1934. At the time they twitched with fear: Who would pay if you could hear for free? In late '38, MacPhail violated the inviolate: The Dodgers would use the wireless. Their voice trailed him from Cincinnati to chat, soft-voiced and evocative. Vin Scully thought Red a palatine. "A cabbie would say, 'That Barber, he's too fair.' " To Bob Costas, he symbolized a borough. "It was a separate city within New York. Red's appeal soared because Brooklynites sensitive about the image as Dees and dems—'I'll

meet ya' at Toydy-toyd and Second Avenue'—were pleased that this eru-
dite man represented them."

Of a given day the Redhead might mix "walkin' in tall cotton" and
"FOB—Full of Brooklyns" with Carlyle and Thoreau. He treated baseball with comity; truth, reverence; the listener, respect. "The human
race," wrote G. K. Chesterton, "to which so many of my readers
belong." Humanity gripped Ebbets Field. From any seat you heard players jabber, saw faces harden, felt tension creep. Said Costas: "Barber was
the voice of that experience. You could walk down streets without a
radio and never miss a pitch because somebody'd have the window open
and Red's voice would loft out. You'd go by a newsstand—the radio was
on. A cab stopped and you'd hear him"—a borough's signet.

"The players were clearly distinguishable," wrote the *Sporting News'*
Harold Parrott of August 26, 1939, "but it was not possible to pick out
the ball." By contrast, you could pick out the Redhead in the second deck,
on Ebbets' third-base side, baptizing TV baseball for fewer than 400 sets
with flickering picture and uneven sound. He was flanked by beery, sweaty
patrons, had no monitor and two cameras, and shilled for Ivory Soap,
Mobil Gas, and General Mills. Making history, he was flying blind.

To Barber, a team would "tear up the pea patch." In 1940, a parole
violator almost tore up plate umpire George Magerkurth. "We were
taunting him," Durocher said of the Dodgers. "It was bad, even by baseball terms." Upon the final out the con attacked Magerkurth before he
could leave the field. "Just rushed from his seat," said the umpire.
"Before I know it he's beating me to a pulp."

The classic fan screams, "Kill the ump!" Colleague Bill Stewart feared
the jailbird might. He freed Magerkurth. Police then hauled the pugilist
to the station house. NL president Ford Frick later fined and suspended
Leo for "inciting a riot." Just another day at Ebbets Field.

In Jack Benny's old TV show, a bank robber accosts our hero. Pointing
a gun, he demands, "Your money or your life." Benny pauses before
replying, "I'm thinking, I'm thinking." Brooklyn thought of baseball

in the last season of an uncertain peace. Urban, it eschewed the farm.

"In '41," said Leo, "every regular came from another club." Kirby Higbee and Whitlow Wyatt won 44 games. Reiser topped the NL in six categories. MVP Camilli led in homers (34) and RBI (120). Reese supplied the glove and glue. "He came here a boy," Barber liked to say, "and wound up a man." Several '40 Bums were beaned. They wore 1941 helmet liners. Catcher Mickey Owen plucked another first—three foul flies in an inning. The Dodgers drew a record 1,214,910. On September 28, they clinched their first title since the last full year of Woodrow Wilson's presidency. More precedent: Brooklyn won 100 games. A writer penned: "Now if we can only win four against the pinstripes."

'Forty-one bred the first Yankees–Dodgers Subway Series. New York won Game One behind Red Ruffing. Wyatt then beat Spud Chandler. Reliever Hugh Casey yielded two third-game runs: Yanks, 2–1. "We're down but not worried," said Durocher, " 'cause we're home and got the crowd." Brooklyn led Game Four, 4–3, in the ninth. Casey retired two Yanks and worked Tommy Henrich to a 3–2 count. Said Old Reliable: "Casey [then] threw the craziest curve I ever saw."

The ball eluded Henrich. Larry Goetz boomed "Strike three!" The pitch knifed off Owen's glove. Mickey was next sighted racing toward the backstop. Henrich reached first base. Joe DiMaggio singled. Casey got two strikes on Charlie Keller, who doubled off the right-field wall. Bill Dickey walked. Joe Gordon doubled. You could hear a sigh: 7–4, New York. Owen vaulted hidebound into baseball's Parthenon of goats. "The condemned jumped out of the chair," one writer said, "and electrocuted the warden." Next day the Yanks won again, 3–1—their ninth world title. The Cathedral of the Underdog played a tired and humbled dirge.

By January 15, 1942, Franklin Roosevelt had drawn *The Four Freedoms,* signed the Atlantic Charter, and declared war "on the empire of Japan." That day he wrote a letter to Judge Landis. "I honestly feel it would be best for the country to keep baseball going," he said. "Here is [a] way of looking at it—if 300 teams use 5,000 or 6,000 players, these players are a definite recreational asset to at least 20,000,000 of their fellow citizens—and that, in my judgement, is thoroughly worthwhile."

To soldiers, baseball left the world alone. Ebbets hailed its first post-'18 twilight game. "It raised nearly $60,000 for the Navy Relief Fund," Harold Rosenthal said. "Even the players paid their way." Camilli made pitchers pay: 26 homers and 109 RBI. A drive by the Reds' Lonnie Frey fell on top of the wall between the scoreboard and foul pole and kept bouncing. "Never came down," said Camilli. "Frey rounded the bases for a homer." Babe Herman '43 hit .330. Tommy Brown, 16, played shortstop in a twinbill against Chicago. The '45ers trained at Bear Mountain, New York, with an incredibly shrinking team. "The war restrictions kept us north," said Durocher, "and we only had 15 players in camp."

On August 13, 1945, Branch Rickey—"El Cheapo" to Dick Young, and "Mahatma" to Tom Meany—and Walter O'Malley and John Smith bought 50 percent of the Ebbets estate for $750,000. Few could discern their effect on baseball's social and geographic core. You *could* see: Dixie Walker (first in RBI: 124) and Luis Olmo (NL-high 13 triples) and Eddie Stanky, Goody Rosen, and Augie Galan (1–2–4, runs: 128, 126, and 114). Respectable, the Dodgers would soon come of age. The journalist Lincoln Steffens once visited the Soviet Union and offered an absurdity. "I have seen the future," he said, "and it works." Brooklyn's future worked around the corner. Jack Roosevelt Robinson was a lion at the plate, a tiger in the field, and "had wounds," said Rickey, "you could not feel or share."

On October 23, Rickey inked Robinson to break baseball's color line. A week later he shipped Jackie to Montreal, Brooklyn's Triple-A affiliate. Baseball's first black player debuted April 18, 1946, with a dinger and three singles. Robinson won the International League batting title at .349. Walker led the parent club: .319 and 116 RBI. Said the unreconstructed Southerner: "Love that right-field wall." Beyond it a gas station serviced clients: Most chased belts to Bedford Avenue. The Bums drew 1,796,824. On May 30, 1946, Boston's Carvel "Bama" Rowell presaged *The Natural*. "Remember when Robert Redford's blast breaks the scoreboard?" said Bob Costas. The Bulova clock broke at 4:25 P.M. Dousing Walker, glass drove old Dixie down.

That September 11, the Dodgers and Reds played 19 scoreless innings. Brooklyn and St. Louis each finished 94–60. Say playoff, and you think Bobby Thomson. The first occurred five years earlier: The Redbirds won the best-of-three. Forget T. S. Eliot. Remember 1916–20–41–46. *October* had become the cruelest month.

SHIBE PARK

For nearly forty years, his voice draped Philadelphia like the Series does October. Byrum Saam became "The Man of a Zillion Words," and listeners felt a link. "Would you please talk a little louder?" wrote a woman from New Jersey. "My radio battery is getting weaker." Saam called the 1938–'54 A's and 1938–'49 and 1951–'75 Phillies. His shield was malapropisms. "Hello, Byrum Saam," began one broadcast, "this is everybody speaking." They seemed a simile for his teams.

Saam's A's and Phillies, respectively, bore a 1,057–1,553 and 2,182–2,842 record. "It wasn't easy when on a Sunday you're down 15 runs, and everybody's at the shore guzzling beer." The statistic weighs, meaningless and all-meaning: He announced more losing games than anyone.

In 1932, Lou Gehrig hit four straight homers. Tony Lazzeri drove in 11 runs one game. Jimmie Foxx and Gehrig cleared the center-field roof. (Double X got his 500th tater September 24, 1940—for Boston!) In 1943, a 65-minute practice wartime blackout halted play. By contrast, the AL lit its first night game in 1939. "The infield," said engineers, "is several hundred times brighter than Times Square on New Year's Eve." Ted Williams shone as bright as any big-league star.

On September 27, 1941, Boston played in Philadelphia—or would have, without rain. No player had hit .400 since 1930. Williams was hitting .3995—.400 in the record book. Manager Joe Cronin urged him to skip the season-ending doubleheader. "You got .400. Sit it out." Ted said, "I don't want it that way." John Wayne was never more colossal on film. Williams and clubhouse attendant Johnny Orlando walked for miles before the game. At 23, No. 9 was morphing from prodigy to legend. Ted whacked a home run and single, then added two second-game hits: 6-for-8, .406, and Cavalry to the rescue niche.

Bill and Eddie Kessler became '30s Everyfan. In 1943, Shibe housed the first night All-Star Game: AL, 5–3. The '52 Nationals had the last rain-shortened 3–2 five-inning laugh. The Phils' Curt Simmons and A's' Bobby Shantz threw four scoreless innings. Saam sighed, wearily. "We had to be interested. You couldn't focus on the local *teams*." The *Sporting News* picked a yearly '38–'49 All-Star squad. Only three teams placed not a single player. "The Browns were one. Guess the other two."

"**B**y now," said Richie Ashburn, "Shibe was comfortable, like an old chair." Until 1935, 20th Streeters sat in their home or on the roof and peered over the right-field wall. "Mack was again losing money, so he tried to stop wildcatters from selling rooftop space." When Connie lost the suit, he "put a 22-foot-high [corrugated iron] barrier" atop the 12-foot wall. Locals called it the "spite fence"—adjective, and verb.

The wall blared schizophrenia. A ball might return toward the infield, or deaden and drop straight down. Ashburn retrieved many in right-center. The Nebraskan hit .308, won '55–'58 batting titles at .338 and .350, yet hit only 29 homers. Some years he seemed to pluck that many from the stands. Number 1 led the NL in chances and had 500 or more putouts a record nine times. He also grasped the franchise's need for an edge.

One day Richie kept whining about pitches. "All right," umpire Jocko Conlan finally said. "You umpire. I'm letting you call the next pitch." Ashburn replied: "You're kidding." Jocko said, "Nope, you call the next one." The next pitch was a foot outside. Ashburn said, "Strike."

Conlan signaled, called time, and went out to dust the plate. Looking up, he eyed the Phils captain. "Richie, I gave you the only chance a hitter ever had in history to bat and umpire at the same time. You blew it. That's the last pitch you'll ever call. You're not gonna' louse up my profession." The 1933–'48 second-division Phils kept lousing up their own.

A 12-foot-wall linked left to left-center. After 1940, a scoreboard draped right field. The original flagstone was replaced by granite. Bricks were painted; pillars cleaned. Numbers doubled back to the points of one's youth: 334 (left), 468 (center), 393 (moving right), and 331 (right). Size fell from 33,000 (1930) to 32,500 ('48). At the time, the diminution felt natural. "In post-war America, baseball clubs were drawing like crazy," said 1998–commissioner Allan H. (Bud) Selig. The '48 Indians lured 2,620,627. At Shibe, only the '46 Phillies even passed one million.

The '49 Phils finished 16 games behind the Dodgers. A 1950 pennant seemed as likely as Mae West singing *The Barber of Seville*. Given history, what ensued astounds: an honest to goodness, praise be, hallejuiah *pennant race*—the Phils v. their patina of fate and insecurity. Freeze America at mid-century. The Korean War darkened. Arthur Miller gloried in *Death of a*

Salesman. Mrs. I. Toguri d'Aquino—"Tokyo Rose"—was sentenced to ten years in prison. Norman Vincent Peale touted inner peace. William Faulkner received the Nobel Prize for Literature. "I decline to accept the end of man," he said. "It is easy enough to say that man is immortal simply because he will end here: that when the last ding-dong of doom has clanged and faded, from the last worthless rock hanging tideless in the last red and dying evening, that even then there will be an inexhaustible voice still talking. I refuse to accept this. I believe that man will not merely endure: he will prevail." The post-'15 Phils had sought merely to endure—till now.

Ashburn topped the 1950 NL with 14 triples. Del Ennis led with 126 RBI. Curt Simmons finished 17–8. MVP reliever Jim Konstanty forged 74 games and a 16–7 record into a rock of ages year. Robin Roberts won 20, the Phillies' most since 1917. (In time, he won 286 games, 234 for Philly, and led in innings [1951–'55], victories ['52–'55], complete games ['52–'56], shutouts ['50], and Ks ['53–'54]). They drew a then–franchise record 1,217,035.

Growing up in Wayne, a Philadelphia suburb, Ned Martin liked the A's. "My dad took me to my first game at Shibe in '32," said the 1961–'92 Red Sox announcer. "Yet I'll never forget '50." Ask any Philadelphian: barbecues and work and PTA begot the Phils. With nine days left, the Nationals had a seven-game lead. Casual fans became addicts. Simmons reported to the National Guard. Eleven-game winner Bob Miller got hurt. Babies were born, and sermons given. Roberts made three starts in the last five days. Marriages were begun, and divorces decreed. The final game—Sunday, October 1—brought Philly to Ebbets Field. "A Dodgers win would tie the race," said Martin. The Phils scored first. Brooklyn's Pee Wee Reese homered in the sixth inning. In the ninth, Ashburn threw out the winning run at the plate. Score, 1–1: Dinners grew cold, and were rewarmed. Dick Sisler clubbed a 10th-inning, three-run, game-winning, pennant-clinching blast. A blizzard of radios knit Center City.

"I'll never forget," mused Martin, "working on the Pennslvania Turnpike and listening to the Yankees beat the Whiz Kids [average age, 26] in the Series." Manager Eddie Sawyer tapped Konstanty to start Game One: New York got two hits, winning, 1–0, behind Vic Raschi. In Match Two, Joe DiMaggio touched Roberts for a 10th-inning (2–1) blow. The

Series moved to Yankee Stadium. Perhaps the turn of parks confused the Phils: Three errors cost, 3–2. "If its and buts were candy and nuts," the saw proclaims, "we'd all have a hell of a Christmas." Game Four evoked All-Fools Day. The Yankees swept, 5–2.

The Phils' (*especially*, the Phils') luck couldn't (and didn't) last. Hitting bottom, the '58ers stayed there through '61. "The A's were just as bad," said Sawyer, but their scent now filled Missouri. Shantz became MVP in 1952. The '54 ALers went 51–103 and drew 304,666. That winter Mack sold them to Kansas City businessman Arnold Johnson. "We just couldn't make a go of it," said Mack, who retired in 1950 and died, at 93, in 1956. Change had a quirky, scattered feel.

Shibe's board of directors renamed the park Connie Mack Stadium. The '54 Phils bought it for $2 million, cleared aisles, and painted box and reserved seats red and pale pink. An in-play batting cage had anchored center field. Distance now fell to 447; the cage hid behind the fence. In right-center, a Ballantine beer scoreboard sign loomed 60 feet above the field. Later, Philly added a 75-foot-high clock. (Both objects were in play). "Don't forget the final change," Saam said. "A see-through Plexiglas that replaced the normal screen behind the plate." It rose upward, abutted a TV booth, then angled toward the roof. "It was like the rest of the park, with its close seats and high walls. Every day was an adventure."

In 1971, Phillies manager Frank Lucchesi malapropped, "Don't you know I'm being a Fascist? You know, a guy who says one thing and means another." It is not facetious to say that in Shibe's last years—few called it Connie Mack Stadium—the need for stability worked overtime.

Jim Bunning helped, winning 224 games, including 100 in each league. Ashburn remained a merlin at the plate. Once Richie fouled a ball that struck a Phillies season-ticket holder in the head. They took her on a stretcher to the hospital. The next day the Samaritan went to visit. The woman's leg was in traction from the roof of the bed.

"Gee," he said, "I knew I got you with that foul ball, but what on earth happened to your leg?"

"Richie, you won't believe this," she explained, "but as they were carrying me off on the stretcher you hit *another* foul ball that hit me and broke a bone in my knee."

Willie Mays was a ballast the Phils could have sailed without. "He owned our park," said infielder Cookie Rojas. "Leave it to our fans. They'd ride us and cheer him." One night Mays was on first when a batter singled to left. Normally the runner stops at second. Mays rounded it and headed for third before the ball reached Don Demeter. "Don got it, looked at Mays," said teammate Bobby Wine, "and Willie slowed down to try to draw the throw. You could see Demeter thinking, 'You're not tricking me. I'll throw to second and stop the hitter.' He did. Willie never stopped running."

Mays scored on a one-hop single to left field. You could excuse a Quaker for thinking that he had seen it all.

FORBES FIELD

By 1943, clubs brandished castoffs, rookies, and men spurned by the armed services. Rosters pulsed with players stamped 4-F. Douglass Wallop wrote, "The game being played on the field was recognizable, but many of the players were not." In Pittsburgh, a U.S. wooden Marine, 32 feet high by 15 feet wide at his feet, stood at parade rest to the right of the scoreboard against the left-field wall. "He was there to salute our World War II effort," said Bob Prince. "It may have been the most bizarre in-play object in baseball history."

Pittsburgh soon added an *object d'art:* a brick and ivied wall from right-center to the left-field line. In left, a 27-foot-high hand-operated scoreboard listed balls, strikes, outs, scores, and pitching changes. Atop it: speaker horns and a Western Union (later, Longines) clock. Seats were blue (boxes), gray (reserved), and green or red (general admission). Beyond third base lay farther-from-the-line bleachers: Many couldn't see the plate. Elsewhere, Forbes Field's beauty was neither clichéd nor Talamudic.

"This became the look," said 1955–'76 general manager Joe Brown. "It's how we remember her—ivy, scoreboard, brick, the batting cage." You also recall a chant of "the bases are FOB" ("Full of Bucs") and "doozie marooney" (extra-baser). In 1936, Rosey Rowswell became a Pirates announcer. They sank the second division 10 of the next 19 years. "In a case like this," said Prince, Rowswell's protégé, "you deflect attention." Rosey and a plump belle called "Aunt Minnie" hyped a '39 KDKA-TV exhibit by entering Forbes in an Austin car.

Aunt Minnie debuted in 1938. A Pirates homer cleared the scoreboard, whereupon Rowswell shouted, "Get upstairs, Aunt Minnie, and raise the window! Here she [the baseball] comes!" An aide then dropped a pane of glass. To listeners, it meant Aunt Minnie's window. "That's too bad," Rosey sobbed. "She tripped over a garden hose! Aunt Minnie never made it!"

Prince arrived in 1948. Rosey subtly changed his tack. "Instead of glass—too messy—I had this big dumbwaiter's tray. On it were bells and nuts and bolts—*anything* to make a noise." A would-be dinger caused Prince to stand on the chair. "When he nodded, I'd drop the tray from about six feet off the floor. On radio, it sounded like an earthquake. And there'd be Rosey saying, 'Poor Aunt Minnie. She didn't make it again.' "

The woman in the Austin car was a faker. Few in Pittsburgh objected to baseball's Empress with No Clothes. Said Prince: "People knew she was fictitious, and didn't care." Upon a homer Prince scrambled to pick up the nuts and bolts. "I had to have the tray ready again, just in case the *next* guy hit one out."

"You got a lot of practice," colleague Jim Woods once said.

"Who wouldn't," he marveled, "with Ralph Kiner around?"

Kiner returned from war in 1946 to become cosmic in Pittsburgh's concourse. He also attended routinely to Aunt Minnie's glass. In 1947, the Bucco blasted eight home runs over four straight games. On July 4, 1951, Kiner exploded for seven RBI in two innings. Kiner '52 wafted 37 homers and asked general manager Branch Rickey for a raise. "I know you hit all those homers," said Rickey, "but we could have finished last without you."

In 1946, Pittsburgh bought Hank Greenberg. It did not tell him to lay down a squeeze. "Home run hitters drive Cadillacs," Kiner famously opined. The Bucs moved pens from foul ground to left field, strung an 8- (later, 12/14-) foot fence to left-center, and shrunk the line from 365 to 335. "The [30-foot] area between the new fence and scoreboard was called Greenberg's Gardens," said Kiner. "Balls landing there were homers." After one year Greenberg retired. His Gardens became Kiner's Korner.

"Through '52, Ralph *was* our team," said Rickey: 294 home runs, including '47–'49's 51 and 54, and *nonpareil* seven straight crowns. Homers didn't win a flag. They did, however, chart oddity. The 1947 Pirates lost 92 games but drew a record 1,283,531. The '48 fourth-placers lured 1,517,021. "After my last up," Kiner laughed, "half the crowd would leave." In 1953, he joined the Cubs. The inner fence came down. It didn't help from '50–'57. "Not once," said Rickey, "did we finish above seventh."

Joe Garagiola rubbernecked their demise. In 1951, St. Louis traded him to Pittsburgh. A year later Joe hit .273. His Bucs finished last in runs, doubles, triples, home runs, Ks, walks, shutouts, ERA—and wins (42–112, 54½ games behind the Dodgers). "It was the most courageous team in the bigs," said baseball's Letterman. "We had 154 games scheduled, and we showed up for every one. We lost eight of our first nine games and then we had a slump. That was probably the only team that clinched last place on opening day of spring training."

Nineteen fifty-three, joked Garagiola, marked the ninth year of Rickey's five-year plan. One day Branch called Joe to his office. "He looks at me with his big, bushy eyebrows. 'By Judas Priest, Joe,' he says, 'we're turning the corner here. We're coming out of the wilderness. And you, my boy, figure in my plans.' " That week, the Mahatma traded Joe G. to the Cubs.

In 1955, Rickey dedicated an 18-foot 18,000-pound statue of Honus Wagner in Schenley Park. Dale Long swapped obscurity for *The Ed Sullivan Show* by homering in seven straight games. On May 28, 1956, before 32,221 at Forbes, Long tried for a bigs-high No. 8 against Carl Erskine. In the fourth inning he whacked a curveball into the seats. "Forbes Field about tumbled down," said Prince. "Long circled the bases and got such a standing ovation that he had to come out of the dugout for a curtain call."

"Common now," colleague Jim Woods observed in 1968.

"Not then," Prince said. "That's what Forbes and the Pirates meant to the Tri-State area." The '58ers soared to second. Danny Murtaugh became Manager of the Year. The Bucs upped capacity to 35,000 through three new field- and dugout-level rows. Many scarfed pizza, fish sandwiches, and a soft drink called lemon blend. The University of Pittsburgh bought Forbes for $2 million. "We were to be allowed," said Brown, "to use it until a first-of-its-kind proposed all-purpose sports complex was built." Before long they would inhabit a different kind of home.

On June 5, 1959, Dick Stuart cleared left-center's 457 mark—another first. Reliever Elroy Face won his 17th straight game. Rocky Nelson once lined to the sprawling garden. "Forbes' size gave fielders more room to run," said writer Les Biederman, "than anywhere else." Willie Mays couldn't glove the ball, but grabbed it with his bare hand. The inning ended. Mays headed for the bench, sat down, and brooked the silent treatment. "Skipper," Willie, distraught, asked Leo Durocher, "didn't you see that catch? I just made a great catch."

"You did?" said Leo, feigning ignorance. "Go out and do it again." He could, at Forbes. Any schoolboy could recite Mays' craft—too, a year where the Soviets shot down a U.S. U-2 plane, torpedoed a Paris summit conference, and enjoyed their leader's truculence. "Only my face is ruddy," Nikita Khrushchev scoffed. "Eisenhower's is white. And [Harold] Macmillan's has no color." In 1960, only the Bucs seemed impervious to the volcanic Mr. K.

YANKEE STADIUM

"I have earned the hatred of entrenched greed," Franklin Roosevelt said, "and I welcome their hatred." The gentry—to FDR, "economic royalists"—returned his bile. Roosevelt was "that man"—a "traitor to his class." Which did they most resent? How they evolved into fall guy, welded FDR to the lower-middle class, or were impotent to respond? In 1936, Roosevelt carried 46 states to Alf Landon's two. "As Maine goes," jeered aide James Farley, "so goes Vermont." Like Joe DiMaggio, so went the Yanks.

DiMag '35 batted .398 for PCL San Francisco. A year later he made the bigs: .323, 29 homers, and 125 RBI. He soon mastered the Stadium's vast center field. "I get the credit," laughed Lefty Gomez. "Until I pitched, they never knew he could go back on a ball." Tony Lazzeri had two grand slams, a third homer, and triple, for a record 15 bases, v. the A's: 25–2. Gehrig seemed abiding: .354, 152 RBI, AL-high in homers (49) and four other categories.

In 1936, the Yankees beat the Giants in the first-since-'23 Subway Series. Distance stabilized: 402 feet, left side, left-center bullpen gate; 415, right side; 457 (formerly 460), deep left-center; 466, left side, center-field screen; 461 (once 490), center; 407 (formerly 429), deep right-center; 344, right side, right-center gate. Cement replaced wood bleachers. "Outfield benches yielded to chairs," said Joseph Durso. Seating curved from 82,000 (1927) via 67,113 ('28) to 62,000 ('29) to 71,699 ('37). What didn't change was the Stadium's one size fits all.

"It's greatest thing," Harold Rosenthal mused, "is that you could hit an inside-the-park homer, 290-foot round-tripper, and 470-foot out." The flagpole stood 10 feet in front of the 461 mark. Once DiMag raced behind it to catch a Hank Greenberg drive. On September 19, 1937, Hancus Pancus drove where not even No. 5 could reach: the center-field seats (a first). DiMag led in runs, homers, bases, and slugging. Could No. 5 bunt? "I don't know," said Joe McCarthy, "nor have I any intention of ever finding out."

The '37 Giants would have loved to. Instead, they lost another Series. Lazzeri hit .400 in his last Classic. "He goes," said Ed Barrow, "rookies arrive"—Tommy Henrich, Joe Gordon, and Charlie Keller '37–'38–'39. On May 30, 1938, an alarum rung: The Red Sox were coming—or was history in the making? The Stadium's largest-ever crowd, 83,533, saw Red Ruffing blank Lefty Grove, 10–0. In June, Joe Louis won a fight *v.* Max Schmeling. "He fought here 11 times," said announcer Don Dunphy. "None bigger than this." The Aryan tumbled at 2:04 of the first round.

On August 20, Gehrig hit his 23rd—and final—slam. A week later DiMag got three triples in the first of a two-for-the-price-of-one: Monte Pearson no-hit Cleveland in Match Two. "They'd played and won six straight double-headers," said Durso. "Break up the Yankees!" huffed 15 of the 16 big-league teams. Their tone hinted more hope than resolution.

Between 1939 and 1951, 11 major-league teams won at least a single pennant. The other five made the first division. Eight times a pennant was decided in the final game. Recalling and applauding the last decade to have a .400 hitter or a pitcher complete more than 35 games in a season or the Indians win a World Series; the first to boast a black major leaguer (Jack Roosevelt Robinson), one-armed outfielder (Pete Gray), and pennant race that ended in a tie ('46–'48); the first/last to have a batter hit safely in 56 straight games and a "Subway [actually, Streetcar]

Series" west of the Mississippi—you marvel at the stories in which base-ball has been rich. Yankee Stadium did not write them all, though a glance shows that no park wrote more.

Jake Ruppert died in January 1939. Barrow replaced him as president. The Yankees won their opener, 2–0, behind Ruffing. History, or hyper-bole? For the first/last time Gehrig and Ted Williams bookended a game. Lou's '38 had been his worst year since 1926. "The next was even worse," Henrich said. "One day he tried to field a ball between first base and the mound, and was all thumbs, no coordination." Gehrig's streak had reached 2,130. McCarthy sensed that Lou must be gravely ill (of amy-otrophic lateral sclerosis, a hardening and collapsing of the spinal cord). Next day the captain acted. "I can't go on like this. Don't put my name in the lineup." Joe loved him like a son. "C'mon, Lou, you'll get over it." Lou insisted. Henrich later said, "Inside, McCarthy was relieved. He knew that Lou was hurting the team, but he'd never take him out on his own."

The Yankees began a series in Detroit. Gehrig took the lineup to home plate, benching himself, a statement read, "for the good of the team." The P.A. announcer said: "Ladies and gentlemen, this is the first time Lou Gehrig's name will not appear in the Yankee lineup in 2,130 consec-utive games." The growd gasped. Gehrig retreated to the dugout. Tears streaked his face. "C'mon, Lou, cut it out," Gomez said, embracing him. "It took 'em 15 years to get you out of the lineup. When I pitch, a lot of times it only takes the other team 15 minutes."

Gehrig retired. In June the Yankees conspired against the record book in a twinbill against the A's: 13 dingers and 53 total bases. On July 4, 1939, Lou gave a speech at the Stadium: "Some may think I've been given a bad break." The peroration: "I consider myself the luckiest man on the face of the earth." The *New York Daily News* blared: "Yanks Split, Lou Weeps, While 61,808 Fans Cheer." Ruth hugged his ex-mate. The Yankees retired No. 4 and later put a monument beside Huggins.

By coincidence, the Stadium staged that year's All-Star Game. Six stripes started; DiMag homered; AL, 3–1, before 62,892. Dartmouth third baseman Red Rolfe led the league in runs, hits, and doubles. No. 5 wed 30 homers, 126 RBI, and .381—last AL righty to clear .380. Was there ever a more-his-own-man? Once Joe was asked, "God, you're beat-ing the Browns, 22–1. Why are you running around like a lunatic?" He replied, "Because maybe there's somebody here who never saw me play."

The Yankees (again) swept the (1939) Classic. Said DiMaggio: "When we walked on the field, we felt they [here, Cincinnati] didn't have a chance." Few did. The '36–'39ers won 16 Series games and lost only three.

In 1939, he became the Voice of the Yankees. His 1964 firing made thousands of Yankees-haters. Walt Whitman wrote, "I hear America singing, the varied caroles I hear." For seven decades Melvin Allen Israel—a.k.a. The Voice—helped baseball sing. Some prayed that an attack of laryngitis would silence him forever. Most thought Mel Allen more compelling than being at the park. All felt that a florist must have decorated his voice.

To Allen, home runs became "Ballantine Blasts" or "White Owl Wallops" that were "going, going, gone." Surpassing moments demanded "How About That!" Red Barber was white wine, crêpes suzette, and bluegrass music. Allen was popcorn, beer, and the U.S. Marine Band. He called 24 All-Star Games and 20 World Series. The Cooperstown '78 inductee sold more cigars, cases of beer, safety razors, and fans on baseball than any broadcaster who ever lived.

DiMag hit .352 in Allen's second year. One day Gehrig visited the Stadium. "Lou was almost bedridden," said Mel. "He came into the dugout and was mobbed. After a while, he shuffled over and sat beside me. Finally, he turned and patted me on the knee. He said, 'I never got a chance to listen to your games before because I was playing. But I want you to know they're the only thing that keeps me going.'" Lou left. Allen began to cry.

At that moment he seemed a Yankee to his pinstriped underwear. Too, the man whose temper menaced jobs, arms, legs, jaws, and possibly life itself. "A bromide said rooting for the Yankees was like rooting for U.S. Steel," wrote Robert Creamer, adding, "Nonsense. There's nothing as wonderful as a team that wins." Their shining city linked the Stadium, with its insatiable bulk, sloping contour, and skim of smoke atop the field, and their 1931–'46 manager.

McCarthy never played in the majors, but played them like a bass. "Twenty-four years as manager, never out of the first division," said Rosenthal. "A .614 percentage"—all-time best. Few doubted that Joe was hard. "What's the score?" he shouted at a player from the dugout. He grew on you, like the scotch he drank talking ball. When Ben Chapman slurred a black patron, McCarthy traded him. Once he entered the club-house, saw a card table, and threw it out. He kept his distance—and strain.

"Sometimes I think I'm in the greatest business in the world. Then you lose four straight and want to change places with a farmer." In 1946, limp and worn, he retired to his farm near Buffalo.

Gehrig died June 2, 1941. That spring Phil Rizzuto entered Barrow's office to sign his first contract. "I didn't know Barrow. I did know that the man being shaved by a guy whom he kept calling Goulash was Barrow." Rizzuto sat silently till Goulash was done shaving. Barrow then snapped, "Young man, what is your trouble?" Phil said he wanted more money. Barrow shouted, "I give you this and no more. If OK, sign. If not, get the hell out of here." Phil signed. Born in Brooklyn, he helped win nine Series as New York's 1941–'42 and '46–'56 shortstop.

The Scooter retired in 1956. A year later he joined the Home of Champions microphone—but few thought of him as a play-by-play man. He stirred as *playactor:* unleashing "Holy Cow!"; hailing birthdays, praising pasta or reading notes, twitting traffic by leaving in the seventh inning. "You forget Phil was so small as a player," said DiMag. "Maybe it's because his reputation was large."

Not at first. Ruffing, Bill Dickey, and DiMag gave him the cold shoulder in spring training '41. Upset, the Scooter asked Gomez if he had done something wrong. "Relax, they're not snubbing you," Lefty said. "They just haven't seen you yet."

DiMaggio became Marilyn Monroe's husband, future Mr. Coffee, and 1939–'41–'47 MVP. He hit 361 homers with 369 Ks, was voted Greatest Living Ballplayer, and seemed always ready with the hospitable play and beguiling gesture. His 1941 is as large as Joe Wood's 1912, Willie Mays playing stickball, or Gehrig's farewell ode. Les Brown and his Orchestra swelled that year's hit parade: "He'll live in baseball's Hall of Fame [Class '55]. He got there blow by blow ['41's 56-game hitting streak]. Our kids will tell their kids his name—Joltin' Joe DiMaggio."

On May 15, he singled off Chicago's Ed Smith. Soon the radio, your

corner bar, a daily paper flacked his streak. In late June, DiMag hit in an
AL-record 42nd straight game. The streak ended at Cleveland. Joe
promptly hit in *another* 16 straight. Gomez beat the Browns, 9–0,
despite walking a most-ever-for-a-shutout 11. The Yanks clinched in
game 136, baseball's earliest terminative. Also abortive: the Series, a five-
game Bombers rout.

More than 69,000 jammed the tiers for 1942 Army–Navy relief.
"Walter Johnson pitched [batting] practice," said Ken Smith. "Ruth
smacked his fifth pitch in the seats." The Series again matched St. Louis
v. New York. They split Games One-Two, then bustled to the Bronx.
"All year a green curtain was put in center," noted Rosenthal. "Each
inning the Yanks used it like a yo-yo"—lowered like a window shade
when hitting. "This gave a good background. When the other team hit,
it was raised to show white shirts." The '42 Series dispatched it to sell
seats. The Cardinals dispatched the stripes.

In 1943, the Allies demanded the Axis' "unconditional surrender."
FDR wrote Churchill, "It has been fun to be in the same decade with
you." Ask, and he received: war bonds, "victory gardens," and more
than 13 million pints of blood. The Yanks roster dimmed: DiMag and
Henrich joined the service. McCarthy didn't miss a beat. The team
trained in Atlantic City, swept an AL record 14 twinbills, and won the
flag by 13½ games. The Series turned on Johnny Lindell kicking the ball
from St. Louis' Whitey Kurowski's glove. "Anything to win," said Marse
Joe. Anything did. Inverting '42, they won in five.

On D-Day 1944, Roosevelt read a prayer over nationwide radio.
America, as community, and FDR, as minister, fused then and evermore.
Abiding: Army's Mr. Inside and Mr. Outside, Doc Blanchard and Glenn
Davis '44, smashing Notre Dame, 59–0, in the Bronx. Ruppert had died
in 1939. His estate gave Larry MacPhail, Dan Topping, and Del Webb
the Yanks, Stadium, Triple-A parks in Newark and Jersey City, and
leases on other minor-league fields for $2.8 million. "They were hot to
sell," said Durso. "Ruppert paid more for the Stadium's 10-acre lot."

FDR died. Hitler shot himself. Japan and Germany surrendered. Douglas MacArthur signed Japan's surrender decree. "We have had our
chance," he said. "If we do not devise some greater and more equitable
system, Armageddon will be at our door." Dynasty stood at the Stadium's.

In 1946, the soldiers of baseball's green and tended fields fed a land starved for peacetime heroes. Baseball broke its all-time attendance record by 80 percent. The players were recognizable again—and 18 million turned out to see them. Six of eight AL teams cracked their single-season high. The Bombers lured 2,265,512. "Five straight years they drew two million," said Dick Young. "Nobody'd ever done it before."

On May 28, night ball debuted at Yankee Stadium before 48,895. "Ruppert thought lights undignified," said Smith. "MacPhail saw cash. So he spent $800,000 for lights." Ex–boy wonder Bucky Harris was hired to manage. His '47ers linked Spud Chandler (2.46 ERA), Allie Reynolds (19–8), Joe Page (league-high 17 saves), and 19 straight wins (tying the '06 White Sox). "We'll beat 'em up ahead," growled the Dodgers captain of New York. Pee Wee Reese's optimism soon sensibly adjured from the fore.

The Series began calmly: Yanks, 5–3, before 73,365. Said Brooklyn's Pete Reiser: "You wouldn't know the nuttiness ahead." Reynolds won, 10–3. The Dodgers then took two of three at Ebbets Field. Excess lit Game Six: record crowd (74,065), longest nine-inning Series game (3 hours, 19 minutes), the Catch (Al Gionfriddo's), and a reprise (by Joltin' Joe). The Brooks led, 8–5, in the sixth: two out, two on, DiMag at bat. He hit toward the 415 sign. "I've seen many greater plays," said Reese, "but I did not expect that one to be made." (Said Barber: "Swung on. Belted. It's a long one! Deep into left-center! Back goes Grionfriddo! [in his last bigs game] Back, back, back, back, back, back! He makes a one-handed catch against the bullpen! Oh, Doctor!") Joe kicked dirt near second. "In all the years I played with him," said Rizzuto, "that's the only time he showed any emotion."

A day later Page beat Hal Gregg, 5–2. "We'll have to wait a while," said Reese after Game Seven—2,939 days till Brooklyn won its first World Series. Larry MacPhail declined to wait. After the final out he quit as Yankees president.

On April 27, 1947, the Yankees held "Babe Ruth Day." Ruth, dying of cancer, could barely speak. Allen introduced him, the crowd unloosed, and Mel yelled, "Babe, do you want to try to say something?" The Babe croaked, "I *must*." He neared the mike, spoke hoarsely, then returned to the dugout. Ruth's trademark camel hair coat and matching cap draped a shell. "He used to sit on the bench with that big cigar," said Rizzuto. "When he wasn't scheduled to hit in an inning he'd just talk to the people in the stands and eat hot dogs in the field."

On June 13, 1948, 49,461 parishioners retired No. 3. "He was so sick," said Rizzuto, "it took two men to lift him." Leaving the dugout, Ruth leaned on a bat like a cane. Greeting him, His Eminence Cardinal Spellman said, "Any time you want me to come to your house for Holy Communion, I'd be glad to do it." Babe smiled. "Thank you, but I'd rather come to *your* place." Next month *The Babe Ruth Story* opened. Ruth appeared in public at the premiere. He died, at 53, on August 16.

"Even in death," said Allen, "Babe drew a sellout crowd." St. Patrick's overflowed. Thousands jammed Fifth Avenue. The Yankees finished third—to New York, an ignominy. They would not troll that depth till the last year of the 1950s.

Some managers burn out like supernovas. Others wear mediocrity like a scarlett *M*. Great skippers never lose their big-league fire. A pyromaniac was Leo Durocher. "It's not how you play the game, stupid. It's if you *win* the game." Charlie Dressen bubbled egomania. "Just keep 'em close," he told his Dodgers. "I'll think of something."

On October 12, 1948, the stripes named Casey Stengel manager. Only once in nine prior big-league years had he placed above fifth. "What are we getting—burlesque?" one writer fumed. No, said another, Joe Reichler, "the most memorable man to ever wear a uniform." Lindsey Nelson smiled. "His 54 years in baseball spanned Tris Speaker and Tom Seaver." The best were 1949–'60's 10 flags and seven World Series. Thanks for the memories: The Yankees fired Casey in October 1960. "I'll never make the mistake," he said, "of being 70 again."

In 1992, Richard Nixon said, "If I had it to do over again, I'd name Casey Secretary of State. The essence of diplomacy is to confuse the opposition. The opposition never knew what Casey was talking about. Stengel *always* knew." Once ex-Tiger George Kell interviewed him for a CBS-TV pregame show. "I had 15 minutes," he said, "and was going to ask him about his entire batting order." A friend later asked about the interview. "Oh, it went fine," said Kell. "But in our 15 minutes, Casey didn't get past the lead-off hitter."

"**A**sk him a question and he'd talk 'bout being a minor leaguer in Montgomery and every club he played with in the minors and fans who gave him dinner before he would answer the question which by now *you'd* forgotten. Oh, yeah, 'How did you like playing under John McGraw?' " Mel Allen paused for breath. Casey was once a minor-league player, manager, and president. Said Allen: "He didn't like it and finally figured out what to do." As manager, Stengel quit as a player; as president, he fired himself as manager; then, Case resigned as president.

Rambling—i.e., Stengelese—hid a street-smart hardness. Stengel and several writers once closed a bar at 3 A.M. At the hotel elevator he greeted the operator and slipped him a baseball. "I got to give this to a kid tomorrow. If any of the guys come in, get him to sign the ball and give it to me at breakfast, will ya'?" The operator agreed. Next morning the man gave Casey the baseball. It bore the names of five Yanks who arrived after 3 A.M. Stengel took the ball, thanked the operator, and fined each $50 for breaking curfew.

Casey hit .400 to beat Ruth in the '22 Series. In 1949, he baptized a monument to Babe in center field. DiMag missed the first 65 games. No regular topped .287. New York had only 115 homers. (The '36–'39ers averaged .174.) With two games left, it trailed by one, closing *v.* Boston at the Stadium. Curt Gowdy was Allen's then-aide. "As long as I live, I'll never forget Yankee fans going crazy. Sox fans roaring after they came down from New England. I've never heard such volume."

On October 1—by chance, Joe DiMaggio Day—Allie Reynolds faced Mel Parnell. A reporter asked Mrs. Rosalie DiMaggio: "Which team are you rooting for?" Brother Tom answered, "Mother is impartial"— unlike 69,551 who filled the tiers. Boston forged a 4–0 third-inning lead. Victory was tangible. Then, momentum swung. New York rallied one run at a time. In the eighth, Lindell's homer broke a 4-all tie.

"Two straight seasons and one game settles it," said Boston's Birdie Tebbetts. "When [general manager Joe] Cronin sends my contract for next year, I'm gonna' specify that I not show until October. It's better to play fresh than tired." Rizzuto's first-inning drive eluded Ted Williams for a triple. Henrich plated a run. In the eighth, New York led, 1–0, when

McCarthy pinch-hit for Ellis Kinder. Four Yankees runs offset three in the Boston ninth. Tebbetts, a tired tying run, fouled out for the last out.

"When they were over, I just wanted to go and hide somewhere," Williams mourned a quarter-century later. The Series again hid from Brooklyn. New York took the third chapter of their serialized novel. Allie Reynolds and Preacher Roe traded 1–0 blankings. The Yanks then swept at Ebbets Field: 4–3, 6–4, and 10–6. Of America's 39 million home radios, an all-time record of 26 million households heard the Cold Warriors duel.

Each American has something central to their life: George Bush, *noblesse oblige;* Adlai Stevenson, language-made-literate; Huey Long, the bruised tailbone of poverty. Stengel's central fact was that he would try anything. If it didn't work, he tried something else. Mostly, he tried platooning.

"I'll never forget '50," said Rizzuto. "Joe Collins was slumping, Henrich was hurt, so Casey put DiMag at first." On August 11, the earth turned flat: Stengel benched DiMag for not hitting. A week later Joe became the first to hit three homers in a game at Washington. Rizzuto fused 200 hits, 125 runs, and wizardry into MVP. "If I were a retired gentleman," said Stengel, "I would follow the Yankees around just to see Rizzuto work those miracles each day."

The Yanks clinched September 29. DiMag was trying to reach .300. One day he lined to shortstop. "Joe heads to center, mumbling to himself as he always did," said infielder Jerry Coleman, "and Yogi Berra fires the ball to second to start the next inning." The throw cleared Coleman's head and hit the Clipper in his injured heel. Joe fell down, got up, and one-hopped a throw to Coleman. "He thinks it's my fault," said Jerry, "so he's yelling, '*Catch* the ball.'" The throw hit Jerry in the knee. *He* fell, writhing. Berra stood sweetly at the plate. Said Coleman: "We either won or lost, there was no second place."

Philly lost a 1–0 Series opener. Reynolds then edged Robin Roberts, 2–1. Back in the Bronx, Gene Woodling, Rizzuto, and Coleman singled in the ninth: 3–2. Rookie Whitey Ford had won nine straight games. He now took Match Four, 5–2. Coleman shook his head. "Winning the Series was fun. Getting there wasn't."

"**I** remember Vander Meer pitching his *second* straight no-hitter," said Mel Allen. "It came at Ebbets Field. Then Reynolds threw two in 1951. It's the second [Boston, September 28, at the Stadium] that rings. Two out in the ninth. Williams pops a foul. Berra drops it. Unbelievably, Ted fouls to the *same* spot. Yogi gets it. No-hitter. Great moments I identify with a particular park."

How to put it? Berra was not a linguist. "If you can't imitate him," Yogi chimed, "don't copy him." Added MacPhail: "He looks like the bottom man on an unemployed acrobatic team." Once the 5–7, 190-pound catcher fielded a bunt and tagged the hitter and runner coming home. "I just tagged everybody," he said of the double play, "including the ump." Dickey helped: "Bill is learning me his experiences." In turn, Yogi helped his team. He hit 358 homers, became 1951–'54–'55 MVP, and owned the Series: most played (14), won (10), games (75), and hits (71). Only Mantle tops his 39 RBI.

Berra '51 had .294 and 27 homers. In July, DiMag muffed a ball. Stengel benched him. Joe's last year became Mantle's first. The Fall Classic portended Mick's luck. Playing right, he tried to avoid Joe on a fly, stepped on a drain cover, tore knee ligaments, and collapsed. Said Coleman: "I thought Mantle'd been shot, the way he went down." DiMag retired. Mickey hit .311 in 1952. John Mize homered in the last of the bigs' then-15 parks. The Series followed. Leading, three games to two, the Bums needed a win. Instead, they got the bum's rush: 3–2 and 4–2. The Yanks had become a verisimilitude *out there,* in the prairies and provinces. "A fan loves the game played well," said Red Barber. No team better fused its blend of outburst and ballet.

McCarthy '36–'39 led New York to four straight titles. In '53, Stengel platooned the Yankees to a fifth in a row. Three players shared first base. Ford was the only pitcher to toss more than 200 innings. Did fit and start pique the Bombers? "When you're walking to the bank with that World Series check every November," Hank Bauer groused, "you don't want to leave. There were no Yankees saying play me or trade me."

New York had an 18-game win streak—and took Series Games One-Two. The Dodgers tied. The Yanks then won, 11–7: Woodling, Mantle, Billy Martin, and Gil McDougald homered. Next day New York led, 3–1, in the ninth; at which point Carl Furillo got a tying homer; whereupon Martin lined his Series-winning 12th hit. "They nice you to death in the season," wrote Dick Young. "They club you in the Series [nine homers to the Dodgers' eight]."

The Yanks had won five straight Series v. Brooklyn. They were also more than ever synonymic with their home.

In 1944, FDR briefly deterred a fourth term in office. "All that is within me," he said, "cries out to go back to my home on the Hudson River." Any player cried out to play on the Harlem River in the Bronx. "If you'd never been to Yankee Stadium, you'd never been in the big leagues," said Bill Fischer, first visiting in 1957. Carl Erskine grew up in Anderson, Indiana, pop. 55,000. In 1949, he visited the Stadium clubhouse recently vacated by the Yanks. Two lockers had uniforms: Ruth's and Gehrig's. "They were sending a message." That day he gaped from the mound at the jammed and rowdy grandstand. "Seventy thousand people. That's more than live in Anderson!" John F. Kennedy called the presidency "the vital center of action." Baseball's was The Home of Champions.

To reach it, a visitor traveled six miles north of 42nd Street. From midtown, cars arrived by FDR Drive. Expressways linked the Stadium to New Haven, Greenwich, and Valley Stream. "Parking facilities are adequate," wrote *Sports Illustrated,* "but fantastic traffic snarls are likely to develop near the stadium both before and after big-crowd games." By contrast, you could take the Sixth Avenue "D" or IRT Woodlawn Road-Jerome Avenue subway. The No. 4 train, on elevated tracks beyond the bleachers, hinted what lay inside. Emerging, you sprinted for the bleachers or took a ramp to, say, the second tier. Best seats: boxes near dugouts, or third deck near the infield. The overhang screened flies at the rear of decks one and two. "Aisle seats are undesirable as latecomers and early leavers block view," said *SI.* "Warning. Some seats numbered in sequence [4–5–6] are actually in different rows." Ample: vendors (martial), concessions (bland), and rest rooms (clean).

On April 19, 1946, the Yankees swapped the third- for first-base dugout. A 20-foot hitter's screen went up in 1953. Later, a Ballantine scoreboard topped right-center field. Below and to its sides a horizontal band of ads crowned the seats: "New Mobil Gas," "Coca-Cola," "Yoo-

Hoo," "Philip Morris," "Seagram's Seven Crown." Backdrops vied: from left-center, triple tiers; a box seat, apartments and water tower beyond the bleachers. Numbers wrote a feel-good shrine: 301 (left pole), 344 (left-center bullpen), 457 (deep left-center), 461 (center), 407 (right-center), 353 (right-center bullpen), 344 (right), 296 (right pole). A late-'40s auxiliary scoreboard covered the 367 and 415 signs, respectively, in right- and left-center field. Size, flags, and shadows *built* the stage. (Left field was baseball's hardest. Said Yogi: "It gets late early out there.") Power *filled* it. Before 1962, 21 ALers hit 46 or more homers in a year; 17 wore the stripes.

Douglass Wallop's book etched *The Year The Yankees Lost the Pennant.* In 1954, the Ol' Perfessor taught a class. The Yanks won a Stengel-high 103 games—eight behind the Indians. Casey kept his humor. The last day Yogi and Mantle played third base and shortstop, respectively. "Welcome," he said, "to my power lineup"—and empty seats. New York drew a worst-since-1945 1,475,161. The '55ers began another streak. Ford threw two one-hitters. Mantle led in walks, on-base, slugging, and homers. The Yanks again met Brooklyn, splitting Games One–Six. Match Seven graced the Stadium. It turned on inning six.

The Dodgers led, 2–0, as Billy Martin walked and Gil McDougald bunted safely. Berra slapped down the left-field line. From left-center Sandy Amoros bolted toward the pole. It helped that he was left-handed. "If he'd been right-handed the ball probably would have dropped to tie the score," said Pee Wee Reese. "Berra would have been on second with no outs." Instead—the Sphinx eroded; the Thames reversed course— "Sandy stuck out his glove hand," said McDougald, "and found that Easter egg," then threw to Reese, who fired to Gil Hodges. Double play Winning pitcher Johnny Podres' take was simple. "Yogi hit that ball, and he made the greatest catch in the world."

In the ninth, Elston Howard grounded out, aptly, short to first: Captain to Quiet Man. The Dodgers won, 2–0—their first world title. Erskine returned to the clubhouse he first visited in '49. "There was a quietness when we first walked in, almost a spiritual feeling. Then someone opened champagne, and the lid blew off." The Perfessor had flunked his first October exam. "We'll be back," he said, and was.

11

HAPPY TALK

On April 12, 1945, Vice-President Harry Truman ended a dry day presiding over the Senate by inviting Speaker of the House Sam Rayburn for a drink. A switchboard operator found Truman at the Capitol and ordered him to the White House. Arriving, he heard numbing news. Eleanor Roosevelt confirmed it: "Harry, the president is dead [of a cerebral hemorrhage]." Was there anything he could do for her? Truman asked. "Is there anything we can do for *you*?" she replied. "For you are the one in trouble now."

Irony followed shock: The first thought was of contrast, not succession. FDR had seemed Olympian. The Rotarian Truman wore double-breasted suits with two-toned wingtop shoes. "To err is Truman," joked sophists. "I'm just mild about Harry." It was said that FDR saved capitalism for the capitalists. Who foretold Churchill's saw? "No one more saved western civilization than Harry Truman."

Truman threw first pitches out left and right-handed—to Yogi Berra, "amphibious." Wife Bess knew how to keep score—the last First Lady till Barbara Bush—and inhaled *The Sporting News*. In 1945, one-legged

Bert Shepard pitched v. Boston. Mickey Vernon '46 hit .353 to win the AL batting title. A year later Democrats and Republicans resumed their annual game after World War II—and announcer Bob Wolff boarded teams whose god-awfulness rivaled the '62 Mets'.

"As I remember," Bob once told colleague Chuck Thompson, "we rarely gave the score of the Senators' games."

Thompson laughed. "That wasn't an oversight, Bob. That was well-planned, believe me."

Never in Wolff's 1947–'60 administration did the Nats snub the second division. The box score: 883–1,270, 482½ games from first. Default glossed creativity. Wolff interviewed scouts and players, season- and other ticket holders, notables and concessionaires. Their sobriquet became "fans in the stands."

One '57 afternoon the Senators won the first game of a doubleheader at Griffith Stadium. Wolff then visited a student of the sport. "I said, 'Sir, I'd like you to be on my show.' He said, 'Sure.' I went on, 'But let's play a game. Don't say your name until we're finished talking.' This was total ad-lib."

Bob began by asking about the Nats' first-game success. Wolff's partner often frequented their yard. "Well, of course," he replied, "being a Washington fan, I thought it was great."

Wolff & Co. spoke for seven minutes. Mused Bob: "He carried it off with a professional's flair, talking about baseball, the Senators." Finally, the climactic parry.

"Are you originally from Washington, sir?" Wolff said.

"No, I'm a Californian."

"What sort of work do you do, sir?"

"I work for the government," said the fan, 44.

"Oh, for the government?" Wolff said.

"Yes, yes, I work for the government?"

"What sort of work do you do, sir?" Wolff probed.

"Well, I'm the vice-president," said Richard Milhous Nixon.

The first president many Boomers recall began the Peace Corps, coined the Alliance for Progress, and drew what a writer called "a picture of "total urbanity." John F. Kennedy, however, was not the president of their late-50's youth. A 1955 Gallup Poll revealed that 60 percent of *Democrats* wanted Dwight Eisenhower as their presidential nominee. His decency lit even the swarmy cave of politics.

Each April players rushed to retrieve Ike's first pitch. In 1958, the Nats' Jim Piersall watched the toss before giving Eisenhower another ball. "Mr. President," he said, "would you sign *this* ball while those idiots scramble for *that* one?" Ike told a friend "that [as a boy] I wanted to be a real major league baseball player, a genuine professional like Honus Wagner. My friend said that he'd like to be president of the United States." Neither got his wish.

Eisenhower was inaugurated January 20, 1953. Eighty days later Mickey Mantle hit the 60-foot-high left-field National Bohemian scoreboard: The first "tape measure" homer traveled 565 feet. "That there Red [Patterson, Yankees publicist]," said Casey Stengel, "got out a measure and found the ball in a back yard"—Perry L. Cool's at 434 Oakdale Street: 391 feet to the bleacher wall, another 69 to the outer wall, and 105 feet across Fifth Street. The homer helped beat the Nats, 7–3. National Bohemian painted an "X" where the ball hit the board.

"I seemed to always call record events—most against the Senators," said Wolff. "Mr. Griffith didn't want any reminder, so he used paint to have the 'X' removed." Chuck Stobbs yielded Mick's behemoth. Later he also threw baseball's longest wild pitch. "His errant throw sailed all the way up to a concession stand, spattering mustard over a fan."

Few Nats failed more grandly than a 1956–'59 utility infielder. Some said Herbie Plews' license plate should read, "E-4–5–6." Others charged he had no license to play. One day hits and errors ricocheted off Herbie's chest, legs, arms, and head. Finally, manager Charlie Dressen left the dugout and called him to the mound. "If I took Herb out of the game it might cost him his confidence. If I keep him in might cost me the game." Plews stayed. Mused Wolff: "If there'd been a crowd, it would have roared."

The next batter hit to Plews, who bobbled, snatched the ball, and nipped the runner. The Senators still trailed in the ninth. Herbie lashed a two-out triple. Nats win. Players sob. "Herbie Plews!" canted Wolff. "Tell me there weren't giants in the land."

Broadcasting at Griffith could fracture or condense the language. "I never had to mention who was winning or losing," said Wolff, "just give the score." Once the Nats trailed by seven runs. The last of the ninth began. On a whim Bob midwived fantasy. "I haven't resorted to this before," he told viewers, "but one of our cameras has a magic ray. If we focus on a fielder, the ray will so mesmerize him that the ball will go through, by, or over him. I should tell you that this demands a concentrated thought process. If even one of you isn't thinking 'hit' at all times, our rays can malfunction."

The camera fixed the enemy shortstop. The batter singled through his legs. The next shot fixed the third baseman. Land o' goshen: The ball escaped his glove. One by one Nats hitters reached safely—"each," Wolff marveled, "after the camera predicted where the baseball'd go." The Griffith crowd was evincing a Tinker Bell kind of faith. The Senators scored six runs: bases loaded, two out, and Mickey Vernon at bat. The two-time batting titleist lined to right. Leaping, the first baseman made a game-saving catch.

For Wolff, shock, then rationale. "I saluted viewers for our almost-miracle," he said, "and mused that maybe one member of our audience had to leave the TV at the critical moment," breaking the spell. In the 1958 movie *Damn Yankees*, the character Joe Hardy sells his soul for a Neverland Nats flag. "Much of it was filmed at Griffith. Art imitates life."

Fifties *baseball* life mixed the quaint and mom and pop. At Griffith, there was nostalgia and love—akin to a gentle protectiveness—for the Old Fox, decent, much-wounded, and as straight and resolute as they came. Clark worked from 9 A.M. to 1 P.M., played pinochle, then shooed friends away. "All day he'd have family, groundskeepers, wall signmakers around him," said Wolff. "At 4 o'clock he wanted privacy." Alone, he heard or watched radio/TV's *The Lone Ranger*. It evoked a simpler time.

"Clark had been brought up in the West," said Wolff. "It brought back memories." TV's Ranger—Clayton Moore—once sent him a birthday telegram. Clark often phoned Wolff in the morning. "It was raining, but Griffith said, 'We're going on, 'cause I want to see a game.' "

He died in 1955. Adopted son Calvin became president. The '56 NL won Griffith's last All-Star Game, 7–3. Nixon dedicated a statue to Clark outside the main entrance on the first-base side. Wolff's aria was more lyric: "The [late '50s] Singing Senators." Albie Pearson, Russ Kemmerer, Truman [Tex] Clevenger, Jim Lemon, and Roy Sievers tuned melody. Howie Devron played accordion. Wolff strummed a ukulele. "People liked us anyway."

"The Senators" graced NBC's *The Today Show* in 1959. Was the age more soft and settled? "Let's suppose that I went up to the Sievers of today and some other guys and said, 'Hey, fellas, you want to join me in a singing group?' " mused Wolff. "Can you imagine? You couldn't print their answer in a book."

For once, history is not debatable. Even a '50sphobe yearned for baseball's remembered and/or reinvented past. The days dwindled down. "We weren't drawing," said Calvin Griffith, "so we made our park more intimate." Center stayed 421. Right was measured, and found to be 320 (not 1926's 328). Others shrank: left, 408 ('51) via 388 to 350 ('57); left-center, 391 through 366 ('54) to 360 ('56). The makeover couldn't hurt: In 1954, the Senators drew 460 *v.* Philadelphia. Carlos Paula led '55 Nats outfielders with *six* home runs. The visitors' pen left foul for fair turf behind a left-field corner fence. New seats beyond the wall filled the gap. Could the Senators reach (or fill) them?

In 1953, Mickey Vernon won a second batting title. The Walking Man—Eddie Yost—five times led the league in walks. Roy Sievers became a wrecking crew: respectively, 106 ribbies (1955), 29 homers ('56), then AL-high 42 taters and 114 RBI ('57), and 38 and 108 ('58). Harmon—Killer—Killebrew's 42 dingers led the '58 AL. Few players were better or more wrongly named.

The gentle Harmon's 573 homers rank fifth all-time. In 1954, at 18, he joined the Nats from Payette, Idaho. "He was a phenom," said Calvin Griffith. Power and reticence forged a Garbo of the game. One day Wolff hatched a scheme. "I said, 'I'll bring you to a father and son game and put you into the game as Mr. Smith. After you hit the ball 10 miles, we'll say, 'That's Harmon Killebrew.' "

Wolff used the P.A. mike to announce a pinch hitter—Harmon in street garb: People didn't recognize him out of uniform. His first three swings preserved anyonymity. Killer swung and missed, then tapped meekly to the pitcher. "Folks," the catcher tipped the bat," Bob explained. "Let's do that again." Washington's Monument proceeded to barely tip the ball.

Wolff's throat rivaled the Sahara. "Harmon Killebrew is the batter but he has a great heart," he ad-libbed. "He doesn't want to lose the only softball you've got. But just to show his power, he'll fungo it and we'll bring it back." Killebrew popped up. "Let's get back to the game," Bob said. "It's getting late." Returning to Washington, the Senators voice consoled his own best subject. "Don't worry. You'll be a Hall of Fame player in hardball. Just skip the softer stuff."

Camilo Pascual did, fusing six shutouts, 185 Ks, and a 2.64 ERA in 1959. Ibid., Pedro Ramos '60, fanning 160. "They were from Cuba, where we had beat other teams in scouting," said Griffith. Still, habits die hard. One Opening Day, subbing for Ike, Nixon watched Baltimore turn a triple play. The '57–'59ers finished eighth in an eight-team league.

Napoleon said, "Ability is fine, but give me commanders who have luck." Luck avenged the Griffiths' final years. *Life* magazine planned a '59 feature on Killebrew. Said Wolff: "They took adhesive tape and put it into every spot at Griffith where he'd homered—then, had a plane take a shot of where and how far the homers went." For days *LIFE* waited for Harmon to go long. Eisenhower came to a game. On cue, No. 3 went yard. The same day—May 26—Harvey Haddix hurled a 12-inning perfect game to KO Killer's cover.

The 1960 fifth-placers drew 743,404 customers—most since '49. "They were bad," noted Wolff, "but they were getting better." On October 27, Griffith said he could not elude the sheriff by keeping the Nats in D.C. Without a hail to the chief, the renamed Twins moved to Minneapolis-St. Paul.

A photo of John F. Kennedy and aide David Powers at the Senators' 1961 home opener shows them reading *The Sporting News*. "It was Griffith's last year, and with the Twins gone the first for our *expansion* Senators," said new president Elwood (Pete) Quesada. Earlier Kennedy had graced WGN-TV's "Lead-off Man Show"—the first U.S. president interviewed on radio at a baseball game.

Vince Lloyd: "Mr. President, have you had an opportunity to do any warming up for this, sir?"

Kennedy: "Well, we've just been getting ready here today."

Lloyd: "Throwing nothing but strikes? Very good."

JFK: "I feel it important that we get, ah, not be a nation of just spectators, even though that's what we are today, but also a nation of participants—particularly to make it possible for young men and women to participate actively in physical effort." Leaving, Lloyd asked about Mrs. Kennedy. JFK smiled and said, "Well, it's Monday. She's home doing the wash."

Before the game JFK threw the first ball past players 15 to 20 feet away to Chicago's Jim Rivera. JFK signed his ball, which Rivera dubbed illegible. He wrote his name again. Said Jungle Jim: "You're all right." Washington wasn't, losing, 4–3. The Nats upped center field (to 426), removed left-field seats (capacity, 27,550), and drafted aging hand-me-downs. Gene Woodling hit .313. Dick Donovan had a league-best 2.40 ERA. It didn't help. Dale Long and Marty Keough batted .249. In May, Boston's Bill Monbouquette Kd an AL night-record 17 Nats. "Five years before and they'd have been great," said Morris Siegel. Instead, they tied for ninth in the new ten-team league.

In spring training catcher Pete Daley lined a ball to left field. Nearing second, he tripped, bounced, and rolled over it, and wound up on his back on the edge of the infield. Laughing, Daley leapt to his feet. "Wowee!" he yelled "What a life!" On September 21, 1961, in a dint of irony, Griffith Stadium's ended: Minnesota 6, Senators 3. They drew a league-low 597,287.

"We can't wait to go to [new 50,000-seat] D.C. Stadium in '62," said Quesada. "It'll be great to be in a new place, with big crowds, that will be cheering as we get better." Last in the American League, the Nats' park was now first in war, peace, and memory. Griffith was demolished in 1965. Howard University fills the lot where Walter Johnson taught Pitching 101.

POLO GROUNDS

Opposing pitchers rarely checked the 1947 Giants. "The window-breakers" homered in 18 straight games, crashed a bigs record 221, placed fourth, but wooed a franchise-high 1,600,793. John Mize smacked 51 dingers. Willard Marshall, Walker Cooper, and Bobby Thomson added 36, 35, and 29, respectively. On July 16, 1948, the Giants fired manager Mel Ott, who was replaced by Leo Durocher, leaving Brooklyn, which tapped Burt Shotton. "Too slow. No hit and run," Leo burbled. "This ain't my kind of team."

"Some Giants fans could never forgive Durocher for having led the Dodgers," Dick Young noted. On April 29, Leo and a Giants fan swapped punches after Brooklyn's 15–2 burlesque. Durocher was charged with assault. Commissioner Happy Chandler suspended him. Leo later was acquitted. Promoted from Jersey City: the 'Jints first black players, Monte Irvin and Henry Thompson. Baseball as looking glass: Thompson '49 faced Don Newcombe—the first black hitter-pitcher duel. In 1950, Boston second baseman Eddie Stanky and shortstop Alvin Dark brought scrap, defense, and "my [Leo's] kind of team." Only at the Polo Grounds: In one game Thompson smacked two inside-the-parkers—*v.* Brooklyn. The Giants climbed from fifth to third: A glow colored Horace Stoneham.

Horace liked to drink, and did not discriminate. He drank alone, with strangers, and with pals. Said Lindsey Nelson: "It is rumored that many deals involving Giant players started and were completed as scotch ran fast and free."

Stoneham's office at the Polo Grounds lay north end east of the Grant Memorial. Stoneham watched the game through a window. The scoreboard loomed above. One day Horace awoke to what he judged a downpour. Water screened the window. A game was scheduled that afternoon. He picked up the phone, called an aide, and said, "Game postponed because of rain."

The aide sputtered, "But . . . but, sir."

"No buts," Horace said, hanging up. He then went back to sleep. That day New York basked in sunlight. Ultimately, we learned why the game was called. "The day was so gorgeous that the crew had decided to wash the scoreboard. Anxious to do a good job, they sent gallons of water up against that structure. Some of it cascaded down to cover the window of his office."

In 1950, Matty Schwab tended Ebbets Field. Stoneham stole the groundskeeper by building an apartment for his family under Section 3 of the left-field stands. Schwab tamed the Polo Grounds. In '51, pitchers Sal Maglie and Larry Jansen tamed the league—46–17. Irvin led the league with 121 RBI. At bat, Don Mueller was termed "Mandrake the Magician." Willie Howard Mays, hitting .477 at Triple-A Minneapolis, reported May 25. God gives us life. Mays gave the Giants' meaning.

Willie went hitless his first 12 at-bats. Durocher heard him crying. "What's wrong, son?" he said, nearing the future Rookie of the Year's locker. Mays, 20, said, "Mister Leo, it's too far for me, I can't play here." Durocher smiled. "Willie, I brought you here to do one thing—play center field. And as long as that uniform says 'New York Giants' and I'm the manager, you will be in center field every day." Next day his first hit, off Boston's Warren Spahn, cleared the Polo Grounds.

In July, Brooklyn swept a three-game series. "We knocked them out," Charlie Dressen crowed about a 9½-game lead. "They'll never bother us again." The Giants then caught a break: Henry Thompson was hurt. Replacing him at third, Bobby Thomson hit .357. On August 7, the Bums led by 13½. What happened next made both parks akin to touring Lourdes—building and praying and nearing, in the wonderwork of pennant races, the last pitch of the year.

Dark shook his head. "Keep in mind what the rivalry was like," said the captain. The foils played each other 22 games a year. Radio and TV coursed each game through the city. Fans rode the subway to the enemy's bailiwick. Police blotters reported how zealots of one team clubbed another's to death. "There were times," added Dark, "we stopped playing to watch a fight in the stands." The Dodgers shortstop took the subway to each park. "In Brooklyn, all the little shopkeepers knew you and wished you luck," said Pee Wee Reese. "Outside the Polo Grounds they'd boo. I'm glad I had the opportunity to play there at the time."

Brooklyn was glad that time was running out. "We never thought they could catch us," Reese mused. New York took 16 straight games. On Friday, September 28, the Dodgers lost and Giants won: each 94–58. Both won Saturday. Next day the Giants beat Boston, 3–2. Jackie Robinson's skidding, diving catch at Philadelphia kept the 12th inning tied. In the 14th his homer forced a best-of-three playoff.

It began at Ebbets Field: Jim Hearn beat Ralph Branca, 3–1; Thomson and Irvin homered. A day later swapped place and result: Dodgers, 10–0, behind Clem Labine. Mays hit into three double plays. A schoolboy knows the next day's plot. Brooklyn led, 4–1, in the ninth. Whitey Lockman's double scored Dark, 4–2: one out, two on. At 3:58 P.M., October 3, off Branca, before 34,320, Thomson lashed a drive into the left-field lower deck.

The Giants won, 5–4—their first flag since 1937. The Scotsman's homer rode waves atop Excalibur, like Pearl Harbor or November 22, 1963. "You have to understand the feeling between those teams zeroed in on each other. All I could think of was that we beat the Dodgers," Thomson said. "I never for a moment thought of anything else but that." Confetti flew. Eddie Stanky wrestled Leo, coaching third, to the ground. In the WMCA Radio booth, amid tension thick enough to chew, announcer Russ Hodges five times cried, "The Giants win the pennant!" and bayed, "They're going crazy! They are going crazy!" and clamored above the hysteria: the Miracle of Coogan's Bluff, the Shot Heard 'Round the World.

Reprise: In 1951, tape recorders were large and rare. Few events were saved. Even fewer laymen had machines. One lived in Brooklyn. In front, he decided to tape the ninth inning. Said Ernie Harwell: "Figured he'd enjoy Russ cry." Thomson homers. The Brooklynite cries. "But he didn't take it personally—in fact, sent the tape to Russ. Russ sent him $10. You can live in Tibet and still have heard Russ' call." By contrast, Harwell on CBS-TV grasped anonymity.

"It's gone!" he said on contact. Ernie then started worrying: Andy Pakfo brushed the left-field wall.

"Uh, oh," Harwell thought, "suppose he catches it." Andy didn't. Arriving home, Ernie was still in shock.

Mrs. Harwell said, "I've seen that dazed look on your face twice in my life. When our first child was born and the day we got married." We accept her word—since '51 TV neither replayed nor kept his call. "To this day only Mrs. Harwell and I know that I did maybe the most famous game of all time."

Ask any Giants fan: Thomson's blast was surrealistic, otherworldly. Thy will be done. In the Series Thy will was rain. The Giants won two of the first three games. "We had 'em [Yankees] on the run," said Dark. On Sunday, October 7, Game Four was washed out. The break gave Allie Reynolds an extra day's rest. He beat Maglie, 6–2. A day later the ALers romped, 13–1. Game Six began the ninth, 4–1, Yanks. Could the Shot be heard again? The Giants tallied twice. Sal Yvars then lined for the final out. Mays hit .182. It would take a while before New York threatened to kill him with love.

Willie entered the Army in May 1952. "We're in first place when he leaves," Durocher said later. "We lose 8 of the next 10." A month earlier Hoyt Wilhelm hurled/won his first game, 9–5, and went long *v.* Boston's Dick Hoover. He never homered in his next 1,069 games. A year later (April 29) Milwaukee's Joe Adcock became the first Polo Grounder to reach the bleachers. Another precedent fixed Coogan's radio booth: tiny, hard to leave or enter, and suspended from the upper deck.

"I hate it," said Hodges. "The worst part is there's no toilet." Russ spelled relief by urinating in paper cups and placing them in a corner. "No one could see them," said Harwell. "It especially helped during long doubleheaders."

One day a visitor accidentally kicked a cup. The liquid leaked into the lower boxes. Soon usher Barney O'Toole stopped by the booth. "Hey," he said, "we're getting complaints from people in the box seats. They said to quit spilling beer."

"Barney," Harwell said, "if it's beer, it's used beer. We'll be careful, but don't tell those folks what really 'hit em."

On April 13, 1954, Mays hit a two-run homer. "He was back from the Army," Durocher said. "It jolted our entire club." The MVP packed a top-this mix: 41 homers, 119 runs, .345, and .667 slugging. Mueller hit

.342. Johnny Antonelli went 21–7. One inning Ray Katt turned Wilhelm's knuckler into a record four passed balls. More baleful was attendance: Milwaukee, 2,131,388; the champion Giants, 1,155,067. "Folks were watching television," said Hodges. "The Polo Grounds was fraying. People around it were getting mugged."

On September 29, Say-Hey mugged the Indians in the Series opener: 2–2, eighth inning none out, two on. Coogan's Bluff matched baseball's deepest center field (483) and shortest right (257). Don Liddle relieved Maglie. Vic Wertz hit high and deep to center. No. 24 raced toward its remotest depth. "I don't want to compare 'em," Mays mused of his play, over the shoulder, to save the game. "I just want to catch 'em." Earlier Leo called Dusty Rhodes "useless." Mays and Thompson walked to start the tenth. Rhodes then pinch-drove a fly 200 feet shorter than Wertz's. Pick another park—Fenway's 302 feet to right, or Bronx's center, 461. Wertz's out goes deep. Rhodes' pop dies. Instead, Dusty struck the right-field seats: 5–2. Next day Rhodes again homered: New York, 3–1. In Cleveland, New York completed the sweep, 6–2 and 7–4. Rhodes had four hits and seven RBI. Leo now thought him useful.

In 1945, Winston Churchill was ousted as British prime minister. "This is an opportunity in disguise," said a friend. Churchill: "If this is an opportunity, it is *well*-disguised"—e.g., Durocher's '55 firing. Attendance fell to 842,112. Mays became the seventh to hit 50 homers. The football Giants traded Coogan's for Yankee Stadium. In March 1956, the Manhattan borough president flayed a windmill: "a 110,000-seat stadium over the New York Central Railroad tracks," said Dick Young, "on a 470,000-foot site stretching from 60th to 72nd Streets on Manhattan's West Side." Cost: $75 million. The idea collapsed. The '57ers placed 26 games behind Brooklyn. Only 653,923 saw the home team fumble. On August 19, Stoneham torched the last 75 years. "We're sorry to disappoint the kids of New York," he said, "but we didn't see many of their parents out there at the Polo Grounds in recent years." Bannered the page 1 New York *World-Telegram:* "It's Official: Giants to Frisco."

Lasts bloomed: Giants' homer (Gail Harris, September 21); victory (9–5, same day, Ruben Gomez v. Brooklyn); game (September 29, Pittsburgh, 9–1); gawkers (Mrs. John McGraw, 1895 manager Jack Doyle, and 11,606 paid mourners); signs ("Stay Team Stay"). The next day's

Herald Tribune blared: "Giants Bow to Bucs in Polo Grounds Finale. Fans Mob Field After Defeat." Added the *Daily News:* "Ghosts of Sports Greats Haunt PG." A two-foot-square piece of sod was yanked from center field for transplant to San Francisco. For baseball, Moving Day had truly come.

EBBETS FIELD

"**N**o other baseball team," Leonard Koppett has written, "generated a richer collection of memories, more closely held by so many people," than the 1947–'57 Brooklyn Dodgers. Gil Hodges. Jackie Robinson. Pee Wee Reese. Billy Cox, his glove turning doubles into slumps. Catcher Roy Campanella, making Flatbush a ping-pong table. Outfielders Duke Snider and Carl Furillo warred with rivals and themselves. In Brooklyn, surnames seemed *de trop*. Oisk, Big Newk, No. 13, and Preach replaced Carl Erskine, Don Newcombe, Ralph Branca, and Preacher Roe. All were family. Said Koppett: "We loved them like our own."

Ebbets Field cross-hatched victory and despair. The 1947–'49 Bums took pennants. In 1950–'51, they lost on the final day. Brooklyn '52–'53 won by 17½ games. In 1955–'56, two more titles and an asterisk: "Four pennants in five years," said Reese—NL best since New York '21–'22–'23–'24. By 1955, the Dodgers had lost seven Classics in a row. Johnny Podres won Game Seven, 2–0, proving that even in the 52nd Oktoberfest a borough could run into luck. "Ladies and gentleman," Vin Scully told his NBC audience upon the last out, "the Brooklyn Dodgers are the champions of the world." Later, a writer asked how he remained calm. "If I'd said another word at that very instant, I'd have broken down crying."

Of their West Coast apostasy, revealed October 8, 1957, but expected like a prison sentence, it must be said: Most saw no cause to leave. Had Brooklyn not drawn a million people a bigs-high *13* straight years? Did Flatbush not revere its team to a *nonpareil* degree? Had owner Walter O'Malley not yapped, "My roots are in Brooklyn"? How could he trade that for a corporate-zombie future of upward mobility and wealth?

Quite easily, as it occurred.

Gladys Goodding—"One d more than God"—played organ at Ebbets Field. Once she serenaded umpires with "Three Blind Mice." On July 23, 1955, Reese turned 37. More than 30,000 of the faithful lit matches as field lights dimmed. "The fans, you joked with 'em on a first-name basis," he said two years before his death in 1999. "You were friends."

Jake the Butcher wore a straw hat and sat behind first base. A rival pitcher failed to pick off the runner. "Late again!" Jake boomed. The Dodger Sym-Phony was a loosely musical group. "Their specialty," wrote Steve Jacobson, "was piping a visiting strikeout victim back to his bench with a tune titled 'The Army Duff.' The last beat was timed for the moment the player's butt touched [the bench]." An enemy might tarry to avoid sitting down. "The Sym-Phony still had that last beat ready on the bass drum."

"It was hard to explain to the uninitiated," said Ernie Harwell. "You had to be there." One day his wife sat down in front of a fan in a T-shirt. Reese led off his first. The man stood up and shouted, "C'mon, you bum. Get a hit."

Upset, Mrs. Harwell tapped the man on his shoulder. "I beg your pardon," she said. "Do you know Mr. Reese?" The man replied, "No, lady, why?"

She said, "If you did, I'm sure you'd find him a very nice gentleman." The man replied, "OK, lady, I'll lay off him if he's a friend of yours."

Billy Cox batted next. The man again leapt to his feet. "Do somethin', Cox. You're a bum." Once more Mrs. Harwell tapped the man. Quickly, he turned around: "Lady, is this bum a friends of yours too?"

Mrs. Harwell nodded. "What about the other bums on this team?" he asked. "I know almost all the players," she said. The man left the seat and walked away. "Lady, I'm moving. I came here to root my bums to a win, and I ain't gonna' let you sit here behind me and spoil my whole afternoon."

'Forty-seven spoiled you on the game. On April 9, Happy Chandler suspended Leo Durocher for the year for "conduct detrimental to baseball." His replacement: scout Burt Shotton. Robinson debuted with no hits and 11 chances. *Time* soon observed: "He seems to hit a baseball on the dead run. Once in motion, he wobbles along, elbows flying, hips swaying, shoulders rocking. . . . He is not only jack-rabbit fast, but about one thought and two steps ahead of every base-runner in the business."

In May, the Cards talked of boycotting Robinson. Some Brooklyn mates demanded his return to Montreal. How would Reese respond? "I was brought up in a poor neighborhood," said the Kentucky Colonel. "I didn't come into contact with black people. I was taught that Negroes were to ride in the back of streetcars, speak when spoken to. [Now] I knew I had to play. I couldn't sign a petition." Baseball blurs envy, ego, and flimflam brass. Reese and Robinson felt a different tie. Jackie braved crayon-scrawled graffiti. An Atlanta letter writer threatened to shoot No. 42 if he played. Reese sidled over in warm-up. "Don't stand so damn close to me. Move away, will you?" Each laughed. The league thought Jackie no laughing matter.

In 1947, Robinson hit .297, scored 125 runs, and became The *Sporting News* Rookie of the Year. Jackie stole home—his first of 19 times. Cincy's Ewell Blackwell had a second straight no-hitter—until Stanky's ninth-frame single. The Dodgers won a third pennant. A record 73,365 saw the Series opener at Yankee Stadium: New York, 5–3. Allie Reynolds beat Vic Lombardi for a 2–0 lead. Critics beat up on the Series—to *Daily News* columnist Jimmy Powers, "The worst we ever saw. It took exactly four minutes short of five dismal hours to play the first two alleged games."

Game Three took longer: a 185-minute/eight-pitcher/9–8 Bums parody. Next day New York seemed ready to take a 3–1 match lead. The Yankees held a 2–1 Game Four edge. Even sweller: Starter Floyd (Bill) Bevens had yielded 10 walks and no hits in his first 8⅔ innings.

Ritual asks you to ignore an at-work-no-hitter. "What I said or didn't say in the booth wasn't going to influence what happened on the field," conceded Mel Allen, airing the Series on Mutual Radio. "But players on the bench think you jinx it by talking. They respect the dugout tradition. It's part of the romance of the game—one of the great things that separates it from other sports, like the seventh-inning stretch or ballparks of different size and field." He halted. "Or the biggest difference of all in a World Series or any other baseball—the lack of a clock."

Game Four required two hours and 20 minutes and tissues to dry moist palms. "Ebbets Field would never forget it," said Red Barber, Allen's colleague, of Brooklyn's 3–2 victory: Baseball was forever caught by time. Mel called the first 4 and ½ innings: "I respected the tradition." Barber, a self-styled "reporter, not a dealer in superstition," did not. Succeeding Mel, he stated Brooklyn's total: one run, two errors, no hits. Allen gasped. The Redhead shrugged. Wild high and inside, Bevens lost the plate.

Carl Furillo walked with one out in the ninth. Spider Jorgensen fouled out to George McQuinn—to Dick Young, "as white as a sheet as he made the catch." Pinch runner Al Gionfriddo stole second. Pete Reiser worked Bevens to a 3–1 count. Yankees manager Bucky Harris walked the potential winning run. Cookie Lavagetto then pinch-hit for Stanky, Eddie Miksis ran for Reiser, and Cookie banged a fastball off the right-field wall. The Dodgers won on their only hit: Series 2-all. Later, Bevens asked a reporter, "Would it have been in [Yankee Stadium's right-field seats]?" Yes: Ebbets' 297-foot fence was 12 inches longer and more than 34 feet higher.

Game Five was less theatric. Bill Shea beat Rex Barney, 2–1, New York. The sixth match tipped, 8–6, to Brooklyn. "Great year, sad end," Shotton mourned on losing Game Seven. He was playing Brooklyn's song.

Al Michaels grew up on Brooklyn's Ocean Avenue. Games began at 1:30 P.M. A quarter and a GO—General Organization—card bought a left-field seat. On weekends the Michaels family sat above the broadcast booth. "My first remembrance in life is looking down into the booth at the back of Barber's head and saying, 'What a job—imagine, seeing every game for free.' "

"Curiouser and curiouser," wrote Lewis Carroll in *Alice In the Looking Glass*. Durocher returned from his one-year suspension. On April 21, 1948, Leo futilely used 24 Bums: Giants, 9–5. Roy Campanella arrived from the Nicetown part of Philadelphia. He hit 242 homers, looked like a sumo wrestler, and became 1951–'53–'55 MVP. In July, Leo vaulted to the Polo Grounds. Ten days later he returned to Ebbets for a game: Schizophrenia washed the borough from Coney Island to Brooklyn Heights.

Next year Robinson testified before the House Un-American Activi-
ties Commission. That night he scored twice and stole home. The '49
MVP led the league in average (.342) and steals (37). Brooklyn won a
last-day pennant. The past assessed the present: The Bums split Series
Games One-Two at the Stadium. "Poi-fect! We got 'em!" a fan told Cox
outside the park. Tell the stripes, winning the next three in Flatbush.
"Habit is a great deadener," wrote Samuel Beckett. The Dodgers' was
killing Brooklyn.

"Our great constant," said Larry King, "was hope." Hodges hit four
homers on August 31, 1950, and finished with 32—and 113 RBI. Snider
broke through with NL-best hits (199) and total bases (343). The
Dodgers had a thing about teasing to the final day. The '50ers lost the
flag, 4–1, to Philadelphia, at home. The Quakers scored first. Reese hit
the right-field wall. The ball kept bouncing on the ledge as Pee Wee
scored: 1–1. Dick Sisler homered off Newk, 4–1, in the tenth. Three
weeks later Branch Rickey sold his share of the club for $1,050,000.
"Comest thou here?" he asked reporters, "to see the reed driven in the
wind?" Walter O'Malley became a "man," said Rickey, in an extempore
pronouncement, "of youth, courage, and desire"—and new Dodgers
president. Ten years later wreckers invaded Ebbets Field and mangled it
to dust.

By the '50s Ebbets forged a Gestalt of memory: left field, 343 ('48),
348 ('53), 343 ('55), and 348 feet ('57); left-center, 351; deep left-center
at the bend of the wall, 393 ('48) and 395 ('54); center, 384 ('48) and
393 ('55); the right side of the right-field grandstand, 376; right-center's
deepest fork, 403 ('48), 405 ('50), and 403 ('55); right-center scoreboard, 344 and 318 (left and right side); right, 297. The Schaefer beer
sign atop the board aped the official scorer. "The 'H' lit up for hit," said
Young, "the 'E' for error."

A visitor could fill any of 32,211 seats. Relievers sat on benches
down the left- and right-field lines. Con: parking. You used the Manhattan Bridge to Flatbush Avenue, or Brooklyn-Battery Tunnel to the
Prospect Avenue Expressway. Most came by subway (BMT to Prospect
Street, or IRT to Franklin Avenue). Pro: seating, especially the first rows
of the center-field grandstand. (Said a writer: "You'll feel like you're

playing shortstop.") Milieu: "No baseball park is more fun," said *Sports Illustrated,* "for the Dodger fan shows his affections or his outspoken displeasure with a continuing riot of noise." Script: Who *wrote* this stuff?

Gil Hodges '51 liked his text: 40 homers and 113 RBI. Robinson and Campy hit .338 and .325, respectively. Roe went 22–3. Newcombe won 20 games. Even the P.A. announcer filled a certain niche. Tex Rickard always wore a sweater, talked from a seat near the Dodgers dugout, and "just said things on the P.A. that made even visitors laugh," said '50s Braves pitcher Ernie Johnson. Of a child, Rickard announced, "A little boy has been found lost." Once Roe left the game. Tex explained: "He don't feel good." Rickard was not a baseball savant. Often Dodgers set him up. Relieving, Johnson was introduced: "Now coming in to pitch for Milwaukee, number 32, Cy Johnson."

Years later Tex said: "Too bad Game Three of the playoff weren't at Ebbets. I'd 'a introduced Thomson against Branca." Where were you for the Shot Heard 'Round the World?

Thomson temporarily delayed the fourth Yankees-Dodgers Series. A year later they picked up where '49 ended. On Bedford Avenue the Faithful queued for standing-room bleacher seats. From a box, Rookie of the Year Joe Black's curveball darted. On October 1, 1952, the righty won the opener, 4–2. A day later New York beat Carl Erskine, 7–1. The Grand Event moved across the river. The teams split Games Three-Four. Oisk then won a taut 11-inning 6–5 assembly. Up, three games to two, Brooklyn was going home. Crowed Charlie Dressen: "We got 'em where we want' em." What Hodges (0-for-21) wanted was a hit. Masses said a prayer. Furillo and Robinson batted .174. The upshot: pinstripes, 3–2 and 4–2. Snider had four homers, 8 RBI, and like Reese batted .345. "Gotta be some day," said Duke, "when we beat the Yankees."

From Ebbets Field, that day seemed more distant than the spires of Manhattan.

The Brooklyn Dodgers Radio Network included 117 outlets from Cleveland to Miami Beach. Begun in late 1950, it whipped Pirates and

Senators ratings, respectively, in western Pennsylvania and Washington. It died after the Dodgers took a hike.

"Most people never knew our games weren't live," broadcaster Nat Allbright said. "Vivid? They couldn't *tell* it was a re-creation. Our mail went to, 'Nat Allbright, c/o Brooklyn Dodgers, Ebbets Field,' and the club sent it to me [at his D.C. studio]. So in the public mind, I was up on Flatbush Avenue." Each park drew a listener in. "The Reds wouldn't draw well, so we'd keep down the noise. Milwaukee—lots of burghers, so we'd have polka music. In the Polo Grounds, we had the crowd noise amplified, fights in the stands, people going wild against the Dodgers—in other words, just like it *was*."

In 1953, it was a team that led the league in runs, home runs, and runs batted in, slugging, fielding, and batting averages, steals, and strikeouts. Furillo and Rookie of the Year Jim Gilliam led in batting (.344) and triples (17), respectively. The Bums had 208 home runs. Five regulars hit more than .300. Campy banged a catching record 142 RBI. Snider bound 42, 126, and .336. Erskine's 20–6 record helped Brooklyn finish 105–49. "You figured," said Reese, "how could we lose?" (Quickly. The Yanks won Games One-Two).

Ronald Reagan tells how a young boy yearned for a gift Christmas morning. Instead, he found a room of horse manure. "Yes," cried the child, "but there must a pony in here someplace!" On October 2, 1953, in chilly sunshine, before 35,270, the largest Classic crowd to elbow its way into Ebbets, Oisk Kd 14 in Game Three to top Howard Ehmke's record (13, 1929). "Here's to mortality," a writer said—and Brooklyn's pony. Next day the Dodgers evened the Series. We had been this way before: New York won in six.

"Think about it," Dick Young wrote. "A stray hit or out and Brooklyn wins each pennant from '49 through '53—and maybe a Series." Instead, Campanella hit .207 in '54; Stan Musial smacked five taters in a May twinbill; and Milwaukee's Joe Adcock used a borrowed bat to homer four times July 31. No good deed goes unpunished. A day later Clem Labine threw a fastball off Adcock's batting helmet. You could hear the crash in the upper deck. Reese hit a career-high .309. Hodges' 42 homers tied Snider's team record. The Duke peaked: .341, 130 RBI, and NL-best 120 runs. Newcombe, returning from the service, went 9–8.

Allbright mused: "I'd say of Don, 'There stands big Newk on the mound, perspiration dripping down his face, firing missiles at the batter.' To the guy at home, I wanted him to think I was sitting in the radio booth, bathing in the sunshine, talking about our team, the Dodgers"— in '54, *sans* title.

In 1955, quiescence dressed America. Said Ike: "Everybody ought to be happy every day. Play hard, have fun doing it, and despise wickedness." The Dodgers were two for three.

Brooklyn won its first 10 games. Newk took No. 20 September 5— and hit a league-record seventh homer. The Series script got lost: New York won twice. Johnny Podres had Flatbush's worst starting ERA. At Ebbets, he turned 23 and took Game Three, 8–3. Brooklyn then tied the Classic, 8–5, Labine relieving. Roger Craig beat Bob Grimm, 5–3; Sandy Amoros and Snider (twice) homered. Whitey Ford took Game Six, 5–1. The Faithful braced. Casey Stengel had won five straight Series. The Bums were 0-for-5 *v.* New York. "Don't worry, Pee Wee," Podres said, mocking history, "I'll shut 'em out tomorrow."

Think of heretical role reversals. Kate Smith becomes Cher. Dan Quayle becomes Mick Jagger. On October 4, 1955, the Brooks became the stripes. Willard Mullin's Brooklyn Bum rejoiced in the next day's *News:* "We dood it! We beat 'em! We beat them Yankees! We spot 'em th' foist two games . . . an' we beat 'em! That Podres! Woil Cham-peens! Me!" The *Times*' John Drebinger tendered a statelier digest. "Far into the night rang shouts of revelry in Flatbush," read his story. "Brooklyn at long last has won the World Series and now let someone suggest moving the Dodgers elsewhere." In two years, someone did.

Podres went deer hunting in the Adirondacks near his Witherbee, New York home. Belatedly, the impact reared. "Hey, Podres," he called into the woods, "you beat the Yankees in the World Series! Where do you go from here?" Would you believe Jersey City?

In late 1955 O'Malley committed the Dodgers to seven '56 home games at single-deck/24,000-seat/Works Progress Administration/named-for-FDR Roosevelt Stadium. "This is part of our effort to spread Dodger baseball," he said. "Jersey City has a long history of minor-league support." O'Malley hoped it would make Brooklyn build a new 50,000-seat domed stadium. Eddie Fisher sang its Opening Day National Anthem. Jersey City Mayor John Grogan threw out the third-game first ball. "Ebbets wasn't big enough," wrote Harold Rosenthal. "No parking, rusting. O'Malley thought they couldn't stay long." Roosevelt abutted Newark Bay and the Hackensack River. Distances were 330 (foul lines), 377 (power alleys), and 411 feet (center field). Wall heights linked 11 (corners), 4 (left- to center field), and 7 feet (right-center to right). A clock topped the right-center scoreboard. The left-center board listed lineups and other games.

The seven matches lured 148,371. "Jersey City had been a Giants farm," said Jack Redding, "and most now booed the Dodgers." Willie Mays became first to clear the plot. Ebbets attendance rose to 1,213,5623. Newk went an MVP 27–7. Snider hit 43 taters. In June 1956, Sal Maglie arrived from Cleveland to no-hit his former Giants. "The only guy," he'd say, "to pitch for all three pre-Mets New York teams." Aging, Brooklyn won the flag on the final day. October reversed '55: Maglie beat Ford, 6–3; Don Bessent, relieving, won, 13–8. "Man, yelled Snider, "we're up, 2–0." The Yankees then won three straight at the Stadium.

Leave it to Robinson: On October 9, he forged Ebbets' last Classic hit, RBI, and victory. For nine innings Labine and Bob Turley dueled scorelessly. Jackie then singled to score Gilliam, 1–0. The 1940–'42 and '46–'57 shortstop of the Brooklyn franchise laughed softly. "Some timing," Reese said. "It was Jackie's last big-league hit." Game Seven is best forgot: 9–0. The Yankees bombed four homers. Newcombe left in the fourth with a 21.21 ERA.

That December 13, Brooklyn traded Robinson to the enemy. He retired rather than join the 'Jints. In January 1957, O'Malley bought a 44-passenger twin-engine airplane for $775,000. "We'll be the first club to have a plane," he said. Added Young: "You could see he was gone." New York City Parks Commissioner Robert Moses touted a 50,000-seat stadium with plastic dome on a 78-acre tract in Flushing Meadows. Said

O'Malley: "We'll not be the Brooklyn Dodgers if we're in Queens." Papers sermonized. Pols tut-tutted. He's bluffing. Ebbets is good enough.

In May, the NL OKd upheaval. "Two conditions," said Lee Allen. "The Giants and Dodgers both had to move to California and ask before October 1 [to ease scheduling]." In August, the Giants announced a move to San Francisco. The Los Angeles City Council approved a 300-acre site in Chavez Ravine: O'Malley must build a park. Designers had already begun. Hodges hit his 13th slam—Brooklyn's last. On September 22, Snider hit Ebbets' last homer. "I loved it," he said of the short right field and 344–foot power alley. Duke was a brilliant fielder, hit 40 homers five straight years, and retired with a Dodgers-high 389 dingers and 1,271 RBI.

On September 3, the Dodgers left New Jersey. Three weeks later they closed Ebbets: 6,702 saw Danny McDevitt blank the Bucs, 2–0. Hodges had the last ribbie. Gladys Goodding played "Auld Lang Syne." Clown Emmett Kelly parodied Mullin's "Bum." Happy Felton and his Knothole Gang met before the game in Brooklyn's corner bullpen.

In 1956, O'Malley sold their park. By and by he sold out Brooklyn. "There's no doubt in my mind," Reese said, "that looking back, O'Malley always intended to leave."

He had not thought so at the time. "Never," he confessed. "I bet a couple players that we'd stay in Brooklyn. They said to me, 'We're moving.' I said, 'Man, what are you talking about? We're drawing over a million people ever' year.' [Since 1945, the Dodgers had outdrawn each NL team.] Those people in Brooklyn would have done anything to keep them—build a stadium anywhere, even on Coney Island."

In "Facing West from California's Shore," Walt Whitman asks, "Where is what I started for so long ago?" He continues, "And why is it yet unfound?"

Ask a Brooklynite to detest a year. He may pick a daybook of Sputnik, the Asian Flu epidemic, and *Leave It to Beaver*. In 1957, a non–New York team won the World Series for the first time since '48. Worse, the Dodgers' and Giants' vacuum spurred a sport long akin to wrestling—except that wrestling had a niche. "Pro football had always been a sorry cousin. Newspapers and TV here had always been baseball, baseball," said Harold Rosenthal. "Now only the Yankees were left. The media needed something to write about." The NFL raised its hand.

Irony: Baseball midwived pro football's surge from hardscrabble sprig to parish sport. *Tragedy:* In 1958, Campanella, 36, was paralyzed in a car accident. Hodges died of a heart attack two days before his 48th birthday in 1972. That October, Robinson died, at 53, of diabetes. Don Drysdale, 56, brooked a fatal heart attack. Gilliam died at 50. *Afterword:* On February 23, 1960, a demolition crew in Dodgers blue and white began wrecking Ebbets Field. Oisk and Branca led 200 pallbearers. Lucy Monroe had sung before many games: Her National Anthem now mimed a dirge. Charles Ebbets would have smiled: Gold-plated bricks sold for $1; flowerpots with infield soil, 25 cents; the cornerstone, $500.

Eight light towers were moved to Downing Stadium on Randall's Island. Right-center's clock tops a board at Asheville, North Carolina's, McCormick Field. In 1963, the Ebbets Field Apartments housing development filled the plat where Jackie darted and Pee Wee parried and Newk played country hardball. I.S. 320 Intermediate School lies across the road. The nearby Jackie Robinson School (née Crown Heights) houses the Brooklyn Dodgers Hall of Fame.

Ask storekeepers, or passersby. "There'll never be another like Ebbets Field," said Pee Wee, gently. "No sir, no way." Richard Nixon once said of Lyndon Johnson, "He died of a broken heart." It is hard not to think that of Brooklyn USA.

CLEVELAND MUNICIPAL STADIUM

At Cleveland's lakeside pen, each night aired a motif: 101 Arabian Knights, Limo Night, Polish Night, Music Knight. Clowns and belly dancers flecked the stands. One night owner Bill Veeck had orchids delivered from Hawaii for each woman visitor. A fan wrote and said he was the average fan who deserved a night. Bill called Joe Early and gave him a car and boat. To then-announcer Jimmy Dudley, the late '40s rivaled Shangri-La. " 'Get the fans interested!' he'd say. Bill stuck S&H green stamps under certain seats. Then, at a signal, everybody closed their seat to see if they'd won. Ever hear eighty thousand seats crash at once?" Pause. "Manhattan never had such noise."

In 1948, Cleveland was loud enough. Gene Bearden and Bob Lemon went 40–24. Lou Boudreau batted .355 with 155 RBI. Veeck signed Satchel Paige, 42, from the Negro League. Satchmo had girls around the league. Once the Tribe was awaiting the train at Boston's South End Station. A woman paraded down the platform. "Hey, baby," Satch finally said, "when you walk you shake that thing just like a caboose." Turning, she spied her man. "Look here, big boy, you ain't seen nothing. You ought to see me when I got a passenger."

Batters saw a hurdy-gurdy. Satch began his motion above the head, passed his knee, and almost touched the ground. One day Paige yielded Tommy Henrich's game-winning blast. The Indians then caught a train. "Hey, Satch," Joe Gordon yelled, "what was that pitch you gave to Henrich?" Paige stopped eating, adjusted his teeth, and said, "I don't rightful know, but he ain't gonna' see it no more." Day, night, and doubleheader crowds of 71,181, 78,392, and 82,781, respectively, broke the AL record. "Man, ain't no park as fun [as Municipal Stadium] when you jam it to them rafters," Paige said. The '48ers drew 33,598 per date.

That fall the Tribe beat Boston (Red Sox, 8–3, playoff, and Braves, Series). In November, Boudreau was named MVP. Barnum Bill had once hinted trading him. Now he hymned: "Sometimes the best trades are the ones you never make."

Cleveland brooked a 12–17 start in 1949. Veeck scheduled a *second* Opening Day. It didn't work: he finished third. Bill buried the '48 pennant behind the center-field fence, then sold the Tribe, bought the Browns, and got them Paige. In 1950, Luke Easter bombed a 477-footer to right-center—Municipal's longest homer. Al Rosen, Lemon, and Early Wynn led the league in dingers (37), wins (23), and ERA (3.20), respectively.

Five times the '51–'56ers placed second. "The Yankees!" Dudley stormed. "Each year they'd pick up Country Slaughter or Johnny Mize. A reserve here, injury there, and we'd have won six straight pennants." In 1952, Bob Feller and St. Louis' Bob Cain one-hit each other: Tribe, 1–0. "Some loyalty," Veeck said of Feller. "It's the fourth time he's one-hit us." A year later Rosen led the AL in homers (43), runs (115), RBI

(145), slugging (.613), and was named unanimous MVP. Nothing beat the Yanks.

"The country is most barbarously large and final," William Brammer wrote in *The Gay Place*. Cleveland was in '54. The Tribe led the league in ERA (2.78) and dingers (156), had an Arthurian Big Four (Wynn, Lemon, Mike Garcia, and Feller won 78 games), and enjoyed Larry Doby's greatest year (32 taters and 126 RBI). Municipal even housed the All-Star Game. Rosen had two homers with five RBI. Doby, pinch-hitting, homered. "The day [11–9 final], crowd [68,751], and hitting [31 hits off 13 pitchers]," said Dudley. "It was like nothing could go wrong."

In August, Cleveland won an AL-record-tying 26 games. On September 12, a bigs-record 86,587 jammed the bowl: Lemon and Wynn spanked New York, 3–2 and 4–1. "All the frustration climaxed," said Lemon. "Stengel was heckled by fans on the train at platforms in Pennsylvania and Buffalo on the way back to New York." The Indians clinched September 18, 1954. Wynn routed Detroit, 11–1, for symmetrical victory 111. "The Indians beat the '27 Yankees' [AL best] 110," Russell Schneider noted. Their record lasted till the '98 pinstripes' 115.

Walter Alston was once asked what he learned in 22 years as Dodgers manager. "You make out your lineup card, sit back, and strange things happen." What was stranger than the '54 Classic? "We had this juggernaut, 'greatest team ever,' top pitching staff," said manager Al Lopez. The Giants had what? Willie Mays, tending the Polo Grounds—e.g. Vic Wertz's Game One poke.

Postscript: Giants sweep. Games Three and Four lured 71,555 and 78,102. Thousands stood behind Municipal's inner fence. "We own the world, then get ambushed," said Dudley. His voice softened. "In some ways the franchise was never quite the same."

In 1542, Charles V, Holy Roman Emperor, said, "I speak Spanish to God, Italian to women, French to men, and German to my horse." The Yankees manager spoke only Stengelese. A *Cleveland News* writer asked him about Lopez's plan to use only three starters in September 1955. Casey thought of Lemon, Garcia, and Wynn. "Well," he said, "I always knew it couldn't be done but somehow, it don't always work." English was Casey's foreign language. The Indians' became hope.

"We got lucky," Veeck cautioned of postwar baseball. "People were looking to spend money, and ours was the only sport." By the late '50s pro football held a sustaining niche. The N.F.L. Browns' Jim and Paul Brown became a rite worth cheering. "They started winning, we weren't, and the crowds weren't there," said Dudley. "Baseball's daily, and twenty thousand in Municipal seemed like ten people." In 1956, Lopez yielded to Kerby Farrell. Attendance fell to 722,256. One day 365 watched the Nats. Ghosts draped its spectral air, short foul lines, and seats rolling away, row upon row, in straight lines.

Insult compounded injury. Herb Score won 20 games in '56. Said Lopez: "Send him to Cooperstown, collect." On May 7, 1957, Gil McDougald's liner careened off Score's right eye, blurring vision. The paladin was never again a star. Replacing him: Rocky Colavito, a slow but fetching slugger. The Rock hit 42 homers as the '59ers matched strength so lyrically with the White Sox that more than three decades of scorched earth later an Ohioan would say, "There was our last hurrah. If only we had known."

Tito Francona thumped .363. Cal McLish won 19 games. The Tribe vied until losing a four-game August series to the Hose. Then, in April 1960, general manager Frank Lane traded a dinger titleist (Colavito) for Detroit's batting champion (Harvey Kuenn). "I'm getting steak for hamburger," he boasted. Few said well-done of dealing Cleveland's greatest pinup since Boudreau.

Increasingly, Municipal became a ghoulish place. In 1960, Ted Williams touched Wynn Hawkins for his 500th homer. Lane swapped his manager (Joe Gordon) for the Tigers' (Jimmy Dykes). Cleveland hosted the '63 All-Star Game. Only 44,160 found its now-74,208-seat yard. The '60–'67 Tribe never drew a million people, missed the pennant by fewer than 15 games, or hinted that faith might breathe past June.

Jerry Coleman shook his head. "The stupor was contagious," said the '63 rookie Yankees announcer. "It was a Sunday, and we were in Cleveland for a doubleheader." Before Game One he asked Birdie Tebbetts if lefties Sam McDowell and Jack Kralick were starting. The Tribe man-

ager nodded. The game starts. His pitcher blanks New York inning after
inning. Coleman is dazzled. "Sam was a strikeout pitcher with erratic
control—but his control this day was astounding."

Soon he discerned why. In the sixth, WPIX–New York telephoned the
booth. "Is that McDowell?" Coleman turns to Dudley and partner Bob
Neal. "Who's pitching?" Jerry says. Bob lip-synchs: "Jack Kralick."
Four decades later the face still dropped. "They were similar in build,"
Coleman said. "But even that doesn't explain why we had the wrong guy
pitching."

McDowell five times led the league in Ks. He liked a slider, heater,
curve, and change—and blame. Once Aurelio Rodriguez hammered Sudden Sam. "I'm in right," said Ken Harrelson. "Ray Foster's in left, and
it's way beyond him." Foster retreated, hit the inner fence, and toppled
over. The ball eluded it, and him. Later, McDowell found his fall guy.
"Hawk, I got to get my behind out of here," he told Harrelson. "I've
been here ten years and never had an outfielder worth a damn."

Some Indians were. In 1963, Wynn won No. 300—and Woodie Held,
Pedro Ramos, Francona, and Larry Brown hit successive homers. Colav-
ito returned to lead the '65 AL in RBI. Sonny Siebert no-hit Washington.
The '66ers won their first ten games. One day Tribe pitchers fanned an
AL-record 19 batters. Luis Tiant '68 became a balladeer: 21–9, 9
shutouts, and Tribe-record 1.60 ERA.

"Know what they were?" said Score. "Consolation, something to
hang on to"—Arcturus or Cassiopeia in Cleveland's mewling, massy sky.

12

WHERE YOU LEAD

They began with—what?—the death of Joseph Stalin, conquering of Mt. Everest, or TV's *I Love Lucy*. Looking back, the 1950s seem artless, even chaste. Even now, something remained, if but a vague recollection, of their shy and sober poise—a closeness that Ronald Reagan, among many from a steppeland generation, felt toward his childhood. "Everyone has to have a place to go back to," he observed. "Dixon [Illinois] is that place for me."

Did such an age exist? It did. You do not reinvent youth. To most, baseball seemed what Reagan deemed America: "Hopeful, big-hearted, idealistic, daring, decent, and fair." In papers (the *Tribune* called the White Sox by first names) and periodicals (like the *Sporting News,* the self-named "Bible of Baseball") and guides and annuals, it was *our* game, bub, and don't you forget it. Even in Chicago? where the White Sox had not, shall we say, found a post-'10s New Jerusalem. "Hell, yes," as Gus Zernial, like Eddie Robinson, smacking 29 homers in the early '50s, would say.

At Comiskey Park, one would no more zing baseball than burn the American flag.

Let us return to hula hoops and Davy Crockett caps and "Your Hit Parade." On the South Side strangers talked baseball. Pubs and restaurants scorned the Cubs. Stands teemed with Andy Frain ushers and kosher hots and beer. The trick was getting there. "Streets jam up and parking lots are inadequate, can handle only 3,500 cars," wrote Robert Creamer. For $50, a season-ticket holder could park daily. Take a cab, Creamer said—15 minutes, or $2, from the Loop. "Or Clark Street car (20 cents) direct to work, or southbound El (from State Street, 20 cents)" to four blocks from the park. Minus: narrow aisles and ramps, a mere dozen rest rooms, and truth in advertising—outfield/corner upper deck "box seats." Plus: clubs finally rewarding a patron's fealty to the game.

The '51–'58 White Sox finished fourth, third five times, and second twice under Paul Richards, Marty Marion, and Al Lopez—the Senor. Capacity shrank to 46,550. More seats were filled: Save '58, attendance topped a million. Billy Pierce packed Comiskey for duels with Whitey Ford. Outfielder Jim Rivera landed from St. Louis. Jim Landis anchored center field. Catcher Sherm Lollar made nine All-Star teams. In '51, a Cuban came via Cleveland to homer in his first at-bat. Orestes Armas Minoso—Minnie—was the Sox' first colored player. At last the Baseball Palace had a court.

A Cooperstown '97 inductee won three Gold Gloves, four times topped the league in hits, and played a bigs second-base record 798 straight games. Nellie Fox was small (5–9), willful (jawing at umpires and tobacco), and allergic to Ks: only 216 in 9,232 at-bats. His infield amigo presaged Garciaparra, Rodriguez, and Vizquel—"the first great Latin shortstop," the Old Roman's son, '57–'59 President Charles Comiskey, said of Chico Carrasquel.

The '50s hailed tater ball. Comiskey accented pitching, defense, and speed. "At some parks, it was like boxing," Lopez mused. "At our place it was like fencing—graceful." Replacing Carrasquel, Luis Aparico became '56 Rookie of the Year. Nine times he won Gold Gloves and led the AL in steals. "Look at his records," said David Condon: most big-league games (2,599) and AL assists (8,016), chances (12,564) and putouts (4,548)—or flair, which was especial.

In 1958, Minoso returned to Cleveland. Arriving was Early Wynn. On August 28, Fox set a record for successive fanless games (98). The record he disdained was Chicago's 39 years *sans* World Series title.

What's in a name? Depends. On March 10, 1959, the Roman's grand-daughter, Dorothy Comiskey, sold her 54 percent of the White Sox for $2.7 million. For the first time in fifty years a non-Comiskey owned Comiskey Park. Bill Veeck shocked many by his presence. Already, Veeck had signed Satchel Paige, brought Eddie Gaedel to bat, and planted ivy at Wrigley Field. The less con than common man was hustler and auctioneer.

On May 26, a helicopter landed behind second base before a game. Four midgets—again, Gaedel—dressed as spacemen leapt out to seize tiny Fox and Aparicio. Later, they gave the tandem ray guns. Fox used his to hit an MVP .306. Aparicio stole 56 bases. Lollar bopped a team-best 22 homers and 84 RBIs. All three won Gold Gloves.

"We beat you, 2 to 1," Fox said. "A big rally meant an infield single, steal, passed ball, and sacrifice fly." The Yankees had won nine of the last 10 pennants. The Sox winning the '59 flag seemed like Monaco taking the Olympics. "No Murderers Row, but hell of a character. A terrific team."

Headlines clashed: Alaska and Hawaii, newly minted states, Fidel Castro, Cuba's new *duce,* and Lunik III, a Russian satellite orbiting the moon. Two scandals rocked broadcasting: Network quiz shows were fixed, and disc jockeys played records for cash. Popular were TV's *Dennis the Menace,* with 49-pound Jay North, and *The Many Loves of Dobie Gillis.* Harvey Kuenn hit .353, Elroy Face went 18–1, and Ernie Banks won a second straight MVP. "Big names, huh?" said Wynn. "Big deal. Our anonymity just made us mad."

On May 1, Early, 39, one-hit Boston, 1–0. "Not bad for an old-timer," growled the 22–10 Cy Younger. Bob Shaw added 18 wins. Turk Lown and Gerry Staley had 29 saves. Veeck built a picnic area under the left-field stands. The Sox broke their attendance mark (1,423,144), took first place on July 12, and clinched September 22, 4–2, over Cleveland. (On the final out Mayor Richard Daley ordered city air raid sirens to hail their first-since-'19 pennant.)

On September 29, Los Angeles beat Milwaukee in a best-of-three playoff. Brooklyn had waited 55 years for a title. California hosted the Series in Dodgers Year Two. It began at Comiskey with a seven-run third inning/Ted Kluszewski two home run/providence-exhausting 11–0 rout. Said a fan: "They should have saved some runs." The next day Chicago fronted, 2–0. L.A. countered on Charlie Neal's blast to left. "What people remember," said Condon, "is the fan dropping his beer" on outfielder Al Smith. The photo won an Associated Press award. Losing, 4–3, the Sox should have been as lucky.

The Series moved to California. Evidently, the Ghost of '19 was aboard. Figure Games Three-Four: Chicago outhit the Dodgers, 22–14, but lost, 3–1 and 5–4. Pitching fiercely, Shaw, Pierce, and Dick Donovan won Game Five, 1–0. Go-go: The Sox scored on a double play. Things should have ended there: At Comiskey, Wynn was shelled 9–3. "What was the difference?" Lopez asked. "[Larry] Sherry," relieving in four games: 12⅔ innings, 8 hits, 0.71 ERA, and two wins.

"It was a great year," said Nellie. Nodding, he grasped a truth. Lollar batted .227. Rivera went 0 for 11. A few key hits would have made it greater.

"**W**hen you come to a fork in the road," Yogi Berra explained, "take it." In 1960, Veeck came to a fork. One road followed pitching and defense. (The '59 Sox hit a league-low 97 homers.) The second read Long Ball Inc. Implausibly, the Hose took the latter. "It was the Series," the Senor mused. "All those guys left on base [43] haunted Bill. 'I'd better get some power,' he said"—and did. It changed the Comiskeys' core.

Minoso, 37, reupped from Cleveland. The Hose acquired Gene Freese, 26, strong and slow, and Roy Sievers, 34, who made Freese seem like Man of War. Prospects left: Norm Cash, Earl Battey, John Romano, John Callison. "Veeck was a present sort of guy," Condon said. "Look at the park." The '51ers put an electronic scoreboard atop the bleachers. Veeck scrapped it for an "exploding" board of fireworks, aerial bombs, rockets, tapes, and pinwheels: "shrieks, crashes, howls," a critic wrote, "that rivaled a train wreck, diving planes, and circus." The board pricked convention. "What is this, Disneyland?" Jimmy Dykes huffed after a Comiskey went yard. In August, twitting excess, the Yanks lit Roman candles after Clete Boyer homered.

The '60 Sox scored 714 runs v. '59's 669. By contrast, when Freese and Sievers caught anything not hit directly at them, car horns sounded all over Illinois. The Sox lured 1,644,460, more than they would till '77.

Veeck painted Comiskey (white) and put names on the back of shirts. (Try Kluszewski.) In 1961, an ailing Barnum sold the team. Wynn began '62 with 292 victories. "Couldn't get past 299," he moaned." On August 16, the Hose hosted Boston. Management ordered buttons stamped "300." Unsympathetic, Bill Monbouquette no-hit Chicago. In July 1963, Wynn finally won No. 300—for Cleveland.

Retiring in 1965, Lopez returned in '68–'69. Leaving Comiskey Park, he closed a frame of Gus and Chico and Little Looie running and Landis fielding and Minnie hitting the ball. Even now, people will retrieve a distant night, under a cloudless sky, with the moon jumping over 35th and Shields. They will hoist a brew. They will revisit Turk and Jungle Jim and Big Klu and Billy Pierce—and hail the dynasty that never was.

MILWAUKEE COUNTY STADIUM

In 1902, Milwaukee's charter AL club moved to St. Louis and became the Browns. At that point the city rejoined the American Association at Eighth and Chambers. "Brewer Field had opened May 20, 1887," said Lee Allen. "A goat grazed the outfield." Winter hatched a skating rink. One season it stabled the Wisconsin National Guard cavalry troop. Always it mimed Milwaukee's melting pot.

"The Irish sat on the right-field side, the Germans on the left-field side," said 1888–'90 pitcher Clark Griffith. "It was a standing rule that the manager had to have an Irish first baseman and a German third baseman." The park became (Otto) Borchert Field after the owner's 1927 death. "By any name," said a writer, "it was kindling wood called a grandstand." Bill Veeck bought the Brewers in 1941, named Charlie Grimm manager, and built a 60-foot right-field wire fence. "We couldn't hit 266-foot homers," he mused. "I don't want other teams hitting 'em either." A year later Veeck used a hydraulic motor to slide fences back and forth. "If the other team has more left-handed power, the entire fence came down for us, and up for the visitor. We could do this without any trouble—and we did it—by reeling the fence in and out between innings. That is, we did it once. They passed a rule against it the next day."

In 1950, Milwaukee broke ground on a $5 million park on 46th

Street off Blue Mound Road: County Stadium had light units attached and was built by public coin. "The AA was OK, but it's the bigs we wanted," said Bud Selig, then 18. "It was a holiday when we heard that baseball was coming [March 18, 1953]." In his novel, *Shoeless Joe,* W. P. Kinsella writes of those who, hearing of the Braves' leaving Boston, gathered "and smiled out at the empty playing field—sat in silence, in awe, in wonder, in anticipation, in joy—just knowing that soon the field would be alive with the chatter of infielders, bright as bird chirps."

Borchert served 195,389 in 1952. On April 14, 1953, the Braves beat St. Louis, 3–2, before 34,359 on Billy Bruton's 10th-frame blast. "Some opener," Selig noted. "In right, the ball hit off Enos Slaughter's glove over the low [4-foot] right wall." The club placed second. Eddie Mathews led the NL in homers (47) and RBI (135). Warren Spahn topped in wins (23) and ERA (2.10). Milwaukee drew a league record 1,826,397.

"The news of the shift had come in spring training down in Bradenton," said pitcher Ernie Johnson. "When we went north to Milwaukee, they had a huge parade and we went downtown. We got there, and people had put up a Christmas tree—in *April*—inside the Schroeder Hotel. Said that since we'd missed Christmas with them, they wanted to celebrate it with us now. There were hundreds of presents under the tree—shaving kits, toiletries, radios, appliances. Ga-ga from day one."

For a glorious few years—so few, in retrospect, they seem almost mythic—Milwaukee became the envy of Baseball USA. Through 1959 it won two flags, barely missed two more, and regularly wooed 2 million–plus. The Braves were the first bigs franchise to change cities in half a century. Their success ensured that it would not be the last.

Burghers brought picnic lunches, arrived early for batting practice, and gave players free gas, milk, and beer. Each year the Braves got cars from dealers rent-free. Spahn won more games than any lefty (363), all but seven for the Braves. He *already* had a car, so fans gave him another—for his family. "It was a small town," said Johnson. "Some of us lived five minutes from the park. When we tried to pay for something the fans wouldn't let us."

'Fifty-four: Joe Adcock tied Ty Cobb's record with 25 total bases in a game v. Brooklyn. 1955: The Nationals erased a 5–0 All-Star Game deficit. Stan Musial pinch-hit in the 12th: 5-all. "Stan, you've murdered my Giants enough in the regular season," jabbed manager Leo Durocher. "Now hit one out of here for me." He did. 1956: Bruton had a league-high 15 triples. Hank Aaron led in three categories, including average (.328). Lew Burdette and Spahn ranked 1–2 in league ERA. Milwaukee lost the pennant on the final day. Braves attendance led the bigs for a fourth straight year.

"[The] rush for tickets to Braves games," mused *Sports Illustrated,* "rivaled only by *My Fair Lady.*" Size left 35,911 (1953) for 43,091 ('54), 47,611 ('70), and 54,187 ('73). The '56ers averaged 30,093 a game. By Opening Day 1957, the Braves sold more than 1 million tickets, luring an NL-high 2,215,404 for the year. Spahn 21–11 threw a league lefty-best 41st career shutout. MVP Aaron led in homers (44) and RBI (132). Red Schoendienst arrived from New York to get 200 hits. The lineup parroted an All-Star team—Mathews, Johnny Logan, Schoendienst, and Adcock third to first; Aaron, Bruton, and Wes Covington right to left; Del Crandall behind the plate.

On September 23, 1957, Aaron's 11th-inning homer off St. Louis' Billy Muffett won the pennant, 4–2. The Braves became the NL's first non–New York City team to win the Series since '46. Game Four whipsawed the Event: Elston Howard's ninth-frame blast gutted a 4–1 Braves edge; the Yanks took a 10th-inning lead; "in our half," said Selig, "Nippy Jones said he got hit by a pitch, showed the ump [Augie Donatelli] shoe polish on the ball, and took first." Logan doubled and Mathews homered: 7–5. Burdette won three games—the last on two days rest. Fred Haney had mocked his righty: "Lew could make coffee nervous." Now the Braves manager spoke with fellow feeling: "If that guy could cook, I'd marry him."

Earl Gillespie was the Braves 1953–'63 prosopopoeia. "The whole phenomenon was hard to put into words," said their mikeman. "We'd go into Forbes Field, and there'd be 30,000. We'd go into Wrigley or Ebbets—parks were packed. It was like a fairy tale—this tiny burg became baseball's capital." Each day the *Milwaukee Sentinel* ran a front-page cartoon. The sketch showed a Brave smiling, weeping, or abiding rain. A doubleheader might flaunt a split head. "Sports is all about *belonging,*" Gillespie noted, "and America took the Braves in their arms."

They embraced in a double-deck, circular ex–stone quarry that sat down and off the road. Tidy streets, church steeples, breweries, and plant smokestacks flecked the neighborhood. For years patients at the National Soldiers Home V.A. Hospital sat outside on Mockingbird Hill, above right field, and watched for free. The Allen-Bradley Clock Tower hovered like the moon. From downtown, you drove 4 miles, or 20 minutes (West Wisconsin Avenue) and parked (among 14,000 spots. A special stadium lot cost $45 a season). Tailgating made the air redolent, say, of Wisconsin v. Purdue. Inside, said a writer: "No stadium is more neutral than County Stadium." Both lines began at 320. Right and left, respectively, became 315 in 1953 and '75. Power alleys grew: 355 ('53) to 362 ('62). Deep alleys ebbed: 397 to 362 ('55). Center traded 404 for 410 ('54) and 402 ('55). Heights rose: left/center 4, 8 ('55), and 10 ('85); right 4, 10 ('55).

"Very neat, rest rooms spacious and heated, concession counters easily available and popular," *Good Housekeeping* in 1957 termed the bigs' first new park since 1932's Municipal. Two levels of chairs soldered one pole to another. Front-row boxes squeezed the infield. "Bad seats are almost nonexistent, but best are in lower grandstand along first or third," said *Sports Illustrated*. "Worst are the four or five rows in the back of the first deck." The second deck overhang sliced fly balls in half. Conceded Gillespie: "You couldn't see half the field." Most saw a family park, drank beer, and gulped baseball's best cuisine: hot corned beef, cheeseburgers, two kinds of hot dogs, grilled cheese sandwiches, cold cuts, and bratwurst on rye.

Outlanders came from most of mid-America. "Braves management slow to call off games in doubtful weather," said *SI* in 1958. "Fans are kept on tenterhooks." Rain was dubbed Perini dew, after owner Lou Perini. In 1961, center-field spruce and fur trees—Perini's Woods—yielded to green-painted bleachers. The Braves also built a picnic area—the Braves Reservation—between third base and left field. The upshot: a hard-hat Pleasantville.

In 1958, Spahn became the first lefty to win 20 games nine times. The Braves again won the pennant. Attendance slipped to 1,971,101. Who cared? Brewtown led the Series, 3–1. "We only needed one win," said Selig. "The key was Game Six. The Yankees scored two in the 10th. We get one back; and can't score the tying run from third." Jibed Casey Stengel after New York's 6–2 Game Seven clincher: "I guess this shows we could play in the National League." A year later L.A. won a best-of-three NL playoff, 3–2 and 6–5. "With wins the last day of '56 and '59," said Haney, "we'd have been in four straight Series."

Aaron '59 led in total bases, slugging, hits, and average (.355). Mathews smacked a league-high 46 homers—seventh of nine straight 30-plus years. No one had pitched a perfect or no-hit game for more than nine or 11 innings, respectively. The Bucs' Harvey Haddix did both May 26, before 19,194, retiring 36 straight Braves. In the 13th, Felix Mantilla reached via error. A sacrifice and a walk to Aaron brought Adcock up. Joe went yard to right-center. Aaron left the field, was passed by Adcock, and both were called out: Only Mantilla scored. "It still hurts," purred Haddix three decades later. "It was a damn silly one to lose." In 1960, Burdette and Spahn *each* no-hit the Phils. Next year Willie Mays hit four homers in a game. "He coulda' made five," said Giants voice Lon Simmons. "Third time up, Mays slammed the ball against the center-field fence. In the ninth, Jim Davenport makes the final out with Willie on deck—and fans boo. Every person in County Stadium thought Mays could park Number 5."

Two days earlier Spahn became second-oldest to pitch a no-hitter. On August 1, 1961, he won his 300th game (and still leads NL lefties in Ks, shutouts, wins, and innings). "It's said he'd walk a player intentionally in a close game and then pick him off—Spahnie's pick-off move is the best I ever saw," Johnson mused. "One night I saw him pick off the runner, umpire, and first baseman at the same time. None of 'em saw the ball coming! Warren'd be upset if you didn't kid him. We used to say that two things helped pick guys off. One, Warren's big nose—'When you move your head, your nose hypnotizes the runner.' Two, he'd have his hat pulled on crooked and they didn't know if he was looking at home or first. There was a story on the banquet circuit that knowing Spahn's move I don't doubt is true. One night he picked a runner off first and the batter swung."

Interest slacked. Milwaukee traded local favorites: Adcock to Cleveland; Bruton, Detroit; Logan, Pittsburgh. Perini sold the club. Attendance fell to 766,921 (1962). Vince Lombardi's Packers became Wisconsin's team. In '63, Spahn became the oldest 20-game winner, tying Christy Mathewson, and had a night at County Stadium. He received a painting of the park: less than 34,000 unpacked it. Aaron led in homers, total bases, runs, RBI, and slugging. The Braves drew 773,018. Milwaukee, no longer suffused with love, watched chairman of the board Bill Batholomay covet a future stadium in Atlanta. "It was obvious that's where they were going," said Gillespie. In October 1964 the Braves conceded they would become the first team to move its franchise twice.

That November, a court order forced the '65ers to linger before skipping town. "We had the unprecedented mess," mused announcer Merle Harmon, "where the Braves had to play an entire year in a city which knew they were losing the club." It was, he said, like two people sharing a house while awaiting a divorce. An NL-record six players on one team had 20 or more homers: Aaron and Mathews (32 each), Mack Jones (31), Joe Torre (27), Felipe Alou (23), and Gene Oliver (21). They drew 555,584, but contended till September. "There were baseball people afraid we'd win the pennant," Harmon said, "wind up in the Series, and County Stadium would be half-deserted."

Be not afraid: The Braves finished fifth. On September 22, 1965, before 12,577, they played their last home game. In eight years, the National League had shed its three most salient teams—Brooklyn, New York, and Milwaukee. "Even when the Brewers came here five years later," Gillespie said, "a lot of us could never forgive baseball its cruelty."

The man called the "Pied Piper of Milwaukee" formed a sad, slow mile. "Every year the Miller Brewing Company did a half-hour Braves highlight film, and we'd show people around the city in boats, on bikes, at sidewalk beer cafes. And there was one common element in these scenes—people had radios on. They were listening to the games," he mused. "Like Brooklyn with the Dodgers, Milwaukee *meant* the Braves. That's what I'll remember."

He was not alone.

MEMORIAL STADIUM

For 38 years, eight was enough. Memorial Stadium (1954-'91) was Baltimore's eighth baseball park. Madison Avenue Grounds housed inner-city matches. Next: Newington Park, then Greenmount Avenue. The great 1890s NL Orioles did much at Union Park to exhilarate their public. The 1901–'02 ALers played at 10th Street and York Road. In 1914, the Federal League debuted and died at Terrapin Park. Folding, it yielded to the International League. Owner Jack Dunn renamed Oriole Park, won seven straight '19–'25 IL flags, and kinged Max Bishop, George Earnshaw, and Lefty Grove. Their haunt joined a single deck, twin tier of outfield ads, left-center scoreboard, and "Gunther Beer" sign—until, on July 4, 1944, a "red glare" in the National Anthem City awoke manager Tommy Thomas at his St. Paul Street abode: "A huge ball of fire swept through the stands."

Embers burned. The '44 O's left for a two-week road trip. Their new built-in-'22 home, football's Municipal (Venable) Stadium, readied for a gentler sport. That fall it wooed 52,000 for baseball's Junior World Series. "By contrast," said longtime columnist John Steadman, "in '44 the [World Series] Cardinals and Browns got only 31,000." The '50 O's hatched a new aviary at Ellerslie Avenue, Ednor Road, and East 33rd and 36th Streets. Name: Memorial Stadium. ("Time Will Not Dim," the entrance scrawled, "the Glory of Their Deeds.") Place: a fine residential neighborhood, on Baltimore's north side, 10 and 20 minutes by car and bus, respectively, from downtown. Look: plain, large, and horseshoed. "Not intimate nor ornate," termed a writer. "From the outside it resembles a large school." Crunch: The Orioles had graced four major leagues ('80s AA, NL, AL, and Federal). The IL seemed old-hat. Said Steadman: "We wanted the bigs."

In 1953, the Anheuser-Busch Brewery bought the Cards—and the Browns' Bill Veeck tried to move to Baltimore. "I knew I'd be outgunned in St. Louis," Veeck said. "I also found I'd be blocked from moving by owners who hated me." That October he sold the franchise for $2,275,000. Next April, Baltimore transformed an absence of 52 years into a kind of cock–a–hoop return. "A gigantic parade," said new Orioles voice Ernie Harwell. "A stirring welcome to Baltimore." It dwarfed the rest of '54.

"We opened the season with eighteen Browns," Steadman said of Baltimore's first post-'02 AL team. "It showed. [They went 54–108]." The '53 Browns drew 297,238. The '54 opener lured 46,354. (Capacity: 47,708. Baseball's sole roofless upper tier wrapped home plate beyond each line.) Foul poles stood 309 feet away. (An 11⅓-foot wall reached the 446-foot alleys). The first year a 10-foot hedge linked left- to right-center. (Center was 445.) "The hedge was beautiful," said the Georgian Harwell. "It rarely entered the area of play."

Chuck Diering robbed Mickey Mantle of a 1954 hedgerow homer. The O's then built an 8-foot wire fence: Jackie Brandt backpedaled and got stuck. The new six-foot wall was padded in 1958 after Harvey Kuenn cut his face. In 1963, Mantle crashed into the lower part and broke his knee. Oddments merged: Huge columns blocked vision around the park. A right-field $152,000 scoreboard had more than 40 miles of electrical wiring and no moveable parts. Foul terrain was more pitcher-friendly than even Griffith Stadium. Bob Turley won the opener, 3–1, v. Chicago. Homering, Clint Courtney and Vern Stephens sowed bum hope: The '54ers hit only 52 dingers. On June 30, Baltimore topped the Browns '22 single-season high (712,918)—and Bob Kennedy hit its first grand-slam.

Pleading, hitters won: Alleys shrunk from 447 in '55 via 405 to 380 and 370 in '62. Center traded 450 for 425 ('55) and 410 ('58). A 14-foot wall later decked each pole, bounced balls toward center, and intersected a 360-foot wire fence. In 1956, Bob Nieman hit safely in 20 straight games. Mantle first cleared the hedge in 1957. Gus Triandos '58 hit 30 taters. On June 10, 1959, Rocky Colavito blasted four: Tribe, 11–8. Still, pitching trumped: 'Fifty-six, Baltimore's four straight shutouts; '58, first O's no-hitter (Hoyt Wilhelm *v.* New York) and *sans* All-Star Game extra-base hit (AL, 4–3); '59, Wilhelm's league-best 2.29 ERA. (Often intrigue laughed last. In 1957, a local law made the O's and White Sox stop at 10:20 P.M. Chicago's Paul LaPalme, up 4–3, faced Dick Williams in the ninth. "It's 10:19. All LaPalme has to do," said Birds manager Paul Richards, "is toss the ball on the screen, game ends." Instead, Williams' homer tied. They replayed the game.) Triandos '59 allowed 28 passed balls. "Hoyt's knuckler did it," said Gus. His reply: "that huge, pillow-like glove" spun by ex-catcher Richards.

The '60 O's came out of nowhere to nearly win the pennant. "We were dead even," said Brooks Robinson, "until the Yankees swept us [four straight in September]." The "Baby Birds" winged it: Chuck Estrada 18–11, Milt Pappas 15–11, Hal Brown 3.06 ERA. Baltimore's record 1,187,849 ranked third in an eight-team league. That winter hitting won again: foul turf ceded to 2,571 new boxes. Jim Gentile's '61 turf was going long: five grand slams; 46 homers, 141 RBI, .302, .646 slugging, and .428 on-base. On September 20, Roger Maris faced Jack Fisher. "He was chasing Ruth ['s home run record], and Commissioner Ford Frick said he had to hit 60 in Babe's 154-game schedule," said Steadman. "This was his last chance." Maris hit 59 that night, and barely missed 60.

Swinging singles. Washington's Tom Cheney fanned a record 21 Birds in a '62 16-inning loss. In 1964, Bob Johnson got an AL-best six straight pinch-hits, Luis Aparicio's 57 steals led the league, and Robinson became the first non-Yankees post-'59 MVP: .317, 194 hits, 28 homers, and Americans-high 118 RBI. The O's led till September, then flagged. On May 2—"Safety Patrol Day"—a 14-year-old was killed, and 46 hurt, when children on a park escalator were crushed against a portable barrier for nearly 30 seconds.

Next year attendance fell to 781,649. The ennui dulled even a sharp-edged visitor. Once a pitcher threw two balls after relieving for Cleveland. Manager Birdie Tebbetts tried to yank him. At that point the umpire reminded Tebbetts that a pitcher must face at least one batter. Birdie smiled and left the mound. "Whereupon every step he looked like a guy swimming the breaststroke," said announcer Chuck Thompson, "you know, flapping his arms in front of him, all the way to the dugout." Later a reporter asked Tebbetts about his Olympic free form. "I was swimming through a sea of my own stupidity," he replied.

"The park was cold, we still relied on pitching," said Steadman. "Ours was still a football town [the 1958–'59 champion Colts]." That puzzlement would change.

[KANSAS CITY] MUNICIPAL STADIUM

As First Lady, Bess Truman listened to baseball on the Truman Balcony. On May 8, 1955, her husband's 71st birthday, the Truman Library in Independence, Missouri, broke ground. A month earlier—April 12: Athletics 6, Tigers 2, before 32,844—Harry, flanked by Connie Mack, threw out the first ball at Kansas City's big-league opener. "The Boss is the real fan," he said of Bess.

In 1923, Municipal Stadium opened as [owner George) Muehlebach Field at 21st and 22 Streets, Euclid Avenue, and 2128 Brooklyn Avenue.

Pitchers loved the ex–ash heap and swimming hole frog pond: left, center, and right field 350, 450, and 350 feet. Through 1950 and '54, respectively, it housed the Negro League Kansas City Monarchs and American Association Blues.

"For years Kansas City was a great Yankees farm club," said *Kansas City Star* sports editor Ernie Mehl. "Mantle, Rizzuto, they all played here." Muehlebach became Ruppert Stadium in 1938. Chicago tycoon Arnold Johnson later bought and renamed it Blues. In 1945, Johnson's friends Del Webb and Dan Topping bought the Yankees. Mehl convinced him that K.C. deserved a club. Johnson, in turn, used Webb and Topping to run interference, bought the A's, and moved them from Philadelphia. Kansas City gave Johnson $500,000 for Blues Stadium, renaming it Municipal.

Johnson bought the Braves Field scoreboard for $100,000, put it in right-center field, and moved the plate 25 feet toward the outfield. (Lengths shrunk, then rose: left, 312 [330 in '56 to 369 in '67]; center, 430 [421 in '56, 410, and 421 in '65]; and left-center, 382 [375 in '57 to 408 in '69]. The bottom of the light tower was in play. Right-center followed the bouncing ball: 382 [387 in '57 to 360 in '63 and 382 in '69]. Ibid., right: 347 [352 in '56, 325 in '65, and 338 in '66]. Wall heights wavered: left, 38.5 ['59] and 10 ['61]; center, 10 ['63] and 40 ['69]; right, 4.5 [plywood '65] to 40 [screen 1966]). Who could foresee in late 1954 that the park would even open? "We'd had a lot of baseball here," said Mehl: NL, AA, and Federal League. "We'd never had so little time to find a home." In 22 weeks, the city rebuilt and double-decked Municipal (capacity 32,561). Over time, the Athletics showed less.

The '55ers finished sixth (Missouri's A's *never* made the first division) and drew 1,393,054 (quadrupling Philly's last year). Vic Power hit .319. Gus Zernial smacked 30 homers. Interest turned to the trivial and profound. Frank Umont became the first ump to wear glasses (Detroit *v.* Kansas City). The A's canceled an exhibition game in Birmingham, Alabama. (A local ordinance barred blacks from playing whites.) Attendance fell below one million, never to return. Skipper Lou Boudreau was fired: Eight succeeded him. In 1958, Bob Cerv had 38 homers and 104 ribbies. On July 11, 1960, the Nationals won the All-Star Game, 5–3, before 30,619. Seven Yankees made the AL team.

"The Yankees! They called us their cousin!" cried 1955–'61 A's broadcaster Merle Harmon. "Johnson kept trading these fine players—Art Ditmar, Bobby Shantz, Ralph Terry, Hector Lopez—the Yankees got every one." The New York Central Railroad shipped Power, Irv Noren, Enos Slaughter, and Jerry Lumpe. In late 1959, Johnson traded Roger Maris to the Big Apple for Norm Siebern, Don Larsen, Hank Bauer, and Marv Throneberry. "Oh," Merle said, "and how the trades goaded our fans." One July night the A's ripped New York for 27 hits. "For once *we* felt like the powerhouse." Self-effacement lit the air. " 'Course, that feeling didn't last for long."

What did was disarray. Through 1960 Kansas City never settled above sixth place. That December, Chicago insurance broker Charles O. Finley bought 52 percent of the A's from the late Johnson's estate. "Cheap! Italicize it," said Harmon. Finley tried to bully a rental reduction. He also blared a baseball sense and showman's yen to please.

In 1961, Lew Krausse got $125,000 to sign. "Really the first great bonus baby," said Mehl, "the first pitcher to start without any minor-league experience." Krausse blanked the Angels on three hits. John (Blue Moon) Odom, signed for $64,000, threw a two-hitter in start two. Catfish Hunter got $75,000. Bert Campaneris arrived from Venezuela. Sal Bando jumped from Arizona State. Alumni Rick Monday and Reggie Jackson led baseball's '65–'66 free-agent draft. "Finley was his own scouting system," said Harmon. "He signed them all." He seemed less adept at winning and drawing. The style was mom 'n' pop, not U.S. Steel.

"We've got nowhere to go but up," eighth-placers once rasped. The '61 A's differed: tied for last in a new 10th-place league. Bill Fischer threw a record 84⅓ straight walkless innings. Only 683,811 found the park, two miles east of downtown. Gino Cimoli had 15 triples. "Municipal loved extra bases," he said, "but hated homers." By 1964, Finley wanted Louisville. The AL told him to sign a K.C. lease or lose the team. Campy, 21, debuted with two homers. So what: The '65ers finished 10th, went 59–103, and played to 528,344.

Campaneris pitched ambidextrously for 1962 Class-A Daytona Beach. One day in '65 he played each position *v.* California. That September 25, Satchel Paige, 59, pitched for the first time since 1953: one hit in three innings. "He stood them on their ears!" said Red Sox broadcaster Ned Martin. Satch was more emphatic. "If you think I'm gonna' throw any place but your letters, shame on ya'!" Finley's shame was the Yankees: He envied, but hated, them.

New York drew Municipal's best crowd, 35,147, August 18, 1962. "What a social occasion," said Mehl. "People from all over Mid-America arrived by car, bus, and train." Many sat on a grass slope that straddled the right-field fence and deeper Brooklyn Avenue Wall. It was too steep to be mowed. Finley imported sheep and dyed them A's green and old. An employee with a shepherd's cap, cloak, and stick managed the animals. "When the Yankees played [selling out]," laughed Bando, Finley put the sheep behind the fence. One day a man accosted him and said he had sat on sheep manure. "My pants are ruined! What you gonna' do about it?" Finley had them cleaned and pressed.

If you can't beat 'em, ape 'em. "[By 1965] Charlie became convinced that Yankee Stadium ['s 296-foot right-field line] had created their dynasty," laughed Hunter. His riposte: the Pennant Porch. Finley built a four-foot-high fence 296 feet from the plate. "Baseball regulations said it had to be at least 325," added Harmon. Defiant, Finley ad-libbed a 325 line. "He then indented it to 296 about five feet from the pole." The AL cried foul. Charlie finally painted "K.C. One-Half Pennant Porch" at the 325-foot pole.

An ex-Athletic smirked. "You don't win pennants by copying another park. Not if one has George Herman Ruth and the other Pee Wee Herman." By now, boxes and bleachers had upped Municipal's size to 33,241. Within two blocks lay 4,500 parking spaces. By bus, car, or taxi it took 10–20 minutes from downtown to the park: "although 30 may be needed," said Finley, "when the Yankees are in town." Seats were bright, ushers kindly, and rest rooms clean. Pizza and grilled hot dogs led the menu. Disabled drivers parked outside a low wall along the left-field line. Others should sit anywhere but the upper deck (far away, like Kansas) and first five box-seat rows ("in mid-summer days," wrote *Sport* Magazine in 1957, "it is quite possible to be baked alive.") In 1961, the home pen was moved from center to "erase the need for the car that used to transport pitchers to the mound." More change followed: Seeing, did you believe?

Beyond right Finley built a children's zoo on an incline. Its cast included a Chinese golden pheasant, German checker rabbits, the mule Charlie O., peafowl, a German shorthaired pointer dog named Old Drum, and Capuchin monkeys. The Kansas City Farmers Market kept them happy. Tigers pitchers once fed the monkeys vodka-soaked oranges. Another time Finley led a young Nebraskan on a tour. "He thinks they're going to the zoo," said Campy. "Instead, they wandered on the field [near center fielder Jim Landis] as the pitch was being thrown." The style was home style: A "Sam's Baseball Parking" sign still spruces a nearby bridge. Finley listened by radio from his Indiana home. He had a soft spot for Paige, ensuring his pension. Groundskeeper Smokey Olson used Charlie O.'s blanket to warm Satch's legs in a bullpen rocking chair.

Some thought Finley *off* his rocker. "Charlie didn't want umpires to have to stash baseballs in their pocket," said A's voice Monte Moore, "so he built Harvey the Mechanical Rabbit," rigged a basket, and buried him behind the plate. "The ump'd point to a ballboy, who pushed a button." The rabbit rose, unloaded stock, and returned to *terra firma*. Finley felt umpires demeaned by cleaning home plate—thus, "Little Blowhard," a compressed air jet. Not everyone knew the brainchild. One batter readied for a pitch. The ump pressed the button. The airjet hissed. Surprised, the hitter leapt up and fell backward in the box.

Little worked. The '67 A's finished last, drew only 726,639, and vamoosed to Oakland. Next year the AL expanded to Kansas City and Seattle. Owner Ewing Kauffman signed a four-year lease at 22nd and Brooklyn. Pitcher Roger Nelson became the No. 1 draft pick. The Royals debuted April 8, 1969, over Minnesota, 4–3, before 35,020. That year K.C. wooed 902,414. Lou Piniella became Rookie of the Year. The '71ers finished second. Oh brother: A year later Ed (Tigers catcher) and Tom (umpire) Haller faced the Royals. "The first sibling act in big-league history," said Hall of Fame librarian Jack Redding.

Everything is relative. In '72, Piniella hit .312. John Mayberry had 100 RBI. The Royals rousted only 702,656. Leaving Municipal, the Yanks' cousin hoped to father a new cachet.

CONNIE MACK STADIUM

In 1957, *Sports Illustrated* critiqued Connie Mack Stadium: "Except for boxes, most seats have at least minor obstruction between you and the game. Management recognizes this, however, and reserved seats especially bad in this respect are held back, except on sellouts when buyer is told it's a 'poor visibility seat.' Only sun seats are in left-field bleachers. Park is clean, brightly painted. Tipping ushers is 'optional.' Rest rooms are clean and modern, but not enough of them for big crowds. Easily accessible refreshment counters [specialty is box lunch with fried chicken]. No beer is sold. Lack of beer in park prompts some Philly fans to bring their own in, and they usually bring plenty. Last season this resulted in at least one near riot when irate spectators (for some strange reason, sedate Philadelphia has the rowdiest clientele in major leagues, as any rabbit-eared player will testify) started to pitch empty bottles down on field."

Gene Mauch hit .270 for the '57 Red Sox. In '61, he changed jobs/leagues as Phillies manager. His Gallipoli was 1964. Nineteen sixty-four. The phrase stands alone, needs no embroidery—a Woodstock or Waterloo, *Sputnik* or Chappaquiddick—so affixed to Connie Mack that even non-Quakers grasp the spoken tone reserved for a drunken spouse or wayward child.

For 73 straight days the Phils gripped first place. Johnny Callison had 104 RBI. Rookie third baseman Richie Allen made 41 errors, but hit 29 dingers. Chris Short finished 18–11. Jim Bunning (19–8) no-hit the Mets June 21—Father's Day. To announcer Byrum Saam: "Perfect day, perfect game." On September 20, the Phils led by 6½ games. They then mimed a greyhound who, lacking food and water, careens toward the end in angst and shock.

Mauch started Short and Bunning in eight of the last 12 games. The Phillies lost 10 straight—a *nonpareil* fold. Headlines blared the Beatles, the Warren Commission, *Mary Poppins,* and Cassius Clay. Philly's concern turned more interior: Its public pursed lips and tightened jaws. Branch Rickey was then St. Louis vice-president: "It's almost incredible. Here is a club that ten days ago had our Cardinal club in the dark recesses. I don't think I've ever seen a group of able-bodied men walk off the field a sadder spectacle."

Connie Mack was living its worst nightmare. By Sunday, October 4, the Reds and Cardinals fronted. Mauch was a game behind. "Last day against Cincinnati," infielder Cookie Rojas said. "If we win and the Cardinals lose [to the Mets], it's a three-way playoff. Cardinals win, they get the pennant." The Phils romped, 10–0. St. Louis frolicked, 11–5. Philadelphia drew a record 1,425,891. A man raised in suburban Wayne returned from a road trip to find a message from his father.

"Baseball had been our bond," said Ned Martin, "and we'd talked about it when I last saw him. He was thin, had several heart attacks." His dad died after mailing a letter. "He'd predicted the Phillies' collapse, which had now come to pass. 'I don't see how they can win,' he said. 'They pitch Short and Bunning on panic and no one else. I'm afraid they're going to crash.' "

Baseball, said a writer, is not a matter of life and death in Philadelphia. The Phillies, he added, *were*.

Nineteen sixty-four marked a Pickett's Charge of pre–Mike Schmidt interest. In 1968, Mauch was fired. "The good news is that he won more games for the Phils than any manager since 1960," mused Saam. "The bad is that he couldn't win one more." Crime rose. The area turned seedy. The '69ers drew only 519,414. Shibe mirrored baseball's then-inferiority complex of stricture and passivity.

On October 1, 1970, its final game graced 21st and Lehigh. Skip nuance. Hundreds of police converged. In the sixth, a batter lofted to left and an oddity rushed the field. "Ron Stone was the [Phillies] fielder," Saam said, "and the fan grabbed him as he was trying to make the catch." Umpires threatened a Philly forfeit. In the 10th, Oscar Gamble plated Tim McCarver with the game-winning run. Phillies fanatics refused to leave. Richie Ashburn shook his head. "The team had tried to stop pillaging by giving souvenir seat slats to each fan as they entered the park. Maybe that would pacify them." Instead, the souvenir became a club. One man removed a toilet bowl. Many ripped seats and raped the turf. "Some seats that survived," he said, "were moved to other fields"—Duncan Park and War Memorial Stadium, respectively, in Spartansburg and Greensboro. In 1971, fire damaged the deserted park. It was razed in '76.

In 1966–'67, Bob Uecker hit a lowly .202 for Philadelphia. He never pointed fingers at his manager and friend. "Mauch stood up for me when no one else would," said Uke. "It never was reassuring to go up in the ninth inning, look into the visitors dugout, and see everybody else in street clothes. Even my mom criticized my play. She'd say, 'Get a job.' "

By contrast, Uke's father was a prism and progenitor of Philadelphia's fear and love. "What a typical Phillies fan. He booed me, too." Ardor, unlike '64, doesn't wilt in the autumn rain.

BUSCH STADIUM

In 1958, Stan Musial had 2,999 hits. The Cardinals wanted the next to occur at home. "We were scheduled to open a series a day later in St. Louis," said manager Fred Hutchinson. "I sat Stan down so he'd get the hit there." The Man is on the bench. Two out, two on, sixth inning at Wrigley Field. Hutch says, "You want to go up?" Musial: "Hell, let's win the game." Pinch-hitting, he lined No. 3,000 into left-center: Cardinals, 5–3. Their train back to St. Louis was besieged at every stop. Musial smiled and waved. "I covered him for 22 years," writer Bob Broeg said, "and in public never saw him make a mistake." St. Louis in July blurs Rio and Tripoli. After a steamy doubleheader, Musial would sign autographs for an hour. "Stan didn't make a fraction of what players get today," Red Schoendienst said. "Doesn't matter. You can't buy class."

Some couldn't rent. Jackie Brandt became baseball's first "flake": i.e., a mate said, ideas seemed to "flake" off his mind and vanish. Once Jackie played 27 holes of golf in 101-degree heat before a twinbill. He later vowed, "I'm going to play with harder nonchalance." Six times the '54–'62ers "nonchalloted" (Dizzy Dean) the second division. (Exceptions: In 1958, Sam Jones led the league in Ks. Ken Boyer '59 hit in 29 straight games. Ernie Broglio went 21–9 in 1960).

In 1957, Busch Stadium housed its second All-Star Game. Ohioans stuffed the voting to elect seven Reds. Even the Man was snubbed. "Then [Commissioner] Ford Frick stepped in," said Broeg, "and named Stan, Hank Aaron, and Willie Mays to replace three Reds." The Nationals lost, 6–5. Airing balls and strikes was a balladeer of sarcasm and passion. It might be! Baseball's Jackie Gleason. It could be! A 1945–'69 reign as the Cardinals red-hot mikeman. It was! Harry Caray, selling Budweiser, sacking pomp, and seeming truant across the land.

"You have to understand what he was to the Midwest of my child-hood," Bill James has written. "In the years when baseball stopped at the Mississippi, [the Cardinals' flagship, 50,000-watt] KMOX built a network of stations that brought major-league baseball into every little urb across the landscape. Harry's remarkable talents were the spearhead of their efforts, and forged a link between the Cardinals and the Mid-west that exists to this day." Over 124 stations in 14 states, Caray exte-riorized the Redbirds retinue—a magical property in Webster, Iowa, and Cleveland, Tennessee, and Lawton, Oklahoma. "Live it up," he crowed. "It's later than you think." Harry defied the laws of probability, longevity, and cirrhosis of the liver. "I never doubted," he said, "that I'd die behind the mike. With my last gasp I'd say, 'Cardinals win!' "

Increasingly, *Busch's* gasp looked inevitable. "A new 55,000-seat sta-dium is on the boards," *Sports Illustrated* wrote in 1961. Most then took a car, parked blocks away, and walked or used a shuttle bus. "Twenty-five minutes from downtown," Broeg said, "or hour from the suburbs." All 30,305 seats were red and green: 21,950 reserved, 3,914 upper-deck box, 2,041 lower-deck box, and 2,400 bleacher. "Best are loge box area on second deck," read *SI,* "which lures carriage trade. Worst are extreme left-or right-field areas of grandstand, both levels, which are left empty." Left field sniffed of Coppertone. The huge Philip Morris cigarette advertisement flaunted a miniature bellhop. Tenor fused beer (draught), hot dogs (grilled, not broiled), and dugouts (baseball's longest)—less elitist than pitchfork-populist.

Like Busch, Musial was sturdy as a post. Life began at 41: He hit .330 in 1962. In '63, Stan announced his retirement and homered in his first at-bat as a granddad. St. Louis went 19–1 to draw within a game of Los Angeles. Said Broeg: "Would Musial go out in a Series?" Middle America held its breath: L.A. arrived for a three-game series. The Dodgers won, 3–1 and 4–0. The Cards then led, 5–4, in the ninth. "Here it comes!" Harry cried of a pitch to the Dodgers' Dick Nen. There followed a soul-wracking silence. "Oh, my God," he said, finally. "It's over the roof."

The Birds finished six games back. On September 29, Stan singled in his last at-bat. Postscript: In 1989, Musial graced a roundtable seminar. The moderator said, "Stan, .331 lifetime, what do you think you'd hit today—watered-down pitching, expansion?" The Man replied, "Oh,

.285, .290." "Stan, you're a modest guy," he jousted, "but what are you talking about, .285, .290?" Stan said, "What the hell, I'm 69 years old."

"There isn't a kid in St. Louis," the *Philadelphia Daily News* wrote in 1984, "who can't tell you the starting lineup of the Cardinals—the 1934, 1944, or 1964 Cardinals." In 1963, their entire infield started the All-Star Game: third to first, Boyer, Dick Groat, Julian Javier, and Bill White. Caray, for one, thought '64 might close the deal. "I can't believe it!" he rejoiced of a pitcher's April double. "Roger Craig has hit the left-center-field wall! The Cardinals are going to win the pennant!" Harry, you thought, would give up Budweiser first.

In June, St. Louis traded Broglio for Cubs outfielder Lou Brock. "Broglio was a veteran," Broeg said. "Brock an unproven kid." Ultimately, the kid averaged .304, had 3,023 hits, and broke Ty Cobb's career stolen-base mark. "They know I'm coming," he said, "but they don't know when." The '64ers came when Philadelphia blew its 6½ game lead. Brock combined .315 and 43 steals. White pounded 21 homers and hit .303. MVP Boyer had a league-high 119 ribbies. Ray Sadecki won 20 games. Bob Gibson went 19–12.

Three Dixieland bands oompahed at Busch Stadium before the Series opener. When one stopped, reserve catcher Bob Uecker snatched its tuba, primed to play, but changed his mind. "What do I have to prove?" he mused. "People already know I have a lot of hot air." Uke then had a brainstorm: Use the tuba to snag fly balls. A few fixed their target. Most clanked off the metal. "Typical," said Uecker. "The Cardinals docked me for a new tuba."

That day Mike Shannon hit the scoreboard off New York's Whitey Ford. Sadecki endured, 9–5. Gibson then lost, 8–3. The Redbirds took two of three games at the Stadium. Jim Bouton won Game Six, 8–3. Gibson took the 7–5 final—St. Louis' first title since '46. "We were all exhausted," said catcher Tim McCarver, "and amazed." Yogi Berra was fired as Yanks manager and replaced by Johnny Keanne, who resigned as St. Louis skipper (O tangled web!), succeeded by Albert Schoendienst, bleeding Cardinals red.

"So good-bye, dear," wrote Cole Porter, "and amen." Sportsman's Park's was a time of last things and final bows. Gibson won 20 games in

1965. Brock swiped 63 bases. That spring, a gunman held up a ticket window, fired a shot, and grazed the neck of a 13-year-old girl sitting near third base. A year later St. Louis swapped one Busch for another: Giants, 10–5, on May 8, in the original's final game. Groundskeeper Bill Stocksick dislodged home plate. A helicopter carted it to the Cards' new home. A band played "Auld Lang Syne." The city soon razed the grandstand. The Hoover Boys' Club and adjacent baseball diamond now fill St. Louis' once–Zion.

CROSLEY FIELD

"In the mid-'50s the Reds were called Redlegs," said Bruce Markusen, Hall of Fame Manager of Program Presentations. "It was the Cold War, and Reds meant Commies." The '56ers warmed a record-tying 221 dingers. Four hit more than the Cardinals: Wally Post (36), Ted Kluszewski (35), Gus Bell (29), and Ed Bailey (28). Frank Robinson added a rookie-record-tying 38. "[Manager] Birdie Tebbetts likes to protest that Redleg hitting isn't as powerful as it looks," wrote Robert Creamer. "But try to get one of his sluggers away from him in a trade and see his red face turn pale." Second baseman Johnny Temple was ready with the beguiling stop. Roy McMillan seemed phantasmagoric defensively—"by far," said Creamer, "the greatest fielding shortstop in [the] game." The Reds finished two games out of first. Forget parking (minimal) or driving (Crosley bordered narrow streets). "Take special 70 cent baseball buses from downtown, Baseball Arrows," urged *SI*. Many did. The team drew a record 1,125,928.

Kluszewski thrice hit 40 or more homers, becoming baseball's Christian Dior. Before 1867, teams wore cricket uniforms with long white pants. George Allard was an amateur Red Stocking. Bertha Bertram owned a clothing store. George placed an order for knee-length pants with white flannel shirts—and bright red stockings. "Her socks," he said, "caused our name." Kluszewski *made* one by cutting sleeves at the shoulder. "We had those heavy woolies," Ted said. "I'd feel cramped." His bare arm-bulging look made women throw propriety in the pit.

In 1958, Adonis left for Pittsburgh. Vada Pinson arrived in '59 to lead the NL in runs (131) and doubles (47). The '60 Reds dredged sixth. That winter pitcher Joey Jay and third baseman Gene Freese arrived by trade. Creamer showed little faith. "Since 1956, Reds have fallen lower and lower," he wrote in March. "It's unlikely they'll fall lower, just as unlikely they'll go any higher." They broke 1–8 to "fall lower" into last. In his book *The Pennant Race,* reliever Jim Brosnan tells how the Crosleys turned inward but not bitter. They won nine straight, took first, and won a doubleheader at Milwaukee. "One of the wins was against [Warren] Spahn," said Brosnan. "It lifted the club." Slowly, Cincinnati reached its greatest juncture since October 1940.

In August, the Reds visited Los Angeles. "[Don] Drysdale was a son of a bitch," said manager Fred Hutchinson. "He knocked Robinson down three times, then hit him and got tossed." Cincy blanked L.A., 6–0 and 8–0. The Reds took first place—for good. Pinson batted .343. MVP Robby merged .323, 37 homers, and 124 RBI. On September 26, Cincinnati beat Chicago, 6–3, to clinch a tie. "We came home," said Robinson, "and then start the drive to downtown from the airport, and thousands line the road."

Fountain Square teemed with carolers. The Dodgers played the Pirates. An L.A. loss meant the flag. "They had loudspeakers doing play-by-play at both ends of the square," said Hutchinson. What they heard—at 11:26 P.M., Bob Skinner's catch, downing the Dodgers—uncorked a jangle of noise in Lynchburg and Loudonville and a blur of past and present in Springdale and Sardinia—joy unmatched since V-E Day.

In 1870, Brooklyn ended the Red Stockings' 79-game winning streak. Owner Aaron Champion wrote a telegram to the Rhineland. "Atlantics 8, Cincinnati 7. The finest game ever played. Our boys played nobly, but fortune was against them. Eleven innings played. Though beaten, they were not disgraced." The Reds were disgraced in the '61 Series. Whitey Ford won, 2–0, at the Stadium. Gordy Coleman then homered, Jay four-hit New York, and Elio Chacon scored the lead run on a passed ball: Reds, 6–2. Back at Crosley, Cincy led, 2–1, through seven. John Blanchard's homer tied the game. Roger Maris' ninth-frame blast won it, 3–2. Games Four-Five sent summer packing: Yankees, 7–0 and 13–5. New York hit seven homers. The Reds batted only .206.

"They called 'em ragamuffins," said then-voice Waite Hoyt by way of postscript. "They would look like a shabby bunch. Then they'd turn it around, not a lot of talent, just heart." Baseball requires a time to return to. To many, 1961 endures, lush and lyric, as a place where one can leave the world alone.

A Dodgers official dubbed the '61 Reds "a conglomeration of castoffs who banded together for one last stand." They fell to third, then fifth. Hoping to reverse the tide was a boy-man from/of Cincinnati. On April 13, 1963, Pete Rose tripled off Bob Friend for his first hit after 11 ups. In November, he became Rookie of the Year. An interstate rose beyond the left-field wall. Blocking it, the Reds topped the concrete fence with 9½ feet of plywood. "The plywood was out of play," said Rose. "But all sorts of problems happened." Cincy covered the home-run line in '65 to make the entire wall in play. In the right-center corner, a vertical line flanked the only ground rule painted on a barrier: "Batted ball hitting concrete wall on fly to right of white line—home run."

Few Jim Maloney pitches reached it in 1963: The righty went 23–7. Many of Pinson's 204 hits *did*. In '64, Robby had 103 RBI. Hutchinson developed cancer, left the club, and died. Attendance fell to 862,466 *v.* '61's 1,117,603—whether because the Reds were dull, or baseball lagged, who can say? Already it had become cliché that baseball was too mild to survive an age of rage and moral *laissez-faire*. Erma Bombeck wrote, "It hasn't happened yet, but it's inevitable. One night [an actress] will lean over the footlights of a Broadway theatre and in the childlike voice of Peter Pan ask, 'Will everyone who believes in Tinker Bell clap your hands?' And the theatre will resound in silence. The silence will record the [end of] faith in America." In 1961, Cincinnati clapped for its village team. By '64, it had lost faith.

The Reds' last years at Crosley were spent hoping for a park—and pennant. "Cincinnati wants a new stadium," *SI* wrote, "but until one comes along [they] will have to put up with . . . [the] smallest in majors." Rose got 200 hits in '65—the first of ten times. Maloney conjured Johnny Vander Meer. In June, he Kd 18, no-hit the Mets for 10 innings, and lost in the 11th. August brought revenge: Maloney no-hit the Cubs. That December Robinson—"an old 30," sniped club president Bill DeWitt—went to Baltimore for Milt Pappas, Jack Baldschun, and Dick Simpson. The '66 Reds slumped to seventh. "Some thirty," tweaked Robinson. He won the AL Triple Crown.

"**M**aybe they should retire the Rookie of the Year award," writer Ken Smith said of Tommy Helms '66 and Johnny Bench '68 joining Rose '63. All saw Henry Aaron's 3,000th hit in 1970 at Crosley Field. "I came to the Braves on business," said the Hammer, "and I intended to see that business was good as long as I could."

Crosley closed for business on June 24, 1970: Lee May's homer beat the Giants, 5–4, in the Park of Firsts' last game. Home plate was helicoptered to Riverfront Stadium. It was hard to be a cockeyed optimist. "We were a little town. You recognized a lot of people," said Hoyt of Crosley Field. "They'd call up to you. At home you could hear 'em on the air."

The Queen City bought Crosley, made it a car pound, and began demolition April 19, 1972. Ex-Redland Field is now an industrial site. Replicas were built at Blue Ash, Ohio, and on a farm near Union, Kentucky. In 1989, Blue Ash hosted the first Crosley Field Old-Timers Game. Nearly 300 original seats recall Schnozz and Big Klu and the acrobat McMillan. The left-center scoreboard catapults a visitor back: last-game lineups list Bench and Rose and McCovey and Mays.

George Bush once sought perspective for his family compound in Kennebunkport. "It's constant," he said of Walker's Point. "It's our rock." Ask a Rhinelander about Oktoberfest, the Cincinnati Symphony, or Proctor and Gamble Company. He will tell you: *Our* rock was Crosley Field.

WRIGLEY FIELD

The 1956–'66 second-division Cubs' rock lay at Addison and Clark. Interest seemed unmoved (by pain) and amnesic (toward calamity). TV was a reason: The '48 Cubs were the first to air their entire home schedule. Day ball was another, evoking a peachy charm. "How fortunate I was," Jack Brickhouse said, "to be in two grand places like Wrigley and Comiskey Park."

"Parks, not facilities," bellowed colleague Vince Lloyd.

"These sterile new stadiums," Jack said. "You don't know whether you're in Spokane or Disney World. No personality. But Chicago's have endured for baseball"—bonding vaudeville and the VCR.

In 1948, 46,951 formed Wrigley's largest paid crowd. The '50–'51 right-field wall was remodeled. New boxes made the screen 60 feet 6 inches from the plate—"same distance," Lloyd said, "as the mound to the plate!" The ivy appeared as close. Roy Cullenbine's hit got tangled in its vines. Trying to find a ball, Roberto Clemente plucked an empty white Coca-Cola cup. "Defeated," Brickhouse said, "you could still be diverted." One way: a pitcher's laureate. "Sad Sam 'Toothpick' " Jones no-hit Pittsburgh for eight innings in 1955. He began the ninth by walking three. Manager Stan Hack trudged to the mound. "Get that blankety blank ball over the blankety blank plate or you're out of here." Jones Kd the next three batters. In '60, Walt Moryn made a skidding catch for the last out of Don Cardwell's Opening Day no-hitter. "First game in a Cubs uniform!" said Charlie Grimm. "Too bad it was downhill from there."

Once a Cub approached Wrigley's batting cage. "Whitey [Richie Ashburn], you hit a lot of foul balls," he told the Phillies captain. "My wife, Madge, and I aren't getting along at all. You know where the wives sit here at Wrigley—why don't you take a shot at her?" Obliging, Ashburn lined a ball his first at bat toward Madge. Her spouse waved a towel: "Whitey, two rows back and one to the left and you got her."

In 1991, *Time* magazine columnist Hugh Sidey observed, "They come from different places [in the Midwest] with a common goal. They want to give birth and grow and love and laugh and die, bonded and sustained by the land, which is the oldest way of life Americans know." At Wrigley Field, two balls came from different places in 1959. Their common goal was to help the Cubs. Bobby Anderson threw a 3–2 pitch to Stan Musial that rolled to the screen. Umpire Vic Delmore ruled ball four. The Cubs yelled that Stan had fouled the pitch. The bat boy retrieved and gave it to P.A. announcer Pat Pieper. "I [then] grabbed it from Pat's bag of balls," said third baseman Alvin Dark. The Cubs never called time-out.

Delmore and catcher Sammy Taylor were oblivious to Dark's search and seizure. Baseball's charm is the unexpected. Taylor got a ball from Delmore. "Go to second," mates screamed to Musial. Sliding, he saw Anderson's throw sail into right-center. "I figure it's the ball in play so I get up and Ernie tags me." (Dark's throw had been caught by shortstop Banks.) The umpire ruled Stan out. Manager Solly Hemus readied a protest—except that St. Louis won. Delmore was asked why he put a second ball in play. "I've been lying in my hotel room looking at the ceiling asking myself the same question and I don't know."

The '59 Cubs enticed 858,255. On any question pertaining to geography the Milwaukee Braves remained their surpassing rival. The two cities lay 90 miles apart. Adherents jammed each other's park. Depending on the day, they met a Wrigley labyrinth of rules. "Follow me," laughed Brickhouse. "A ball's a homer if it hit the top of the railing or screen above the bleacher wall and dropped between the screen and wall"—also, hitting the railing or screen to land in the seats. "If a ball stuck in the screen or in the vines, it was a double"—also, landing/staying under grates in left or right. Jack inhaled. "If a ball went in or under grates on either side of home plate and remained there it was one base on a pitched ball and two bases on a thrown ball."

Bob Lillis got a single when bleacherites doused L.A.'s Frank Howard with peanuts and made him miss a fly. Rookies of the Year glimmered champagne-in-the-making. Billy Williams '61 hit 25 dingers. He retired with 426, a then-NL record 1,117 straight games, and swing that made the complex simple. Ken Hubbs '62 set a bigs mark for successive *sans* error games (78) and chances at second base (418). "He died in '64 [at 22, in a plane crash]," said Brickhouse. "Typical."

The '21–'70 Chicago Bears were annual tenants at Wrigley Field. "Picture this," said Brickhouse, their longtime voice. "Temporary bleacher seats were put on the left-field grass in front of the brick wall. The north end zone ended 18 inches in front of the bleachers." The southeast corner of the south end zone hung in midair over the top step of the first-base dugout. "You catch a pass, disappear into the dugout, then reappear." In 1971, the Bears reappeared at Soldier Field.

Up: The first Telstar Satellite hookup televised a 1962 Cubs game to Europe. Wrigley hosted its second All-Star Game: AL, 9–4. In '67, Ferguson Jenkins won 20 games for the first of seven times. That July 2, the Cubs took first that late in a year for the first time since 1946. "Forty-two thousand going berserk," said Mr. Cub. "The greatest thrill of my life." The Cubs finished third and nearly drew a million. Said Bill Veeck: "The city fathers declared a holiday."

Down: In 1963–'64, an eight-foot-high by 64-feet-wide wire fence—a.k.a. the Whitlow Fence, for front-office head Robert Whitlow—topped the center-field wall. "It will help the hitters background," Whitlow said. Instead, it thwarted 10 homers—mostly, the Cubs'. In September 1966, a lowest-ever 440 watched. The '67ers put AstroTurf over the center seats. (Vines replaced it in the '90s.) "Imagine," added Santo, "phony grass in Wrigley. Obscene!"—like swapping Brock for Broglio in 1964.

On April 8, 1969, before 40,796, in Chicago's last at-bat, pinch hitter Willie Smith cleared the right-field wall for an Opening Day 7–6 euphoria-inducing win. Banks (106 RBI), Glenn Beckert (.291), Don Kessinger (.273), and Ron Santo (123) formed the league's best infield. Williams topped Musial's 895 consecutive games played NL streak. On August 19, Ken Holtzman yielded no hits for eight innings. Hank Aaron then drove to left. "It was gone,' " said Hank. "But it hit Wrigley's shield of wind, came back, and Billy [Williams] caught it." Plenty of nothin': no hits and Holtzman Ks.

The Confines had rarely seemed friendlier. Reliever Dick Selma, waving a towel, spurred the Bleacher Bums. By June 1, the Cubs were 32–16. They led New York in mid-August by 9½ games. Santo began clicking heels upon each victory. Wrigley drew a record 1,674,993. Ahead lay the New Jerusalem when the Chicago Nationals became the best baseball team on earth. Who imagined that the Mets, benign as a housebroke pup, would go 38–11 while the Cubs—addled, exhausted—froze, like artifacts, in shock and disbelief? Chicago finished eight games behind. Ironically, milking ardor for any dog that was under, it became America's most beloved team.

In 1970, Sweet Will had a career-high 42 homers and 129 ribbies. On May 12, Banks lined tater 500 over the left-center wall. "Banks hit a trademark place," said Brickhouse. "Wrigley's the only park where it's harder to hit a homer down the line than 40 to 50 feet into fair ground['s 368-foot power alleys]." At that point, curving toward home, bleachers protrude into the field—the 357-and 363-foot left-center and right-center wells.

A year later Jenkins became the Cubs' first Cy Younger. In 1983 he retired, 284–226. By '91, another first: a Canadian in Cooperstown. "All this," marveled 1966–'72 manager Leo Durocher, "despite spending ten years at Wrigley Field." An old blues adage fanned: "If the Cubs didn't have bad luck they'd have no luck at all."

FORBES FIELD

Name a season. Nineteen twenty-seven denotes Murderers Row; '34, the Gas House Gang; '45, the last Cubs pennant; '68, the Year of the Tiger. Which was better—1961 (Yankees) or '76 (Big Red Machine)? Could *anyone* be worse than the '99 Cubs' barely more wins (67) than Sammy Sosa homers (63)? In 1960, Pittsburgh oozed with an almost tropical density of "Beat 'Em Bucs" and "The Bucs Are Going All the Way" and an all-time Forbes Field attendance record of 1,705,828 and a surreal World Series.

The Pirates won 23 games in their last at-bat. Cy Younger Vernon Law went 20–9. Elroy Face moored the pen. MVP shortstop Dick Groat hit a bigs-high .325. Second baseman Bill Mazeroski honed the double play. "When he pivoted," mused Law, "the ball looked like it took a U-turn." First basemen Dick Stuart and Rocky Nelson had 30 homers. Bill Virdon lit center field. In right, Roberto Clemente batted .314, drove in 94 runs, and threw out a league-best 19 runners. Wrote Les Biederman: "The 1960 Pirates were something special."

On September 25, the Buccos won their first flag since 1927. They opened the Classic ten days later v. New York at Forbes. The Yankees won Games Two, Three, and Six 10–0, 16–3, and 12–0. Bobby Richardson set a Series mark for most RBI in a game (six, Game Three) and Series (12). Whitey Ford threw two shutouts. The stripes outhit (.338–.256), outhomered (10–4), and outscored (55–27) the Bucs. Novas blur: Virdon's leaping catch off Yogi Berra; diving stops by Don Hoak and Mazeroski; Mantle, batting righty, clearing Forbes' 436 right-center mark.

October 13 broke mild and sunlit for a Good-God-Almighty, one-frantic-play-after-another Game Seven. Pittsburgh led, 4–0 (by way of Nelson's first-inning homer), trailed, 7–4 (via Berra's three-run poke), and scored five eighth-frame runs. Gino Cimoli singled. Virdon slapped a grounder to Tony Kubek. "A sure double play," said the shortstop, "except the ball hit something, came up, and hit me in the throat." Groat and Clemente singled: 7–6. Hal Smith's three-run "electrifying homer," read the *Pittsburgh Press*, "turned Forbes Field into a bedlam."

Four Yanks singles scored two runs in the top of the ninth inning: 9-all. At 3:36 P.M., Mazeroski led off the bottom. Ralph Terry threw a slider, Maz clubbed it toward left-center, Berra retreated to the 406 mark, and the ball cleared the wall. In California, Bob Costas, 8, retired to his room. "I took a vow of silence. My initial vow was not to speak until opening day of the 1961 season. That impracticality dawned on me quickly. But I kept mute for 24 hours—protesting this cosmic injustice."

On October 18, Casey Stengel was fired. By then, a hangover still hooded bars, mail routes, and screened-in porches, where one radio after another heard Bob Prince cry, "We had 'em all the way!" dub Forbes's infield "the alabaster plaster," or hail a distant blast, "You can kiss it good-bye!" Four decades later, even a Yankees fan recalls the leaves and splashing hues and spooked-up days that cradled fancy. If Bogart means *Key Largo*, baseball can mean year.

By default, Maz's shot sustained a decade. It is true that: Willie Stargell blossomed in 1966 (.315, 33 homers, and 102 RBI). Prince dubbed Virdon "the Quail," Hoak "Tiger," Harvey Haddix "the Kitten," and Stargell "Willie the Starge." He now coined a hex—the Green Weenie, a hot dog painted green—that Tri-Staters bought at stores, shook at rivals, and hung on car antennae. It almost worked. The Bucs finished three games behind L.A.

It was also true that: The '61–'69 Pirates five times flunked the first division. Increasingly, The Wonder That Was Clemente—to Prince, "Arriba" a.k.a. "The Great One"—greased their creaking gate. No. 21 had 3,000 hits, five times led outfielders in assists, and won four batting titles and a dozen Gold Gloves. His pinnacle was 1966: .317, 29 taters, 119 RBI, and MVP. In '67, Clemente batted a career-high .357. He ran like Secretariat, hit like Ali *v.* Frazier, and "treated baseball," wrote Roger Angell, "like a form of punishment on the field."

Forbes closed June 28, 1970, before 40,918, the Bucs' largest crowd since 1956, in a doubleheader *v.* Chicago. "The Cubs won Forbes' first game [1909]," said general manager Joe L. Brown. "Now the Pirates returned the favor [winning, 3–2 and 4–1]." Their new field had Tartan turf, football sight lines, and an upper deck nearer the troposphere than plate. "The Pirates were stupid, but not unique," added Costas. "As amazing as it seems, teams of the '60s and '70s wanted something new—they couldn't grasp what in parks like Forbes they already had." Mourners did, heisting soil and seats and numbers from the scoreboard.

Fire singed Forbes Field July 17, 1971. Wreckers soon crumpled it. Today home plate, in glass, keys the University of Pittsburgh's Forbes Quadrangle, a large graduate school classroom and office building. A plaque notes where Maz's homer left the park. A red brick path traces the left-field wall. Patches of the center and right-center wall conjure the Waner Bros. and the in-play batting cage. Arriba hovers at Mervix Hall—once right field. The ex-alabaster plaster tops Roberto Clemente Drive.

"I often come back here," Prince said in 1983, two years before his death. "I love what it had"—haze and horizon, pleasant, nearly golden, with pews so near the field that, observing players, you could almost know what they were like. At Schenley Park, memory comes unbidden like a postcard from the past.

13

THE WONDER YEARS

If you couldn't fantasize about being Mickey Mantle in Ike's and JFK's America—forget it, man, you were squaresville, freaked out, out of it (but good). "I wish I was half the player he was," Al Kaline said of No. 7's 1956 Triple Crown (.353, 52 homers, and 130 RBI). Added Casey Stengel of the '56-'57-'62 MVP: "Mantle was better on one leg than anybody else on two."

Like Ruth, No. 7 shunned nuance. On April 17, 1953, Mick wafted the first "tape-measure" homer. In 1956 and '63, he hit the Stadium's third-deck facade. Among Mantle's World Series marks: dingers (18), runs (42), and RBI (40). He made 20 All-Star teams, four times topped the AL in homers and slugging, and twice hit 50 taters. Bunting, Mick could race to first in 3.1 seconds. He swung to go yard. "Not once did I not try to hit it out of the park."

Teresa Brewer's song, "I Love Mickey," spoke to/for most baby boomers. No one could run faster, hit farther, or was hurt more often. "His threshold of pain," said Mel Allen, "was one reason teammates—[Tony] Kubek's a case—idolized him." In 1961, he played despite a hip abscess.

"I'll never forget the Series," said Kubek. "You saw blood oozing through the uniform." Between games of a double header the trainer unwrapped bandages and massaged Mantle's legs. "The circulation came back," said Bobby Richardson. "He'd amaze everybody by coming back on the field."

Mick's father and grandfather had osteomyelitis, a degenerative bone disease. Thomas Wolfe thought he would never die. Mantle thought he would die by 40. Mike Garcia was asked how to pitch Mantle in a close game. His reply hailed the Okie in New York. "Easy. You don't."

Pollster George Gallup says Americans would rather relive the 1950s than any decade of the century. At home, Ike felt that "the road to success must be down the middle." Abroad, forging summitry, he believed that "open skies" could open hearts. At baseball's '56 summit stood old icons and new names. Ernie Banks blasted 28 homers. "Without him," jibed Jimmy Dykes, "the Cubs would finish in Albuquerque." Duke Snider, Stan Musial, and Hank Aaron led in homers (43), RBI (109), and average (.328), respectively. The Man hailed Warren Spahn. "I don't think Spahn will ever get into the Hall of Fame. He'll never stop pitching."

In 1956, Mantle seldom stopped hitting. On May 18, he homered a record third time from both sides of the plate. Twelve days later—Memorial Day—he almost hit a fair ball out of Yankee Stadium. "A couple inches, and he's the first. [The Nats'] Pedro Ramos is pitching," said Bob Wolff. "The ball is rising when it hit the copper frieze." The homer was No. 20: No one had hit that many before June. Chimed Ramos: "If it had not hit the roof, it would have been in Brooklyn."

In August, Yankees general manager George Weiss added Enos Slaughter to the roster. Country's stage was soon phantasmagoric: the last Subway Series. The Classic opened at Ebbets Field. It seemed like '55 again: The home team (Brooklyn) took Games One-Two. Ibid., Three-Four: Bombers, 5–3 (Slaughter hit a three-run blast) and 6–2 (Mantle reached 12 rows above the 407 sign). "It wouldn't have gone over the fence at Ebbets Field," mused Roy Campanella. "Might have gone *through* it, though."

Don Larsen mimed Churchill re: Stalin's Russia—"a riddle wrapped in a mystery inside an enigma." Said Stengel of the 6-foot-4 Hoosier: "He can be one of baseball's great pitchers when he puts his mind to it." On October 8, 1956, before 64,519, Larsen used no windup, needed only 97 pitches, and threw the first Series no-hitter—and perfect game since Charlie Robertson '22. Dale Mitchell's called last strike—Babe Pinelli jabbing the air; Berra's leap into Larsen's arms—has been reshown more than *The Longest Day*. Pee Wee Reese was the sole batter to go 3–2. Only three Dodgers neared a hit: Jackie Robinson, second inning, lashing off Andy Caray's glove to Gil McDougald; Gil Hodges, fifth, lining to Death Valley; Sandy Amoros, the next batter, hooking foul to right.

Hodges' rip would have cleared Ebbets' 351 sign. "In those days," wrote Stan Isaacs, "there was hardly a street corner analysis that wasn't replete with speculation of how the day's particular battle might have gone had it been played in the other ball park. A drive to left-center in Yankee Stadium would have been a home run in Brooklyn; a home run down the short right field in the Stadium would have hit the high fence at Ebbets field. It made a difference." Next day Robinson's hit beat Bob Turley, 1–0. Don Newcombe had been shelled in Game Two. "I want to beat them more than anything else in my life," he said before Match Seven. "I won't rest until I do." Newk left trailing, 5–0. Fans taunted him. Yogi Berra (two two-run homers) *owned* him: 9–0.

The 1947–'56 Subway Series draped 39 games. "They [Brooklyn–New York] had played each other so often, it seemed safe to assume that everything possible had happened. What more could happen?" Isaacs wrote. "Larsen had an answer. He strolled to the mound and retired twenty-seven straight Dodgers. That effort must have destroyed the script maker. There was nothing else to say. So the Yankees and . . . Brooklyn never played another World Series after 1956, at least for the price of a subway ride."

By 1957, baseball bliss meant a meeting with the points of its past: The Yanks won another pennant. Infielder/outfielder Tony Kubek became AL Rookie of the Year. His hometown, Milwaukee, split Series Games One–Six *v.* New York. The Braves' Lew Burdette then beat Larsen, 5–0.

"Only 61,207 saw the finale," noted Harold Rosenthal. "The day before the Dodgers announced their exit. There was a bitterness in New York." It showed in '58: Attendance fell to 1,428,348. Stripes daubed the league: Bob Turley 21–7; Whitey Ford, 2.01 ERA; Ryne Duren, 20 saves; Mantle, 42 homers and 127 runs. Stengel's ninth AL title tied Joe

McCarthy. Again Casey met Milwaukee: behind, three games to one, he turned to Turley, who blanked Burdette, 7–0, and saved Game Six, 4–3. Next day Stengel relieved Larsen in the third: Bombers, 6–2.

"Robert can pitch for me anytime," caroled the Perfessor. Stengel's song soon rang off-key.

Compare the Yankees' 1950s and early '60s. Anomaly: 1959's 79–75 worst-record since 1925. Continuum: Yankee Stadium. "Forget Ralph Lauren," said Dick Young. "The most famous pinstripes were the Yanks'." In 1960, Roger Maris led the league in RBI (112) and slugging (.581. Mantle had 94 and .558.) The Mick topped in runs (119), homers (40), and total bases (294. No. 9 was No. 2: 98, 39, and 290, respectively). As a boy my favorite player was second baseman Bobby Richardson. Dad called him "a fine family man and Christian gentleman." Germane to me was Bobby's smooth sailing on the double play. He hit .252 in the season. In the Series No. 1 had a record 12 RBI. How did Pittsburgh win its first world title since '25? "The question," said Abraham Lincoln, "is not whether God is on our side, but whether we are on God's side."

If you were a Yankees fan, God loved you in '61. Ralph Houk replaced Stengel. The Bombers had 109 wins and a record 240 dingers. Six players hit 20 or more: Maris, 61; Mantle 54; Bill Skowron, 28; Berra, 22; John Blanchard, 21; Elston Howard, 21 (hitting .348). "Dial M for Murder," Allen cried. "If he beats Ruth ['s 60]," vowed Commissioner Ford Frick of Maris, "he must do it in the same [154] number of games." Roger smacked No. 59 in Game 155. (The Yanks played one tie). On October 1, he knifed Tracy Stallard for 61. "Holy cow! What a shot!" Rizzuto said of the fourth-inning/163rd and final-game/right-field blast. Maris, relieved, had exorcised a ghost. "If I never hit another home run, this is one they can never take away from me." He hit 117 more. They never did.

Maris encored as '61 MVP. Ford went 25–4. Luis Arroyo 15–5 had 29 saves. Churchill spoke of "The Terrible Ifs": Yanks defense became a rival's. Like Maris and Mantle, catcher Howard was a star. "Moose at first, Kubek and Bobby up the middle, [Clete] Boyer at third," said Allen. "Ft. Knox had more holes." The Yankees drew a most-since-'51 1,747,725. Mick's thigh infection shelved him for the Series. The Yanks barely noticed, outscoring Cincinnati, 27–13. Ford passed Babe Ruth's Classic streak of 29⅔ scoreless innings.

Allen sighed. "For pure excitement, the day in and out thrills that lift baseball, there may not have been a season like it. Nor, by the way, a team as great as the '61 Yanks."

Sixty-two was a fine play that opened the night after *Hamlet* closed. Richardson got 209 hits and his second of five Gold Gloves. Mantle got the MVP. Ralph Terry led the league in wins (23), starts (39), and innings (298⅔). "I came into the Series [v. San Francisco] with a bad record ['60–'61 0–3]," he said. "You rarely get a second chance." Terry lost Game Two, 2–0. Larsen, now of 'Frisco, not New York, took Match Four, 6–2, at the Stadium on the sixth date of his perfect game. Terry won and Ford lost Games Five-Six, respectively, tying the Series. The Yanks then beat Jack Sanford, 1–0, for title No. 20. "What people remember is rain [for three days before Game Six]," said Willie Mays. The Series ended October 16, lasting 13 days, longest since the '11 A's–Giants. Of '63 a New Yorker recalls a shot, two pitchers, and a team in late bloom.

Mantle hit 536 career homers. None orbited like his 11th-inning/8–7 winning/May 22, 1963, leviathan. "It was still rising when it hit [the facade] two feet from going out," said Allen, "like a plane taking off." The *New York Times* diagrammed the ball. Bill Fischer pitched it. "Six feet over and it would have killed somebody waiting at the station." Right fielder George Alusik didn't move when Mick uncoiled. Next day Fischer said, "You showed me up. Why in the world didn't you turn around or do something—act like you had a chance to catch the ball?" Alusik said, "I wasn't concerned about trying to pretend. I was worried that the ball was hit so hard it'd strike the concrete, knock blocks off, and come down and kill me."

The ball hit the overhang before the TV camera spied it. A Harvard physics professor gauged the flight at 620 feet *sans* facade. "Nobody could do that but Mantle," said Bob Costas, "just like nobody was as famous for a two-strike drag bunt with the infield back." In 1991, Costas entered a Manhattan restaurant after an NBA telecast. It was empty except for two people—Mantle and Billy Crystal, in a corner. For the next four hours Costas and Crystal rehashed No. 7's career. "The whole time Mickey's saying, 'Shoot, I don't remember that, damn, did that really happen, holy sh . . . ' ya know. He *did* it. Billy and I *remembered* it. Tells you something right there."

Stengel nursed the son of a Queens saloonkeeper during the regular season. "I never got more than 33 starts," Ford said. Houk let him pitch. Whitey '61–'63 started 113 games and went 66–19. "Watching him," said Terry, "was like watching a pitching textbook in the flesh."

Once Ford summoned Blanchard to a meeting on the mound.

"What's wrong?" asked Blanchard.

"Nothing," said Whitey.

"Then why bring me out here?"

"Because," said Ford, "I figured you could use the break." Opponents did. The Chairman of the Board won 236 games, lost 106, and had a century-best .690 winning percentage.

Ford '63 went 24–7. Howard became the A.L.'s first black MVP. The Yanks' Grand Event was short (four games) and stunning (a Dodgers sweep). Mantle laughed. "For years Whitey had been the Series. [Records: wins (10), losses (8), starts (2), opening-game starts (8), innings (146), strikeouts (94), walks (34), and scoreless innings (33⅔ straight)]. Then Sandy Koufax comes along"—twice beating Ford. The dynasty was breaking up.

In 1964, Mantle got his 2,000th hit and 450th dinger, homered lefty/righty for a record 10th/final time, and linked 35 homers/111 RBI. On life support, the Yankees won pennant 29 on the next-to-final day. The Series opened at St. Louis: one win apiece. The return east had a bite to its panache. In Game Three, Mantle put Barney Schultz's first ninth-frame pitch in the upper deck. "That's Mick's 16th Series homer, surpassing Ruth," cried NBC's Curt Gowdy of its 2–1 *touché*. Next day the Bombers led, 3–0. Ken Boyer smacked a sixth-inning/game-winning (4–3) grand slam. Tim McCarver was St. Louis catcher. "I still see him nearing third and brother Clete getting in the baseline and almost intentionally forcing him to run behind him as Kenny whacked him on the ass," he said. "It was like Clete saying there's more to life than a Series." The Yanks hoped so. St. Louis won two of the last three games.

In August, CBS had bought 80 percent of the Yankees for $11.2 million. "Think of it. Yogi's 15th Series, Mantle's 12th, Ford's 10th—all last," said Gowdy. Berra, replacing Houk as manager, was fired, replaced by Johnny Keane. The Bombers had graced 15 of the last 18 Series. They now went into mothballs. The closet closed.

The '65ers fell below .500 for the first time since 1925. In September, 50,180 hailed Mickey Mantle Day on his 2,000th game. Mel Stottlemyre, 20–9, became the first pitcher since '10's Deacon Phillippe to hit an inside-the-park-slam. More typical: 6-foot-7 and 255-pound Frank Howard's grenade off Steve Hamilton. "It went over the roof, but barely foul. Nobody's hit a ball like that," said Clete Boyer. "You had to see it to believe it." Ibid., 1966. Houk replaced Keane. New York drew only 1,124,468; on September 22, the Stadium had its smallest-ever crowd (413). The Yanks finished 10th. Ghosts lurched around the tiers.

Understandably, a broadcaster avoided whenever possible anything germane to the score. "It was easy," Joe Garagiola jested, "to drift to subjects outside the park." On occasion he returned. In May 1967, Mantle touched Stu Miller for his 500th homer. From a distance you winced: Where were the *Yankees?* To children weaned on Ford and Mantle, explain Jake Gibbs and Horace Clarke.

The 1930 stripes hit .309 v. '68's .214. Memory mocked the slingshoters in the flesh. Mick retired in 1969. The Yanks retired No. 7. "I always wondered how someone who was dying could say he was the luckiest man on the face of the earth," he told 60,000. "Now I know how Lou Gehrig felt." Bobby Murcer hit .331 in 1971. In '72, New York lured less than a million—966,328—for the first time since '45. The football Giants primed to skip town. "They headed to New Jersey," said Harold Rosenthal. "New York recalled the Dodgers and baseball Giants. They weren't going to lose the Yankees." New 463 and 433 signs draped the alleys. The Stadium exterior changed from green to white. Seats and pillars were painted blue. "The trouble went deeper," added Rosenthal. "Seats and aisles were too narrow. The infrastructure and amenities stank."

The solution was Ruthian. The '73 Yankees closed his house. Shipbuilder George Steinbrenner and friends bought the team for $10 million. Ron Blomberg became baseball's first designated hitter. Attendance leapt to 1,262,103. On September 30, 32,238, including Ruth's and

Gehrig's widows, watched the last game: Yanks 8, Detroit 5. Thousands stormed the field. Dirt and grass and bases vanished. The Yanks left for Shea Stadium, signed Catfish Hunter, and finished second and third. The Stadium began a $100 million facelift.

In October 1973, Alan Hague of New Milford, Connecticut, and a cousin drove to Yankee Stadium. Several blue wooden seats lay behind the right-field gate. Hague gave a guard $50. Arriving home, an uncle laughed: "What are you guys going to do with those pieces of junk?" It seemed an allegory for the past ten years.

MEMORIAL COLISEUM

An October 1959 cartoon showed a Brooklynite crying at Ebbets Field. The text quoted Ernest Thayer's *Casey at the Bat*. "Somewhere the sun is shining, somewhere hearts are light." At that moment the Bums were hosting the World Series v. Chicago. "Somewhere" meant baseball's most bizarre chalet.

The Los Angeles Memorial Coliseum was modeled after the 50,000-seat Roman Colosseum, built in A.D. 82. (Two stones from Rome and the Altis in Olympia, Greece, graced the peristylum atop the right-center bleachers at one end of the oval.) The ex-gravel pit, armory, agricultural park, and museum opened in 1923. It expanded to 74,000 for the '32 Summer Olympics. "Before that it housed saloons, livestock, and burlesque," said *Los Angeles Times* columnist Jim Murray. Later, it portended Walter O'Malley's Alley a.k.a. Chinese Theater.

Brooklyn's anti-Christ at first eyed the Rose Bowl. Armageddon: Its design aped the *Polo Grounds*! "Ten rows would have been removed in right and left to deepen the lines to 300 feet, and center field would have been 460," Dodgers announcer Jerry Doggett noted. The field would have been symmetrical (home plate in one end zone; center, the other) and box seats put behind the plate (and along first and third). Instead, O'Malley spurned Pasadena for L.A. "Twice we'd been close to getting big-league ball," said Murray of the 1941 and '53 St. Louis Browns. "First, the Japanese bombed Pearl Harbor. The second time the L.A. Coliseum Commissioner told baseball to get lost." O'Malley's choice at Exposition Boulevard, Merlo Avenue, Santa Barbara Avenue (now Martin Luther King, Jr., Drive) and South Figueroa Street made Ebbets Field look sane.

"The problem is that the Coliseum was a football and track and field place[debuting with '23 USC]," explained Vin Scully. "And football and baseball demand different configurations." The Dodgers carved sunken dugouts, a wire screen, and huge tunnel behind the plate. O'Malley spent $200,000 for three banks of lights to illumine the infield. The four-foot-high concrete wall around the field forged the right-field line (301/300 feet '58–'59). The wall veered to form a right-center Fenway belly: 390 and 333 in '59—"it was so far, they brought it in," said Doggett—and 340 in '60. An 8-foot-high inner fence moored right-center: 440-375-394-380 ('58-'59-'60-'61. Center was 425 [420 '59]. Duke Snider panted for Brooklyn.). The fence intersected the concrete left-center wall: 425 (417 '59). A Sahara divided the fence and bleachers. The catch was intimacy: Ebbets oozed; the Coliseum flunked.

Ask a New Yorker to recall Memorial Coliseum. He will curse the tiny left-field line: 250 ('58) and 251 ('59). O'Malley built a tater-dimming '58–'59 40–42-foot-high screen. The Screen a.k.a. Bamboo Curtain/Great Wall of China reached 140 feet to left-center (320), angling to the ground at 348. (Its cables, towers, and wires were in play.) Some feared for Ruth's 1927 record. Publicly, Babe's ex-ghost shrugged. "I do not think his record is in particular danger," said Ford Frick. "Foul lines are not especially important where home runs are concerned. The other distances in left-center and right determine the number of homers." Privately, he winced. "He had this absurd idea," said Murray, "to build a *second* screen 333 feet from the plate in the *stands*. If you clear both screens, it's a homer; the first, a double. Happily, the California Earthquake Law forbade its creation."

The USC Trojans worked out before the Dodgers. "It was the first time baseball played there," laughed Pee Wee Reese. "They could have told us what we had in store." First-base stands almost touched the line. By contrast, third's lay off Catalina Island. Said third baseman Jim Gilliam: "I'd run a mile and still not see a fan." The rim lay 110 feet from ground level. The field lay 33 feet below. Baseball seemed so otherworldly—back rows needed binoculars to spy home plate—that many brought radios to *hear* what they couldn't *see*.

In 1950, Scully began at Ebbets Field. Ultimately, he was named "the most memorable personality in franchise history." His voice used the transistor to beguile, explain, soothing, then regressing. "People were so far away," he said, "that I guess I gave them some connection with the game." They gave him a cyclopean audience.

"Until '58 the closest big-league ball we'd ever had was sixteen hundred miles away in St. Louis," said Murray. "So the Dodgers had a selling job to do, and Vinnie more than anbody did it." Writer Rick Reilly asked, "Does Los Angeles love Vinnie? Vinnie doesn't *do* the Dodgers. Vinnie *is* the Dodgers. Forget video. From April to October, Scully's musings drift up from every traffic jam and outdoor café. He may be the single largest influence on transistor radio sales in Los Angeles."

In 1960, spectators serenaded umpire Frank Secory. "It was a particularly dull game," Vin said, "and so I started looking through the press guide and noticed that it was Frank's birthday. So I said over the radio, 'I'll count to three and everybody yell, 'Happy Birthday, Frank.' "

Scully: "One, two, three."

The Coliseum's cast of thousands: "Happy birthday, Frank!"

The Dodgers had televised each game at Ebbets Field. In California, O'Malley banned all free home TV. The reversal gave Vin a deep and abiding leverage. It boosted attendance, which buoyed interest, which accented radio, of which Scully was a wizard. His script merged the Coliseum's absurdities, improbabilities, and preposterous cant.

On April 18, 1958, a Nationals-record 78,682 packed its opener. "Giants–Dodgers. What a way to start!" said Scully. "After tying the game in the ninth, Jim Davenport was called out for failing to touch third." L.A.: 6–5. There but for the grace: In June, the "Dodger Referendum" to let the city sell 300 acres of Chavez Ravine to O'Malley passed by only 24,293 votes. "If this bill fails, the Dodgers will leave Los Angeles," yapped NL president Warren Giles. Instead, the seventh-placers drew 1,845,556 v. '57's 1,028,556. Snider dropped from 40 to 15 homers. Roy Campanella broke his neck in a car accident that left him paralyzed in both arms and legs. On May 9, 1959, the bigs' largest-ever crowd, 93,103, cheered Campy, wheeled by Reese from the tunnel. Upon a signal lights dimmed and each person lit a candle. "Baseball's only bigger crowd," said Hall of Fame librarian Jack Redding, "was in 1936 [Berlin's Olympia Stadium, before 108,000, for a U.S. amateur game]."

The Coliseum bulged August 8, 1959: 90,751 (67,132 paid) *v.* Milwaukee. Three weeks later 82,974 watched Koufax K a record-tying 18 Giants. Charlie Neal and Wally Moon each zapped a league-high 11 triples. Snider had 23 homers and 88 RBI. On September 15, "[Milwaukee's] Joe Adcock cleared the screen but the ball struck a girder and lodged in an overlapping wire screen," observed Scully. "The umpires ruled it a double. Then they ruled it a homer when fans shook the screen and the ball landed in the seats behind. Then they reversed themselves." Adcock never scored. L.A. won in the 10th inning. "If it's a homer, the Braves win the pennant by two games." Instead, they tied (86–68). L.A. took a best-of-three playoff, 3–2 and 6–5.

Don't judge a book by its cover. Chicago won the World Series opener, 11–0. In Game Two, L.A. nipped Sherm Lollar at the plate to kill a rally: 4–3. The convention moved west. The White Sox stranded 11 runners, losing, 3–1. Next day Gil Hodges parked a pitch over the Screen: 5–4. Koufax then lost, 1–0. The Coliseum rocked to record crowds of 92,394, 92,650, and 92,706. "There was so much to disturb us," said the Sox' Luis Aparicio. "The white-shirted background, the noise, coolie hats everywhere, those crazy dimensions." The Dodgers won Game Six, 9–3, at Comiskey Park, and the Series, four games to two. Each winning player got a record $11,231 share.

O'Malley bought Chavez Ravine in February 1960. "He overpaid [$494,000 for $92,000 valued property]," Murray wrote, "while his team underplayed [fourth]." The Angelenos drew an NL-record 2,253,887. Most drove from downtown: 10 minutes in light traffic; 30, peak. Parking helped: 5,100 and 3,000 state- and private-owned spots. "For big crowds, people would rent their front lawns." As many as 500 vendors patrolled the cyclops. "We frown on gratuities," Allied Maintenance warned ushers. "A man caught accepting tips is given a couple of days off to remember." Scrubs sold the Coliseum's charbroiled hamburgers and French-dip sandwich (roast beef and ham).

Sales zoomed on a Giants visit. "Later, the rivalry faded," Doggett said, "but at first it was like back east." Willie Mays hurt the Dodgers—except when Jocko Conlan umped. "Jocko was a great umpire who for some reason wouldn't call Willie safe," mused Murray. One night habit whipsawed L.A.. John Roseboro homered over the right-center inner fence. Coliseum lighting was oxymoronic: Jocko couldn't see the ball. "Did it go over the fence?" he asked Mays. "No," Willie answered, "it went through a [nonexistent] hole in the fence." Roseboro got a ground-rule double. Another Dodger later led off third. A fly followed to right fielder Felipe Alou. "Alou lost it in the sun," said manager Walter Alston, "but Mays covered so much ground that he caught the ball in straightaway right, threw to the plate, and kept the guy from scoring." A writer asked if the play was planned. The only plan—Mays—was God's.

"Historically, we shall be proven right," O'Malley said of moving to Los Angeles. By the end of 1961 the Coliseum had drawn 8,400,676 since '58. *Vindication?* It was *absolution*. That August 16 the Dodgers wooed an NL-twi-night-doubleheader-high 72,140. Koufax set a league Ks record (269, topping Christy Mathewson's 267). The Coliseum closed September 20: Sandy over the Cubs, 3–2, in 13 innings, before 12,068. O'Malley didn't care. Flacks were already terming his next home "baseball's Taj Mahal."

SEALS STADIUM

In 1958, the Giants swapped Coogan's Bluff for steep-pitched Seals Stadium. A Hamms Brewery belched nearby. A breeze blew from right to left. San Francisco scheduled mostly afternoon matches. Bayholders wore coolie hats to block the sun. Candlestick Park would be ready—when? Until then, Giants-watchers had airy, if thimble, fun.

Stu Smith worked for Giants radio flagship KSFO. "Seals was a San Francisco trademark, and this town is protective of its heritage," he said. "The park had charm and history." The Pacific Coast League Seals won or shared 14 pennants or playoff titles, including 1957. Joe DiMaggio and Lefty O'Doul grew up and played there. The '46ers' 670,563 outdrew the '57 Giants.

"Why didn't the Giants expand Seals and stay there?" a reporter asked Smith in 1975.

"There was talk, but there wasn't much parking. The problem was even if you, say, doubled its capacity, where would you put the club during renovation?"

Before 1958, ads dotted the left and left-center-field wall. A pavilion abutted the right-field fence. The hitter's backdrop keyed center's. "We needed more seating," said 1958–'78 and 1996–voice Lon Simmons, "so we put bleachers in left and left-center. The overflow crunched between them and the fence." The new park sat 22,900. Lengths careened: left and left-center, 365 and 376 (361 and 364 '59), respectively; left and right of center, 404 and 415; center, 410 (400 '59). Seats further right (397) jutted toward the infield. Right measured 355 (350 '59). A Longines clock topped the scoreboard. On April 15, 1958, Ruben Gomez retired the Dodgers' Gino Cimoli in Seals' NL debut. Daryl Spencer whipped the first homer; Giants win, 8–0; 23,192 booed L.A.

"If this kid doesn't make it," Horace Stoneham said of Orlando Cepeda, "I'll give the franchise away." Baghdaders cheered Baby Bull and Jim Davenport and Felipe Alou. "[Unlike Willie Mays] they weren't New York's," said Smith. "They matured here." In '58, Cepeda coupled 96 RBI and NL-high 38 doubles. Stu Miller's 2.47 ERA led the league. Mays linked 350 total bases, 11 triples, 208 hits, a career-high .347, and league-best 31 steals and 121 runs. The Giants placed third—"their first of 14 straight years[longer than any New York skein] over .500," added Simmons. Attendance almost doubled to 1,272,625.

Cepeda had a wild and violent swing. Willie McCovey was a phenom. On July 30, 1959, he reported from Phoenix hitting .372. Stretch went 4-for-4, including two triples, off Robin Roberts, finished with 13 homers, 38 RBI, and .354 in 192 at-bats, and became Rookie of the Year. The Bull and Say-Hey hit .317 and .313, respectively. Sad Sam Jones and Johnny Antonelli went 40–25. That year the Bay Area sold more than 500,000 transistors. The fuss led one holdout to mutter, "Good God! People will think we're like *Milwaukee* or something!" Smith forged a half-smile. "You'd walk down the street and hear baseball from a dozen directions. A restaurant—they'd have it on. Go to the opera—people wearing earplugs. Because we played so many games in the afternoon, it just flooded offices, bars, cable cars. Women, especially, went batty. In a supermarket, they'd hear the game on a radio at the meat counter, and wouldn't leave for the vegetable aisle until, say, Duke Snider fanned."

In September 'Frisco led the league. A city quivered. Where would the *Series* go? Seals was too small. The new park wasn't ready. The homestanders finished third, wiling 1,422,130, or 81 percent of capacity. "There was innocence to this bandbox," said Simmons. "People loved it." Their next home earned more contempt than Don Drysdale beaning the Bull.

CANDLESTICK PARK

No park had more pseudonyms: the Stick, Cave of the Winds, Wind Tunnel, Croix de Candlestick, and North Pole. Few bore more pain or seemed amnesiac toward charm. How did Candlestick Park a.k.a. 3Com Park become baseball's most ridiculed locale? The old-fashioned way. It earned it.

That, of course, was not the Giants' plan. San Francisco's first baseball game inked February 22, 1860. Its sally toward the bigs began almost a century later. In November 1954, voters backed a $4 million bond issue for a new park "contingent on the city getting a big-league team." By May 1957, Mayor George Christopher asked for surveys of possible sites. Contractor Charles Harney offered ground at Candlestick Point, overlooking San Francisco Bay, noted for jagged rocks and trees that rose like candlesticks. "In eight months," he said, "we'll have it built." Harney got $30 per square foot to scrap 300,000 feet of the Bay View Hill. Horace Stoneham toured the point with Christopher and said, "No cold, no wind, no problems." Groundbreaking started at the first bigs park built exclusively of reinforced concrete. Problems soon swung away.

Property owners fought widening streets for traffic. In September 1958, a grand jury probed hanky-panky. Said a writer: "There is some question about the payment for Harney's land." Teamsters struck, delaying seating. Opening receded to at least '59. In January 1960, the City Fire Prevention Bureau called Candlestick a "fire trap." A month later the Giants moved to their seaside home, five miles south of downtown, named in a contest by the City Recreation and Parks Commission. "Two months before the season started," Stoneham sniffed, "and we're using the players clubhouse for our temporary office."

When it opened, said Simmons, Candlestick had already fizzled. "They asked why it was put on the water, where it was as cold as anywhere in the city, terrible wind. 'Jesus,' you know, 'is that all there is?' "

California's then-governor disagreed. "San Francisco has always been a city of giants," Edmund G. (Pat) Brown said April 12, 1960—Opening Day. "Now we have a home for them." First pitcher: Sam Jones. Batter: Joe Cunningham. Hit: St. Louis' Bill White. Homer: mate Leon Wagner. Score: S.F., 3–1. Mays singled and tripled for three RBI. A crowd of 42,269, including Mrs. John McGraw, Vice-President Richard Nixon, and Ford Frick filled the 42,533-seat plot. Some parked in lots built by leveled rock outcroppings in the bay. Many came by helicopter, yacht, or cabin cruiser. All saw a rivalry-renewing rhubarb.

"Foul poles should be parts fair and foul," said Giants skipper Bill Rigney. "Later Dodger Stadium opened['62]. Its foul poles were screwed up—all in foul territory. Candlestick opens, and they're screwed up in an opposite way—all *fair*!" Consulting Rig, the umps were told to get off. "If you don't like 'em there, get a shovel," Rigney said. "Dig a hole, and put 'em where you want 'em." The '60ers drew 1,795,356. Mays' three triples in a game set a bigs record. Juan Marichal threw a one-hitter in his debut. The Stick became a belly laugh.

The Point was cold at night. Thus, Stoneham played most games by day in "the only heated open-air stadium in the world." Candlestick built a natural-gas fired boiler system for 20,000 reserved seats. The 35,000 feet of 0.75-inch pipe didn't work. One man sued because "I had to leave my seat during several rallies because my feet were freezing." Stoneham said the Giants hadn't built the system: A jury awarded $1,597. Spencer Tracy hoped to inherit the wind. The Giants sought to junk it. Wind skirted Bay View Hill, blew from left-center toward home, then swirled toward right-center. "A natural wind tunnel," said Cepeda. Mays said Candlestick cost him 150 homers. A lefty, on the other hand, liked drives in the air.

The early park was symmetrical: lines, 330; alleys, 397; center, 420. A cyclone fence stood 10 feet around. By 1961, wind forced Stoneham to cut Death Valley: center, 410; left-center, 365. "A fence was strung up[from left-center to left's pole]," said announcer Russ Hodges. Bleachers sat more than 30 feet beyond. A homer into No-Man's Land drew children, panting for the ball. "The irony is that O'Malley had convinced Stoneham to come here—'a gold rush,' he promised," Simmons laughed. "Soon O'Malley had beautiful Dodger Stadium, and Horace had this dump."

The sun shone, then vanished. A visitor traded lotion for a fedora. "That damn wind," said McCovey, "keeps blowing peanut shells in my eyes." Caps flew off players' heads. Birds dive-bombed pitchers. Hot dog wrappers fused in the outfield corners. Stoneham, desperate, ordered a study. "Changing the shape of the stadium would not only change the directions of the winds," it read. "If the winds had been checked before construction, the stadium might have been shifted a few hundred yards to a more comfortable site." Great, said Horace: At two years of age, Candlestick was obsolete.

Two tiers of plastic fold-up seats stretched from one corner to another. The lower level sloped more gradually. "If anyone is too tall," wrote the San Francisco Chronicle, "they block your view." Foul turf was mammoth. Almost every seat was too far from the field. "There was hardly anything good about it," said Simmons. "If it's cold at the [Oakland A's 1968–] Coliseum, it's bitter at Candlestick. If it's a breeze at the Coliseum, it's a gale here. In most parks, you got fans that say on a gorgeous night, 'Let's go out and see a game.' It's a pleasant time. When the Giants won, they drew—but nobody went out to Candlestick for a pleasant time."

In 1961, general admission seats raised size to 43,765. Most were filled: The Stick's first eight years averaged 1,537,506. "The trick was to look *past* the park," said columnist Bob Stevens. "A lot of clubs have nobody worth going to see. Then, we had almost too many." Start with 23 years, 3,283 hits, 660 homers, and .302 average; 11 Gold Gloves, four World Series, and record-tying 24 All-Star Games; four slugging, four homer, and two runs scored titles; and the basket catch, coiled swing, and *mot* "Say-Hey." Ernie Harwell has called baseball for 54 years. "I'm often asked," he said, "who's the greatest player I ever saw. My answer is Mays." Four and six times, respectively, he led the league in steals and smacked 40 or more homers. In center, said Ralph Kiner, "Willie's where triples go to die."

One night a two-out ninth-inning pop headed to shallow right. Felipe Alou charged in, and Chuck Hiller back. Mays knifed between them, caught the ball off the ground, and sprinted toward the dugout. Cepeda laughed: "They're [Alou and Hiller] both lookin' for it [ball] and Willie's in the shower!" Another game was scoreless in the eighth. Mays led off first base. Jim Ray Hart singled to left. Normally, the runner stops at second. Mays tore toward third. Houston third baseman Bob Aspromonte took the cutoff throw and glared at the left fielder. "It's like he was saying," said Simmons, " 'How can you let this guy go to third on a hit to left?' " The glare spurred Mays toward home. "He wasn't trying to steal, there's no error, the ball was a single—and Mays scored from first!"

Marichal won, 1–0, high-kicking like Gwen Verdon by way of Gower Champion to hurl a no-hitter, twice lead the NL in complete games and shutouts, make 10 All-Star teams, win 20 games five times, and finish 243–132 with a 2.89 ERA. Relieving, Juan debuted in '58 Class A: bases loaded and none out. The Dominican, 18, spoke little English. The shortstop translated his Spanish to manager Buddy Kerr. "Juan wants to know where you want him to throw the ball." Kerr answered, tongue in cheek: "Well, low and outside corner is pretty good." Nine outside and low strikes later the prodigy left the mound.

Once Marichal blanked the Dominican's Air Force team, 1–0. It drafted him the same week. Later he lost, 1–0, and was tossed in the Air Force brig. The *Giants* did less losing after 1960. In '61, Mays got a bigs-high $85,000, led the league with 129 runs, and went yard four times in a game. The third-placers' 1,390,679 trailed only L.A. Cepeda bloomed: .311 and NL-best 46 homers and 142 RBI. Ultimately, Cha Cha batted .297, lashed 379 homers, and entered Cooperstown in '99. McCovey's plaque lists 18 grand slams, 1969 MVP, and 521 dingers. Said Stevens: "Our guys were so good, you almost forgot the weather."

In 1961, Candlestick hosted its first All-Star Game: NL, 5–4, on 10th-inning hits by Hank Aaron, Mays, and Roberto Clemente. "Household names," said Simmons, "but what people remember is reliever Stu Miller, balking in the ninth. A gale came up and moved Stu an inch or two." Headlines blared: "Miller Blown off Mound!" It was better to blow off the Dodgers. The '62ers read "The Miracle of Coogan's Bluff" like an understudy miming Streisand.

On September 30, Mays's 47th dinger edged Houston, 2–1. The

Giants then turned on the radio. The hated Scully coursed from Chavez Ravine. Gene Oliver's homer beat Los Angeles, 1–0, and forced a best-of-three playoff. 'Frisco coasted in Game One, 8–0. The Dodgers then won baseball's then–longest-ever nine-inning game—4 hours and 18 minutes—8–7. L.A. led the decider, 4–2, in the ninth inning. "All that effort for what?" Mays remembered thinking. Actually, so the Giants could score four runs: 6–4. A walk scored the clincher. Willie flung the final out into Dodger Stadium's seats. "A City Goes a Bit Whacky," blared the *Examiner*. More than 70,000 jammed the airport. Jack Sanford went 24–7. Mays led in homers (49) and total bases (383). Recalling '51, the Stonehams met the Yankees in the Transcontinental (née Subway) Series.

"It's a relief—to win [6–2, before 43,852 at Candlestick] and have it over with [his Series scoreless streak at 33⅔ innings]," said Whitey Ford after the opener. The Giants tied, 2–0: Sanford winning and McCovey going long. The teams then twice traded wins. New York led Game Seven, 1–0, in the ninth. Matty Alou pinch-dragged a bunt single. Ralph Terry Kd Felipe Alou and Hiller. Mays then lashed into the right-field corner. "The grass was wet," said Willie, "or it would have got past [Roger] Maris."

Manager Ralph Houk grilled his pitcher. Should Terry pitch to McCovey or walk him, filling the bases, and face right-handed Cepeda? In 1960, the righty had yielded Bill Mazeroski's Series-winning poke. "[Now] my heart was in my throat." McCovey ripped his first pitch to right—far enough, but foul. He took a ball, then lined to second baseman Bobby Richardson. "A foot either way, we win," said Willie. The unfairness seemed of a piece with the park.

Jon Miller, 11, was sitting in a dentist's chair. "Given the pain that Candlestick gave us," he said years later, "it was the right place to be." The future Giants voice grew up in nearby Half Moon Bay. "Friends would say, 'Let's go surfing.' " Jon's response: "Hey, I got a big series [on the baseball board game, Stratomatic]. Dodgers and Giants finally meet at Dodger Stadium—first place for grabs. If there's any way I'd be with you—but hey."

Jon fixed on becoming the next Russ Hodges. The real Russ was, shall, we say, an epicure of hooch. "Here's what we'll do," he told colleagues. "If we win the game we'll drink because we're happy. If we lose

we'll drink because we're sad. The only way we won't drink is if we tie."
One night Giants catcher Hobie Landrith's extra-inning throw sailed
into center to tie a game. Moments later the curfew hour struck. Said
Hodges: "We're just gonna' break a rule."

Warren Spahn hoped merely for a break. On July 2, 1963, Mays dingered, 1–0, for Marichal over Spahn—the NL longest-decided-by-a
homer game (16 innings). McCovey bashed a league-high 44 taters. Juan
went 25–7, had a 2.41 ERA, and no-hit Houston. A year later Masanori
Murakami became the bigs' first Japanese.

Hodges chanted "Bye, bye, baby!" upon each homer. The Giants' peopled an orphanage. In 1964, Cepeda and Jim Ray Hart had 31 apiece.
McCovey smacked 39 in '65. That season Mays' best in a Burma Road
of years linked MVP, NL-high homers (52), on-base (.399), and slugging
(.645), and league record for taters in a month (17, August).

On August 17, Marichal batted v. Koufax. John Roseboro was catching. "He threw the ball back too close to my ear," said Marichal, who
promptly clubbed him with the bat. The fight that then ensured was worthy of Flatbush or the Polo Grounds. (Batman was suspended eight games
and fined $1,750.) "The rivalry!" said Miller. "It was alive on the field and
in the stands." E.g., the '65–'66 Giants almost, but not quite, beat L.A.

Mays hit homer 512 (passing Mel Ott as NL leader) and 534 (tying
Jimmie Foxx as then-righty big). Go figure. On July 3, 1966, Atlanta
pitcher Tony Cloninger had two grand slams and 9 RBI. Marichal and
Gaylord Perry were 46–14. The Giants finished second. Flower children
dotted San Francisco. Mike McCormick won the '67 Cy Young award.
Attendance fell from 1,657,192 to 1,242,480. The Giants finished second. In 1968, Marichal led the league in wins (26), innings (326), and
complete games (20). On September 17–18, Perry and St. Louis' Bay
Washburn no-hit each other's team. The A's invaded the Bay Area from
Kansas City. The Giants finished second, drawing 837,220. "Bye, bye,
baby" seemed a wake, not tune.

WRIGLEY FIELD (LOS ANGELES)

Watching television in late 1959, I turned to my grandfather and asked
which show he liked best. He removed his cigar and thought a moment.

I expected him to name *Gunsmoke* or *Bonanza*. Instead, he said, "Guess I like that *Home Run Derby*," taped at Los Angeles' Wrigley Field. The program aired weekly that offseason. One show blared Colavito v. Mantle; another, Killebrew and Mays. Host Mark Scott died after the first year's taping. It remains a Woodstock for baby boomers. We remember. We were there.

Actually, we would have been in the then-22,000-seat park at Los Angeles' Avalon Boulevard, San Pedro Street, and 41st and 42nd Place. Center (412) and the lines (340 and 339) suggested *big*-league derby. "Why do you tape it here?" Scott was asked of Wrigley field. He said: "The fences aren't that high [14½ feet from left to center; 9 right]. Even more, alleys are a breeze [345]." Home runs must bloom for "Derby" to thrive.

In 1921, William Wrigley, Jr., bought the PCL Angels. They played at Washington Park till Los Angeles refused to build an underground parking site. The Cubs squire then designed a new $1.1 million park: "It will be a miniature version of Chicago's North side." Ivy covered the outfield wall. An in-play light tower anchored left-center field. Bleachers decked right-center. A trademark office tower abutted the grandstand behind home.

Wrigley West was dedicated September 27, 1925. The junior Cubs buoyed the PCL into the '50s. "Under the rules of the time, they had territorial big-league rights to the area," said Jerry Doggett. Walter O'Malley swapped his Ft. Worth Texas League club for the Angels—and park. "It was preparatory to his moving to Los Angeles," Doggett added. What might have been: a '57 sketch likened Wrigley to the Polo Grounds— enclosed, twin-tiered into left and right field, and center-field seating. "But it was too small," said Jim Murray. O'Malley chose the Coliseum.

In 1958, the Angels transferred to Spokane. The American League panted for the nation's third-largest town. On October 21, 1960, Nixon and Kennedy staged their last debate. Six days later the AL's ended: It jumped to 10 teams (adding L.A. and Washington) and adopted a 162-game schedule (playing each team 18 times). A group headed by singing cowboy Gene Autry and ex–football star Bob Reynolds bought the franchise. By spring 1961 *Sports Illustrated* wrote: "News from the Angels camp was wholesome and happy. The players were hustling like mad, spirit was at a frenzied peak, the weather was delightful. It was one for all, all for one, and we're gonna' win our share."

The Angels started 1–7 on the road. The home opener was a bust:

Twins, 4–2. Tom Morgan then won, 4–2. First expansion pick Eli Grba went 11–13. Fences shared—and shared alike. Five Halos hit 20 or more homers: Leon Wagner (28), Ken Hunt (25), Lee Thomas (24), Steve Bilko (22), and Earl Averill (21). Albie Pearson revived dead-ball subtlety (.422 on-base). Most were as discreet as the San Andreas fault. Wrigley's 248 dingers set a big-league record. (Oddly, Roger Maris hit just two there of 61). Attendance flagged: 606,510. Only the Yankees filled their well (19,930 August 22; the '33 Angels v. Hollywood drew 24,695).

The last weekend typified L.A.'s malaise. The Halos beat Cleveland, 6–1 and 11–6. Furious, Tribe general manager Gabe Paul fired manager Jimmy Dykes. Ryne Duren then lost Wrigley's final, 8–5, his 13th defeat, before just 9,868. Wagner and Bilko homered. "It'd be great for softball," Duren said years later. Today its plot houses the Gilbert Lindsay Park. Does *Home Run Derby* waft across the infield? Here's to slug-at-all-cost ball.

METROPOLITAN STADIUM

Like the field of dreams in W. P. Kinsella's *Shoeless Joe,* two big-league parks rose from a cornfield. Keokuk, Iowa's Perry's Park, home of the National Association Westerns, opened in 1875. Metropolitan Stadium rose from rivalry: Minneapolis and St. Paul, on opposite sides of the Mississippi River.

St. Paul got a jump with the '84 Union Association. By 1902, both cities joined the American Association. "The Saints played at Lexington Park," said longtime writer Halsey Hall, "the [Minneapolis] Millers, Nicollet Park." Nicollet treated pitching like Billy Graham does sin. In 1935, Joe Hauser bopped a then-record 60 homers (50 at home). Most cleared right (280 feet) or right-center field (328). The Saints won nine flags before leaving Lexington in 1956. A year earlier the Millers dumped Nicollet.

"By now," Hall mused, "both cities were thinking majors." The Saints went marching to $2 million 10,000-seat Midway Stadium. Minneapolis chose $4.5 million 18,200-seat Metropolitan Stadium—the Met—at Cedar Avenue, West 78th Street (later, Killebrew Drive), 24th Avenue South, and a cornfield. "It was only partly done," said Horace Stoneham, buying the Millers in '48, "because of an explosion and two fires."

He called it "the finest minor-league park in the country, and there are not over two in the majors that are better." Among them: neither Ebbets Field nor the Polo Grounds.

"We thought they might come here," Hall said of the Giants. Squabbling hurt. "We had two cities with minor-league parks that wanted ball." Each needed a *big*-league den. Midway was too small. The Met lay between the Twin Cities. A 1957 exhibition lured 21,687. "I liked the park," boomed Senators owner Calvin Griffith, "the people, how they don't have a lot to do." In October 1960, the Nats of Washington since 1901 became the Twins. To the capital, they looked like a two-headed monster.

Like L.A.'s Wrigley, the Met was a *hitter's* park. Left field measured 329 (330 in '62, 344, 346 in '67, 330, and 343 in '77). Left-center traded 365 for 360 in '66, 373, 350, 346 ('76), and 360 ('77). Hurlers survived by pitching straightaway: deep left-center 402 became 430 in '65, 430 in '68, 410 in '75, and 406 in '76. Deep left-center and right-center corners tailored 430 '65 (left, 406 in '75). Center field dealt 412 for 430 ('76), 425, 410, and 420 ('77); right-center, 365, 373 ('68), 365, and 370 ('77); right, 329 for 330 in '62. "You tried to pull," said Harmon Killebrew. Right field's 330-foot sign lay near right-center. "That had to mean the pole was actually less." The ball carried well—and needn't carry high. Center's wire fence stood eight feet tall. (Left's and right's rose from 8 to 12.)

The Met became a *family* park. "Down-home," said Hall, and built in stages (30,637 in '61 through 45,959 in '75). The triple-deck cantilever had no posts, a few out-of-the-way seats, and a skeletal feel. Mused Hall: "You could see this was once minor league": two tiers from right to third base; pavilion beyond the bag; third deck behind the plate; single and two-tiered right- and left-field bleachers; and center scoreboard. Buses served the Twin Cities. Most came by car. The parking lot had 14,000 slots. Andy Frain ushers patrolled the stands (no tipping). Farmers and businessmen and women with curlers filled the Midwest meeting place. Cows grazed beyond the bleachers.

The *regional* park exteriorized Northland ball. Three 50,000-watt radio stations—WHO, Des Moines; WOW, Omaha; and flagship WCCO, "The Good Neighbor to the Northwest"—berthed a network of 55 stations in seven states and an extra 15 in the Rocky Mountain area on weekends. "You'd go to the parking lot on Saturday or Sunday," said 1961–'66 voice Ray Scott, "and there'd be license plates from Colorado, Idaho, Wyoming to Illinois." Few dreamt that the Twins would one day move inside. "It was a time when baseball was relatively new, and thus tremendously popular," said Hall. "Plus, we had a lot of big-namers, and the game here bombed away."

Their brigade debuted in the Bronx: 6–0, behind Camilo Pascual, April 11, 1961. The Met opened April 21, before 24,606: The *expansion* Senators, 5–3! It combined longing (for homers; Killebrew hit 46 and Bob Allison 29; lengths were measured and announced) and belonging (the 1955–'60 Nats drew 2,722,790; the '61ers alone, 1,256,723.). Baltimore's Jim Gentile hit grand-slam homers in successive innings. Griffith would have traded his right arm for a left arm. One day lefty Ralph Lumenti was flinging darts. A Twins scout marveled, "No control—but what a fastball." Lumenti proceeded to walk three batters. The scout said, "If they ever move the strike zone to high and outside we're seeing a future Hall of Famer." Later, Killebrew faced Don Drysdale in an exhibition. A fastball decked him—"feet up in the air, bat flying," said Scott, "never said a word." Killer rose, froze the bat, and homered. Eight years he hit 40 or more—573, in all. "Harmon never gave Drysdale the benefit of a dirty look—just rounded the bases and touched the plate."

In 1962, Killebrew paced the AL in dingers (48) and RBI (126). He and Bob Allison became the first mates to grand-slam in the same inning. Pascual topped in complete games, Ks, and shutouts (with teammate Jim Kaat). First baseman Vic Power won his fifth of seven straight Gold Gloves. The Twins hosted 1,433,116, placed second, and led till a Yanks July 8–10 series. The '63ers got A.-L.-high: Allison (99 runs), shortstop Zoilo Versalles (13 triples), Killer (45 homers and .555 slugging), and team taters (225). Pitching failed: The Twins drudged third, then sixth. Tony Oliva fronted in five categories, including average (.323) in 1964. In '65, the *Griffiths* fronted.

"A pennant [in year five]," Calvin blew. "If I knew it would come this soon, I'd have moved years ago." Mudcat Grant's 21 wins led the AL Ibid., Oliva's .321 and MVP Versalles's 308 total bases, 12 triples, and 126 runs. On July 11, the Twins trailed New York, 5–4, in the ninth.

"The Yankees were champions, but on the ropes," said Killebrew. "We were in first, and had won the previous two games." He homered: 6–5. In New York, I was listening: The dynasty was dead; my radio seemed to quiver. Two days later the Met hosted the 1965 All-Star Game: Harmon homered to the second deck—"Killer Country." NL, 6–5, before 46,705.

The Series was as close. Grant beat Drysdale, 8–2: Don Mincher and Versalles homered. Kaat clipped Sandy Koufax, 5–1. "What helped," Twins manager Sam Mele said, "was Allison's great catch off Jim Lefebvre [diving near the left-field line]." The Dodgers won three straight at home. Grant's Game Six dinger evened the Classic, 5–1. "We are all mortal," John F. Kennedy said in a nuclear test ban treaty address. Not Sandy. On two days' rest he won Game Seven, 2–0, before a Met's-largest 50,596. (Its smallest crowd, 537, watched the A's September 20.)

There they go again. The '66ers popped a record five homers in an inning—Rich Rollins, Versalles, Oliva, Mincher, and Killebrew. Dean Chance '67 won 20 games and no-hit Cleveland. Rod Carew became Rookie of the Year. Killer linked 44 homers and 113 RBI. The Met packed 1,463,258, more than it had before, or would ever again, and lost the flag the final day. Luis Tiant '68 Kd 19 Twins in 10 innings. The A's Jim Hunter's perfect game crowned a Griffiths' season-long batting slump. Mele, fired, recalled how scout Del Wilber had scavenged for pitchers. Spying a comer, he locked him in a room. "Sam," he phoned Mele, "I've found the greatest young pitcher in America. I wouldn't have believed it if I hadn't seen it. He struck out every man who came to bat—27 straight. Only one guy even fouled a pitch off. The pitcher is here with me. What should I do?" Mele didn't blink. "Sign up the guy who got the foul," he said. "We need hitters."

Minnesota found them in 1969. MVP Killebrew had 140 RBI. Carew's seven steals of home tied Pete Reiser. The AL split into two six-team divisions. The Twins' Billy Martin won the West in his first/sole year as manager. Baltimore swept the new best-three-of-five League Championship Series. Next year Cy Young Jim Perry went 24–7. Oliva hit .327. Cesar Tovar once played each position in a game. In '70, he led the league in doubles and triples, but kept forgetting signs. Finally, coach Vern Morgan said, "I've got an idea. If you [manager Bill Rigney] want Tovar to steal and I'm giving him the sign, why don't I call his last name three or four times and that'll signal him to go to second on the next pitch." Said Rigney: "We've tried about everything else. Let's give it a shot."

Tovar promptly reached first. Rigney flashed the steal sign. Morgan said, "Tovar, look alive—c'mon, Tovar, find your position—atta' boy, Tovar, let's go." Cesar asked the first-base umpire for time. "Vern, I've been with this club for five years," he said. "How come you don't call me by my first name?"

Footnote: The 1970 Twins won the West. Baltimore again swept the playoff. In '71, Oliva's .337 led the league, Killer hit homer 500, and attendance fell below a million. Announcer Larry Carlton vowed the '74ers would reach that level: "If not, I'll return half my salary." The last day of the year he entered the booth. Pat Rickey of the St. Paul *Pioneer* was, as they say, unmoved. "Well," he told broadcaster Herb Carneal, "your partner might be in a little financial trouble if the Twins don't draw 345,000 today." He didn't give back a dime.

In 1977, Carew won his sixth batting title (.388), led in hits, runs, triples, and on-base, and became the Twins last AL MVP. (He batted over .300 15 straight years, averaged .328 lifetime, and retired with 3,053 hits.) "How good was he?" said Bud Selig. "Only Cobb, Gwynn, and Wagner won more titles"—eight. (Carew led again in '78). Mike Marshall '79 graced 90 matches. Ken Landreau '80 hit in 31 straight. The Met aged gracelessly: Griffith scrimped on upkeep. In 1981, broken railings in the third deck threatened patrons. Construction quickened on downtown's Hubert H. Humphrey Metrodome.

The Met closed that September 30—Royals, 5–3, before 15,900—and was razed to build the huge Mall of America, the nation's largest retail and amusement park. (Plaques mark home plate and Killer's longest homer). "If we remember it," Harmon mused, sadly, "it's because it was the first modern park to be torn down."

POLO GROUNDS

"After '57 you could see soccer, hoops, midget auto racing, and boxing," said the *New York Daily News'* Dick Young. "Even the AFL

[American Football League] Titans. Just no baseball." Some mocked New York as an NL town. By contrast, Mayor Robert Wagner forged a five-man committee chaired by Manhattan native, Georgetown University Law School graduate, and corporate lawyer William A. Shea to get a team.

The Reds, Pirates, and Phillies rebuffed him. In response, Shea named the eight cities, including New York, of the third major—Continental—League. "Branch Rickey was its president," said official baseball historian Jerome Holtzman. "It had heft. Threat of player raids and anti-trust suits spurred the National League to expand in 1962." At a 1960 huddle, NL owners told Shea that New York's team depended on a park. He phoned Wagner at midnight. "You've got to send a telegram to each owner promising that the city will build a new ball park." Wagner did.

In 1961, George Weiss became Mets general manager, Casey Stengel left retirement to manage, and the New York State Senate OKd $55 million for a new stadium in Queens. Work began on Flushing Meadows Park—and the NL expansion draft. "They went for old players from the Dodgers and Giants," mused Young. "Roger Craig, Gil Hodges, Charlie Neal." Their temporary home was even older: The city spent $250,000 to gussy up the Polo Grounds. Groundskeeper Johnny McCarthy painted predecessor Matty Schwab's apartment pink, built lockers and a shower, and called it the Pink Room. Howard Clothes gave a boat to any player hitting its outfield sign. "The [postwar] Giants had kept the walls free of ads," said Young. "The Mets put ads back. Not much else had changed." The real change was on the field.

Each year affects a certain thought and feel. In 1962, John Steinbeck won the Nobel Prize for Literature, John Glenn became the first American to orbit the earth, a Californian stormed, "You won't have Nixon to kick around any more," and the first Negro student enrolled at the University of Mississippi. It linked punch (the AL hit a record 1,552 homers) and speed (Maury Wills stole another record 104 bases) and a certain haughty charm. "I've got one way to pitch righties," snarled Don Drysdale—"tight." Willie McCovey told pitchers how to keep him in the park: "Walk me. Prize me." A New Yorker could be forgiven for prizing NL baseball, as attempted by the Mets.

"**T**he '62 Mets were the last age of innocence," vowed Lindsey Nelson. "They played for fun. They weren't capable of playing for anything else." In February, Nelson and colleagues Ralph Kiner and Bob Murphy decided to shadow Stengel. "We're training in St. Petersburg," said Murphy, "and we find he's indefatigable. He was over 70 years and running us into the ground!"

Said Nelson: "I learned soon that Casey couldn't care less what you had to say. At his age, he'd met every person he was interested in meeting. Being around him was egalitarian—no one had an identity." Names were less vital than a .250-hitting shortstop. Stengel confused Nelson and pitcher Bob Miller. "Miller goes tomorrow and Nelson pitches the next day," he'd say. Joe Pignatano arrived in August as bullpen coach. The first night the phone rang in the seventh. "Get Nelson up," Stengel said. Pignatano knew Lindsey was a broadcaster: "I also knew I wasn't going to argue with Casey." He took a ball, put it on the bullpen rubber, and said, *"Nelson!"* Miller got up and started throwing. *"I'm* Nelson!" he said.

The Perfessor is said to have pled, "Can't anybody here *play* this game?" He mused, "We got to work on the little finesses—the pickoff of the runner with runners at first and second, and on the first baseman holding a runner, breaking in and back to take a pickoff throw." That day the Mets lost, 17–1. Casey saw the light, not liking what he saw. "The little finesses," he conceded, "ain't gonna' be our problem."

Potboilers still hail the early Mets. "I tell the stories myself," said Nelson. "But they were gruesome years. Thank heavens for Stengel. He spread more happiness than anyone I've ever known—because he was doing exactly what he wanted to. I remember a sellout the first year and Casey standing on the dugout steps in disbelief. He said, 'We are frauds for this attendance, but if we can make losing popular, I'm for it.' "

The Mets were, too, and strove to please.

They lost their first game to St. Louis, 11–4. "Casey was giving the opening-day lineup," said Nelson. "He got through the names of most of the players until he got to the right fielder. Then he stumbled and fell over his name, chatted on as only he could and finally said, 'And when he hits the ball he rings the ball, and that's his name, Bell' "—Gus—touching the Big Apple's need for a ready and unifying eloquence.

A day later the Mets opened at Coogan's Bluff: Bucs, 4–3. They began 0–9, brooked a 17-set losing streak, and roused hilarity at 40–120. Roger Craig and Al Jackson finished 10–24 and 8–20, respectively. Until 1962, only Joe Adcock had reached its bleachers. Chicago's Lou Brock and Milwaukee's Henry Aaron joined the list. "They were 60½ games out of first," yapped Young, "and 18 out of *ninth*." The '63ers crawled to 51–111. A recording here, transcript there, photos and cartoons reemerge like yelps on the *Titanic*. Craig lost a record-tying 18 straight. Rod Kanehl got 50,000 King Korn trading stamps for the Mets' first grand slam. Jimmy Piersall ran his 100th career homer *backward* around the bases. Murphy sighed: "As bad as we were ['62–'63 91–231], few teams had as many legends."

Craig was hardship's poster child. Once McCovey pulled two pitches into Coogan's right-field seats. Stengel neared the mound. "At the end of next year they're tearin' down this place," he said. "You keep throwin' inside fastballs, they're gonna' have a head start in the right-field stands." Marv Throneberry became Marvelous Marv. "He never made the same mistake twice—always different ones," Kiner mused.

"Ashburn was a rarity," Nelson noted of the Mets as Methuselah. "His talent wasn't in the past tense," hitting an Amazins'-high .306. The ex-Phil anchored center. Spanish-speaking Elio Chacon played shortstop. Frank Thomas was not a gazelle in left. The triad often merged when a fly headed for short left-center. "I got it!" Ashburn would holler. Thomas then stopped as Chacon ran into Richie.

After a time Ashburn sought bilingual Joe Christopher. "How you do say, 'I got it' in Spanish?" Joe said, "Try 'Yo la tengo.' " A pop fly soon headed for the Bermuda Triangle. The three players converged. Ashburn yelled, "Yo la tengo, yo la tengo!" Chacon stopped. *Thomas* ran into *him*.

Catcher Hobie Landrith was Stengel's first expansion pick. "If you ain't got no catcher," Casey explained, "you get all passed balls." Once Hobie homered down the short foul line. "Ain't that somethin'!" Stengel jabbed of the '64 move to Shea Stadium. "Just when my fellers learn how to hit in this ballpark they're gonna' tear the thing down." Kiner interviewed another catcher for his first pregame TV show. He began with a softie. "Choo Choo, how did you get that nickname?" Coleman: "I don't know." A writer asked, "What's your wife's name and what's she like?" Coleman treated the question like a spitball. "Her name is Mrs. Coleman, and she likes *me,* bub."

The puzzle was how New York would like the Mets. The '62–63ers drew 922,530 and 1,080,108, respectively—"amazing," said Murphy, "given our atrocity." Inevitably, two teams packed the Grounds. On May 30, 1962, 54,360 hailed the Bums; 43,742 greeted the Giants June 1. "Other teams didn't draw," Kiner said, "but fans watched and listened." By 1963, the Mets radio/TV audience beat the Yankees—akin to a spavined nag beating Man o' War.

That year the Mets visited Yankee Stadium for the Mayor's Trophy Game. "It was an exhibition," said Nelson, "and Stengel's first trip back to where he'd been fired. He *despised* the Yankees—and so did our fans. My wife and two daughters came with their cowbells and horns and the Yankees confiscated their stuff, like anybody else with noisemakers, at the gate. The Yankees were world champions. Fifty thousand people were there that night and forty-nine thousand rooted for the Mets."

The Mets led in the sixth inning. Stengel called for a reliever. The bullpen coach said, "[Ken] MacKenzie? [the Mets' Harold Stassen]." Stengel said, "No, Carl Willey [3.10 ERA]." Nelson fell back on memory. "Casey was using our best pitcher to nail down an *exhibition.*" Mets win, 6–2. The area aped Picadilly Circus on V-E Day. "I have never seen *anything* like the fans that night. It took me two hours to get to the Triborough Bridge." Traffic gnarled. Bystanders—the New Breed—flung confetti. "David had killed Goliath. But that's what Stengel brought to the Mets."

September 18, 1963, brought a final blow: Phillies 5, Mets 1. The wrecking ball that felled Ebbets Field struck Coogan's Bluff in 1965. The city's Board of Estimates voted to build 1,700 housing units. "Low-cost," laughed Nelson, "like Marvelous Marv." A plaque denotes Matty and Mel and King Carl and The Shot Heard 'Round the World. Reading, you sense a Metsian sense of *déjà vu.*

In 1962, Ashburn was voted team most valuable player. The season ended with Pignatano hitting into a triple play. Richie took his prize, a boat, home to Philadelphia. He took it out on the Delaware River, where it sank.

COLT STADIUM

To grasp Colt Stadium meant knowing Texas—its peach orchards and berry fields and streams, falling away in endless sequence— and everywhere impatience with limits of any kind. There was nothing peewee about H. Roy Hofheinz: by turn, Houston mayor, county judge, and president of its 1962 expansion NL baseball team. Hofheinz begot the Astrodome—'65's "the Eighth Wonder of the World." Its forebear was the Colt .45s' 1962–'64 home, 32,601-seat Colt Stadium a.k.a. Mosquito Heaven. "Our grounds crew," vowed general manager Paul Richards, "will regularly spray between innings." Texas-sized insects bombed like Stukas over Warsaw.

The expansion draft occurred October 10, 1961. Casey Stengel said, "The Mets is great—they give everybody a job just like the WPA." By contrast, Richards tried to return his merchandise, trading *rosters* with the '61 last-place Phils. On January 3, 1962, groundbreaking skipped shovels for used .45 caliber blanks. The team trained at Apache Junction in the Arizona Desert south of Mesa. "Geronimo's warriors had roamed here," said voice Gene Elston. "The way our club played, you'd think he warred on us." Talk later hinted of a curse. "Possibly, it wasn't wise to train in the shadow of Superstition Mountain where Indian spirits and an old Dutchman's ghost were said to guard a lost gold mine."

The Colts opened Mosquito Heaven April 10, before 25,271 at the East/West Utility Road, North Stadium Drive, South Main Street, and Kirby Drive. First pitcher: Bobby Shantz. Batter: Chicago's Lou Brock. Hit: Houston's Bob Aspromonte. Homer: Roman Mejias. Score: .45s 11, Cubs 2. A single deck tied the foul lines. Bleachers draped right and left field. The 30-foot-high left-center to right-center Phillips 66 scoreboard bookended a dark backdrop. The ad-littered fence stood 8 feet high. Eight light standards towered. "Especially important," said Elston, " 'cause it's too hot to ever play in the day."

Symmetrical lengths were deep: lines, 360; alleys, 395; center, 420; corners to each side, 427. A stiff breeze blew from right to home. The '62ers hit a league-low 105 homers, finished eighth, but outdrew the Mets (924,456 to 922,530). "Our newness," explained Richards, "plus the characters we had."

Aspromonte set an NL-record for third basemen with 57 straight errorless games. In 1962, businessman Bobby Maduro wanted to put a Triple-A team in Colts minor-league territory (Jacksonville). His money lay in a Cuban bank. Maduro owned minor-league outfielder Jim Pendleton. "Give us Pendleton," Richards said, "and we'll give our rights to Jacksonville." One night Jim neared third on a hit to right-center. "All of a sudden," mused Richards, "he stops, restarts, and scores." Was he hurt? The umpire and catcher began laughing. "Jim lost his cup. It fell out when he rounded third, rolled down his pantleg, and was hanging around his knee about the time he hit home."

George Brunet (2–7 '62–'63) played for 26 professional teams. The A's once traded the lefty to Milwaukee. The Braves publicist's wife intercepted a phone message telling him to "pick up that brunette from Milwaukee at the airport." Brunet's prime was past by Houston. At 19, Rusty Staub's was ahead. One day the first baseman told pitcher Hal Woodeshick, "I'm going [toward the plate] on the first pitch so whatever you do, throw to the batter." Woodeshick nodded. Rusty charged. Hal then threw to first, almost hitting him in the ear.

Hofheinz made the traveling party wear cowboy clothes on the road. "I still remember," said Richards. "Blue western outfits with black cowboy boots gilded in orange, black cowboy hats, and belt buckle embossed with a pistol with 'Colt .45's' on it, an orange tie, white shirts with red and blue baseball stitching." Players gaped. Onlookers hooted in airports and hotels. Finally Richards asked Hofheinz to deep-six their duds.

Larry Dierker was a Houston pitcher. "I was afraid of him," he said of Dick (Turk) Farrell. "No matter how parched I was, I wouldn't go for a Coke across the locker room because I'd have to pass his locker." In 1962, Farrell lost 20 games, Kd 203, and made Peck's Bad Boy look tame. "He'd pull pranks, put snakes in lockers, give guys the hot-foot," said Woodeshick. Once Hank Aaron lined a drive that hit Farrell in the forehead, bounced off, and was caught by outfielder Jimmy Wynn for an out. "Explains a lot," said '62–'64 manager Harry Craft. Harder to explain: Houston's reverse Midas luck.

In 1962, outfielder Al Heist stepped in a hole and broke an ankle, ending his career. Pitcher Jim Umbricht died of cancer in '64. Walt Bond later fell to leukemia. Don Wilson was accidentally asphyxiated in his garage. "Think of our marquee names," said Elston. "Bobby Shantz, Robin Roberts, Pete Runnels, Nellie Fox, Joe Pepitone, Jim Bouton, Eddie Mathews, Don Larsen, Bo Belinski. How come our whole didn't match the parts?" Spirits roiled over usurping Apache Junction.

Both sides now: Colt Stadium's largest (30,027, June 10, v. Dodgers) and smallest (1,638, September 8, Mets) crowds shared 1962. A year later the Colts drew 719,502, Don Nottebart no-hit the Phillies, and Houston staged the bigs' first Sunday night game (June 9, 3–0, over Giants). "We got an exemption," Hofheinz explained, "because the days were so beastly hot." In 1964, Ken Johnson allowed no hits one night v. Cincy: Reds, 1–0, on an unearned run. The team had a league-low 70 homers. On September 27, the .45s blanked L.A., 1–0, before 6,246, to close Colt's run. You looked next door and saw the future in its facade.

DODGER STADIUM

In late 1956, the Dodgers toured Japan. Walter O'Malley liked the ground-level suites—"dugout boxes"—between each dugout. They became part of Dodger Stadium. Too: five tiers of seating, red infield and warning track clay, and palm trees beyond the outfield. "I want to build the perfect park," he pledged. Designers still heap praise on baseball's Taj Mahal.

Like Saul, the Dodgers boss knew his Damascus Road. "I was flying over it in a helicopter," he said of Chavez Ravine, two miles from center city, a hilly, depressed region peopled by squatters and goats. O'Malley especially liked how several freeways merged nearby. He bought 166 acres of land, a referendum narrowly backed the sale, and the Dodgers and city signed a deal. Suits vied to block the park, and lost.

O'Malley lit a cigar ten years before his death. "It wasn't easy," he remembered. "The squatters and a goatherd had to be evicted." One family slugged U.S. marshals on a visit. Groundbreaking lit September 17, 1959. Fused: 21,00 precast concrete units. Removed: more than 8 million cubic yards of land. Delayed: Opening Day, by landslides and further lawsuits, past 1961. Busted: the budget, twice the $12 million estimate. "This will be a memorial to the O'Malleys," Walter said of baseball's first privately financed park since Yankee Stadium. In 1962, outfielder Lou Johnson saw it for the first time: "My first thought," he said, "was that this was Heaven on earth."

Taj O'Malley a.k.a. O'Malley's Gold Gulch opened April 10, 1962. Wife Kay threw out the first ball. First pitcher: Johnny Podres. Batter/hit: Reds' Eddie Kasko. Homer: mate Wally Post. Score: Cincy, 6–3, before 52,564. The park pooled Santa Ana Bermuda grass, 16,000 parking spots, and a Brooklyn twist. "The foul poles were all in foul territory. How could you hit a home run?" said Jim Murray. The NL ruled them fair. "Next year the plate moved so that poles *were* fair." Architect Emil Praeger's initial 85,000-seat design fully enclosed the outfield. O'Malley scratched it for single-tier bleachers, a grand view of downtown L.A. and the San Gabriel Mountains, and 56,000 capacity. "Forget new parks opening since '92," Murray added. "Except for them, this is the only park whose size hasn't changed." Unchanged: its era of Good Feeling.

A visitor found the terraced lot nearest his seat. ("One parking level for every deck," crowed O'Malley.) Entering, he took outdoor steps and escalators to orange-red, gold, and Dodger blue seats. The top deck wrapped from first base to third. Others passed the poles. Pitchers liked the lengths (330, lines; 380, alleys, 380 [370 '69, 385 '83], and center 410 [400 '69]) and large foul turf. A 10-foot (8 '73) wooden fence tied left-and right-center. Bullpens perpendicular to the field split bleachers and foul-line seats. A 3¾-foot steel wall linked them to the corner. What might have been: The original plan included a fountain in center field. The scoreboard touted Farmer John's and Phillips 66. The concrete infield spun wacky hops. The mound was said to be higher than other parks'. The sky was blue; temperature, warm; aisles and seats, spick-

and-span. Even the address screamed *baseball:* 1000 Elysian Park Avenue, after the game's first park, Hoboken's Elysian Field.

Early-'60s Los Angeles was sprawling, bereft of a focal point, and stocked with emigrants. "When you talk about Los Angeles, you're talking about the drifter. Californians aren't in contact with their neighbors," Theodore H. White, quoting a local politician, wrote in *The Making of the President 1964.* "Out here, people are lost. They have no one to talk to. And the doorbell-ringer has an importance far beyond his normal pictorial quality. Those who win elections [or baseball audiences]—they've reached out and touched." Broadcaster Vin Scully became a doorbell-ringer, exalting baseball since the Grand Army of the Potomac staged its last reunion (1950). He sounded like, well, a friend you would want to talk to. The Taj O'Malley became your focal point, and its voice your new-town tie.

The 1962–'65 AL Angels were O'Malley's tenant. One day Baltimore changed pitchers at Chavez Ravine. (Said Halos owner Gene Autry: "We never call it Dodger Stadium.") Fans began to applaud. Orioles voice Chuck Thompson told himself, "Wow, these are really great fans here in California, cheering Baltimore." Next day the O's change pitchers. Fans applaud. Thompson says, "What in the world is going on?" Binoculars fixed the stands: A light went on. Thousands of Angelenos were wearing ear-plugs. "But they weren't listening to *our* game," said Thompson. "They were tuned to the *Dodger* game, clapping when *they* scored runs!" Millions seized Scully's offer to "pull up a chair."

In 1962, the Dodgers pulled a record 2,755,184. Cy Young Don Drysdale went 25–9. "He had to work a little harder," said catcher John Roseboro, "but he was about 100 percent meaner than Sandy Koufax, and everybody knew it." Koufax '60 walked 100 in 175 innings. A mate called "[even] batting practice like Russian roulette with five bullets." Planets then realigned. In '62, Sandy Kd 18 Cubs. Tommy Davis linked a league-leading .346 and franchise-high 153 RBI. MVP Maury Wills—to Scully, "The Mouse That Roared"—swiped a record 104 bases. 'Frisco tied for the flag in Game 162. "[Best-of-three] playoff, huh?" said L.A. coach Leo Durocher, who had been this way before. On October 3—

"D," for "Dat" Bobby Thomson, Day—"The Giants [again] win the pennant!" 6–4: as in 1951, scoring four in the ninth.

The Dodgers had blown the flag. The 1962 Angels nearly won it, ending third. A Yankees game wooed 53,591. The Halos lured 1,114,063 (but just 3,292,244 through '65). Leon Wagner welded 37 homers and 107 RBI. Minutiae: Albie Pearson .304 in '63; Dean Chance '64 (20–9, league-best 1.65 ERA, and 11 shutouts); '65 far-from-the-madding crowd (566,727. One game drew 476.). The Angels had one-fourth of O'Malley's gate, but paid 50 percent of toilet paper, and cut and watered the grass. Autry owned hotels. "I'd have a hell of a time getting people who rent my rooms to water the posies. It's the responsibility of the landlord." O'Malley thought him a sponge. "The Angels play as many games in our 'hotel' as we do. Are we supposed to let everything die when they're at home?"

In 1965, the Angels changed their name to California and suspended a pitcher for slugging an L.A. writer. On May 5, 1962, Bo Belinsky had no-hit Baltimore, 2–0. He was tall, dark, handsome, and said to be a little on the wayward side.

"Bo really didn't like baseball, possessed little talent, and only stayed with the game because it enhanced his social life in Fantasyland," said announcer Harry Kalas." One night he graced a party. Said a friend: "Bo has some girls, gets drunk. We got back just in time to catch the team bus to the park." Modern marvels: Belinsky proceeded to throw nine shutout innings. His mind, unlike arm, lay elsewhere. In the fifth, a mate traded Bo's left-for a right-handed glove. "It's a long walk from the dugout to the mound at Dodger Stadium, and out ambles Bo not realizing he has a righty's glove. He toes the rubber, starts to warm up, and finally grasps the crime."

My first fielder's glove was a Belinsky model. I begged my dad, "Can't I trade it for a Koufax?" Sandy's speed blinded hitters. The curve dropped off a shelf. No pitcher had thrown three no-hitters. Mr. K threw four, including a September 9, 1965, perfect game v. Chicago. From 1962–'66, Koufax went 111–34, won the 1963 MVP and '63-'65-'66 Cy Young Awards, and pitched like no one had, or is likely to. 'Sixty-two: NL-low 2.54 ERA. '63: bigs-best 25–5, 1.88, 306 Ks, and 11 shutouts. '64: Nationals-leading winning percentage (.792) and ERA (1.74). '65: bigs-high 26 wins, .765 percentage, 2.04 ERA, and 382 Ks.

'66: 27–9, 317 Ks, and 1.73 ERA. He then retired due to elbow arthritis. "I don't regret for one minute the 12 years I've spent in baseball," Sandy said, "but I could regret one season too many." One writer mixed film and stage. "He left at High Noon, a Hamlet in mid-soliloquy."

In 1963, Ron Perranoski went 16–3. Frank Howard hit 28 dingers. Tommy Davis' .326 gilded the league. The Dodgers tickled 2,538,602, hit only .251, but had a 2.85 ERA. "It was the opposite of Brooklyn," said Scully. "There they'd club you to death. Here it's a single, steal, ground out, score on a fly." To Bob Uecker, they played for keeps. "We'd rate 'em like divers. A pitch under the chin, hold up a sign, '5'. Fastball in the ribs—'10'. That was their secret. They'd only score three runs a game—but *you* couldn't score three in a *series*. The weird thing is that I hit over .400 against Sandy. There he was, the greatest stuff since Doubleday—and I'd hit a home run or smack a double. Talk about a travesty. That alone should have kept him out of the Hall of Fame."

The Flatbush/L.A. Dodgers boast 38 Famers, eight Cy Young, 10 MVP, and 16 Rookie of the Year Awards, 18 flags, and six world titles. In 1963, their Series matched sport's Caesar and Pompey. Sandy won the opener, fanning a record 15. (Harry Bright Kd for the final out.) Johnny Podres and Drysdale then beat the Yankees, 4–1 and 1–0. Game Four packed the Ravine. "Mantle batted against Koufax. Sandy threw a fastball, then that hellacious curve that dropped out of the sky," said Roseboro. "Then he hit him with a high fastball around the letters. Mick didn't swing at a pitch. He looked back to me and says, 'How in the hell are you supposed to hit that stuff?' "

Howard blasted the first ball into Dodger Stadium's second deck: 1–0. Mantle then tied, 1-all. In the eighth, first baseman Joe Pepitone's error gave Sandy a 2–1 win. A *sweep,* of the *Yankees?* For those recalling Brooklyn, the simple thought amazed.

The '65ers blared baseball's first switch-hitting infield: Wes Parker, Jim Lefebvre, Wills, and Jim Gilliam. On September 1, Cincinnati led by half a game over the Dodgers and Giants. San Francisco then won 14 straight. L.A. riposted: 13 in a row. The Dodgers hit .245, clinched on the penultimate day, and went forth *v.* Minnesota. "Sandy sat out the

[Series] opener because of Yom Kippur," recalled manager Walter Alston. Minnesota took Games One-Two. Back home, Claude Osteen beat Camilo Pascual, 4–0. Drysdale won, 7–2. The image lingers of Twins catcher Earl Battey, chasing a pop, hitting his neck against a railing. Koufax was Koufax: 7–0. Minnesota won Game Six. The Twins had been blanked only thrice all year. Sandy blanked them a second time, 2–0.

The decline began. In 1966, Koufax's last victory clinched the flag at Philadelphia. Baltimore then swept the Series: 5–2, 6–0, and 1–0 twice: Willie Davis made three errors in Sandy's final game. Wills and Tommy Davis were peddled. The '67ers collapsed to a worst-since-'05 eighth. Attendance fell from 2,617,029 to 1,664,362. "Five years they had 2 million or more," said Jim Murray. "Now it seemed they were playing to the groundskeeper."

Only Big D remained. In 1968, he pitched 44 straight scoreless innings, then hit Dick Dietz with the bases full. "He didn't try to get out of the way," said umpire Harry Wendelstedt, "so I voided the hit." Dietz made out. The streak endured. In June, Drysdale's 58⅔ scoreless innings broke Walter Johnson's record (56, in '13). Tiers pulsed, then stilled: L.A. drew a worst-ever 1,581,093. Big D's retirement as its winningest pitcher (209–166, 2.95 ERA, and 2,486 Ks) didn't help. Neither did Willie Davis' 31-game hit streak, Al Downing's 20–9, or Don Sutton's 2.08 ERA in 1969-'71-'72, respectively. The Dodgers lost a division on the final day to—*San Francisco*. In 1969 and '73, Willie Stargell cleared and reached, respectively, the right-field pavilion roof. The gate cleared 2 million for the first time since Mr. K.

O'Malley, replaced by son Peter, retired as president in 1970. The team retired the numbers of Koufax, Robinson, and Campanella (10 in all). Tom Lasorda joined the team as Alston's coach and successor. "I want my team to think baseball the way my wife shops," he bayed, "24 hours a day." The ex-Brooklyn lefty brought Ron Cey, Bill Russell, Dave Lopes, and Steve Garvey from the farm—ultimately, baseball's longest-running infield. The Angelenos again were getting good.

THE COOKIE-CUTTERS

1962–'91

'14

UP ON THE ROOF

In the early-'60s meridian of baseball temples, few dreamt that a player would one day say, "When I'm at bat, I can't tell whether I'm in Cincinnati, Philly, or St. Louis." Richie Hebner hated cookie-cutters more than Madonna flouts modesty.

As we shall see, yeasting began in Washington. It then corked up the seaboard. In 1964, the Mets dealt the '62–'63 Polo Grounds for Shea Stadium. "No one will ever know," said Casey Stengel, "how the craziness of the Grounds park made them people fall in love." The New Breed scribbled messages on bed sheets. Exhibitionists waved placards before the roving camera eye. The chant of "Let's Go Mets" pierced the ancient grandstand. Metsomania became a favorite allegory of the time.

Shea's "Metsies" missed Coogan's Bluff's daybook of variety. In 1965, Houston fled Colt Stadium for the sterile Astrodome. A year later the Braves moved to Atlanta–Fulton County Stadium—generic, with vast foul ground, and seats in another county. St. Louis swapped one Busch Stadium for another multisport lookalike. "In these places, you feel alone," recalled the Cardinals' Stan Musial. "No corners for balls to take strange hops. No odd shapes where anything can happen."

In 1968, the A's left Kansas City for the heavy night air and Gulliver foul turf of the Oakland-Alameda County Coliseum. The '70–'71 Reds and Phillies traded Crosley Field and Shibe Park, respectively, for Riverfront and Veterans Stadium. Then, like dominoes, Seattle occupied the Kingdome, the Expos changed Jarry Park for gaping Olympic Stadium (the Big O, as in zero), and Minnesota fled Metropolitan Stadium for the tomblike Metrodome.

"You'd be kind," said former Phillie Mike Schmidt, "to say they had the charm of a parking garage." *Hallo* to sport's invasion of the body snatchers. One by one, football stadiums raided baseball's soul.

Dwight Eisenhower read Louis L'Amour, ate TV dinners, and danced to Fred Waring and the Pennsylvanians. America's 1961 presidential inaugural augured change. Black Marian Anderson sang "The Star-Spangled Banner." Robert Frost prepared a preface to his poem, "The Gift Outright." John F. Kennedy outdid both: "Let the word go forth," said the new president, "from this time and place, to friend and foe alike, that the torch has been passed to a new generation of Americans."

Soon the torch would pass to a new generation of ballparks. Increasingly, planners sought "super blocks" close to freeways, gorged by parking, and uncurbed by streets. They would help sport's oil and water coexist. "Looking back," said Hall of Fame president Dale Petroskey, "we see that the demands of baseball and football are mutually exclusive." The schizoid made the pastime inert, and dull.

Author Bruce Markusen shook his head. "In this era baseball started losing its way," he said. Whyfores merged: Few '60s parks were forged by a city grid. "Form followed function," said architect Ludwig Mies von der Rohe. "Less [symmetry of shape and length] was more." Computers and steel design helped concrete better cantilever, build multiple tiers, and extend seating distance. Football's rectangle left baseballphiles far from the field. Loge seats surfaced, often hanging beneath a deck. "The result," said architect Joseph Spear, "was to further push stands away." A final fillip, "column-free" design, made decks remote and limited the roof. "Welcome," said Spear, "to more rain and little enclosure."

On April 12, 1962, District of Columbia Stadium became just the second new AL park (after Minnesota) since 1932 (Cleveland's Municipal). "It had great football sightlines," said *Washington Post* columnist Shirley Povich, "and was formal, pretentious, and cold." The Redskins loved the Senators' new park.

"I'm leaving you in first place," Kennedy quipped to Nats general manager Ed Doherty after 42,143 opened D.C. Stadium: Senators 4, Detroit 1. Arkansas Democrat Oren Harris had introduced a bill to build it with public funds. Kennedy agreed: "[It] will be an enduring symbol of the American belief in the importance of physical fitness and of the contributions which athletic competition can make to our way of life."

The city's Fine Arts Commission oversaw public sites. "D.C. Stadium [in the southeast section]," a release read, "will be on direct line with the United States Capitol and the Lincoln and Jefferson Memorial." Thus, light towers were banned, and arcs tacked on its curved, dipping roof. Wrote a critic: "It looks like a wet straw hat." The plot strayed from Griffith Stadium like Ike v. JFK. D.C. was larger (43,500 capacity), circular (two decks caged the field), symmetrical (lines, 335; alleys, 385; center, 410), and uniform (seven-foot wire fence). Skip your glove: Outfield seats pocked the upper, not lower, deck. Bullpens straddled the fence and back concrete wall. "You couldn't get as involved as at Griffith," said P.A. voice Phil Hochberg. Life was easy, but antiseptic: 24 ticket booths, 45 rest rooms, 28 concession stands, 14 15-degree pitched ramps, 13,500 parking spaces, and air-conditioned dugouts with overhead lights. Heat oozed. The ball zoomed. No portholes broke concrete. "Griffith was baseball," said Povich. "This was not."

A visitor entered past monuments on the left (north) and right (south) side to Clark Griffith and Redskins owner George Preston Marshall, respectively. The first year six feet of leveling sank sections of left and left-center field. The '62 Nats sank to 10th place. *Pro:* Tom Cheney Kd 21 Orioles in 16 innings. The '63ers beat Cleveland, 7–2, in the bigs' 100,000th match. *Con:* Attendance plunged to 535,604. "It was a tightrope act," said Senators voice Dan Daniels. "Washington's unique. At the park, like on radio, there were government workers from every state in the audience—fans cheering for the teams Washington was playing. You couldn't be a rooter, and yet there were a lot of fans pulling for Washington." Usually, they pulled in vain.

The Nats lacked bigwigs like the Mets' Marv Throneberry. They did, however, resemble him: 178–307 in '62–'64. "People still resented Calvin Griffith's [1960] move [to Minnesota]," said columnist Morris Siegel. "They were also tired of decades of incompetence." Willie Tasby rode by train when weather threatened. Dick Donovan loved routine: Teammates learned not to sit where he laid his glove between innings. Danny O'Connell hit three homers in 729 at-bats. He also brooked a bad back. A mate accused him of malingering. "Listen," he said, "with this back I'd like to see you try to get laid."

In May 1963, Gil Hodges was named manager. Said Siegel: "He fretted quietly when his players threw to the wrong base, missed the cutoff man, screwed up rundown plays, and misran the bases—which happened about every game." Former Dodger Rube Walker became pitching coach. One day his ex-mate aced a birdie. Walker said, "I'm gonna' write a book on the life of Gil Hodges entitled *Nice Guy, My Ass.*" Outfielder Jim King shared Rube's earthy air. "I hope my wife's not in the bathtub when I get home," he said after a one-week road trip. Hodges asked why. "Because I don't want to get this new suit wet."

Frank Howard was 6-foot-6, 255 pounds, and easily the Senators' most popular player. Once he went deep 10 times in 20 ups. Thrice Hondo hit 44 or more homers and drove in more than 105 runs. He retired in 1973 with 382 homers and 1,119 RBI. Howard's blasts were ballistic. "That's where they landed," Frank said, sadly, of upper-deck seats painted white. "It's one of the few things left that remind you there was baseball in Washington."

On September 26, 1965, the Twins won their first pennant, 2–1, in an exquisite irony of team and town. "They clinched in D.C.," said Povich. The near future took a more abiding turn. Washington was more than 70 percent black. Emmett Ashford '66 became the bigs' first black umpire.

In 1968, Martin Luther King, Jr., was murdered. Riots tore more than 250 cities. Opening Day was postponed a week. The 82nd Airborne Division and National Guard patrolled the streets and park.

Vice-President Hubert Humphrey tossed two first pitches to outfielder Hank Allen and coach Nellie Fox. Hondo homered in six straight games. Robert Short became team president. His brainstorm was naming Ted Williams manager. The Yankees had drawn a D.C. record 48,147 August 1, 1962. In April 1969, they packed 45,000, including President Nixon, for Williams' Nats debut. That July the bigs turned 100. Players met Nixon at the White House. An All-Star dinner honored the Babe and Joe DiMaggio. Rain postponed the All-Star Game: The NLers later won. The Senators finished fourth and wooed a highest-since-'46 918,106. Songwriter Paul Simon: "But I would not give you false hope." D.C. did, reclaiming last. Short began courting Dallas–Ft. Worth. Denny McLain '71 went 10–22. Curt Flood left after 13 games for Denmark: "I will continue my [anti-trust reserve clause] suit." In time, it U-turned the game.

"The bright day is done," wrote Shakespeare, "and we are for the dark." Darkness pieced September 30, 1971. "By now," Siegel said, "Short had announced he was going to Texas." Hondo homered into the bullpen in the sixth inning. "They thought it was my last time up," he said. "The ovation shook me when I batted." The Nats led, 7–5, with two out in the ninth. A goodly part of the crowd then stormed the field. Vandals stole bases, took home plate, and swiped letters from the scoreboard. Park police mimed Barney Fife. At 10:11 P.M. umpire Jim Honochick forfeited to New York, 9–0. Paul Lindblad lost a save. *Postscript.* The Senators became the Texas Rangers. The Padres, Giants, and A's almost moved to Washington. The Redskins owned the city. Baseball's colony rivaled exiles in a foreign land.

In 1968, D.C. was renamed Robert F. Kennedy Stadium. On July 19, 1982, 29,196 peopled RFK for an old-timers game. "By now it had a football configuration," said Hochberg. Left and right, respectively, stood 260 and 295 feet away. Former White Sox shortstop Luke Appling, 75, homered off Warren Spahn: The noise ferried you back to Hondo's last blast.

Exhibition games teased baseball's return. The '87 Mets-Phillies abided a 24-foot-high left-field wooden fence. Povich shook his head. "It's sad, the greatest game reduced here to one game a year." In 2000, Commissioner Bud Selig ordered a study: Would a D.C. team hurt the nearby Orioles' attendance? JFK said, "I'm leaving you in first place." Washington is still unsure if baseball has left it for good.

SHEA STADIUM

"Don't cut my throat," Casey Stengel told his barber after a bizarre Mets loss. "I'm saving that for myself." Casey once thought that managing was easy. "What the hell is it but telling the umpires who's gonna' play and then watching them play." By late 1962 he wondered. "I don't ask how we lost 120 this year. I ask how we ever won 40." A new park might change their lot.

Shea Stadium, named for William Shea, flanked the 1939–'40 and '64–'65 World's Fair site in Flushing Meadows. "Without Bill," said businessman Bernard Gimbel, "whose enthusiasm was responsible for the support of newspapers, sportswriters, and fans, there would have been no new Met Stadium." The $28.5 million park sat 55,300, had 10,000 parking slots, and gushed with firsts. Said New York City parks commissioner Newbold Morris: "Shea Stadium is the first of its size to have such an escalator system carrying patrons to every seating level. It is the first capable of being converted from a football gridiron [AFL Jets] to a baseball diamond and back by means of two motor-operated stands, moveable by underground tracks. It is the first in which every seat in the permanently fixed stands is directed at the center of the field, and not a single column obstructs the spectator's view." Shea had a 1,500-seat restaurant, 20 snack bars, and 54 public rest rooms. What it lacked was a spitspot of charm.

"The Polo Grounds had its tiny lines and vast center field," said Harold Rosenthal, "and its death valley and high walls." Shea was symmetrical: lines, 330 (marked), 341 (actual), and 338 (1979); alleys, 371; and center, 410. Other lengths marked 358 and 396. Corner walls were 16⅓ feet high (4 wire above brick: later, falling to 12⅓ brick '65 and 8 wood '79. Alleys and center stood 8.) An 86-foot-high by 175-foot-long clock-topped Stadiarama scoreboard loomed 25 feet beyond right-center. A rare projection screen showed color slides at night—"a big deal in the '60s," wrote Dick Young. LaGuardia airport sprawled nearby. Bobby Bonilla later wore earplugs to blot noise—and boos.

Shea abutted Grand Central Parkway and Flushing Bay. Wind and cold could rival Candlestick. "The park was open," Rosenthal explained, "and it came in from center." Seats formed a four-tiered broken circle from one line to another. Foul turf hugged the lowest deck, sloping gently to the field; the top three rose almost vertically. "The lower boxes were on rails that moved into position for football [also originally, soccer]. This left you too far from the action," said Young. "Up top, you were too high. Everything was too set back."

It was nearly worse. "The park was designed to completely enclose and expand to 90,000," Rosenthal noted. "In late '64, they decided to ditch that but attach a dome and 15,000 more seats." An engineering study killed the plan. Shea agreed. "New York fans are entitled to fresh air, certainly on Saturday and Sunday afternoons and nice nights." They still are, four decades later.

E *Pluribus Unum.* Shea was christened April 16, 1964, with Dodgers Holy Water from Brooklyn's Gowanus Canal and Giants Holy Water from the Harlem River at the point it passed the Polo Grounds. Next day it opened. Some watched *gratis* from a walkway of the Willets Point subway station. Others drove. Roads clogged around the park. Many left their cars and returned to $15 parking tickets. The pregame starred ex–Dodgers and Giants: Bill Terry, Frank Frisch, Zack Wheat, Max Carey. Mets lose, 4–3, to Pittsburgh. First pitcher: Jack Fisher. Batter: Dick Schofield. Hit/homer: mate Willie Stargell. Crowd: 48,736. A *New Yorker* cartoon soon showed several dejected Mets entering the dugout. A bystander says, "Cheer up. You can't lose them all."

On May 26, the Mets scored 19 runs against the Cubs. A caller asked WABC Radio, "Yeah, but did they win?" (19–1). That week they played a doubleheader v. San Francisco. The second game—Mets bow, 8–6—took 23 frames and a record 7 hours, 22 minutes. A crowd of 57,037 began the day: 5,000 were left at 11:25 P.M. Willie Mays played shortstop for three innings. New York cashed a triple play. Banner Day included "Mongolia Loves the Mets" (in Mongolian), "Eamus Metropoli" ("Let's Go Mets" in Latin), and "E=mc2" (Errors equal Mets times customers squared.) On Father's Day, Jim Bunning pitched the first regular-season perfect game since Charlie Robertson '22. Mets second baseman Ron Hunt started Shea's All-Star Game. Philly's John Callison won it, 7–4, on a ninth-inning homer. The Mets outdrew the *Yanks* by 429,959.

"How do you top a year like that?" Lindsey Nelson said. You don't (for a time). The '65ers got no hits in 10 innings off Jim Maloney—and won. Said John Lewis: "No one was ever so glad to homer [11th, 1–0]." Stengel retired (of a broken hip). The Mets wowed 1,932,693 (New York NL high). "Shea had all the conveniences—great parking, easy to get to, a protoype of the modern stadium," Nelson said. "It opened all of Long Island to the Mets market. Dodger fans hadn't wanted to go to the Polo Grounds. They came here. And in a sense Mets fans were like Ebbets Field's." Yankee Stadium mimed the Louvre on Sunday. Shea mixed Mr. Met (team mascot), Miss Rheingold (beer sponsor), and the city's National League lilt.

Its signature entered the '66 Hall of Fame. "Them Metsies," Stengel rasped, "is the hope of America." For the first time they left the cellar. 1967: Tom Seaver 18–12 became Rookie of the Year. '68: The Mets soared to 73–89. Beyond: Tug McGraw, Bud Harrelson, Jerry Koosman, and Ron Swoboda sniffed respectability. "Haltingly, like a child, you could see newcomers throw off habits—in their case, bad players," said Nelson, "and learn social graces like how to hit and catch and pitch. Still, there wasn't even a hint of what was to come. I thought that they'd stay near the basement forever."

Miracle, or metaphysical? Were the Mets a recompense for Marvelous Marv, or God's reprisal against O'Malley? In 1969, men first walked on the moon. The Mets walked on air. On April 11, Tommie Agee became first to reach Shea's upper deck. In July, Seaver retired the first 25 Cubs. Jimmy Qualls' looper wrecked a perfect game: Mets, 4–0, before a record 59,083. "I guess it shocked him," said Young. "[After '69] Qualls had one more hit." In September Chicago invaded Shea. "Just before the first pitch," Seaver laughed, "a black cat came over to the Cubs leadoff batter in the on-deck circle," staring like a witch doctor, then slunk to Chicago's dugout and hissed at manager Leo Durocher. Seaver won, 7–1. The crowd sang, "Good night, Leo." A day later the Mets snatched first.

The moon was in the seventh house: The Cardinals' Steve Carlton Kd a record 19; Swoboda smacked two two-run homers: 4–3, Mets. They clinched September 24, 6–0, v. St. Louis. "That night," said Nelson, "someone asked, 'Gil [manager Hodges], how did this happen? Tell us what this proves.' He sat back, stared, and spread those meat hands wide. 'Can't be done,' he said, and this giant, gentle man just laughed." The '62–'68 Mets five times dredged last. "No way," Lindsey said, "any of us could have believed that the butt of everybody's jokes were finally going to win. We'd always been an unbelievable team—but now we were *winning* the improbable games. Carlton, Qualls. Al Weis, a banjo hitter, homering to beat the Cubs. Or the madness of the clincher."

Seaver 25–7 took Cy Young I. Koosman went 17–9. Cleon Jones batted .340. Agee hit 26 homers. New York wiled 2,175,373. The 100-tolers then swept Atlanta in the first League Championship Series, 9–5, 11–6, and 7–4. A country stirred with implausibility. The Mets faced Baltimore in the Series. "We are here," said Brooks Robinson, "to prove there is no Santa Claus." The O's won Game One, 4–1. Koosman evened the Classic, 2–1. Elves awoke. Game Three moved to Shea. Agee homered and made two diving catches: Mets, 5–0. The North Pole warmed. Seaver led Game Four, 1–0, in the ninth, one out, tying run on third. "Brooks Robinson lined a hit to right-center," said announcer Bob Murphy, "except that Swoboda made the catch of his life." The 1-all run scored, but the O's rally died.

Tenth inning: The Mets' J. C. Martin bunted with two runners on. Pitcher Pete Richert's throw struck Martin on the wrist; the ball bounced wildly; the winning run tallied. "I'll swear to my dying day Martin ran out of the baseline," said Orioles manager Earl Weaver. Plate umpire Shag Crawford differed. Santa readied for the trek. Next day the O's led, 3–0, when Jones claimed to be hit on the foot. Hodges retrieved the ball, pointed to shoe polish, and swayed the ump: Clean took first. Donn Clendenon promptly homered. Infielder Weis had not dingered in five years at Shea. In the seventh, he dented the left-field auxiliary board: 3-all. Jones and Swoboda doubles and a double O's error KOd Baltimore: 5–3. At 3:16 P.M. the New York Mets—baseball's Tiny Tim—won the 66th World Series. "To me," Swoboda said in 2000, "it is still a fairy tale."

NBC's Nelson aired the clubhouse party to a nation that after hearing of baseball's death—too slow, unhip, and '50s—found to its delight that the patient lived. He then drove around Manhattan. "I told my wife and kids, 'If we don't go into town, we'll have missed the celebration.' So we did and it was marvelous. Dancing in the streets, throwing confetti. Once in a while a cop would recognize me and go wild. It's a cliche, I know, but this was—if there has ever been such a thing—a once-in-a lifetime happening."

Santa slid down the chimney. A ticker-tape parade topping Lindbergh's snaked through Manhattan. M. Donald Grant was asked what it meant. Said the Mets chairman of the board: "Our team finally caught up with our fans."

For years '69's glow remained, a perceptible, inexplicable thing. It lit much of 1970. On April 22, Seaver fanned the last ten Padres to tie Carlton's 19. The Mets drew a record 2,697,479. McGraw said he didn't need amphetamines because "just being left-handed is like taking a greenie a day." A reporter asked if he liked artificial or natural turf. "I don't know," said McGraw. "I never smoked AstroTurf." He dubbed his fastball the "Lady Godiva. There's nothing on it."

In 1972, McGraw had 27 saves. Jon Matlack became Rookie of the Yeear. Hodges, 48, died of a heart attack. Yogi Berra replaced him. Mays returned to Shea as a Met—and homered in his debut. The '73ers limped to a 34–46 start. "Mr. Grant gave a pep talk," said McGraw. "When he stopped I started yelling, 'Ya' gotta' believe!' " Seaver's fourth straight league-low ERA helped—and fate. On September 20, 1973, Shea honored Mays. "Willie," he choked, retiring, "say good-bye to America." The game reached the 13th inning. "[Pittsburgh's] Dave Augustine hit a drive that struck the top of the wall, bounced straight up, and came down into my glove," said Jones, throwing to Wayne Garrett, whose relay nabbed Richie Zisk. New York won the game and NL East—"not bad," Nelson laughed, "for an 82–79 record." Cincy took the West, splitting LCS Games One-Two. On October 8, the Yom Kippur War raged in Israel. Spiro Agnew fixed to resign as vice-president. Pleased: "nattering nabobs of negativism," "effete corps of impudent snobs," and "vicars of vacillation."

Pete Rose thought vacillation nuts. In Game Three, he slid hard into second base. Shortstop Harrelson completed a double play. The pair then began wrestling. Both benches cleared. Returning to left field, Rose met debris from the grandstand. Shea's P.A. voice pled for calm. NL president Chub Feeney warned of forfeit. Berra, Seaver, Jones, and Rusty Staub approached the offending throng. "We told 'em," said Yogi, "they was only hurting the team."

The crowd got with the program (too, New York, 9–2). Rose's next-day poke tied the playoff at two games each. Seaver won Match Five, 7–2. Said Jones of another pennant: "Praise the Lord." Alas, a Second Coming skipped this outfit *sans* .300 hitter, 20-game winner, or driver-in of 100 runs. Oakland began the Series by winning, 2–1. The Mets then took a record 4 hour and 13 minute 10–6 grotesquerie: Mays fell chasing a routine fly. At Shea, New York won two of three games. The peroration was gloomier: A's, 3–1 and 5–2.

The Mets had swung from tenth (in a 10-team league) to first. They now swung back in a Metsian sort of way. On September 11, 1974, St. Louis won, 4–3, in 25 innings. Joe Torre hit into four double plays v. Houston on July 21, 1975. Seaver fanned 200 for a record eighth straight year. In 1977, Grant traded the three-time Cy Younger. Tom Terrific retired with a 311–205 record, 2.86 ERA, and NL-righty high 3, 272 Ks.

The '77–'78–'79ers finished last. Ghosts peopled 126th Street and Roosevelt Avenue. New York, New York was again a Yankees, Yankees town.

ASTRODOME

A February 1960 newsreel etched Ebbets Field's razing. "And now it's 'Play Ball' again, but not the sort Dodger fans cheer, as wrecking ball hit Bums dugout. This time Ebbets Field itself is struck out." Ballpark tradition Kd in the 1960s and early 1970s. *Exemplum*: Houston, the Space City, hatched a space-age home.

"The day the doors on this park open, every other park in the world will be antiquated," Branch Rickey said in late 1964. A publicity release added: "The world's first air-conditioned, domed all-purpose stadium, sitting like a precious jewel in southwest Texas, was constructed by the citizens of Harris County at a cost of $20.5 million, plus $3 million for the land on which the site is located at a total cost of $31.6 million for the entire project including access routes and parking"—and leased for 40 years to Houston Sports Association, which owned and operated the NL Astros.

The Harris County Domed Stadium rose to thwart Houston's rain, humidity, and mosquitos. Said creator Roy Hofheinz: "It soon became an emblem of the state."

The Dome on the south side of official Houston was the bigs' second "covered stadium." Hall of Fame librarian Jim Gates laughed. "The first concerned the '30s Negro National League New York Cubans. They literally played *under* Queensboro's 59th Street Bridge in New York City." It was the second "indoor" plot. The 1888 Downtowners beat the Uptowners, 6–1, inside Philly's State Fairgrounds building. Other firsts claimed that bigger is better. The 9½ acre, 715-foot diameter had baseball's first covered roof, which measured 642 feet across, peaked at 208 feet above second base, and had 4,796 clear panes of glass, $4.5 million air conditioning, a 6,600-ton cooling capacity, 72 degree temperature, enough plumbing for 40,000 persons to wash their hands, footlights that used enough power to illumine a town of 9,000, and "baseball's [first] exclusive sky boxes, a place for relaxation and entertainment," said a video. "This is really some kind of baseball."

Actually, sky boxes shunted baseball. "People were there to socialize, make deals," said then-Governor John B. Connally. "The baseball was incidental." Roger Kahn later wrote of "telephones, radios, bars, and furniture ranging from French Provincial to Texas Gauche." Each fully-carpeted box housed 24 to 30 people and linked ice makers, refrigerators, rest rooms, catered hors d'oeuvres, and closed circuit TV. You might kibitz about the size (46,217), five tiers (team colors orange, lemon-yellow, and raspberry red), configuration (seats swiveled to house football), and isolation (boxes sat eight levels above the field).

Even the name pealed Texasspeak. "We had a pact with the Colt Firearms Company," said former vice president Bill Giles. "But when Hofheinz wanted to market novelties under the same name, the firm threatened to sue." The Aero Space Center defined Houston. The .45ers became the Astros—hence, Astrodome. Colt Stadium was razed into part of a 30,000-car parking lot. Nearby, Hofheinz built four hotels, a convention center (Astrohall), and amusement park (Astroworld). Inside, he forged a Countdown Cafeteria, Trailblazer Restaurant, imitation Sidewalk Cafe, and VIP suite with *faux* medieval chapel. "I'll pray for pitching," said manager Luman Harris, who soon prayed for calm.

On April 8, 1965, the Astros played a seven-inning game against their Triple-A Oklahoma City farm club. Gene Elston brought baseball to the lonely towns and booming cities of the scopic Southwest. "From the start fielders had trouble with flies," said the Astros voice. "The problem was the ceiling—its 5,000 plastic windows and steel grate guides a foot and half apart. When a fly hit this jigsaw background, the light and dark made it impossible to judge." A night later the Dome opened with an exhibition: 47,878 gaped. Connally threw out the first ball. First batter/hit/homer: Yankees' Mickey Mantle. Score: Astros, 2–1, in 12 innings, on Nellie Fox's hit. Twinbills then followed v. the Yanks and O's. Day glare made flies clear to radar, not men. "We've had a billion dollars worth of publicity and can't jeopardize it," Hofheinz told general manager Paul Richards. "If the game turns into a farce, refund the money of any dissatisfied fans."

The Dome opened for real April 12. Twenty-four of 26 U.S. astronauts got a lifetime bigs pass. First pitcher: Bob Bruce. Batter/hit: Phillies' Tony Taylor. Homer: mate Richie Allen. Score: Chris Short checked Houston, 2–0.

Soon, glare checked real grass.

A '65 story about Bob Lillis shows the infielder comparing a pair of sunglasses to see "which will cut back glare." Neither: Hofheinz thus applied a blue translucent acrylic to the roof. "This killed the problem of not seeing fly balls," said Elston. "But daylight coming into the stadium was cut," killing the Tifway 419 Bermuda grass bred for indoor use. The offshoot can hardly be overblown: phony turf. Edgar Ray's book, *The Grand Huckster,* claims that grass' demise secretly pleased the Judge. He saw the Dome hosting auto and motorcycle races, rodeos, and conventions—a multipurpose place.

"This schedule," said Elston, "required a harder, more durable surface." From St. Louis the Monsanto Company unveiled artificial grass (here, *AstroTurf*). On April 18, 1966, it abutted the Dome's dirt infield. By 1971, it draped the entire field except dirt sliding pits. At one point in the '80s 11 of 26 big-league parks flaunted what hitters loved (the ball laid rubber), fielders hailed (no bad bounces), and the public damned (grotesque). "I don't want to play on no place my horse can't eat off of," said Richie Allen. Suddenly, watching grass grow had a new appeal.

The Dome presaged in another sense: It became the NL's least power-friendly home. Lines measured 340 feet (later, 330 in '72, 340 in '77, 330, 325, 330, and 325 in '94). Alleys seemed a moonshot away: 375 (390 in '66, 378 in '72, 390, 378 in '85, 372, 380, and 375 in '94). Center field varied: 406 (400 in '72, 406 in '77, and 400 in '85). Ibid., wall heights: left and right 16 (12 in '69, 10, 19.5, and 10 in '92); center, 12 (10 in '77). The '65 Mets accused Houston of lowering the temperature to help its offense. "Sure didn't help our drives carry," mused Elston. "Look at the homer figures." No Astro has led the league.

A sock-happy Texan found distraction in space-garbed ushers, lower-deck shoeshine stands, and carousel of ground rules. A ball hitting a foul speaker was out if the fielder caught it. The P.A. speaker was in play 117 feet up and 329 feet from home. Mike Schmidt hit it in June 1974. "Another boon to pitchers," he said. "It would have gone 500 feet." On April 28, 1965, the Mets visited the Dome. Lindsey Nelson called play-by-play in a gondola suspended over second base.

"What about my man up there?" Casey Stengel asked umpire Tom Gorman.

"What man?" Gorman said.

"My man Lindsey. What if the ball hits my man Lindsey?" Gorman looked up and shrugged. "Well, Case," he said, "if the ball hits the roof, it's in play, so I guess if it hits Lindsey, it's in play."

"How about that?" Casey later said. "That's the first time my man Lindsey was ever a ground rule."

That year another beef fixed the Eighth Wonder of the World. "Want big?" said Giles. "It's 300 tons, cost $2 million, is 474 feet long, has 14,000 lights, and more than one-half acres of computer-sequenced lights." The world's largest scoreboard made Bill Veeck's exploding board look like chalk in the Roman Colosseum. It had something for everyone, if you liked the 'Stros.

Left-center and right-center message boards flanked the Astros insignia. Above it, lights flashed, cannons boomed, and cartoon cowboys hailed a homer. "But only Astros homers!" laughed Giles. "Anway, the Dome lost charm when it ditched the scoreboard [1990] to put in 10,000 lousy football seats." Visitors found the *scoreboard* lousy. A relieved pitcher was parodied by a figure entering the shower. Tears stained his cheek. The shower filled with water. Funereal music played. Finally, only two eyeballs shone through the dark.

The board shouted "Charge" with serial regularity. Once Cubs pitcher Bill Paul turned his back until noise abated. The umpire told him to pitch. Said Giles: "It is [our] job to make every game as entertaining as possible." Ump John Kibler ruled against the Astros on one play—and ejected Bob Aspromonte on another. The board swelled, "Kibler Did It Again." Crew chief Frank Secory quickly phoned league president *Warren* Giles. "This is an attempt to incite the fans. That's about as low as you can get." Dad told son to act his age.

On April 24, 1965, Aspromonte became the first Astro to go Dome yard. Willie Mays hit homer No. 500 off Don Nottebart. Joe Morgan lashed a franchise-best 12 triples. Home attendance nearly tripled to 2,151,470. Next year Mike Cuellar had a second-to-Koufax 2.22 ERA. In June, Sandy beat Houston, 5–2: A Dome-high 50,980 watched. By 1967 the house count dipped to 1,348,303. Jimmy Wynn—The Toy Cannon—homered thrice in a game. The likeness lingers of Morgan and Sonny Jackson leading off first: Board images of go-go dancers urged them to steal. Don Wilson tossed the Dome's first no-hitter. Houston placed ninth for the fourth time in five years. "I like to win big, or lose big," Connally often said, "but what's the sense of losing small?" The '68ers finished tenth.

That April 15 the Astros beat the Mets, 1–0, in 24 innings, on Al Weis' error off Al Spangler's grounder. By then, a certain actor was three sheets to the wind. "That game set a ton of records [e.g., longest complete NL and bigs night match] but John Wayne didn't see them. He was in town to make a movie," said Elston. "Our radio booth was next to the Astrodome Club where people ate and had a bar. The last time I saw him was the 23rd inning. They had to carry him out of there." The first 1–0 All-Star Game drove you to drink: 20 Kd; Mays scored an unearned first-frame run.

In 1968, Wilson's 18 Ks v. Cincinnati tied Feller. Third baseman Doug Rader .267 was not exactly an altar boy. He used the locker room as a driving range. A writer asked Larry Dierker, "How come nobody took Rader's golf clubs away?" He said, " 'Cause they wanted to live." Rader urged Little Leaguers to digest bubble gum cards. "You eat the information, and become a better player." Later he told them to eat the bases and home plate. Once Rader, Morgan, announcer Harry Kalas, and his dad, a minister, played golf. By the rear nine Doug's language had turned blue. "Dougie, ease off [on profanity]," said Morgan. "Don't you know Harry's dad is a minister?" Doug brightened. "Mr. Kalas, I didn't know you were a minister. Jesus Christ!"

Less godly: the '69 Astros, fifth in a six-team West. On April 29–30 Jim Maloney and Wilson, respectively, no-hit Houston and Cincinnati. In 1970, J. R. Richard debuted by fanning 15 Giants. Their manager knew hitting, rarely contended, and reaped small respect. On the bus Harry Walker sat with a hat over his head. To the rear players caroled the once-batting champion.

"Now Harry Walker is the one that manages this crew," went a verse. "He doesn't like it when we drink and fight and smoke and screw. But when we win our game each day, then what the hell can Harry say?" The kicker: "It makes a fellow proud to be an Astro."

BUSCH STADIUM

Lyndon Johnson made even a Republican proud November 27, 1963. "We have talked long enough in this country about equal rights," he said in his first address as president to Congress. "We have talked for 100 years or more." St. Louis talked long about building a park to revive downtown. It talked into the early 1960s. At that point Cardinals owner Anheuser-Busch pledged $5 million. More followed—and a city referendum to clear a 30-acre tract of land. Ground broke May 24, 1964, near four current U.S. interstates. Eight blocks away a Gateway Arch rose on the banks of the Mississippi to hail taming the Wilderness. "St. Louis turned 202 in 1966," said writer Bob Broeg. "The ballpark was its soul—baseball, its heart."

In 1985, Peter Gammons called St. Louis "the best baseball town in the world. For more than the first half of this century, as the western and southernmost team, they were the club of the heartland from Raleigh to Memphis, Mobile to Little Rock, Omaha to Dallas, because the games on KMOX grew to become baseball's first, foremost, and most powerful. From any of the eight states that border Missouri all the way down through Mississippi—the Cardinals draw weekend trippers. The Cardinals are the *real* America's Team." Baseball tied liturgy and benediction. Streets and factories blared big-league talk. Redbird waves of loyalty splashed shirts, shorts, and hats. "The color, the nonstop roar. A Cardinal crowd is the only place in baseball that resembles a college football game," wrote Bob Burnes. If only the ballpark could seem as Promethean as the clientele.

May 12, 1966, Opening Day. Cardinals Nation cheered a cross of Sportsman's Park and the age's whitebread clones. Like Houston, parking bulged: two stadium garages, small plots, and multistory lots. Public transportation was something to take or leave. Like Shea, Busch Stadium was symmetrical (330, lines; 386, alleys; and 414, center), multipurpose (NFL Cardinals), and *sans* specialty (no bad bounces off the 10½-foot outfield fence). "The '60s parks favored alley hitters," said Broeg. Fast forward: the '81–'91ers placed last in homers each year but one. On the other hand, Busch was better than later lookalikes: *That* was the wonder.

Ardor helped. "The Greeks had their Parthenon, the Quakers their meeting houses and the colonists their village greens," *Sports Illustrated* noted. "St. Louisans have Busch Stadium." Their 141,500-square-foot, 49,275-seat park lay almost 30 feet below street level. Unlike in Houston, grass was real. Unlike in D.C., seats rimmed the fence. An upper level enclosed the park. Two lower tiers wed the plate to each pole. A two-section, 35,000-light, $1.5 million scoreboard bisected bleachers. (An electronic redbird fluttered upon a Cards homer or seventh-inning stretch.) The organ liked Busch's "King of Beers." Connecting arches angled inward at roof level 130 feet above the field. "They gave a distinctive look," said adopted St. Louisan Bob Costas. "The arches made Busch seem more traditional than other parks."

By Opening Day, the Gateaway arch towered beyond left field. Broeg laughed: "The message board didn't work, the elevator service wasn't up to speed, and the clubhouse wasn't done." Most of St. Louis' largest sports crowd, 46,048, didn't care. First pitcher: Ray Washburn. Batter: Atlanta's Gary Geiger. Homer: mate Felipe Alou. Score: Cardinals, 4–3, on Lou Brock's 12th-inning hit. On July 12, Busch (a.k.a. Civic Center Stadium [1966] and Busch Memorial Stadium [1966–'83]) hosted the All-Star Game. The temperature registered 105 degrees and 130 on the field. Tim McCarver scored the 10th-inning decider: Nationals, 2–1, before 49,936. Honorary coach Casey Stengel was asked about the park: "Well, I must say that it sure holds the heat well."

The '66 Swifties wooed 1,712,980. The '67ers roped 2,090,145 and a pennant. Lou Brock led the league with 52 steals and 113 runs. Curt Flood and McCarver batted .335 and .295. Orlando Cepeda—Cha Cha—had .325 and league-high 111 ribbies, named the Cards "El Birdos," and became clubhouse leader and first unanimous league MVP. One day the team bus readied to leave for the park. Manager Red Schoendienst said, "Everybody on? We're ready to go." Bob Gibson was pitching. "No," he shouted. "Cepeda isn't on, and we're not leaving till he gets here." Gibbie broke his leg, clinched the flag v. Philadelphia, and thrice beat Boston in the Series. "Not bad," said Broeg, "26 strikeouts and a 1 ERA." Next year Brock hit 14 triples. Mike Shannon had a team-high 79 RBI. Flood took his sixth of seven straight Gold Gloves. Gibson abided another planet.

"I'm asked the greatest left-handed and right-handed pitchers," said Harry Caray. "Easy. Koufax and Gibson. You can have the rest, and wouldn't have a chance." Batters didn't in 1968. Gibbie led in complete games (28), shutouts (13), Ks (268), and ERA (1.12, yielding only 38 earned runs). The Cy Young/MVP finished 251–174, fanned 3,117, won nine Gold Gloves, and became the first pitcher to hit two Series homers. He hated between the lines. In 1965, mate Bill White was traded to the Phils. Gibson threw at his head. He pitched like an egg timer. Once McCarver asked Bob to slow down. "What are you doing here?" he snapped. "Go back behind the plate—only thing you know about pitching is that it's hard to hit." A manager told Tim to brake Gibbie's pace.

Said McCarver: "But he *likes* to work fast." Finally he took a few steps, yelled at Bob, and beat a path back home. Pitching coach Barney Schultz was afraid to near the mound. "What can *you* teach *me*?" Gibson shouted. "You were a knuckleball pitcher. I throw fastballs"—e.g., October 2, 1968.

Five years earlier to the day Koufax had set a World Series mark by fanning 15 Yankees. Gibbie Kd 17 to beat Denny McLain, 4–0, in Game One's "pitching duel of the century." Said the principal: "I'm never surprised at anything I do." He took Game Four, 8–1, for a 3–1 Cardinals lead. Detroit then won twice. Game Seven surprised: Gibson lost, at home, *v.* Mickey Lolich, 4–1. Baseball soon shrank the strike zone and dropped the mound by five inches. Burnes sighed. "Gibbie had taken all the fun out of the game."

A 1968 statue of Stan Musial, coiled, eying the pitcher, was unveiled outside Busch Stadium. (Others honor Brock, Jack Buck, Dizzy Dean, Gibson, Rogers Hornsby, Red Schoendienst, and Enos Slaughter.) "Ironically," said Broeg, "Stan never played there." Walt Whitman wrote *Leaves of Grass*. Next winter Busch deserted grass. "Summers in St. Louis are hell," said Broeg. "The grass gets splotchy. So they put in phony grass with a dirt infield [in 1977 becoming sliding pits]." In '71, Gibbie threw his sole no-hitter. Joe Torre parlayed a league-high .363 and 137 RBI into St. Louis' then-12th MVP.

The Cards moved center field to 410 and back to 414, then strung an 8-foot inner fence from left-center to right-center. Alleys became 376, center 404. "The artificial stuff and fence hurt the look," said Costas. "This had been a *baseball* park. Now it looked less so." Outhomered, St. Louis yanked the fence in 1977. "The long ball," said KMOX talk host Jack Carney, "isn't the Cardinals anyway."

ATLANTA–FULTON COUNTY STADIUM

Say Atlanta. "You think of Hank Aaron, the thin air, the name Launching Pad," mused the Georgian Ernie Harwell. "It's hard not to think of homers." Forgotten: In 1866, a writer dubbed the amateur team "Atlantas" the "finest team in the world." It proceeded to lose to the "Gate City Nine," 127–29, in a four-hour, 30-minute game. Shamed,

Atlanta disbanded, then revived in 1885. "Welcome to professional baseball," wrote *Atlanta Constitution* managing editor Henry W. Grady. Soon he became Southern Association president.

His Crackers graced Peters Park, Brisbane Park, the Show Grounds, Piedmont Park, and 1903's Ponce de Leon Park—said Grady, "named after the amusement park that gave its name to Ponce de Leon Avenue." A 1923 fire razed the wooden chapel. Replacing it: a concrete 15,000-seat kirk. Ponce's scoreboard loomed 462 feet from home plate. Fronting it: a magnolia tree. "It seemed not just the park's symbol," said Harwell, "but the baseball South's."

Earl Mann became president in 1934. In '49, he built a hedge from left to center field. "It cut down the distance," added Ernie. "It also created controversy. A catch in the hedge was legal. If the fielder crashed through, it's a homer." The Crackers won flags, bred icons, and packed the greenhouse. Many sat atop a four-deck series of right-field signs. In late 1959, Mann gave the SA his franchise. Atlanta mayor Ivan Allen, Jr., raised the bar in '64. "I have the verbal commitment of a major-league baseball club to move its franchise to Atlanta if we have a stadium available by 1966." Quickly the board of aldermen backed an $18 million stadium complex, in a downtown urban renewal area, ¼ mile from the state capitol. Most hinted at the Milwaukee (née Boston) Braves. By coincidence, they soon signed a new Triple-A affiliate: Atlanta's Crackers.

Atlanta–Fulton County (a.k.a. '65–'74 Atlanta) Stadium rose near where the old South died. The park joined Capitol Avenue and Fulton, Pullman, and Washington Streets (later, Interstates 20, 75, and 85). General Sherman headquartered on a ridge during the Battle of Atlanta. Yankee, schmankee. Georgia welcomed the invading Braves. Their teepee anchored 19.4 acres, was 751 feet in diameter, and had a 10,000-car parking lot. Few were filled in 1965. "A judge ruled that the Braves could move, but had to play that final season in Milwaukee," said *Atlanta Constitution* columnist Furman Bisher. "So the Crackers played there instead." The enclosed circular Thompson and Street Company–designed park housed 51,000 (later 50,893 '66 via 53,046 '85 to 52,007). The field lay 33 feet below street level. Light standards were mounted on the roof. Riblike ventricles circled the exterior. Inside, you found a dud.

Lengths were pedestrian: lines, 325 (330 in '67); alleys, 385 (375 in '69 and 385 in '74); and center, 402 (400 in '69 and 402 in '73). A six-foot wire (later 10 partly/fully Plexiglas) fence linked the poles. Forget heisting homers: Bullpens paralleled the fence. Behind them a 22-foot outer wall trimmed the lower deck. "Color ads [also, right-center main board] often decorated it," said Aaron, ironic, since bigs color paled. A matrix board fronted the roof in center field. Foul ground was enormous. Three levels of plastic rimmed the yard. "Florida seemed closer than the upper tier," added announcer Milo Hamilton.

"For the Braves," said a wag, "it all seemed perfect—for the [NFL] Falcons."

On April 12, 1966, the Braves debuted at Fulton: Pittsburgh, 3–2, before 50,761 (season attendance: 1,539,801). Preview of coming attractions: Atlanta's Joe Torre (twice) and the Bucs' Joe Pignatano and Willie Stargell homered. Tony Cloninger, of Lincoln, North Carolina, pitched all 13 innings. "Tony would have given his right arm to win," mused Torre. "Many felt it was never the same." That July 3 Cloninger smashed two grand slams, had nine RBI, was relieved, and won, 17–3. "One day he pitches all the way and loses. Another day he slugs like Ruth," added manager Bobby Bragan. "Anyone who says they know baseball is hallucinating."

The Braves coaxed Hamilton that year from the White Sox. "They were looking," he said, "to create an image." It often seemed that the Braves had not the slightest thought what that image was. "There was a novelty at the start," mused Torre. "One day there were about forty-five thousand people in the stands. You could hear a pin drop. Fans just didn't know what to do at a game—it was such a contrast to Milwaukee." Red Georgia clay splotched the infield, warning track, mound, and around the plate. The park also sported Indian biases and deities.

Big Victor, a totem pole–styled model, warmed Fulton in 1966. The '67ers dealt him for a real Indian in tribal garb—Levi Walker, Jr., a.k.a. Chief Noc-A-Homa—in a teepee on a 20-foot square platform behind the inner fence. By 1978–'82, it usurped 235 left-center seats between aisles 128 and 130, rows 18–30. "This caused a crisis," said 1976–announcer Skip Caray. "For years the Chief was a staple, dancing, hoot-ing, signing autographs. In '82, the Braves got in a pennant race. They needed the seats, and yanked him." Directly the Braves hit the skids. Noc returned. They made the playoff. The L.C.S. again loomed in August 1983. Again the chief was bumped, and Atlanta slumped. Noc returned September 16, retiring in '85.

Enduring: long ball waves of imagery. Atlanta lies more than 1,000 feet above sea level—the bigs' highest pre-Denver park. The Launching Pad led the league in homers ('70-'71-'72-'73: 211, 186, 174, and 205, respectively). Rico Carty, Mike Lum, and Orlando Cepeda '70 homered thrice in different games. Atlanta ripped four dingers in a '71 inning. Dave Johnson's 43 homers set a '73 bigs record for second basemen. For the first time three players hit 40 on a team—Johnson, Darrell Evans (41), and Aaron (40). Intrigued: much of the Confederacy. Baseball's largest single-team TV network joined 22 stations in six states. Lacking: fidelity to *being there*. By 1972, attendance fell to 752,973.

Felipe Alou topped the '66 NL in total bases, hits, and runs. In '67, Aaron smashed his only inside-the-parker. The '68 Teepees finished fifth. Next year the league split into two six-team divisions: 1,458,320 watched Atlanta win the West. Phil Niekro went 23–13. For the fourth time Aaron bashed 44 taters. The Braves even turned seven (men) into three (outs). Cubs Don Kessinger and Glenn Beckert people third and second base, none out, Pat Jarvis pitching. Billy Williams hits to Cepeda, who steps on first. The ball leaves Cha Cha for the shortstop, catcher, second baseman, and finally Jarvis. Pat tags Beckert, then turns toward third. "All of a sudden I see [second baseman Felix] Millan moving there," said Jarvis. "He's trying to tag Kessinger before he can get back." Jarvis throws to Millan, who tosses to outfielder Carty at third. Carty tags out Kessinger. For those of you scoring, 3-6-2-4-1-4-7. Triple play! The season ended two days later.

The LCS ended quickly: Mets 9–5, 11–6, and 7–4. Next year Hoyt Wilhelm, 46, pitched his 1,000th big-league game. Carty led the league in average (.366) and on-base (.456). Aaron got hit 3,000. In 1971, No. 44 whacked his 600th homer. "Move over, Babe," Harwell would write, "Here Comes Henry." Fulton installed an 80-year-old calliope organ. Manager Luman Harris sang the blues, replaced by Eddie Mathews, followed by six skippers through '78. Fulton hosted the All-Star Game: Nats, 4–3. Niekro no-hit San Diego. On July 21, 1973, Aaron bashed

No. 700. What was Joe Friday's badge number on TV's *Dragnet?*—714. Aaron's first '74 swing, off Cincy's Jack Billingham, tied the Babe. He then primed to cross a most Ruthian line.

Aaron never went yard 50 times in a year, as Babe did, or 60, like Ruth in '27. He did bop more than 30 and 40 homers, respectively, 15 and eight times. Said Stan Musial: "He thinks there's nothing he can't hit." The Silent Man tied efficiency, grace, and skill: third all-time, games played (3,298), behind Rose and Yaz, and hits (3,771), behind Rose and Cobb; second, times at bat (12,364), trailing Rose, and tied with Ruth, in runs scored (2,174), trailing Cobb; first, ribbies (2,297), total bases (6,856), and extra-base hits (1,477). "Eclectic," says *Webster's,* means "selecting from various systems, doctrines, or sources." Hank selected three Gold Gloves, six years stole more than 20 bases, and led the NL in batting twice—and four times homers and RBI.

On April 8, 1974, a drizzly night in Georgia, Aaron walked his first up before a Fulton-high 53,775. In the fourth, he arced a low slider toward the sky. "He's sitting on 714," Hamilton began. "Here's the pitch by [Al] Downing . . . swinging. . . . There's a drive into left-center field! That ball is gonna' be . . . outta here! It's gone! It's 715!" clearing the inner fence into reliever Tom House's glove. "There's a new home-run champion of all time! And it's Henry Aaron! Henry Aaron's coming around third! His teammates are at home plate! Listen to this crowd!" Noc-A-Homa erupted. The stadium shook. Mates hoisted Aaron on their shoulders. The Hammer embraced his parents and wife.

The rest was anticlimax, like World War I post–Verdun. (Atlanta marked Aaron's longest Fulton poke, No. 557, in seat 107, upper deck.) The '75ers scattered 534,672, less than Wisconsin's lame-duck adieu. On September 8, only 737 eyeballed the Astros. That winter Ted Turner bought the team. The Braves spent the next four years sweeping the West cellar.

ANAHEIM STADIUM

In 1955, Disneyland opened in Anaheim, California. By 1964, the suburb boasted 150,000 people—and 6 million in a 30-mile radius. "It is young and growing," said Mayor C. L. (Chuck) Chandler. That August he broke ground on the Angels' new park with owner Gene Autry and builder Del E. Webb. From Disneyland, two miles away, a fire engine carried Mickey Mouse, Goofy, and Pluto to give skipper Bill Rigney a pennant. Even Los Angeles mayor Sam Yorty, arriving by helicopter, hoped to buck the Halos' new idyll. "If we had [your] foresight and been able to build a ballpark that you are doing, we would still have the Angels."

Anaheim Stadium, a.k.a. the Big A, replaced 148 acres of corn, alfalfa, and orange and eucalyptus trees. "I'm proud that my construction company will build this," said ex-Yanks co-owner Webb. "I've tried to observe the right and wrong of every stadium in the country. We want to get all the right things in this one—and leave out all the wrong things." A monthlong strike slowed work. Picketing forced another four-day stop. Saving Webb: 200 laborers, working till 2:30 A.M. in the final week. It was easy to get there: Three entrances bled off major freeways.

The Big A was small (43,000). Outside split-level homes dotted block after block. The San Gabriel Mountains splashed the backdrop. Palm trees rose beyond center field. The park's namesake $1 million 230-foot A-frame scoreboard dwarfed left. A giant halo atop it, built by Standard Oil of California, bordered a ground-level parking lot for 12,000 cars and more than 200 buses. You took two escalators, four elevators, and ramps to varied-colored levels. Then, it hit you. Unlike Fulton, here was a baseball-*only* park.

"To decide our distances," Webb began, "we tested both air density and wind at normal game times [1:30 and 8 P.M.]." The haunt was symmetrical: lines, 330; power alleys, 375 (369 in '73, 374, and 370 in '89); deep alleys, 386; and center, 406 (402 in '73 and 404 in '79). Heights, however, varied: lines to each pen, 4¾ feet (steel); gates 10 (wire) and 9 (padded in '81); most of the fence, 10 wire (7-foot-10-inch wire in '73 and padded in '81); and left-center between 386 and 406, 7½ (padded in '81).

The $24 million den had a living-is-easy feel. "Baseball isn't Armageddon," said Webb. "We've built this park to have fun." Three tiers wrapped around home plate beyond the lines. Sightlines were, oops, divine: The highest row sat 109 feet above the field. At RFK, the outer wall kept you from plucking homers. Anaheim's low corner fences pitted client *v.* fielder. Its brochure touted "convenience, comfort, and cour-

tesy." The bluegrass looked lusher than Kentucky's. The Big A opened
April 19, 1966. To many, it seemed Anaheim's *second* magic world.

Marcelino Lopez threw the opening pitch 20 minutes late. "A broken
water main flooded a nearby highway," said Autry. "What do we get? A
massive traffic jam." Other firsts. Batter: Chicago's Tommie Agee. Hit:
Halo Jim Fregosi. Homer: mate Rick Reichardt. Score: White Sox, 3–1,
before 31,660. The Angels placed sixth. Attendance tripled to 1,400,321.
A year later America got its first real glimpse of Disney West. "The Big A
was a hitter's park," Webb said. Sadly, its '67 All-Star Game began in
late afternoon. Sun and shadow waylaid hitters: a record 30 Kd. Tony
Perez's 15th-frame homer gave the Nationals a 2–1 win.

A year later George Brunet tied thrift (2.86 ERA) and loss (league-
worst 17). Rigney then yielded to Harold (Lefty) Phillips, for whom English was a second language. Once the Angels led Minnesota by a run:
ninth inning, two out, bases full. The batter grounded between shortstop
Fregosi's legs. Next day the skipper leaned against the batter's cage,
malapropping, "That's water over the bridge."

In 1970, Clyde Wright entered the National Association of Inter-
collegiate Athletics (NAIA) Hall of Fame. That night the Angels pitcher
no-hit Oakland, 4–0. Sullen, immature, and prescient of Albert Belle
Alex Johnson won the Angels' only batting title (.329). Phillips benched
(five times), fined (29), and suspended him in '71. "A judge later said
Alex had been 'emotionally incapacitated,' " said Wright, "and that he
should be treated the same as a physically disabled player." Johnson got
back almost $30,000 in salary. The Angels soon got a *wunderkind*.

By 1972, Jim Fregosi combined one Gold Glove, six All-Star teams,
and franchise lead in games, at-bats, runs, hits, doubles, triples, and total
bases. The Mets swapped Nolan Ryan hoping to close their third-base
revolving door. Instead, Ryan, 24, became pitching's Ulysses. On Closing
Day 1973, he Kd 16 Twins, in 11 innings, to top Sandy Koufax's single-
year 382. Ryan '73–'75 no-hit Kansas City, Detroit, Minnesota, and Baltimore. "He was wild enough to keep you loose," said new mate Frank
Robinson, "and strong enough to fan you."

Signs read "Big A K Country." It was also walk country. Eight times
Ryan led the league. "Later he got control," said Robinson, "and

became the total package." It nearly arrived in '77: The Express led in complete games and strikeouts and Kd 19 in a game. Rigney had been the Cowboy's manager for 8½ years. In 1978, Fregosi became the seventh post-'68. Said Autry: "We'll just keep changing till we get it right."

The Soviets invaded Afghanistan. Jimmy Carter confessed shock, embargoed sales of grain and technology, and boycotted the 1980 Moscow Summer Olympics. The exiled Shah of Iran entered the U.S. for medical treatment. Forces of Islamic leader Ayatollah Khomeini seized 63 Americans at the Embassy in Teheran. U.S. power had flown the cage. Angels' power slew their '79 division. Don Baylor had 36 dingers, led the AL in RBI and runs, and became California's first MVP. Brian Downing hit .326. Rod Carew arrived to add .318. The Angels cajoled a record 2,523,375. Baltimore grabbed a 2–0 best-of-five playoff lead.

The Big A then hosted its postseason opener: Autrys, 4–3, on a ninth-inning walk, dropped fly, and Larry Harlow's double.

Later, Richard Nixon dropped by the clubhouse. "He was living in [nearby] San Clemente," said Autry, "a terrific fan, came to a lot of games." He came next day, too. It didn't help: 8–0, O's.

15

DOWN ON MY KNEES

"There's no there there," Gertrude Stein said famously of Oakland. Perhaps she meant the bigs before 1968. The Pacific Coast League played Oakland from 1903–'57. Its field, Oaks Park, in nearby Emeryville, was small and special. Bleachers began 10 feet off the ground. "That way," said owner J. Cal Ewing, "we can avoid a white hitters' backdrop." The clubhouse also had a washing machine. "If you want to look neat on the field," said trainer Red Adams, "you have to start from inside out." In 1948, Casey Stengel won the pennant with "Nine Old Men." The team averaged 34 years old. The park was older. "Every time a ball hit the left-field fence," said ex–NL batting champion Ernie Lombardi, "the boards fell down." The Oaks soon became Vancouver's. For a decade, the NL Giants boomed across San Francisco Bay. Then, in late 1967, Charles O. Finley left Kansas City for a park 15 miles from Emeryville, at the C. W. Nimitz Freeway and Hegenberger Road. Divide and conquer may work in politics. It nearly killed baseball in the Bay.

Public cash built the Oakland–Alameda County Coliseum for the AFL

Raiders. It was symmetrical (the '60s: what else? lines, 330; alleys, 378 [later, 375, 372, and 367]; center, 410 [400 in '69, 396, 397, and 400 in '90]) and had foul ground to Berkeley. "Balls kept getting caught," said '68 skipper Bob Kennedy. "Cost you 10 points a year." (No Oakland A has won a batting title.) Tall grass stemmed triples. Heavy night air punctured would-be dingers. The backstop—a notch in the stands—lay a league-high 90 feet from the plate. "The Coliseum," said a writer, "is easily the AL's most pitcher-friendly park." Set in the ground like a concrete pillbox, barely visible from the freeway, its exterior fit the neighborhood, plain and rough.

"No cable cars or great skyline," said Bay native Jon Miller, "just train tracks and warehouses." You descended to the ticket window. Next door a complex housed skating, hoops, and hockey. The Coliseum a.k.a. Mausoleum was stark, outside and in: no brick, arch, roof, or sculpture. Capacity housed 50,000. Three tiers reached beyond each line. A single 7,000-seat bleacher deck trimmed the 8 (10 in '81) foot outfield wall. A green hill lay beyond it. "Given the park's sterility," read the *Oakland Tribune,* "you focus on the hill, not field."

The Coliseum premiered April 17, 1968. First pitcher: Lew Krausse. Batter: O's' Curt Blefary. Homer: mate Boog Powell. Score: Baltimore, 4–1. First ball: thrown out by Governor Ronald Reagan. "One thing I'm sure of," he said of Income Tax Day, "is that a lot of you paid your taxes." Boos rained from 50,164. Reagan smiled. "Up to a few moments ago, I was happy to be here." Straight off, the A's practiced hand-to-mouth. Mule mascot Charlie O. stepped from a luxury van, stopped at each base, and bowed. Tennessee Ernie Ford and a marching band readied for the Anthem. "But Finley couldn't negotiate an agreement on live music with the union," said announcer Monte Moore. "We played a recording." Finley's $1 million right-field scoreboard flopped for several months. The pitcher's mound lay on a steel shell for Oakland's soccer team. The exposed shell was covered between innings. "Opening Night had sort of a wing-it feel," Charlie fessed. A worse feel: empty seats.

"Finley thought you could create new fans in the Bay Area," said writer Bob Stevens. Instead, he stole the Giants'. In 1968, both clubs drew 1,711,069 v. the '66 Stonehams' 1,657,192. (Oakland's 837,603 barely topped '67 Kansas City.) Many missed the franchise's first .500 year since 1952. Bert Campaneris led the league in hits and steals. On

May 8, Catfish Hunter faced the Twins' Rich Reese in the ninth: 6–0, two out, and full count. "Reese fouled off a bunch of pitches," said Moore, "then Kd for the AL's first perfect game since 1922." Next year the A's installed the 24-foot-high and 126-foot-wide "Finley Fun [computer score] Board" with cartoons and other graphics. It had loads to cheer (in '69–'70, Reggie Jackson's 47 dingers, Sal Bando's 113 RBI, and Vida Blue's '70 no-hitter: "Youngest to no-hit anyone [21]," Finley noted, "since Daffy Dean") and few to celebrate. The '70ers drew 788,232. Blue pitched before 4,284.

"Charlie was hung up on his color scheme—white, gold, and kelly green," said Hunter. "I remember one home opener had gold-covered bases." Ironically, marketing gold would have reaped more green. "Charlie had only one scout, carried his briefcase, worked in Chicago," said 1970 announcer Harry Caray. After high school, this son of a steelworker entered the mills, sold insurance at night, formed a company, and was a millionaire by 35. Finley badgered grounds help, phoned the dugout, hatched trades, and had a reverence for talent developed here. Bando and Campaneris moored third base and shortstop. Joe Rudi, Rick Monday, and Jackson formed the outfield. Gene Tenace caught Blue and Hunter and Odom and Ken Holtzman. Harry laughed. "Charlie let me use his penthouse on the lake [near Oakland]." The A's soon seemed to the manor born.

Blue '71 burst like Vesuvius: 24–8, 8 shutouts, 1.82 ERA, and MVP. Oakland won the West, drew 914,993, and lost the LCS to Baltimore. One night AL booh-bahs had dinner in Jack London Square. Casey Stengel, 81, began giving tales the "Stengel treatment." Suddenly, the mule Charlie O. entered, wandered to Casey's table, and nudged the Ol' Perfessor, by now slightly wasted. "A very remarkable horse," Stengel mused. "He hasn't seen me for a year, and still remembers." The A's remembered Game Three's attendance: only 33,176. Said an Oakland pitcher: "Maybe we should move back to Kansas City."

'Seventy-two began with a players' strike, closed in a classic Classic, and forgave how only Rudi hit .300 for Oakland. Campy led in steals for the sixth/final time. Catfish won 20 games for the second of five straight years. Cooperstown '87 retired 224–116 with a 3.26 ERA. "He was our guy," said manager Dick Williams. "No one like him could win the big one." Few could equal Rollie Fingers' handlebar mustache. Once Finley voided a major pay hike by giving Fingers a year's supply of mustache wax. Rollie repaid him in '72–'74 (61 saves). The A's fought like other teams played pepper. "So what else is new?" said Fingers of a Jackson–Billy North brawl. "Being on this club is like having a ringside seat for the Muhammad Ali–Joe Frazier fights."

The '72 A's beat Detroit, 3–2, in the playoff opener before 29,536 at the Coliseum. A day later 31,088 saw Lerrin LaGrow hit Campy, Bert throw his bat, and Oakland romp, 5–0. The Athletics won the fifth/final game, 2–1. Next: Cincinnati. Tenace hit five homers in the regular season. October's Hero twice went yard to start the Series. Next day Rudi robbed Dennis Menke of a game-tying dinger. Said Joe: "I didn't think I had a chance." (The A's did, 3–2 and 2–1.) The Classic moved to Oakland: In Game Five, Johnny Bench went to an eighth-inning two-on and-out 3–2 count. Williams pointed to first base. Bench readied, Fingers set, and catcher Tenace rose. Said Bench: "I thought they were putting me on"—until Fingers kicked, Tenace crouched, and Bench took a called third strike. "I'll never be set up like *that* again." On October 22, the A's won Game Seven, 3–2, and their first world title since 1930. Fingers relieved in six games. Tenace had four homers and nine RBI. "Mr. Finley has been wonderful to me," vowed Williams." Twelve months later, he yearned to punch Charlie in the nose.

The movie *The Way We Were* lit 1973. The A's preferred *One Flew over the Cuckoo's Nest*. Blue, Holtzman, and Hunter each won 20 or more games. MVP Jackson led the league in homers, RBI, runs, and slugging. Finley finally hit a million—1,000,763. Fewer heard. A college station anchored his radio network. "You could barely catch games 10 miles from the Coliseum," said Moore. "We bragged about our network stretching to Hawaii. One day a guy calls. 'Honolulu? How about *here*?'" On October 11, Oakland blanked the Orioles, 3–0, before 24,265, to win the LCS "How bad is this?" said Fingers. "Walk-up play-off tickets are a breeze." Next: Mike Andrews made two errors at second. Finley tried to disqualify him; whereupon Kuhn reinstated him; at which point Andrews sued Finley for libel and slander. New York led, three games to two, upon the Event's return to Oakland. Hunter beat Tom Seaver, 3–1. The A's then won, 5–2: Campy and Jackson homered.

"First team since the ['61–'62] Yankees to win back-to-back Series," Finley bellowed. Added Williams, resigning: "He's a raving maniac. A man can take only so much of Finley."

Finley tried seven second baseman in 1974. He also minted the "designated runner." Neither changed Alexander Cartwright's core. Hunter went a Cy Young 25–12. The A's won their fourth straight West. Baltimore again fell, in four. Fingers and Odom fought a day before the Series. Five stitches closed a cut on Rollie's head. "The record is 15," he said, "held by many." The first all-California Classic was less absorbing: A's in five. The final-game crowd littered the Coliseum. "For some reason the crowd started throwing litter at [Dodgers outfielder] Bill Buckner," said Hunter. As play stopped, Rudi saw reliever Mike Marshall cease warming up. "In a case like this," said Joe, "you expect the pitcher to throw a fastball." Marshall did. Joe planted it in the seats: A's, 3–2.

JACK MURPHY STADIUM

"**P**eople don't know how good the PCL is," a onetime miner named H. V. (Hardrock Bill) Lane said in 1935. "There's Oakland, or San Francisco." Next year he moved the Hollywood Stars to San Diego, renamed them Padres (for a nearby mission), opened 9,100-seat wooden Lane Field (WPA-built), and set out to make baseball count. Lane's team housed Bobby Doerr and Vince DiMaggio (later, Minnie Minoso, Al Rosen, and Luke Easter). A rookie left Herbert Hoover High School to slosh homers in the drink. "Hell," said Ted Williams, "the ocean was only 100 yards from the plate." A single deck linked the lines. The park had no roof, or foul screen. Easter hit the 500-foot center-field scoreboard. The '49ers drew a record 494,780. In 1957, C. Arnholt Smith bought the Pads for nearly $350,000. Shiver me timbers: Termites were eating Lane Field. Smith soon built 8,200-seat Westgate Park. One cloud nagged: San Diego wanted big-league ball. The sky cleared in 1965: The City Council approved a multisport villa.

A referendum backed the $27.5 million kirk in Mission Valley. The San Diego River coursed through the ballpark site: Engineers diverted it. They then moved 2.5 million cubic yards of dirt. San Diego Stadium boasted 1,715 massive pieces of precast concrete in 2,345 different shapes, some weighing 39 tons. Its address asked absolution: 9449 Friars Road.

Doors opened August 29, 1967: Detroit Lions 38, hometown Chargers 17. A February 1968 open house hailed a different sport: 15,000 ogled 47,634 seats, Santa Ana Bermuda grass, uniform length (lines, 330; alleys, 375; center, 420) and 17½-foot concrete outfield wall. The park resembled a box with three sides. Five foul-turf tiers tied the left and right-field corners. Four half-enclosed the site from left to center field. Bleachers speckled right. A large scoreboard stood behind them. Breakdown: 6,394 lower box, 8,183 reserved, 1,918 press level box, 11,224 upper box, and 19,915 general admission seats.

"In '68," noted then–Hall of Fame librarian Jack Redding, "the Padres [in their new park] led the minors in attendance." On May 28, San Diego joined the Nationals. Dodgers G. M. Buzzie Bavasi became expansion president. Ex–L.A. coach Preston Gomez was named manager. Said Bavasi: "We'd might as well imitate the best." How would the Pads do 120 miles from Chavez Ravine? "We'll walk," said Bavasi, "then we'll run." San Diego was America's 15th-largest city, each decade doubling its post-'40s population. "We've got wealth, a booming area, tradition," said Smith. The Pads seemed sure to draw.

They debuted April 8, 1969, v. Houston. A visitor drove between two steep Mission Valley ridges, about 8 miles from the Pacific, near Interstates 15 and 8. He parked (18,000 slots), approached the stadium, and gasped at six odd futuristic concrete swirls. "Walkways surrounding the stadium," mused Smith, "to drop you off at each level." Escalators between the swirls accessed the park. Inside, checkerboard-cut grass bathed the field. "It was everywhere," said 1972–voice Jerry Coleman. Grass replaced dirt on each side of both lines. Corner pens bisected them. "Only park," bragged Bavasi, "where a foul can be caught out of sight of the umps and players." It was lovely to look at—save empty seats. Only 23,370 saw the opener (Padres, 2–1). First pitcher: Dick Selma. Batter/hit: Jesus Alou. Homer: San Diego's Ed Spezio. Through 1973 the Pads lured a high of 644,273. "It was a ghost town," Smith conceded—but why?

"You've got ocean to the west, Mexico to the south, desert to the east, and [Dodgers voice Vin] Scully to the north," said announcer Bob Prince, spurning a Padres offer. Pick a reason: bad marketing; bad team;

L.A. hovered like smog. 'Sixty-nine was wretched: 52–110. A year later Dock Ellis no-hit San Diego and Tom Seaver Kd 19. Now and again the gloom left. In 1972, Nate Colbert became the first Pad with 100 RBI (including a record 13 in a doubleheader v. Atlanta). Always, it returned.

In early 1974, Smith sold the Padres to a Washington, D.C., buyer. Files were packed, new uniforms sown. On January 25, McDonald's founder Ray Kroc saved them for San Diego. The Padres opened—and stank. Kroc grabbed the P.A. mike to snarl, "This is the most stupid ballplaying I've ever seen." Next day he apologized. San Diego couldn't grasp why. "The reaction," said Coleman, "was, finally, a guy who wants to *win*." It took a while. Like '69–'73, the '74ers placed last. Attendance nearly doubled to 1,075,399, breaking highs for opening day, single day, twin-bill, night, and season.

By 1976, Randy Jones went 22–14, tied Christy Mathewson '13's mark of 68 straight *sans* walk innings, and won the Cy Young Award. Gaylord Perry (21–8) became the first Cy Younger in each league in '78. That season the Krocs drew a record 1,670,107, hosted the All-Star Game, and cracked .500 for the only time in their first 15 years. Dave Winfield led the '79 NL in RBI (also, S.D. six of his first seven years). The '80ers boasted a record three 50-steal men. Tony Gwynn '83 hit safely in 25 straight games. Shakespeare wrote, "Fair and foul." The Padres' fairest blessing became baseball's foulest bird.

One day in 1974 a 5-foot-4, 125-pound journalism student at San Diego State heard that KGB Radio needed someone to wear a chicken costume. Ted Giannoulas needed the $2 a day. Soon he was giving kids candy Easter eggs upon entering the San Diego Zoo. The job ended, and brainstorm began. Giannoulas asked if he could wear his henhouse costume to a Padres game. Team and station nodded. Before long he warmed fields across the land. "There was no grand plan," he laughed. "It was the laughter from the grandstand that carried me onto the field." Ultimately, the San Diego Chicken bespoke the Pads. KGB later fired him. "I wanted more control over my career," Giannoulas said after winning a patent suit. Ted rehatched in 1979 before a sellout crowd.

"I had to change the costume," he mused, "but it's the soul that counts." In 1981, the park became Jack Murphy Stadium—said Kroc, "he beat the dream to get us big-league ball"—for the late *San Diego Union* sports editor. From 1966–'71 baseball opened 15 new plots. Most were multipurpose. "Some baseball parks were wrecked before they opened," said Rod Carew, "by trying to accommodate football." Others (e.g., San Francisco, Anaheim, and Oakland) foundered afterward. The Murph was "Chargerized" in 1983–'84. Three decks enclosed the field from left-center to right-center. Capacity soared to 58,671. "Adjust for football," said Bavasi, "and wreck for baseball, no matter what you do." The '82 Pads built an 8½-foot inner fence. Center dropped to 405. Alleys became 370. Each line nested 327 feet from the plate. Poles (329) separated them and the outer wall. "Hit a homer," said Kroc, "and see the ball go foul at the pole." The Pads moved home five feet toward the backstop, erected a black hitting backdrop, and put ivy on the wall. Nothing restored the Murph's rapport.

Television compounded boredom. "The two shots that matter most are center field's [baring pitcher, batter, catcher, and umpire] and from behind home plate [showing the entire field]," Coleman explained. "They supply a ballpark's feel." At Wrigley and Fenway, fans sat in field-level boxes behind the plate. The Murph's high wall precluded their TV look. Worse: its home-plate camera. Tiger Stadium's caressed the hitter. By contrast, the Murph's seemed as yonder as the Hollywood Hills. "So high," a producer added, "the players looked like ants." For a time it mimed how the big leagues looked to Canada.

JARRY PARK

Discounting Brooklyn, the bigs first played a foreign country April 14, 1969, at Montreal's Jarry Park. The audience wore Gallic garb, devoured corned beef and pastrami, and sang "O Canada" and "The Happy Wanderer" in French. Left and right field stood 340 feet from the plate. Alleys: 368. Center: 415 (later, 417 and 420). An 8- (later, 5) foot wire fence bordered the outfield. A single deck wrapped home plate to each corner. Bleachers peopled left. Home runs found a public pool in right. The public address announcer made baseball bilingual. Pitchers became *lanceurs,* the shortstop an *arret-court,* a balk the *feinte irreg-uliere.* Beer was largely Molson. Seats were largely backless. Binoculars were a must: Women were the most ooh-ah in the league. Modern banks flanked old churches and museums. The streets blared European inns and shops. The Continental effect was dizzying.

"You know, 85 percent of the people up here speak French," announcer Byrum Saam said that first year. "But they're nice people any-way." A writer added: "Baseball in Montreal is interesting, but uneven." Five minor-league teams failed from 1890 to the mid-'20s. In 1928, redress: The International League returned; Delorimier Downs a.k.a. Montreal Stadium/Hector Racine Stadium opened. Cost: $1.5 million. Place: Montreal's East Side. Crowd: sellout 17,757. The single-tier park liked lefties ("Right was 295 [left 340]," said 1950–'53 Royals manager Walter Alston) and pennants (eight). Delorimier became Brooklyn's con-veyer belt: Don Drysdale, Carl Erskine, Jim Gilliam, Roy Campanella, Carl Furillo. Jackie Robinson won the IL batting and RBI titles in 1946. Don Newcombe, Duke Snider, and Sam Jethroe won the '48 Junior World Series. In 1956, Brooklyn sold Delorimier for $1.25 million, but leased the park. The franchise died in 1960. Montreal reverted solely to hockey's Canadiens.

In 1967, Canada held its centennial. Expo '67, "Man and His World," dwarfed New York's '39–'40 World's Fair. Scales fell from base-ball's eyes. "They suddenly looked at us," said Gerry Snyder of the Mon-treal Executive Committee, "and saw a cosmopolitan, not backwater, place." The '68 NL gave Montreal an expansion team. Warned president Warren Giles: "On condition that a suitable site is found for opening in 1969." The team picked Expo '67's 25,000-seat Autostade. The city spurned $7 million for a roof and 12,000 extra seats. Mayor Jean Dra-peau became involved. Giles and pols clashed on different sites.

By August 1968, the league primed to retract its bid. Then, one day Giles and Drapeau visited a 3,000-seat park in northwest Montreal, near Jarry, Faillon, and St. Lauren Streets. Giles smiled. "It was minutes from a subway, less than a mile from an expressway, and 200 yards from a commuter railroad." Capacity rose to 28,456. Jarry would house the Expos—till when?

Montreal chose Maury Wills, Mudcat Grant, Manny Mota, and Jesus

Alou in the expansion draft. It debuted April 8, 1969, beating the Mets, 11–10, at Shea. Drapeau and owner Charles Bronfman cried during "O Canada." Six days later they returned to Parc Jarry.

"**T**he first time I knew the Expos were special," said 1969–2000 voice Dave Van Horne, "was that home opener. The frost hadn't yet come out of the ground. When you stepped on the dirt portion of the infield it was like standing on a sponge—three, four inches deep. The field's so bad runners actually took their lead off first by stepping on the infield grass to run to second. Yet no one complained. They knew what a moment it was for Canada and major league baseball—the first game played outside the continental U.S." *En famille* 29,184 watched an 8–7 Expos victory: More stood on snow beyond right field and watched for free. In their ninth game Bill Stoneham no-hit the Phils. "Some guys spend a career and don't call a no-hitter," said Van Horne. "Sort of foretold how whatever this franchise would be, it would never be dull."

Small size bred early buying. "This was a God-send," recalled Snyder, "since it meant that on game day you didn't stay home because of our cold and snow." Early-'70s Montreal boasted 1,214,300 people. The '69-'73ers *averaged* 1,263,452. "Our percentage of seats filled," he continued, "was nearly 60, with the Dodgers, the highest in the league." A breeze lofted dingers to left-center field. In '71, Jarry's 153 homers only trailed Atlanta. An Expophile enjoyed—and learned.

Radio carried play-by-play in French and English. Said player-turned-voice Ken Singleton, "Lots of people turned down the [French TV] sound and listened to us on radio. Kept you on our toes. It made me feel good walking down the street in Montreal and a gentleman comes up and says in halting English, 'I learn something new each day.' " The Expos drew from Quebec, Vermont, eastern Ontario, and Upstate New York. The English Canadian Broadcasting Corporation also piped them to Brandon, Manitoba, and Saskatoon, Saskatchewan. "The Expos were Canada's Team," said Singleton, "a decade before the Braves were ours."

The '69ers finished last, lost 110 games, and allured 1,212,608. Rookie of the Year Coco Laboy had a baseball name to rival Wayne Terwilliger. *L'Expos* traded for Houston's red-haired Rusty Staub. In 1970,

Le Grand Orange had 94 RBI. Jarry packed 1,424,684. Willie Mays got his 3,000th hit. The city pledged a park. Those knits were made for plunking: Ron Hunt was hit a bigs-record 50 times in 1971. A year later Stoneham no-hit the Mets. The city pledged a park. One night, broadcasting at 2 A.M. Quebec time, Van Horne "asked folks to write, and we'd give an autographed Expo ball to the one farthest from St. Catherine and Peel Streets. The winner was in Timmins, Ontario. More than 400 listeners wrote."

In late 1973, the Expos tied for the NL East lead: 34,331 overflowed Jarry v. Philadelphia. Mike Marshall hurled in a record 92 games. Singleton became the first Expo with 100 ribbies. Rookie Steve Rogers had a 1.54 ERA. The Jarrys turned five: The city pledged a park. President John McHale had heard it all.

"We were told that we should have a covered stadium for the 1972 season," he said. "That's what the mayor told us when we were given the franchise. We get a reprieve each year when the matter comes up at league meetings. The league has the right to revoke the franchise. Our toughest decision is when to call a game. These are tough decisions and only will become easier or be eliminated entirely when we move into a domed stadium."

For the first time Montreal failed one million in '75. Its first manager resigned. "We need a new park," said Gene Mauch. He was old school, disliking facial hair. Steve Renko once grew sideburns. Gene said, "Steve, I see the sideburns are down and the ERA is up." They disappeared.

The '76ers were last in average, ERA, and the NL East. Only 646,704 trooped to Canada's Ebbets Field. (Jarry was razed in the mid-'80s.) Its final game, September 26, Phils, 2–1, lured 14,166. A new park awaited in the city's French quarter. The Expos soon yearned for home.

SICK'S STADIUM

As in Montreal, "It was Seattle's first try in major league baseball," said pitcher Jim Bouton of 1969. "You might even call it sick." Actually, Sick's Stadium tied beauty and history. Seattle graced the 1901–'02 and '07 Northwest League and 1906 and '19–'68 PCL. Alumni included Earl Averill, Lew Burdette, Babe Herman, and Maury Wills. By 1969, over

2½ million peopled the Central Puget Sound area. It brandished back country and lovely lakes and an aircraft economy. How could baseball fail?

In late 1968, the AL Pilots drafted their expansion team. It was long on name, and age. Steve Barber trekked from Baltimore. Gary Bell left Fenway Park. Others forged a past All-Star team: Tommy Davis, Rich Rollins, Don Mincher, and Diego Segui. "Take five years off their ages and we'd have been great," said Pilots manager Joe Schultz. "Damn it. We didn't have those five years." What they had was an interim home.

Sick's Stadium was originally named for Emil Sick, longtime PCL Rainiers owner, and called Sick's Stadium, for a local beer. It opened June 15, 1938, at Empire Way South, South Bayview Street, Rainier Avenue, and South McClellan Street. Like Forbes Field, bleachers flanked the left-field line. Four light towers topped the roof. A single deck housed 15,000 seats between the bases. A '69 visitor could see Mount Rainier in the distance—and the Pilots panic over Opening Day.

On April 11, Sick's joined Seals Stadium and Wrigley Field as PCL–turned-big-league parks. "We just got a late start," said co-owner Dewey Soriano, understatingly. Seven thousand seats and the left-field wall were unfinished. He explained: "The carpenters weren't done." Only 14,993 saw Seattle beat Chicago, 3–1. Many watched outside through the fence (8 feet tall in left and right, 12½ center). Bleachers cut lengths (left, 305; alleys, 345; corners of each side of center, 405; center, 402; and right, 320) and upped size (25,420 by June). "Hell, we didn't have many big crowds," said Schultz, "but what we had was a mess. The rest rooms didn't work"—insufficient water pressure—or vision.

"The visiting broadcaster," said Baltimore's Chuck Thompson, "looked down the first-base line. All you could see was center field, shortstop, right field, first and second baseman. But you know how I had to follow anything that went by the third baseman into left field? A mirror was hung up—you had to look into it and refract the play." Seattle's *record* needed refracting: 64–98.

The Pilots drew only 677,944. Their largest crowd—August 3's 23,657—cheered mostly for the Yanks. Mike Hegan hit .292. Tommy Harper's 73 steals led the league. Seattle lost its last home game, 3–1, to Oakland, before 5,743. The Pilots looked locally to sell. "We couldn't find anybody," said Soriano. On April 1, 1970, a bankruptcy court sold the team to Milwaukee for $10.8 million. Bouton later eulogized it in his landmark *Ball Four*. "Damndest way to be remembered," said Schultz. For Seattle, it seemed strike three.

FENWAY PARK

Tom Yawkey smiled. "It's nice that Montreal, San Diego, places like that have teams," the Red Sox owner said in 1970. "But we've got the tradition, and amazing years you remember." Too, Detroit and Chicago with their boxy Midwest barns.

Return to 1940: Only England stood between Adolf Hitler and the abyss of a Fascist age. Addressing the House of Commons, its new prime minister, Winston Churchill, thundered: "Let us therefore brace ourselves to our duties, and so bear ourselves that, if the Britist Empire and its Commonwealth last for a thousand years, men will say: 'This was their finest hour.' "

Assume that baseball lasts another *hundred* years. The Red Sox may win a Series; Bill Clinton will fall again, Richard Nixon rise again, and Jupiter align with Mars; Newt Gingrich may become a social worker, Jane Fonda a patriot, and the Rolling Stones retire; Jim Bakker might rejoin the ministry, Billy Graham become a rabbi, and Madonna a nun; Pete Rose may scream *apologia,* Bob Uecker find the front row, and National League return to Boston—all this will occur before baseball knows a finer hour than Nineteen hundred and sixty-seven.

"We played well in the last two months of 1966," pitcher Darrell Brandon said. "We thought we had a chance the whole season long." Few did. Boston lost 535 games in 1961–'66. The 100-to-1 '67ers then wrote "one of baseball's great rag-to-riches stories," Joseph Durso wrote, by winning their first post-'46 flag on the final day. Broadway's *Man of La Mancha* starred "The Impossible Dream." Fenway Park's transfixed a region.

In 1967, Matty Alou hit .330 or over for the fourth straight season. Child's play: Jim Lonborg Kd another batter. Roberto Clemente won the NL batting title at .357. Who cares? Yaz just went deep. Violence marred more than 200 U.S. cities. Thousands protested Vietnam policy by marching on the Pentagon. Arson, sit-ins, and bombings split campuses where panty raids once seemed bravura. The Red Sox took a fractured time and briefly made it whole.

"**W**e'll have only one chief," said new manager Dick Williams. "All the rest are Indians." July '67 marked the rubicon. Boston trailed by six games at the break. Next day it left Logan Airport for a 10-set road trip. The earth turned flat. The Great Salt Lake became fresh. The Sox won every game, then returned: Ten thousand greeted them like Lindbergh at Le Bourget Field. Once Reggie Smith hit with the bases loaded. "A guy is listening," Williams said, "and refuses to enter Sumner Tunnel. Soon hundreds of cars are backed up tuned to the game." Pilots from Boston to Nova Scotia traced a Sox West Coast trip by lights in homes below. By August 2½ games split five teams. At that point the Red Sox traipsed nearer death than a gentle game should go.

Freeze August 18: Tony Conigliaro batting against Jack Hamilton. "He threw inside," said No. 25, "and I moved my head back so quickly the helmet came off." The ball caused a grotesque wound around Tony's eye. Out a year, Conig returned in '69 to a record Fenway Park opening crowd—35,343. He later had a heart attack, went into a coma, and died at 45.

The Sox fell behind California, 8–0, two days after Tony's injury. Fenway was silent; the bottom was falling out. Jerry Adair homered in the eighth: Boston, 9–8. Detroit had won its last pennant in 1945. On September 18, at Tiger Stadium, Dalton Jones stroked a tenth-inning game-winning blast. The poke meant a two-game swing. Neither patrons, cheering, nor announcers, speaking, believed what they were seeing. Still, analyzing the contenders—Detroit had Al Kaline; Minnesota, Tony Oliva; the White Sox, pitching—a Townie had little choice but to sniff, "No way."

Your response fell back on the left fielder with the encyclopedic name.

"**I** never saw a man have a season like him," Williams said of Carl Yastrzemski's MVP/Triple Crown .326, 44 homers, and 121 RBI. One day, he beat Cleveland with his third of seven Gold Gloves. Another knifed the Angels with his arm (topping AL left fielders with 13 assists). Yastrzemski led in five other categories. He warred with different weapons in the Season of The Yaz.

"One week left!" Williams said. "Four teams within 1½ games." By Thursday, September 28, advantage Twins—a game ahead with two left at Fenway—Saturday and Sunday. Stores closed. Churches opened. Most of New England knew the truth and consequences. Boston won, 6–4: The teams were tied. Whoever won Sunday would make a playoff. (To force it Detroit must sweep California.) The Twins led, 2–0, in the sixth. Lonborg then bunted safely. Two hits filled the bases. Yaz singled to center field: 2–2.

The Twins resembled the late '40s Sox. On one hand, they could club you to death. On the other, defense was not a strength. Ken Harrelson hit to shortstop Zoilo Versalles, who hesitated and was lost: 3–2. Two wild pitches and a muff gave Boston a 5–2 lead. In the eighth, Bob Allison lined to the corner with two out, Oliva on first, and Harmon Killebrew on second. No. 8 threw to second base. Out! Allison—and the Twins' year— died.

In the ninth Rich Rollins batted. "The pitch . . . is looped towards shortstop. Petrocelli's back, he's got it!" announcer Ned Martin cried. "The Red Sox win! And there's pandemonium on the field! Listen!" We are, more than three decades later.

As the ball settled in Rico's glove, students and workingmen and housewives on the field became a wave, hundreds of bodies rocking, collectively and ecstatically. "I was terrified," said Gentleman Jim. Inside the clubhouse, mates turned on a radio. Detroit trailed, 8–5: second game, ninth inning, two on, one out. "[Dick] McAuliffe's at bat," marveled Tigers manager Mayo Smith. "Hasn't hit into a double play all year. All of a sudden it's 4–6–3, game over, pennant lost." The Sox no longer had to ape Churchill. "He is a modest man," he said of Clement Attlee. "But then, he has much to be modest about."

The October 2 Boston *Record-American*'s cover blared: "CHAMPS!" above a drawing of two red socks. Next, the World Series—climactic, or was it? 'Sixty-seven's followed a surreal year. Boston linked 12–4 Jose Santiago, Rico Petrocelli's 17 homers, and Lonborg's Cy Young 22–9 and 3.16 ERA. The Cards, said Williams, "have an All-Star team." Bob

Gibson beat Santiago, 2–1, in Fenway's first Series game since October 11, 1946. Anticlimax indeed.

Game Two was more like it: Lonborg one-hit St. Louis; Yaz twice went yard. El Birdos won Games Three/Four behind Nelson Briles and Gibson. Gentleman Jim won Game Five, 3–1. The Occasion returned to Fenway, where Boston bats revived. Yaz, Reggie, and Petrocelli homered back-to-back-to-back. Q: Name the youngest pitcher to start a Series game. A: Gary Waslewski, reaching inning six with a 4–2 lead. Game, Boston, 8–4; and Series, 3-all. Next day Gibbie and Julian Javier homered. Lonborg pitched with two days' rest. The Cards belted him around the lot, 7–2.

St. Louis relived Brock's seven steals and Gibson's three victories. The Sox replayed an Ozymandian year. In 1966, Fenway housed 811,172 customers. The '67ers set an all-time record—1,727,832. "Karl Marx, who said religion was the [people's] opiate, would have revised himself had he watched the Red Sox unite to throw off their ninth-place chains," the *Boston Globe*'s Bud Collins wrote in 1967. "The Red Sox are the opiate right now, Karl, baby, although you might classify them as a religion."

Not bad for one year's work.

TIGER STADIUM

On January 1, 1961, the new Tigers owner renamed his park. "Full circle," John Fetzer said of Bennett via Navin through Briggs to Tiger Stadium. Ditched: more than 4,000 scorecard pencils, 2,300 pennants, and 4,500 Briggs souvenir buttons. Few guessed that the Tigers would draw 1,600,710, win 101 games, and almost beat the Greatest Team since Murderers Row.

"The club planted a screen from right 100 feet into right-center," Ernie Harwell began. "For that one year [also, '44], you had to clear it for a homer." Not hurt: lefty Norm Cash, hitting a bigs-high .361. Rocky Colavito had 45 homers and 140 RBI. Al Kaline batted .324. Frank Lary went 23-9. "Mantle and Maris outhomered Ruth and Gehrig in 1927," said Harwell. "What's amazing is that we almost beat the Yankees the pennant."

The Tigers crashed New York for a September 1–3 series. Hordes jammed the tiers. Detroit trailed by 1½ games. "The first night the Lions had a preseason game scheduled back in Detroit," said manager Bob Scheffing. "But interest in the Tigers was so high that the Lions postponed their game so people could stay home and watch the series on TV. [The Yankees won, 1–0, 7–2, and 8–5.] We're talking baseball at its best"—Detroit's last real gaiety until the '60s' next-to-final year.

On June 24, 1962, the Tigers and Yankees began at 1:30 P.M. Golf games commenced, and ended. Barbecues were lit, and doused. A crowd of 35,638 consumed 32,000 hot dogs, 41,000 bottles of beer, and 34,500 bottles of pop. The match was 7-all after 21 innings. Jack Reed then hit his only career homer: 9–7, Yanks. The madding crowd: 43 players, 39 hits, more than 600 pitches, three seventh-inning stretches, and baseball's longest game (7 hours). In the top of the 20th, an Ontario sportswriter announced, "I've got to leave."

"Where are you going?" a colleague asked.

"My visa just expired"—or hope? The '63 Tigers fell to fifth. A year later attendance dove to 816,139. In 1967, a riot tarred Detroit—43 died. Three games were moved to Baltimore. "The Tigers were a constant," said Harwell. "They tried to keep a city sane."

Earl Wilson and Denny McLain went 39–27. Catcher Bill Freehan won his third straight Gold Glove. Kaline took his 10th. Upon McAuliffe's last-game double play the crowd rushed the field. The Tigers scattered to their muse. Later, Detroit's owner penned a note: "John Fetzer has just died. This is his ghost speaking."

Entering 1968, you were unsure if the Tigers would win the pennant—or their city would collapse. Men purchased firearms. Housewives bought triple locks. Would stores be looted? Would smoke again swirl around Tiger Stadium? As Martin Luther King and Bobby Kennedy were murdered, unrest tore 168 cities, and America seemed a carnage—no one knew.

Baseball does not mirror life. It *can* assuage a wound. "A strange thing happened [in 1968]," Joe Falls wrote. "The ball club . . . started winning games. . . . Each game seemed to produce a new drama. As the streets began to heat up, people began staying in at night to listen to the games on radio. . . . And when the team was at home . . . there was . . . a place to go. A place where it was exciting. A place where a guy could let off steam."

Ironically, '68 blew the whistle on baseball's larger sense of fun. Yastrzemski's .301 won the AL Batting title. Gibson's 1.12 ERA was the lowest in NL history. Don Drysdale threw a record 58⅔ straight scoreless innings. *For shame,* moaned the Ghosts of Campy, the Duke of Snider, and other boppers: Len Gabrielson led the '68 Dodgers with *ten* home runs.

"For a lot of people," Harwell mused, "The year was a sleepathon." What piqued was why a decade after the Mick, Big Klu, and the Rock of Colavito, no one could *hit* the ball? "Westward look," Clough said, "the land is bright." Baseball looked to Michigan. Jim Northrup bombed four grand slams. The "Tiges" won 40 games after inning six. Their ancient franchise smashed its all-time gate—2,031,847. The patient was baseball. Its placebo was Detroit.

"That following winter they lowered the mound and reduced the strike zone—anything to restore offense. For them, the Year of The Pitcher [hereafter, TYOTP] was the year to forget," said Harwell. "Here no one *wanted* to forget. Every night a Gates Brown [.468 pinch hitter] or Tom Matchick [hitting a two-out, three-run, ninth-inning blast to beat Baltimore, 5–4. Said Mayo Smith: 'The final nail'] would do something amazing to help us win."

McAuliffe led the league in runs. Left fielder Willie Horton hit 36 dingers. Freehan caught 155 games and led receivers with 17 double plays. Hank Greenberg hit 306 homers for Detroit. In May, Mr. Tiger pinch-hit a record No. 307.

Kaline '53-'74 trekked to Detroit straight from high school. "He grew up in a Baltimore working class family," said Freehan. "Never flashy. Just great year after year."

In 1955, Kaline, 20, became the AL's youngest batting champion. He totaled 3,007 hits, including 399 homers, and made 18 All-Star teams. No. 6 never hit more than 29 dingers, but at 36 played 129 straight errorless games. "I really don't care what people say," he said. "Self-centered people are the only ones who worry about what other people say." People who knew called him the best right fielder of our time.

Harwell's breeding masked a nonpoker-faced heart. "I loved a ball in that right-field corner at Tiger Stadium. Al'd race over, catch it on two hops, turn, fire the ball to second, and the guy would be out or have to stay at first. I see it all—and Al hasn't played in twenty years."

In 1968, he buoyed Mickey Lolich (17–9). John Hiller's 2.39 ERA moored the pen. Aloft: the man later suspended three times, termed "not mentally ill" by Bowie Kuhn, and sentenced to prison for racketeering. Denny McLain was an aspiring organist, self–proclaimed "character," and prospector before the crash—the first pitcher since Dizzy Dean to win 30 games in a season (31–6). "In his own wild way," wrote Falls, "[he] created every bit [as much] of an impact as Cobb or Cochrane did in their greatest years."

McLain unanimously won the Cy Young and MVP Awards. On September 14, he faced Oakland at Michigan and Trumbull. Reggie Jackson homered twice: A's, 4–3. Pinch-hitting for McLain, Kaline walked to start the ninth. McAuliffe popped out, but Mickey Stanley singled him to third. Northrup bounced to first. Kaline broke for home. Danny Cater's throw was late: 4-all. "I'll never forget it," said McLain. "The infield in, Horton up, and Jim Gosger playing shallow in left." Willie singled over his head. Stanley scored.

Pleased: 33,688, an NBC "Game of the Week" audience, and McLain, winning No. 30. Rewarded: Mickey Mantle. "Hit this one!" Freehan yelled later that week. Denny grooved Mick's 536th/final homer. Relieved: the Tigers, clinching their first pennant since '45. Score: aptly, in TYOTP, 2–1, over New York.

"We needed a Detroit win or Baltimore loss to wrap it up," Harwell recalled of September 17. He got both: Baltimore lost; Don Wert's hit scored Kaline in the ninth. A columnist wrote, "In story-book style, the Tigers won it. Then the fans poured from the stands; they caved in the left-field screen and overran the field, starting a celebration that lasted almost until dawn." Then-teenager Lary Sorensen helped paint it. "For years I kept a piece of sod from that night in my refrigerator," said the 1977–'88 bigs pitcher. Tiger Stadium evoked the most overwhelming sense of coming home to some locale that belonged.

The World Series began October 2. Baseball hoped to redeem the year. Gibson blanked McLain. Lolich then beat Nelson Briles, 8–1. The Series moved to Tiger Stadium: some home-field edge. Earl Wilson lost. Gibbie again beat the Maestro, 10–1. Columnist Jimmy Cannon pronounced: "I never saw anyone play so bad in the World series. They're [the Tigers] stinking out the joint is what they're doing." Jose Feliciano sang the Game Five National Anthem in a folk-rock vogue. St. Louis scored three first-inning runs. "All over," said Cannon. Right.

Kaline had waited 16 years for a Series. Smith wanted him to play— but where? Stanley and Northrup patrolled center and right. "If you lose," wrote Theodore Roosevelt, "lose while daring greatly." Benching Ray Oyler, Mayo moved Stanley to shortstop; Northrup, center; and Kaline, right. The Cardinals led Game Five, 3–2, when Horton threw out Lou Brock at the plate. Detroit clawed from behind to win a 5–3 match—Al drove in the deciding run; Lolich won again; Tiger Stadium was in an uproar. McLain tied the convention at three games with a 13–1 blitz.

On October 10, Gibbie faced Lolich. Scoreless innings multiplied. Shadows lengthened. Tonsils dried. Lolich picked Curt Flood and Brock off base in the sixth. An inning later Gibson retired the first two Tigers. Cash and Horton singled. Northrup lined to center. Flood moved in, retreated, and slipped. The ball cleared his head, scoring two. Tigers win, 4–1. Smith basked—a brief blur of Mack, McGraw, and Stengel. Conga lines blurred. Block parties erupted. Thank-yous began. Detroit had breathed life into baseball's corpse.

COMISKEY PARK

In 1962, owner Arthur Allyn renamed Comiskey White Sox Park. New wrinkle wed burlesque. Joe Horlen '67 no-hit Detroit. That September the Hitless (.225) Wonders printed Series tickets. "We're in first and only

have to face Kansas City and Washington—the league's worst teams,"
said Horlen. "Five games left, and we lose 'em all." It would be a while
before the Hose vied again.

Hoyt Wilhelm pitched in a record 907th game. Allyn installed an
inner fence (335 lines; 370 alleys; 400 center) in 1969. "By now some
teams had all-AstroTurf fields," said writer Dave Nightengale. "Leave it
to Chicago—artificial infield next to outfield grass!" A year later the
Sox lost 106 games and averaged six thousand per date. "Fans were
afraid of the park [especially the ¼ mile walk from the subway el
stop]," mused Bill Veeck. "Little coverage, less concern about the
team."

In 1971, ex-Cardinals voice Harry Caray became the Sox radio/TV
announcer. Inheriting a hemophiliac, he was asked to stanch the blood.
Terrific, the 1970 Oakland announcer told himself: What a draconian
way to revisit the Midwest. Looking back, the wonder is that the
Comiskeys survived. One day 511 watched the Red and White Sox.
"There were years," said Veeck, who rebought the team in 1975, "when
Harry was all we had."

Caray had owned St. Louis. He became a patch of folklore at 35th
and Shields. The '71 Sox lured 833,891 v. '70's 495,355. In 1973, a
record 55,555 watched a May 20 doubleheader against the Twins: The
fifth-placers drew 1,316,527 to "the world's largest outdoor saloon."
Seats going first were in the upper deck under Caray's booth. His "It
might be! It could be! It is!" of a homer was already Chicago's *selah* and
amen. Looking up, you heard Harry now warble a mix of *Messiah* and
"Maggie May."

"There's only one song I know the words to," Caray said. "I've
always sung it, but nobody had ever heard me." Let us visit a '76 seventh-inning stretch. Organist Nancy Faust is playing "Take Me Out to
the Ballgame." Caray starts singing *sotto voce*. Spying him, Veeck lip-
synchs the words. The next night he covertly hides a P.A. mike. "All of a
sudden," roared Caray, "my voice comes roaring back at me with everyone else." Later he asked, "Bill, what was that about?" Veeck said, "I've
been looking for 40 years—and as soon as I heard you, I knew you were
the guy I was looking for."

Caray was flattered. Caruso never sounded better. Veeck then applied a lance. "As soon as I heard ya' I knew that any fan knew he could sing better and'd join in." Harry's jaw dropped. "If you had a *good* voice," Bill continued, "you'd intimidate them and they wouldn't take part." Instead, he grabbed the P.A. mike and bellowed, "All right, lemme' hear ya', everybody!"—never letting interest die, even when the Pale Hose *did*.

On one hand, Ken Brett's 10 wins led the '76 Pale Hose. By contrast, Bill Melton hit 33 homers in 1971—the first Sox to top the league. Balding Wilbur Wood knuckled his way to four straight years of 20 wins. In 1972, Dick Allen smacked a team-record 37 dingers, posed for an *SI* cover with a cigarette in his mouth, and won the MVP. "Think of the irony," Sox pitcher Jim Kaat urged. The Comiskeys had spent 40 years— 1919–'58—in the wilderness. Mates soon dubbed Allen "Moses." He led them from oblivion, if not to the Promised Land.

Allen loved taters, horse racing, and two-hour games. "You pitching, old-timer?" he asked Kaat, who threw like he was double-parked. Once Dick blew a double play to key three Tribe runs. "Old-timer, sorry about that. I'll get those back for you." Allen belted two two-run homers. A '74 gale whipped toward the infield. "Not a man alive," said Kaat, "could hit one out. Dick hits it to left-center field—upper deck." Allen had a good sense of priority. Hyping his movie *M*A*S*H*, Elliot Gould visited Comiskey. Allen asked, "Old-timer, who is that?" Kaat told his friend. Dick—Don't Call Me Richie—was unimpressed. "Yeah, but can he hit a slider?"

The Bicentennial Hose lost 97 games. Veeck lost $670,000. "No one could have imagined," said Bill, "that the next year we'd come up like we did." Austerity/free agency spun the '77 "Rent-A-Player." The Sox broke their attendance mark (1,657,135), gained a signet ("South Side Hit Men"), and forged baseball's curtain call (after homering). The Royals visited in August. The first-place Sox were losing: 5–3, eighth inning, two on. Eric Soderholm promptly found the seats. On a whim Faust razzed the Royals with a forgotten rock anthem that now drapes more high school and college matches than blue prose or "The Star-Spangled Banner"—"Na na na, hey hey hey, kiss them good-bye."

In September, the Sox said good-bye to first, finishing 12 games behind K.C. "An incredible year," Veeck remarked. "So much better than everything before and that was to come."

Postlogue: Veeck II renamed White Sox Park Comiskey. Minnie Minoso returned as coach. Down came the center wall: Numbers again read 352-440-352. Players dressed in black jerseys that aped pajamas with matching shorts: You pined for pinstriped Gothic "Sox" 1951–'68, '71–'75, and 1991–. Clowns and dancers specked the stands. A visitor could sample beer halls under stands behind the plate and left-field Bull Ring and right/right-center Bullpen I and II picnic areas. "Buttered All Over" Popcorn Eddie greased cholesterol and sales.

"There was an eccentricity, a jerry-built quality," wrote Richard Lindberg. Some seats faced center field. Right's hung above left's. The outfield foul lines were water hoses, painted white and flattened. Enduring was a patchwork charm: speaker horns on the bleacher wall; a wall clock to the flagpole's left; noise, booze, and belly mixing "people, strange places, and things resembling a drive-in flea market," a writer said, "taking place at the same time with a world ethnic food festival." The park's symmetrical exterior resembled Charles Comiskey's. The Roman hated to spend money. Veeck despaired of having it.

On July 12, 1979, Bill asked fans to turn in disco records. Hundreds stormed the field using LPs as frisbees. Twice Veeck booked rock concerts to raise cash. By September, the outfield resembled the terrain at Antietam. "The irony," said David Condon, "is that Comiskey had great groundskeepers"—Roger, Gene, and Emil Bossard. They a) painted baselines to keep Sox bunts fair; b) cut grass short or long, respectively, for fielders with great or small range; c) watered or added clay and gasoline and burned ground before the plate for Sox or rival sinkerballers; d) lowered enemy bullpen mounds below uniform height to upset a pitcher's rhythm.

"What was needed was someone who flew around in Lear jets and operated under the protection of a tax shelter," Lindberg wrote. "Sensing the inevitability of it all, Veeck began looking around for such a person." In 1981, he sold the team to a group headed by TVS Television Network founder Eddie Einhorn and Chicago real estate syndicator

Jerry Reinsdorf. Forget kitsch, heart, and camp. "We're going to clean up Comiskey, open it to families," Reinsdorf chimed, jabbing Veeck. "Baseball is more than a park full of drunks."

Caray took that personally, joining the Cubs in late 1981. Veeck died in 1987. Free agency killed him sooner.

16

WHERE'S THAT RAINBOW?

However vague and selective memory may be, there is no trick to note which team suffered most by leaving one park for another. Savor the foliage, navigate the drawbridge, and sight the Allegheny and Monongahela Rivers becoming the Ohio. The skyline etched here and high-tech. Across the water cable cars climbed drop-dead hills. In 1985, *Rand McNally* named Pittsburgh our most livable city. Then the Pirates' hull of concrete and sameness hit you—a joyless, awful park.

That, of course, was not the Buccos' wish. The plot itself oozed lore. Kilbuck Island, named for a Delaware chief, had housed Indians, swayed the French and Indian War, and "then saw its backchannels fill with silt," said the *Pittsburgh Press*. On April 25, 1968, Mayor Joseph Barr broke ground for a new municipal complex. Erik Sirko's original design foresaw "a Stadium *over* the Monongahela." (Boats would pass beneath.) It never happened, nor a planned complex of office buildings and businesses by the Allegheny. Forbes Field rose in four months. Three Rivers Stadium took two years, cost $55 million, and was hardly worth the time, or price.

The 50,326-seat fort screeched multipurpose: symmetrical (340, 385, and 410), large foul area, and TartanTurf. A 10-foot wooden fence ringed the outfield. "The outer wall," recalled then–general manager Joe L. Brown, "was 342 feet down the line to 434 in center." The flagpole was attached in left-center field. Pens behind a low wooden fence filled each corner. Three levels of plastic chairs enclosed the park. A plurality (17,287) formed the upper deck. A center-field scoreboard topped the first outfield tier. Sight lines favored the Steelers, who soon ruled the city. "Why?" a reporter asked Bob Prince in 1980, "would the Bucs leave Forbes Field?"

"In '58, the team sold Forbes to the University of Pittsburgh for $2 million," said the Pirates voice. "The school wanted to expand its graduate facilities. The Pirates could use Forbes until a proposed all-purpose stadium was built." He paused. "The club also wanted a bigger place to play."

"Why didn't they expand?"

"They didn't realize what they had. When the Pirates left Forbes Field, they took the players away from the fans—you were near them, had the real smell of grass. It was easy to get to. You had the high wall in left, right-field bleachers—so unique. So what if girders needed replacing? You could do it, add bleachers for more seats. But when they went downtown, geez, the park is hard as hell to get to, it takes forever to leave after a game."

Three Rivers was scheduled to open May 29, 1970. Labor tiffs delayed it to July 16. First pitcher: Dock Ellis. Batter: Reds' Ty Cline. Hit: Pittsburgh's Richie Hebner. Homer: Reds' Tony Perez. The Bucs christened Forbes '09 by losing to Chicago, 3–2. Cincy won by the same score before 48,846. '70's first 40 dates at Forbes drew 386,907. Three Rivers' 39 wooed 955,040 (total: 1,341,947, v. '69's 769,369).

Four regulars batted over .300. Ellis no-hit San Diego, later conceding he took LSD before the game. Wilver Dornel Stargell owned a Kentucky Fried Chicken franchise in Pittsburgh's Hill District. Cried Prince: "C'mon, Willie. Let's spread some chicken on the Hill!" Stargell hit four of the first seven balls into Three Rivers' 70-foot-high upper-deck yellow seats. The Bucs won the East—their first title since 1960. Cincy swept the playoff. The '71ers drew a more arresting 1,501,132. Bob Gibson threw the first no-hitter in Pittsburgh's suzerainty. Stargell's 48 dingers led the league. Baseball's oldest *mot*—"Away, play to win; at home, to tie"—flowered July 15. Thrice San Diego led in extra innings: Each time the Bucs tied. "All season, every season, I gave everything I had," said Roberto Clemente, giving now. In the 17th, he homered to reprove the saw.

Clemente batted .341. Bob Robertson had 26 homers. Danny Murtaugh won his second straight division. The '71 LCS v. 'Frisco began with a split. The Bucs rafted home, drew only 38,322 and 35,487 for Games Three-Four, but won the playoff. The Series commenced badly: Baltimore, 5–3 and 11–3. Said Stargell: "You would have thought the Pirates were nothing more than the invited guests." Added Ron Fimrite: "There was no doubt that the Pirates were on the verge of extinction. They could only hope that the escape from Baltimore to their carpeted home would offer them a chance to recoup, or at least die less ignominiously." Steve Blass won, 5–1. Next day Three Rivers hosted the Classic's first prime-time game. "We wanted to reach working-class people," said Commissioner Bowie Kuhn, "let them see games at night." The Bucs lit the scene, 4–3, before 51,378. On October 17, Clemente homered, hit in his 14th straight Series game, and keyed the Game Seven 2–1 decider. The Three Rivers organist played "Jesus Christ Superstar" when Arriba batted. Said reliever Dave Giusti of his glove, arm, and .414 artillery: "It is a shame that it took the 1971 World Series before people said, 'Hey, this guy is one of the greatest ever to put on his uniform.' "

Clemente got hit 3,000 off New York's Jon Matlack in his last regular-season game—September 30, 1972. Stargell spread 33 chickens. The Pirates drew their first playoff sellout—50,476, Game One, v. Cincinnati—and took a 2–1 match lead. The Reds won the last two at Riverfront. A worse loss seared New Year's Eve: Clemente died, in a plane crash, at 38, trying to help victims of the Nicaraguan earthquake. Said Kuhn: "He had about him the touch of royalty" (also, four batting titles, .317 average, and 12 Gold Gloves). In 1994, a statue was dedicated outside Three Rivers on Roberto's 60th birthday. "He *was* the Pirates," a fan noted, "and they were different without him."

Clemente was inducted at Cooperstown in 1973. That year Hall of Fame '88—"Pops"—tied 44 homers, 119 RBI, and .646 slugging.

Stargell retired with 475 dingers, 1,540 ribbies, and 2,322 hits. He also swayed men in blue. Once the Bucs put Stargell's name in the fourth and sixth lineup spots. Padres skipper Alvin Dark shrewdly waited till Willie doubled and the second Mr. Stargell hit. "Look it," Dark brayed to plate umpire Doug Harvey. "We got two Wilver Stargells in the game at one time!" Harvey fixed his scorecard, Stargell, and the hitter. "Well, Mr. Dark, I know who Wilver Stargell is and I know he's not at home plate now. Therefore, no matter what the line-up card says, Stargell's hitting fourth and this man up for the second time is hitting sixth—and I don't care *who* he is!"

Stargell hit .301 in 1974. Three Rivers hosted the All-Star Game: NL, 7–2. It even waved babushkas, a Slavic term meaning handkerchief. The Bucs played one night in Atlanta. "Ladies, we need your help," Prince said on the air. "We got a Ladies Night when we get home. Why don't you bring out your..?" He wanted to say hanky, but couldn't find the word. "Why don't you bring your babushka and wave it?" An official was aghast. "They'll never know what you mean." The team returned to Pittsburgh. Thousands trooped to its isle. Two Pirates reached base in the first inning. Prince intoned, " 'Come on, ladies, wave your babushkas,' and they start going wild. We get a run in, and I say, 'See, that's what Babushka Power is all about.' "

The Bucs won the East by 1½ games over St. Louis. So how come they drew only 1,110,552? "What's troubling," said Brown, "was the trend. In the late '60s we, the Reds, and Phillies drew about the same. We all move into a new park and contend. Soon they're outdrawing us, 2 to 1." '74: Murtaugh again won the East, but lost the playoff to L.A. '75: Manny Sanguillen hit .328. Rennie Stennett went 7-for-7 for the first time since Wilbert Robinson 1892. As in 1970, Pittsburgh lost the LCS to Cincinnati. John Candelaria—"the Candy Man—Kd 14 in Game Three. The Pirates receded to the Tri-State periphery.

"Five divisions in six years," said Prince, "and we still can't draw." Candelaria pitched the Bucs' first home no-hitter. Murtaugh died. A Pirates shortstop bred the (Mario) "Mendoza Line [.200]." The '77–'78ers finished second. Dave Parker won two batting titles—and became MVP. The Lumber Company morphed into "Lumber and Lightning." Attendance flunked a million for the first time since '69. A guest visited the Allegheny Club's 12 Romanesque statues, plaque noting Babe

Ruth's 714th homer, and 8-by-12 foot "406" chunk of Forbes' brick wall. Increasingly, you yearned for the real McCoy.

"If we have shortcomings," wrote Mao Tse-tung, "we are not afraid to have them pointed out and criticized because we serve the people." The '79ers served Pittsburgh. Chuck Tanner managed like an artisan. The Bucs led, 5–3, as 'Frisco's Jack Clark outlegged a two-out ninth-inning bunt. Switcher Darrell Evans and Mike Ivie batted next. Tanner switched righty pitcher Kent Tekulve to left field, southpaw Grant Jackson relieving. "If Darrell reached, Kent would pitch to Ivie," he said. Evans flied to—where else?—left field. Stargell became league co-MVP with Keith Hernandez. The Bucs plucked the East, swept Cincinnati, trailed Baltimore in the Series, three games to one, and rallied, 7–1, 4–0, and 4–1. Phil Garner hit .500. Wilver added .400, 7 RBI, three dingers, and a Series record 25 total bases.

"He was our father," Garner said of Pops, awarding stars for the Bucs' Cap Anson hats. The club rotated nine gold, black, and pinstriped combos. "Stargell," said a Series writer, "looks like a canary." Three Rivers brooked varied patches of turf color. Clashing inner and outer walls' seemed color-blind. Cold evoked the football Browns and Steelers. No Series site was more grotesque than Pittsburgh's in '79.

RIVERFRONT STADIUM

"He may live long," the British statesman Edmund Burke said of a colleague, "he may do much, but he can never exceed what he does this day." Who will exceed the Big Red Machine? The 1970s Reds fused four pennants, two World Series, and only one losing year. "I don't manage this team," said Sparky Anderson. "It's managed by Rose and Morgan and Bench and Perez. I'm just a cheerleader." Said early-'70s mikeman Al Michaels: "These Reds were perhaps the best there ever was"—a dowry of Louisville and Zanesville and Muncie and Marietta. The club was so good that you overlooked the park.

"No old-time feel," Michaels said of Riverfront Stadium. "Such a departure from Cincinnati." To get there, a visitor parked across the Ohio River in Covington, Kentucky, crossed the historic John A. Roebling Suspension Bridge, and entered the field atop an underground garage. "The only place in baseball," wrote the *Cincinnati Enquirer,* "you travel up to see a game, then down to go home." A 12-block radius plied more than 20,000 parking slots. Many took buses to 1½ blocks from the park. Interstates 71 and 75 fed outlanders into future Pete Rose Way. All crowds have personality. Riverfront's was family, old-school, and regular-fellow. Like Three Rivers, it was symmetrical (330, 375, and 404), multipurpose (NFL Bengals), and cookie-cutter. Field seats knit one pole to another. Three pasteled upper levels enclosed the 51,050-seat plot.

"The top has the most seats," read the *Dayton Daily News,* "and are popular because of the price. But there is no bleacher atmosphere, and all you see is the fielders' backs." A 12-foot (later 8) wooden fence rimmed the meadow. The Reds fanned precedent by putting metric distances (100.58, 114.30, and 123.13) on walls and installing an all-Astro-Turf field. "Pittsburgh, St. Louis, the Giants, Houston had a dirt infield," said Pete Rose. Cincy's dirt only filled cutaway sliding pits. Saving Riverfront was the sheer splendor of the team.

On June 30, 1970, Bowie Kuhn left a cab, ran into a player, and walked to the Reds' new home. Riverboats strewed the water. Horns pierced the air. "You guys outta here! The gates open soon!" a construction foreman shouted. The commissioner was amused. "I didn't expect to be recognized," Kuhn said, "but I thought everyone recognized Pete Rose." The opener portended (full house), or did it? (Braves, 8–2). First pitcher: Jim McGlothlin. Batter: Sonny Jackson. Hit: mate Felix Millan. Homer: Hank Aaron. Crosley Field's last 34 dates drew 567,937. The move to Riverfront swelled the ledger board: 1,235,631 in 43 dates. "It was the novelty," '73–'78 president Bob Howsam said of the team record 1,803,568. It was also the Reds.

"I was a naive young man of 35," said Anderson of 1970. "I had so much enthusiasm. It never occurred to me that we might lose." Bobby Tolan's 57 steals led the NL. First baseman Tony Perez had 90 ribbies at the All-Star break. MVP catcher Johnny Bench bound 45 homers and 148 RBI. Cincy won a franchise-best 102 games, took the West by 14½, and earned the byname Big Red Machine. Riverfront hosted the All-Star Game. In the 12th, Rose led off second: 4-all. "[Jim] Hickman lines a hit," recalled Perez, "and here comes Petey. [Indians catcher Ray] Fosse had the ball." Rose decked him, dislodging it and Fosse's future. The Reds swept the LCS, 3–0, 3–1, and 3–2. More precedent: Baltimore won the first World Series game on pseudo-turf. "I remember two things," said Kuhn. "The disputed play. [The Reds lost a run, losing, 4–3, on plate umpire Ken Burkhart's phantom-tag out call of Bernie Carbo.] The other is the rain." The field looked like German measles.

Next year Cincy abided its sole '70s losing season. Philly's Rick Wise compounded pain: first to pitch a no-hitter and homer twice. That winter second baseman Joe Morgan landed from Houston. "I told [then-G.M.] Howsam," said Anderson, " 'You have just won the pennant.' " Bench was again MVP. Five of the first six best-of-five L.C.S. ended in three games. '72's extended whoopee. Game Five braced Riverfront: Bucs, 3–2, in the ninth. "One and two," Michaels said of Bench, leading off. "The wind [by Dave Giusti] and the pitch . . . Change, hit in the air to deep right field! Back goes Clemente! At the fence! She's gone!" Two Reds singled. With two out, Bob Moose threw a wild pitch, George Foster scored, and Cincy gained the Series.

Classic imagery went deep: hirsute *v.* bare-faced/Kiwanis *v.* camp/gray and white v. green-and-gold. Oakland took a two-game lead. The Reds rallied near their first post-'40 title. Game Seven took a different road: A's, 3–2, before a Cincy record 56,040. The '73ers forged the first of eight straight 2 million years. (The Mets won the playoff.) On April 4, 1974, Hank Aaron smacked Ruth-tying homer 714 at Riverfront. Cincinnati placed second. "We were so close," Anderson said, "But people were saying we couldn't win the big one"—until '75.

Its Reds won 108 matches—and the West by 20. Each regular had more than 45 ribbies. MVP Morgan could beat you with his glove, speed, and bat, and did—.327, 67 stolen bases, 132 walks, and 94 RBI. Perez '67–'77 drove in 90 or more, retiring with 1,652, 2,732 hits, and 379 taters. Cincy topped the league in swipes and bigs in fielding. Shortstop Dave Concepcion bred the AstroTurf bounce throw to first. Jack Billingham, Don Gullett, and Gary Nolan each won 15 games. "We had a great bullpen [50 saves]," said Anderson, who answered to "Captain Hook."

Sparky swept the playoff, 8–3, 6–1, and 5–3, then beat the Red Sox. A year later the encore MVP bonded .320, 27 homers, 111 RBI, and 60 steals, retiring with 2,517 hits, 449 doubles, 96 triples, and a then-second-base-high 266 dingers. "Morgan did everything," said Michaels. He also had help. George Foster's 121 ribbies led the NL. Ibid., Rose runs (130), hits (215), and doubles (42). Ken Griffey had 37 infield hits. Cincinnati led the bigs in 11 categories. Five regulars hit over .300. Four wore Gold Gloves. The Reds again won the West, swept the LCS, and beat the Yanks four straight. "First to not lose a playoff or Series game," said Michaels, "and first NL [post '21–'22] to win back-to-back Series." Keeping score: 5–1, behind Gullett; 4–3, on Perez's single; 6–2, Dan Driessen homering; and 7–3, Bench dinging twice. No. 5 hit .533, had six RBI, and became Series MVP.

"If the other team was one or two runs ahead," he said, "they were in trouble." Old-timers knew its cog. "I have never seen anybody who handled the glove like Bench," Casey Stengel mused. Cooperstown '89 won 10 Gold Gloves, caught 100 games a league-record 13 straight years, and hit 389 dingers, including a then-record 327 as a catcher. "Where do you stop with his team?" Michaels said. "I remember when I was young. Catching was a non-glamorous position—the tools of ignorance. The worst kid was told to catch because he put all of this stuff on. John changed all that—the quickness, catching one-hand." In 1999, he was voted baseball's greatest all-time catcher.

VETERANS STADIUM

In 1787, Benjamin Franklin looked at the president's chair and observed that he had often wondered during Philadephia's "long hot summer" whether the sun painted on the chair was rising or setting. "But now at length," Franklin concluded, "I have the happiness to know that it is a rising and not a setting sun." Like Riverfront, Veterans Stadium rose in the late 1960s and early '70s. In Philadelphia, the sun set on baseball of a human scale.

"For many winters Phillies have talked of playing in another part of Philadelphia or even in New Jersey," *Sports Illustrated* wrote in 1961, the year they sold Connie Mack Stadium to a New York realty firm. They soon expected to open a new park, but haggling reared. A South

Philadelphia site was picked near 100,000-seat John F. Kennedy Stadium. Two bond issues passed. Ground broke October 2, 1967. Delay followed roadblock. The cost rose to $49.5 million. Veterans Stadium—"The Vet"—was dedicated April 4, 1971, on 14 acres six miles from Connie Mack. It had the old park's home plate. "Too bad," said a writer, "it didn't have its heart."

Parking was ample (14,000 slots), but dingy (a 12-foot-high fence boxed cars). Others rode the subway from 15th and Market to Broad and Pattison, then walked half a block. The new park was rounded, but rectangular—to architects, an "octorad." Vertical columns fused the ground and roof. Statues of Connie Mack and a sliding runner graced the exterior. Inside: *not* your grandfather's 21st and Lehigh. Lengths were symmetrical: (330, lines; 371, alleys; 408, center). Capacity totaled 56,371. As in Pittsburgh, plastic seats enclosed the bowl (70 percent in foul ground: the rest, a huge upper tier.) Atlanta-style, pens linked an inner fence and outer wall. The cement turf caused a run on ground-rule doubles. Said ex-Phil Richie Ashburn: "We originally started with a 6-foot wooden fence"—adding a '72 six-foot Plexiglas top. Antipodal was early '71's tarp over the right-field wall. "The ball would hit the plastic," said owner Bob Carpenter, "drop down, and die"—not unlike the Phils.

The '71–'73ers hugged sixth in a six-team division. "It's a good thing that we had a new stadium to look at," said Ashburn, "since there wasn't much on the field." The Vet opened April 10, 1971: Two miles of ramp, eight sets of escalators, and four elevators carted Pennsylvania's largest baseball crowd (55,352). The Phils preferred glitz. A helicopter dropped the ceremonial first pitch to catcher Mike Ryan, who bobbled, then snatched, it. Another year Hugo Zacchini carried it through the air from a cannon. Thrice Kite Man dropped the ball, once crashing the seats. Other deliverers included a high diver, parachutists, and Dave Merrifield, holding the trapeze bar under a helicopter. In 1976, a horseback rider galloped from Boston to hail the Bicentennial, then gave the ball to Rocket Man, who jetted around the Vet.

Its exploding scorecard was not finished by Opening Day. "The first homer [Phils' Don Money] had to depend on the crowd for noise," said publicity czar Bill Giles, migrating from Houston. First pitcher: Jim Bunning. Batter: Expos' Boots Day. Hit: Larry Bowa. Score: Philly, 4–1. Attendance nearly doubled to 1,511,223. Deron Johnson homered in four straight ups. Giles mounted a Liberty Bell from the fourth level in center field. On May 16, 1972, the Phils' Greg Luzinski struck it for the first/final time. The Bull bought tickets for youth groups, filled his left-field "Bull Ring," hit 307 homers, and talked freely to reporters. Traded for Wise, Steve Carlton mimed a locked-up room. "He'd take batting practice, come in, and enter a trance-like state before a game," said catcher Tim McCarver. One night McCarver lost his temper and began screaming at Lefty about his motion. Next day he apologized. "That's OK," said Carlton, airily. "I wasn't paying attention to you, anyway."

Baseball paid attention in 1972. On August 17, Carlton won his 15th straight game. The unanimous Cy Younger led the NL with 30 complete games, 310 Ks, 346 innings, 1.97 ERA, and 27 victories—of the Quakers' 59! A Vet banner hailed "Super Steve" on winning: "Try It, You'll Like It." Philly seldom tried. Manager Frank Lucchesi held a meeting to scold players. "I've been reading things in the papers," he began, "that you guys—so-called anonymous sources—have been saying about me and I want you to know that nobody makes a *scrapgoat* of Frank Lucchesi." The scapegoat was fired: Successor Danny Ozark also bombed English 101. The Phils once brooked a losing streak. "I give up," he said. "Those games were beyond my *apprehension*."

Ibid., Carlton. Ultimately, he Kd 4,136, took four Cy Youngs, and won 329 games. In '73, Super Steve lost 20. *Pitcher* Ken Brett homered in four straight games. A year later Mike Schmidt made the Vet a faint outpost of faith. "He came up, and you could see the skill," said Carlton. "But he'd swing and miss wildly, or make an error and berate himself." Schmidt's 36 homers led the league. He and Luzinski smacked 72 in '75. The Bull and Dave Cash had an NL-high 120 RBI and 213 hits, respectively. The Phils placed second, had their first .500 year since '67, and called forth a record 1,909,2333. Bob Boone keyed catching. Larry Bowa made shortstop hermetic. "Two thirds of the world is covered by water," wagged broadcaster Ralph Kiner. "The other third is covered by [center fielder and 'Secretary of Defense'] Garry Maddox." The sun began to rise.

How good was team morale? "*Morality*," huffed Ozark, "is not an issue here." The '76 Bicentennial, however, was. The Vet hosted the All-Star Game: 63,794, including President Ford, saw the Nationals romp, 7–1. Schmidt's 11 April homers set an NL best. The 101–61 Phillies won the East. "For years, luck ran against us," said Ashburn. "Not now"—well. Once they put two runners on. Maddox smoked the Cardinals' Al Hrabosky's pitch to center field, where Bake McBride made a diving catch. Schmidt lined up the middle. The shortstop made a sprawling second out. Luzinski then smashed a drive that Hrabosky deflected and retrieved for a game-saving out. Later a reporter asked Cardinals manager Red Schoendienst what he thought. "Well, I thought we had everybody played right except maybe Al was a little shallow on Luzinski."

The LCS was less funny: Cincy swept. Next year Philly again won 101 games, including 13 straight, and split playoff games One-Two with L.A. The Quakers led Game Three, 5–3, two out, none on, in the ninth: 63,719 rattled their concrete shell. "Maybe they were thinking World Series," said Ozark—until Vic Davalillo, 38, drag bunted safely (umpire Bruce Froemming blew the call), Manny Mota, 39, doubled to left (Luzinksi juggled against the wall), and two more singles gave the Dodgers a 6–5 crusher. Next day Carlton lost, 4–1. The Vet wilted in the rain.

"Artificial turf is never pretty," observed 1971–announcer Harry Kalas. The Vet's cut-out turf was gross. "It got bare, worn, hard." Rain splotched it. The Phillies patched it. The '78ers lost the playoff. A year later Schmidt bopped 45 homers. Pete Rose deplaned from Cincy. Philly won a 23–22 arabesque. Fired, Ozark hadn't won enough. The Phillie Phanatic blared warm and fuzzy: "a big blur of fur," one writer called the pear-shaped, green-haired, elephant-nosed mascot. "He's as personable [dancing, cartwheeling, and riding a motorcycle] as the Vet is cold." A record 2,775,011 bought its good seats (box, left- and center sun, general admission behind the plate) and bad (left-field section 35, row 14, seat 13: The upper tier blocked flies).

"We prayed our heads off," a 78-year-old nun said of 1980. The Quakers kept the faith: Bake McBride .309, Carlton 24–9 Cy Young, and Schmidt 48 homers, 121 RBI, and unanimous MVP. Play ended Sunday, October 5. Friday the Phils beat Montreal, 2–1, to lead by a game.

On Saturday Schmidt's 10th-inning drive clinched their fourth post-'75 division, 6–4. The LCS began at the Vet before 65,277. The Bull slammed a two-run homer: Phils 3, Astros 1. Owner Ruly (Bob's son) Carpenter sighed. "We've waited a long while," he said of Philadelphia's last pennant (1950). "Hopefully, not long to go." Houston won twice in extra innings. Philly answered, 5–3, in 10. Baseball as roller-skating: Game Five careened into walls. Houston fronts, 5–2. The Phils score five eighth-inning runs. Astros tie, 7-all. Maddox plates Del Unser with the tenth-frame/flag-waving/drought-ending run. "Yes, We Can!" blared reliever Tug McGraw.

The Series began by accentuating the positive: Philly, 7–6 and 6–4. Kansas City won twice and led Game Five, 3–2, in the ninth. At that point the Classic turned. Unser and Manny Trillo drove in runs; McGraw beat Dan Quisenberry, 4–3. Back in Philadelphia, the homesters took a 4–1 edge. In the ninth, McGraw, again relieving, loaded the bases. Frank White fouled near the first-base dugout. Catcher Bob Boone touched but dropped the ball. Rose, nearby, caught it with his bare hand. At 11:29 P.M., the 97-year-old Phillies won title one. "World champions of baseball!" Kalas roared of McGraw fanning Willie Wilson for the final out. "It's pandemonium at Veterans Stadium! All of the fans are on their feet. This city has come together behind a baseball team! Phillies are world champions! This city knows it! This city loves it!"

Schmidt hit .381 with 7 RBI. Wilson had a Series record 12 Ks. Mounted horses and canine cops flecked the field. Next day the real wingding hailed a rising sun. A million Quakers jammed the team parade.

ARLINGTON STADIUM

Forget Philly's brotherly love. Neighbors crashed pro ball in the 1886 Texas League: Ft. Worth, in the "Prairie" area a.k.a. Hayne's Park near downtown; Dallas, trading Gaston Park for Gardner Park and Burnett Field. In 1950, the Eagles lured a minors-high 53,578 to the Cotton Bowl. "It was the pre-game show that got 'em," bellowed Dizzy Dean by way of self-congratulation. "Cobb, Cochrane, Home Run Baker, Speaker, and Ol' Diz" in Dallas duds."

By 1959, the Ft. Worth Spurs of the AAA American Association hoped for a new major—Continental—League. The Texas Legislature OKd a Bi-County Sports Committee to raise $9.5 million in bonds for a big-league park. (Voters must approve, and did.) It berthed Arlington, between Dallas and Ft. Worth, on 137 acres north of the former Arlington Downs race track and near Six Flags Over Texas amusement park.

To save money Turnpike Stadium was built in a natural bowl, 40 feet *below* street level. "No excavation, except to connect dugouts directly with dressing rooms, would be necessary," said Arlington mayor Tommy Vandergriff, "if the stadium were enlarged to seat more than 50,000." The outpost sat 10,000, parked 2,500 cars, and was symmetrical (325 alleys, 400 center). Sod was laid, and lights installed, the night before the opener. Don't peak too soon: The Spurs drew foul lines in pregame practice.

"It had a personality," said Vandergriff. You entered at the top of the park. Wind blew toward home plate. "It was warm, and humid, which actually helped homers since the air's not as dense." For a time some thought Washington Senators owner Robert Short dense for adopting Texas. Ignore the pipedream Continental: In late 1971, the 11-year-old Senators became the Texas Rangers. Distances tied 330 (poles), 400 (center), and 380 (alleys, also 370 in '74, 383, and 380 in '82). An 11-foot fence ringed the outfield. Turnpike was renamed Arlington Stadium. "Turnpike is thought too bush league," wrote the *Dallas Morning News,* "and the Mayor refuses to use his name."

Foul turf was modest. Seating waxed: 20,000 ('70), 35,185 ('72), 41,284 ('78), and 43,508 ('85). The bottom level yoked each pole. A second tier approached them. Plaza seats put you behind the plate. "It was jerry-built," admitted Short. "Stands were jammed in where there was room." In each corner several rows 12 seats across almost touched the field. Above them and around the outfield: the bigs' largest (18,000-seat) section of aluminum bleachers. Missing: a roof, or nearby buildings. "There's nothing to enclose the park," Short noted, "or in the vicinity to provide perspective. You couldn't nestle into the neighborhood. There *wasn't* any." The effect: small, not intimate.

Vandergriff threw out the first ball at Arlington's April 21, 1972, inaugural. Traffic swamped two toll plazas on the Dallas–Ft. Worth Turnpike. Slowly, 20,105 arrived. Manager Ted Williams exchanged howdies.

Frank Howard bombed a first-inning homer: Lenny Randle had four RBI; Rangers, 7–6, over Kansas City. A night later they drew 5,517. The season totaled 666,974: D.C. had nearly done as well. First Texan: "We have two seasons." Second: "Football and spring football." Baseball would have to feel its way.

In 1973, it got a break. The Rangers drafted top-rated free agent David Clyde, 18, a pitcher, from Houston's Westchester High School. On June 28, he started v. Minnesota before Arlington's first sellout, 35,698, leaving ahead, 4–2. Leads were rare: The '72–'73 Rangers finished last. "The breakthrough," rued Short, "was the year I sold [1974]": Jeff Burroughs (25 homers, 118 RBI, and .301), MVP; Ferguson Jenkins (25–12, 2.83 ERA), Comeback Player; and Mike Hargrove ("Human Rain Delay"), Rookie of the Year. Dave Nelson stole second, third, and home, in one inning. Texas finished second, courted 1,193,902, and turned manager Billy Martin into Connie Mack. It didn't last: The '75ers sacked him for Frank Lucchesi.

Shortstop Toby Harrah started Texas' first triple play. Buddy Bell became the first ALer to get 200 hits and *not* bat .300. The Angels scored a league-high 13 runs in a frame. "The Eyes of Texas Are Upon You": Randle, breaking Lucchesi's cheekbone; catcher Jim Sundberg, a six-time Gold Glover; Jenkins, the fourth pitcher to win 100 games in each league (others: Cy Young, Jim Bunning, and Gaylord Perry). Legends in time, or mind? Skippers Don Zimmer's, Doug Rader's, and Bobby Valentine's clubhouse was not always pacific. One teammate pointed an eight-inch knife at Jim Norris' stomach. The pitcher was later asked how he stayed calm. "I knew by the way he was holding the knife," said Norris, "that he didn't know how to use it."

KAUFFMAN STADIUM

"One of the things about these concrete donuts is that they were no longer built by one person," author Michael Gershman railed about the early '70s. Unlike Shibe Park, cookie-cutters "had some absolutely atrocious, safe-as-hell corporate name. Riverfront Stadium. Sounds like a god-damned housing development. Three Rivers Stadium. Veterans Stadium." By contrast, Ewing M. Kauffman (née Royals) Stadium hailed the owner/name of the Kansas City Royals. The 40,613-seat miter was also the sole baseball-only park built between 1962 (Dodger Stadium) and '91 (Comiskey II). Said Kauffman: "We kept the faith" in a dead-end age of ballpark handiwork. There are worse ways to be recalled.

In 1967, Jackson County voters backed a $43 million bond issue for a big-league sports complex. "They didn't want a *single* multipurpose site," recalled George Brett. Royals rose to keep the then-Athletics. It didn't work: Charlie Finley left for California in 1968. Baseball then expanded to K.C.'s '69–'72 Municipal Stadium. On April 10, 1973, 30,464 braved 39 degrees to open the Harry S Truman Sports Complex. Royals and football's Arrowhead Stadium stood side-by-side.

The park was symmetrical: poles, 330; alleys: 375, (385 in '90 and 375 in '95); center, 405 (410 in '80 and 400 in '95). It cost a strike- and weather-delayed $70 million. Worse: the AL's first all-phony turf. "The Royals are a small market. Artificial turf cuts rainouts," Kauffman stated. "We need to draw from hundreds of miles away." Opening Day preferred the score—12–1 over Texas—to worry. First pitcher: Paul Splittorf. Batter: Dave Nelson. Homer: John Mayberry. Steve Busby threw K.C.'s first no-hitter (also, bigs' first *sans* pitcher batting [designated hitter]). Royals hosted the All-Star Game (NL, 7–1) and drew 1,345,341 (almost doubling '72's Municipal). "Overall," said Brett, a rookie, "you had to like what you saw."

Outlanders liked a baseball-high 22,000-slot parking lot. "You get there by taking Interstate 70," a brochure read. "You can see inside the stadium from your car." The sea of red wowed a passerby. Three tiers soared above the infield. "In a sense it was like Veterans or Three Rivers," said Gershman. "Near new freeways, good parking, the phony turf, the same dimensions." The contrast lay *in*side: not a bad seat in the house.

The top two decks wrapped home plate to each pole. A lower tier curled around them to pens perpendicular to the field. Each seat faced second base. "No matter what your ticket," said architect Joseph Spear, "we want to make you [part of the game]." Its cynosure topped an incline beyond the 12-foot (9 in '95) outfield fence: A $2.7 million 12-story high crown-shaped scoreboard bore the Royals insignia and used more than 16,000 light bulbs. Beneath and to one side a 322-foot-wide water complex cost $750,000. "One 10-foot waterfall descends from an upper cascade pool which serves as a background for two water fountain pools," Spear explained, "each 40 feet wide, and ends in front with five 10-foot-high horseshoe falls." Water rose as volume swelled. Nineteen pumps circulated 70,000 cubic feet. Nearly 700 500-watt lamps lit as many as 50,000 gallons sailing skyward at a time.

Royals housed the first fountain—and a team of defense, alley pop, and speed. "Our outfield pulls back quickly from the poles. We've got a big sort of National League park," said Whitey Herzog, becoming manager in 1975. K.C. led the AL in triples for six straight years. In '76, Brett trumped in triples, total bases, hits, and average, edging mate Hal McRae, .333–.332, on a final at-bat bloop. "I just punched to left," Brett recalled. The ball fooled Minnesota's Steve Brye, hit the turf, and became an inside-the-park homer.

The Royals won the '76 West—K.C.'s first bigs title. Infielders Fred Patek and Cookie Rojas partied by crashing the fountain. The LCS aped pinball: New York in five. "We were young," said Brett. "We knew we'd we back." In 1977, second baseman Frank White won his first of six Gold Gloves in a row. Jim Colborn no-hit Texas. Four regulars tied more than 20 dingers and 80 RBI. Dennis Leonard (20–12), McRae (54 doubles), and Patek (53 steals) led the league. The gate turned beatific (record 1,852,603); September, deific (bigs-post-'53-high 16-game win skein); October, Beelzebubic. (The Yanks again stood in the Series door.) K.C. took a 2–1 game playoff lead. "We're coming home, we're up," said Brett. Mid-America was atwitter. New York won, 6–4. The Royals led Game Five, 3–2, in the ninth. "They hit us with three," said ex-Yankees outfielder Herzog. "It went slow motion." Patek cried in the dugout. Kansas City again seemed a cousin. (Ibid., '78. Brett homered thrice in Game Three, but New York won the playoff.)

Retrieve how-close, oh-but, what-might-have-been. For a long time Amos Otis led the team in games, at-bats, runs, hits, homer, RBI, and steals. Brett and McRae ranked 1–2 in '78 doubles. In '79, Brett became only the second ALer with 20 doubles, triples, and homers. Willie Wilson whipped a most-since-'25 five inside-the-parkers. "A lot of things came into play," said Jim Frey, replacing Herzog in '79. "The outfield padding is soft, so balls can stay there. The corners curve, so the caroms are unpredictable. The warning track is hard, so balls bounce high and hit past the outfield."

In 1980, Brett hit, period—on August 17, reaching .401. Could No. 5 become the first .400 batter since the Kid? He missed 45 games, but had 24 homers and 118 RBI, finished at .390, and was voted MVP. "He was a one-man warrior," said Frey, but not one-man team. Leonard won 20 for the third time in four years. Dan Quisenberry saved 33 matches. Wilson won a Gold Glove, had a then-record 705 ups, and got 230 hits—100-plus righty/lefty. The playoff began on cue: Royals, 7–2 (Larry Gura over New York's Ron Guidry) and 3–2 (Leonard, before a K.C. record 42,633). The Bronx Zoo hosted Game Three: Yanks, 2–1, in the seventh. Brett's three-run titian then hit the upper tier.

"One moment," said Frey. "It threw off all that frustration"—almost. Philadelphia grabbed a 2–0 game Series lead. On October 17, K.C. won Match Three, 4–3, at Royals: Brets and Otis homered. Next day Willie Aikens homered in and to the left of the right-field pen: 5–3. Game Five countered: Quakers, 4–3. Philly's concrete donut rocked to a 4–1 clincher.

"We climbed another step," said Brett, hitting .375. Ahead: the final rung.

MILWAUKEE COUNTY STADIUM

Milwaukee was still climbing. Its hike began amid '60s EST, Zen, spiritualism, globalism, "Do your own thing," "If it feels good, do it," "Honk if you want peace," and "Don't trust anybody over 30." Bud Selig's upheaval was less public: On April 12, 1966, he was listening to KDKA, Pittsburgh. "The Atlanta Braves were playing their first game. Bob Prince opened by saying, 'Welcome to Pirates baseball. We're a long way tonight from Milwaukee, Wisconsin.' And I began to cry." In a sense, Shakespeare was a Wisconsonite. "The fault lies not in our stars but in ourselves. (Milwaukee's '53 adoption)." The gates had opened: Arcadia was greener on the other side. Dominoes fell: Browns, to St. Louis; A's, Kansas City (then Oakland); Dodgers and Giants, California; Senators, Minnesota; new Senators, Texas; Milwaukee, like Sherman, marching toward the sea.

County Stadium became a shell. On August 27, 1966, Fox Cities and Wisconsin Rapids played a Midwest League game. The 1968–'69 AL returned extempore for the first time since '01. Chicago played nine and 11 games, respectively, in Milwaukee, averaging 29,494 and 17,880. Would it move to Wisconsin? Expansion passed. Selig formed a local group. "We'll go anywhere," he said, "for a team." In March 1970, Seattle neared bankruptcy. Its Pilots became the Brewers. "We had a week to get ready for the season." Long lines again queued for Opening Day.

County (re)opened April 7 before 37,237. First pitcher: Lew Krausse. Batter: Angels' Sandy Alomar. Hit: mate Alex Johnson. Homer: Bobby Knoop (April 10). Score: California, 12–0. Bob Bolin won the Brewers' first game. Milwaukee served only 933,690. Time had wracked culture and convention. Baseball was no longer king. The Braves' rape stung: Milwaukee was chary, if not cynical. Said '70–'80 voice Merle Harmon: "You weren't going to be hurt again."

In 1972, George Scott ("Boomer") left Boston to wear second basemen's "teeth" (beads and shells) around his neck. A year later Milwaukee briefly took first place and passed a million—1,092,159—for the first time since 1961. Robin Yount cracked the '74 lineup. Third baseman Don Money played a record 86 *sans* error games. "Twenty years since our *last* All-Star game," said Selig in 1975: 51,480 watched a Nationals' 7–5 conquest. Slowly, the feeling came back. Too, No. 44: On April 11, 48,160 cheered Aaron's return from Atlanta. Cooperstown '82 retired with 755 homers (420 for Milwaukee). The Boomer's beat went on: AL-high homers (36), ribbies (109), and total bases (317). George Bamberger became '78 manager. Bambi's Bombers grand-slammed a record thrice in their first three games. Larry Hisle had 115 RBI. Milwaukee drew 1,601,406.

Twinklings mused: '79, Gorman Thomas' league-best 45 dingers; '80, Cecil Cooper's .352; '81, Rollie Fingers' Cy Young/MVP, second-half title, and five-game Division Series v. New York. (The Brewers lost.) "It took a while," said Harmon, "first to get back near the mountaintop, then for fans to get excited." Milwaukee got there in 1982.

On August 27, the A's' Rickey Henderson stole four bases to break Ty Cobb's single–season record (118). Another first dotted County: Fingers' 300th save. Pete Vukovich (18–6) won a Cy Young. Molitor led in runs. Thomas and Ben Oglivie smacked 73 dingers. (The Brewers hit 216). MVP Yount battled .331, had 114 ribbies, topped in total bases, doubles, and slugging, and smacked two homers and a triple to win a last-day title. The Angels took a 2–0 playoff lead, 8–3 and 4–2. The LCS then reverted to baseball's once–capital: Milwaukee, 5–3 and 9–5. Game Five wooed 54,968. It was like '57: The rafters rocked and benches shook. Cooper hit in the seventh: two on, bases full, 3–2, Halos. "I'll never forget him," said Selig, "with his hands, pushing the ball down." The liner fell: Brewers, 4–3.

The World Series began in St. Louis. Only the Brewers, romping, 11–0, showed. Molitor's five hits set a record; Yount added four. The Cards won two of the next three games. In Match Five, Robin, homering, again got four hits: Brewers, 6–4, before County's largest crowd, 56,562. The Classic returned south and west: St. Louis, 13–1 and 6–3. "A stadium pep rally," read the *Milwaukee Sentinel*, "will welcome the Brewers home [after Game Seven]!" Yount entered on his Harley-Davidson motorcycle. Chants filled the tiers: "MVP" and "It just doesn't matter." What did: loyalty (1974–'93), durability (only three treks to the disabled list), and longevity (.285, 251 homers, 1,406 RBI, and 3,142 hits).

"Growing up, I saw a lot guys play their whole career in one city," said stand-up comic, movie/TV actor, and '72– Brewers voice Bob Uecker. "With today's money, they don't need to. One of the last one-town players will be Yount. Not an Aaron or Mantle in talent, but no guy meant more." The ex-player became his own best material. By contrast, "Yount didn't say much, didn't need to, had sense to retire when his skills started fading. I think of Robin when I drive to County Stadium off the Interstate into that huge parking lot. People with hibachis. Weddings with guys in tuxedos."

Mr. Baseball paused. "It's what baseball lacks—a sense of community—and Robin helped build it."

MEMORIAL STADIUM

"**T**he greatest player I ever saw," said George Kell. "He looked like a guy who'd run over his own grandmother." Added Brooks Robinson: "We were a good ball club until we got Frank. He made us a winner." Frank Robinson left Cincinnati for Baltimore in December 1965. Straightaway he led baseball's 1966–'83 top-of-the-ladder team. Robby began May 8, 1966, off Luis Tiant, hitting the first fair ball out of Memorial Stadium. "Every game," added Orioles voice Chuck Thompson, "you saw this flag marked HERE beyond the left-field seats." His Triple Crown marked another first-since-Mantle '56: .316, 49 homers, and 122 RBI.

Boog Powell added 34 homers and 109 RBI. Shortstop Luis Aparicio, second baseman Davey Johnson, and center fielder Paul Blair were foolproof up the middle. Jim Palmer won 15 games. "His fastball exploded," said writer John Steadman, "out of those white houses beyond the center-field fence." The O's clinched September 22. Attendance climbed to 1,203,366. The Dodgers won that "other league." Said Brooks: "They expected to own us."

He and Frank crushed Game One homers off Don Drysdale at Dodger Stadium. Moe Drabowsky, fanning 11, yielded 1 hits in 6⅔ innings: O's, 5–2. Jim Palmer (20), Wally Bunker (21), and Dave McNally (23) blanked L.A. for a Series-record 33 straight innings. Blair's 430-foot blast won Game Three, 1–0. Next day Frank's fourth-frame dinger beat Big D: 54,458 roared; Blair caught the final out. The tenant swept the floor.

"**L**ooks more like football bowl than ballpark," *Sports Illustrated* wrote of Memorial. It had 5,500 parking slots. Private lots flanked nearby streets. Entering, a visitor sniffed a mix of ramps, grass cut in three directions, left- and right-field bleachers, and three tiers in a semicircle. He might sashay toward a) lower boxes with back supports; b) the east side for sun; or c) upper deck, framing Baltimore. "Fans take it easy going up steep 'cardiac ramps.' View of game and city from the heights is novel and interesting." Ditto, Stu Miller, losing a 1967 no-hitter to Detroit; Earl Weaver, replacing Hank Bauer next year as manager; and the 109–53 '69ers. The Apostles' Creed cites the "quick and the dead." Minnesota was the latter in the first best-of-five LCS: 4–3, 1–0, and 11–2. Brooks batted .500. He hit .053 in the Series. "God wanted the Mets," laughed No. 5. "Who am I to argue?"

In 2000, baseball named the '70 O's its fifth-best-ever team. Palmer forged a 2.71 ERA. McNally and Mike Cuellar went 48–17. Powell had 35 dingers and 114 RBI. Three players wore Gold Gloves. Eight homered in double figures. The Birds won 108 games, drew only 1,057,037, and again thrashed Minnesota, 10–6, 11–3, and 6–1. "Can you believe it?" Weaver said of Game Three: 27,708 half-filled *SI*'s "football bowl." The Series v. Cincinnati presaged A&E's *Biography*. The Orioles won the opener, 6–5: lingering, B. Robby, robbing Lee May from foul ground. Game Two: O's, 6–5. In Game Three, McNally became the first Series pitcher (and twelfth batter) to slam. Brooks combined .429, two homers, six RBI, and two diving stops in the 9–3 Game Five clincher. Said Johnny Bench of the Series' MVP: "If we'd known he wanted a car so badly, we'd have chipped in and bought one."

Some players breed babies out of wedlock. In Baltimore, they are named for a man mother never met. On September 17, 1955, Robinson got two hits in his first game. He entered Cooperstown in 1983—to May, "the human vacuum cleaner." In 1977, Memorial's largest baseball crowd (51,798) jammed Brooks Robinson Day. He recalled being a rookie: "I don't think I would want one day to change." Records link best fielding average (.971), chances (8,902), assists (6,205), putouts (2,697), double plays (618), and Gold Gloves (16). "Brooks played a very simple game," mused Chuck Thompson. "Hit it to him and he'd catch it—on grass, artificial turf, concrete pavement, a marsh, in a swamp. Throw it to him, and Brooks hit it": 268 dingers and 2,848 hits.

His final homer spiked 1977. "It was a cold rainy night, 'bout 7,000 people," Thompson continued. "Brooks pinch-hit a homer to win the game. What followed was among the craziest acceptances of a homer I've ever seen. The spectators ran down to the railing trying to get as close to the field as they could. Maybe they sensed this was Brooks' last blast. Whatever, this tiny crowd made as much noise as I've heard at a World Series"—*the* World Series being 1970's. Brooks abhorred losing to the Mets. In late '69 he affixed a tag to his luggage: "Brooks Robinson, 1970 World Champions."

Thompson learned baseball in a home, owned by his grandmother, that boarded Connie Mack. "One of the first things I noticed about Brooks was when I was trying to interview him. Soon, he began interviewing me. When fans ask for an autograph, he complies while finding out how many kids you have, where you live, how old you are, and if you have a dog"—like his '71ers treated the league.

"We knew how important '71 was," said Brooks. "Win it all, and people might talk dynasty." The court held Frank Robinson (500th homer), Merv Rettenmund (.317), Don Buford (99 runs), and *nonpareil* pitching. On September 26, Palmer became the fourth starter to win 20 games, joining McNally (21–5), Pat Dobson (20–8), and Cuellar (20–9). "Only one other team ['20 White Sox] ever did that," said Weaver. The O's again won 100 games, swept the A's, and took a 2–0 game Series lead. The Pirates then won Games Three–Five. "[In Game Six] it's the tenth, 2-all, one out," said Steadman. "Frank had bad legs. He walks, dashes to third on a single, and barely beats the throw to third with a belly-flop." Brooks then flew to shallow center. Heaving, Frank slid between catcher Manny Sanguillen's legs. Pittsburgh took the 2–1 final. Said Brooks: "We won the two World Series we should have lost ['66–'70], and lost the two we should have won."

That winter F. Robby was traded to the Dodgers. He averaged a career .294, scored 1,829 runs, batted in 1,812, missed 3,000 hits by 57 and 600 homers by 14, and became the first black to manage a bigs team. The '72 O's hit .229. *Dynasty* was canceled. The '73–'74ers lost the playoff to the A's. In '75, Palmer wed league-best wins (23), shutouts (10), and ERA (2.09). He won a team-high 268 games, had a .638 percentage, and never yielded a slam. The outfield changed: alleys 385 to 375 ('76), 378, (376) ('80), and 378 ('90); center, 410 to 400 ('76), 405, 410 ('78), and finally 405 ('80).

In 1977, Ken Singleton batted .328. P.A. voice Rex Barney swooned upon each foul, "Give that fan a *contract*!" The seventh-inning stretch swayed to John Denver's "Thank God I'm a Country Boy." Weaver's tomato plants bloomed down the left-field line. Yogi Berra said of streaking: "I couldn't tell if he was a man or woman. He had a bag over his head." One night rain delayed the game. A man shed his clothes, cleared the railing, ran to second base, and slid on the tarp into third. Security hustled him to the first-base dugout. The man leaves for the poky. Raising his right hand, plate umpire Nestor Chylak separates his thumb and index finger by an inch. "There were 27,000 in the park," said Weaver, "and every one of 'em roared."

Ultimately, the Earl of Baltimore won six divisions, four flags, and the '70 Series. He kicked dirt, taunted players, and badgered umpires. Weaver was bantam, profane, and proud. "I'll never forget the night someone gave Earl a double-billed cap," laughed Brooks, "so he could argue with umpires any way he turned." Once, suspended for three games, he vowed to not hound players till they lost. The O's won twice, then bowed. Said Earl: "I knew the pressure would get to you." Another night an Oriole fouled deep to left. Weaver pounds the dugout wall. "Damn it, should be one to nothing." Next pitch, same place. Weaver is apoplectic. "Damn it, should be one to nothing." Next pitch, same spot, but fair by a foot. Weaver is beside himself. "Damn it, should be *three* to nothing." Hot, Earl never yearned to seem cool.

Outfielder Pat Kelly became a minister. In the late '70s, he homered, touched home plate, raised his right arm, and pointed skyward. "What's this pointin' all about?" Weaver asked. Kelly said, "Earl, without the Good Lord up there, I wouldn't be able to do that." Jibed Earl: "Kel, the Good Lord didn't do too much for the guy who threw the ball, now did He?"

Once Pat exhorted mates, "We should walk on the righteous side, that's the way to live." Weaver happened by. "Isn't that right, skip?" Earl looked at him. "Kel, a walk with the bases loaded would be just as good."

"In one summer," John Steadman later said of 1979, "Baltimore became a baseball town." The Birds' new radio flagship took to hyping "Orioles Magic." They began winning games in an "Orioles Way." Memorial became "Birdland," or "The House at 33rd Street." Bill Hagy, a taxi driver in Section 34, twisted his body to spell ORIOLES atop the dugout. Attendance soared from 1,051,724 to 1,681,009. Recalling '71—15,000 empty seats marred the Series' last two games—you sang, swung, and cheered.

Mike Flanagan went a Cy Young 23–7. Singleton bopped 35 dingers. John Lowenstein won the playoff opener by homering, 6–3, v. California in the 10th. Baltimore then won, 9–8, lost, 4–3, and took the pennant, 8–0, behind Scott McGregor. The Birds took a 3–1 game Series edge over Pittsburgh. In Game Seven, Willie Stargell U-turned an O's lead with a two-run blast. Said mate Dave Parker: "Why shouldn't Pops win it for us? The man is a legend." The Birds would have settled for the humanity of a K.

Old hat: Steve Stone's 25–7 earned the Orioles' sixth Young since '69. Eddie Murray topped '81 Americans in dingers and RBI. A year later Cal Ripken debuted at third base, played every inning, and became Rookie of the Year. The last weekend Baltimore won three games v. Milwaukee to forge a tie: 33rd Street rocked with true believers. Weaver had announced his retirement. Would a Series delay it? "We win our last game, and [would have won] the pennant," he said. Instead, Milwaukee won; 51,642 roared afterward for Earl. Next April the O's held an Opening Day rally at Inner Harbor. Fifty thousand jammed boats, filled blocks, and chanted O-R-I-O-L-E-S. Announcer Jon Miller arrived that spring from Fenway Park. "People ask, 'How do Oriole fans compare to the Red Sox?' " he said in 1995. "I think you should ask, 'How do Boston fans compare to the Orioles'?' "

Few years compared to '83. Ripken hit .315, led in runs, hits, and doubles, and became MVP, edging Murray. "Already he was a local boy [coach Cal Ripken's son]," said Steadman. "Now he was making history [first to win back-to-back Rookie of the Year and MVP]." Joe Altobelli was named Manager of the Year. The bugle charge stirred a record 2,042,071. Chicago took the playoff opener. Mike Boddicker and Flanagan replied, 4–1 and 11–1. Tito Landrum's 10th-inning blast decreed

Game Four. The Birds then won the "Interstate 95" Series *v*. Philly, four games to one. A year later the Orioles Way shuffled north and west.

TIGER STADIUM

"**N**ineteen eighty-four," repeated then–Tigers manager Sparky Anderson. "People here were still obsessed about '68, just wondering if we'd win again." Al Kaline hit a '68 Series .379. Norm Cash batted .385. Mickey Lolich fused a 1.67 ERA MVP award, and three complete-game victories. "You all thought I was an improbable hero," the lefty said, "but I came sneaking through." In 1971, the beery motorcylist led the league at 25–14. "Finally, somebody knows who I am."

We already knew Reggie Jackson. The A's' DeMille swung *v*. Dock Ellis, hit the right-center light tower, and spun a '71 All-Star dinger to rival Williams '41. "Homers were the place's core," said Kaline of Tiger Stadium. "Reggie's blast and the others' [Hank Aaron, Johnny Bench, Roberto Clemente, Harmon Killebrew, and Frank Robinson]." The AL won, 6–4, ending an eight-game streak.

On October 1, 1972, Detroit led Boston by a half-game. "The schedule!" scolded Boston's Carl Yastrzemski. "The [early-season players'] strike made us play one less game than the Tigers": the half-game meant nothing. More than 51,000 packed the opener of The Corner's season-ending trio. "Whoever took two games," recalled Yaz, "would win the pennant." One old warrior—Kaline—homered. Another countered in the third. Two Sox reached base. Yastrzemski drove to center over Mickey Stanley's head. Tommy Harper scored easily. Luis Aparicio lost his balance, fell, retreated, and found Yaz at third: two men on base. Boston should have led, 2–1. Instead, Yastrzemski was out. Score: 1-all.

"They lost it there [4–1]," said Lolich." Next night Detroit took the East. It faced Oakland in the LCS. The A's won twice. Joe Coleman Kd 14 in Game Three, 3–1. Waterloo, said Nelson, was "a close-run thing." Oakland led Game Four, 3–1, in the 10th: The Tigers tallied thrice, tying the playoff. Blue Moon Odom then won, 2–1: 50,276 filled the bowl. "What a series," said manager Billy Martin. "Three one-run games, two extra innings," and the A's first title since 1931.

On July 15, 1973, Nolan Ryan no-hit Detroit. Cash proceeded to ditch his Louisville Slugger. "He had a leg from a clubhouse chair as a bat," said Kaline. "The ump didn't notice until the first pitch was thrown," then made Norm replace it. "Why?" Cash huffed. "No difference. I'm not gonna' hit Ryan anyway." Kaline, who could, became the first ALer since Eddie Collins to get 3,000 hits. Attendance fell to Detroit's lowest since '63.

Talk hinted of leaving downtown. Owner John Fetzer vetoed a suburban dome. "This franchise belongs to the inner city of Detroit," he said. "I'm just the caretaker." Soon an antic species owned Tiger's aviary.

In 1976, rookie Mark Fidrych became "The Bird," after the *Sesame Street* character—talking to the ball, prancing on the mound, and jamming big-league stadia. He was unaffected and different; his lure passed baseball boundary. On June 28, Detroit's chickabiddy faced the Yankees on network television. What a Saukeville/New Bedford/Made-in-USA storyline.

"We were so delighted," said ABC's Warner Wolf. "The game was sold out because of him. It's all you heard, how he acted, talked, patted the mound like a gardener." Fidrych won, 5–1; 47,855 made Tiger quake. He then acknowledged the first nationally televised sports curtain call. "Folks," Wolf exulted, "they're not going to stop clapping until the Bird comes from the dugout. . . . Fantastic! Mark Fidrych is born tonight on coast-to-coast television."

Fidrych 19–9 grasped priority. At the All-Star Game he asked President Ford if his son, Jack, a then-soap actor, could arrange a date. The Bird became Rookie of the Year (like '78 second baseman Lou Whitaker, retiring with 2,369 hits, a .275 average, and three Gold Gloves. Shortstop Alan Trammell, '77–'96, tied 2,365, .285, and seven. Said Joe Falls: "They became an institution." It enhanced another. One night Ernie Harwell said, "That foul was nabbed by a guy from Alma, Michigan." Whim turned ritual. Before a game bystanders pled, "Hey, Ernie, let a guy from Hope grab one"—or Puptown or Richfield Center. As a boy I recall thinking that Harwell had a lot of friends.

Ernie cited Casey Stengel. Once a prospect told him, "I'm a great player." Casey said, "What are your credentials?"

He said, "My senior year in college I hit 40 home runs. I knocked in 85 runs. I was a pitcher, threw five no-hitters, had a 1.30 ERA, and I run the 100-yard dash in 9.7."

Casey was amazed. "Don't you have any weaknesses?" The player said, "Well, I do lie a little." Re: Harwell, few Michiganders complained. In 1977, the original press box burned. General manager Jim Campbell complained about the *time*.

"I wish this [fire] had happened five months from now," he said. A reporter asked why. "All of 'em [writers] would have been in there." After eulogy, rebirth.

Anderson became skipper in 1979. In '84, "Bless You Boys" swept Michigan like courage, London's Blitz. Detroit started 35–5—only the fourth team to lead its league or division each day. Lance Parrish had 33 homers. Trammell hit .314. Willie Hernandez went 9–3, saved 32 games, and took Cy Young/MVP. A concomitant benefit: Tiger drew 2,704,794 to break its all-time attendance record. The playoff *v*. Kansas City ended quickly: 8–1, 5–3, 1–0. Enter the '80s winningest pitcher—162–119. Was Jack Morris arrogant? "Yes," said Anderson, "but he's like a high-strung racehorse, a great thoroughbred who'll bite you if you come near him."

Morris took the Series opener, 3–2. San Diego replied, 5–3. The Event moved east. A record 11 walks caged Game Three, 5–2. Morris threw his second complete game, 4–2: edge, Tigers, three games to one. Next day Detroit fronted, 5–4, in the eighth. Kirk Gibson came to bat: two on, one out. Gibbie had already homered. Sparky now tried a ploy. "Five bucks you don't hit one out," he yelled from the dugout. Furious, Kirk signaled to double the bet. Goose Gossage threw. Gibson hit the right-field upper deck. "It was ours," he said after dancing around the bases, arms pumped like pistons. "That's why it took so long [reaching home]. Everybody knew we had it."

Thugs burned cars, smashed windows, and assaulted passersby on the final out. Motowners rushed, crushed, and clutched the field. The Padres' Jerry Coleman keyed CBS Radio's post game show. "In Detroit it's only about 30 feet from the field to the booth—so somebody picks up the idea of target practice. It's not enough they've just beaten the

Padres—this adds insult to injury. We close the screen, and I fall on my hands." Coleman nearly sent the Tigers his dry cleaning bill.

WRIGLEY FIELD

Detroit that night seemed coming apart at the seams. A Chicagoan felt its pain. The optimist sees half a glass of water and says, "It's half-full." The pessimist says, "It's half-empty." The Cubs fan says, "When's it going to spill?"

In 1972, Burt Hooton no-hit the Phils. The Cubs then returned to form. Longtime Oriole Milt Pappas had a perfect game with two out and two strikes in the ninth. He tossed two pitches that, depending on your view, missed or caught the corner. Bruce Froemming called them balls. The batter walked. The next popped up. Pappas had the no-hitter. A day later Milt caught his prey. "Bruce, why didn't you call one of those a strike because that's what they were—and you'd have made history by calling a perfect game."

Froemming said, "Milt, if I did that I wouldn't a' been able to live with myself."

Pappas said, "So how do you live with yourself on all the other lousy calls you make?"

By 1975, the Cubs had shunned October since the year Harry Truman became president. Pittsburgh romped, 22–0. Bill Madlock won two batting titles. Rick Monday hit 32 homers and had 107 RBI in '76. The Mets' Dave Kingman hit the third frame house on the east side of Kenmore Avenue. "If the ball had carried three feet higher," said Cubs skipper Jim Marshall, "it would have gone through a window and smashed a TV set [on which a Naomi Martinez was watching Kingman]." Three days later Mike Schmidt smacked four homers at Wrigley Field: Phils, 18–16. In this parlor of a park, the wind was blowing out.

"I often wondered," said Schmitty, "how I'd have done if I played here." Wonder is self-fulfilling. Nightmare on Addison Street: On May 17, 1979, the Phils and Cubs combined 11 homers, 11 doubles, 11 hurlers, and 50 hits. Now-Cub Kingman homered thrice (ending with an NL-best 48). Schmidt's two included a 10th-inning clincher. Cheaper by the dozen: Phils, 23–22.

"**O**ne of the prettiest parks in the majors," read *Sports Illustrated.* "No light towers mar skyline." Day baseball grasped mellowspeak. "Best place to sit is behind home plate in upper deck. All the spacious box seats are angled toward diamond to eliminate stiff necks, and all are filled with wide, comfortable chairs." A visit led back in time: cat-walks near each pole; 15–16 feet high left- and right-field wall; 11-foot-4-inch wall from left- to right-center; "Chicago Cubs" sign and bleacher entrance behind the scoreboard; numbers culled from mem-ory—355, 400, 353 (and 495 on a rooftop across Sheffield). Rest rooms were clean; concessions, large; ushers, unwilling to hammerlock a customer. You inhaled hot dogs, pretzels, Italian beef—and baseball's Bali Hai.

In 1980, Bill Buckner won the batting title. His Cubs finished last. A year later the Tribune Company bought the team. "The Wrigley family was constant," said Bill Veeck. "You worried about change." At first the Trib soothed: no night ball! Enter a subsidiary. For years, WGN-TV flung the Cubs into every corner of the city. It now became a superstation beaming their schedule by satellite. "Once the Cubs belonged to the North Side," a writer said. "Now even North America isn't big enough. Cable television has made the Cubbies more than a home-town team."

Overnight, the '84 Tribunes swapped one paradigm (bungling) for another (America's Cubs)—sadder but wiser losers who won their first flag since 1945. Forget "the most ridiculed, least imitated sports fran-chise of your lifetime," wrote columnist Bob Verdi. Marvels merged: a first-place team ("Part of the Cubs' charm," said *USA Today,* "is how bad they have been for so long"); SRO yard (record 2,107,655); and cable, packing the Cubs wagon. Driving: Holy Cow! God broke the mold *before* He made Harry Caray.

In 1982, Caray left Comiskey Park for Addison and Clark. "Cable made me a household name," he conceded. In Idaho, Cubs Power Fan Clubs took root like spuds. The Costa Rica Key Largo Bar flagpole flew the Cubs and City of Chicago pennants. "Cubs win! Cubs win!" Harry called a late-season triumph. "The Good Lord wants the Cubs to win!" Stars: Leon Durham (96 RBI), Rick Sutcliffe (Cy Young 16–1), and MVP Ryne Sandberg (114 runs, 19 triples, and 200 hits). Millennium in the morn: September 24, 1984, 8:49 P.M., Central Time. "One more and it's over. The Chicago Cubs will be the new Eastern Division champs!" Harry crowed from Pittsburgh. "It's in there. Cubs are the champions! The Cubs are the champions! . . . The fans are getting on the field! . . . Now our lives are complete!"

A writer for Governor Thomas E. Dewey once formed "The Brave Twisted Smile Club." Beer and sympathy. The Cubs forced the "Die Hard Fans Club." Chicago blitzed San Diego, 13–0, in the playoff opener. Steve Trout then beat Mark Thurmond, 4–2. "Two played, two down," said Padres manager Dick Williams, "and not too good." Sadly, the LCS was best-of-five, not-three. San Diego won, 7–1 (over Dennis Eckersley); 7–5 (on Steve Garvey's ninth-inning poke); and 6–3 (blowing a 3–0 edge; Leon Durham's error scored the tying run).

"All my life, I've believed in miracles," said Ronald Reagan. "And now after 39 years of waiting the miracle is happening." Almost. One more victory would have matched Chicago v. 1907-'08-'35-'45 foe Detroit. "We should have known," a writer said, bitterly. "These are the Cubs." Bud man, or Cub fan, we still loved '84.

KINGDOME

Wrigley's opposite was "the worst baseball arena *ever*," *Newsday*'s Marty Noble huffed of the Seattle Kingdome. "It is a large mausoleum that gives its guests the impression of being a poorly lit, damp basement with a beat-up, old pool table in the middle. Let it rot." It imploded in March 2000. By then, balls had struck speakers, hit roof support wires, and entangled red, white, and blue streamers. The roof leaked. The gray look and quiet feel led a visitor to call it the Tomb. Even Seattle couldn't wait for the joint to fall. One Mariners official urged selling detonating plungers for the Kingdome's razing. "Let 'em partake in the act. A lot of people would pay money. Everyone wants to see it blown up."

Actually, the problem lay outside. "Summers here," said announcer Dave Niehaus, "come to us from God." Seattle borders Puget Sound and the Cascade Mountains. Ferry boats link green covered islands. Victorian homes speckle Capitol Hill. Must-sees include Ivar's Old Clock Tower, Union Station, and Pike Street market. "It's traditional and eclectic," wrote the *Seattle Post-Intelligencer*, "and above all has charm." The Kingdome was none of the above.

"Baseball had been played outdoors in Seattle since the early 1900s [Northwest League]," said the Hall of Fame's Jack Redding. After the AL Pilots left Sick's Stadium, a dome was thought needed to best rain, house football, and counter memory—but where? Consensus firmed on downtown's southern perimeter. Groundbreaking used a symbolic gold home plate. "This is the place," puffed a King County executive. Ultimately, it sat 59,438 (football 65,000), parked 4,000 cars (private lots held 30,000), hosted concerts and exhibitions, and cost $67 million. "Money is like manure," said industrialist Clint Murchinson. "If you spread it around it does a lot of good. But if you pile it up in one place it stinks like hell."

Manure stank from Opening Night (April 6, 1970). Official ball: U.S. Senator Henry Jackson. First pitcher: Diego Segui. Batter: Jerry Remy. Hit: Don Baylor. Homer: Joe Rudi (all Angels, winning, 7–0.) Attendance: 57,762. In time, King Country Stadium boasted Hoody's peanuts, center-field Diamond Vision, and schooner cannon shots hailing a Mariners homer. Necessities were the problem: poor sight lines, few up-close seats, and no sky or grass.

"**Y**ou can play five or six years on turf and another five or six on grass and there's no comparison," said '81–'86 M's outfielder Dave Henderson. "The turf and the concrete seem like 10 years. The grass seems like five years." From the start Niehaus' "My, oh, my" and "It will fly away" fashioned baseball's Northwest Opening. He coveted an open roof. "There are no elements, no effect on the ball. Going indoors is a pain in the ass on a beautiful day. Say it's 75 degrees, clear skies, I'm sitting on my deck watching the boats race up and down the lake, listening to the birds in the background, and I can see beautiful Mount Rainier. Oh, for a place like Fenway Park. You can see the grass grow, Fenway smells, you can see Ted Williams, Babe Ruth playing there. I genuflect when I walk through the gates."

In 1977, 1,338,511 came, saw, and panted for Puget Sound. A red tartan track rimmed the field. Foul ground swamped the lines. Upper deck's section 32, row 18 loomed 617 feet from the plate. Distances were reachable, if not seeable: left, 315 (324 in '90 and 331 in '91); left-center, 375 (365 in '78, 357 in '81, 362, and 376 in '91); deep-left center, 385 (389 in '91). Center skewed from 405 to 410 ('78), 405, 410, and 405 ('91). Deep right-center swapped 375 ('90) for 380 ('91). Right-center shrank: 375, 365 ('78), 357, and 352 ('90). Right hugged 315, 316 ('78), 314, and 312 ('91). (The 11½-foot high wood fence marked '77–80 distances in feet and fathoms: one fathom equals six feet.)

"From the floor," said the *Post-Intelligencer*, "the [acoustical] ceiling looks like thousands of bricks." It was built to dim the echo of dinky crowds. Designers knew their team. The 1977–'84 M's once drew a million. "People knock Seattle as a baseball town," said Niehaus. "I say, 'You fans don't owe the Mariners anything, they owe you a team.' " John Montague tried, retiring an AL-tying 33 straight hitters in 1977. A year later the M's lost a still-record 104 games. The '79ers hosted the All-Star Game: NL, 7–6, before 58,905. Bruce Bochte hit .316. On June 5, Willie Horton's would-have-been 300th homer struck a support wire for a single. (Four nights later he smacked it on "Willie Horton Night.") Reliever Dave Heaverlo shook his head. "There was always something weird."

Far out was the steel and concrete web suspended from the ceiling. Seventy-five red, white, and blue streamers were hung to help infielders track flies. Instead, pop-ups brushed them. Fifty-nine wires and 14 loudspeakers made each play a venture. Numerous balls struck speakers and remained in play (e.g., Ken Phelps' grand-slam). Others smacked the foul-ground NBA SuperSonics' speaker. Ruppert Jones' foul lodged above the first-base dugout. Dave Kingman made out by hitting a left-field roof wire. In 1981, the three outfield speakers were raised from 102 to 135 feet above the field. An added spin: 42 air-conditioning ducts, 16 in fair ground, 26 foul, blowing air toward the field. Bert Campaneris once touched Heaverlo for a homer. "The press asked me how he hit it so far," said Dave. "I told the truth, 'The air conditioning must have been blowing out.' "

Seattle had a losing record its first 14 years. "It was so quiet," said right fielder Jay Buhner, "you could hear the fans talking about you."

Oddments kept the small core of loyalists wandering back to "Puget Puke."

Maury Wills was the Mariners' '80–'81 manager. He and his girl friend left one exhibition game to fly to Los Angeles. "They just wanted to go there," explained Niehaus. Another day grounds help extended the batter's box a foot toward the mound. Jibed ump Bill Kunkel: "Maury wanted to give his guys an advantage against the A's curveballs." He was fined $500 and suspended for two games.

Wills was not exactly a workaholic. Once, entering the clubhouse, he saw two bystanders. "Fellows, what batting order should I use—why don't you just make out the lineup for tonight's game?" Maury was fired after submitting a lineup card showing two players at the same position. In 1981, California real estater George Argyros bought the club. Seals and Croft sang, "Summer Breeze." That May 27, Lenny Randle's turned personal. A batter bunted toward Randle, playing third. "The King-dome's flat on the base paths," he reasoned. "I knew the ball would go foul." Lenny decided to help. "I still see Lenny on all fours trying to blow the ball foul," mate Tom Paciorek laughed, "and the umpires, scolding him." For 22 years batters scolded Gaylord Perry's spitballer. Perry returned the bile.

In 1980, the then-Ranger Perry began clicking a Kingdome camera. Its owner objected: The pair almost came to blows. "What happened next," said announcer Mel Proctor, "was out of Peter Sellers." The photographer brought assault charges. Police arrived. A rumor flared: Perry would be arrested on the final out! The Rangers reacted more quickly than Clouseau. "They got Gaylord to the airport, stashed him in the truck-loading van, and put him on the plane." Cops weren't convinced, handcuffing pitching coach Fred Koenig. "Same height as Gaylord, bald." Ultimately, police uncuffed him, scurried to the airport, and missed their man. My, oh, my. Gaylord had flown away.

OLYMPIC STADIUM

We come now to the Edsel of baseball parks—actually, Citroën, since most Quebecers speak French. The Citroën is bizarre, otherworldly, and technically inept, except to groupies. Unlike Olympic Stadium, however, it lures, not repels. Not even your *grandmere* could love the cavernous Le Stade Olympique. If the Expos flee Montreal, blame the Big O, as in zero.

"Why do all the most beautiful cities have the most awful dumps?" asked a friend. "Seattle, Montreal [and later Minneapolis]." Blame accident, stupidity, and luck. Each conspired to breed a corpse.

We forget: Baseball thrived during Jarry Park's 1969–'76 suzerainty. "I chose one [another] road," wrote Robert. Frost, "and that made all the difference." Jarry was small and elfin. Olympic mimed a hangar and/or shape ship: Concrete walls bowed out, then in, then curved back to almost meet. Open: the roof's small oval hole. "Officials promised to cover it with a retractable dome," recalled Expos then-president John McHale. Instead, the *promise* turned retractable.

Jarry Park meant *L'Expos*. Olympic Stadium evolved for the '76 Summer Games. An all-weather tartan track circled the field. ("You could see the track and field lines," a player laughed, "even on the warning track.") Three tiers of seats loomed a province from the mound. Capacity was 60,000: surface, AstroTurf; foul turf, large; distance, symmetrical. Lines veered from 325 through 330 in '81 to 325 in '83. Alleys were 375. Center remained more or less 404. A 12-foot interior fence fused the poles. Olympic's back wall towered an extra-base hit beyond. "In between was this blackness between the outfield and building shell," said McHale. Its no-man's land nicely characterized the park.

Parking was seldom a problem near 4549 Avenue de Coubertin: Canada's largest indoor parking garage lay under the stadium. On April 15, 1977, many took Metro trains from downtown to the nearby subway station. The game proved a bomb. First pitcher: Don Stanhouse. Batter: Philly's Jay Johnstone. Hit: Expos' Dave Cash. Homer: mate Ellis Valentine. Score: Philadelphia, 7–2. Reviews were worse.

"Your eye is caught by the tower [556 feet, one foot higher than the Washington Monument: 50 stories high angled at 45 degrees], the world's tallest inclined structure," wrote a columnist. It tied sections 766 and 767 in left-and right-center, respectively, and could be scaled in two minutes in a 90-passenger car. The tower was built (here Olympic gets hideous) to cover the oval hole (checking rain and snow) with a 60,696-

square-foot, 50-ton, silver-topped, orange-bottomed, retractable dome (linked by 26 white cones). It flopped. The roof took 25 minutes to lower or raise, froze when wind topped 25 miles an hour, and wasn't finished till 1987. Ultimately, a faulty generator made it impossible to open. "You can't win," wrote a columnist. "Put the roof on, and it keeps out the cold but makes it sterile. Open, and it rains." The roof seemed futuristic, bland, and vapid, unlike Montreal.

For a time it didn't matter. Andre Dawson became 1977 Rookie of the Year. Attendance more than doubled to 1,433,757. Willie Stargell hammered a 535-foot tater. The '79 Expos placed second. A year later Bill Gullickson, 21, Kd a rookie record 18 Cubs. Ron LeFlore's 97 swipes led the NL The Phillies eliminated Montreal the next-to-final day. "They were interesting players," said manager Dick Williams. "You almost forgot the park." Tim Raines stole a rookie 71 bases in 1981. The 'Spos won the second-half East, beat Philly in the intradivision series, and went forth against L.A. The teams split LCS Games One–Four. The decider wooed only 36,491 to a strike-soured Big O. It began the ninth 1-all. Rick Monday then took Steve Rogers into the center-field abyss. "The most memorable moment in Montreal baseball." Williams laughed, "and it happens *against* us."

In 1982, Al Oliver led the league in doubles, hits, RBI, average, and total bases—and wasn't MVP. Montreal hosted the first non-U.S. All-Star Game: NL, 4–1. The '83ers drew a record 2,320,651. Raines led the league in on-base and batting. Tim Wallach had 123 ribbies in 1987. Dawson seven times topped 20 homers. Gary Carter thrice hit 31 or more. (They rank 1–2 in Expos dingers, respectively, with 228 and 215.) The Mets' Darryl Strawberry lipped the roof. The Expos lost, 1–0, to L.A. in 22 innings. Mascot Youppi—"the only warm thing about the Expos," wrote *La Presse*—was ejected from a game. Part of a 55-ton concrete block in the upper deck collapsed in September 1991. The Expos finished their home schedule on the road.

"You began to ask if the franchise was collapsing," said voice Dave Van Horne. Seals from a pregame circus refused to leave the field: The grounds help couldn't catch them. An 18-wheel truck capped a pregame parade by crashing through the fence. Another night 500 high school bands misplaced their musical scores. "I keep seeing the plaque and statue of ['46 Royal] Jackie Robinson," Carter added, "and wondering what he would think." Slowly, the Citroën tried to start.

"How do you improve this place?" a writer shrugged of the O. Barely. The Expos moved home plate nearer the backstop. Field-level VIP stands rose behind it. "They had cupholders," said President Claude Brochu, "and were bigger than '70s seats." New bleachers abutted the right- and left-field fence. The team stopped selling other seats: size dropped to 43,739. A center scoreboard blared ads and video. Felipe Alou became manager. Son Moises hit .339 in 1994. That August 12, the Expos' .649 winning percentage led the bigs. "Some luck," Brochu mourned. "That day the strike kills our season." It cost Montreal nearly $16 million.

The '95ers made $40,000 but dredged last with a mere $10 million payroll. Henry Rodriguez had 36 homers a year later. In 1997, Pedro Martinez Kd 306, won the Cy Young Award, and left. Mourned Felipe Alou: "We just can't afford him." Attendance dropped to 914,717. Was Montreal a hockey town? Plexiglas shielded midlevel row one. Labatt's put a Noise-Meter above right field to measure—what? Vladimir Guerrero's 1999 fused .316, 42 homers, and 131 RBI, broke eight club records, and lit the top 10 in 11 NL categories. The Expos drew fewer than 10,000 per game. Green lights went on in Charlotte, northern Virginia, and Washington, D.C. Grace: the Big O's smoked meat, Kojax Souflaki, and Cordero wine. Was it saving? Only a new park could keep baseball from skipping to *les Etas-Unis*.

"We cannot stay here," New York art dealer Jeffrey Loria said in '99 on becoming new majority partner. Key was pressure: The legislature must build a new park. Instead, it dawdled. Loria didn't help. "People keep telling me that television and radio are promotional tools," he said. "This is not a public charity. I want more money." He didn't get it.

The 2000 Expos were blacked out on TV and English radio (like Guerrero's .345, 44, and 123). "No local team baseball on TV is a difficult concept to grasp," said Brooklyn-born *Montreal Gazette* columnist Paul Hickey. The '01 home opener drew 45,183. The next 27 dates averaged 7,776. One night a movie company renting space at Olympic Stadium tested special effects equipment. Smoke from a machine billowed beyond the right-field fence. "The Expos future in Montreal is hazy," said *Baseball Weekly*. "But last weekend, so was the here and now." Loria disagreed. "Montreal is a great baseball town," he said, "and can be again." Not at sepulchral Le Stade Olympique.

Forget applause. At the Big O, locals often cheer by kicking seats in front of them. "Tradition," custom said. The seats, of course, were empty. Seat abuse? Team abuse? The real abuse is the park.

EXHIBITION STADIUM

Toronto's first baseball park cost $7,000, sat 2,000, and flanked the Sunlight Soap Works on an eight-acre plot near Queen Street and the Don River. A local writer liked its outfield fence. "[It] will tax the acrobatic talents of the smartest to surmount." Sliding doors on three sides "would be used by the players to recover baseballs when hit over the fence, which is not likely to happen very often." Those wacky Canadians cheered opening-in-1886 Sunlight Park.

In 1891, Toronto left organized ball. Five years later it joined the Eastern (then, International) League. The '97ers moved to Hanlon's Point. "To get there you had to dodge railroad traffic at a [level] street crossing," said former Hall of Fame historian Lee Allen, "and then take a ferry to the island." A picture of Queen Elizabeth II once spruced hockey's Maple Leaf Gardens. Maple Leaf Park was scheduled to open May 9, 1910. God *didn't* save the King: Edward VII's death delayed it a day. The Leafs beat Baltimore, 4–3, before 13,000. Next year Babe Ruth smacked his first professional—and sole minor-league—homer off the Leafs' Ezra Johnson. A plaque exists today.

In 1926, Toronto reclaimed the mainland. Opened: Maple Leaf Stadium, capacity 20,000, on Bathhurst Street. Hired: comedian Nick Altrock, for its June 18, 1934, night debut. "He went on too long," said Allen. Play began at 10 P.M. "Then came a vendors' brawl in the seventh inning." Play ended after 1 A.M. Pleased: later football and hockey owner Jack Kent Cooke. His '52 Leafs placed fourth, but crammed 440,000. "We're major league," Cooke said, four times trying to buy a team. A special committee urged the Canadian National Exhibition to up size to 64,000. The City Parks Committee conjured a nearly 40,000-seat park. Said Cooke: "It's the biggest step ever taken toward bringing

major league baseball to Toronto." In 1965, businessmen floated a suburban domed stadium. Both plans died.

RIP, Maple Leaf, expiring September 4, 1967. Metro Council chairman Paul Godfrey recalled: "Toronto had simply outgrown minor-league
ball." A new dome scheme rose, and fell. Finally, in 1974, the Council
voted $15 million to expand CNE Stadium to 40,000 (55,000 football).
Bowie Kuhn called Toronto "a success waiting to happen." It almost
happened *tout de suite*. Toronto was once called "The Good City." It
awoke to January 1976 good news. "Giants Agree to Sale," read the
Globe and Mail. "Toronto Warms Up for Baseball." Plot: The ex-
McGraws acepted $13.25 million from Labatt Breweries, Vulcan Assets
Commission, and Canadian Imperial Bank of Commerce. Footnote: The
sale needed a green light from 9 of the other 11 NL teams. Instead,
'Frisco fused money, lawsuit, and court injunction. The Giants stayed.

The AL sighed, giving Toronto a 1977 expansion team. The head of
Toronto's Irwin Toy Ltd. soon brayed: "People all over Canada feel an
addiction for the team." A contest bred the name Blue Jays. Their
insignia fluttered across the land. Sold: by Irwin, $10 million in hats, jer-
seys, and other bric-a-brac in 1977.

A bonanza, eh? Except for the team and park. The expansion Jays lost
107 games, but drew 1,701,052. They were consistent, placing last in
the '77–'81 AL East. Toronto's winning percentage was .359. "There
was no reason to listen," said radio's Tom Cheek, "except for the novelty of big-league ball." Daily Cheek and Early Wynn amused their new
"home and native land."

One night a young man dropped a foul pop. A moment later a second
neared him. His girlfriend made a one-handed catch to save another
boo-boo. "Can you believe it?" Cheek boomed. "*He* boots it and *she*
catches it." Cooed Wynn, "She probably knows all about his hands."
Once Early drove his motorcoach from Florida. An accident in Coon
Hollow, Tennessee, delayed the arrival. On the air Wynn recalled how,
driving down a hill, he looked out the window and saw his front wheel
rolling beside the road. "Your life must have flashed before your eyes,"
Cheek said. "What was going through your mind?"

"Tom, I was recalling the lines of that song," popular in the 1970s. " 'You picked a fine time to leave me, loose wheel.' "

Opening Day 1977 evoked TV's *Sergeant Preston of the Yukon*. Chicago lost, 9–5, before 44,649. Doug Ault homered twice, and was seldom heard from again. Al Woods pinch-dingered in his first bigs up. Snow fell off the lake. The windchill hit 10 degrees Fahrenheit. "The only major league game ever played with snow covering the entire field," said manager Roy Hartsfield. A Zamboni borrowed from the hockey Leafs repeatedly cleared the turf. Any Canadian could share: CBC-TV linked Grand Pre and Dawson City.

As a baseball park, CNE was a football shrine. "It just took a while to get used to," said Hartsfield of 300 acres of Exhibition Park. Shops and restaurants prospered. Frisbees and picnicking knit the tidy grounds. Most took the bus and subway. Stadium and city lots managed the rest. A block away Lake Ontario welcomed boats—and seagulls. "They buzzed the park after games," said outfielder Bob Bailor, "after the scraps were discarded." In 1983, Dave Winfield's warm-up throw killed a seagull. "They say he hit it on purpose," said Yankees manager Billy Martin. "They wouldn't say that if they'd seen the throws he's been making all year. It's the first time he's hit the cut-off man." Law-abiders briefly proposed the slammer. Actually, *CNE* belonged there—for impersonating a park.

I t began with foul lines, bases and dirt squares, and infield/outfield plastic. Each was implanted on the Canadian Football League Argonauts' field. "You thought the [L.A.] Coliseum was bad," said a writer. "At least it had real turf." The Jays' linked the west end zone to the 35-yard line (right-field fence). Yard lines to the east zone paralleled the fence. Seats flanked each sideline behind the outfield and first base. "The only decent seats were on the third-base side and behind home," said Cheek. "You could at least see the plate. All the others looked away." Few outfield seats were sold right of football's midfield. By 1979 the right-field scoreboard showed the Jays hitting bottom: 53–109. The '80ers lost fewer than 100 for the first time.

A visitor opened Labatt's beer and silver linings: Hector Torres hit the

Jays' first grand slam; John Mayberry smacked 30 homers; Otto Velez went deep four times in a doubleheader; Toronto turned its first triple play. In 1977, Jerry Garvin picked off 22 runners. That year Earl Weaver forfeited a game by yanking his O's off the field. "The umps," Hartsfield explained, "refused to remove a tarp in our [baseline] pen." A year later 24 Jays hits KOd Baltimore, 24–6. Dave Stewart led the league in shutouts, complete games, and innings in 1982. The next year Toronto led in batting and slugging. The '84ers cracked 2 million. Crowds clapped softly. Said a player: "They're the quietest in the league." Between innings they stood and stretched. "Maybe they think the first period is over."

The Jays' preamble ended in 1985. George Bell and Jesse Barfield drove in 179 runs. Reliever Dennis Lamp went 11–0. Dave Stieb's 2.48 ERA led the league. (He retired as Toronto's winningest pitcher: 175–134). The Jays took their division. The enlarged best-of-seven LCS opened at CNE. Toronto soon led, three games to one. K. C. then drew three of a kind. Barfield's 40 homers led '86 Americans. Ibid., Jimmy Key's '87 ERA (2.76) and Bell's RBI (134, parlaying .308 and 47 dingers into MVP). The wind blew out September 14: A record 10 taters beat Baltimore, 18–3 (Ernie Whitt, 3; Bell and Rance Mulliniks 2 each; Lloyd Moseby, Rob Ducey, and Fred McGriff). The Jays lured a record 2,778,429. Few could believe how they proceeded to blow the East. "We've got it in the bag, and then lose four straight the last week," said Cheek. "Still, we're up by one with three games [v. Detroit] left. A win'll force a playoff." Some sunlight: Toronto lost each by a run.

In 1988, Stieb threw two no-hitters for 8⅔ innings. "Each time a guy gets a hit," he said. "The story of our team." Exhibition's ended May 28, 1989: Jays 7, White Sox 5, before 46,120. At each game the seventh-inning stretch blared a homey number. "Okay-okay, Blue Jays-Blue Jays," it went. "Let's play—let's play BALL!" They would, and do, two miles and a roof away.

17

THE IMPOSSIBLE DREAM

"What an awful time for baseball parks," Michael Gershman said of the mid-'70s. "Thank God there was more to the game." Baseball is subjective: What appears vanilla to me may seem like chocolate to you. By any taste, the 1975–'86 Red Sox played three of arguably the five greatest games of television's, or Modern America's, age. By rote: Game Six of the 1975 World Series, the '78 playoff against the Yanks, and Game Six of the '86 Oktoberfest. (The other two: Bobby Thomson's poke and Bill Mazeroski '60.) Never before was the Republic so attached to the Boston American League Baseball Company.

TV in our place and time is America's tribal meeting place. Forty-eight percent in a 1964 Lou Harris survey named baseball their favorite sport. Seventeen did in early '75. The bigs did little marketing. Pro football played the networks like a cello. Many of baseball's best teams drew poorly, played far from New York's electronic core, and/or had a mausoleum of a park. In TV's creative colony, network ball became a leper.

"That was the talk," Bowie Kuhn said. "Baseball was dying." Re-enter a sort of yeasty Eastern turbulence. The '75–'86 Sox helped America refind the game. In 1975, more than 124 million watched all or part of the Boston-Cincinnati Series. Game Seven of the '86 Mets-Yawkeys Classic was seen in 34 million homes, luring 81 million of the devoted and curious—easily, baseball's most-watched-ever game.

"It helped," Kuhn said of going back to its future. "You love to see up-close, roaring fans." Without besmirching the latter, televised games at Olympic Stadium rival a stroll through K-Mart. On the other hand, the plot at Lansdowne and Yawkey increasingly bespoke the sport. "The Red Sox mean Fenway," said NBC director Harry Coyle, "and Fenway means great TV. It's got the loud fans and weird nooks and low grandstand and up-close shots. The key to baseball on television is intimate camera angles. Forget the new parks. Fenway's the best."

"The Sox always need pitching," mused ESPN-TV's Peter Gammons. "In '75, they had youth, too." Youth meant the "Gold Dust Twins"— rookies Jim Rice and Fred Lynn—flanking Dwight Evans: Boston's best outfield since Duffy Lewis, Tris Speaker, and Harry Hooper.

Baseball's wild card devalues its pennant race. By contrast, '75's regular season fused name and deed. On June 19, Lynn (.331, 21 homers, 105 RBI: first same-year MVP/Rookie of the Year) had three homers and 10 ribbies at Detroit. Rice (.309, 22, and 102) was so strong he broke his bat while checking a swing.

The A's paraded Reggie Jackson, Sal Bando, and Joe Rudi in the playoff. Reading, you thought Boston limited to Ancient Mariners (Luis Tiant/Carl Yastrzemski) and Baby Huey (Rice/Lynn). The balding, bulging, cigar-in-the-shower-smoking, pirouetting-as-he-threw El Tiante won the opener, 7–1. Said Jackson: "Tiant is the Fred Astaire of baseball." Boston again won, 6–3. The series moved to Oakland. Yaz threw a runner out and kept another from scoring: Sox, 5–3, to sweep. No. 8 hit an LCS team-high .455. Spying a calendar, you spotted a mistake. The year should read 1967.

Boston's upset began a fall that roused time zones from Fenway. The World Series opened October 11. Cincinnati fielded an All-Star team— four Hall of Famers (Sparky Anderson, Johnny Bench, Joe Morgan, and

Tony Perez) and two might-bes (Dave Concepcion and Pete Rose). None helped in Game One: Tiant, 6–0. Next day Boston led, 2–1, when rain doused the seventh inning. "[Bill] Lee was hot," said the Sox' Dwight Evans. "The delay broke his rhythm." Three ninth-frame hits broke the Townies' back, 3–2.

The Series moved to Riverfront: Events dwarfed its gray and concrete bowl. The Reds grabbed a 5–1 lead. Concepcion and Cesar Geronimo homered back-to-back (first Series time since '67 Game 6). Evans' ninth-inning blast tied: 5-all. Next inning Geronimo reached first. Catcher Carlton Fisk then threw Ed Armbrister's bunt into center. "Armbrister interfered [with Fisk's attempted force-out]!" screamed manager Darrell Johnson, charging plate umpire Larry Barnett. "Forget it!" Barnett cried. Morgan singled for the winning run. A night later Boston's best pressure hurler since Ruth threw 163 pitches: Luis, 5–4. Game Five went to Don Gullett, pitching, and Perez, homering twice: Reds, 5–2.

Had play ended there, we might recall it as limply as 1959's White Sox–Dodgers (L.A., in six). The Classic returned to Boston. For three days it rained. The delay was thought to ebb interest. Instead, it upped pressure. Cincy led, 6–3, in the eighth. Lynn got a single and Rico Petrocelli walked. Pinch hitter Bernie Carbo topped a 2–2 pitch, then arced a memorable, epochal, implausible blast: 6–6. Farce and daydream careened near midnight. Lynn popped to short left in the ninth with the bases loaded and none out. Third-base coach Don Zimmer told the runner, "No, no!" Denny Doyle thought Zim yelled, "Go, go!" George Foster doubled him at the plate. With Ken Griffey on base, Morgan pulled an 11th-frame curve toward right—good for a triple or home run—except that Evans raced back, grabbed the ball, and completed a double play.

The game turned four hours. Fisk led off the twelfth and belted Pat Darcy's 1–0 pitch to left. "When there is a game that means something," wrote Dave Anderson of Game Six, "baseball is the best game of all." Memory freezes Fisk, draped against the night, swinging and lancing the ball and employing hand signals and body English to push or force or pray the ball fair. It caromed off the pole for a game-winning, Series-tying, Falstaffian drive. "I went home," said Anderson, "and I was stunned."

Sparky returned for the finale. Boston led, 3–0, until Rose upended Doyle on a potential sixth-frame double play. Fisk then ordered a curve to Perez. Instead, Lee tossed a blooper: Tony cleared the screen. Rose singled to tie the score. In the ninth, reliever Jim Willoughby yielded to a rookie.

Cincy won on a run more redolent of Dead Ball than the Big Red Machine. Griffey walked, was sacrificed to second, moved to third on a ground out, and scored on Morgan's game-winning lob. The loser, Jim Burton, pitched one more bigs game.

Anderson called Game Six "a keeper." It was also a changer. Fenway's first Series night game presaged baseball's all prime-time Classic. A then–record 75,890,000 watched Cincinnati win the 4–3 decider. On Madison Avenue, the game escaped TV's critical list. The reaction shot of Fisk changed sports coverage. Even Fenway changed.

"In the Series Lynn hit the center-field concrete wall and crumpled to the grass," recalled Ned Martin. In 1976, owner Tom Yawkey padded the wall base, replaced left-field's tin with plastic, shrunk the built-in-'34 board by dropping NL scores, and moved it 20 feet to the right. Novelties included a new press box and center-field commercial messageboard. (In 1982–'83, private suites rose atop the left-and right-field stands.)

"At the time," said Gammons, "the change was seen as meteorological," not commercial. Fenway's wind had blown in and out. The new press box and board made currents ricochet. Even numbers spelled change. The distance to Fenway's left-field pole—315 feet—was like the rock at Plymouth Point. In 1997, the Sox revised it to 310. It was like waking up and being told that one plus one equals three.

Zimmer was Boston's fine 1974–'76 third-base coach. As '76–'80 manager, he remained a fine third-base coach. Some call Game Six of the '86 Oktoberfest the Dante of Sox damnation. Others disagree: It could only have been decreed by God. By contrast, '78 wrote "the apocalyptic Red Sox collapse," wrote the Boston Globe's Dan Shaughnessy, "against which all others must be measured."

On July 20, the 62–28 Townies led the Yanks by 14 games. Anguish then built toward the "Boston Massacre." On Thursday, September 7, a four-game series began at Fenway. By Sunday, the Yankees had outscored the Sox, 42–9, outhit them, 67–21, and won 15–3, 13–2, 7–0, and 7–4. New York led 12–0, 13–0, 7–0, and 6–0. It was sad, grotesque, and mesmerizing. The Sox fell 3½ games behind. Perversely, they then turned and won their last eight. When Pope Paul I died, a Boston TV station teased its upcoming newscast, "Pope Dies, Sox Still Alive."

The season ended October 1: Tiant beat Toronto, 5–0; Cleveland, New York, 9–2. Both clubs were now 99–63. Next day Fenway Park would host a one-game playoff for the AL East title.

Ghosts surfaced from 1948.

The Sox were glad to be playing baseball. The Yankees were glad to be playing Boston. "When you were the Yankees, you just handled the Red Sox," Reggie Jackson said later. Yaz nailed Ron Guidry for a first-inning homer: 1–0. Boston later added a run. The Yanks then turned their first of several screws. With two on, spray hitter Lynn pulled the ball into the right-field corner—a double except that Lou Piniella was there, but why? "[Catcher Thurman] Munson told me Guidry's slider was slowing up, acting like a curveball."

Bucky Dent, .244, hit with two out and on in the seventh: Boston, 2–0. He fouled Mike Torrez's second pitch off his foot. In pain, Dent asked for time. Another turn: On-deck hitter Mickey Rivers noted a small crack in the bat, ditched it, and gave Dent another bat. Torrez threw, Dent swung, and Fisk sighed. "I thought, 'We got away with that mistake pitch.'" Earlier Jackson's drive had dropped off a shelf into Yaz's glove. The wind now blew *toward* the wall. "I saw Yaz looking up," said Fisk, "and I said, 'Oh, God.'"

Fenway rivaled a dark, unseen room: New York, 3–2. Each team scored twice. Next: the final turn, wrote Gammons, of "the Red Sox–Yankee competition [that] reached a peak of intensity rare even in that legendary rivalry." Rick Burleson drew a one-out ninth-inning walk. Jerry Remy's liner blinded Piniella in the sun. Somehow Lou stemmed a flag-winning inside-the-park home run.

Two runners perched. Rice had a gemstone of a year—46 homers, 139 RBI, and 406 total bases—the only ALer to top 400 since Joe DiMaggio '37. He flied out. Yaz approached the plate—his final chance for a World Series ring.

You can't stop the clock, Boswells say of baseball. Fenway's stopped as No. 8 wafted Goose Gossage's second pitch toward third baseman

Graig Nettles. "I was trying to will the ball to stay up," said Fisk. Irreversibly, it came down.

In 1979, Yaz got hit 3,000. Wade Boggs later won '83-'85-'86-'87-'88 batting titles. Seven years he had 200 or more hits, climaxing in '85's team-record 240. Boston finished 81–81. Dick Stuart would have understood.

In 1985, Boston's best mound prospect in 30 years brooked shoulder surgery. A year later Roger Clemens mimed Joe Wood in '12: 24–4, 2.48 ERA, and Cy Young/MVP. On April 29, he left off-Broadway on a dank night at Fenway. Said the Rocket, fanning a record 20 Seattle Mariners, 3–1: "The strikeouts just kept coming." As usual, the Sox played station-to-station ball. Don Baylor clubbed 31 homers. First baseman Billy Buckner tied 18 homers and 102 RBI—Oh, irony! a favorite.

"Fans loved Buckner's gutting it out," shortstop Spike Owen said of ankles hurt, rebuilt, and gouged again. The Sox won their first AL East in 11 years. Billy Buck caressed the final out. Amid cold fish and glamor boys, the Hub and the man with the gimpy gait and high-topped shoes seemed thoroughly warmed.

The '86 Sox, Angels, Mets, and Astros won their divisions by husky margins. Baseball then began an extended stretch as it has barely been played before—a Ferris wheel of drama. "It is baseball at its summit," wrote Newsweek's Pete Axthelm. "[Even now], millions are still savoring their rendezvous with baseball at the pinnacle. It leaves you breathless."

Boston edged the Angels in the L.C.S. It then faced a team "[whose] MTV video has more stars than hands across America," wrote the Washington Post, "[which is] another reason they present opponents with special problems." The Mets won 108 games, won the playoff, and entered the Series as a 2 and ½-to-1 favorite. In 1948, New York had helped force a playoff. New York '49–'78 applied the choke. Would the snake charmer still seduce the snake? "History, hell," glowered Red Sox manager John McNamara, who should have been more careful.

The Classic began October 18. Bruce Hurst became Boston's first lefty since Ruth to win a Series game, 1–0. The Yawkeys draped Shea with 18 Game Two hits: 9–3. In '46, Joe Cronin said, "We'll handle this [Series] back at Fenway." The Sox, up two games, flew home. What was there to handle? Len Dykstra, for one. Tip O'Neill threw out Game Three's first ball. Dykstra hit Oil Can Boyd's third pitch downtown: New York, 7–1. Gary Carter, for another. Next night he homered twice: Mets, 6–2.

When Hurst won Game Five, 4–2, Boston neared its first world title since 1918. "Is this the threshold of a dream or the eve of destruction?" Shaughnessy wondered. "Are baseball's heartbreak kids finally going to keep a promise, or are they just setting you up for one final apocalyptic, cataclysmic fall?" The region of Cotton Mather, Jonathan Edwards, and hope turning to Calvinist tragedy replaned for Shea Stadium—and once more approached the abyss.

It began rather commonly, as epic theater goes. Boston took a 2–0 Game Six edge. The Mets scored twice. The Sox' Marty Barrett then scored on a seventh-inning force play. As in a tragic play, moments portend disaster. Rice, lumbering, thrown out at the plate—Boston stranding 14 runners. In the eighth, ahead, 3–2, Clemens sustains a blister on his pitching hand and leaves—Calvin Schiraldi relieving. With the bases loaded, McNamara lets left-handed Buckner bat against southpaw Jesse Orosco. Billy Buck lines to center—leaving his sixth, seventh, and eighth runners of the night. In the bottom half, the Mets score the tying run.

At 11:59 P.M., Dave Henderson bashed a 10th-inning ball off a *Newsday* left-field billboard: Sox, 4–3. He reached the dugout as the Shea clock read midnight. Boston scored a fifth run—insurance, except that Sox policies rarely redeem—even when two Mets flew out, the Shea message board prematurely blazed, "Congratulations Boston Red Sox," Hurst was named Classic MVP, the World Series trophy and twenty cases of Great Western champagne entered the Boston clubhouse, and New England, believing that it had seen the worst, was ungently disabused.

One out would win Game Six. All season Dave Stapleton had replaced Billy Buck in late innings. Not tonight. One out would win the Series. Carter slapped a hit to left. You recalled that night's NBC-TV pregame guest: Dick Casey, 92, scribe of the '18 World Series. "Every day since," he said, "I've prayed to God that the Red Sox would win one more World Series before I die, so now I guess I'm going to die soon." Kevin Mitchell singled. Ray Knight went to 0–2. One strike would end the drought. Knight singled, Carter scored, and Mitchell took third. A friend said to Gammons, "They're going to do it. Just when we thought that we had been freed at last, they're going to create a way to again break our hearts that goes beyond our wildest imagination." Boston led, 5–4. Shea was throbbing. McNamara ditched Schiraldi for a once-comer turned hard-luck kid.

Bob Stanley had thrown only one wild pitch all year. His fifth toss to Mookie Wilson—the 13th pitch that could have won the Series—knifed off Rich Gedman's glove, scored Mitchell, and tied the game at 5. Knight reached second. Wilson fouled off four pitches. "So the winning run is at second base with two out!" NBC's Vin Scully said. "Three and two to Mookie Wilson! . . . A little roller up along first . . . behind the bag . . . It gets through Buckner! Here comes Knight! And the Mets win it!" It was enough to make you a Yankees fan.

Even Metsies sensed what lay ahead. "After they lost the sixth game," Knight said, "you knew the Sox wouldn't win." Game Seven was rained out Sunday. Next night Keith Hernandez hit in the sixth inning with one out, the bases full, and Boston up, 3–0. "I told myself, 'if Keith makes out, Boston wins," Sox announcer Joe Castiglione said. "If he gets a hit, the Mets will win.' " He singled, scoring two. As reliever Sid Fernandez glowed, New York scored a 3-all run, and Knight bashed a seventh-frame blast, the inevitable pronounced itself: The Sox would lose their fourth straight Series. Later Dwight Evans shook his head. "I don't believe in history, but maybe I'm starting to. Sixty-eight years is a long time—1918 was a long time ago. It does make you wonder."

Dick Young covered the 1950s Every Year Is Next Year Brooklyn Dodgers. Now, he saluted its dreamstuff fall: "The four divisional races were a drag. Not one hot finish. Then, two breath-holding playoffs and one excruciating see-saw World Series. Always, it seems, the game has something to redeem it. As The Natural said, contemplating the end of his career: 'God, I love baseball.' "

So did Red Sox Nation, often against its will.

YANKEE STADIUM

America in the wake of Watergate had a quirky bent. Leisure suits dressed a gender. With a burst of fireworks a million people hailed the country's two-hundredth birthday by watching a grand flotilla of tall ships in New York Harbor. Twenty-nine persons died of a mysterious ailment called Legionnaire's Disease after staying at Philadelphia's Bellevue-Stratford Hotel for an American Legion convention. A writer wagged: "They wouldn't rather be in Philadelphia."

By 1976, baseball had begun an age that, years later, as Washington Irving wrote of the Hudson Valley, "[still] holds the spell over the minds of the people"—tying, as it did, the end of a plantation order (under free agency, athletes could play an option year and sign with another team), familiarity (the Yankees and Dodgers won five of six '76–'78 divisions), domination (only five clubs won titles), and the first AL playoff game in 30 years.

It fused show (Chris Chambliss' playoff poke), myth (Dent's soul-crushing dinger), and Charlie Finley's bulky, bellowing successor as baseball's Bad Boy (G. M. Steinbrenner, Boss George). Said Yanks manager Billy Martin: "One [Reggie Jackson] is a confirmed liar, and the other [Steinbrenner] is convicted." Did Dodgers owner Peter O'Malley *really* say: "How sweet it is"? He *should* have. The 1978 ex-Bums became the first to draw more than 3 million.

The '76 pinstripes lured 2,012,434 to rebuilt Yankee Stadium. On one hand, it rode a gravy train. More police patrolled a better-lighted area. Walkways circled the park. A giant Louisville Slugger under the stadium sign reached skyward. "It was as big as a ticket booth," said Phil Rizzuto. "You met visitors at the bat." Tiers and outfield walls hued blue. New seating under the upper deck almost put you on the field. Seats were plastic, not wood. Sight lines were better; aisles and walkways, wider; concessions, choicer. "Name it, we have it," a brochure read. Beer and ribs and pizza and Spanish: The new Stadium was slimfast hell. Four ad screens crowned the bleachers. "One has the line score, another updates on other games, a third balls and strikes. The last [ultimately, Diamond Vision] has photo, instant replay, and Yankees history." The organ never sounded clearer. P.A. announcer Bob Sheppard crossed Alexander Scourby and James Earl Jones. On the other hand, this *couldn't* be the Stadium, but *was*.

The new shrine yapped heedless, needless. *Moved:* the facade, above the bleachers, from around the roof. *Shrunk:* bleachers. A black tarp covered center field. *Hidden:* slabs (Gehrig, Ruth, Huggins, and later

Mantle and DiMag) and plaques (Barrow, Berra, Ruppert, Dickey, Stengel, McCarthy, Munson, Ford, Gomez, Maris, Reynolds, Howard, Rizzuto, Martin, Sheppard, Mel Allen, Don Mattingly, and Pope Paul VI and Pope John Paul II, saying Mass in 1965 and 1979) in Monument Park behind an inner fence. *Lost:* the 450-foot circus catch, inside-the-parker, or drives ricocheting around the stones. Said Stengel of a blast behind the monuments: "Ruth, Gehrig, Huggins, *someone* throw that damn ball in here now."

The misbeat went on. The vast meadow waned. Center field dipped from 463 in '67 through 417 in '76 via 410 in '85 to 408 in '88. Left-center: 457 to 430 in '76 to 411 in '85 and 399 in '88. Left-center pen: 402 to 387 in '76 and 379 in '85. Right-center: 407 to 385 in '76. Right-center pen: 367 to 353 in '76. Foul lines swelled: left, 301 to 312 in '76 and 318 in '88; right: 296 to 310 in '76 and 314 in '88. Pop-fly homers and dinger-robbing ebbed. "In the old Stadium, Al Kaline would perch on the low right or left-field wall," said Mantle, "leap and spear the ball." Heights varied: left and right, sub-four feet; left-center and right-center, almost eight; center, 14. The new inner fence was 8 feet tall; actually, left to right, 8, 7, and 10, because the outfield sloped.

"In the old Stadium, the outfield look was beautiful," said Bob Costas. "This took away some of the the mystique." The inner wall seemed like subdividing the White House lawn. "They could have rebuilt the stands," he added, "and still kept the dimensions. Instead, they hurt the classic look"—for what?

Capacity dipped to 54,028. The Stadium reopened April 11, 1976: Yankees 11, Twins 4, before 52,613. Some drove, fought for auto space, or parked at the nearby Grand Concourse. Others stepped on the subway platform and peered toward right-center field. "Another change," said Costas. "The exterior wall was now so high you couldn't see above it." Bob Shawkey hurled the first ball. Graig Nettles smacked 32 homers. New York won the AL East.

"Post-season!" said Martin. "It's been a while." The Royals split LCS Games One–Four. Game Five quivered. Yanks lead (6–3); George Brett smacks a three-run dinger (6-all); Chambliss leads off the ninth by homering to right-center (New York's first flag since '64). He was mauled, plucked at, accosted, crushed. "I never touched the plate." The umps didn't care. "You look at the years since World War II," said Rizzuto after Cincy swept the Oktoberfest. "They're [Reds] maybe the best." He smiled. "If you don't count '61."

New York had last won a Series in 1962. The '77ers drew 2,103,092, again took the East, and won 100 games for the first time since '63. The Stadium staged an All-Star Game: Nationals, 7–5. Sparky Lyle parlayed 26 saves into Cy Young. "If I played in New York," said Reggie Jackson, "they'd name a candy bar after me." He came from Baltimore to meet the Dodgers for the rounders title of North America. "How big was it?" jabbed ABC's Howard Cosell. "The opener led our *news*cast." The Yanks took three of the first five set-tos. Game Six reverted to New York.

Thurman Munson reached in the fourth. No. 44 pulled Burt Hooton into the right-field seats. Mickey Rivers singled an inning later. "Reg-gie! Reg-gie!" lined Elias Sosa's fastball into "Ruthville"'s lower deck. Jackson again hit in the seventh. Charlie Hough tossed a knuckleball. Reggie knocked it 450 feet off the tarp. "Three straight homers!" Cosell brayed. "[Including Game Five] Four straight swings. Four straight homers!" He batted .450 with a Series-high five homers. Mr. October a.k.a. "The straw that stirs the drink" became Class of Cooperstown '93.

In 1978, Ron Guidry forged the AL's best non-MVP year: 25– 3, 1.74 ERA, and .893 percentage. Bob Lemon replaced Martin: Improbably, he won the flag. The stripes again beat K. C. Once more, with feeling: The Dodgers took Series Games One-Two. At the Stadium, Nettles' glove saved at least six runs: Guidry, 5–1. L.A. led Game Four, 3–0, when a throw hit baserunner Jackson. "It scored a run, led to more, changed everything," said Lemon. "The Dodgers still say he tried to get hit." The Bombers won their 22nd Series. "Three flags in four years. We thought we'd keep winning," said Bucky Dent. Their next title kept till '96.

In 1979, a gas shortage after Iran cut America's flow of oil bred long lines, high prices, and unemployment. At Camp David Jimmy Carter queried aides, Cabinet members, and solons. He emerged to give a talk—to Ted Kennedy, the "Malaise" speech—that addressed a crisis of the spirit. Carter had vowed a season in the sun. Like the fourth-placers, his presidency wilted in the rain. Martin replaced Lemon. Munson, 32, died in a plane crash. A night later 51,151 hailed the catcher. In 1980, New York won 103 games and drew a record 2,627,417. The Royals finally squared round holes and oblong: K.C. in three.

Next year New York led the East at the strike, beat the Brewers in the division playoff, swept Oakland in the LCS—and lost the Series to L.A. A 1994 Gallup Poll asked America to rate the '80s: 3 to 1 felt well, not ill. It forgot to ask the Yankees, fourth or worse in '82-'87-'88-'89.

Exception: On America's star-spangled day (July 4, 1983), in its capital arena (Big Ball Park), before Richard Nixon (in the Boss' box), and Mel Allen on play-by-play ("Will he do it? This crowd is standing! This crowd is wild!"), rivals sang Yankee Doodle. Dave Righetti pitched the stripes' first no-hitter, 4–0, v. Boston, since Larsen '56. Rule: July 24. Brett wafted a ninth-inning homer for a 5–4 victory; was called out because pine tar on his bat topped 18 inches, violating Rule 1.10 (b); and aped "Once it was lost, now it is found." For the first time AL president Lee MacPhail overruled an ump. The game resumed August 18. Hal McRae made out to end K.C.'s ninth. Dan Quisenberry retired the Yanks 1-2-3 before 1,245.

Martin was twice fired and hired. Yogi Berra replaced him in 1984. By George: A year later he signed, axed, and inked Billy again. Don Mattingly became the AL's first post-'77 non-title MVP. That August Tom Seaver won game 300 at the Stadium. "I was so nervous today," he said, "I felt like I was levitating." Next year Righetti saved a record 46 games. Mattingly '87 smacked a bigs-high six slams. Who was the enabler? Steinbrenner hired/fired Martin for the fifth/final time.

The '89 stripes darned last. Martin died in a car accident. New York finished second in '93–'95. "Some luck," said then-skipper Buck Showalter. "In '94 we were first [70–43] when the season ended [August 11, the players' strike]." Paul O'Neill's .359 won the batting title. In 1995, Mattingly retired with 2,153 hits and 222 homers. Managers shunned stability—13 in Steinbrenner's first 23 years. "Nothing personal," he said. You could hear Billy snorting, "Pa-leeze."

DODGER STADIUM

Chavez Ravine rivaled the Bronx in name-dropping: Sinatra, Danny Kaye, Don Rickles, Doris Day. In 1974, they fawned over Bill Buckner

(.314), Steve Garvey (All-Star and season MVP), and Cy Younger Mike Marshall (bigs-record 106 games). L.A. led in homers (139) and ERA (2.97), won the LCS (over Pittsburgh), and dropped the Series. Davey Lopes stole a big-league-high 38th straight base in 1975. On April 25, 1976, two strays tried to burn a U.S. flag at Dodger Stadium. "It's like yesterday," said Vin Scully. "[Cubs outfielder] Rick Monday stopped and snatched the flag they were about to light." Overnight he roused the heartland. Walter Alston retired after seven pennants, four world titles, and a 2,040–1,613 record. "It says something," said Peter O'Malley, "that Walter's only the third to manage the same team for 20 years [23, joining McGraw and Mack]."

The fourth bled Dodger Blue. "The first time I saw [Tom] Lasorda he was catching batting practice," Monday recalled. "Thirty minutes later, I saw him on the mound throwing batting practice. Thirty minutes later, he was in the outfield with us. I thought, who *is* this guy?" The '77ers made history with four 30-homer men—Garvey, Ron Cey, Reggie Smith, and Dusty Baker. L.A. renewed it October 1977–'78, losing to the Yanks. Enduring: In '78, Game Two's Bob Welch v. Jackson. The Dodgers led, 4–3, ninth inning, two out and on. "He's up there an eternity," said Scully. "Classic drama." Reggie fanned on the ninth pitch.

In 1929, General Motors director John Raskob wrote in *Ladies Home Journal* of saving and investing. "I am firm in my belief that anyone not only can be rich but ought to be rich." Walter O'Malley, who died August 9, 1979, agreed. A year later his ex-Bums hosted the All-Star Game: 4–2, Nationals. The Dodgers unveiled a Diamond Vision scoreboard. Two large screens aired line scores, lineups, replays, and baseball shorts. "The power in our entire complex," an engineer said, "equals that used by the city of Seattle." Don Sutton powered his last Dodgers pitch, retiring with 100 Ks for 21 straight years. "It's his consistency," said Lasorda, ignoring another trend. The Angelenos had lost a playoff or World Series in 1966-'74-'77-'78-'80.

An (un)little child shall lead them ('81 L.A.). On April 9, rookie Fernando Valenzuela debuted by blanking Houston. Soon Fernandomania embraced a physical burgeoning in all its diversity. By May 20, No. 34 tied four shutouts, a 5–0 record, and 0.20 ERA, and was batting .438. Hispanics jammed the park. More record-keeping: a million customers in 22 home dates. L.A. led at the strike, won the Intradivisional Series, and split L.C.S. Games One–Four v. Montreal. The O'Malleys took the decider, 2–1, on Monday's ninth-inning blast. "We had the feeling," said Jerry Reuss, "that this might be our last chance." Fat chance, it seemed. The Yankees grabbed a 2–0 game Series lead. "We're too good to lose again," said Lopes. Pride precedeth the unfall. Game Three: Cey's diving catch keyed a 5–4 conquest. Four: Jay Johnstone homered: O'Malleys, 8–7. Five: Pedro Guerrero and Steve Yeager went deep, 2–1. L.A. won the 9–2 final.

Lopes' trade ended the eight-year infield. Replacing him: Steve Sax '82, the Dodgers' fourth straight Rookie of the Year (others: Rick Sutcliffe, Steve Howe, and Fernando). They lost the West on the final day but wooed 3,608,881, more than they ever had, or have again. Garvey's NL-record games streak ended at 1,207. The '83ers took the division. Inverting '77–'78, they lost the playoff to Philadelphia. A year later Dodger Stadium housed baseball in the Summer Olympic Games: More than 385,000 paid. In 1985, Guerrero tied .320 and 33 homers; Orel Hershiser, 19–3 and 2.03 ERA; Lasorda, pasta and bravado.

"I'm on a sea-food diet," said Major Tom. "I eat all the food I can see." St. Louis led '85's now-best-of-seven LCS, three games to two. L.A. fronted in Game Six, 5–4, at Chavez: ninth inning, one out, two Cardinals on. Lasorda and pitcher Tom Niedenfuer communed on the mound: Should they pitch to Jack Clark? Clark reached the bleachers: 7–5. "When I die I want the Dodgers schedule put on my tombstone," said Lasorda. "That way I'll be working for the Dodgers when I'm gone." Lasorda was working later. Niedenfuer sat, shattered, by his locker. "Tom came over and said we wouldn't have been there without my [19] saves," he said, "that I should talk to the media—be a *Dodger*." Lasorda was still talking in '88. L.A. won the MVP and Cy Young: Kirk Gibson and Hershiser, Lasorda's 23–8 "Bulldog." The Dodgers won the playoff v. New York. The Series scent of '74: Oakland opened at Dodger Stadium.

Return to Game One, A's, 4–3, two out in the ninth. NBC field voice Bob Costas is planning the postgame interview. "Gibson is injured, supposedly unable to pinch-hit, and by all accounts not even in the dugout." Costas sees Kirk enter the trainer's room to practice swing.

Coach Ben Hines says: "He's got one good swing in him." Lasorda replies, "All right, if we get to the ninth spot, we'll go." Dennis Eckersley walks Mike Davis. Alfredo Griffin leaves the on-deck circle. Gibson limps to the plate like Walter Brennan, fouls off several pitches like Hank Aguirre, then pinch-hits into the right-field pavilion. Gaped Scully: "In the year of the improbable, the impossible has happened!" Exulted Lasorda: "Whoever the good Lord has for a scriptwriter, I'm giving him a raise."

NBC's elegaic next-day feature likened Gibson to *The Natural*. "Look at that," said Costas, "and tell me there's anything wrong with baseball on television when it's done by people who care about it." There was little wrong with a) Fernando and Dave Stewart's same-night no-hitters (June 29, 1990); b) Dodger Stadium's first rival perfect game (Dennis Martinez, July 28, 1991); and c) annual attendance near or above 3 million. In '89, Hershiser became the first player to get $3 million yearly. Next season Ramon Martinez matched Koufax by fanning 18 Braves. Lasorda platooned like Stengel one night v. Houston: Third baseman Jeff Hamilton was the losing pitcher; Fernando played first. "How come the '94 strike couldn't have come later?" said Lasorda. "We were in first when it happened." He won an eighth division title in 1995. Atlanta swept the opening round.

"Tradition matters more to us than most clubs," said Peter O'Malley. The Dodgers' linked Lasorda, harpies and hangers-on, glitzy cars, drop-dead women, and the Straw Hat Man, cigar-chomping scout Mike Brito. "You see him on TV," said Scully in 1999, "standing behind the plate in the dugout box, radar gun in hand, checking each pitch." At the park, you checked Pizza Hut, Carl's, Jr., grilled "Red Hot" spicy dogs, and TCBY yogurt in mini-Dodger batting helmets. The Outfield Bar near the food court hailed wine and beer. A peanut vendor tossed bags in the loge level like Magic Johnson in the paint.

In 1996, Lasorda had a heart attack and retired. A year later Mike Piazza hit .362 with 124 RBI. In '99, St. Louis' Fernando Tatis hit two slams in an inning. O'Malley sold the team. Fox, buying it, ordered blue game jerseys, louder music, and attitude. A history mural draped the outfield wall. "We've got the players from Koufax to Robinson," said an official. "This is a way to honor them."

Honoring 2000. Gary Sheffield tied Duke Snider's homer record (43),

Eric Karros added 31, the Dodgers tied for second (with Arizona), and boxes replaced ground-level seats behind the plate.

Change, or tradition: "Heaven on earth," said former outfielder Lou Johnson, remained baseball's Athens in the sky.

CANDLESTICK PARK

"Go back to the ['57] move west," said Jim Murray. "Who'd have thought the Dodgers would thrive, and the Giants sink?" In 1968, the A's arrival split the Bay Area market. "The Giants started losing a lot of fans," said Gaylord Perry. They also brooked debauchery.

The football 49ers wanted out of Kezar Stadium. Mayor Joseph Alioto urged a $50 million multipurpose downtown park. Baghdaders hooted. Alioto then asked the Board of Supervisors and Recreation and Parks Commission to expand and "improve" Candlestick. Willie McCovey was already good enough: '69 NL MVP. Willie Mays got dinger 600 and hit 3,000. The $16.1 million overhaul greeted 1971. A new escalator carried you from the parking lot. Artificial turf replaced grass. Moveable seats served football. The park was enclosed, turned into a bowl, and enlarged to 58,000. "That wind!" roared manager Charlie Fox. Architect John Bolles' boomerang-shaped concrete shell was guaranteed to stop it. Instead, it dove, swooped, swirled.

Murphy's Law. The makeover wrecked Candlestick—at baseball's expense. Announcer Lon Simmons started laughing. "The 49ers wanted the expansion. It made the park less intimate. So who pays? The city slapped a surcharge on *baseball* tickets!" Horace Stoneham was funding his own suicide. San Francisco lost the '71 LCS to Pittsburgh. It soon almost lost the team. Mays joined the Mets. Jim Barr retired 41 straight hitters. One year Bobby Bonds bonded 43 steals and 39 homers. Another, Ron Bryant won 24 games. Attendance crashed to 519,987. Houston's Bob Watson scored baseball's one millionth run at Candlestick. Broadcaster Al Michaels joined the Giants. He inherited much to be caustic about.

"This team doesn't care if it wins or loses," Michaels scolded the Giants in June 1974. "The players show a complete lack of respect for the manager." One night he disclosed attendance. "That's 1967," he told listeners. "There are 1967 people here tonight. That's a great year . . . 1967 . . . a great year for Ingelnook Wine. Not so good for the Giants, however." On September 16, 1974, 748 forged Candlestick's smallest-ever crowd. Another night Michaels went to break. "The score at the end of six innings is San Diego 9, Giants 4. Unfortunately, the Giants are playing in German."

The mid-'70s rivaled Stalingrad. Rumor bound the Giants for D.C. or Denver. Stoneham tentatively sold the team to Labatt Brewery of Toronto. Mayor George Moscone cajoled businessmen Robert Lurie and Arthur (Bud) Herseth to match its price. Little changed: The '77ers baited only 770,056. Then, in a combustible 1978, Bill Madlock hit .309, Jack Clark had 98 RBI, and McCovey returned to hit homer 500 as Comeback Player of the Year. The club's brief, unlikely contact with first place segued back to Seals Stadium's simpler kind of happiness.

"One small step for man. One giant leap for mankind." In early 1979, Lurie replaced fake with real grass. Walter Haas bought the '81 A's from Charlie Finley and began a bottom-line kind of marketing. "For the first time," said Simmons, "it was the A's that people began to talk about in this area. You saw Oakland caps on the street. Crowds were great. Today, whichever team is on top is the team that draws."

"Which wasn't true, say, in the early '70s," a reporter said.

"Oh, no," said Simmons. "Even in their lousy years the Giants were this region's team"—e.g., Closing Day '82. Joe Morgan smacked a three-run homer to rob L.A. of a playoff.

The 1984 All-Star Game hailed a silver anniversary. "In 1934," said Lurie, "Carl Hubbell struck out five straight men." He threw out '84's first ball: Nationals, 3–1, before 57,756. Mike Krukow later became the Giants' first post-'73 20-game winner. By '87 manager Roger Craig wanted pitchers to "Hmmm, baby!" A record 1,917,179 watched the Giants win the West. (St. Louis took the LCS.) Capacity rose to 62,000. Many got the Croix de Candlestick: "a marketing pin," said the *Chronicle*, "given to fans at the end of night extra innings—a Purple Heart for braving the wind and chill." You recalled Joe Torre: "It was great going there in July and freezing your butt off. Mays would hit balls to left and, man, they wouldn't go anywhere. I was catching one day, and Felipe Alou hit a ball that went out of the park—and came back."

At thirty, Candlestick finally hit 2 million (2,059,701 in '89). League-leaders: Scott Garrelts (2.28 ERA), Robby Thompson (11 triples), and MVP Kevin Mitchell (47 homers and 125 RBI). 'Frisco beat the Cubs in a five-set LCS. The final wooed a record 62,084. Will Clark hit .650. *Sic transit gloria.* (Thus goes the glory). He batted .250 in the Series *v.* Oakland. The A's fronted, 5–0 and 5–1. The Event moved to Candlestick. October 17, 1989, broke clear, and warm. "By local notion," said Michaels, a resident, "earthquake weather." At 5:04 P.M. Pacific Time, Al was keying ABC's pregame show. Suddenly, he shouted, "We're having an earthquake." The picture died.

For 30 seconds a 7.1 Richter Scale quake rocked the region. Ruptured gas lines blazed the Marina area; part of the Nimitz Freeway collapsed, crushing cars on the lower deck; a Bay Bridge upper span section fell onto the lower level; 67 died. At Candlestick, generators quickly revived the picture. Said ABC's Tim McCarver: "Everyone remembers where they were when the earth split wide." The crowd filed out quietly. Players' wives and children sought safety on the field. Commissioner Bart Giamatti had recently died of a heart attack. Successor Fay Vincent now postponed "our modest little sporting event." It resumed 10 days later: The A's swept, 13–7 and 9–6, before an all-time low Series audience (16.4 Nielsen rating/29 share v. '88's 23.3/39). The wonder was Candlestick: It shook, but stood. "Thank God for its being entirely of concrete," said Michaels. For three decades the Stick had been likened to a funeral parlor. "In the ultimate test," amended McCarver, "it saved human life."

Could Candlestick save baseball's? On June 4, 1992, San Jose voters spurned a referendum to build a park. That August the Giants were sold to Tampa investors. NL owners blocked the deal. It was '76 again: The Giants had one foot out the door. Moscone had saved them: Now, a season ('93) did. John Burkett and Bill Swift won 43 games. Rod Beck saved an NL-second-ever-best 48. Barry Bonds left Pittsburgh to hit .336, lead in homers and RBI, and become MVP. The Giants led the West, trailed Atlanta, rallied, but lost the West by a game.

"You win 103 games," mused manager Dusty Baker, "and don't even make the postseason." Next year baseball baptized the wild card. To many, 1993 remains The (Last) Great Race.

Brace yourself. The '93ers almost outdrew L.A. A record 2,606,354 trekked to Candlestick by rail, bus, boat, or car. Traffic clogged U.S. 101, the near north-south highway, into almost 10,000 parking slots. What didn't change: Only the 'Jints accessed a clubhouse. A visitor must cross the field to the right-field shed. What did: the JumboTron, and guest dugout finally heated. The area dimmed. San Francisco backed Aquarius v. Main Street. "Take Me Out to the Ballgame" deferred to the Rolling Stones.

Acreage shrank: center, 410 feet to 400; right, 335 to 330 in '91 and 328 in '93. New owner Peter A. Magowan put seats between left's bleachers and new 8-foot fence. In 1961, the Stadium Club offered salad ($1.50), steak ($4.25), and Giant burger ($1.85). We are what we eat: The '90s tied Polish sausage, garlic-chili French fries, nachos, vegetable burritos, and sweet dough pretzels. The Giants had five world titles, 17 flags, and 43 Hall of Famers. "We also have more restaurants per capita," said a friend, "than any city. We've got money, and intend to keep it." It would not spend a cent on a *new* old park: Four times Bay voters killed public financing of a Camden Yards or Jacobs Field.

Matt Williams hit 43 homers in 1994. "Only the strike," said announcer Ted Robinson, "kept him from possibly beating Maris." Baghdaders shrugged. Pols tut-tutted. "This city thinks highly of itself," a columnist wrote. "Losing baseball wouldn't crush its self-image." The '97ers won the West, but lost the LCS to Florida. A year later Bonds became the first to link 400 steals and homers. San Francisco dropped a wild-card playoff. Its hand, however, won the pot: 40,800-seat Pacific Bell Park.

On Sunday, September 26, 1999, the Giants announced their all-time team. The final series capped "Tell It Good-bye Week," after Simmons' calling card. Candlestick closed Thursday v. Los Angeles: Dodgers, 9–4, before 61,389. Mays threw out the first ball. Sun washed the dowager.

The Stick was contrary to the end: You vainly sought a teary eye, or twitching jaw. Most were glad to see her go.

ATLANTA–FULTON COUNTY STADIUM

Ditto-head, Atlanta's ash heap: By the mid–'70s, you could sit in the press box and *literally* count the crowd. Braves owner Ted Turner hyped camel relays, bathtubs on wheels, home plate weddings, and an ostrich race. "You know what they are?" he said. "You have a wagon behind an ostrich and a broom in your hand. Put the broom to the ostrich's right eye and he goes left—to his left, he goes right." One day he and Tug McGraw rolled baseballs from home to first and third base, respectively—with their nose. "Geez, look at your nose," a friend told Turner. "Yeah," he said, "but I won"—something Atlanta did less than utter a good word about Ulysses Grant.

Houston knuckler Joe Niekro hit the only homer of his career: It beat brother Phil, 4–3. The '77 Braves lost 16 straight games. Turner became skipper, lost, 2–1, and was fired by Chub Feeney. "We have a rule," explained the NL president, "that prohibits a manager from owning even part of a team." Willie McCovey bombed his 500th homer in 1978. Andre Dawson homered twice in an inning: Expos, 19–0. One night Atlanta's Buzz Capra and Biff Pocoroba forged the battery. The Padres' Gene Richards broke for second. Biff's throw hit Capra in the forehead and bounced almost 100 feet in the air. Buzz collapsed on the mound. Announcer Skip Caray could barely speak. "Capra was a friend and I was afraid he might be dead—but it was so typical of our team that I couldn't help laughing." Rare glimmers lit August 1, 1978 (Larry McWilliams and Gene Garber stopped Pete Rose's 44-game hit streak) and September 26, 1979 (Phil Niekro beat Joe for win 20). "Jesus, history on *our* side," chirped Turner. "Second time brothers won 20 games in the same year."

Ultimately, Phil won 318, lost 274, and four times led the NL in complete games and innings. Said Joe: "That knuckler could get anybody out"—except Dave Parker. Once Phil and Caray went to dinner. "How the hell do I get Parker out? My knuckler's not working," Niekro said.

"Skip the knuckler," Skip replied. "Why don't you throw your blooper ball and see what happens?" Twice Niekro threw a knuckeball. Parker lined out and singled. His third up Phil tossed another knuckler, looked at the booth, and waved. The next pitch was a blooper that Parker hit 400 feet. Later Dave whacked a lob 390.

"Both were caught!" Caray laughed. "Niekro takes my advice, Parker bombs two balls almost 800 feet, and I can still say, 'I told you so.' "

Cable television lured a wider audience for '80s baseball. In turn, baseball drew new subscribers. "It really made [Atlanta's] WTBS the first superstation," said Turner, using the Braves to woo local system operators. Satellite coverage bred "America's Team."

Its breakthrough was 1982. "Till now TBS was just one cable offering," said announcer Ernie Johnson, a soft-spoken Vermonter. "People weren't aware how daily exposure could make a die-hard Brave fan out of someone in Nevada who'd never been near Georgia." Atlanta won a bigs record first 13 games. Suddenly, people were aware. "One man," said Johnson, "said the streak was the 'two-by-four' which hit America between the eyes." A Storm Lake, Iowa (pop. 8,814), billboard read, "The Atlanta Braves: Iowa's Team." In Valdez, Alaska, the Nanook Chapter of the Braves Fan Club pooled cash, bought a screen, and renamed its saloon the "Braves Lounge." An average of 1 million viewers watched each game. "What excited was what cable might become," said Caray—to columnist Frank Dolson, "the greatest thing to happen [to baseball] since Bat Day." By the 1990s, Turner's cable service reached more than 50 million homes.

Weigh the forest against the trees. On one hand, Niekro went 17–4, the Braves drew a record 1,801,985, and Dale Murphy became Most Valuable Player in 1982. On the other, St. Louis swept Atlanta in the LCS. A year later 2,119,935 packed its bowl. Murphy was named back-to-back MVP. *Boston Globe* columnist Robert Healy once noted "that Yankee trait of competing hard, then picking your opponent up off the floor." The '84 Braves tried to floor the Padres. On August 12, Pascual Perez plunked Alan Wiggins in the back. Perez had four at-bats. Each time the Pads decked him. The dust-up vaunted two bench-clearing brawls (including several fans) and 19 ejections (including both regular and replaced skippers). July 3, 1986, was even sloppier. The Mets scored five to Atlanta's two 19th-inning runs: 16–13. The game ended at 3:55 A.M. Fireworks began at 4:01. "It was so late many thought the city was under attack," said Turner. Bob Horner hit four homers in a game. A fly by Dion James killed a dove and became a double. The Braves dropped to last in 1987 (also '88-'89-'90). You remembered '82. Where had the dream gone wrong?

Baseball is the oldest and greatest talking game. The Braves' god-awfulness recalled a yarn. The home first baseman was stinking up the joint. He Ks in the first inning. A blowhard behind the dugout starts yelling. The batter fans in the third. "Bum," says the fan, "you can't hit, go back to the minors!" The first baseman Ks again in the ninth. The fan outjabbers Bugs Bunny. The batter proceeds to climb on the dugout. "I'm not gonna' hit you—just tell a story," he tells the magpie. "When I was a boy I was brought up on a farm and we had a jackass and I treated him horribly. My dad used to tell me, 'Don't whip that jackass so bad. The way you're hitting him, someday his spirit'll come back to haunt ya.' I never believed my daddy until today."

'**N**inety-one began an age that Atlanta likened to, say, the '10s A's or '50 Yankees. "This is the team of the decade," said Turner. Would the laugh be on him? The Braves wooed a record 2,140,217, dashed a last-week L.A. lead, and clinched the flag on the penultimate day. MVP Terry Pendleton led in hits (187) and average (.318). Tom Glavine won 20 games for the first of three straight years. Pittsburgh led the LCS, three games to two. Steve Avery and John Smoltz then won Atlanta's first flag, 1–0 and 4–0.

The Braves had come out of nowhere. The early Series sent them back: Minnesota, 5–3 and 3–2. Mark Lemke's 12th-inning hit took Game Three, 5–4, in/for Atlanta. Next night he tripled in the ninth, scored the 3–2 winning run, and tied the Series. Lemke hit two more triples in Game Five: 14–5. The Event returned to Minnesota. The Twins' Kirby Puckett won Game Six, 4–3. The final dueled zeroes. In the seventh, Lonnie Smith singled. Pendleton drove to the left-center wall. Said manager Bobby Cox: "Lonnie gets deked [by infielder Chuck Knoblauch] that there's a play at second," slowed, stopped at third, and was left: Twins, 1–0, in 10, Jack Morris beating Smoltz. Three matches went extra innings. Five ended one-run. Even the "Tomahawk Chop" chant seemed exhausted. Sadly, it revived.

Yin was Atlanta's past. (Charlie Leibrandt got his 1,000 K. "I thought I'd keep it, so I rolled it back toward the dugout." He forgot to call time. The runner took second. Said Turner: "Shit, like the bad old days.") Yang was the '92 playoff. Pittsburgh led, 2–0, in Game Seven. Pendleton doubled to lead off the ninth. David Justice reached on Jose Lind's error. Sid Bream walked to load the bases. Ron Gant's fly scored a run: 2–1. Damon Berryhill, walking, reloaded them. Brian Hunter popped out: two out. "Up comes this banjo hitter [Francisco Cabrera]," mused Turner, "and he lines a single" to score Justice and Bream: 3–2. As Bream slid, people in the Atlanta booth began pounding Caray on the back. He never knew it. "I didn't feel it, my concentration calling the play was total. All I knew was Frank's hit meant the pennant." Stick a fork in him. He's numb.

Atlanta lost the Series to Toronto four games to two. Again the clincher left you bleary. The Blue Jays led, 4–3, in the 11th inning. "Otis Nixon makes out bunting," a writer marveled, "with the tying run on *third*!" Yin and yang: The '93ers jammed 3,884,725—"more in a week," said Cox, "than we used to get in a month." They also lost the playoff to Philadelphia. Good things come to those: In '95, Atlanta finally squared the circle. Fred McGriff became the ninth big to hit 30 homers for seven straight years. Greg Maddux won a fourth Cy Young in a row. The Braves beat Colorado in the Division Series, swept the LCS v. Cincinnati, and took the Series over Cleveland—their first title since '57. Glavine won twice, including a 1–0 decider. Marquis Grissom hit .360. "Hell," said Turner, "first team to win Series in three different cities."

A year later Smoltz led the NL in Ks, innings, percentage, and wins (24). A new park rose next door. Atlanta swept the DS, trailed the LCS, 3–1 (to St. Louis), took Games Five–Seven, and opened the Series in New York (winning, 12–1 and 5–0). The Classic moved South: Yanks, 5–2 and 8–6. On October 24, 1996, the stripes' Paul O'Neill made a running, straining catch to save Match Five, 1–0, take a 3–2 game edge, and close the wigwam. A visitor left Cobb, Aaron, and Niekro, littered aisles, and a raucous P.A. system. "Only stadium to end with a World Series game," crowed Turner. That is not how its baggage is recalled.

18

LOOK WHAT YOU'VE DONE

"Three straight titles! ['72–'74]," Charlie Finley bellowed of baseball's first three-peat since the '49–'53 Yankees. "Take that away!" Baseball tried. Catfish Hunter charged that Charlie owed him salary from 1974. An arbiter agreed, ruling him a free agent. In 1975, a bigs-record four pitchers threw a combined no-hitter: Vida Blue, Glenn Abbott, Paul Lindblad, and Rollie Fingers. The Finleys lost the ALCS to Boston. Fingers, Bert Campaneris, Reggie Jackson, and Joe Rudi left. The '77ers hit the cellar. "What is it with this team?" said Rudi. "Connie Mack breaks 'em up [in the '10s and '30s], now this." Oakland lost 108 games in '79. Attendance collapsed to 306,763: One game drew 653. Oilman Marvin Davis tried to move the A's to Denver. The Coliseum Board blocked the sale. Stadium toilets and the scoreboard went on the fritz. They seemed a metaphor for the team.

"Not a gentleman," said Bertrand Russell, referring to Anthony Eden. "Dresses too well." In 1980, the Haas family of San Francisco bought the A's for $12.7 million. Could its Levis Strauss company regroom the A's? Rickey Henderson swiped 100 bases. A 1981 players' strike led baseball to crown split-season titleists. The A's won the first half, swept K.C. in a playoff, and lost to the Yankees in the LCS. Tony Armas' 22 homers co-led the league. Eight straight A's singled to start one game. Crime (his) bore punishment (ours): "Crazy George" Henderson hatched the wave. A year later Rickey's 130 steals broke Lou Brock's mark of 118. "Billy [Martin] Ball" wowed a record 1,735,489. Raiders president Al Davis bolted for Los Angeles. For the first time A's caps and jerseys eclipsed the Giants'.

"I came over here [from San Francisco] in '81," said Lon Simmons. "The Raiders' leaving changed everything, made the Coliseum a baseball place." Three billboards rose behind the bleachers. Left field's aired events and future series; right's, line score; Diamond Vision, highlights, crowd shots, and *This Week In Baseball*. Cartoons showed the A's hitting other teams. Outside, you hailed the A's Swingers band, dressed in green and gold. Inside, Oakland bought baseball's best high-tech stereo: Van Morrison had people dancing in the aisles. "With football gone, we can do anything we want," said manager Tony La Russa, hired in 1986. What he wanted was to rebuild a team.

The farm system bore Jose Canseco, Mark McGwire, and Walt Weiss—1986-'87-'88 Rookies of the Year. Big Mac, Jose's "Bash Brother," hit 49 homers in '87. Dave Stewart won 20 games during four straight years. La Russa switched Dennis Eckersley to relief. The Coliseum hosted its first All-Star Game: NL, 2–0, in 13 innings, before 49,671. "We're building a puzzle," said La Russa. Pieces fused in '88. Canseco led in homers (42), ribbies (124), and slugging (.569). Eck had a league-best 45 saves. Pinch-runner Gene Nelson became the first AL pitcher to steal a base since Blue Moon Odom. Other Oakland firsts: 14 straight wins and 2 million attendance.

The A's swept Boston in the LCS. "Another three-year pennant streak [like '29–'31 and '72–'74] began," noted announcer Monte Moore. Game One swung the Series. Canseco grand-slammed at Dodger Stadium, but Eckersley yielded Kirk Gibson's ninth-inning thunderbolt: "That home run was good for baseball," said Eck, "but not for me." A year later Stewart, Mike Moore, and Storm Davis went 59–27, Oakland licked

Toronto in the playoff, and the Series v. San Francisco crushed fire (earthquake) and ice (A's sweep).

" 'Ninety may have been our best team," said La Russa. Bob Welch 27–6 won Oakland's third Cy Young. Henderson became the franchise's eighth league MVP. The Coliseum packed a record 2,900,217. " 'Seventy-nine," jibed Dave Parker, "seemed a hell of a time away." Dueling sweeps: the A's v. Boston for their 15th flag; Cincinnati over Oakland in the Series. "Considering that they were defending champions, and how heavily they were favored," said historian Jerome Holtzman, "it's among the most stunning upsets since [Mays/Rhodes Giants v. Cleveland] '54."

On May 1, 1991, Henderson's 939th steal topped Lou Brock. That night Nolan Ryan pitched no-hitter number seven. "The Express" accepted kudos with Gary Cooper modesty. Henderson mimed Muhammad Ali. "Brock was a great base stealer, but today I'm the greatest of all time." The A's time was ending, though few knew so at the time. In '92, they won the West but lost the playoff to Toronto. "First to worst!" cried the '93ers. The Haas family sold the team to businessmen Steve Schott and Ken Hofmann. McGwire bashed 52 homers in 1995. Alas, his new Coliseum oozed sterility. "How bad is the makeover?" read the *Tribune*. "It makes the old Mausoleum look good."

Blame the Raiders' '95 return to Oakland. Al Davis demanded luxury boxes and 22,000 new seats. The city caved: "They showed no loyalty to the A's," said Moore. "They screwed 'em—anything to get football back." The hash turned surreal. Construction proceeded *while* the A's, say, played Cleveland. "Jackhammers were going off," said 1996–manager Art Howe. "Outfielders couldn't hear how hard the ball was hit." The facelift made Oakland open '96 at Las Vegas' 9,353-seat Cashman Field. A 20-to-22-foot fence trimmed the outfield. Fifty-six billboards, including Caesar's Palace, broke a big-league record. Usherettes danced the polka between innings. Picnicking graced a berm beyond the field.

"It was minor league," said Howe. He returned to find *six* outfield tiers—"Mt. Davis"—marring the Coliseum. "We couldn't sell 'em," said Schott, "so we covered them up," cutting '91's 47,450 revised size to

39,875. Enclosed, the park blocked the old view of the East Bay hills. Power alley walls rose 18 feet to abut the bleachers. "To each side it's eight feet," said a writer. "It looks like an elephant in heat." Ben Grieve became the A's fifth Rookie of the Year in 1998. The '99ers crashed 235 homers. (Matt Stairs, John Jaha, Jason Giambi, and Grieve whacked 38, 35, 33, and 28.) A year later Oakland bopped 239, won the West the final day, and nearly beat the Yanks in the Division Series. Giambi was voted MVP: .333, 43, and 137. "The sole consolation of the renovation was its blocking the wind, helping homers," Howe said. Empty seats showed the price.

The Coliseum menu offered barbecue, Chinese food, soft-serve ice cream, and veggie burgers. "The food is great," mused announcer Ray Fosse. "The players are getting better." Not enough ate, or watched. Five times the 2000 A's were outdrawn the same day by their Triple-A affiliate, the Sacramento River Cats. Oakland's 1,728,888 placed 11th in its 14-team league. "It's depressing," said Stairs even before the '01 A's trailed Seattle by 20 games in June. Don't worry about sections 103 and 131 behind the foul pole. Good seats could be had any day. "They'd climbed so far from the '70s," said Simmons, "only to fall back into the hole."

In June 2000, the A's asked Bud Selig for tentative assent to move to Silicon Valley. "If they receive it," wrote the *Contra Costra Times*, "they'll talk further with a group wanting to build a privately financed stadium" in Santa Clara. Getting even: The A's hoped to leave Mt. Davis before long.

EDISON INTERNATIONAL FIELD

"What is it about football?" an Angels fan snapped in 1980. "Why can't they leave us alone?" That year the Rams left the Coliseum for Anaheim. The Big A was enclosed, swelled to 67,335, and became the Bigger A. Moved: the Big A's base and scoreboard, to the *parking lot* and left-field facade, respectively. Wrecked: the baseball feel. Three decks now ringed the outfield. Sections 60 and 70 wore a cheesy hitters' tarp. An inner fence linked the pens. Behind it, the outer wall grew ivy. Six doors were labeled "warning track," "slim material," "screen clay mounds," "raw clay," "sand," and "equipment." Ex–Babe Ruth roomie

Jimmie Reese was Angels hitting coach. In 1980, his closest friend left the Big A for Texas. "Today, there's no warmth, companionship," Reese said a season later. Did he mean the park, or the Halos *sans* Nolan Ryan?

In '82, Gene Autry signed a Ruth legatee. Reggie Jackson later hit Gehrig-tying homer 493. He circled the bases, gave his bat to Jimmie, and kissed him. "Embarrassing," said Reese. "That bat he homered with? When he hit it, he cracked it. That's how strong he is." Jackson's 39 dingers co-led the '82 AL. Rod Carew hit .319. Brian Downing drove in 109 runs. The Angels won the West, drew 2,807,360, and attacked the inner fence. "[Fred] Lynn hit it while chasing a ball," Reese mused. "It fell down, Lynn made the catch, and crashed [into] the area between it and the outer fence." The umpire ruled an out. Said manager Gene Mauch: "It was as if Lynn had caught the ball and fell in the seats."

It seemed for a time that the pennant would finally fall in Autry's lap. California took a 2–0 match LCS lead. Milwaukee swept Games Three–Five at County Stadium. "During the playoff we sold out the World Series for St. Louis," rued Mauch. He likely burned his tickets. The Halos began to be perceived as a kind of Orange County Red Sox. Mike Witt threw an '84 perfect game v. Texas. "I'm glad it's over," said Carew of his 3,000th hit. Jackson targeted a myth, not number. "When I was growing up, we had to root for the black players like Mays, but I always admired Mantle," he confessed. Four days before turning 40, Reggie's 537th homer passed the Mick for sixth place all-time. "What a thrill, just to be mentioned in the same breath." California often left you breathless. That was not always its intent.

The '86ers linked Witt's 18–10, Gary Pettis' 50 steals, and Donnie Moore's 21 saves. Don Sutton won his 300th game. Mauch won another division. The now-best-of-seven playoff began Tuesday, October 7, at Fenway. Good karma: Witt won the opener, 8–1. Next, Boston's Bruce Hurst frolicked, 9–2. The Halos won Friday, 5–3. In Game Four, the Sox led, 3–0, until the Angels scored two ninth-inning runs and loaded the bases with two out and a 1–2 count. Future reference: One Sox strike would win the game. Instead, Calvin Schiraldi struck Downing in the ribs, tying it. Bobby Grich's hit gave California a 3–1 game lead.

" 'History,' Stephen said," wrote James Joyce, " 'is a nightmare from which I am trying to awake.' " Boston led Game Five, 2–1, when Grich drove to center. Dave Henderson raced back, nearly made the catch, but knocked a two-run homer over the wall. California led, 5–2, in the ninth. Now-Sox Don Baylor went deep: 5–4. One out would win a Halos flag. Mauch yanked Witt for Gary Lucas. Lucas hadn't hit a batter in six years. His first pitch plunked Rich Gedman. Replacing him, Moore faced Henderson. The count went to 2–2. The Sox had one strike left. Champagne chilled in the Angels clubhouse. Moore threw a forkball. Henderson's two-strike, two-out, two-run poke etched man bites dog.

"This is supposed to happen *to* us," said a Soxaphile, "not *by* us." It almost did. Grich hit in the ninth with the bases full, one out, and one run in. He and DeCinces failed to plate another runner. Henderson's 11th-frame fly scored the winning run, 7–6. "Still the best game I've ever seen," ABC's Al Michaels said. "So many twists. Take [Sox reliever Steve] Crawford [pitching innings 9–10]. Ninth guy on a 10-guy staff, trying to save a pennant. Afterward, he says, 'If there was a bathroom on the mound, I'd have used it.' Baseball has the unlikeliest heroes. One day: Crawford's moment in the sun."

The Angels' had receded, though it is doubtful that Mauch knew. Boston took Game Six, 10–4. It then won the team's first winner-take-all game with a division flag, pennant, or World Series at stake since the year Fenway was built. "What can you say?" manager John McNamara asked of the Sox' revival. "You know what the poets say: 'Hope springs eternal in the human breast.' " Not in Anaheim: It was '82 again.

In July 1989, Donnie Moore committed suicide. Agent David Pinter said, "Ever since Henderson's homer, he was extremely depressed. He blamed himself for the Angels not going to the World Series." It was a feeling, and event, with which both teams could sympathize.

Ross Newhan sighed. "In a way," the *Los Angeles Times* writer said, "this franchise hasn't recovered [from Henderson's *touché*]." The '87 Halos fell from first to worst. Mauch resigned. Mark Langston and Witt no-hit Seattle, 1–0. Happy: In 1997, the Walt Disney Company bought the team and renamed it Anaheim. Mo Vaughn arrived from Boston. Grumpy: The '95–'98 and '91-'94-'96-'99ers, respectively, blew a late-season lead and finished last. Dopey: In 1999, Tim Salmon readied for a fly until a beach ball sailed past his head. "There have been 500 beach balls on the field this year and one has to drop right in front of my outfielder," said manager Terry Collins. "I hope they had a good time in the outfield." Sleeping Beauty: The park revived. A good time again filled the seats.

In 1995, the Rams deserted Anaheim for St. Louis. Suddenly, the chance arose to (re) remake the Big A. Disney hired the architectural firm of Helmuth, Obata and Kassabaum (HOK Sport). "They'd built Coors Fields and Camden Yards," said Disney CEO Michael Eisner. Anaheim Stadium evolved into Edison International Field. The "new" park largely mimed the original. HOK scrapped the two top outfield tiers. The A-frame scoreboard returned behind the left-field fence. The inner wall became a memory. Capacity dropped to 45,050. Good sight lines got better.

"If you like the sun, try the first-base side [or right and center bleachers]," said president Tommy Tavares. All outfield seats now angled toward the plate. The Halos added suites, a third-base Stadium Club, and food courts. Hot dogs, funnel cake, and cinnamon rolls complemented Mexican, Japanese, and Italian food. More arresting: the Big A's new look. Disney wed Busby Berkeley and Frank Lloyd Wright. Sculptured bats and caps trimmed the exterior. A showy water fountain flowed beyond center field.

In 2000, the Angels installed a muraled outfield fence. Darin Erstad (team-record 240 hits) and Troy Glaus (79 extra-basers) shelled it. Glaus's 47 homers led the league. Vaughn, Garret Anderson, and Salmon added 36, 35, and 34, respectively. Four Halos had 100 or more RBI. A year later Anaheim plodded to a .500 start. Power paled. Attendance fell. Disney offered the club for sale. No one met the $240 million price. "Don't worry. Maybe we'll even get to expand the wall," said Tavares. "It's got Fregosi, Ryan, and our history"—patchwork, teary, and unique.

"We want to get all the right things in this one—and leave out all the wrong things," contractor Del Webb said in 1966. More than three decades later, the Angels had.

ASTRODOME

The Astors, however, hadn't. "One lousy first-division finish in our history. You looked for interest elsewhere," voice Gene Elston mused in 1978. Trading Joe Morgan to Cincinnati didn't help. "We missed him," said Elston, "even before he was ['75–'76] MVP." Reliever Joe Sosa became the first Astro to homer his first at-bat. "It will never rain inside the Astrodome," went the line. Punch line: "What about outside?" On June 15, 1976, a deluge kept umpires and the Pirates from reaching the Dome. "Rain out, Astrodome" seemed oxymoronic. Similarly, pitcher J. R. Richard's mind and arm. "I was having trouble [pitching]," he recalled, "when I felt something on my shoulder and I looked up and here was this bird." The reporter seemed puzzled. J. R. continued. "This bird was evidently sent down by God and he told me to straighten up and go out and win this game and that's why I turned things around." The reporter asked, "What kind of pitches were you using to make the change?" Richard said, "Shit, I'll tell 'ya." One day an announcer interviewed him. "If you had to throw a pitch in a tight situation, what would you throw?" J. R. said, "Well, I'd throw him a slider"—Richard then put a hand on his groin, adding, "I'd put it right in there, cock high."

In 1977, Cesar Cedeno stole over 50 bases for the sixth straight year. Next season Jose Cruz batted .315. Ken Forsch no-hit Atlanta in '79. "History," said '76–'82 skipper Bill Virdon. "He and Bob became the first brothers to pitch no-hitters." Richard's 313 Ks set a righty high. He was hospitalized in July 1980, tried to throw, braved a stroke and surgery to remove a blood clot, and never pitched in the bigs again. Houston drew a record 2,278,217, most till '98, and won the '80 West in a playoff with the Dodgers. Its first postseason became a keeper. The Astros and Phils split Games One-Two. The LCS then moved south and west. Niekro pitched 10 scoreless innings. The reacquired Morgan tripled and scored on Denny Walling's fly: 1–0, in 11. "Two left at home, one win, bingo," said Morgan. "You have to like our chances."

You'd like them more with a little luck. "If our luck was any worse," said Elston, "you'd think we were the Cubs." 'Stros pitcher Vern Ruhle nabbed Garry Maddox's liner and started a Game Four triple play. Said Virdon: "That's until umpire Doug Harvey ruled that time was called before the third out occurred." The Astros later took a 2–0 lead—before Gary Woods was put out for leaving third early on a fly. The run cost a pennant: Phils, 5–3, in 10. "What a series," Morgan mused. Four games went extra innings. Houston led Game Five, 5–2, trailed, 7–5, tied, 7-all, and lost on Maddox's 10th-inning double, 8–7.

"We'll climb that final step," chirped Virdon. The Dome is dead. The Astros are still climbing.

In 1981, Nolan Ryan passed Early Wynn as all-time walk leader. That September he faced the Dodgers on NBC's "Game of the Week." Virdon smiled. "All the greats have a sense of timing." Ryan pitched a *nonpareil* fifth no-hitter. The split season matched first- and second-half winners: Houston beat L.A. twice, then lost. Capacity rose to 47,690. In '83, Nolan became baseball's all-time K king, besting Walter Johnson's 3,509. Joe Niekro won game 200 in '85. Next year Cy Young righty Mike Scott led the league in shutouts (5), innings (275⅓,) ERA (2.22) and Ks (306). On September 25, fanning 13, he pitched a no-hitter to clinch the West. "Shakespeare," chimed Houston reliever Charlie Kerfeld, "couldn't have written it any better."

Drama segued to the LCS. Scott won Games One and Four. New York led, however, three to two. Mentally, they trailed. "Scott had so dominated us [fanning 19 in 18 innings]," said Mets manager Davey Johnson. "If we lost Game Six, he'd face us tomorrow." Ahead lay what Tim McCarver called "the most tiring game I have ever been part of, either as a spectator or player." 'Stros lefty Bob Knepper led, 3–0, in the ninth. Right-handed Mookie Wilson came to bat. Johnson defied strategy by pinch-hitting Len Dykstra. "A lefty," Knepper mourned, "and he triples!" The Mets tied: 3-all. Inning followed inning. Scott lingered like Banquo's Ghost. New York took a 4–3 14th-frame edge. Billy Hatcher then *re*tied by homering inside the left-field pole. Sixteenth: Mets front, 7–4. The crowd stills. Scott's shadow pales. "But our bullpen was tired," said Johnson. "Our best guy [Jesse Orosco] had already gone nearly three." Houston again rallied: 7–6, two out, two on. The count went full. The noise made indoor ball seem almost comely. Kevin Bass missed a breaking ball. Said a writer: "An inside World Series would have to wait [till Minnesota '87]."

"After the game," wrote *USA Today*, "players and fans on both sides shook their heads in disbelief and appreciation." Said the *New York Daily News:* "It was about as lovely as the most lovely sport in the world can be. Rapture! Congratulations to all!" Try consolation. Ryan's 2.76 ERA led the '87 NL. The '89ers beat the Dodgers in 22 innings—and seven hours and 54 minutes. The Dome faded. Animals patrolled the field. An employee said, "You see cats hanging around first base and the pitcher's mound. During a stadium tour, the cats were looking at us like, 'What are you doing, invading our home?' I've heard stories of cats running from rats." Bleakness dimmed the mind. One day Yankees owner George Steinbrenner called general manager Lou Piniella to his office. "Go down and look at Bass [as barter for Dave Winfield]. Don't go through the press entrance, don't go in the press room, don't use any credentials. Just go incognito." Steinbrenner paused. "Number one, Lou, wear a raincoat. Number two, wear a hat and sunglasses and sit in the bleachers so nobody notices you." Piniella hit the, uh, roof. "George, you're out of your mind—it's the Astrodome—*indoors*! They'd put me in a cell if I went down there in that disguise." Increasingly, it was hard to disguise the Dome as a '90s baseball park.

Capacity rose to 54,370. Supports blocked some outfield general-admission seats. In 1992, George Bush was nominated for reelection. The Astros suffered a club-record 26-game road trip—"kicked out of our park," sniffed Jeff Bagwell—for the Republican National Convention.

Darryl Kile no-hit the '93 Mets. Bad luck: Houston trailed Cincy by a half-game when the strike KOd '94. Bagwell averaged .365, homered twice in an inning, led the league in runs, total bases, and RBI, and became MVP. Craig Biggio topped in steals and doubles. "When sorrows come they come not as single spies," wrote the bard, "but in battalions!" '97: Bagwell bombs 43 homers. 'Stros win the NL Central. Atlanta sweeps the Division Series. '98: Houston hits a DS .182 and loses to San Diego. '99: Mike Hampton wins 22 games. Billy Wagner gets 30 saves. The Dome's last regular-season game dots October 3: Houston 9, L.A. 4, before 52,033.

Memory strayed: Only Jimmy Wynn, Doug Rader, and Andre Dawson reached the fifth deck. The '99ers could have used them. Bagwell

and Biggio went 4 for 32 (.125) v. Atlanta in another blue Division
Series. The Braves took Game Four, 5–3, in 12 innings. (Houston blew a
bases-loaded, no-out boon.) Atlanta took the final, 7–5 (October 9,
before 48,553). "What a way to close the Dome," said Bagwell. "Losing
a third straight postseason." The Space City's Eighth Wonder had
become baseball's Lost In Space.

BUSCH STADIUM

The '70s Cardinals seemed lost as well. "Treading water," wrote Bob
Burnes. Bob Gibson became the second pitcher to K 3,000. Lou Brock
led the NL in steals eight of nine years. "People don't remember his highest Series average ever for 20 or more games [.391, including '68's
.414]," Bob Broeg added. They recall his start and glide. In '74, Brock
broke Maury Wills's single-season (104) and Max Carey's NL career
(740) steals record. By then the AstroTurf had paled, often hiding the
ball. One night a batter went deep. Phillies announcer Byrum Saam
couldn't see. "There's a ground ball to shortstop," he said, mistakenly,
"and it's gone!" The '76ers faded to fifth. Attendance fell to 1,207,079.

A visitor could still relive the Cards' feeling of possibility. A St. Louis
Sports Hall of Fame boasted photo, trophy, an entire area on Musial,
and model of Sportsman's Park, built from 15,000 pieces to a one-eighth
inch per scale. By '85, Brock entered baseball's Hall. In 1977, steal 893
broke Cobb's record. Lou later got hit 3,000 and swiped his 938th and
last base to pass 19th-century Billy Hamilton. Bob Forsch tossed Busch's
first no-hitter in '78. Al Hrabosky—"The Mad Hungarian"—stalked
behind the mound, conversed *sotto voce,* smacked his glove, and
restabbed the rubber. Garry Templeton became the first switcher with
100 hits each way. Another first: co-MVPs in '79: Willie Stargell's Bucs
won the Series; St. Louis' Keith Hernandez led the NL in batting doubles, runs, and batting average. In 1980, Ken Boyer was scrapped as
manager. His successor had a crew cut, answered to "White Rat," and
liked small, not long, ball. On one hand, he loved Cardinals Nation. On
the other, he thought it strange St. Louis hadn't won a Series in 13 years.

"You tailor your team to fit your park," said Whitey Herzog. "We've
got the artificial turf, the long distances." Whitey Ball would flaunt aver-

age, defense, and speed. In 1982, Ozzie Smith arrived to reinvent short-stop. Lonnie Smith fused .307, 68 steals, and a Nationals-best 120 runs. Bruce Sutter forged a league-high 36 saves. St. Louis won the East, beguiled 2,111,906, and swept Atlanta in the LCS. The Cardinals trailed the Series, three games to two, to Milwaukee. Herzog then won, 13–1 and 6–3. The Event ended with Sutter fanning Gorman Thomas. "That's a winner! That's a winner!" cried Jack Buck. "A World Series winner for the St. Louis Cardinals!"

They almost won in 1985. Willie McGee hit an MVP .353. Rookie of the Year Vince Coleman swiped 110 bases. John Tudor had a 1.93 ERA. A record 2,637,563 painted Busch red. The playoff v. L.A. tottered at two games each. "What we'll remember is Coleman," said Bob Costas. "Busch's automatic tarp machine mashed his leg, ending his post-season before Game Four." In 2,967 bigs at-bats, Smith had never—as in, well, *never*—hit a homer batting lefty. In Game Five, he launched a 2-all ninth-inning drive off Tom Niedenfuer. As "The baseball flew out toward the right-field fence, seemingly pushed by the roar from the crowd," wrote the *Miami Herald*'s Bob Rubin, "a mystical, magical transformation took place in Busch Stadium. The ballyard by the Missis-sippi became the land of Oz."

St. Louis won the decider, 7–5, met Kansas City in the "Interstate 70" Series, took a 3–1 game edge, and led Game Six in the ninth. Umpire Don Denkinger's blown call helped K.C. win, 2–1. Game Seven: Royals, 11–0. "Winning teams win it all," Herzog said in '87. Coleman stole 101 bases. Jack Clark had 106 RBI. The Birds upped seating (53,138), used it (record 3,077,122), rallied in the LCS (John Tudor and Danny Cox blanked the Giants in Games Six-Seven), then lost the World Series' last two games. "They were at [Minnesota's] Metrodome," said Broeg, "a home-run hitter's park. What played at Busch didn't always work elsewhere." Like beer, Whitey Ball seemed an acquired taste.

By now Busch had acquired a middle-age sheen. Add, subtract, do up, do over. The AstroTurf was replaced by grass. The right-field board yielded to extra seats. St. Louis affixed a two-foot-high chicken wire fence to the alleys. "This way no question," said Herzog, "whether the outfielder catches the ball." Owner August Busch died in late 1989. Next year Herzog resigned, McGee won another batting title, and St. Louis placed last for the first time since 1978. One season ('91) Lee Smith saved 47 games. In another ('92), the alleys, center field, and outfield fence dipped to 375, 402, and 8 feet, respectively. "A litle manicuring," said author Rob Rains. "A rose bed was planted between the bleachers and wall."

Gregg Jefferies hit .342 in 1993. That September 7 Mark Whiten had four homers and 12 RBI v. Cincinnati. "I'm not used to this," he said. "I've never hit more than 15 homers on *any* level for a *season*." Bulking up: The Wizard homered in successive games for the first time in his 16-year career. On July 14, 1994, Smith broke Luis Aparicio's shortstop record for assists. In '53, Anheuser-Busch had bought the club. It now sold to St. Louis banker Andrew Baur and William DeWitt, Jr., who came full circle: DeWitt's dad had owned the Browns.

Brewery tie-ins vanished: the Clydesdales, Budweiser wagon, and "King of Beers." Likewise, Smith retiring in '96: His legacy bound dazzle, backflips, and 13 straight Gold Gloves. "It's like with Ozzie leaving," said Broeg, "the Cardinals said, 'OK, we'll swap speed for power.'" They ditched fake turf, planted the real McCoy, and put bullpens in left- and right-center field. Between them: bleachers and a backdrop. Above: a new scoreboard, axing 3,000 seats.

The club closed part of the upper tier: flags now salute its eight retired numbers. In 1997, another future Hall of Famer arrived to, well, resuscitate the game.

METRODOME

One night in 1968 Mel Allen began chattering about literature and geography on a broadcast out of Minnesota. "This is the land of ten thousand lakes," he said. "They have these picturesque names." Mel then began to repeat them. When his partner injected baseball, Allen paddled to Lake Hiawatha, site of Henry Wadsworth Longfellow's poem, "The Song of Hiawatha." Was the colleague familiar with the poem? Mel asked. Wearily, he muttered that he was. "Let's see, how does it go?" said Allen, reciting the first 37 lines.

Baseball at Metropolitan Stadium set senses churning. By contrast, its successor—sterile and antiseptic Hubert H. Humphrey Metrodome a.k.a. Minnedome, Bounce Dome, Hump Dome, Homer Dome, Hubie Home, Thunderdome, or pre–air conditioning Sweat Box—is the American League's all-time bust.

The Metrodome cost $2 million under budget and opened April 6, 1982, at 401 Chicago Avenue South, just east of downtown Minneapolis. First pitcher: Pete Redfern. Batter: Seattle's Julio Cruz. Hit and homer: Twins' Dave Engle. Score: M's, 11–7, before 52,279, including Mrs. Muriel Humphrey Brown, widow of the former senator and vice-president. The Dome pleased the Twins' drawing radius. "The market isn't big," said President Calvin Griffith, "so folks now drive from Iowa and the Dakotas without fear of rainouts." Its fixed roof blocked rain, but wasted the Northland's clear, mild summer.

"Minnesota leads the nation in fishing licenses," said Harmon Killebrew. "The waters are legendary for their beauty." The Met was homey, pleasant. The Dome had short gray walls and a white fabric roof. A shuttle bus carried burghers. Cars parked at street meters or private lots. Some lots accessed walkways over the Mississippi. A visitor passed tidy grounds, opened well-marked doors, and entered a bare-boned department store. "Get fans in, let 'em see a game, and let 'em go home," an official said. "That's all we want from a stadium." The 54,711-seat capacity later became 55,883 '89 and today's 48,678. Many upper-deck seats are no longer sold.

Lengths hugged a power hitter: left, 344 (343 in '83); left-center, 385; center 407 (408 in '83); right-center, 376; and right, 327 feet. Fences formed a patchwork. Left vacillated: left 7, then 13 in '83 and 7 in '94. Center remained 7. Right leapt to 13 and 23 in early and late '83—the "Trash Bag," a 16-foot-tall tarp atop 7-foot concrete wall. "It's awful," Mickey Hatcher said of the hefty bag and 7,600 retractable football seats perched 40 feet high behind the fence. Foul ground was slight. Bullpens flanked the lines. In early 1984, Griffith sold to local banker Carl Pohlad. Minnesota drew a record 1.5-plus million. The '85ers hosted the All-Star Game: NL, 6–1. Gary Gaetti once cracked 34 homers. Kirby Puckett won his first of six Gold Gloves. "Didn't matter," said Yanks manager Billy Martin. "It's the place folks notice."

Faux grass (Sport Turf) led Martin to protest a game. "The junk is the sport's worst field. The ball bounces so high, it turns pop fly singles into ground-rule doubles." In 1987, the Dome junked it for light grayish-green AstroTurf. Some improvement: "On TV," said Mel Allen, "you can't see a contrast between the field and ball." Sight lines were grand— for the NFL Vikings. Left-field line seats faced the right-field fence! "To see home you have to turn your body and neck completely around," wrote *Baseball Weekly*'s Bob Nightengale, "and make an appointment to see the chiropractor in the morning." The Dome was the only bigs park *sans* field-level seats. Instead, two levels rose almost vertically. The upper enclosed the entire field. The lower tied one pole to another. Left-field bleachers sat behind a Plexiglas shield. "You have to sit up in the stands, or the glass blocks your view," said Nightengale. "There are only a few places from where you can see up-close [first and second deck sections 119 and 132 and 220–229, respectively]." A writer penned, "The whole place looked like a tinker toy set, designed for everything but baseball."

Like the Kingdome, in-play speakers made fielders wary. Dingers increased with air-conditioning off. The curved wall behind the plate bounced wild pitches and passed balls toward first. Seats were cramped, aisles few, and the P.A. announcer loud. Poor lighting made flies MIA. Left field's spartan scoreboard paled, say, v. Houston's. "We were so proud that this park came in under less than we'd thought," a reporter wrote. "We didn't care that it shows." Worst: the air-supported Teflon roof, peaking at 195 feet. In 1983, snow collapsed the roof and postponed a game v. California. Another stopped for nine minutes when a rainstorm swayed the roof. Toronto catcher Buck Martinez caught Randy Bush's carom for an out. Detroit's Rob Deer hit Teflon in two straight ups: The shortstop snatched each. A ball rose *through* the roof on May 4, 1985.

The A's' 6-foot-6 Dave Kingman was batting off Frank Viola. "Kingman would mostly strike out or homer," said announcer Joe Angel, "but his upper cut would also hit unbelievably high pop-ups." Viola threw. Kingman's hit soared toward the ether. A false ceiling below the metal roof had ventilation holes barely larger than a baseball. "Once the ball gets past a certain point," Angel noted, "you lose it and look at fielders to find it." Angel looked at Hatcher, circling behind first. "Soon the entire team is running around 'cause they don't know where it is! Nobody knew what was going on—never happened before or since."

Forthwith the umps call time. In time, they find that the ball cleared a hole to lodge atop the ceiling. Kingman gets a ground-rule double. Hatcher decides to catch a ball dropped from the roof. "The law of gravity," he later jibes. "What goes up has to come down." Afterward a Twins official drops a ball through the hole. It starts to dart and knuckle. Hatcher raises his glove, but misses. The ball doesn't, hitting Mickey's toe. Something about the Metrodome caused mental moorings to rip away.

One St. Patrick's Day Hatcher arrived at the park in Florida with his face, neck, arms, and hands painted Shamrock green. Mates chortled. Is he a package, or what? Hatcher began taking flies, at which point his skin began to burn. The pain turned unbearable. The paint was dimming oxygen. An ambulance carted Mickey to the hospital, where doctors removed it. "The most I do [now] is paint by number," he said in 1986. The most the '87 Twins did was tickle 2,081,476, coin the Homer Hanky, and "sire decibel levels," a writer said, "normally associated with jet air craft takeoffs."

Puckett batted .332. On August 30, his six hits, including two homers in six ups, tied the nine-frame high. Minnesota won the West and the LCS. The World Series opened with its first inside match: Twins, 10–1, behind Viola. Bert Blyleven encored, 8–4. At Busch, St. Louis swept Games Three–Five. "Home is home, though it be never so homely," said scholar John Clarke. The homely Dome was home, howling so loudly that Cards fielders wore earplugs. The Twinkies won Game Six, 11–5: Puckett had four hits. Viola then beat St. Louis, 4–2, for Minnesota's first title. Steve Lombardozzi batted .412. Kirby added a team-high 10 hits. A year later he averaged .356, Viola went a Cy Young 24–7, and the Twins became the first ALers to draw 3 million. Up: In '90, Puckett won the batting title. Down: That team crashed to last.

Detroit's Jack Morris grew up in St. Paul. "If I had one wish," he said, "it'd be to come back and finish here." The '91 free agent returned to go 18–12. Scott Erickson won 20 games. The Twins and Toronto split playoff matches One and Two at the Thunderdome. The Jays then lost the LCS at home. Kirby batted .429, but had only three hits in the first five Series Games: Twins, 5–2 and 3–2; Atlanta, 5–4, 3–2, and 14–5. Said Puckett: "Talk about home cooking." The host won each. In Game Six, he tripled, robbed Ron Gant of a dinger, and hit the Event's fourth game-winning overtime homer: 4–3. The decider was grander. Morris threw 10 scoreless innings. Dan Gladden led off the Twins' 10th by doubling. Chuck Knoblauch bunted him to third. Two walks filled the bases. Gene Larkin then pinch-singled over the drawn-in outfield: 1–0. Five, three, and four games were won, respectively, by a run, in extra innings, and in the last at-bat.

Perspective is all. "Maybe they should have stopped this game [and Series] after nine innings," said Atlanta's Mark Lemke, "and cut the trophy in half."

Kirby led the '92 AL in hits for the fourth and final time. The Twins beat Cleveland, 5–4, in a 22-inning game. Dave Winfield left Toronto to get hit 3,000. "The Dome's had more guys collect that hit [Eddie Murray '95 and Cal Ripken 2000]," owner Pohlad noted, "than any park." In '94, Erickson threw Minnesota's first no-hitter since Dean Chance '67. Their Everyman retired with 207 homers, 2,304 hits, and a .318 average. "I don't have a choice," Puckett said of a damaged retina. The Twins retired his number, joining Killebrew, Tony Oliva, Kent Hrbek, and Rod Carew. "No doubt," said broadcaster Herb Carneal. "He's our most popular Twin." Knoblauch and Paul Molitor '96 each hit .341. Brad Radke was 20–10 in '97. The Dome had little else to bare.

A bored guest snarfed burgers and onion rings at concessions behind the plate. A kids novelty meal offered chips, soft drink, licorice snack, and hot dog in a Twins-logoed pail. A health-food stand had garden salads, vegetables and dip, and Thelma's frozen lemonade. More bracing: Bavarian, cinnamon, garlic, and plain pretzels. "Wally the Beerman" vended your favorite brew. Business briefly closed May 30, 1998: a storm snapped the cable tying the 45-foot right-field pole to the roof.

A temporary 10-foot pole replaced it. The Twins needed to replace the Dome. Attendance fell to 1,165,980, then 1,059,715. The '99 and '00ers finished last. Pohlad agreed in principle to sell to a North Carolina businessman. Funding collapsed for a new park near Greensboro. A *Star Tribune*/KMSP-TV Minneapolis poll affirmed bad blood: by 68 to 12 percent, no to public help. Said Pohlad: "We have to have aid to build a park." In 2001, Knoblauch played left field at the Dome for the first time since requesting a trade in 1998. Fans pelted him with coins, hot dogs, and golf balls. For 12 minutes his Yankees left the field. Twins manager Tom Kelly left the dugout to chide the miscreants. "Please stop throwing things!" P.A. man Bob Casey told the crowd. "Now quit this!" The '01 Twins won 41 of their first 65 games. "Doesn't matter," said Pohlad. "Without a new park we can't make more money. No money, no new players. No players, no compete."

The Twins once regaled Bismarck and Burlington with a family feeling of respectability, good manners, and pluck. They now read like Alexander Dumas: trapped in a (here concrete) mask. "We never should have built it," a fan was quoted about the Metrodome. "Here we are in the Land of Ten Thousand Lakes, and we're drowning in a grave."

KINGDOME

On May 6, 1982, in another dome, Gaylord Perry won his 300th game. "No one wanted the ol' boy," he drawled of Seattle signing him in spring training. Churchill afer El Alamein: "Now, this is not the end. It is not even the beginning of the end. But it is perhaps the end of the beginning." Gaylord ended the start of Mariners anonymity. "Little by little," he said, "people began to know who we were."

In 1982, Seattle climbed to fourth. Alvin Davis became '84 Rookie of the Year. Three times Mark Langston led the league in Ks. Harold Reynolds' 60 steals led the '87 AL. "Think of it," chirped M's voice Dave Niehaus, "their first offensive leader in history!" Visitors proved unwelcome guests: Rickey Henderson's 100th steal; Rollie Fingers' 300th save; Texas' Perry tossed for doctoring the ball. "Cain't believe it," he said. "First time in my career." The '84ers finished last. In '86, Boston's Roger Clemens Kd 20 Mariners in a game. One year Seattle ended with four straight victories. Manager Dick Williams wasn't fooled. "Know what?" he told a friend at the airport. "We're still horseshit."

Seattle tried making defeat more palatable; in 1982, adding a 23-foot-high right and right-center field wall (the Walla Wall, after Walla Walla, Washington). "It will become baseball's second-highest in-play wall," read a brochure, "after Boston's Green Monster." (A 123 feet by 11½ old-time scoreboard later framed the barrier.) The '90ers moved the plate 10 feet toward the first-base dugout to make the field asymmetrical. Alleys changed slightly: left-center, 357 ('81) and 362 ('90); right-center, 357 and 356. Papers jeered the "Homer Dome." Nothing kept the M's from six times placing last.

"When today stinks," Williams jibed, "you look at tomorrow." In 1990, Randy Johnson tossed the M's' first no–hitter. Seattle signed Ken Griffey, Jr. 19, son of the Reds outfielder. On August 31, father and son played in the same outfield after Cincinnati dropped Griffey, Sr. The Mariners' luck still rivaled Charlie Brown's: Matt Young yielded a hit after 1⅓ frames on "Guaranteed No-Hitter Night." A year later the M's finally reached .500 (83–79), drew a record 2,147,905, and had a player (Griffey) hit (a franchise-high) .327. In '92, Nintendo president Hiroshi Yamauchi bought the team. He had never seen a Mariners game. Edgar Martinez later won Seattle's first batting title (.343). Chris Bosio no-hit Boston. Johnson's 308 Ks set a new league high. Griffey went yard in a bigs-tying eighth straight games.

"I'm often asked about how good Junior can be," said Niehaus in 1993. "I say the best player who ever lived—bar none." He had debuted in Oakland, doubling off the wall. Later Griffey smacked his first King-dome pitch for a homer. "He says he's not a home-run hitter—but his homers average over 400 feet," Niehaus added. "He'll have many chances to break Maris' and Ruth's records, and I think he will."

Griffey might have, in 1994, had the strike not intervened. He broke Ruth's high for most homers before July (31). His grand slam graced the last pre-strike match: Forty homers in 111 games! Sadly, the dome remained dreary, its carpet still zipped together, laid out by the grasshopper machine. Four 15-pound tiles fell from the roof 30 minutes before a game *v.* Baltimore. One nearly plunked Cal Ripken. Said Griffey: "We can't go on like this."

In 1995, the Mariners asked the state legislature for moolah for a new park. Pols unleashed a belly laugh. The Emerald City shrugged. "We didn't have leverage," said a team official, "which is what politicians understand." The M's then proved that in their 19th season a franchise could get a break. Seattle beat the Angels, 9–1, in a West playoff. Briefly, it forgot the NFL Seahawks. Ahead: the best-of-five Division Series. New York won the opener, 9–6: Griffey homered twice. The Yanks' Jim Leyritz's 15th-inning blast took Game Two, 7–5. Johnson won the King-dome's first postseason game, 7–4, before 57,944. A day later the M's scored five eighth-frame runs: Martinez's slam tied the series, 11–8. The house stood between pitches. In two weeks Seattle had become a base-ball town.

Game Five showed why a fan abides glitz and greed and attitude. The Yanks led, 4–2. Seattle tied in the eighth. Lou Piniella then inserted a weary Johnson. "He'd pitched two days earlier," the M's manager said. "But he was the best we had." New York led in the 11th, 5–4. Martinez then lashed a double down the line. Sliding, Griffey beat the relay throw: 6–5. "I thought for a moment," he said, "the noise would blow the roof off." (Seattle would have liked the open-air feel). Griffey whipped five dingers. Martinez hit .571, but only .087 in the LCS (Cleveland won, in six). The legislature now OKd $320 million. "Once in a while," says Piniella, "I'll be sitting at Safeco Field [opening 1999] and I'll think of why we're here. It was 1995."

The '96ers hosted baseball's first March (31) Opening Day. Griffey had 49 homers and 140 RBI. Shortstop Alex Rodriguez's first full year con-jured Cronin, Wagner, and Banks (league-high .358, 54 doubles, and 141 runs). Johnson, 20–4, Kd 19 White Sox in 1997—the first to fan that many twice in a year. Junior topped in homers (56), RBI (147), runs (125), slugging (.646), and total bases (393)—the AL's ninth unanimous MVP. Attendance leapt to 3,192,237. "No longer can you show up on game day," said the *Post-Intelligencer,* "and get tickets." Many flew from Idaho, Oregon, Utah, and Montana. "For the first time," added Griffey, "we became a regional team."

In '97, Seattle won the West, lost the Division Series to Baltimore, and began to ask about Griffey and Rodriguez. "Even with attendance up," mused an official, "we're still a small-market team." Could the M's afford

Seven Up Forever, *Bill Purdom.* Who didn't fantasize about being Mickey Mantle? In 1956, No. 7 won the Triple Crown (.353, 52 homers, and 130 RBI). Off Pedro Ramos, Mantle hit the facade of Yankee Stadium. No one came closer to clearing its roof.

Yankee Stadium Panorama, *Andy Jurinko.* 1964, Mantle hits toward left-center. The Stadium at high meridian: triple tiers, short foul lines, Death Valley, in-play flagpole, facade, and monuments in center field. Mid-'70 renovation defaced its look.

Yankee Stadium Diptych, *Joseph Golinkin.* The Big Ballpark in the Bronx became sport's premier arena. Note the '36 World Series flag, Lou Gehrig singling, and No. 3, George Selkirk, in the on-deck circle. (Babe Ruth's No. 3 was later retired.)

County Stadium Classic, *Andy Jurinko.* Milwaukee became baseball's 1950s capital, as Joe Adcock's single wins '57 World Series Game Five. The Braves later left for Atlanta. The Brewers played here from 1970-2000.

timore Memorial Matinee, William Feldman. In 1954, the Browns moved to Baltimore. The Orioles' new nest was [*i*]n, horseshoed, and hoisted three Series and six pennant flags.

veland Municipal Classic, Andy Jurinko. The 1932-93 Indians played at Municipal Stadium. Giant (74,208 seat) [*c*]e reaped pygmy luck. The Tribe's only title came in 1948, *v.* Boston, shown here.

avez Ravine Triptych, Andy Jurinko. In 1962, the ex-Brooks found El Dorado in the five levels and surpassing beauty [*of*] Dodger Stadium. L.A. tied Koufax, Wills, Fernandomania, and attendance in excess of 3 million a year. The stadium [ha]sn't aged a day.

Twilight at Shea, *Andy Jurinko*. Since 1964 the Mets have played a pop fly from LaGuardia Airport. Shea was loud, four-tiered, and symmetrical. In 1969, men first walked on the moon. The Mets won their first World Series. Which was the real miracle?

Spirit in Saint Louis, *William Feldman*. "The Greeks had their Parthenon," wrote *Sports Illustrated*. "St. Louisians have Busch Stadium." The park was remodeled in the '90s. September 8, 1998, Mark McGwire hits home run No. 62.

Astrodome's Greatest Moment, *William Feldman.* In 1965, the Astrodome became the first air-conditioned, indoor stadium and a pitcher's Eden. In 1986, Mike Scott no-hit the Giants to clinch the N.L. West. The Dome closed in '99.

Seven One Five, *Bill Purdom.* Atlanta-Fulton County Stadium became a multi-sport prototype: vast foul turf, no idiosyncrasy, seats a time zone from the field. On April 8, 1974, Henry Aaron hit a silver lining: home run 715 to break Babe Ruth's mark.

Oakland Coliseum Matinee, *Thomas Kolendra.* In 1968, the A's moved to Oakland. They still lack a park befitting the team. The Oakland Coliseum sits in the ground like a concrete pillbox. This etches 1994.

First Camden Pitch, *Bill Purdom.* In 1992, Camden Yards began baseball's trip back to the future. Its brick, steel, and in-play board mimed classic parks. The urban area buoyed it. Result: The Ebbets Field of the bigs' '90s U-turn.

First Jacobs Pitch, *Bill Purdom.* Opening in 1994, Jacobs Field became Cleveland's new prism and progenitor. Light towers mimicked toothbrushes. The inside mixed quirk and charm. The Tribe sold out a record 455 straight games. Municipal what?

Rebirth in Seattle, *Bill Purdom.* All thirteen parks opened since Camden Yards have sought to out-do it. Safeco Field came closest. Its roof resembled a carport. Inside swam a sea of dark-green seats. A writer said: "The Mariners did it right."

Rebirth in Detroit, *Bob Novak.* In 2000, Detroit left Tiger Stadium for Comerica Park. The spacious site tied a Ferris wheel, carousel, and dancing water. Only 127 homers were hit there that first year.

Rebirth in Houston, *Bill Purdom.* "Can there be such a thing?" asked Houston's owner, "as too much excitement?" He said no: e.g. Enron Field's berm, pillars, left-field porch, in-play flagpole, and train to hail Astros homers. *S* called it "Field of Screams."

Rebirth in San Francisco, *Bill Purdom.* In 2000, the Giants opened the first privately-funded baseball-only park since Dodger Stadium. Pacific Bell Park had 40,800 seats, 188-foot-long wall, and 309-foot right-field line. Behind it dingers splashed into McCovey's Cove.

them? Griffey became the second-youngest to hit 300 taters in '98. Rodriguez joined Barry Bonds and Jose Canseco in the 40/40 steals/homers club.

Seattle soon cheered the Kingdome's looming exit. No more falling tiles! Forget in-play speakers! Let the sun shine in! Said Niehaus: "I'm not going to feel sad about leaving." The curtain fell June 27, 1999. First, Junior launched a three-run blast; later, the then-nine-time Gold Glover cleared the fence to rob Juan Gonzalez; 56,530 watched the M's beat Texas, 5–2. In March 2000, the world's largest concrete dome structure collapsed in a controlled implosion. "It took less than 20 seconds," read *Baseball Weekly*, "for 5,800 gelatin-dynamite-filled holes to reduce the 24-year-old arena to rubble."

KAUFFMAN STADIUM

By then, the Royals castle was 27. Said then-G.M. Herk Robinson: "It's like Dodger Stadium. It hasn't aged a day." You recalled how Willie Wilson (.332) and Hal McRae (133 RBI) led the '83 AL; George Brett's T-85 Marv Throneberry-model bat oozed pine tar; and rain delays bred thousands of sawed webworm moths. A frogman cleaned the right-center pond. The A's and Yankees more often than not sold out. Box and reserved seats teemed for even the Brewers. Left field promised a George Hamilton tan. A heartlander mixed barbecue beef and local Boulevard beer. After each game a water show took 9 minutes, 58 seconds. Middle America loved the Royals becoming king of the hill.

In 1985, Brett had .335, 30 homers, and 112 RBI. One K.C. official said: "They should put one sentence on his tombstone: 'He ran 'em all out.' " Mates believed in team, baseball, and an honest day's work. Cy Younger Bret Saberhagen went 20–6. Wilson lashed 21 triples. "Ain't nothin' easy," said Andy Griffith as TV's Ben Matlock. K.C. won the West by a game, then trailed Toronto, 3–1, in the '85 LCS. "In the old [best-of-five], we'd be dead," said manager Dick Howser. "We've still got a chance," winning three straight. "The War Within the State" followed: St. Louis, 3–1 and 4–2. No team had won a Series after losing the first two games at home. Saberhagen countered, 6–1. The Cards replied, 3–0. Danny Jackson kept K.C. alive, 6–1.

St. Louis led Game Six, 1–0, in the ninth. The Royals' Jorge Orta led off by rolling to first baseman Jack Clark. Todd Worrell took the throw and beat Orta to the bag—except that Don Denkinger called him safe. Steve Balboni then popped out near the dugout—except that Clark lost the ball. The Cards still led—until a passed ball, intentional walk, and pinch-hitter Dane Iorg's game-winning hit. "It's a situation you dream about as a child," said Iorg. A night later Saberhagen threw a five-hitter. Darryl Motley went yard. Brett batted .370, doubling St. Louis' .185. The Royals still display their World Series trophy in section 107.

"Howser is to Billy Martin," said ABC's Al Michaels, "what the Salvation Army is to the SWAT team." A brain tumor took his life in 1987. Kevin Seitzer whacked a team record six hits in a game *v.* Boston. Saberhagen won another Cy Young in 1989. Ageless: Brett, 37, only big leaguer to win batting crowds in three decades—1976 (.333), '80 (.390), and '90 (.329). Timeless: the 13-time All-Star, getting hit 3,000 September 30, 1992. "All fame is fleeting": Brett was promptly picked off first—the sole player with 3,000 hits, 300 homers, 600 doubles, 100 triples, and 200 steals.

Kauffman died in 1993. The park became his namesake. In '94, the Royals shortened outfield turf (by 10 feet) and fences (12 to 9 feet high). A year later groundskeeper George Toma finally got high on grass. "I'd always thought it unusual," said Brett, "that baseball's best in his field only had to maintain the cutaway [base] areas and Baja [125-foot forest beyond left center]." Toma mixed five strains of bluegrass and one kind of rye. The park mixed the JumboTron video-display board, amusement area with pitching booth, Royal Courtyard picnic and music area, and Fan-A-Gram, timing 14 tarp crew members. "They go like nuts," said 1997– manager Tony Muser, "cleaning up the infield [after the fifth inning]."

Jeff Montgomery became K.C.'s all-time saves leader. Carlos Beltran became '99 Rookie of the Year. That September Carlos Febles, Jermaine Dye, Joe Randa, and Johnny Damon dotted the AL's top seven triplers. "No team had that many in the top 10," said Robinson, "since the '66 Bucs." A year later Mike Sweeney had a club record 144 RBI. Damon's 136 runs led the league. "The idea has always been to get a full roster of guys who hustle and hit to the alleys." Keep the faith, like the ballpark. Most Royalists asked little more.

MILWAUKEE COUNTY STADIUM

Like Kauffman, Milwaukee's berghoff evolved, quaint and tangible, a rear window on Ike's America. By 1983, Bob Uecker's front row was full (even section 21, row 35, seat 1, abutting a brick chimney. You only saw right field). "Ah, those fans," he said, "I love 'em." The decks wrapped beyond the foul lines. Bullpens perpendicular to the field split two bleacher sections. Behind them a scoreboard flashed a clock, Brewers logo, score, and instant replay. A huge beer keg and small shack dwarfed it. Upon home-team dingers "Bernie Brewer" slid into the barrel. A special bus line brought doyens from Eau Claire and Madison. The Brewers drew a Milwaukee record 2,397,131. Most devoured subs, Italian and Polish sausage, fresh-dough pizza—and bratwurst "secret stadium" red sauce. Bob Costas became its salesman.

"The secret sauce has a formula that's in a vault that makes it taste like another planet. Put beer on the grill and seep it in sauerkraut," said NBC's '83–'89 "Game of the Week"er. "On camera I'd say it's now an official game because we have the bratwurst. We'd [Costas and Milwaukee native Tony Kubek] have to alternate play-by-play because one of us would have a mouthful. This became semi-legendary, especially in Wisconsin, to where the concessionaire at County Stadium sent vats of bratwurst to my home in giant industrial size. I'd get jars of the secret sauce, but also letters from Cub fans who were insulted that I didn't say Wrigley Field had better hot dogs."

One day a true believer named Ma Pesh wrote to Costas from Stevens Point, Wisconsin. "Ma wants to challenge me to a bratwurst-eating contest. He enclosed a Polaroid and the guy had to tip the Toledos at about 430. Ma wears bib overalls, he's got a big head, looks like Junior Samples, and claims he holds the record for County bratwurst consumption. Says he consumed the most brats in a game between the Brewers and Orioles in August 1972—and that this was even more surprising because before then he'd never eaten well against Baltimore. You know, what do ya' say? I wrote back and he wrote back to me and now we're pen pals."

Ma loved County's curiosa. Bonnie Brewer, in Bavarian beer hall garb, sweeping bases and whomping umpires with her broom; the seventh-inning stretch (a polka band played "Roll Out the Barrel"); the on-deck circle, warmed by water bottles. The '86ers froze in sixth place. "It's

'87," said Bud Selig, "and we're a consensus choice to finish last." Instead, Milwaukee won its first 13 games to tie Atlanta's streak ('82). Its Eden was Juan Nieves' April 15 masterwork v. Baltimore. "This is incredible," the Puerto Rican southpaw said of the Brewers' first no-hitter. "I wish my mother was here tonight. I'd squeeze her to death."

Paul Molitor forged the AL's longest post-DiMaggio hit streak (39 games; final average, .353). In September 1988, the A's' Jose Canseco formed the single-year 40/40 club (homers/steals) by swiping second in Milwaukee. "I got nervous [only] when I was going for the fortieth steal," he said. "My legs locked." Locked in memory: 1990, Nolan Ryan victory 300; Cecil Fielder, County's longest blast (502 feet); Molitor '91, leading in runs, hits, and triples; September 9, 1992, Robin Yount's 3,000th hit. Selig retired numbers 19 (Yount), 34 (Rollie Fingers), and 44 (Aaron; later, Molitor 4). In 1993, a nearby Harley convention drove seagulls from Lake Michigan into the park; at which point, they began nesting on the outfield; whereupon Gus the Wonderdog was hired to dispatch them.

The '94ers switched to the AL Central. The next year Milwaukee drew only 1,080,560. Realignment closed its circle: The '98 Brewers joined the Nationals—said Selig: "Our hearts were always there." They finished last, but lured 1,811,548. By then, the Wisconsin legislature had approved a sales tax to build a domed stadium in County's parking lot. "We just can't compete against the other new parks," said Selig. The Brewers' final game was scheduled for October 3, 1999. A lighted numeric sign visible from the freeway counted the days until Miller Park opened. It read 261 when a 567-foot crane, lifting a 400-ton piece of the retractable roof, collapsed July 14, 1999. The crane hit another, landing on the roof's first-base side.

Three ironworkers were killed: William DeGrave, 39, of Kimberly; Jeff Wischer, 40, of Waukesha; and Jerome Starr, 52, of Milwaukee. Damage neared $75 million. The Stadium Board voted to delay the park's debut until 2001. "I understand this may disappoint many people," chairman Robert Trunzo said. "But we will not compromise safety." Opening Miller immediately after the 2000 All-Star break was pondered, then dropped. "Too expensive," said an official. The deadline would take 1,200 workers working 58 hours weekly for 42 weeks.

'Ninety-nine's last game had sold out months earlier. It lured hundreds on a dank, funereal day. September 28, 2000, marked real *finis*: Reds 8, Brewers 1, before 56,354. The postgame bill starred Aaron, Spahn, Fingers, Yount, and 39 other ex–players and managers. Play-by-playmen Uecker, Merle Harmon, and Earl Gillespie emceed. Scaffolding still rose in County's parking lot. "Can't wait," said Selig. A parking lot had never seemed so grand.

SHEA STADIUM

"**F**ifteen years had passed," James Fenimore Cooper wrote, " 'ere it was in the power of the Deerslayer to revisit the Glimmberglass." By 1983, six years had passed since Tom Seaver, returning from Cincinnati, pitched the opener at Shea.

The first-day crowd was its largest since 1968. A Diamond Vision replay board moored left-center. "Great shorts between innings [e.g., *The Three Stooges*], lots of replays," said Lindsey Nelson. The P.A. system treated silence like a leper. A small bleacher area housed picnic groups. A church spire beyond center shaded the Mets Magic Top Hat. "When a Met homers," explained voice Bob Murphy, "a red Big Apple rises out of the black hat, which looks more like a big kettle." Seaver assessed shorter lines (338) and fences (8 wood) than, say, 1973. "Left was always a hoot," he said. "Early on ['64], a ball down the line could bounce fair, roll foul into the corner where they stored football seats, and still be in play. Worse, a railing topped the fence." Some drives grazed it for a homer. Others caromed into play. "It was so controversial the Mets painted an orange homer marker. That didn't work, so [in '79] they built the inner fence."

*Un*changed: The right-field board listed lineup, batting order, number, position, and line score. The lighting was still awful; walkways, dingy; sight, dim in the rear loge and mezzanine. "The deck above is the problem," said Dick Young. "Its overhang blocks the scoreboard and leaves you guessing on fly balls." The facade still showed players in varied pose. A visitor still arrived by subway train No. 7, or Long Island Railroad Port Washington line. Inside, you found a familiar on-air voice: Ralph Kiner, calling Howard Johnson Walter Johnson, Marv Throneberry Marv Strawberry, Gary Carter Gary Cooper, and Milt May Mel Ott. One day the Mets unveiled a new sponsor, American Cyanamid. He said, "We'll be right back after this word from American Cyanide." In September 1983, reliever Bert Graff entered his first bigs game. Kiner couldn't see his number. Partner Tim McCarver wrote Graff's name on some paper. Kiner promptly told his audience, "I beg your pardon, Frank Graff is in the game." At that point McCarver wrote "Bert." Kiner observed that "Frank Bert" was pitching. McCarver began to shake his head. Kiner amended, "Check that, it's Bert Frank."

The '83ers drew 1,842,695. Darryl Strawberry became Rookie of the Year. Davey Johnson became manager. Threads began, ebbed, reappeared: The ex-O made '69's final Series out. In 1984, Dwight Gooden Kd 16 Bucs to break Herb Score's rookie mark of 245 (total 276). He topped the league a year later in wins, Ks, innings, complete games, and ERA. New York won the '86 East by 21½ games. The Mets and Astros split LCS Games One-Two. Len Dykstra's ninth-inning two-run poke took Match Three, 6–5. Houston's Mike Scott won next day, 3–1. Casey Stengel would have loved Game Five. "It is my consideration that them pitching duels where the hitter ain't powerful ain't so forgot," he said. Gary Carter's 12th-inning single scored Wally Backman: 2–1. The Metsies won Game Six—and the World Series.

By default, their afterword seemed as mild as a church cotillion. David Cone went 20–3 in '88. "Darryl! Darryl!" 's 39 dingers led the league. The Mets enticed a record 3,055,445, won the East, and beat the Dodgers 10 of 11 games. The LCS became an antigen: L.A. in seven.

The seesaw resumed: second ('89–90) to last ('93). Anthony Young lost a bigs record 27 straight games. John Franco got his 253rd save—a bigs lefty mark. Guests were gorging better (knishes, Kahn's hot dogs, Carvel ice cream, and New Amsterdam beer) and enjoying it less ('94's gate barely hit 1.1 million). Todd Hundley's 41 homers broke Campy's single-year mark for catchers. Scratch old rivalries, and sparks fly. In 1997, baseball retired Jackie Robinson's No. 42 on the silver date of his debut.

"This is the perfect place," Selig said at Shea: Mets beat L.A., 5–0; 54,047 included widow Rachel Robinson. That June 16 the Mets beat the Yankees, 6–0, in their interleague investiture. A year later John Olerud hit a franchise-best .354. A beam collapsed in the Bronx, making the Yanks play at Shea. "For the first time this century," said historian Jerome Holtzman of April 15, "One park hosted two games for four different teams": day, Yankees, 6–3, v. Anaheim; night, Mets 2, Cubs 1.

In 1999, the Mets unearthed, if not a pennant, baseball's DNA—"the wild card"—its new code for life. "We're in first place in August," said manager Bobby Valentine. "Next month we lose seven straight, then come back from the dead [winning a 5–0 playoff over Cincy]." Mike Piazza had .303, 40 homers, and 124 RBI. Armando Benitez saved 22 games. Olerud (.298), Edgardo Alfonzo (.304, 27, 108), Robin Ventura (.301, 32, 120), and Rey Ordonez (like Ventura, a Gold Glover) sealed the infield. Todd Pratt's Game Four 10th-inning blast won the Division Series. The LCS parodied '62 v. '69. The Braves swept Games One–Three. The Mets a) took Game Four, 3–2, on Olerud's eighth-inning hit; b) won the 4–3 15-frame Game Five on Ventura's over-the-fence slam "single" (mates mobbed/kept him from the plate); and c) trailed, 5–0, tied, 7-all, led, 8–7 and 9–8, and lost Six, 10–9.

"Theatre doesn't get better than this mad week of games," wrote Dorothy Rabinowitz in the *Wall Street Journal*. (Actually, 2000 wasn't bad: the Yanks July 7–9 Subway Series; Division Series and LCS v. San Francisco and St. Louis, respectively; and first all–New York Oktoberfest since 1956. '01 broke worse: sub-.500 in June.) Was Shea colder than a front of Arctic air? At such moments the Metsies seemed as warm as a Bermuda breeze.

JACK MURPHY STADIUM

"**U**nfair!" wrote a late-80's San Diego columnist. "The Mets have two magical years ['69 and '86]. We don't even have one." 'Eighty-four came close. The Padres won the West (by 12 games) and nearly hit 2 million in attendance (1,983,904). Steve Garvey and Graig Nettles keyed the corners. Goose Gossage ruled the pen. Tony Gwynn, a bottle-shaped San Diegan, won his first batting title (.351). America then hoped the Pads would fall on their LCS face. Said Tony: "We were the bad guys" v. Chicago. They quickly reeled: Cubs, 13–0 and 4–2. Ed Whitson won San Diego's first postseason game, 7–1. The playoff turned on Garvey's one-out, two-run, Game Four poke. "In a game that absolutely defies description," Pads voice Jerry Coleman cried, "Steve Garvey, in the ninth inning, hit one over the 370-mark, and the Padres beat the Cubs, 7 to 5!"

The Cubs led the decider, 3–0. San Diego tied the score on Leon Durham's seventh-inning error. Gwynn and Garvey then knocked in three runs: 6–3. "We've come a long way, baby," rejoiced manager Dick Williams. The Murph's largest crowd (58,359, v. smallest, September '73's 1,413) agreed. The Series is best forgot. Detroit took the opener, 3–2. Kurt Bevacqua's three-run dinger won Game Two, 5–3. The Tigers swept at Michigan and Trumbull. The Padres hoped their loss would not forge H. G. Wells' "the shape of things to come." The '85ers broke 2 million. Eric Show yielded Pete Rose's Cobb-crushing hit 4,192. Rookie Benito Santiago hit in 34 straight games. Gwynn won the '87–'88–'90 batting titles. Mark Davis became the Padres' third Cy Younger. San Diego reclaimed last.

On August 30, 1988, L.A.'s Orel Hershiser yielded a run. He then threw 59 straight scoreless innings to break Don Drysdale's 1968 mark (58). The final 10 stung San Diego. "There's a drive to right field!" said Coleman. "He's going to put it away! Oh, doctor! History was born right here at San Diego!" Just: The Murph became the first big-league park to honor a Negro League player. Inept: The Claw, snatching homers between the inner fence and outer wall. "This guy'd sit in the first row," said Gwynn. "He had a rod with a claw on the end. You'd lower the claw and it would collapse on the ball." A mural behind the right-field scoreboard showed thousands cheering—what? Profane: The actress Roseanne (Arnold/Barr) butchered the National Anthem. The Padres twice finished last and flunked a million. Sacred: Gwynn got six hits in a game ('93) and hit an NL best-since-'30 .394 ('94). Enduring: a 1949–'57 Yankee and World War II and Korean Marine, Coleman seemed sprung from Mrs. Malaprop via Casey Stengel to Ol' Diz.

"On the mound is Randy Jones," he related, "the left-hander with the Karl Marx hairdo." The batter lined deep to center. "Winfield is going back . . . back . . . he hits his head against the wall. It's rolling toward second base." The runner tore around first base. "He slides into second with a stand-up double." Meanwhile, "Rich Folkers is throwing up in the bull pen." Some liked John Grubb, pursuing a fly. "He's under the warning track, and he makes the play." Others preferred Jesus Alou "in the on-deck circus." A hitter lined "a shot up the alley . . . oh, it's just foul." Evolution, however, went yard. "Sometimes big trees grow out of acorns. I think I heard that from a squirrel." Jerry once worried about Colemanisms. "Not any more," he said in 1992. "Now I figure they add to my sex appeal."

In December 1994, John Moores and ex–O's president Larry Lucchino bought the Padres. They sought a less provincial air. "The Republican ['96 National] Convention kicked us out of our stadium," said Lucchino. "So we went to Monterey [Mexico, v. the Mets] because we were trying to become a regional team." Estadio Monterey housed the bigs' first game outside the U.S. or Canada. It held 27,000, had 310-foot lines, and resembled the Murph. Music hailed each K, and fireworks each homer. Fernando Valenzuela won the first game of "La Primera Serie," 15–10. San Diego teemed with Spanish-speaking people. "We're the only team next to the border," said Lucchino, starting Spanish oral and written ads, "and we'd ignored them for years."

Tradition sells: The Pads revived their swinging Friar mascot. Ibid., service. San Diego bought a 24-by-33 foot JumboTron, closed the top outfield deck, built field-level seats behind the plate, made each Friday Family night, and put an 86-foot-long by 9½-foot-high board atop right field's fence. (Lefties must now clear a 17½-foot barrier.) Capacity became 48,639. The scene mixed beach balls and bathing suits. "We have to be more intimate," Lucchino said. The P.A. rotated Top 40 and organ music. The Stadium Club served season-ticket holders. A plaza-level Sports Club offered food and a dozen imported beers. Gourmets gravitated toward deluxe sausages, fish taccos, corn on the cob, and Randy Jones' barbecue stands. "You gain weight," said the ex-pitcher, "but what a way to go." Increasingly, the Pads hinted that they might leave the Murph.

In 1994, Ken Caminiti became the first to homer lefty-righty thrice in four games. The Nationals' '96 MVP set team highs for homers (40), RBI (130), and slugging (.621). San Diego dropped the Division Series to St. Louis. Gwynn won a Wagner-tying eighth NL batting title (.372). The park was renamed Qualcomm Stadium. On April 19–20, 1997, Hawaii's Aloha Stadium booked the Cardinals and Pads. "Construction was going on," said Moores, "so we moved a series." Franchise-setting: Greg Vaughn and Trevor Hoffman's 50 dingers and 53 saves, respectively, in 1998. The Padres won 98 games; took the Division Series, 3–1, over Houston; and upset Atlanta, 4–2, to win the pennant. The Series was as flinty as '84: a Yankees sweep.

Lucchino was unfazed. "What the season did was bring back baseball," he said. That November a referendum passed to build a downtown park. "I hope I see it," said Gwynn, then 38, who retired in 2001. On August 6, 1999, he batted in Montreal. At Qualcomm, a crowd of 8,000 chanted his name and hailed hit 3,000—a single to right-center.

"It's awesome!" said Anthony Greene, 10, watching the game free on a giant-screen television. Fireworks spouted. Sports bars joined the fling. A week later nearly 61,000 jammed Qualcomm upon Gwynn's return. He replied like Mr. Padre: two two-run dingers. Life begins at 40. In 2001, Gwynn and Rickey Henderson became the first 40s mates in the same outfield since Detroit's 1945 Doc Cramer and Chuck Hostetler. Henderson, 42, set the all-time walk record (2,063). Pro: Dave Winfield entered Cooperstown—the first Padre with their emblem on his plaque. Con: A swarm of bees on the right-field auxiliary scoreboard halted a Pads-Dodgers game. They didn't stay long enough: L.A., 5–4.

"We'll forget stuff like that, but never Number 19," said Billy Howe of Pacific Beach of Gwynn. Will we say that of the Murph?

19

SHOW ME

I attended Allegheny College, 90 miles north of Pittsburgh, in the early 1970s. A decade later I returned to Meadville, Erie, and Oil City. Even old friends ribbed how the Bucs might be leaving. Pittsburgh without its *Buccos*? Better Foster Brooks without his booze. Bill Madlock won '81–'83 batting titles. Willie Stargell's No. 8 was retired. (Also, Bill Meyer 1, Ralph Kiner 4, Bill Mazeroski 9, Pie Traynor 20, Roberto Clemente 21, Honus Wagner 33, and Danny Murtaugh 40). The '84–'85ers finished last. Attendance crashed to 735,900. Abiding: upper-deck seats, painted white to recall Stargell's blasts.

The city helped a local cartel buy the Bucs. AstroTurf replaced Tartan Turf. Bleachers bridged the inner and outer walls. Capacity rose to 54,499. Bless the beasts and the Pirates: Skunks were said to dwell in the belly. Shortcomings waxed and waned. The '88ers drew a record 1,866,713. Father and son reunion: Bobby and Pittsburgh's Barry Bonds' combined 408 dingers passed the Bells (Gus and Buddy) and Berras (Yogi and Dale). In 1990, Bonds and Bobby Bonilla had 234 RBI, Doug Drabek became the team's second Cy Younger, and attendance finally cracked 2 million. The L.C.S. repeated '70–'72–'74: Cincy planked the Bucs.

"First, we score five runs in the ninth [tying the Cubs, 7-all]," manager Jim Leyland said of April 21, 1991. "They get five runs, we get six [in the 11th]—baseball's greatest extra-inning comeback." Playoff tables turned: Pittsburgh led Atlanta, three games to two, then lost Six and Seven at Three Rivers. Bonds '92 minded the Bucs' jibs: 34 homers, .624 slugging, and NL MVP. Again they drowned in the LCS high tide: the Braves scored thrice in the ninth to win Game Seven, 3–2. Bonds joined 'Frisco. The '95ers finished last. Belly-up seemed around the bend. Then, in 1996, Kevin McClatchy, 32, bought the team. Soon hope no longer sank hull down. By '98, Kevin Young had 27 homers and 108 RBI. A year later Brian Giles added 39 and 115.

Could the Bucs again fit in Pittsburgh's emotional luggage? "Everyone has an emotional attachment to Forbes," said McClatchy. "We have to make Three Rivers more baseball-friendly." At each base the Bucs planted a patch of grass—"hallowed ground"—from fields where Clemente played. Up went a Sony JumboTron video board, two out-of-town boards beyond the outfield wall, and tarp on its upper deck. Size shrunk from 58,729 to 47,972. A Tri-Stater could still buy a ticket minutes before the game. Best value: upper terrace boxes. Best tan: third base to left field. Best seat: $75 on-field "Batter's Box" behind the plate. Best call: "Get your cold beer!"—Becks, Amstel Light, and Pittsburgh's Iron City. Good eats involved cheese steak, pastrami, specialty sandwiches, and fillets on a Kaiser roll.

Tailgating graced the small stadium lot (4,000 cars). "In our new field [opening 2001]," McClatchy said, "it'll be more of an event." The Bucs augured a future $45 million payroll $v.$ '98's $13.7. It couldn't jump too soon. The '00ers finished 69–73. On Friday, September 29, Stargell was honored at the confluence. That Sunday 55,351 saw the Cubs close it, 10–9. Willie the Starge threw out the last first pitch. Sister Sledge sang the national anthem—or was it "We are Family"? A high-flyer in a jet-propelled backpack carted home plate to new PNC Park. "It's part of our continuity," mused McClatchy, "the ties that bind us back to when baseball first came to Pittsburgh."Upon its 2000 end Seattle's Kingdome imploded. Let's raise an Iron City to Three Rivers' '01 like demise.

RIVERFRONT STADIUM

Ask Pittsburgh. The 1976 Reds could hit, pitch, and lure—a record 2,629,708. Parts of the Machine then began leaving—Tony Perez '77, to Montreal; Pete Rose '79, to Philadelphia; Joe Morgan '80, to Houston. George Foster became '77 MVP: 52 homers and 149 RBI. Tom Seaver, acquired from New York, threw Cincinnati's first Riverfront no-hitter. Rose got hit 3,000. The Reds bided their longest-ever game: "We played 3½ innings," said Sparky Anderson, "and we had 3½ hours of rain delay." Game called: 12:47 A.M. Time per inning: 80.6 minutes. Cincy's bigs-best 66–42 record failed the '81 playoff. "It's unfair," bawled Foster. "Why penalize us because we didn't win either [half of the strike-spun split season]?" Uh, Reds management led the strike. A Riverfront record regular-season 53,790 honored Johnny Bench in 1983. Rose replaced Vern Rapp as [player/]manager. His first at-bat hymned a Golden Oldie. Charlie Hustle belly-flopped into third.

To many, Rose by now defined baseball. "Every day," said Morgan, "was his seventh game of the Series." An auto dealer named Marge Schott bought the club. Her '85ers pulled 1,834,619. On September 11, Cincy hosted San Diego. Pete led off the first. "Two-one pitch from [Eric] Show," Ken Wilson told a TV audience. "It's into left-center! There it is! Rose has eclipsed [Ty] Cobb [as baseball's hit leader]! That's hit 4,192! . . . This city [47,237] mobs its native son." The night sparked bottle rockets. Rose embraced son Pete. "Clear in the sky, I saw my dad, Harry Francis Rose, and Ty Cobb. Ty Cobb was like in the second row. Dad was in the first." *Time* magazine went yard: "It took Pete Rose two decades and more, just a blink and a nod on the eternal baseball schedule, but he has come to both a paramount moment in his game [passing Cobb on the 57th anniversary of Ty's last at-bat] and a place of moment in any enterprise. By the numbers and beyond them, he is what he does. Rose *is* baseball"—it seemed.

Charlie Hustle was born in Cincinnati. Dave Parker moved there as a child. In 1986, he slammed 31 taters. Riverfront hosted the '88 All-Star Game: AL, 2–1. That September Tom Browning became the first Red to hurl a perfect game. The game took 1:51—a lifetime to L.A. Browning was asked if President Reagan had called. "No, but he's from the West Coast. I guess he's a Dodger fan." Rose loved his sport's tradition: "Players who don't know its history got no business playing it." Ignorance, he said, cheapened baseball. A 1989 skeleton from the Reds' closet did.

The commissioner's office began to probe whether Rose had bet on baseball. "I would go into hell in a gasoline suit to play ball," Pete had said. Lawyers and detectives ferreted. The noose tightened. Rose's sanctuary was the game. A 1950s song said, "The music goes round and round." The August 3 Reds did: 14 runs and 16 hits in the first third of an inning. "Now I know what blitzkrieg is about," said Houston manager Art Howe. Records: most hits, singles (12), and batters with two hits in an inning (7). It could have been worse: Houston got the last two outs to leave the bases jammed.

Three weeks later Rose pled *nolo contendere* to gambling. Commissioner Bart Giamatti felt it conceded guilt, and banned Rose lifetime from the sport.

Some sniped good riddance. Many could not forget his career: 4,256 hits in 24 years; a bigs-record 3,562 games and 3,215 singles and 14,053 at-bats; NL high 746 doubles; and three batting titles. "His not entering the Hall of Fame," said Harry Caray, "is the worst thing that's ever happened." Among Cincy's best: 1990, starting 9–0. Eric Davis blasted 24 homers. Relievers Randy Myers, Rob Dibble, and Norm Charlton became "The Nasty Boys." Browning went 15–9. Riverfront now seated 52,392: 2,400,892 sat and often stood. On May 22, manager Lou Piniella intentionally walked a bigs-high seven Cubs. "Dawson [Andre, passed five times] wasn't going to beat us." Few did. The LCS v. Pittsburgh evoked '72: Four one-run games hinged on Reds defense. "We've shown America," said Piniella, "what Cincinnati fans have known all year."

Still, most thought the defending champion A's a dynasty—until Davis smacked a first-inning Game One hellion. Cincy won at Riverfront, 7–0 and 5–4. "What I remember is Mickey Hatcher," said Piniella, "tying the [second] game by scoring after his [Series record] seventh straight hit." The A's braced to revive in Oakland—until Cincinnati swept, 8–3 and 2–1. Hatcher levitated: .750. Jose Rijo won twice and had a 0.59 ERA. A week later the Reds visited the White House. Said President

Bush: "Maybe you [Rijo] can lower interest rates." Hope fell instead.

The '91ers lost 12 straight games. Schott had long treated dog Schottzie like a dear aunt or lost child. "Hell," said a player, "she put her in the team photo, lets dog shit stain the field, coos to her—sick." In 1993, baseball banned Schott for racial slurs. Browning fled Wrigley Field in uniform to watch from a nearby rooftop. "It's a long season. I couldn't take it any more," he said. Reds attendance fell. It became easier to get a second-level infield or upper-deck seat behind home plate. "Great sense of the action there," said writer Hal McCoy. Always available: Riverfront's top six rows, sold game day. A Sony JumboTron replaced two screens hung from the roof. Organ music recalled Brooklyn's Gladys Goodding.

Something old: Rhineland melts, brats, a cheese coney hot dog, and Cincinnati chili, drenched by Hudepohl-Schoenling's local beer. New: name, Cinergy Field (displacing Riverfront in 1997); numbers, retired on the outfield wall—1 (Fred Hutchinson), 5 (Bench), 8 (Morgan), 18 (Ted Kluszewski), 20 (Frank Robinson), 24 (Perez), and 42 (Jackie Robinson); grass, restored in 2001. Blue: In 1999, Sean Casey hit .332, Greg Vaughn belted 45 homers, and Barry Larkin became a 10-time All-Star, but Cincy lost a wild-card playoff game: 5–0, Mets. Borrowed: baseball's Valentino, arriving from Seattle. "I can't wait to be where my dad played [and now coached]," said Ken Griffey Jr.

Ticket lines queued around the block. Griffey counseled prudence: "I'm not the new Big Red Machine." He was right: The 2000 Reds placed second. By now, their next home—The Great American Ball Park—was rising next to Cinergy—"so close," said Griffey, "that they got to cut distances and remove seats from left to right-center field." Capacity fell to 39,000. Lines and alleys became 325 and 371 feet, respectively. A 32-foot-high wall was put in dead center (now 393, not 404). "The problem," noted Cox News Service, "then became that the wall isn't high enough to make a complete backdrop for hitters trying to pick up the ball out of the pitcher's hand." The wall became 40 feet, topping Fenway as baseball's highest. Said Cox: "It will be the biggest, baddest wall in all of ball."

The Machine had been biggest, baddest, too. You could almost hear Sparky chanting: "It never occurred to me that we might lose."

VETERANS STADIUM

"**L**ook only at the facts," Bertrand Russell said. Facts vexed in the year that baseball stopped. The '81 Phillies drew less than 2 million for the first time since 1975. The Carpenter family sold the team. The split season bore the Intradivisional Series; no game v. Montreal drew more than 47,384. In 1787, Ben Franklin compared a rising and setting sun. Rising: Steve Carlton, first lefty to K 3,000; Mike Schmidt's encore MVP 31 homers and 91 RBI; and Pete Rose's league-high 140 hits. On August 10, Rose's 3,161st hit hailed the Strike's end before 60,561 at Veterans Stadium. "Not bad," Pete mused of his NL record, passing Stan Musial, "but the big one's ahead"—Ty Cobb's 4,191.

In 1983, the Phils turned 100. Their starting lineup totaled 301 years. Joe Morgan and Tony Perez joined Rose. "We're the Wheez [not Whiz] Kids," said Little Joe. Rasping, they took the East. If it ain't broke: Schmidt (homering) and Lefty (with Al Holland) won the play-off opener, 1–0. L.A. answered: 4–1. Philly then took Games Three and Four, 7–2. "We've got as many pennants [two in five years] since I've been here," boasted Rose, "as they had [in the prior 95 years]." The Phillies also won the "I-95" Series opener, 2–1. (Baltimore promptly took four straight.) Rose hiked to Montreal. Garry Maddox retired with eight Gold Gloves. Carlton took his 241–161 Phils record to San Francisco. The Vet expanded to 66,271. Also swelling: Schmidt, eight times leading in NL homers. In 1986, the Dayton Flyer won a 10th Gold Glove, led for the final time in taters and RBI, and earned his third MVP.

"Once he threw wildly to first base," recalled Richie Ashburn, "raced over there, got the return throw [from the first baseman], and tagged the runner who overran the bag." On April 4, 1987, off Don Robinson, perhaps the best-ever third baseman became the 14th big leaguer to whack 500 homers. "You couldn't write a more perfect script," he said of his two-out, three-run, ninth-inning blast to beat Pittsburgh, 8–6. "When you're a little kid playing ball each day, this is the kind of thrill you dream of." By 1988, only Schmidt remained from the '80 Phils. He retired with 548 homers—then-seventh all time. The team later retired Mike's 20 (also Ashburn 1, Carlton 32, and Robin Roberts 36).

Rising/setting. The '88–89ers finished last. In 1990, Len Dykstra led the NL in hits (192). Terry Mulholland pitched the Vet's first no-hitter. "When it rains," he laughed, "it pours": Tommy Greene no-hit Montreal in '91. Capacity fell to 62,382. 'Ninety-three attendance hit 3,137,674. Out of the blue Philly won the East. Dykstra's 143 runs led the league. Atlanta took a 2–1 game playoff edge. The Quakers countered, 2–1, 4–3, and 6–3. For a time the Series parodied the LCS: Toronto led, two games to one. Ahead, 14–9, the Phils lost Match Four, 15–14, and ultimately the Classic. "I've seen better baseball," said columnist Phil Mushnick, "in Little League."

In 1995, Jim Eisenreich hit .361. Scott Rolen became '97 Rookie of the Year. Attendance dropped to a lowest-since-'73 1,490,638. One thrice-delayed game ended at 4:40 A.M. Another night the Phillie Phanatic invaded a broadcast booth, climbed on the ledge, and mugged his way around the stadium. It cost $120 to propose marriage on the scoreboard. A new downtown park would cost more.

"It's [more revenue] the only way we can compete," said former President Bill Giles. "Our fans are tough, knowledgeable, loyal, the best in baseball. They deserve better"—place, and team. In 1999, fans named the '80 Series their most abiding memory. (Rose was later barred from a reunion.) That September the Reds pounded an NL-record nine homers in a game. The 2000 Phillies again placed last. Under *tease*: The '0lers held first place in June. Franklin's "long, hot summer" now seemed tropical. The sun set behind Philly's sad-sack bowl.

ARLINGTON STADIUM

It had already for several parks. At Arlington, a huge Lone Star State–shaped scoreboard rimmed the stadium from one pole to another. Billboards seemed as numerous as miles in west Texas. The seventh-inning stretch blared "Cotton Eye Joe." The Diamond Vision's *William Tell Overture* evoked TV's *Lone Ranger*. Before the game and between innings the Ranger galloped across the screen. A Lady Ranger escorted guests to their section. They might recall Mickey Rivers '81 (.330) or Charlie Hough '80–'90 (knuckling to 139–123) or Larry Parrish '82 (grand-slamming a bigs-high thrice in one week). The scoreboard base stood 512 feet from the plate. In '86, Parrish, Pete O'Brien, and Pete Incaviglia took aim. The Rangers finished second. The gate burst to 1,692,002.

In 1989, a group led by the then-U.S. president's eldest son, George W. Bush, bought the team. Ruben Sierra led the AL in RBI, triples, total bases, and slugging. Attendance broke 2 million—the first of five straight years. In 480 B.C., Pindar wrote: "Words have a longer life than deeds." He never met Nolan Ryan.

Ryan entered Cooperstown July 25, 1999. His career evoked a Pecos Brigadoon: 27 seasons, 324–292, and 5,714 Ks. Six times he fanned 300, including '73's 383. He struck out 1,176 different *players*, including 21 Hall of Famers. Ryan first pitched for Texas in April 1989. On August 22, lost in thought, he drove past Arlington Stadium, U-turned his car, greeted Commissioner Bart Giamatti, and thrilled the park's second-largest crowd (42,869, v. July 23, 1983's 43,705. Its smallest: 2,513, September 21, 1973).

At 8:32 P.M. Central Time, Ryan fanned Rickey Henderson for strike-out 5,000. Broadcaster Merle Harmon called the K. "To get 5,000, a pitcher would have to average 250 a year for 20 years, and it ain't gonna happen. I had laser prints made of my score sheets and had every player and umpire in the game sign it." Later, partner Mark Holtz left through the Rangers dressing room. Ryan was alone riding the stationary bicycle. "Nolan, I can't believe you're not out celebrating!" he gaped. Ryan smiled: "Mark, I'm in my forties and if I don't ride this bicycle, I won't get ready for my next start. I got to ride a bike for 45 minutes after everybody else leaves the day I pitch."

In 1990, Ryan pitched victory 300. Next year No. 34 fanned 16 *v.* Toronto for his record seventh and last no-hitter. Sniped the Jays' Joe Carter: "This should be illegal." Ryan topped the AL with fewest hits per game (5.31). The Express retired in 1993. "It's time," he said, "to give up the ghost. Let the younger kids try." Juan Gonzalez's 46 homers led the American League. On October 3, the Rangers lost their last game at Arlington Stadium, 7–4, to Kansas City before a record day crowd (41,074). Ahead lay The Ballpark in Arlington. Few would confuse the two.

MUNICIPAL STADIUM

Did you hear the one? In 1964, Indians outfielder Chico Salmon knocked Don Zimmer's drive through a hole in Cleveland's right-field wall. "I touched it," he said. "I just couldn't catch it." Another hit: '74's "Discount Beer Night." The Tribe tied the score in the ninth. After hundreds rushed the field the umpires forfeited the game. Fog postponed another match. "That's what you get," said Boston's Dennis (Oil Can) Boyd of Municipal Stadium, "when you build a ballpark by the ocean."

To reach it, you walked or took a cab or shuttle bus ¼ mile past train tracks and empty buildings to the north rim from Public Square. Semicircle stands rose from the parking lot. A white facade covered the park's outer shell. In three places the shell became a ticket booth. Atop one booth mascot Chief Wahoo loomed, bat and face cocked. Entering, you found a concession stand—"specialties: pizza and fish sandwiches," a writer said—and passed grime and debris to the picnic area (formerly, garden) behind center field. An old-timer might find numbers changed: alleys, 400 feet ('65), 390, 395 ('68), 385, and 391 ('91); center, 408 ('66), 407, 410, 400, 415 ('90), and 404 ('92).

"Best place to see the game is behind home plate and along first- and third bases in upper and lower decks," wrote *Sports Illustrated*. "Ramps to upper decks are very steep and it's a long climb for most people. If you sit in the center field bleachers, bring along . . . binoculars. You'll be a long way from home plate." The *Plain Dealer* added: "What a wonderful place. You start with a bleacher seat. By the fifth you grab a box." Ushers were as drowsy as the never-above-fourth '69–'93ers. In 1970, Detroit's Cesar Gutierrez went 7-for-7. The gate bottomed at '71's 591,361. Twelve managers got a pink slip, not gold watch. On April 8, 1975, baseball's first black (player/) manager, Frank Robinson, homered in his first at-bat.

Gaylord Perry won 24 games in 1972. Joe Carter thrice topped 100 RBI. In 1993, Albert Belle fused 38 homers and a league-high 129 ribbies. "That's it," said announcer Herb Score, "all we had to show for thirty years in the wilderness." A data processor, John Adams, sat in the bleachers and beat an old wooden drum in splendid isolation. "This is a fantasyland," he said. "It's a magic place where I can escape. If I didn't have this thing"—the drum—"I'd still come." Boston's Carl Yastrzemski had, shall we say, a different take: "I hate this place. All I hear is that damned pounding drum."

Talk heightened of a move. The city finally OKd a new park—ultimately, named Jacobs Field. Capacity dropped to a final 74,483. Pitchers Steve Olin and Tim Crews died in a '93 boating accident. The cement hulk housed its final game: White Sox, 4–0, before 72,390. It was razed in 1998 for the reborn NFL Browns' new home. "Tear Fenway down, and there'd be a riot," said Score. "Knock Wrigley, and you'll go to jail. Not Municipal," shunning hope in the dreary lakeside somnolence.

COMISKEY PARK

In 1981, Carlton Fisk joined the White Sox. "This [team] was baseball's Rodney Dangerfield," said owner Jerry Reinsdorf. "No respect. Carlton changed the way people saw us." Rookie Ron Kittle hit 35 dingers in '83. La Marr Hoyt went 24–10. Manager Tony LaRussa coined "Winning Ugly." Comiskey Park hosted the All-Star Game: AL, 13–3. "Some night," said Chicago native Fred Lynn, smacking the Game's first grandslam. "Fifty years to the day [July 6] since the series started here, and we break our 11–game losing streak." The Sox clinched the West on September 17, 1983.

Baltimore took a 2–1 game lead in the best-of-five playoff. On October 8, 45,477 South Siders tried to stay execution. Chicago had 10 hits and no runs through nine innings. O's reserve Tito Landrum then homered into the wind. "It hurt," Fisk said of the 3–0 loss. "But we figured we'd get back." Remember 1917–'19: Sox polarity rivaled Sybil's. Detroit's Jack Morris no-hit the Hose. Fisk's 37 set a bigs mark for catcher homers in a year. The '86–'89ers fell to fifth and seventh. Comiskey turned eighty July 1, 1990: New York's Andy Hawkins lost a 4–0 no-hitter. Steve Lyons was even stranger. One night he reached first base. Forgetting his place and mind, the Sox infielder began to pull down his pants to remove loose dirt. Thousands gasped. Lyon's face reddened. A nickname—"Psycho"—rose.

Mercifully, Closing Day neared. Comiskey turned dowager: loose wires, chipped asphalt, broken floors. Diamond Vision anchored the scoreboard, as dissonant as the wave at Wrigley Field. Paint mimed makeup on a weary face. In 1990, the park brooked a record 7-hour, 23-minute rain delay. "The Rangers weren't coming back, the Sox were in a pennant race," said writer Jerome Holtzman, "and they didn't want to move the game to Texas." The game was postponed. On September 30, the Baseball Palace dimmed: Sox 2, Seattle 1, before 42,849. "THANKS for the Memories," read the board. "Comiskey Park, 1910–90."

Joni Mitchell sang, "They paved paradise to put up a parking lot." A garage fills the lot where Little Looie, the Mighty Mite, and Old Aches and Pains shared a city's joy, worries, and confessions of the heart.

MEMORIAL STADIUM

Return to a mid-'80s Seat Cushion Night. TV cameras panned Memorial Stadium. P.A. mikeman Rex Barney said, "OK, hold up your seat cushions." At that point player-turned-broadcaster John Lowenstein threw his cushion toward the field. Like lemmings, a good part of the crowd tossed theirs. Play was stopped, and Brother Lo scolded. It was a feeling with which the last-place '86ers could identify. On September 14, 1987, the Blue Jays smacked a bigs-record 10 homers v. Baltimore. The '88 Birds lost 21 straight games to start the year. The streak topped the '06 Red Sox and the 1916 and '43 A's: "What I remember," said Barney, "is how people stood by us. [50,402 packed Fantastic Fans Night.]" It was like '54 again—except that now the region cared. The '89ers reversed flow, placing second. Cal Ripken's '91 river ran through 34 homers, 114 RBI, and league-high 368 total bases.

In June 1989, the Orioles broke ground on Orioles Park at Camden Yards. On Sunday, October 6, 1991, Detroit won, 7–1: Cal banged into a Memorial-closing double play. Postgame started. A chauffeured limousine removed home plate and carted it downtown. Since 1955, Chuck Thompson had covered the O's. "The field was cleared. First, the background music began from 'Field of Dreams' [over the P.A. system]. Then Brooks [Robinson] emerged from the dugout to take his position at third base—followed by Frank [Robby] in the outfield, followed by Jim Palmer. This is how the Orioles said good-bye to Memorial Stadium—asking all former players to come back to Baltimore. The crowd didn't know, hadn't expected, this. When it happened, they were stunned."

More than 75 players trotted to their position in period unies. "Scattered around the field—no introduction, just music, and that music kept rolling. I looked with binoculars at fellows like Brooks and Boog Powell—and they were, like me, drained. It was hard to keep from breaking down completely. The thing is there was no cheering—none. Instead, thunderous applause—and enough tears for a river."

Later, walking to his car, Thompson saw a sea of red-eyed love. "There's no crying in baseball" daubs art, not life.

SkyDome

Frank O'Connor, the Irish writer, told how, as a boy, he and his friends explored the countryside. Often they came to an arched wall. If it seemed too high, or hard to hurdle, they removed their caps and flung them over the wall. They then had no choice but to follow them. Toronto's SkyDome forced baseball to follow. Its terminus: the world's first stadium with a retractable roof.

"This showed the future," said architect Roderick Robbie, creating SkyDome with project engineer Michael Allen and Toronto-based engineers. Domed stadia kept out bad weather. By contrast, fans wanted out during July's sun and breeze. The riddle piqued the Stadium Corporation of Toronto. Its answer flung caps over the '90s: a car with a convertible top. "A roof that opens gives you the best of both worlds," crowed the Toronto *Globe and Mail*. It debuted June 5, 1989: 43,378 crowded the circular 50,016-seat, five-tiered four-paneled orb. First pitcher: Jimmy Key. Batter/hit: Brewers' Paul Molitor. Homer: Jays' Fred McGriff. Score: Milwaukee, 5–3. Few noted the AstroTurf/sliding pits/symmetrical 328, 375, and 400 field. The crowd's something on the brain was size.

The apex reached 310 feet (the Kingdome's was 250, Astrodome 208, Metrodome 186, and Big O 172). A 31-story building, 516 elephants, or eight Boeing 747s could fit inside. SkyDome's concrete would form a sidewalk from St. Louis to Toronto. The roof alone weighed 11,000 tons, enough to build 3,772 cars, and presaged cable TV's *Home Improvement*. More than two hours before the game two large panels began sliding toward the north end. A third section crossed the perimeter to nest inside. The process took barely 20 minutes, and cost $500 Canadian. "When the roof is opened," said Michael Allen, "91 percent of the seats are exposed to the sky." Open, sesame, however, could fan. The first home stand it began to rain. The Jays shut the roof, which jammed without closing. "There we are," said announcer Tom Cheek. "It's raining only on the batter, catcher, and umpire. The game was postponed." Another night millions of gnats invaded. Umpire Don Denkinger ordered the top closed. The bugs were not a monkey wrench: Toronto loved its new-age digs.

That first year McGriff hit 36 dingers. The Jays drew an AL-record 3,375,883. On September 30, NBC-TV aired its 981st and final "Game of the Week" at SkyDome. The Jays' 4–3 AL East clincher over Baltimore ended baseball's TV arcade. Oakland vaulted to a 2–0 game LCS advantage. Toronto's Jimmy Key then won, 7–3. A day later Jose Canseco became the first to reach the fifth deck: A's, 6–5. They won in five. 'Ninety's Dave Stewart and Dave Stieb, respectively, threw Sky-Dome's and Toronto's first no-hitters. Attendance leapt to a bigs-record 3,885,284. "Like the Dodgers," marveled then-President Paul Beeston, "you couldn't get a seat."

Most took the Young-University-Spadina subway to Front and Bay Streets. Others rode a bus, peddled (tracks housed bicycles), or drove (14,000 lots rimmed the park). The CN Tower—"the world's tallest free-standing structure," read brochures—dwarfed the area. Baseball artwork marked the facade. Inside walkway art scrawled worker names. SkyDome hosted the '91 All-Star Game: AL, 4–2. The Jays cracked 4 million: a big-league first. On October 2, Joe Carter's two-run, ninth-frame single gained entrée to the LCS (another four-game defeat). "Some home-field edge," said manager Cito Gaston. "We lose all three [games at SkyDome] against the Twins, like '89."

By contrast, '92's cap cleared the wall. Dave Winfield, 40, left California to knock in 108 runs—baseball's oldest 100-RBI man. Jack Morris, 21–6, fled Minnesota. The Jays' 10 straight hits *v.* the Twins tied an AL high. On October 14, Juan Guzman waved the Jays' first flag, 9–2, over Oakland. The Series v. Atlanta began badly, 3–1. Ed Sprague's ninth-frame dinger took Game Two, 5–4. The Jays came home: an umpiring muff blew their triple play; Candy Maldonado's hit beat the Braves, 3–2; 51,813 saw the Classic's first non-U.S. game. Key won, 2–1. Atlanta replied, 7–2, at SkyDome. Avenging ex-Angel Winfield doubled for a 4–3 Game Six/11th-inning/Series-winning blow.

"Some people didn't like a Canadian team winning the Series," said Gaston. They liked 1993 less. For the first time three mates ranked 1-2-3 in batting: John Olerud, Paul Molitor, and Roberto Alomar. On September 26, 50,518 raised SkyDome attendance to a still-AL high 4,057,947. The Jays again made the Series. Act One: Toronto, 8–5, Al Leiter winning. Two: Philly, 6–4. Three: Jays, 10–3, behind Pat Hentgen. Act Four combined T-ball and *Kansas City Bomber*. "There's the score [Jays, 15–14], time [Series record 4:14], and records [29 runs]," Cheek mused. Exhausted hitters skipped Game Five: Phils, 2–0. The Classic returned north. Again balls splattered around the Dome. Toronto fronted, 5–1. Philly rallied, 6–5. Mitch Williams began the Jays' ninth by walking Rickey Henderson. Molitor singled an out later. Carter lashed "Wild Thing" 's would-be third strike down the left-field line over the 10-foot canvas fence. Jays win! Carter leapt wildly around the bases. Hockey's heart had become baseball's capital.

"It won't last," said Maple Leafs president Cliff Fletcher, correctly. It was a gas at the time. Right-center's 115-by-33 foot JumboTron forged the world's biggest video display board. "To eat is human," said Charles I. Copeland, "to digest divine." Cuisine seemed sacramental. The Sight Lines Club restaurant topped center field. The Hard Rock Cafe graced deep right. The 650-seat Windows on SkyDome offered tickets, lunch or dinner, and homers clanking off Plexiglas. Take your pick: corned beef, Italian sausage, and Chicago Gyros. Molson's and Labatt's beer filled tap and bottle. North America's largest McDonald's berthed the 11-story, on-site, 348-room SkyDome Hotel. Seventy rooms overlooked the field. One couple forgot to close the blinds. "They're making love," said Cheek. "Forget my radio. The park is focused on *their* play-by-play."

Debit: No grass or bleachers. "[Fifth-level] seats were so steep you could get nose-bleed," a writer said. No grass or bleachers hurt. On TV, the high home-plate camera made players look like specks. Asset: SkyDome was huge, multipurpose (seats circle, not flank, the lines), yet more intimate than, say, Seattle. "There's so much to keep you busy," chimed Allen. "You don't have to like baseball to be entertained." It worked till the '94ers placed last, had their first losing year since 1982, and bore the strike. "It hurt every city," said Beeston. "Because we were at the top and didn't have other towns' baseball roots, it hurt us worse." Suddenly, you could get tickets minutes before a game.

In 1995, two 30-pound roof tiles fell and hurt seven patrons. "This was a hitter's park, with the AstroTurf and gaps," said general manager Gord Ash. Now pitching reared. Hentgen won the '96 Cy Young. (Also, Roger Clemens '97–'98—the only pitcher ever to win five. He then skedaddled to New York). Shawn Green hammered 42 homers and was traded to L.A. A year later David Wells won 20 games. Carlos Delgado bound .344, 41, and 137. Six other Jays had 20 or more blasts—Tony Batista (41), Brad Fullmer (32), Jose Cruz (31), Raul Mondesi (24), Shannon Stewart (21), and Darrin Fletcher (20). Attendance crashed to 1,819,886. Large pieces of metal siding and insulation fell from the roof, postponing an '01 game. Boston's Manny Ramirez bombed SkyDome's longest homer—491 feet. The Jays were no longer Chavez East.

"The city seems to have developed a take-it-or-leave-it attitude toward everything but the beloved Maple Leafs," columnist Stephen Brunt wrote. "The novelty value of the stadium fully wore off. Ticket availability led to more ticket availability—no reason to buy ahead if you know you can always walk up and get a seat." Said Jays marketer Terry Zuk: "[SkyDome] was built at the height of big buildings. We missed the wave [Camden Yards] by three years."

The *Globe and Mail* observed: "The roof has become the Jays' symbol—is it open, or closing?" No matter. Baseball would never double back to before its cap neared the wall.

COMISKEY PARK II

The White Sox' abode is Eddie Fisher, who had and then lost Elizabeth Taylor; Richard Nixon and Bill Clinton, throwing greatness in the can; and ESPN founder Bill Rasmussen, who sold his network before the getting was truly good. Put another way, the new Comiskey Park *could* have been Camden Yards. As we shall see, the Yards "restored the faith in the future of baseball architecture," wrote Ron Fimrite, "a craft dis-honored in the 1960s and early '70s by the erection of all those symmet-rical look-alike multi-purpose stadiums." We know the old Comiskey Park. The old Comiskey was a friend of ours. The new is not the old—and surely not Camden Yards.

Revisit the late 1980s. Sox owners Eddie Einhorn and Jerry Reinsdorf yearned to move to western Florida. Illinois governor James Thompson lent a caring ear: "I will bleed and die before I let the Sox leave Chicago." The first baseball-only park since Royals Stadium '73 soon bloomed across the street from old Comiskey '10–'90. Like Camden, Comiskey II was designed by HOK Sport. One became baseball's K-Mart—the other, its Bloomingdale's. "Comiskey opened 12 months earlier," said Bob Costas. "Given how they look, you'd think 12 years." The difference: vision. Camden looked forward, the South Side park, back.

Comiskey aped Royals' curved (8-foot-tall) fence, pleasant feel, and symmetrical shape: lines, 347 feet; alleys, 383 (375 in '92); center (400). The Sox copied Comiskey I's grass (eight different strands), center-field exploding scoreboard (140 by 30 feet), and rose-colored precast con-crete exterior. Brick arches evoked its windows. "Old Comiskey's open-ings brought the neighborhood into the park," said Bill Veeck's son Mike. "You saw outside. The new [park] kept the neighborhood out"—gas stations, parking lots, and homes. The $135 million cabash bound a glass-enclosed Stadium Club, diapering stations in men's rest rooms, and Comiskey, Sr.'s infield dirt. Two tiers wrapped around the plate beyond each foul line. A single bleacher deck connected them. Hitters liked the blue backdrop in center field. "It had everything," mused Veeck, "but a soul."

Seats abutted Camden's left-field fence. "It's great," said then-O's head Larry Lucchino. "Fans and fielders fighting for balls." Comiskey's stood six feet behind the fence. Said a Sox official: "We want to keep specta-tors from interfering"—but why? No field-level boxes sat behind home plate: the center-field TV shot lacked personality. Worst was Comiskey's steep upper deck. "Old Comiskey had poles, which pushed upper-deck seats toward the field," Michael Gershman. "New Comiskey didn't have any. Seats were so far back as to be useless for viewing." Climb the second-deck grandstand. II's *first* row was *farther* from the plate than I's *last* row—and top seat almost *twice* as high above the field. Old Comiskey's roof enclosed the park. "The new roof was smaller," said Veeck, "didn't wrap you back to the field." Also absent: Camden's varied fences, short and long distances, in-play boards with varied angles, and carnival around the park. Said an early Comiskey visitor: "It feels like going to the library."

Eighty residential buildings crumbled to build new Comiskey. Its frame rose during I's last year. A '91 wrecking ball doomed the relic. "Many a happy day I spent in this place. I thought it would be here forever," confessed an 80-year-old regular. "I'm a grown man and I almost want to cry." On April 18, 1991, 44,702 (capacity 44,321) attended Opening Day. Thompson hurled the first ball. First pitcher: Jack McDowell. Batter: Detroit's Tony Phillips. Hit and homer: Tigers' Alan Trammell and Cecil Fielder, respectively. They led, 16–0, by the fourth (final score). Frank Thomas clubbed the Hose's first home tater. Wilson Alvarez no-hit the Orioles in his first bigs start. Attendance leapt from barely 2 million to a franchise high 2,934,154. The *New York Times* reporter Isabel Wilkerson shrugged. "If the old Comiskey was Luke Appling and Crackerjacks, a South Side Roman Coliseum, II is grilled chicken and frozen yogurt, a factory new Disneyland in a field of warehouses and bungalows."

The '93ers stormed the Matterhorn. Jack McDowell's 22 wins led the league. Thomas was voted MVP: 41 homers, 128 RBI, and .317. Carlton Fisk passed Bob Boone for most games caught. Bo Jackson's September 27 homer v. Seattle won the West. Prophetically, fewer—2,581,091—took the el, No. 35th Street bus, or Interstate 94 and Dan Ryan Expressway. The LCS opened at Comiskey: 7–3, Toronto. "[NBA Bulls owner] Jerry Reinsdorf chose that day to comment on Michael Jordan's supposed retirement," said ESPN's Peter Gammons. "The Cubs had always owned Chicago. Now the Sox were upstaging themselves"—losing the playoff, four games to two.

In 1994, Thomas became the first back-to-back AL MVP since Roger Maris '60–'61 (.353, 38, and 101; he later won a batting title and hit at least 35 homers five straight years). By '96 attendance fell to 1,676,403.

There goes the neighborhood: Albert Belle became baseball's first $10 million a year man in 1997. Nineteen Sox Kd v. Randy Johnson. Interleague play began: The Cubs jammed Comiskey. Its 90 sky boxes teemed, and six kennels bulged. Reinsdorf joked: "Sure, we take dogs. We try to serve everybody." The Bullpen Sports Bar mixed loyalty and ice. Said a bartender, "There were more Cub than Sox fans." The food court—Old Roman Plaza, after Charles Comiskey—sold lemon chill, frozen yogurt, and peanut butter sandwiches. Toothsome: Tex-mex, Maxwell Street–style pork chops, and grilled kosher hot dogs. "Too bad," said Einhorn, "we can't host the Cubs 81 times a year."

In 1998, Belle had .328, 49 homers, and 152 RBI. Magglio Ordonez bloomed a year later: .301, 30, and 117. Neither made Chicago their kind of town: The '99ers drew 1,338,351, or 17,616 per date. Said reliever Bill Simas: "The Cubs have something going that we don't have: atmosphere and location." Einhorn hinted he might demolish part of the "incredibly steep upper deck," said Associated Press, "that is [perhaps] better suited for skiers and mountain goats."

Posthaste the Hose won the '00 West. James Baldwin finished 14–7. Ordonez had 126 ribbies. Thomas big-hurt the league: .328, 43, and 143. The Sox linked a club-record 216 dingers and 978 runs, drew 1,947,799, or 841,722 less than Chicago's NL diadem, and lost the LCS to Seattle. The '01ers lost 29 their first 43 games. Oakland's Eric Chavez hit Comiskey's longest homer, an estimated 500 feet, over the right-field seats.

By then Einhorn announced his facelift: shorter fences (left, 330; left-center, 377; center, 400; right-center, 372; and right, 335); bleachers rimming the outfield wall; and seats stripped from the upper deck. Go further! Soxaphiles taunted him. Put boxes behind the plate, make the outfield quirky, tear the upper deck in half, and look to the south and east.

Andy Griffith once wrote a monologue, "What It Was, Was Football." What Comiskey Might Have Been sold out nightly in Baltimore.

BACK TO
THE FUTURE
1992–2000

20

BEEN TO CANAAN

Ignore intimacy! Make *us* a cookie-cutter! cities blared in the late 1960s and 1970s. It is clear that baseball did not realize what it had. For two decades multipurpose plots entombed the Pastime. Then, with hope blearier than the '62 Mets, an unlikely savior rose.

From 1954 to '91, the Baltimore Orioles played in a place of vanilla look and feel. Built for the transplanted Browns, Memorial Stadium paled like yellow B movies. "They didn't want them good, they wanted them Tuesday," said a bromide of the time. Right about Hollywood, it conveyed the Birds' roost, too.

Memorial Stadium was uncovered, double-decked, horseshoe shaped, and aped a football bowl. Few saw then how with play-by-play cloaking Baltimore—on summer nights, with car windows down, you could drive by front stoops and candy stores and not miss a pitch—its new park would become the Ebbets Field of baseball's 1990s U-turn.

Ironically, Eden stemmed from the NFL. In March 1984, its Colts skipped Baltimore for Indianapolis. Stunned, the Maryland Stadium Authority vowed to keep the city's once-second sport. "The Colts had owned the town," said *Washington Post* writer Richard Justice. "Now baseball was all it had." The O's promptly spurned cookie-cutters. "The message from the Chesapeake Bay was clear from the outset," said chief architect Joseph Spear of Helmuth, Obata and Kassabaum (HOK Sport). "What the Orioles and the Authority had in common in doing was to set a new standard."

The new park flew largely from the Birds' then-president. Larry Lucchino had grown up in Pittsburgh. "I loved Forbes Field," he said. "I'd seen how the Pirates suffered when they left it for Three Rivers." Some in Baltimore wanted a new baseball-football stadium. The Orioles refused. "We saw that the franchises that were the most successful, the ones that were truly great," mused Lucchino, "all had baseball-only facilities."

HOK Sport agreed. In 1983, a small group of architects had founded the firm. "The idea was laughed at," said Spear, who designed '73's Royals Stadium. "That an architectural company could thrive by designing only sports facilities." By 1988, revenue passed $7 million. That year HOK's 19,500-seat Pilot Field opened in Buffalo. It screamed elan, fit into downtown's grid of urban alleys, and set a Class AAA attendance record. "They walk into a town and spend time there before they give you anything," said Indians senior vice president Bob DiBiasio. "Rather than handing you some boilerplate stadium that they want to build you, they look at the architecture in a city and the landscape of a city, and they work off it." Practice makes perfect: Pilot presaged Camden Yards.

Ironically, HOK's initial design resembled Comiskey Park's. Lucchino hated it. "We said we don't want that kind of facility. We want to do something that is distinctive, that is more like a traditional old ball-park"—but where? Lucchino, O's owner Edward Bennett Williams, and then-Mayor William Donald Schaefer wanted downtown. HOK looked at more than two dozen baseball-only sites in and around Baltimore. "The public was asked for input," said Spear. "Ultimately, we thought if the park was downtown, people would make a day of it." That summer, the O's razed an 85-acre parcel parallel to turn-of-the-century trolley tracks, near the historic Camden Railroad station of the Old Baltimore and Ohio, a short fly ball from the Inner Harbor.

"That's really its genius," said Michael Gershman. "For once, they didn't build it at the intersection of two interstates. It was built in the city. The city was part of the ballpark. The ballpark was part of the city."

Thirteen big-league parks opened in the next decade. Each pined to match Oriole Park at Camden Yards.

"Like magic, the clout makes the clouds roll by," said a 1920s newsreel. "The Bambino is back. The season rushes on."

Like magic, the Yard—few call it "Oriole Park"—opened April 6, 1992. First ball: President George Bush, saying, "Baseball is the most democratic sport. Of course, it's also the most republican," bounced it on a hop. First pitcher: Rick Sutcliffe. Batter: Indians' Kenny Lofton. Hit: Tribe's Paul Sorrento (also, the first homer, two days later). Score: Orioles, 2–0. I sat in the upper deck and inhaled nouveau and tradition. "It is the best plan for a major league baseball park," said the *New York Times*' Paul Goldberger, "in more than a generation." *Time* magazine termed the Yard "one of the 10 best designs of 1992." My view was more prosaic: Here was the perfect park.

Let Oakland's seats half-circle the foul lines. Camden's squeezed them like fuzz on a tick's ear. Let Veterans suffer wall height uniformity. The Yard morphed 7 (left and center) into 25 (in-play right-field board). At Riverfront, a no-man's land split the seats and inner fence. Camden's left-field bleachers met the wall. "About a dozen times a year," said Lucchino, "you'll see fielders reach into the stands and grab a homer." At the Astrodome, fences gently curved. The Yard began at 333 (left), receded gradually to 364 (left-center), jumped to 410 (deepest left-center) and center (400), ebbed to right-center (375), and dropped off the shelf (318, right). Columnist John Steadman measured left-center field at 352, center 397, and right-center 363. Let cookie-cutters plant phony turf. Maryland bluegrass gleamed. Foul territory was minute. Pitchers termed Camden a homer palace. Actually, the palace crowned the game.

In 1781, French general Le Comte de Rochembeau and his troops camped there en route to Yorktown. Throngs camped in 1992 at the then-46,500-seat park. On June 22, the Yard boasted its 12th straight sellout. The O's counted 3,567,819 paid v. '91's 2,552,753. The stadium lot housed 5,000 cars. Another 30,000 lay nearby. Baltimore Metro plunked fans at Camden Station. Some sailed to Inner Harbor Marina, three blocks away. All entered through wrought-iron gates and arched portals. Memorial Stadium was hot dogs, National Bohemian beer, stripper Blaze Star, and jazz. Camden was less rowdy than a baseball carny. "They took the best of the old parks," hailed Brooks Robinson, "and put it into one."

An arched red-brick facade mimed old Comiskey Park. Left field was triple-tiered like Yankee Stadium. Right-center seats echoed Fenway's. The center scoreboard and ivied backdrop leapt from Mr. Cub. The right-field wall recalled Carl Furillo playing caroms at Ebbets Field. "Its scoreboard is emblematic of the park," said Gershman. "Camden's is traditional," linking ads, blurbs, and out-of-town scores. A standing-room area topped it. Behind right and center the longest building on the eastern seaboard, the 1,016-foot-long and 51-foot-wide 1898 brick B&0 Railroad Warehouse, enfolded the park, like houses around Wrigley Field.

"Some wanted to tear it down," said columnist and O's board member George Will. "Instead, they refurbished it [housing sports bars, eateries, souvenir stores, and O's offices]. It became part of the park, made Camden seem intimate." Between the park and Warehouse a 60-foot promenade extended Eutaw Street. You could shop, read brass plates denoting homers, and imagine balls hitting the building, 432 feet from the plate. (Ken Griffey, Jr., finally struck it in the '93 All-Star Game Home Run Derby. The AL won the game, 9–3.). Smoke wafted from Eutaw's Boog's Barbecue. "Hell, at my age," said Powell, 60, in 2001, "what better than to talk a little ball, cook beef, and make some bucks?"

Disraeli said, "What we anticipate seldom occurs. What we least expected generally happens." Unexpectedly, Camden went back/forward to real ball. Back: Babe Ruth's birthplace lies two blocks from the park. Plow center field and find the ex-406 Conway Street site of a saloon, Ruth's Cafe, owned by Babe's father. (A large Ruth statue showed the Babe wrongly wearing a *right*-handed fielder's glove). Light banks rose from the roof (and warehouse). Each aisle seat wore an 1890s Orioles logo. An upper-deck sun roof ringed the plate from left field to the right-field corner. Beyond center the skyline embraced the park. "It's like

Ebbets and Wrigley," said Steadman. "The community *becomes* the team." P.A. announcer Rex Barney moved from Memorial Stadium, his "Thank youuuu!" a rite.

Forward: The hard-of-hearing could dial "hearing assistance channels" at their seats. The playing field sat 16 feet below street level. A double-faced clock, seen from outside and inside the park, topped the right-center field board. In left-center, double-tiered pens showed relievers warming up. A grounds crew shed lay in front of the bleachers. "What a great ground rule," said O's then-voice Jon Miller. "Balls hitting the roof and bouncing back onto the field were a homer."

A Baltimorean wanted to know: Could Camden's witching power prove catching? The '92ers won 22 more games than 1991. Mike Mussina's .783 percentage (18–5) led the league. A year later Cal Ripken passed Ernie Banks for most homers by a shortstop (278). More vitally, Peter Angelos bought the club for a record $173 million. In 1994, the O's and Angels bombed a then-record 11 homers: Baltimore, 14–7. Mickey Spillane's Mike Hammer said: "I'll make a note." Ripken played his 2,000th game.

On September 6, 1995, ESPN visited the Yard for another O's-Halos shebang. The Angels were retired in the fifth inning; at which point the game turned official; whereupon the crowd went nuts. "We were just coming out of the strike," said Miller, "and baseball needed some good news"—Ripken's 2,131st successive game, passing Gehrig. Repeatedly Cal tipped his cap. Applause deafened. Finally mates Rafael Palmeiro and Bobby Bonilla yanked him from the dugout to begin a hand-shaking/high-fiving peregrination around the park. The warehouse banner changed from "2-1-3-0." Cal also homered: O's, 4–2. In time, he returned to third base after 2,216 straight games. "What's left?" a reporter asked. "Win a pennant," Ripken said. The Birds' last: 1983.

They might have in '96. Eddie Murray hit his 500th dinger. The O's bombed a bigs-record 257: Brady Anderson 50, Palmeiro 39, Ripken 26, Roberto Alomar 22. The last week Alomar spit at umpire John Hirschbeck, was suspended, appealed, and homered to clinch the wild card. Baltimore won the Division Series in four games v. Cleveland. (Alomar singled and homered to tie and take the decider.) The O's then split Games One-Two of the LCS at New York. "We're going home," said Anderson. The Yanks proceeded to make the Yard seem less home than jail—5–2, 8–4, and 6–4. A year later the Birds won the East, jammed a record 3,711,132, beat Seattle in the Division Series, and lost the LCS to Cleveland.

On September 29, 1998, Ripken's streak ended at 2,632. "He came to me [before the O's last home game]," said manager Ray Miller, "and he said, 'That's it.' " The calendar stood still: Ripken batted .340 and got hit 3,000 in 1999 and 2000, respectively. Albert Belle joined Baltimore to hit for distance and snarl on command. The '99–'00ers fell to fourth. Before 2001—"too many bad teams," Steadman said of dwindling crowds—tickets seemed as elusive as a flag. Season tickets were capped at 27,500: A waiting list topped 8,000. Many tried scalping, or radio and TV. Save the team, what was there to beef about? (Perhaps Angelos' '01 moving home plate seven feet toward the backstop. It hurt the O's, not rivals: They hit only 8 homers in the first 19 games.) Not pizza, quesadillas, Chespaeake Bay crab cakes, and more than a dozen imported beers. Bad seats were rarer than an Orioles reliever who retired the side.

Each December the First Pitch event let you tour the park, visit Santa Claus, buy single-game tickets, and hail retired numbers: 4 (Earl Weaver), 5 (Brooks Robinson), 20 (Frank Robby), 22 (Jim Palmer), 33 (Eddie Murray), and soon 8 (Ripken). At Camden, each *game* still seemed like a first pitch. Baseball's U-turn endures.

THE BALLPARK IN ARLINGTON

Term Yankee Stadium baseball's most famous park; Wrigley, gorgeous; Brooklyn's Cathedral of the underdog, beloved. Camden may be its most *important*. "When all seemed lost," said Bob Costas, "along it came to knock into owners' heads why baseball thrives," spurning failure (fixed domes, fake turf, and homogeneity) for success (idiosyncrasy, closer-is-better, and smaller-brighter, woven into the community).

In 1991 Texas began a stab to match the Yard. The City of Arlington OK a half-cent sales tax hike to raise $135 million. Private cash would add another $56 million. The club hired HKS, Inc. (Dallas) and David M. Schwarz Architectural Services (Washington, D.C.). Their charge: a complex of two artificial lakes, Riverwalk area of shops and eateries, and Falstaff in the saddle of a park. "Other parks were built in a neighborhood," said then–general partner George W. Bush. "We put ours in the plains. Our thought was to build the neighborhood around the park." Building began April 2, 1992.

Camden Yards opened four days later. Ronald Reagan: "How do you insult a pig by calling it a pig?" Rangers: How do you better the perfect park? They commenced by borrowing: Like Camden, the field lay below street level. Like Wrigley, lengths varied: left field, 332 (later 334), left-center, 388; center and deep right-center, 400 and 403; right-center, 381; and right, 325. Nooks recalled Ebbets Field. Right-field touted The Home Run Porch's columned upper-deck overhang. Was this Detroit? Or Brooklyn: A sign read, "Hit It Here and Win a Free Suit."

"We had to be careful," mused former president Tom Schieffer. "We didn't want to have ivy on the wall *and* a green monster *and* a home run Porch—a conglomeration. We said, 'Let's think why those things are special in other parks and build on ideas generated.' " They built like Caesar straight out of Marco Polo by way of Sam Houston because this, after all, was Texas.

At The 49,166-seat Ballpark in Arlington, even grass spurned subtlety, imported from Combine, three hours away. A visitor off the Nolan Ryan Expressway parked in one of nine color-coded lots. "All bear the name," said Bush, "of a giant historic figure from Texas' birth age"—the 1830s and '40s. Each lot fed the Rangers Walk of Fame, ringing the park, that sketched team history. "Each panel has the roster of a given year written on the bricks." Buying one, guests could sign their names. Baseball-shaped lamps lit the upper concourse. A red brick and home-grown granite facade flaunted cast-stone carvings, 35 longhorn steer heads, and 21 Lone Star emblems. Texas murals linked the upper and lower arches. Behind right a 17,000-square-feet Legends of the Game Museum contained lithographic art and 7,000-square-foot Children's Learning Center. The park's brand towered beyond center: a four-story office building of Cajun twist, steel trusses, wrought-iron decor, and glass walls. It housed shops, ticket windows, businesses, and team offices, linked left-center and right-center, and enclosed the squared complex with beveled corners. "Everything points inward," Bush said. "The place feels smaller than it is."

It opened April 11, 1994. First pitcher: Kenny Rogers. Batter and hit: Milwaukee's Pat Listach. Homer: mate Dave Nilsson. Score: Brewers, 4–3, before 46,056. On April 26, wind stopped the game for 45 minutes. (A 42-foot by 430-foot screen to curb it topped the office building.) Jose Canseco homered thrice with 8 RBI in a game. Rogers pitched the bigs' 14th perfect game—and first by an AL lefty. By August, the Rangers' humdrum .456 percentage led the West by a game. "Then the strike hit," said Schieffer. The five levels emptied: lower deck and suite, club level, and upper deck and suite. A year later Arlington hosted the All-Star Game: National, 3–2, on only three hits (all homers). Frank Thomas' struck a luxury box. "The strike had ended earlier that year," Costas continued. "The irony is that the baseball was retrieved by [players head] Donald Fehr's nine-year-old nephew."

Texans watched from office balconies, often distracted from the game. A white overhang rimmed their building; state-of-the-art scoreboard topped the Porch; hand-operated board framed the left-field wall. Beyond center, an incline pleased hitters (backdrop) and kids (chasing dingers on the grass). On either side, Arlington Stadium seats forged bleachers. The visiting bullpen divided them and the left-field stands. Texas' pen fixed right-center field. The wall around it angled. "We tried to be eccentric," said Schieffer. "It meets right at 381, jogs again at 377, and meets the fence at 407"—The Ballpark's deepest point. A tunnel between the Porch and right-field line filtered light on the field.

Box seats were a pickoff throw—some, 44 feet—from first and third base. Less close, but glitzier: luxury suits, named for 122 Hall of Famers, priced up to $200,000. Knothole tickets let you peer through a hole in the right-field fence. Anyone could wolf hot dogs, pizza, and smoked meat from the Rangers smoke house. A Sports Grill serviced the Porch. The Ballpark bakery served cookies and other food. "We have everything," boasted Bush, by now Texas governor, "except a pennant."

The '96 Rangers won their first division title. Punch was Lone Star–style: MVP Juan Gonzalez (47 homers and 144 ribbies), Dean Palmer (38 and 107), Rusty Greer (.332 and 100), and Kevin Elster (24,

99). Texas won the Division Series opener, 6–2, v. New York. The Yankees then took three straight. Gonzalez hit five homers; the Rangers, .218. The '97ers lured a record 2,945,228. Bobby Witt became the first AL pitcher to homer in 25 years. On June 12, The Ballpark housed the first inter-league match. Ryan and Willie Mays threw out a first ball: Giants, 4–3. Next year Gonzalez rivaled San Jacinto: 175 RBI and a second MVP. Rick Helling went 20–7. Texas won the West, and again met the Yanks. Sweeping, New York cloned Santa Ana at the Alamo.

"I'm so bored with it all" were Winston Churchill's last words. In '99, Gonzalez wed .326, 39 homers, and 128 RBI, and was traded. Rafael Palmeiro exploded: .324, 47, and 148. Ivan Rodriguez evoked Dickey, Cochrane, and Bench. "Only catcher ever to get 30 homers [35], 100 RBI [113], and 100 runs [116]," said manager Johnny Oates—also, Texas' third MVP since '96. "We'll get there," vowed Bush, though it was not easy to see how, or when. Bored: The Yankees *again* swept the Division Series. The 2000 Rangers plunged to last.

Owner Tom Hicks bought Seattle's Alex Rodriguez for $252 million. It didn't help. Texas opened v. Toronto April 1, 2001, at Hiram Birthorn Stadium in San Juan—Puerto Rico's first bigs game. Lines were 313 and 313; alleys, 339 and 350; center, 398. A full house (19,950) watched: Jays, 8–1. The Rangers thudded to a 23–43 start. In May, Oates resigned. The Ballpark still evoked hope as wide as the sky and as green as winter oats. This, after all, was Texas.

JACOBS FIELD

"The only question judging Three Rivers, Riverfront, and Three Rivers Stadium," laughed ex-big Darrell Evans, "is which to detonate first." By contrast, comparing the Yard and The Ballpark in Arlington was akin to Derek Jeter v. Nomar Garciaparra. Where was A-Rod? Then, in 1994, the Indians replaced 74,683-seat Municipal Stadium with a park antipodal in its charm.

First party: "Be grateful for what you have." Second party: "Be grateful for what you miss." Critics jeered when voters spurned a downtown domed stadium: That Cleveland, what a loser, mistake on the lake. "We'll go another way [referendum]," vowed Richard E. Jacobs, who brought the Tribe with brother David in 1986. Jacobs Field became the prism of team and town. It sat 43,863, bordered three streets, and was a dome's antithesis.

Municipal long rocked with silence. Jacobs doubled back to an earlier age. On soft, springy-green afternoons, Ohioans could sit anywhere at 1910–'46 League Park and watch without binoculars. "You were right on top," said Herb Score, the Tribe's onetime slingshot of a southpaw. "It was a more intimate feeling they had with the players and the game."

The Jake went yard a cityside away. From Public Square, Tribers walked, drove, or took the Regional Transit Authority bus. Seventeen thousand spaces dotted a 10-minute radius. "It was dispersed intentionally," said Jacobs. "We're trying to create businesses all over downtown." The park's framework was open, with accent areas of buff brick, Atlantic green granite, Kasota stone, limestone, and glass. "It displays its bones, tendons, and ligaments," wrote architecture critic Steve Litt, "like the bridges that span the Cuyahoga River." Vertical light standards mimicked large white toothbrushes. A white steel rim topped the roof. "The combination is telling," said Jacobs. "The brick and downtown setting say urban. The open architecture is Cleveland—a steel town at heart."

Yesterday Once More: A huge bronze statue of Bob Feller adorned the Indians Square entrance. *Imagine:* sitting there on three-foot-high granite blocks that spell "Who's On First?" *People:* The front office occupied a separate building behind left field. Concourses teemed with pennants, archives, and Tribe photos. "Great moment" signs dotted the park—e.g. Len Barker's '81 perfect game.

Rocky Colavito would have loved the 325-foot left-field porch. Al Rosen played too soon: left-center measured 368. By contrast, Score would embrace Jake's mini-Monster: a 19-foot-high wall knitting the left-field pole and deep left-center (410). The wall's out-of-town scoreboard fronted bleachers and "baseball's largest [220 feet wide and 120 high] free-standing scoreboard" of ad and video. From the board it angled to 8 feet past center field (405) via right-center (375) to the right-field pole (325). Three sharp angles caromed hits.

Center's "Back Yard"—a four-tiered tree and shrub picnic area—oversaw the Indians' elevated pen. (The visitors' occupied the right-field corner). To its right, bleachers beckoned strong man Jim Thome. Farther right a three-tiered stand inverted Camden Yards. Four luxury decks tied one deck to another. The skyline loomed behind left and center field. A sign in left's standing area read "10th Man Society." Another counted straight sellouts (455, ending April 2001; president Larry Doland hung a plaque among retired numbers behind the right-field grandstand).

On April 4, 1994, Dennis Martinez threw the Jake's first pitch to Rich Amaral. The Mariners' Eric Anthony first went long. Indians: 4–3, in 11. Eddie Murray later homered righty/lefty for a record 11th time. Albert Belle tied .357, 36 homers, and 101 RBI. At the strike Cleveland trailed first-place Chicago by a game. "We'd been so awful for all these years," said Score, "and suddenly get good." The '95ers went 100–44, crammed 2,842,745, and clinched the Central September 8. Belle turned ballistic: 52 doubles, 377 total bases, .690 slugging, and franchise record 50 homers. David Bell, father Buddy, and granddad Gus forged the bigs' second three-generation family. The Tribe swept Boston in the Division Series, beat Seattle in the LCS, and lost World Series Games One-Two to Atlanta.

Game Three shook the Jake: Murray's 7–6 11th-frame single gave Cleveland its first Series "W" since TV's *Toast of the Town*, Mohandas Gandhi died of an assassin's bullet, and Harry Truman called the GOP "gluttons of privilege." The Braves endured in six: That winter the Indians sold out an entire season ('96). Score laughed: "First time. Included standing room above the left-field scoreboard."

Forget Armani: sellouts wore the besotted, beloved, gap-toothed grin of mascot Chief Wahoo; Belle's 148 ribbies led the league; the Tribe lost the '96 Division Series. John Adams—the Tribe Drummer—moved from Municipal. Cleveland housed the '97 All-Star Game: Catcher Sandy Alomar went deep to beat the NL, 3–1. The Indians won their third straight division. The beat went on.

"Four outs," said Yankees manager Joe Torre of 1997. "Four lousy outs from winning [the DS]." Alomar homered to tie Game Four. (The Tribe won, 3–2, and Game Five, 4–3). On October 15, Tony Fernandez's 11th-inning blast won the LCS over Baltimore. The World Series juxtaposed: Florida, age 5, v. the AL charter Indians. Cleveland took Matches

Two-Four-Six. Game Seven broke even a neutral's heart. The Marlins tied in the ninth, 2-all, winning on an 11th-frame hit. The Indians hit .291. "Who gives a shit about average?" manager Mike Hargrove huffed. "It's runs that count." Consolation: The '95 and '97 Jake hosted more Series games (six) than Municipal (five, '32–93).

"Look in my face; my name is might-have-been," said Dante Gabriel Rossetti. "I am also called No-More, Too late, Farewell." Manny Ramirez had 45 homers and 145 RBI in 1998. Shortstop Omar Vizquel won his sixth straight Gold Glove. The Central was again a breeze. (Cleveland '95–99 won by a combined 81 games). Scalpers were in the money: bleachers, middle-level mezzanine, even obstructed views in the upper left and right-field corners. The Tribe again won the first playoff round, 3–1, v. Boston. The Yanks then took the LCS. A Wahoo fell back on the Jake. The downtown site was warmer than Municipal, yet breezier. "It's the open spaces in the outfield," said Score. "They keep winds swirling [usually toward left]."

The Jake helped rebuild downtown Cleveland. Many wondered when the Tribe would win it all. Not 1999. It scored 1,009 runs—first over 1,000 since the '50 Red Sox. Ramirez's 165 RBI broke Hal Trosky's team-high 162. Richie Sexson, Thome, and Roberto Alomar had more than 120 apiece. Different script, common end. The Indians led the Division Series, 2–0. Boston then won three straight. A year later Cleveland missed the playoffs. In 2001, Thome became its all-time home run leader. "At Municipal, we'd have been glad to contend," mused Jacobs. "Now we want more." They already had it. Its name was Jacobs Field.

PRO PLAYER STADIUM

In March 1988, the O's and Dodgers played an exhibition at Miami's $115 million fully enclosed open-air Joe Robbie Stadium. "The [NFL Dolphins owner's] name tells you the problem," Blockbuster Video chairman H. Wayne Huizenga later said. "It's a football place."

In 1990, he bought 50 percent of the gridiron plat at 2269 N.W. 199th Street. (Huizenga bought 100 percent in '94, renaming it Pro Player Stadium.) He got an NL expansion team, began spending $20 million, and set out to convert 200 luxury suites, club seats, and football sight lines into a ready-for-baseball park. "Our upper-deck outfield seats are too far away," Huizenga said. "So we'll cover them [with a blue tarp]," cutting capacity to 41,855. Nothing could cover lower-level seats between the infield and poles. "They're great," said the Miami *Herald*— "for the Dolphins [fixing the 50-yard line in center field]." Best seats: along the baselines (sold on season basis) and right- field corner (day of game). The problem was size: Even large crowds got lost. The '93 rookie Marlins enticed a still-record 3,064,847.

Most came by car. (Huizenga added 7,500 spaces: total 23,000). The lot also handled 254 buses (Metro-Dade-Transit Agency) and a helicopter. Palms trees flanked two swirling ramps at each corner of the park. Three statues graced the main entrance—Robbie, former Dolphins coach Don Shula, and Casey of *Casey at the Bat*. Few expected what lay inside. "We'll give this a baseball feel," said Huizenga, "not make it an afterthought." An 8-foot-wall ringed the outfield. Above it a 202-foot-long by 17-foot-wide clock-topped out-of-town scoreboard—the Blue Blocker, or Teal Monster—linked left-center to inside the left-field pole. (In 1993, Atlanta's Ryan Klesko crashed into the wall and knocked several letters off the board.)

To its right the wall jutted forward to form a notch—the Bermuda Triangle, 434 feet away. Dead center measured 410; alleys, 380; right, 345; left, 330. Single-deck bleachers bound right-center and right's pole. Seats were painted orange. Trim hued teal and blue. "On Opening Day the sky was light blue," said play-by-playman Joe Angel. He introduced each Marlin: Reliever Bryan Harvey became "a man with almost as many saves as John the Baptist."

A month earlier Charlie Hough, 45, threw Florida's first-ever pitch. "[He's] into his motion," Angel began the exhibition, "and the first pitch in the history of the Marlins is a knuckleball, high *and* low, ball one." Hough now readied for the Real McCoy. L.A.'s Jose Offerman led off. Charlie threw a foot outside the plate. Umpire Frank Pulli called a strike: 42,530 roared. Hough then flung one even wider. Again Pulli struck. "Anywhere the pitch was," said Angel, "Frank was going to inaugurate this place with a strikeout." Offerman fanned. First hit: Marlins' Bret Barberie. Homer: Dodgers' Tim Wallach. Jeff Conine got four hits;

Hough, a 6–3 victory; Harvey, his first of 45 saves. Joe DiMaggio threw out the ceremonial first ball. "Here I win the game," said the slow-speed Hough, "and DiMag [then 78] throws harder than I do."

Conine smacked Robbie's first grand slam. Catcher Benito Santiago started the Marlins' first brawl. In 1996, Gary Sheffield bound 42 homers and 120 ribbies. Kevin Brown's 1.89 ERA led the league. Al Leiter Kd 200, threw Florida's first no-hitter, and enjoyed the poor lighting around home plate. For the fourth straight year Florida flunked .500. Attendance fell to 1,746,767. "We can still make it here," said Huizenga, adding a second JumboTron board, interactive Sports Town food, drink, and games complex, and new drainage system. (One year South Florida rain delayed 16 games). He also spent a bundle for new '97ers: Bobby Bonilla, Moises Alou, Alex Fernandez, Jim Eisenreich, John Cangelosi, and manager Jim Leyland.

On June 10, Brown no-hit San Francisco. In September, Bonilla's two-out, two-strike, ninth-inning slam beat Colorado, 9–6. Florida won the wild card. The Division Series was another last-frame hoot: Edgar Renteria's Game One single topped the Giants, 2–1. Next day Sheffield scored a ninth-frame decider: 7–6. Fernandez then won, 6–2. "A sweep!" said Angel. "We thought that was it." Actually, it augured the LCS v. Atlanta. Huizenga untarped the upper deck. In Game Five, Livan Hernandez had a playoff-tying 15 Ks. Brown won the Game Six clincher, 7–4. The Series with Cleveland was even closer. Craig Counsell's one-out ninth-inning sacrifice fly tied Game Seven, 2-all. In the 11th, Florida filled the bases with two out. Renteria lined a single past Charles Nagy's glove—"at age five," marveled Angel, "we're the champion"—its reign, as brief as Pro Player's four Series crowds (each 67,000-plus).

Huizenga broke up the Marlins in a '98 firesale. "You can't make money," he said, "in this free-agent mess." Later, he sold the club to commodities trader John Henry. "People go to Pro Player," conceded Henry, "largely to cheer the opposition." The Giants' Barry Bonds cleared the scoreboard to reach 400/400 homers/steals. Four homers on September 1-2, 1998, gave Mark McGwire 59. Florida beat Tampa Bay, 8–4, in interleague play's first All-Florida match. Few cared. Suddenly, Pro

Player seemed as hip as Glenn Miller, Mitch Miller, and Mrs. Miller combined.

The '99ers reeled a new low 1,369,420. Sales of Cuban coffee, the *Medinoche* sandwich, and *arepa,* a Latin dish of two grilled corn-bread pancakes stuffed with mozzarella cheese, fell. "It used to be that you couldn't compete well without a ballpark," said Henry. "Now you can't even afford to go into arbitration in the situation we're in." Florida drew 7,101 and 6,955 against the Padres. Pro Player throbbed to a *Red Sox* victory. "Why are they *against* us? It feels as if we should be wearing gray uniforms," said Preston Wilson (31 homers, 36 steals, and 121 RBI) of his 2000 third-place Marlins. "I'm embarrassed."

In 01, A. J. Burnett threw the Marlins' third no-hitter. No matter. In Miami, seldom had baseball and football more rivaled Venus and Mars.

WRIGLEY FIELD

"Let's say we get a park," a Marlins fan said. "It won't buy tradition. You can't morph into Tiger Stadium, or be a Gas House Gang." No snap of the fingers could evoke "Let's play two." In June 1984, the Cubs and Cardinals met at Wrigley Field in NBC's Saturday "Game of the Week." Even now, said Bob Costas, Chicago cab drivers will spot him and lower a window. " 'Hey, Bob. The [Ryne] Sandberg Game.' That's what they call it—and it's almost two decades ago."

The Cubs trailed, 9–3 and 9–8. St. Louis' Bruce Sutter—"then untouchable," said Costas—pitched the ninth. Sandberg homered to left-center: 9-all. An inning later Willie McGee put the Cards ahead, 11–9. The first two Cubs made out. Bob Dernier walked. Sandberg batted with four prior hits. "Boom!" said Costas. "He homers again, the identical spot. The same fan could have caught the ball." Thousands of Redbirders gasped. The rest of Wrigley shook. "That's the real Roy Hobbs, at least today," Bob cried on NBC, "because this can't be happening. It doesn't make any difference if it's 1984 or '54—just freeze this and don't change a thing." The Cubs won, 12–11. To Costas, it remains "a telephone game—the kind you're watching and say, 'Who likes baseball as much as me?' and start calling all over the country."

In 1985, 2,161,534 answered. The Wrigleys added seats to the catwalks and a wire basket to the left-center- to right-center wall. "No more confusion about if a ball found the stands," mused President Dallas Green. On September 8, Pete Rose singled for Cobb-tying hit 4,191. "Wrigley," he said, "keeps making history." In 1987, Andre Dawson did, too. The first last-place MVP's 49 homers united Wrigleyville. Fake sun split it. "For years, neighborhood activists kept lights out of Wrigley," said Mike Veeck. "They went to court, said it would wreck the area." Finally, network TV made baseball drop the hammer.

"The Commissioner's Office said if the Cubs were to win a division or pennant and make the Series," recalled Harry Caray, "they needed to present games at night [more revenue]." Otherwise, baseball would move their postseason to Milwaukee or St. Louis. "What would have happened," he added, "if the Cubs won a pennant and you had to go to St. Louis? Mass riot." As it was Chicago nearly popped a cork. Ernie Banks and Billy Williams tossed out first balls at Wrigley's August 8, 1988, night debut. NBC attended; rain washed it out. Next night Cubs win! 6–4.

The new pact limited night games to 18 a year. "Good!" boomed Caray, "because don't forget what made the Cubs. Generation after generation, a kid leaves home, gets on the el, gets off at the park and watches the game. By 6 he's home and can you imagine his excitement when he gets there!" Sandberg going yard. Fergie fanning the side. *The Music Man*: "Pick a little, talk a little" between father and son. "Kid grows up and has his own kids," Caray said, "same thing happens. Day ball made the Cubs so lovable. More clubs should explore how."

In 1989, the Cubs added a food court, built a new press/broadcast booth, and affixed 67 luxury boxes to the bottom of the upper deck. The clubhouse was redone. A new ticket office rose. Mark Grace batted .314. Sandberg led the league in runs (104). The Cubs won the division after brooking a slump. At that point a patron of their mediocrity named Ken Foxx parodied *Macbeth*: "Anson, Chance, and Wilson, Hartnett, Hornsby, Brown, and Grimm / hex the Mets, the Birds, and Expos/stand behind the Cubs and Zim. Double, double, toil, and trouble/ fire burn and Cubbies bubble. Eye of newt and raven beak/ presto, it's a winning streak. So heed this curse from Bill Veeck's vines. Our Cubs are the champs of '89."

The playoff was a hash: Giants, in five. A year later Sandberg became the first second baseman to hit 30 dingers back-to-back. In 1992, Greg Maddux went 20–11, won his first Cy Young, and began a trip to Georgia. Karl "Tuffy" Rhodes hit three homers in all of 1993. On Opening Day '94, he went deep thrice off Dwight Gooden. Bleacher cultists kept them, but threw back other teams' dingers. "A custom," said writer David Broder, "part of Wrigley's charm." Their public was still put to purpose. The NL's smallest park yearly made its top half in attendance. Sadly, the law of averages seldom reached the field.

Caray shook his head. "This isn't a Humpty Dumpty who's moved from one town to another. It's a great name in baseball—the Chicago National League Baseball Team. Unbelievable—half-a-century without even being in the World Series?" The '90–'96ers made the first division once. Baseball spurns transiency. The White Sox beat the Cubs in the 1906 World Series. The Cubs darned the Hose, 6–3, in '97's interleague debut.

In May 1998, Kerry Wood fanned 20 Astros to tie the record. Ultimately, he became Rookie of the Year (13–6 and 233 Ks). Surpassing: the Sosa-McGwire marathon. Suddenly, a nation said, "Baseball's been very, very good to me."

BUSCH STADIUM

The 1994–'95 strike revealed owners and players more as bottom-dwelling Hessians than protectors of the sport. The percent of 1990–'94 CBS poll respondents who said they cared about baseball fell from 61 to 39. A *U.S. News* survey asked Americans their favorite sport: 17 per cent said baseball v. '48's 39. The strike aborted years, mangled records, and killed the Series for the first time since 1903. Baseball became the Flying Dutchman. 'Ninety-eight became Port Reborn.

"By then, baseball had already come back a little," said Bud Selig. In 1995, Albert Belle hit 50 homers in a 144-game schedule. At least two players whacked that many in each of the next two years. "Power helped revive the game," added Cardinals voice Joe Buck. (Too, Cal Ripken, interleague play, and the '96 champion Yankees.) It also buoyed the Red-birds, whose revival then seemed clearer than the game's. The '96ers won the Central, blared "30" (Ron Gant homers; Dennis Eckersley saves,) and almost won the LCS (leading Atlanta, three games to one). Mark McGwire left Oakland July 31, 1997. On August 6 he smacked his first Cardinals dinger (career 365). By Closing Day Mac's 58 dingers tied Jimmie Foxx '38 for most right-handed homers in a year. The Swifties bagged 2,634,014 visitors. A year later they broke their fran-chise high (3,195,021).

Believers filled boxes, reserved, general admission, and same-day bleacher seats. A new picnic area—"Homers Landing"— overlooked the left-center pen. The discerning fan came with a thirst and glove: a lower-concourse food court wed bratwurst and burgers; Budweiser washed hot dogs and burritos; The Hot Corner on level two pleased even a vegetar-ian. Pleasing to all was No. 25. Mac joined the Redbirds unsure of St. Louis. "I'd always played in the American League," he said, "but the fans are wonderful. I wish everyone could play here." By 2000 Edgar Renteria, Fernando Tatis, Fernando Vina, and Jim Edmonds, among others, did: Forfeiting free agency, each signed a below-market-value pact to play in St. Louis.

Later, *Sports Illustrated* wrote: "McGwire is almost solely responsible for this era of unprecedented interest in the Cardinals [and baseball, with Sammy Sosa]." It began as America swung to '98's Great Race. A writer said: "They are stopping the world with their magic, record-assaulting, home-run blasting summer." Bars, stores, and water coolers rediscovered baseball's winnowing force for good. "You couldn't go anywhere," said Selig, "and not be assaulted." The Cubs' Sosa had never hit 40 dingers: On June 30, he smacked No. 20 of the *month*. On Labor Day, Big Mac hit No. 61, passing Ruth. The next night Fox TV showed baseball's apotheosis, 34, red-haired and bulging, try for the crusher. At 8:18 P.M. Central Time, McGwire faced Chicago's Steve Trachsel—fourth inning, two outs, bases empty—and lined the first pitch down the left-field line.

"It wasn't his typical moon shot," said manager Tony La Russa of Mac's 341-foot 62nd dinger. "It went out so fast." I was flying to New York. The pilot announced McGwire's Maris-breaking drive. Passengers began applauding. At Busch, 43,688 pilgrims, fireworks, and history burst. Mac missed first base, tagged it, and was hugged at the plate by his mates and 10-year-old son. Sammy embraced his foil. On September 12, Sosa ripped homer 60. Next day he hit No. 61 and 62 out of Wrigley's quaking, pulsing yard. McGwire's 490-foot monster hit the roof-styled "Budweiser" house at 3701 Kenmore Avenue. Dave Kingman had hit 3705 Kenmore's Blue house 525 feet from the plate: Mac and Sammy neared it. Each Cubs telecast showed a yellow house at 1032 Waveland. A Sosa shot entered the open window of a second-floor apartment. Rooftoppers paid $100 a head, limit 100 per game. Said manager Chris Niro: "It's like sitting below the upper deck of Busch Stadium"—a site Mac and Sammy dented, too.

Sosa's 66th took the lead September 25. McGwire then melded fact, myth, and miracle: 5 homers in his last 11 ups. Sunday (Closing Day) Big Mac faced Montreal's Carl Pavano in the seventh inning. The SRO crowd rose. Signs dappled: "McGwire, You Are the Man." Mac whipped No. 70 over the left-field wall. "I have no words to describe what he has given us this season," said La Russa. "He has given us incredible moment after moment."

McGwire led the world in homers, walks (162), on-base average (.473), and slugging (.752). "The irony is," he said, "it's the Cubs who made the postseason." Trachsel beat the Giants, 5–3. in a wild-card playoff. Atlanta swept the Division Series. You can look it up: Sosa was first in runs (134), RBI (158), and total bases (416), second in homers (66) and slugging (.647), and elected MVP. Ahead: a can you believe/so there/top that '99. Somehow, he almost did.

"The second installment of their Home Run Race didn't receive the same hype," a writer said. Sosa didn't give a hoot, becoming first to hit 60 twice (63.) Meanwhile, other "moments" gripped Missouri. Mac hit career homer 499 August 4, 1999. Next day, driving to Busch, "I had the same feeling I had when I hit 62." In the third, Big Red took Andy Ashby 451 feet. "The sixteenth to get 500," wrote Bob Broeg, "and the one to do it in the fewest at-bats [5,487 v. Ruth's 5,801]." Tony Gwynn cheered Mac's hike around the bases. "I love all his ritual," said Mr. Padre, "landing at the plate with both feet, the [fake] gut-punches [to mates], the high-fives." Going yard was catching. Next up McGwire hit a 479-foot blast off the scoreboard near his number in the lineup.

A week later 145,635 packed Busch for a three-game series: Chicago v. St. Louis. Were they Big Mac and Swinging Sammy, or Valentino and Barrymore? "Both knew," said Bob Costas, "one would always invoke the other." The fourth-placers wooed more than 3.2 million. "You play for the Cardinals, you're a part of royalty," said ex-Redbird Joe Torre. It seemed impossible for a sport to matter more than baseball in St. Louis.

In 2000, McGwire passed Mickey Mantle (homer 537) and Willie Mays (64 multi-dinger games trail only Ruth). The Cards won the East, beat San Francisco in the Division Series, and dropped the LCS to the Mets. Hurt, Mac only pinch-hit in postseason. Darryl Kile finished 20–9. Edmonds left the Big A to whip 42 homers and own center field. St. Louis drew a record 3,336,493: 41,191 per date. It also proposed a new downtown park.

"They saw what lesser baseball cities had done. This was their response," said Broeg. "Put a Camden Yards in St. Louis, and it will own the Midwest"—or was that Wrigley Field?

WRIGLEY FIELD

The '99 Cubs drew 2,813,854, 93 percent of capacity. "With Boston [going] and Detroit gone," said Cubs Vice-President Mark McGuire, "it will leave us as the one and only real deal." Forget no Series flag, or losing nine straight postseason series ('18-'29-'32-'35-'38-'45-'84-'89-'98). "Wrigley is what everyone else is trying to copy."

The Cubs ended 1999 feeling that anyone can have a bad century. They would make do at Wrigley in the next. "People think of it and Fenway as being the same size. Not true," said Earl Santee of HOK Sport. Wrigley was two acres larger, had 5,000 more seats, and boasted nearly 200,000 more square feet. Some decried its age. Others, parking: The Cubs owned fewer than 2,000 spots. More mourned having to spend $800,000 yearly on infrastructure. Why stay? How could a new Wrigley match the old? Thus, luxury suites reaped more than $5 million yearly. One concession stand with two lines equals 22 "points of sale": Wrigley's post-'81 leapt from 22 to 220. "We've put in a large concession area in the upper deck, built a patio on the roof." They joined the Stadium Club, Friendly Confines Cafe, and Sheffield Grill.

Some teams hate sidewalk and rooftop parties. The Cubs *encouraged* them. "The neighborhood experience around the ballpark," McGuire said, "is very much a part of Wrigley Field." Music is claimed to be the universal language. The Cubs' language is Wrigley's lure. On March 28–30, 2000, they turned against America's erect-a-wall/isolationist/avoid foreign-entanglement heart by playing the Mets in Tokyo. "Wrigley sells us abroad," said Trachsel of baseball's first regular-season games outside North America, "so let's expand the sport."

On May 11, the Cubs and Milwaukee played the NL's longest-ever game—4:22. (Their season was longer: 65–97. Sosa wed .320, 50, and 138.) Another first: Chicago's Glenallen Hill's homer *hit* the roof across Waveland. More precedent: A May 16 fan swiped catcher Chad Kreuter's hat, virtually every Dodger hit the stands to reclaim it, and 19 (later, 12) players, coaches, and a bullpen catcher were suspended and fined. In '01, Tribune Company raised bleacher prices to $20: Each game sold out. The Cubs rocked L.A., 20–1—its worst loss since leaving Brooklyn. Sosa hit his 400th homer. Jon Lieber and Kerry Wood threw consecutive one-hitters. Turning 60, George Will wrote: "I shall be 67 on the centennial of the Cubs' last World Series victory. Something to live for." Leave it to the Cubs. In June, they led the Central.

That month the team announced an '02 reworking: stadium advertising, 215 field seats behind the plate, and 2,100 new bleacher seats along Waveland and Sheffield Avenues. "We are committed to staying in Wrigley Field," noted McGuire, "but we have to do somethings to compete." A Waveland ballhawk shook his head: "The park won't change. This is where I met all my friends," said Dick White. "It's like a family. This is my social life." *Wrigley's* life is rich, not worn—tender, brimming, human, and humane.

Philip Bess, associate director of the Andrews University Division of Architecture, recently wrote "The Old Ballparks Were Better." Bess lives two miles from where he watches about 15 games a year—the upper deck at Addison and Clark.

"Here are fifty reasons why the old ballparks were better than today's new stadiums: 1) They were part of normal neighborhood life. 2) It was possible to live across the street from the ballpark. 3) It was possible to have or patronize a business across the street from the ballpark. 4) Ballpark-generated economic activity extended broadly through the neighborhood. 5) It was possible to go to school or to church within a quarter-mile of second base. 6) If you drove from out of town and parked, you didn't have to walk to the ballpark through a sea of cars. 7) It was possible to ride your bike or take public transportation to the ballpark. 8) It was possible to walk to the ballpark from home. 9) Old ballparks were physically constrained by existing urban street and block conditions. 10) They had smaller seating capacities and fans sat closer to the game. 11) There were real bleachers and more of them. 12) Fans in the upper deck had regular opportunities to catch a foul ball. 13) Fans would walk from one side of the ballpark to the other, in both the lower and upper decks, without ever losing sight of the playing field. 14) Old ballpark quirks and asymmetries were site-determined and dramatic. 15) Fans could see a 300-foot home run and/or a 440-foot out—sometimes even in the same park. 16) Fans could see a home run break a building window. 17) Fans could see a home run go into the street. 18) Fans in the upper deck didn't need oxygen tanks. 19) There was no right-field home run "porch" that isn't a porch. 20) Office buildings beyond the outfield fence were outside the park. 21) Fans could sit during a rain delay under the upper deck or under a real roof. 22) Fans could hide behind a post if their team was playing lousy. 23) The occupant of the upper-deck seat next to you was never a mountain goat or a St. Bernard. 24) Old ballparks were paid for by team owners rather than taxpayers. 25) They were physically smaller by a third and less costly (in today's dollars) by more than half. 26) That $200 million in tax money for today's typical new stadium with a retractable roof was available for twice as much education and recreation, police and fire protection, street improvements and public transportation. 28) Every game was played outdoors on grass. 29) Old ballparks were made to focus attention upon (rather than divert it from) the game. 30) Fans could get away from television for three to four hours. 31) No electronic advertising. 32) No rotating advertising. 33) No one told fans when to clap or cheer. 34) No loud music after the national anthem, except during the seventh-inning stretch. 35) No 'dot' races. 36) No cigar bars. 37) No swimming pools.

38) No hair salons. 39) Real people occupied (and were visible in) the scoreboard. 40) Old ballparks did not flaunt class differences in their architecture. 41) Luxury suites had to be retrofitted into old ballparks—they were an afterthought, rather than the ballparks' reason for being. 42) Business networking and political schmoozing had to be done out in the open. 43) Food was delivered by vendors rather than waiters. 44) A family of four could go to a game for less than $100. 45) There were double-headers on Sundays. 46) The best playing field configuration in baseball today is Fenway Park. 47) The best place to see a baseball game today is Wrigley Field. 48) The closest upper-deck seats in baseball today—where Tom Boswell learned from watching Jack Morris the meaning of changing speeds—are in Tiger Stadium. 49) Fred Merkle failed to touch second, Babe Ruth called his shot, Jackie Robinson stole home, and Ted Williams homered in his last at bat in old ballparks. 50) Finally, old ballparks didn't require market-analyst recommendations to be called 'ballparks.' But don't take my word for it. Just come see a game at Wrigley Field."

TIGER STADIUM

In 1986, Detroit Mayor Coleman Young urged a new downtown dome: By 2–1 a *News* poll disagreed. A year later the Tigers won the East, banged a next-to-'61 Yankees 225 home runs, and lost the LCS. In '89, Tiger Stadium joined the National Register of Historic Places. Renovation braced its belly. "It's like Wrigley. It's got character," said Ernie Harwell at the time. Added Sparky Anderson: "Forget those pens. [Relievers burrowed down each line. Said '90s pitcher Todd Jones of the pillbox a.k.a. Submarine: 'It's a weird feeling. You're *of* the game, not *in* the game.'] Except for that, what's there not to like?"

As at Comiskey, groundskeepers grew grass long to help the club. Ground rules were a pip. A drive above the yellow flagpole line became a homer. "A fair ball off the bullpen roof," said Al Kaline, "is a double." Home plate faced toward right-center. "It was hell on umpires. Pitchers got outside strikes." The overhang was Tiger's calling card. "You think you're gonna' catch it," added No. 6. "Then it hits up top." *He* hit seat railings in the right-field a.k.a. Kaline Corner. "I went to the hospital so often they took out 10 or 12 of those seats." By contrast, straightaway built a playhouse for a triple or inside-the-parker. Almost anything could happen, and did.

One day Baltimore was hitting. Frank Robinson and Paul Blair led off first and second base. The batter lined to right-center. "Way to the flag-pole's right," said Frank. "Nobody's going to get this." Blair wasn't sure. He stopped, saw the ball drop, then left for home. "He caught up to me," said Paul. Pity catcher Bill Freehan: Blair and Frank slid to the first and foul side of the plate. Both scored at almost exactly at the same time.

"Strangers felt like guests," said Harwell. Even his booth rivaled pin-ball. Luis Polonia fouled a pitch back that hit the Oakland TV stage manager on a shoulder. Polonia hit him again—next pitch, same shoul-der—leading A's voice Ted Robinson to wave a towel. Between innings a visitor could kibitz. Once Reggie Jackson cleared the roof. Next up, he whistled toward the broadcast booth. Looking down, Bob Costas saw Jackson pantomime tying his shoe.

"Reggie's telling me that when we're back on the air, he's gonna' enter the batter's box, call time-out to pretend to tie his shoe, and give us time to discuss what he did last time up and show his replay." He, and Bob, did. Singling, Reggie then pointed to the booth. " 'Hey,' as if to say, 'it's all a great show.' Only in Detroit could you be heard at the plate."

Meanwhile the Tiger Stadium Fan Club hectored city hall, the state leg-islature, and team to save its home. The Cochrane Plan would build pri-vate suites, gird the infrastructure, and widen aisles and seats. Were they visionaries, or innocents unabroad? Let Baltimore build a Camden Yards. *Here* was an original.

With Fenway, Michigan and Trumbull became the oldest site—"and longest continuously used place," said Harwell—"in professional sport." It headlined punch. Cecil Fielder became the first Bengal to clear the left-field roof. (Others: Frank Howard, Harmon Killebrew, and Mark McGwire.) Fielder hit 51 dingers in 1990. Six times Tiger led the

'82–'92 AL in homers. "Later they *lowered* the outfield fence," laughed Kaline. "When it came to runs, fans could never get enough."

New owner Mike Ilitch spent $8 million to build "Tiger Plaza, among our new areas," a brochure read, "[with] 208 menu items." The team was less easy to digest. The '93ers drew 1,971,421. The next three years flunked 1.2 million. In 1995, Lou Whitaker and Alan Trammell played in their record 1,914th game together. Detroit retired four numbers: 2 Charlie Gehringer, 5 Hank Greenberg, 6 Kaline, and 16 Hal Newhouser. It could not forestall new old parks—the Jake, a Coors Field.

Ilitch insisted that rebuilding would be quixotic. Too costly. Little parking. The structure sagged. Posts and luxury boxes could not coexist. Cramped concourse, peewee leg room, and archaic press box merged. "Worse than high school," Willie Hernandez mocked the team's 1,500-square foot locker room. Assume renovation, the Tigers said. Where would they play? In the meantime, the debate talked past, not to.

"**W**e've always been proud," an official said, "of our advertisement-free park." By the '90s ads dotted walls and the sub-upper deck. A piece of facade broke and hit the stands. The area grew dingy. "It is a hulking old building in a ratty part of town," read the *Washington Post*, "an architectural hodgepodge of no particular distinction, a crazyquilt of aluminum siding, sagging wood, rusting iron girders and—now the team finally admits it—more than 10,000 obstructed seats." The Fan Club won a referendum to ban public funds and formed a group hug around the park. "Adults," said Hall of Famer George Kell, "embracing bricks and mortar." Many understood.

"You see the different colors," manager Larry Parrish said of dugout paint. "You have the dark blue at the top, then you get other shades of blue from other years, then shades of green, and then other colors, and then, well, you're at the wood. You're back at the beginning"—1912. John McHale, Sr., became Tigers general manager in 1958. His son was now president. "Not much has changed in this office since my father had it." As a boy, team photographer Mark Cunningham visited with his mom. "We didn't have a car, so we'd take a bus to the Michigan State Fairgrounds and then the train, and then we'd still have to walk half a mile or so from the old station. Sometimes we'd bring my friends. Their parents . . . had cars, but they liked coming with my mother and me better. It was more exciting."

Ilitch completed funding for $289 million Comerica Park. Clubbers took him to court, and lost. Late 1999 became an Irish wake: "fitting," said Harwell, "since this used to be Corktown, an Irish immigrant neighborhood." Tatters vanished: a box armrest; signs from the clubhouse. Even players got Tiger's charm: dugout bunkers, low clubhouse ceiling, and sink in a long tunnel from the clubhouse to field. Here they stopped to unzip their fly. "You'd always do this during a game," one said. "Saved you from going back to the clubhouse."

The Tigers chose an all-time team September 26, 1999. The next day they closed the joint down. "I love this place," said Harwell. "But it's . . . time to move on. People will get used to it." Not all. Vicky Schering brought her seven-year-old son from Michigan's Upper Peninsula. "I came here with my dad, and he came with my granddad. And this is where I was going to teach my son about baseball, but now he'll just see it to say good-bye. Why do they have to do this to us?" Tiger Stadium's 6,911th and last game sold out in 33 minutes. Current Tigers shook hands and signed autographs. Ex-players introduced children and grandchildren in a picnic area.

Kaline and George Brett exchanged lineup cards. Someone waved a sign: "Never forget." Kansas City's Carlos Beltran led off. So many bulbs blazed that home plate umpire Rocky Roe noted, "It was like looking into the Milky Way." Detroit starters wore the number of an all-time Bengal. Kim Garcia, wearing Greenberg's No. 5, homered. Center fielder Gabe Kapler wore no number: neither had Ty Cobb. Robert Fick's No. 25 hailed the late Norm Cash: 43,356 hailed his rooftop slam. (Detroit won, 8–2.) Fick thought of his late father. "I gave him a wink," he said of Tiger's last dinger, "because I knew that he was there." Emotion was palpable. Grown men cried.

Later, 65 ex-Tigers formed a chronological line from the flagpole to plate. The flag was lowered and passed from one player to another. "Behind me stands over 70 years of Tigers history," said Elden Auker '34, giving the flag to Brad Ausmus '99 for Comerica. "Never forget us, for we live on by those who carry on the Tigers tradition and who so proudly wear the olde English D." Home plate was dug up, and moved.

Born in nearby Pontiac, Kirk Gibson said: "This is the story of baseball in Detroit going down right here. My childhood. My dreams. This is where my dream came true."

The most popular man in Michigan said good-bye over the household's P.A. microphone: "Farewell, old friend, Tiger Stadium," said Harwell, voice breaking, lights dimming. "We will remember." We do.

FENWAY PARK

In early 1987, Joel Krakow of the Newton, Massachusetts, Captain Video Store unwrapped a shipment that included the 1986 World Series highlight film. He knew where to place the tape—the horror/science fiction section. A year later the air felt settled by a Wilsonian itinerary. Boston won a second flag in three years for the first time since 1916–'18. (Oakland swept the playoff.) On August 6, 1989, Carl Yastrzemski joined Ted Williams, Joe Cronin, and Bobby Doerr on the right-field facade. Their retired numbers scrawled a taunt: 9-4-1-8, the month of the Sox last crown.

The '90ers led second-place Toronto by one game with one left: Boston 3, Chicago 1, two out, ninth inning. The crowd recalled '86's Ray Knight: one strike to go. Two White Sox reached base. Ozzie Guillen then sliced to right. "If the Gods truly had it in for the Boston Red Sox, [Tom] Brunansky would have lost Guillen's drive in the full moon that hung over Fenway Park," wrote the *Chicago Tribune*'s Andrew Bagnato. Instead, his tumbling grab clinched the East and sent the Yawkeys forth against the A's.

For those who recalled 1988, the playoff wrote a script already banned in Boston. The Sox lost the series, 4–0, scoring one run in each game.

As we will see, Fenway bred scions from Coors Field to Pacific Bell Park. Each had luxury suites, hip cuisine, and a warp-speed cash register. In response, the Red Sox renovated restrooms, built energy-efficient lighting, heating, and cooling, and put a metal awning roof above the left- and right-field roof seats. Suddenly, Fenway's lure had a catch-up '90s gloss.

Mo Vaughn helped: '95 MVP. Boston met Cleveland in the first wild-card-spun Division Series. "Maybe we should stop playing on October 1," mused Mike Greenwell after the Sox' 11th straight playoff loss. In late 1996, Roger Clemens bolted for the phony turf, devalued coin, and somnolence of SkyDome. His dowry: '86 MVP, '86–'87–'91 Cy Young, 1986–'90–'91–'92 ERA and '88–'91–'96 Ks title, respectively, and single-game strikeout high (20, tied by '98's Kerry Wood).

"Dan Duquette wants robots," Clemens said. "He drove me out." The Red Sox general manager called Roger washed up at 34. At 23, a U.S. Olympic team walk-on homered in his first full game. "The dream came through," said '97 Rookie of the Year Nomar Garciaparra: "It could have ended there, and that would have been enough." That winter Nomar inked a seven-year deal. Thinking changed: To leverage a *new* high-revenue Fenway, Boston would have to win. The Sox hatched a rebuilt sub-bleacher batting cage, 25-foot Coca-Cola contour bottle on the screen, and Wally the Green Monster presaging the apocalypse. A *mascot,* at *Fenway*? Next, Vaughn would be asked to leave.

In 1998, he was. "Mo's rejected our final effort," said Duquette. "It looks like he'll play somewhere else [Anaheim]." The acquired from Montreal Pedro Martinez had a 19–7 record. Nomar hit .323. "It's a small step," he said of the wild card. "We understand that." On September 29, a bigger step approached: the Division Series with Cleveland. The Sox won the game, then brooked a *new* three-game postseason losing streak. A fan could only marvel at their massy, light and dark, bewitching and enduring pull.

The '98 Red Sox Yearbook posed questions to honor their new mascot. Below, Wally wonders—and responds.

Questions: 1) How tall was the original left-field wall when Fenway opened in 1912? 2) What was the name of the 10-foot grassy rise that fronted the wall? 3) What part-time left fielder hit 11 homers in 1918 and 29 homers in 1919? 4) What year was Fenway's current left-field wall built? 5) How tall and wide is it? 6) From what material is the wall made? 7) What was the most popular feature of the new wall in 1934? 8) What year was the screen installed above it? 9) How are balls retrieved from the screen? 10) What year was the left-field wall painted green? 11)

What year were lights added above the wall? 12) What year was the first television camera used inside the wall? 13) What year was the old scoreboard renovated? 14) What size and weight are the number placards used in the scoreboard? 15) What is the biggest number on either a hit or a run placard? 16) What is the highest number placard ever used for a half-inning? 17) Whose initials are spelled out in Morse code dots and dashes on the scoreboard? 18) What year was the protective padding installed along the base of the wall? 19) What three Red Sox left fielders won awards as the American League MVP? 20) What is the length down the left-field foul line from home plate to the wall?

Answers: 1) On Opening Day, April 20, 1912, the wall measured 10 feet tall. 2) Duffy's Cliff, named after Sox left fielder Hugh Duffy. 3) Babe Ruth, topping the American League each year. 4) The current wall was finished in time for the 1934 season. 5) It measures 37 feet, two inches high by 240 feet wide. 6) Concrete. Prior to 1934, it was made of wood. 7) A long scoreboard which showed inning-by-inning results of each major-league game. 8) The 23-feet, 4-inch high screen was added in 1936. 9) A Fenway grounds crew member climbs a ladder next to the scoreboard. 10) In 1947, after the ad tin advertising signs on its facade were removed. 11) In 1947, in time for Fenway's first-ever night game of June 13. 12) Luckily, the 1975 World Series, which caught Carlton Fisk's twelfth-inning Game Six homer. 13) In 1976, it was reduced in size by about half and moved 20 feet to the right. 14) Hit or run placards are 16 inches (three feet). Others are 12 by 16 inches (two pounds). 15) These placards go up to the number 19. 16) Seventeen—the number of runs the Sox scored in the seventh inning on June 18, 1953. 17) Longtime team owners Thomas A. (T-A-Y) and Jean R. (J-R-Y) Yawkey. 18) 1976. The wall's tin facade was also replaced with a plastic covering. 19) Ted Williams (1946–49), Carl Yastrzemski (1967), and Jim Rice (1978). 20) 310 feet, changed from 315 feet after a re-measurement in 1995. Where there's a wall, there's a way—and a sudden magic place to treasure.

In 1998, Fenway hosted the Jimmy Fund's Fantasy Camp. For $1,250 you got 15 swings at the Monster and "a chance," read *ESPN Magazine*, "to tell your grandchildren how you felled the behemoth with one mighty stroke." The task was to smack the ball at a minimum speed of

72 miles per hour at an angle of 45 degrees. Nomar etched how: "Remember to stay back." Added third baseman John Valentin: "And swing out your ass."

In 1999, batters did. Fenway hosted the Home Run Derby prior to its last All-Star Game. (Mark McGwire swatted 13.) A woman in 1952 said of Ike's election, "It's like America has come home." Ibid., the Game. Nearly 40 all-Century team nominees were introduced. Ken Griffey, Jr., gravitated to Willie Mays. Curt Schilling left the pen to meet Mike Schmidt and Robin Roberts. "I couldn't help myself," he said. "This was one of the greatest moments in the game's history." Tony Gwynn, on the disabled list, flew from San Diego: "I finally got to see it! Fenway!" Was the eight-time batting champion 39, or nine?

Before the game Ted Williams, 81 and frail, rode a golf cart down the warning track, along the boxes, around the plate, and toward the mound. All-Stars rushed to greet him. Fenway bid to tumble down. Baseball's Grand Old Man asked McGwire, "Do you ever smell the wood burn?" of bat hitting ball. Rafael Palmeiro refused to leave. "The game can wait. That's the chance of a lifetime." Larry Walker noted tears in Ted's eye—and his. Saint Francis of Assisi said, "Give me a child until he is seven, and you may have him afterward." Seldom has baseball seemed more sure and certain of its place.

When the Red Sox run a pennant race, their lure expands until a goodly portion of the land cares whether at last they will oust a vengeful deity. The '99ers unexpectedly drew another wild card. Nomar's .357 won the batting title. Martinez blurred Walter(s) Johnson/Mitty: 23–4, 2.07 ERA, and Cy Young. (A year later both repeated.) Cleveland went up, 2–0, in the Division Series. Love those Sox: They won Set Three, then staged a 24-hit/Valentin seven RBI/highest run total/23–7/largest margin of victory in postseason history. Martinez, hurt in Game One, hurled six hitless last-game relief innings: Sox, 12–8. The *Globe*'s Kevin Paul Dupont surmised: "The Yankees will be seeing a most unexpected visitor."

The LCS U-turned from the start. Boston led, 3–0. New York countered. Catcher Jason Varitek dropped a throw (3-all), ump Rick Reed called a Yawkey out at second ("I blew it," he said. "[Yankee Chuck]

Knoblauch wasn't in the act of throwing. He just dropped the ball. I feel awful"), and Bernie Williams homered. (Yanks, 4–3. The Sox felt worse.) Game Two: Boston led, 2–1, but stranded 13 runners, missed two homers by a foot, and lost, 3–2. Said New York's David Cone: "We've caught some breaks."

Set Three matched Martinez, 27, v. Clemens, 37—or was it Gibson and McLain? "That's how big this is," said Peter Gammons as 33,190 jammed Fenway. "Who owns this house?" Seats went for $1,200. Posters read: "Cy Young v. Cy Old." Clemens left in the third. The crowd mocked: "Where is Roger?": Sox, 13–1. A night later ghosts merged: Galehouse, Torrez, Larry Barnett. Boston made three muffs. Tim Tschida blew another call. Skipper Jimy Williams was ejected. Fans then threw bottles. The Yankees briefly left the field: game, 9–2, and series, 3–1.

George Steinbrenner accused Williams of "inciting" the crowd. Jimy replied: "When Georgie-Porgie speaks, I don't listen." Two errors, two Bombers dingers, and 11 left on base fused: stripes, 6–1. Boston's 10 errors set an LCS record. "Too bad," said Nomar, "it happened the first time we and the Yankees met in postseason." Errors, bad umpiring, and nonautomatic in the clutch. Read Red Sox 101.

YANKEE STADIUM

In 1996, Joe Torre became Yankees manager. Augury began May 14: Dwight Gooden tossed their 10th no-hitter. New York took the East, beat Texas in the Division Series, and led LCS Game One, 4–3, in the eighth. Derek Jeter hit toward right. Baltimore's Tony Tarasco awaited the ball. "All of a sudden," he said, "this kid [Jeffrey Maier, 12] puts his glove over the fence and steals it." Umpire Richie Garcia ruled home run. The O's blew their top. AL president Gene Budig denied the protest. Said Tarasco of the Stadium: "Merlin must be in this house."

Bernie Williams homered in the 11th: 5–4. New York lost, 5–3, then plucked three at Camden Yards. The World Series opened in the Bronx: Braves, 12–1 and 4–0. Game Three: Cone beat Tom Glavine, 5–2. Game Four's utterance scrawled an enduring twist. Atlanta led, 6–0. Jim Leyritz's poke tied the game. Wade Boggs' 10th-inning walk won it. Game Five: Yanks, 1–0.

"For months, Torre's brother [ex-Brave] Frank had been trying for a heart donor," wrote Phil Pepe. "The day before [the final] Frank got a heart." New York got Game Six, 3–2, and the Series, 4–2. Next year it won the wild card, but lost the first playoff round to Cleveland. "The bear bit us," said Torre. Actually, they were hibernating.

January 1998. Waving a finger, Bill Clinton says, "I did not have sexual relations with that woman, Miss Lewinsky." The Torres became the anti-Clinton: honest, selfless, real. Cone went 20–7. The Yanks acquired David Wells for Jimmy Key: Boomer won 18 and threw a perfect game. Williams' .339 took the batting title. New York drew 2,949,734, won an AL record 114 games, and swept the Division Series. "Maybe we should skip it," said Rangers manager Johnny Oates, "and go directly to go." Torre went to the LCS (beating Cleveland) and Series (sweeping San Diego). Final record: 125–50. A year later the Yankees went to 3 million for the first time—3,293,659, or 40,662 per date.

Talk quieted of leaving the Bronx. "It's the fiber of what baseball's supposed to be," said announcer DeWayne Staats. SI's Rick Reilly disagreed. "The Yankee fan is an overdog-loving, Everready-chucking, bandwagon-hopping, fair-weather, brownnose, puck-lipped human goiter." By contrast, Bob Costas liked their small ball/long ball. "People relate to them because of their resourcefulness," he said in early 1999.

It began with Torre, missing 36 games with prostate cancer. He returned May 18: The Yanks took first for good. Steinbrenner had axed Yogi Berra as '85 manager. Angry, No. 8 stayed away. DiMaggio died in 1999. Calling Yogi, Boss George apologized. On July 18, the Yanks family communed. "It's the history," said Cone. "Joe gives Yogi a ['98] Series ring." Phil Rizzuto, Whitey Ford, Gil McDougald, and Bobby Richardson circled the catcher. Berra then crouched to receive Don Larsen's pregame toss.

"Mr. Larsen," Cone asked, alluding to '56, "are you going to jump into Yogi's arms?" Larsen laughed. "You got it backward. He jumped into mine." Berra caught the pitch and gave his glove to Joe Girardi. Joe then used it to call Cone's perfect game v. Montreal. The last out crested a laying-on of hands. Orlando Cabrera popped to third baseman Scott Brosius. Cone pointed skyward, dropped to his knees, and clutched his head in disbelief. "Maybe there is something to Yankee mystique and the magic to the ballpark," he said. Added Girardi: "I don't want to be superstitious but so many great things happen here, you wonder."

Roger Clemens won his 17th straight decision. Jeter exploded: .349 and 134 runs. Williams hit .342. Orlando Hernandez went 17–9. Mariano Rivera had 45 saves. "We played as a team," said Torre, and grieved. A franchise-high 17 fanned v. Pedro Martinez. The fathers of three players died. Atlantans hailed their "Team of the Decade." In the World Series, the "Team of the Century" swept.

Yankeetime, and the winning was easy: 4–1 and 7–2. Glavine led Game Three, 5–1. Said Cone: "I thought I'd have to pitch Game Six." Chad Curtis and Tino Martinez homered. Chuck Knoblauch's game-tying tater bounced off Brian Jordan's glove. Curtis went deep again, winning, 6–5. Clemens beat Greg Maddux, 4–1, to sweep the Fall Event. The post-'62ers won two Series in 33 years: Torre took three, tying Miller Huggins, in four. "Look at his [Joe's] 12 straight Series wins [tying 1927–'28–'32], or back-to-back sweep, the first since '38–'39," wrote *TV Guide*'s Phil Mushnick. "Unlike Stengel and McCarthy, he had to win two playoffs to even *reach* the Series."

Said the *New York Times*: "It is impossible to think of any other franchise . . . like this one." A columnist chimed: "In a perfect world we'd all be Yankees."

Atlanta's razing led some to pomp. "Best dynasty ever!" one wrote. Berra flashed his Series ring. "They still have to get five other rings," Yogi mused of his ten world titles. In 1923, mah-jongg swept America. The Yankees won. In 1951, Truman fired MacArthur. The Yankees won. In 1999, Clinton dueled Ken Starr. The, well, you get the point. "They've been baseball's great constant," wrote Joseph Durso, "and one of the country's"—their house, sport's brightest light, a Capella or North Star.

The right-field porch still wooed a lefty. The alleys were still a sprayer's friend. Unlike, say, 1966, the discerning vied for tickets before the season. Get your first-deck boxes, or third-level upper deck. "Forget 'em if you got vertigo," said a friend, "but you view the entire field." From the top row—Uecker Country—see New Jersey, the Hudson, Empire State Building, and World Trade Center. Wear a helmet in seats along the left-field line. Between innings try the food court, "Fries in the Sky," and Sidewalk Cafe. Inhale eight international coffees. A populist sampled Beers of the World.

Heckling still forged a visitor's Gehenna. "Haalee-eee Berr-rrry!" the crowd mocked Cleveland's David Justice of his divorce from an actress. (2000 targets: Oakland's Randy Velarde, making baseball's 11th unassisted triple play, and Pedro Martinez, blanking Clemens, 2–0, in an ESPN Classic). Other language outraunched HBO's. Said Cleveland's Travis Fryman: "There's a certain air of intimidation." The air of history was more sublime. Ruth reappeared with Gehrig. Yogi found Larsen's arms. At shortstop, the Scooter dove, or was Derek leaping? In center, specters loomed, fused, evanesced.

In 1999, the usual suspects (Yankees) took the usual parade (down Manhattan to City Hall). Said Torre: "This stuff never gets old." Groupies shrieked: Jeter as Jagger. Babies wore pinstripes: Teach 'em when they're young. Mayor Giuliani gave 55 identical keys to the city to players, coaches, officials, and workers. Later, they taped *The Late Show With David Letterman* to unveil "The Top Ten Things the Yankees Have Always Wanted to Say." Number one was Torre's "I was rooting for the Braves."

In 2000, a rainout bred a July 8 Yankees-Mets doubleheader: afternoon, at Shea; night, the Bronx. "This will mark only the fifth time [last since 1903: Brooklyn Superbas v. New York Giants]," wrote Jason Stark, "two teams have played each other in different ballparks on the same day." Naturally, the Yankees swept. They ended the season 3–15, but edged Oakland in the Division Series and beat Seattle in the LCS.

"Now they [Mets and Yankees fans] can spill beer on one another," Lou Piniella said of the first Subway Series since 1956. The Yanks spilt more: 4–3, 6–5, 2–4, 3–2, and 4–2. "Three world championships in a row," bannered *Baseball Weekly*, "four in five years," and 26th overall. In 2001, Clemens passed Walter Johnson, Gaylord Perry, and Don Sutton as baseball's fifth all-time Ker (3,535). Torre became the sixth stripes skipper to win 500 games.

Ol' Reliable, or Bernie Baseball. Marse Joe, or the Ol' Perfessor. From facade via shadow through tombstone to Death Valley, the Stadium 'r' us.

21

ROCKY MOUNTAIN HIGH

I magine two strangers beached on a South Sea isle from Tajos, New Mexico, and Butte, Montana. They differ in age, race, income, and religion. Their common denominator: the Colorado Rockies. "For years," said President Jerry McMorris, "the Rocky Mountains was only minor league"—the 1948–'92 AAA Bears and Zephyrs. "A whole region missed the big leagues." Its niche changed upon 1993 National League expansion.

The 1993–'94 Rockies played at Mile High (a.k.a. '48–'67 Bears) Stadium, off Clay, West 20th Street, and Elliott Streets, and Interstate 25. Distances were homer-happy: left to right, 335, 375, 423, 400, and 370. A 10-foot padded fence trimmed the outfield. "The thin air," said '93–'98 manager Don Baylor, "made it Little League." Capacity fit the NFL: 19,000 (1960) via 43,103 ('75) to 76,037 ('76). Twenty-one thousand movable seats changed Mile High from football to baseball. The grass field was heated to spur yearlong growth. Our strangers loved the "first fully distributed sound system," a brochure read, with "near stereo quality sound" of any U.S. stadium. The Rockies hoped to avoid a requiem.

"Coming in, our challenge was the [chief tenant] Broncos. They owned the region," said McMorris. "How do you compete?" Colorado lost its first two games in New York. Mile High's Opening Day—April 9, 1993, v. Montreal—drew the NL's regular-season largest crowd (80,227). Play-by-play man Charlie Jones had called Wimbledon, the Super Bowl, Seoul and Barcelona Olympics, and '86 World Cup final. "The Rockies first-ever opener was as big as those combined," he said. "For 30 years the Rocky Mountain region had been baseball's bridesmaid—and now the big leagues were here . . . it was an ode to joy."

Eric Young led off the Rockies' first inning by slamming a tater. Said Jones: "You could hear the roar in California." Young didn't homer again in '93 till Mile High's last game. (Other firsts: pitcher: Bryn Smith. Batter: Montreal's Mike Lansing. Hit: Young. Score: Colorado, 11–4.) The Rockies braved a bigs-worst ERA (5.41), set a record for first-year wins (67), and flaunted a baseball high 4,483,350 (nearly 57,000 per game). "Rain, snow, cold, sun, they came all over the region," mused Baylor. Charlie Hayes had a league-high 45 doubles. Andres Galarraga fronted at .370. A year later the Big Cat, hitting .319, broke his hand. By August 11, the third-placers had already wooed 3,281,511. They lost the final Mile Highfest: Atlanta, 13–0.

"Next day the strike hit," said McMorris, "so we never really got to salute Mile High in the proper fashion." Actually, Mountain Time Zoners still do. They pack its successor.

COORS FIELD

Not invented here. Coors Field swiped Mile High's brainchild: twenty-three hundred upper-deck game-day bleacher seats—$1 kids and seniors, $4 all else: bring a glove, and binoculars. "We could sell them [a.k.a. the Rockpile] in advance like we do everything else," said an official. "But the spur of the moment fans matters. So we sell 'em hours before the game, and you should see the jostling."

Coors was intended to seat 43,000. Mile High tossed that number off a peak. "We saw all those big ['93–'94] crowds," said McMorris, "and we figured we'd better add some seats [size, 50,200]." The former site of a 1876 railroad depot revived a 25-square block historic district named lower downtown, or LoDo. The Rockpile fixed Denver's skyline. First base/right field espied the Rockies beyond left field. Retro red brick, Colorado sandstone, and exposed green girders flanked restaurants, shops, lofts, and art galleries. "It looks like a warehouse," McMorris said of Coors, "and it's made the area come alive."

History: A dinosaur bone was found during Coors' shafting. Things other than they seem: Lengths suggested a pitcher's park (left, 347 feet; left-center, 390; deepest left-center, 420; center, 415; right-center, 375; deepest right-center, 424; right-field corner, 358; and right, 350). Fact: Coors aped pitch 'n' putt. Said Don Baylor: "The ball just carries [about 10 percent higher then the same ball hit at sea level]." Upper deck row 20 was painted purple to mark 5,280 feet—one mile above sea level. A manual board framed a 14-foot right-field wall. Elsewhere, the 8-foot fence trimmed a pitcher's Bellevue. Foul turf was the bigs' smallest. Sharp angles turned gappers into triples. "That means we have to play deep," said right fielder Larry Walker, "which means hits fall in front of you." Grumbling skipped fans: They couldn't get enough.

Coors opened April 26, 1995. First pitcher: Bill Swift. Aptly, the Mets' first batter, Brett Butler, slapped a homer. Dante Bichette's three-run 14th-inning blast foretold: 11–9. Many of the 47,228 parked in the stadium's 6,000 spots. Another 40,000 spaces studded a 20-minute radius. Some had bought a brick inscribed in an outside plaza. The main entrance was topped by a clock tower. The sunken field lowered Coors into the area. Three tiers linked one line to another, then spread to right-center field. To its left, bullpens sat side-by-side. Further left, a water spectacular draped a tree and rock-covered plot. Beyond it a backdrop fattened averages.

A huge scoreboard atop the left-field seats hoisted a latticed steel-framed light standard. "It resembles tracks," the *Rocky Mountain News*' Tracy Ringolsby said of stanchions from LoDo's railroad history. Others crowned the rim in right-center and along each line. "Even the lighting is great," Baylor jibed. "Anything to help score runs."

On June 25, 1995, Andres Galarraga became the first big to homer in three straight innings. On July 3, he got six hits v. Houston. That September the Big Cat gave Colorado four 30-homer men (Bichette a league-high 40 [and 128 RBI, 359 total bases, and .620 slugging], Walker 36 [101 ribbies], Vinny Castilla 32 [90, .309], and Galarraga [106]). "Only the ['77] Dodgers," said McMorris, "ever had that." Two days later John Vander Wal broke a single-year mark with pinch-hit 26. The Rockies packed 3,390,037, won the wild card, but lost the Division Series opener, 5–4. "Some ninth inning," mused Ringolsby. "[Atlanta's] Chipper Jones homers." Rockies pitcher/pinch-hitter Lance Painter then Kd with the bases full. Next day the Braves scored four in the ninth: 7–4. At Atlanta, two 10th-frame runs reprieved Colorado, 7–5. Game Four went 10–4, Braves.

"Our third season!" McMorris said of postseason. "We'd like to make it a habit." Galarraga tried in '96: 47 homers and 150 RBI. Castilla had 40 and 113. Ellis Burks added 40, 128, and .344. "Only the second team," mused Baylor, "to have three guys hit 40 each." On July 12, the Rockies trailed San Diego, 9–2, after 6½ innings. Small potatoes: Colorado, 13–12. Offense took September 17 off: L.A.'s Hideo Nomo no-hit the townies. Attendance hit 3,891,014. Some habit: The '96–'97–'98 Rockies finished third twice and fourth. Galarraga's 140 ribbies led the '97 NL. Walker became MVP: .366, 130 RBI, 49 dingers, and first National with over 400 total bases since Aaron '59. A year later he won the batting title (.363). Coors housed the '98 All-Star Game: AL, 13–8. "Typical pitcher's duel," said the Hall of Fame's Bruce Markusen. "Most hits by a team [19, tying 1992] and total runs [21]."

Mark McGwire went 510 feet in batting practice. In 1999, Walker won another title (.379) and became the first NLer to win the percentage Triple Crown (average, slugging, and on-base) since Musial '48. Pedro Astacio's 17 victories tied a team record. "He also pitched seven complete games," said announcer Wayne Hagin, "a Rockies record not just for a year—a career." Coors' ERA yearly led the league. In '99, 303 homers broke its own record (271); pitchers ceded an NL-most-since-'30 1,028 runs; and four Rockies cleared 100 ribbies (like '96–'97). A year later Todd Helton combined .372, 42 blasts, and 147 RBI. Said Vin Scully: "You don't need an official scorer at Coors Field. You need a certified public accountant."

Between dingers a Mountain Timer might dig the lower-level concourse mural and playground, 90 percent crushed lava/10 percent red

clay warning track, and any of 35 concession stands. Taste buffalo burgers and deep-fried oysters. Try peanut butter and jelly sandwiches from
the main-level kids' stand. Visit baseball's only on-site microbrewery.
The leader, of course: Coors. "I can't think of any place nicer to see a
game," a bystander routinely observed. Yes/yet: Check almost any score.
Some pitching might be nicer.

TURNER FIELD

Facts, John Adams said, are stubborn things. "The Team of the ['90s]
Decade" won a single World Series v. the Yankees' three. Similar house
praise bathed Atlanta's Turner Field—"The Ted," after owner Ted
Turner. "It's the best of the new old ballparks," Braves announcers were
heard to chant. Fact: It was pleasant, more theme park than baseball
field, and a league behind Camden Yards.

Turner rose from Atlanta's 1996 Summer Games. "Olympic Stadium
was built with two things in mind," said general manager John Schuer-
holz. "First, the Olympics. Then it became our permanent home." In
1996, Atlanta–Fulton County Stadium was razed next door to become a
parking lot (8,700 available spots). Olympic then segued—"downsiz-
ing," read accounts—into Turner Field. Temporary bleacher columns
girded the fence around Monument Grove plaza. Atlanta-Fulton statues
greeted a visitor: Hank Aaron, Phil Niekro, Ty Cobb sliding into third.
Five retired number statues fronted the brick and limestone facade: the
Hammer, Nucksie, Warren Spahn, Eddie Mathews, and Dale Murphy.
Turner's mix made Fulton seem philistine: museums, luxury suites,
shops, restaurants, ATM machines, and even day-care centers. Adjacent:
an entry area of photo kiosks, retail store, Hall of Fame and Museum,
Chop House restaurant, and video wall. Monitors carried every in-
progress big-league game.

Turner opened April 4, 1997, near the state capitol, by the hub of
three freeways. First pitcher: Denny Neagle. Batter: Cubs' Brian McRae.
Hit: Braves' Chipper Jones. Homer: mate Michael Tucker. Score:
Atlanta, 5–4, before 50,062. "Welcome," said broadcaster Skip Caray,
"to the new heart of the South." Ventricles linked lush grass, small foul
turf, a 20-foot-below-street level field, and 42-foot-tall Coke bottle. "It

spews fireworks and advertises Atlanta's major business," added colleague Ernie Johnson. "This place doesn't miss a trick." The '97ers
missed few.

Kenny Lofton hit .333. Neagle's 20 wins led the league. Atlanta
crammed 3,463,988, won the East, swept the first playoff round, and
lost the LCS to Florida. A year later The Team of the Decade again communed with consummation: Greg Maddux, NL-best 2.22 ERA; Andres
Galarraga, 44 homers; and team-record 106 wins, including Tom
Glavine's league-high 20. Glavine won Atlanta's sixth-since-'91 Cy
Young. It again swept the Division Series (Chicago) and lost the LCS
(San Diego). "We're running out of time," said Maddux. The Ted's
50,528-capacity wasn't running out of seats: Only one playoff game
topped 43,100.

Three tiers flanked foul ground past each pole. Left-center and right-
center bleachers flanked the backdrop. Atop them, a scripted Braves
emblem over the trademark tomahawk crowned the scoreboard. Robots
chanted the Tomahawk Chop to distraction—theirs, and yours. Red,
white, and blue splashed the interior. Niceties dotted: the city skyline
alight at night; Coca-Cola's sky field 22,000-square-foot pavilion area;
Fulton's old out-of-town board atop the left-field Stadium Club; center's
with a 100-foot Aaron image. (His likeness graced each seat and an
enlarged main entrance photo.) Even cuisine left Fulton in the dust:
gourmet ice cream, Italian food, vegetable quesadillas, a hummus platter.
"You're very close to everything," said Ted Turner. "There's so much to
do." Little translated to the kinetic tube.

Atlanta used '80s television to baptize "America's Team." Ironically,
Turner Field looked better off-air. On TV, fences seemed symmetrical.
(They nearly were: left, 335; left-center, 380; center 401; right-center,
390; right 330). The uniform 8-foot height lacked Fenway's Monster, or
even Camden's right-field wall. Worse, the TV-savvy Braves endured
baseball's most God-awful camera coverage. "In your living room, the
home-plate camera shows the entire field, makes a park seem intimate or
distant," said *Baseball America*. "Turner's is baseball's highest and most
remote. [Other contenders: Arizona, Cincinnati, Cleveland, Detroit,

Oakland, San Francisco, Texas, and Toronto]." At home, it seemed like you were watching from another county.

Tomahawkers wondered: Would "Team of the Decade" vanish? In '99, Maddux went 19–9. Brian Jordan had 115 ribbies. Jones was voted MVP: .319 and .45 dingers. The Braves won their fifth straight Division Series: At Turner, 20,024 unsold tickets marred Matches One-Two. "We and the Mets kept going back and forth," said Cox of LCS Game Six, which finally packed the Ted (52,335). Throats clutched. Drinks flowed. Bedtimes were postponed.

The 11th inning began 9-all. Leading off, Atlanta's Gerald Williams doubled. Bret Boone bunted him to third. New York's Kenny Rogers purposely passed Jones and Jordan. Andruw Jones then walked to plate the pennant-winning run. The Series is best-forgot: Yankees, 4–1, 7–2, 6–5, and 4–1. Atlanta hit only .200. (At least Turner Field sold out.) That winter reliever John Rocker insulted gays, minorities, and New York City in a *Sports Illustrated* article. Commissioner Bud Selig suspended him. The Ted's 2000 All-Star Game wooed a worst-ever 10.1 rating/18 share. St. Louis whacked the Braves in that fall's Division Series. Rocker was traded in 2001.

"If it's not one thing, it's another," Rosanna Danna Danna huffed in *Saturday Night Live*. Turner Field was a kick up close. TV boredom stained it. Camden Yards eclipses the sum of its parts. Somehow the Ted's doesn't equal them.

BANK ONE BALLPARK

A cemetery plot in Tombstone, Arizona, reads: "Here lies Jack Williams. He done his damndest." The Arizona Diamondbacks did their's. Bank One Ballpark—"the BOB"—sat 49,075, cost $335 million, filled 1.3 million square feet, and had a pool, jaccuzi, and retractable roof. "We had to put folks inside," said majority owner Jerry Colangelo. "It can get up to 120 degrees on a summer day." More than 4 miles of cable in a pulley system helped two 200 horsepower motors open or close the roof. Each half of the roof's three movable trusses telescoped over a fixed end truss. BOB's damndest inveigled sun without heating its concrete and metal support system. Air conditioning did the rest. It could drop the temperature 30 degrees in three hours. At night, bring a jacket.

Colangelo got the NL expansion team in 1995. Minority investors included Nike's Phil Knight and comedian Billy Crystal. They hired the firm that designed Boston's Fleet Center and Atlanta's Olympic Stadium. Ground broke at downtown Jefferson Street between 4th and 7th Streets. The NHL Coyotes' and Colangelo's NBA Suns' America West Arena stood across a parking lot. Nearly 20,000 spaces studded the neighborhood. Transit buses stopped nearby. "It's easy as hell to get to," Colangelo suggested of the less dome than airport hangar. Jack Williams would think it populist.

Take the warehouse area, outside plazas and walkways, and red-brick facade, green steel, and southwest-styled design. The main entrance terra-cotta rotunda floor display hailed the state of Arizona. Another kicker lay inside: a retractable roof sports site with God's, not fake, turf (shade-tolerant DeAnzon Zoysia). The Sun Pool Pavilion splashed 415 feet from home behind the right-center fence. "You can rent it for [swimming pool/hot tub] parties," said Colangelo. For sale: the beer garden, restaurant (down the left-field line), Stadium Club (right), and tiered picnic area (beyond center).

"We entertain," said manager Buck Showalter, "but the focus is on baseball," e.g., March 31, 1998, the 'Backs' Opening Day. First pitcher: Andy Benes. Batter/hit: Colorado's Mike Lansing. Homer: mate Vinny Castilla. Score: Rockies, 9–2. On April 5, ESPN aired Arizona's first victory, 7–2, v. San Francisco. David Dellucci's 12 triples led the league. Benes threw a no-hitter for 8⅓-innings. Chicago's Mark Grace became first to slosh the pool. Record: 65–97. Attendance: 3,602,856. Most filled the 80 percent of steep-pitched five-tiered seats that circled home from one pole to the other.

Corner pens welded the grandstand and left- and right-field bleachers. "Only park," said Showalter, "where a ball to either pen can be a homer—or foul." The BOB was asymmetrical: left, 330; alleys, 374; and right, 334. The wall rose from 7½ feet (right- and left-center 413) to 25 (center 407). It had a period dirt track between the mound and plate;

scoreboard above each pole; and concourse of shops, concessions, pho-tographs, and baseball monitors. The kids' concession stand sold maca-roni and cheese. A farmer's market vended fruit and vegetables. Ads topped the outfield like daisies in a field. Between them a giant board blared a frenetic JumboTron. On either side square panels opened and closed. "Gotta' love it," said Colangelo. "Open, they're a number. Closed, they're an ad." In 1999, Mark McGwire's 510-foot batting prac-tice shot bounced through an open window. The 'Backs countered: 35 more victories than '98. Puffed Showalter: "Baseball's largest-ever sin-gle-year improvement."

Randy Johnson's 6-foot-10, sphinxlike face, and marauding fastball forged a '98 Cy Young NL-leading 2.48 ERA. (On May 8, 2001, the Big Unit Kd a record-tying 20 Reds in nine innings: He left tied 1–1.) Also fronting: Tony Womack (72 steals) and Luis Gonzalez (206 hits. In April '01, he had a bigs-record-tying 13 homers). Four '99ers topped 100 RBI: Matt Williams (142, and 35 homers), Jay Bell (112 [38]), Gonzalez (111 [26]), and Steve Finley (103 [34]), Arizona won the West. Before 49,584, the Division Series opened at the BOB. New York's Edgardo Alfonzo slammed in the ninth: 8–4. Next night Todd Stottlemyre evened the best-of-five, 7–1. The Mets took a 9–2 laugher. Arizona led Game Four in the eighth—but lost a run when Bell was thrown out at home. The Mets tied at 3—after Womack missed John Olerud's eighth-inning fly. In the 10th, Finley leaped for Todd Pratt's drive to center—and barely missed his series-ending 4–3 blast.

"I jumped as high as I could," said the Gold Glover. "I just couldn't get it." Damndest try, and park. You could see Jack Williams smiling.

TROPICANA FIELD

The name implied sun, breeze, and Ricky Ricardo. The place meant a dark, sterile "park," said *Sports Illustrated,* "that has all the ambiance of a warehouse." Floridians seek outside's peaceful, easy feeling. The Tampa Bay Devil Rays foreswore it for a doughnut-shaped home. Trop-icana Field did afford a grand view of the Sunshine Skyway bridge. Sadly, it required that you stand on the roof.

The problem: timing. "We built it [a.k.a. Thunderdome or Florida

SunCoast Dome] before the trend began to open air, tiny ballparks," said Devil Rays CEO Vince Naimoli. "Other clubs then talked of moving here." The late '80s White Sox declared for western Florida. Chicago kept them by building Comiskey Park II. Seattle bit, then balked. In 1992, Naimoli's group bought the Giants for $115 million. NL owners blocked the sale. "Some teams were sincere about moving here," recalled the local businessman. "Others used us for leverage." On March 9, 1995, Naimoli received a $130 million AL expansion team. The Rays then set out to gloss their 1.1 million square-foot facility.

They began by building a 900-foot ceramic walkway—1,849,091 colored tiles etching the beach, sun, and sea. Music, stage lighting, and sound system buoyed the walk: play-by-play recalled Thomson, Fisk, and Maz. You entered a rococo eight-story main rotunda on Tropicana's east side, redolent of Ebbets Field, facing the main parking lot. (The Teflon-coated translucent 6.5-degree slanted roof, visible from Interstate 275, was lighted orange after Rays home wins.) Lengths resembled Brooklyn's: left, 315; alleys, 371; deepest left-center, 415; center, 407; and right, 322. A 9½ foot fence rimmed the outfield. A full house sat 43,819. The apex slid from 225 feet (above second base) to 85 (the center-field wall). Rotunda/schmunda. Hilda Chester would not have recognized the joint.

Point: AstroTurf 12 grass covered most of the field. Counterpoint: It *looked* like grass. The Devil Rays installed baseball's fifth dirt infield (like the 1966–'77 Astrodome, '70–'72 Three Rivers, '70–'76 Busch Stadium, and '71 Candlestick). "We didn't want cheesy cutouts," said manager Larry Rothschild, fired in 2001. "This is a *baseball* park." It opened March 31, 1998; 45,369 attended. First pitcher: Wilson Alvarez. Batter: Detroit's Brian Hunter. Hit: mate Tony Clark. Homer: Tigers' Luis Gonzalez. Score: Visitors, 11–6. The Rays spurted to a 10–6 start. Quinton McCracken set an expansion high for hits and outfield assists. Rookie pitcher Rolando Arrojo became Tampa Bay's first All-Star. It wasn't much, miffing few. The last-placers baited 2,506,023. "We're big-league, after all these years," said Naimoli. It seemed enough, for now.

"Let me entertain you," Ethel Merman sang in *Gypsy*. The Rays strived. Tropicana brandished batting cages, pitching machines, and miniature golf. Above left field: The (1,339-seat second-deck) Beach. "What's there?" said a visitor. "What isn't?"—palm trees, a spa, restaurant, and bar. The retail Center Field Street area knit the Budweiser Brew House, Cuesta-Ray Cigar Bar, and The Batter's Eye restaurant. The latter's backside turned backdrop. "Its tinted windows hide the diners," Naimoli explained, "and is just right for a batter." Sight lines eclipsed the Metrodome's. Lighting left Pro Player in the dark. "[So] what's the use of worrying?" mused songwriter George Asaf. The Devil Rays worried that their baseball was inside.

Four cable rings, or catwalks, upheld the roof. Hitting them, were drives homers or out of play? The highest two were unreachable. The others bred dirt-kicking/breast-beating/game-protested beefs. On May 2, 1999, Jose Canseco's blast landed on the "B" ring catwalk and didn't come down. (He got a double.) That September he put a franchise-record 34th homer on the roof of The Batter's Eye. (Fred McGriff added 32.) The '99–2000 Rays drew 756,456 and 955,971, respectively, fewer than 1998. One '01 game wooed a franchise-worst 11,056. Commissioner Selig scurried to Florida. What gives? he asked. Naimoli's response: "We're not convenient to the bulk of our potential base."

Tampa's 285,000 population topped St. Petersburg's 260,000. St. Pete, however, housed Tropicana Field. Twenty-six years remained on the lease: Naimoli spoke of breaking it. "We need some old-fashioned baseball," a columnist wrote of the self-hyped "Ballpark of the 21st Century." The Rays got some August 7, 1999. Wade Boggs needed three hits to become baseball's 23rd 3,000 player. "All I could think of was Little League," he said of growing up in Tampa. Singling twice, Boggs thought of Cobb and Clemente. In the sixth, the five-time batting champion faced Cleveland's Chris Haney. "I was just trying to hit the ball," Boggs said, "after all, I'm the spray hitter." Instead, he whelped a 372-foot dinger. "How about that?" he said later. "First to reach 3,000 with a homer!"

The near-SRO (39,512) crowd erupted. Boggs pumped his fists and high-fived first-base coach Billy Hatcher. "Billy had said that he wanted to kiss me on the 3,000th so I just ran on by him so I didn't have to kiss him." Rounding second, he pointed upward and blew his late mother, killed in a 1986 car accident, a kiss. Nearing home, Boggs again pointed, then smooched the plate. "Before I touched it, I blew another one and something ran through my mind to say, 'Go ahead and kiss that thing. You stepped on it enough, you might as well kiss it.' "

Generations hugged: Boggs, mates, father, wife, and 12-year-old son Brett, the Devil Rays batboy. Said Wade: "His godfather is George Brett," a fellow 3,000er. At that moment even inside baseball seemed baseball, after all.

SAFECO FIELD

In August 1999, the Indians readied to leave Cleveland for Seattle. Their skipper was asked if Safeco Field would surpass the Kingdome. "This room," said Mike Hargrove, pointing to his Jacobs Field office, "would be better than the Kingdome." Intimacy helped: Safeco sat only 46,621. The field was fairer. "That other field," mused pitching coach Stan Williams, "was a terror for our pitching." Dimensions: left field, 331; left-center, 390; center, 405; right-center, 386; and right, 326.

Arched windows and brick facade aped Camden Yards. Outside staircases echoed Turner Field; left-field roof, Wrigley Field; right-field restaurant, SkyDome; bleachers, Jacobs Field. Even better: the look from the NBBJ Seattle-designed upper deck bound the city skyline, Space Needle, Elliott Bay, Mount Rainier, Olympic Mountains, and pastiche of ferries, cargo ships, and sunsets from Albert Bierstadt. Trains rumbled by the park. Whistles spiked each inning. "This is what a baseball park *should* be!" ESPN's Jon Miller blared one Sunday night. It should be— for the cost.

In 1995, voters spurned public funding. The state legislature then approved a half-cent prepared food and rental car tax. A year later its public authority chose a site on 9.59 acres south of the Kingdome at Royal Brougham Way, South Atlantic Street, and First and Third Avenues South. The Mariners shortly signed a lease through 2019. On June 4, 1998, a Seattle bank bought naming rights: $1.8 million annually for 20 years. Ground broke. The M's pledged $75 million. "Famous last words," said Seattle city council member Cynthia Sullivan. Budgeted at $320 million, Safeco was to open in 1999.

The *Boston Globe* later caught its charm. "New stadium equals big crowds, and new luxury-box revenue equals better, more expensive players, which ultimately equals on-field victories, pennants, and eternal 'big-league bliss'—all with real grass." The problem was price: Overruns began. The budget rose to $417 million. Mariners owners demanded $60 million more in public cash. King County said no. Safeco would open on time—if the M's paid the bill.

It/they did. A July 15, 1999, countdown proceeded to 7:05 P.M. Jamie Moyer threw the first pitch to San Diego's Quilvio Veras. First hit: Padre Eric Owens. Homer: Seattle's Russ Davis (two games later). Score: M's lose, 3–2. A ferry horn, blue and white confetti, and amnesia filled the air. "Seeing this place," said Sullivan, "you forgot how much it cost [ultimately, $517 million]." From Interstate 5, Safeco resembled a huge postmodern insect. Up close it aired steel cutouts of players hitting or fielding. A large bronze sculpture, "The Mitt," etched a baseball glove with a hole in the middle. The main concourse circled between box and terrace seating. You could leave a luxury suite (all sold out) via lower-level "personal [seat license] boxes" (as much as $25,000 yearly) through field-level stands (up to $175 a game, including private bar and restaurant) to bleachers (left field $7; center $5) and not miss a play. "Even the highest seat [right-field corner Section 306, Row 25, Seat 1] lets you read the jersey's name and see 'em breathe," said announcer Dave Niehaus.

Perceived waste made Safeco's color scheme (green) ironic. Grass dressed the field five and two feet, respectively, below street and sea level. Four decks linked right-center and the left-field pole. "It's all here. It's gorgeous," said M's manager Lou Piniella, paroled from the Kingdome. An out-of-town scoreboard graced the left-field wall. Bleachers topped it. To the right pens touched left-center field. Center and right each tooted two bleacher areas. The main scoreboard boasted a video screen and matrix board. "Wait till high definition TV signals are available," said an official. "We'll even show that."

Bigs first: Play-by-play boards along each line. "Jeff Fassero 95 mile per hour fastball," one might read. Another: "Rodriguez grounded out, Griffey struck out, Martinez doubled." Other pieces: team store, picnic and children's area, baseball museum, upper-level swimming deck, and "Hit It Here" Cafe. Thirty-eight concession stands and carts, respectively, offered barbecue, teriyaki, fish and chips. Some boasted a North-west or baseball theme: e.g., Sliders Sushi Bar and The Grounds Crew Express.

About 40 percent of Dome attendance sprung from beyond King County. Safeco's neared 50. "They're the Northwest's, not Seattle's, team," said Niehaus. A retractable roof would ensure Spokane of an M's game being played. It covered 8.75 acres, weighed 11 tons, had enough steel for a 55-story skyscraper, could brook 70-mile-per-hour wind and seven feet of snow, lay 215 feet above the field, and opened in 20 minutes. (Other Safeco numbers: nine elevators, 11 escalators, 4,988 light fixtures, 1,231 doors and gates, 1,400 foundation piles, and 25 miles of pipe.) Open, three panels nested above the right-field grand-stand. Shut, it stopped rain, opened to each side, and resembled a giant carport. "If it's cold outside," said *Baseball Weekly*'s Tim Wendel, "you'll still feel it."

Seattle air is often moist and thick. "The ball travels in Denver because of the thin air," an M's official said. "Seattle is the opposite." The Kingdome mimed a shooting gallery. (In '99, pitchers had a 6.14 ERA). Safeco esteemed the bunt, bullpen, and hit and run. Griffey, Jr., hit 56 taters in both '97 and '98. His first at Safeco came July 18. "I don't worry about it," he said of length and carry. "I just hit it. Once it leaves my bat, I have no control over where it goes."

Randy Johnson left for Houston in 1998. The M's said overruns would preclude signing Griffey. "I feel used up in this stadium thing," he said. In 2000, Junior was traded to the Reds. Would free agent All-Star shortstop Alex Rodriguez follow? Could even Safeco—'99 attendance, 2,915,908—let small-market Seattle best Boston and New York? It helped: The '00 Ms drew 3,148,317, won the wild card, and beat Chicago in the Division Series. A-Rod had an A+ year: .316, 41, and 132. The Rangers then inked him to a $252 million pact. A-Who? The 'Olers broke Atlanta's 1996 record with 20 April victories. Ichiro Suzuki left Japan to hit safely in 15 and 23 straight games. Seattle's 52–15 start forged baseball's second–best–ever 67–game record.

"The relative advantage of a new stadium has diminished," said author Andrew Zimbalist. "When each team has a Camden Yards, you can't get a $30 million revenue advantage." For the time, advantage,

Mariners. "They may have gone $100 million over budget," wrote Tracy Ringolsby, "but the Mariners did it right."

Better than the Kingdome? Hell, almost a Camden Yards. "We'll always have Paris," Bogart tells Bergman. Let Seattle always have Safeco Field.

COMERICA PARK

In December 1998, Comerica Inc., a Detroit-based bank, paid $66 million over 30 years for naming rights to Motown's new den. Comerica Park would lie north of town, across from the Fox Theater on Woodward Avenue, east of Tiger Stadium. It cost $295 million—$115 million, public cash; the rest, Tigers owner Mike Ilitch—and sat only 40,000 patrons. "Seats close to the field," growled Ilitch. "Only 15,000 in the upper deck." The seats were slat-backed and dark green, like pre–repainted Tiger Stadium. To see them you passed an area redolent of a zoo.

A 25-foot-long by 15-foot-high Tiger with a raised paw statue bearded the main entrance on Witherell Street. Four more perched on a parapet. Two guarded the Grand Circus entrance. Thirty sculpted Tiger heads, a lighted baseball in the jaw, protruded the beige, orange, and mottled green facade. You roamed the Hall of Fame Museum Walk (six 25-foot-high bats, pictures, and other bric-a-brac) through the main concourse (twice Tiger's width) to a sunken field (26 feet below street level). Then, it hit you: This was not your father's park.

For one thing, more than 100 private suites served the rich and/or famous. Three parlors thrived: The Ballpark Club, lower-deck Tiger Den Lounge, and upper-deck club lounge. The 100-foot circular Big Cat Court, behind first base, starred a merry-go-round carousel. "The trick is," said Ernie Harwell, "kids ride [30 hand-painted] tigers, not horses [also, two wheelchair-accessible chariots]." Beyond third: a 50-foot Italian-made Ferris wheel with 12 baseball-shaped cars, and Beer Hall/Brushfire Grill. A theater starred Greenberg, Cobb, and Kaline. You wanted to hand it to HOK Sport, Detroit's SH&G, and the Rockwell Group of America. Cushioned "club" seats. Indoor pitching and batting practice. Even diaper-changing areas. All seats wider than Tiger Stadium's. "[The designers] got it all," said a Tigers catcher shortly after the opening, "except that the object in baseball is to score."

Tiger offered bread and circuses. "Chicks dig the long ball," went a 2000 Nike commercial. Comerica banned a long-ball feed. "It's a beautiful park," said two-time MVP Juan Gonzalez, joining the '00 Tigers. "It's just too big. I've already hit a lot of balls that would be easy home runs in lots of other parks." The *Wall Street Journal* read: "The franchise has declared war on home runs [In Comerica's first month, baseball hit a then-record 931], believing that as exciting as they are to fans, they aren't always the best thing for the sport." It also wished to help Detroit pitchers, shellshocked at The Corner.

Comerica's left-field wall measured 345 feet (v. Tiger's 340). Right's 330 topped Michigan and Trumbull's 325. Center field was actually shorter (420 v. 440). The alleys were its headache:at Tiger, 365 and 370; Comerica, 398 and 380. "Left-center, nearly 400!" said the White Sox' Frank Thomas. "You can just see the Tigers cracked." Even Detroit's Doug Brocail said: "I pray they move in the fences next year. I mean, I pray they do. This ballpark is killing us." Brocail was a *pitcher*.

Comerica opened April 11, 2000: First pitcher: Brian Moehler. Batter: M's' Mark McLemore. Hit: mate John Olerud. Homer: Ironically, Gonzales, fleeing to Cleveland in 2001. Score: Detroit 5, Seattle 2. The Tigers brooked a bigs–high 15 shutouts. Comerica sported only 127 home runs. Final attendance, however, hit a best-since-'84 2,533,752. "It's old-timey baseball," said reliever Todd Jones. "Detroit finally built a stadium that would have made Cobb proud. Just too late for him." Actually, not quite.

Stainless steel 12-to-13 foot tall statues of Willie Horton and Hall of Famers Cobb, Gehringer, Greenberg, Newhouser, and Kaline, atop a granite pedestal, flanked the left-center wall. Tiger Stadium's flagpole was still in play. Twin 40-foot-long by 27-foot-high Tigers, each weighing 5,000 pounds, crowded baseball's largest scoreboard (202 feet wide by 147 feet tall) with video replay and color matrix board, high above left. You viewed it from the street (like skyline from the park). "Tiger was enclosed," Ilitch noted. "This opens to the city." Too, the center-field fountain, 22 feet above concourse level, synchronized to music.

"It's a beautiful park," Harwell said. "Wonderful sight lines, a real sense of Detroit"—and the dead-ball age. The Tigers atop the score-board growled, eyes lighting, upon a Bengals homer. Laryngitis struck in Comerica's first year.

ENRON FIELD

Skip the polygraph. I will tell you no lies. I love the brick behind home plate, and steep berm in center field. I love the short left-field porch, and in-play flagpole to decapitate a fielder. I love Union Station's roof, left-center pillars, and 1860s life-size, 48,000-pound coal locomotive and steel tender that punctuates an Astros dinger. I love the park that is everything the Astrodome was not. I love the bells and whistles and architectural quirks. I love how *Sports Illustrated* wrote: "[Astros owner Drayton] McLane [and HOK of Kansas City] has built a ballpark with more nooks and crannies than an English muffin, with angles and wide spaces that will create doubles and triples, action everywhere . . . a ball-park of idiosyncrasies and intrigue." I love the 12-foot-tall model of a Conoco gas pump in left-center field. Said McLane: "We'll keep track of our homers." I love the arched left-to-center wall. Scrap Comiskey Park. Return to the drawing board for SkyDome and Comerica. Give the Metrodome leavetaking and lights out. I love the majors' "Ripley's Believe It or Not! museum of the arcane," as described by *SI*. I love Enron Field.

"The Astrodome was so antiseptic," McLane said in April 2000. "The crowds were so quiet . . . if you got a 3–0 lead, the game was over." Houston's began when a 1996 task force urged that Harris County spend $625 million to build a new downtown baseball park and arena and refit the Dome. The Astros and NBA Rockets threatened to leave the South's largest burg. (The football Oilers would, to Tennessee.) For months McLane hinted of a move to suburban Washington, D.C. Finally, he vowed to stay if voters OKd a park. They did, barely, November 5, 1996: McLane would now see if baseball could click. "I remember going to the Astrodome when we'd have crowds of 12,000," he mused. "Houston is the fourth largest city in the United States, and we were still a small-market team. Why was that? High school football in my home-town [Temple, Texas] draws more people on a Saturday night than we did." He would build it. Would they come?

Ground broke November 1, 1997, on downtown's east side at Crawford and Texas Streets, next to historic Union Station, near the George R. Brown Convention Center. Parking lots were razed, or kept. (More than 2,000 spaces were enclosed or reserved on site. Off-site parking within a ½-mile radius: 25,179.) A naming fee turned The Ballpark at Union Square in Houston to Enron Field, after a gas and electricity company. HOK Sport began to design the $250 million, God's (actually, 419 Tifway Bermuda) grass, brick and limestone, retractable-roof plot. They had a willing client. McLane yearned to reproduce, wrote *Sports Illustrated*, "a number of eccentricities from old-time stadiums." E.g. Fenway's wall (left fielders play on or near the warning track), Tiger Stadium's flagpole (near dead center, about 430 feet from home), and 10-foot grassy knoll with a 30-degree slope (Crosley Field). "The one feature I'm surprised I got included is the hill in center," said Tal Smith, president of baseball operations. "I always figured someone could come along and take it out of the plans." In May 2000, the Reds' Ken Griffey stumbled on Tal's Hill trying to catch a triple. It reminded him, he said, of growing up in Cincinnati.

HOK began on time and track. First, it made Union Station's arched brick wall Enron's outer barrier from dead center to the left-field corner. Tracks atop it moved the $65 million roof. (Panels measured 120 by 537 feet to 242 by 589 feet, had a movable area of 271,500 square feet, stood 242 feet high, weighed 5,000 tons, could be opened in 12–20 minutes, and then nested over the right-field seats.) The wall, in turn, oozed vagary. "Field dimensions are dictated by site restraints. It was a problem," said HOK project manager Earl Santee of left-center's 362 feet, "because the wall closed us in," becoming a fan's joy and pitcher's horror house. "There'll be plays when I'll say, 'I've got it . . . oops,' " said outfielder Daryle Ward. (Grabbing it: longhorners in the 800 Crawford Boxes atop the 21-high by 128-feet-long, old-time, hand-operated scoreboard.)

Left field's pole hovered 315 feet from the plate. "The wall's height makes hitting homers a little harder," said Santee. (Little: Enron broke the Dome's '99 homer total in 37 games. The 'Stros smacked an NL record 249, including 131 at home. Jeff Bagwell and Richard Hidalgo bombed a franchise-high 47 and 44, respectively. Not coincidentally,

Houston drew a record 3,056,139.) To its right the boxes ended in straightaway left. The wall then dropped to 10 feet, veered left by 90 degrees, recessed for almost 30 feet to 362, and took a 90 degree *right* turn toward center field (436). Left-center pillars preceded the berm, flagpole, and right-center pens (373). A seven-foot bleacher wall extended to the pole (326). Right's third-deck megaboard flashed scores, ads, and stock quotations. Standing roomers mobbed the left-center arches and balconies.

A giant knothole: Enron's 550-foot glass wall—said Santee, "The world's largest sliding glass door"—gave passersby a peek. Four tiers tied the poles. Right field boasted terrace dining. "Can't wait," said one fan, "for a homer to hit my barbecue." Concessions included Tex-Mex and items from each visiting city: e.g., cheese steak via Philly. Enron paraded sixty suites, 300-seat Diamond Club, air-conditioning, a kids' play area, and three main entries.

The 138-foot-tall home plate tower on Texas Avenue flanked the east ingress. Most entered through the gussied-up Station of cafés, retail shops, team offices, and a tour theater. Its roof housed renting partiers. "We got the idea," said Santee, "from people watching Cubs games from roofs across the street from Wrigley." A Texas Limited Excursion train deposited many at the park. "This city was a turn of the century railroad town. We wanted to reflect that," mused McLane. Quickly its *leitmotif*—Fenway's wall, BOB's swimming pool—became the re-created 1860s engine on the track atop the left-field wall. "A giant crane pulled it up in two sections."

An ex-actor was the engineer. "What you have to try do is anticipate the home run," Mike Kenny said. "This is a big locomotive, so it really doesn't jump to 60 miles an hour in a hurry. If I see a ball that looks like it's going out, I start to get the train moving right then. When I'm sure it's gone, I start ringing the bell and turning on the side effects."

New York opened the Astrodome with an April 12, 1965, exhibition. The Yanks kicked off Enron, too: Houston, 6–5, March 30, 2000, over Texan Roger Clemens. The regular season opened April 7: Phillies 4, Astros 1. "Can there be a thing," McLane said, "as too much excitement?" *SI* thought not of its "Field of Screams . . . It is a ballpark in which the ball not only can fly over the fence, but also bounce off the fences [Enron's had 21 angles] and roll forever." Upon each victory Kenny crossed 800 feet from center field to the left-field corner. Whistles tooted. Bells rang. Heard: more than 8,000 watts of sound.

"All of this for a win," said broadcaster Milo Hamilton. "Imagine what the train would do someday if we take it all." In Enron Field, perhaps Houston already had.

PACIFIC BELL PARK

In 1999, the Giants and Padres staged "Turn the Clock Ahead." Players wore hats and jerseys suggestive of 2021. Positions were renamed: shortstop became "intermediate station," left field "left sector." The Giants then moved the clock back to the bigs' first privately funded baseball-only park since Dodger Stadium '62.

Pacific Bell Park, named for a phone company, opened April 11, 2000, on a waterfront site (SOMA, for South of Market [Street]) bounded by King, 2nd and 3rd Streets, and China Basin. First pitcher: Kirk Rueter. Batter and hit: L.A.'s Devon White. Homer: mate Kevin Elster. Score: Dodgers, 6–5. "After years of cold weather at Candlestick/3 Com Park, Giants fans can enjoy warm days at Pac Bell," wrote ESPN's Peter Gammons. "It's hard to say what's best about the place, except that it is in San Francisco." The brick-clad, HOK-designed plat cost $319 million: $134 million from charter seats and naming, sponsor, and concession rights; $170 million, bank loan; and $15 million, city tax financing. Like Candlestick, it was built to endure earthquakes. Likeness starts there, and ends.

"Small is beautiful," said British economist E. F. Schumacher. Pac Bell filled a tiny 12.8 acres. "HOK told us that the China Basin site would be worth the challenges," Giants executive vice president Larry Baer recalled, "because of the way it makes the Bay part of the game of baseball in San Francisco." Public transportation interlocked the Bay Area: Muni Metro street cars and trolleys, CalTrain, BART (Bay Area Rapid Transit), buses, and ferries. Pac Bell fronted San Francisco Bay. The Giants wanted you to hop or walk. A dissident could park in among more than 10,000 spaces. "Everything is precious in this part of town," added owner Peter A. Magowan. "Size, land, development."

Nearly 30 restaurants surrounded the park. Near the main entrance: a life-size statue of the Say-Hey Kid. Pac Bell's address: 24 Willie Mays Plaza. Other numbers: 40,800 (capacity), including 63 (luxury suites), 1,500 (field seats), and 5,200 (club seats), 48 (feet, front row, to plate), 15–20 (bullpens behind first and third base), and 45 (degrees HOK turned Pac Bell's design to block the wind).

"The original design had better views of the Bay Bridge," said Baer. The switch warmed a visitor: High seats behind the plate cut a southwest breeze. The China Basin Channel paralleled right to center field. "The reason was the water," Magowan said of right's 309-foot foul line. "We had to get an exemption for the fence. We had nowhere else to go." Pull hitters liked the NL's shortest porch. Pitchers, however, could survive. A 188-foot by 25-foot barrier yoked the line to right-center (420, up to 55 feet longer than Candlestick; the final 80 feet dipped to 20 feet, 5 inches). A brick wall topped the 8-foot fence. "It's got all sorts of stuff on it," said right fielder Barry Bonds. "You don't know if it'll drop down or ricochet away." Other heights spurred nook and cranny: 8 left (335) to center field (405); a 19-foot length peaked at 11 in left-center (364).

Four tiers boomeranged the plate from one pole to another. Bleachers dotted left and center. Above them a Coca-Cola–sponsored interactive area let kids walk inside a Coke bottle, sit in a huge fielder's glove, and play in a mini-Pac Bell. A live video board blared their picture: Hey, Mom, that's me! In right, a 35-foot-wide public access walkway linked the bay and arched exterior. Homeless? For three innings peer from the Portwalk behind the wire-mesh fence. Wrote Gammons: "One man watched, then went outside, and caught a striped bass off the pier." Inside, food was pricier: Mexican, chowder, sushi, and sourdough. A Cha Cha Bowl, for Orlando Cepeda, mixed jerk chicken, beans, and rice.

On May 1, Bonds became the first to splash McCovey's Cove. Portuguese water dogs trained by Don Novello, a.k.a. *Saturday Night Live*'s Father Guido Sarducci, left their barge to pluck homers from the drink. Also letting loose: the Old Navy Splash Landing. Said Magowan: "A 14-foot-tall mechanical player named 'Rusty' goes back and forth on a track to celebrate." Four canons launched water 100 feet in the air. A right-field sign totaled Giants drives to the channel. "What a great sight," Vin Scully said in the opening series. "To look out there and see all the yachts [and kayaks and fish boats and freights], and the people sprawled out on their decks with their TV and drinks, it was unbeliev-able"—a floating sports bar in right field.

A hand-operated scoreboard topped left field. The main board topped straightaway center. The '00ers sold out before the season started: total, 3,315,330. Jeff Kent (.334 and 125 RBI) was voted MVP. 'Frisco won the West, but lost the Division Series. Bonds became the 17th to whack 500 homers. "Not a bad start," he winked of 2001: four straight dingers, five in two games, six in three, eight in five, and a record 38 in the Giants' first 71. You couldn't get a ticket for 90 straight games. It was like '58 again: a *baseball* city, slightly bonkers. "When we got into this venture, people asked, 'Is San Francisco a baseball town?' " said Baer. "For us, the question has been answered." Gammons' take was even rosier. "For a fan, this may be the best park ever built."

THE ROAD NOW TAKEN

2001–

22

YESTERDAY ONCE MORE

"What I don't understand is the lack of imagination in ballpark design," Bart Giamatti said in 1988. "Why can't we build an angular, idiosyncratic park for a change, with all the amenities and conveniences, and still make it better than anything we have?" Baseball did. Camden Yards begot Arlington via Phoenix through Detroit. In 2001, Milwaukee and Pittsburgh boarded their train. Cincinnati, Philadelphia, and San Diego will likely join them by 2004. Future baseball-only plots may also dot Boston, Miami, Minneapolis, Montreal, and New York. All recall Giamatti: "When this is complete," he said of the Yard, "every team will want one."

Sameness and Murphy's Law soiled, say, 1965–'91. Veterans equaled Three Rivers equaled Riverfront. By contrast, new old Escurials were fashioned to fit the game. Begin with baseball's smallest, oldest, and most lyric park. Fenway Park links the Triangle, Williamsburg, right-field belly, Pesky Pole, and Yawkeys' morse code. "This is the capital of baseball," chimed the Phillies' Curt Schilling. What could equal Fenway? The Red Sox had a thought.

"The Sox tell us that they need luxury boxes, gourmet concessions stands, nicer bathrooms, and more high-priced seats," the *Boston Globe*'s Charles A. Radwin wrote in 1998. "What they don't need, they say, is Fenway Park." Fenway's pull kept the faithful coming and sponsors queuing. Parks like Camden Yards turned that specialty on its head. By aping it, they devalued it.

Early in 1998, general manager Dan Duquette announced but would not detail a "spectacular plan" to replace Fenway. A year later the *Globe* said that the Sox would at some point build a new park abutting it on a triangular 14-acres parcel boarded by Yawkey Way, Brookline Avenue, and Boylston Stret. The ersatz plot would "look and feel like Fenway" and rise over several years while the Sox closed their 1912 cafe.

Revenue would stem from ticket and luxury box seats and probably a private partner. "We need a new park," Duquette said. "Our fans complain about narrow seats and lack of modern amenities [rest rooms, ticket windows, and concession stands]. Without corporate boxes, there's no way to get money to compete." Most knew how the Yard and other new parks threatened Fenway. All grasped that Fenway, if razed, would shroud its successor. "Build a new park, if you must," said broadcaster Ken Coleman. "Get your new deck, loges, better amenities. But keep the outfield as it is. This is what people see on TV, how they know Fenway—from one pole to another, don't change a thing."

Could fans warm to another park? *If* it's Fenway, the Sox replied. On May 15, 1999, team CEO John Harrington affirmed the *Globe* report. "It will be a larger Fenway," he said, choking tears, "and incorporate its best features." Home plate would move 206 yards, and Pesky's Pole to the new right-field line. Copied: the Green Monster, Triangle, right-field pens, left-field ladder, arches, and brick facade. "The Red Sox have thought things through this time," said the *Globe*'s Dan Shaughnessy. "If they can do what they say they are going to do, they'll be going new— without going modern." Proposed capacity: 44,130, including 100 luxury suites and 5,000 club seats. Lengths: same (save right field: 307, not 302). Said Duquette: "Our fans indicated they like the dimensions like they are."

A red seat would show where Ted Williams' 502-foot homer landed at

Fenway I. Long-time switchboard operator Helen Robinson would switch lines. The Citgo sign would still gleam beyond left-center. Most of Fenway would crumble on the new field's opening. The original manual scoreboard, part of the wall, infield, and facade would become a museum (flanking a new Sox Hall of Fame, baseball museum, and learning center). Rumble, say, to 2005. Walk from Kenmore Square down the old third-base line to a game. Diamond Vision would top the monster; field lie 20 feet below street level; right's scoreboard crown two-tier bleachers; foul turf *decrease*! "If the Sox'd varied from Fenway more than this," wrote a columnist, "the cry would have killed a new park."

A question coursed: Could cash be raised?—ultimately, private $362 million (more than any club has invested) and public $312 million for design, land acquisition, construction, infrastructure, and parking (2,760 spots). The state legislature OKd funding in July 2000. "They did their job," wrote the *Globe* in early '01. "Now the pressure is on the Sox." Manager Jimy Williams shrugged. "I think I got the best shower in baseball. I'll take that shower I got and put it in the new park. The rest of it I'll leave up to them."

The new Fenway was designed by Helmuth, Obata and Kassabaum. By 1997, HOK's $64 million revenue topped its eight major rivals. Facilities included Coors, Enron, and Jacobs, Hong Kong Stadium, Sydney's Stadium Australia, hockey's Nashville Arena, aping an open music box, and the new Pirates hull, opened in 2001.

In 1995, Pittsburgh created a Forbes Field II Task Force. A year later it chose a Northside site, a parking lot from Three Rivers Stadium, to retrieve the past. The new park (PNC, after a bank) knit Federal Street, East General Robinson Street, East Stadium Drive, River Avenue, and North Shore Drive, between the Fort Duquesne and Sixth Street (renamed Roberto Clemente) bridges. One hundred and forty feet beyond right field the Allegheny River flowed slowly to the sea. The Clemente bridge was to be closed on game day. A Tri-Stater would walk across. Live music would hail arrivers by riverboat. Said Pirates president Kevin McClatchy: "We're trying to make the bridges and river part of the experience."

Experience taught HOK and Pittsburgh's L. D. Astorino what *not* to re-create. "People never accepted Three Rivers Stadium," said broadcaster Lanny Frattare. "This is our chance to make up for a [Pirates] mistake made in 1970 [scorning Forbes Field's alloy of sight, sound, and feel]."

Sight. Brick, steel, terra-cotta tiled plasters, masonry arches, corner pens, 16 light towers, and flat green-roof evoked the '09–'70 dinghy. PNC's 21-foot right-field wall hailed No. 21. (Like Forbes, heights varied: left, 6; left-center and center, 10. Left-field line, 325; left-center, 389; deep left-center, 410; center, 399; right-center, 375; right line, 320). Clemente's and Honus Wagner's statues emigrated from Three Rivers.

Sound. "Wherever you are," said McClatchy, "you'll hear the bat, ball hitting glove, players swearing." The first double-deck park built since County Stadium sat an NL-low 38,365: 18,171 seats filled the lower deck; club boxes lay only 50 feet behind the plate. The upper tier had 11,061 grandstand pews—the highest, just 88 feet above the field. Other seats included: bleachers (2,648), outfield reserved (1,845), suite level (1,048), Pittsburgh baseball club level (2,507), and left-field deck seats (202).

Feel. A 42-by-24-foot scoreboard domineered left field. Jagged sandstone formed the wall behind home plate. "I love this place," said catcher Jason Kendall, "but if a ball gets by me, it could carom anywhere." Fans could picnic on the center-field terrace. A first-base terrace featured "Tastes of Pittsburgh." Two-tiered bleachers linked left and left-center. The Brew Pub decked the roof. "For so long we didn't know if we'd get this done," said McClatchy. "It is part of a larger effort [to raze Three Rivers, build a new Steelers stadium, expand the Convention Center, and build a new Development Center] to open downtown to the world."

PNC debuted with two exhibitions with the Mets. Said Bucs infielder Pat Meares: "This is as good as it gets." The park officially opened April 9, 2001. By dint of irony, Willie Stargell died earlier that day. Many left flowers at his 12-foot bronze statue. Said Chuck Tanner: "Now, every opening day at PNC Park . . . is Willie Stargell Day." The opener lured 36,954: Cincy, 8–2. "Just like Three Rivers," Tanner laughed. "The Reds won its first game, too." First pitcher: Todd Ritchie. Batter: Barry Larkin. Hit and homer: Reds' Sean Casey, a native Pittsburgher. "I was thinking about getting the first hit and I never thought about the first home run," said Casey. "It's amazing. I watched so many games at Three Rivers."

The Bucs' hull cost $228 million: The view of downtown and the Allegheny River seemed worth it. In March 2001, the Coast Guard warned dinger-seekers not to dive into the drink—443 feet from home plate. "It's a dangerous environment," said an official. Added another: "There are large vessels in the area." A three-story atrium, Hall of Fame, and glass-paneled second level opened PNC to Pittsburgh. "When they tore down Forbes," Bob Prince said, "they took the park away from the neighborhood." The Pirates have more or less reclaimed their park.

"The reward of a thing well done is to have done it," said Ralph Waldo Emerson. The reward of Milwaukee was to get Miller Park done. In November 1996, ground broke on its 42,885-seat natural-grass, retractable-roof arcade. "First, we had financial [political] problems over funding," said Bud Selig, whose daughter, Wendy Selig–Prieb, runs the Brewers. Opening Day receded to April 2000. On July 14, 1999, a 480-foot crane collapsed, killing three workers. Next day Selig attended the opening of Seattle's Safeco Field. "I wanted to be here because this is so critical to baseball in general and the future of Seattle," he noted, eyes brimming. "But I hope that all of you will understand that my heart is back in Milwaukee."

Miller Park filled County Stadium's center-field parking lot. The HKS, Inc., Dallas-designed brewhouse lay two miles from downtown (between the Menominee River, Stadium Freeway, Story Parkway, Interstate 94, General Mitchell Boulevard, West National Avenue, and the National Soldiers Home). "We wanted it near public highways, and enough parking so that folks could tailgate," said Selig. Thirteen thousand spaces fired beer and bratwurst. "It's one of many ties between the parks." (Another: Milwaukee's Hunzinger Construction, which built County Stadium.)

Miller Park cost fifty times County's $5 million. The Brewers paid $90 million. A five-county, 0.1 percent sales tax offset the rest. Another $72 million in public cash doctored 260 acres, "Things like freeway location, new exits and roads, more lighting, landscape," noted Selig-Prieb. Miller had a pub, open air patios and walkways, Hall of Fame, and children's area—and enough steel and concrete for a 50-story building. Poles put one County Stadium deck atop another. Miller spurned them for a split-bowl plan. Tiers slightly overhung: field, 11,700 seats and 20 sky boxes; loge, 12,650; club, 4,150 and 50 sky boxes; terrace, 14,385. "It brings fans close to the field without columns," said Brewers manager Davey Lopes. A $50 million, 10.5 acre, seven panel, closing-in-10-minutes roof harbored you from the cold.

Early returns piqued worry. The roof leaked, and was patched. A piece of temporary vinyl tarp fell off. Things got better. The White Sox opened Miller with an exhibition. On April 6, 2001, its first NL year began. President Bush's first ball to Lopes bounced in the dirt. "The split finger," said Bush, "is not meant to reach the plate." First pitcher: Jeff D'Amico. Batter: Reds' Barry Larkin. Hit and homer: mates Sean Casey and Michael Tucker, respectively. Score: Brewers, 5–4, on Richie Sexson's eighth-inning blast. Crowd: 42,024. Closed: the roof. Open: the interactive area "Big League Blast." Native: Selig, like Bush throwing out a ceremonial first pitch. Transplanted: Mascot Billy Brewer and sausage races, from County Stadium.

"You never know," said Selig, "whether a park will favor hitters or pitchers." We know. Thirty-one homers dented Miller's first nine games. On April 28, Milwaukee's Geoff Jenkins went deep thrice. Next day he homered twice—the 22nd player to hit five in two games. "It's the alleys," he said—371 and 374 feet v. County's 392. Lines were 344 and 345 v. 315, center 400 v. 402. Heights: right-field line, 6 feet; left field to right-center, 8. The seven panel, 12,000-ton roof opened or closed in 10 minutes. Miller became North America's only fan-shaped convertible roof park. Forget County's ancient scoreboard: Miller's had a 48-by-37-foot color replay board. In June, the Brewers sold their 2.4 millionth ticket, breaking the '83 franchise record of 2,397,131.

Miller denoted Milwaukee's blue-collar, hardworking, draft-drinking cast. "Can we get back to when the Braves first came here?" said Selig. "Our roof'll help people come from the hinterlands." The reward might be a '50s "Happy Days" Milwaukee. "You couldn't go anywhere without baseball affecting your life."

In 1956, two markets that believed in work, God, family, neighborhood, and a reverence for authority finished a combined three games behind Brooklyn. "German descent, traditional values, very cautious," said Hall of Fame librarian Jack Redding of Milwaukee and Cincinnati. "Change takes a while to happen." e.g., Miller Park and the Reds' new home.

In March 1996, Cincinnati backed a half-cent per buck sales tax hike for new baseball/football stadia. The combined budget: $544 million. (By 2000, the *Bengals'* park topped $450 million.) NFLers scored on first and long. "They got the money first," said the *Cincinnati Enquirer,* "because they had their plan in place and worked the politicians." By contrast, Reds owner Marge Schott apparently viewed spending cash—hers, and taxpayers'—as unconstitutional. Debate began, and hardened. Most boosted a Broadway Commons location. Schott liked a river fort between Firstar Center and Cinergy Field. "Games can be played [at Cinergy] while the new park's built next door," she tooted. "Our outfield stands gradually can be removed to make room." Schott loved the common site. "No new land will have to be bought." Voters backed the plan.

The HOK-designed field will be named the Great American Ball Park, after the Great American Insurance Company, owned, like the Reds, by the Linder family. It links Broadway, Interstate 71, Pete Rose Way, Johnny Bench Boulevard, Mehring Way, the railroad tracks, and the Ohio River. The design plops home plate 568 feet from the water. Said *Baseball Weekly:* "The muddy water is probably safe." A plaza, Crosley Terrace, will feature a peewee field and statues of noted Reds. "Rose'll be at third, Perez at first," said architect Joseph Spear. "Fans'll say, 'I'll meet you at Johnny Bench.' "

The Ballpark will have grass and a special marker where Rose's 4,192st hit landed. "It'll be within a 'Rose garden,' " touted voice Marty Brennaman. "Engraved bricks around it will honor donors." Other hits: steel, a brick exterior, cast stone base, outfield berm, 316-foot right-field porch, 42,000 capacity, including 20,000 field seats, and 2003 debut. "Close your eyes," said general manager Jim Bowden. "The new park will play like Crosley. Things here don't change."

They soon may in San Diego. A 1998 referendum endorsed funding for a $476 million downtown park, two blocks from San Diego Bay, near the San Diego Convention Center, bordered by 7th Avenue, K Street, 10th Avenue, Harbor Drive,, railroad tracks, and rerouted Imperial Avenue. The Padres' proposed new rosary: size, 42,000. Lengths: left, 334; left-center, 367; center, 390; deepest right-center, 411; right-center, 387; right, 322. Design: HOK. Hope: a Ballpark District of offices, homes, and retail shops. President Larry Lucchino helped plan Camden Yards: "The park is key," he said, "to turning a seedy area into a year-round jewel."

The first stone was thinking local. Street-level arcades conjuring early-Spanish missions knot a palm court, jacaranda trees, and water malls. Two hundred-foot towers would light the park and house luxury suites and lounges. L Street would become a pedesterian mall. Nearly 4,000 could stand or sit on a grass incline beyond center field.

"We're aiming for milling around [and real capacity of nearly 46,000]," Lucchino said. By contrast, the seating bowl would have separate parts. "The [two-tiered left- and right-field] bleachers and grandstand will all be individual sections," added broadcaster Jerry Coleman, "each facing the pitcher's mound." Right field would boast a kids' entertainment zone and theater. Beyond left, the Western Metal Supply Co. would be so close that its corner might be painted yellow—said Spear, "our standard foul pole." Also batting: a Padres Hall of Fame and 250-seat auditorium.

"A fight over the environmental effect slowed us for a time," said Lucchino. Too, the city, unable to issue bonds to finance its $225 million share. "We've got to suspend work on the park," Lucchino rued in late 2000, "till we get this straightened out." By 2004, he hopes, the Pads' jewel should be hid no more.

"I wasted time," said Shakespeare, "and now doth time waste me?" In 1997, then-Expos president Claude Brochu touted a new downtown retractable-roof park to be built two blocks south of hockey's Molson Centre, near Montreal's old train station, between Rue Peel, Rue de la Montagne, Rue St. Lacques, and Rue Notre Dame. L'Expos would raise $80 million of the estimated $250 million cost. The city and province of Quebec quickly kiboshed public aid. "When we're closing hospitals it's not certain that we're going to open stadiums," said Quebec premier Lucien Bouchard, "especially when there's a big one there already [Olympic Stadium, age 25, and still in debt]." The city returned to the Canadiens, and baseball to the ledger board. Labatt Brewery signed a $100 million pact ($40 million in naming rights).

Ultimately, Brochu sold to art dealer Jeffrey Loria. Crisis: revenue. "We'd like to be in 30th [in the majors]," jested Loria, "not 80th." In 2000, he proposed a $180 million plan. Labatt would have 64 corporate boxes, field-level dugout loges, and nearly 300 seats between the dugouts. Forget the Yard and Jake. The 'Spos spurned retro: no brick, quirks, sharp angles, or park as player. Labatt was to be oval, symmetrical, and enclosed by transparent exterior glass. "People can focus on what's going on in surrounding streets and public squares," said Loria. Unknown: whether the AXOR Group-design would accent the field. "We're in a battle for the survival of baseball in Montreal," said aide David Samson. Groundbreaking for the 36,287-park adjourned past 2000. Would the bigs move their first team since 1971? "I hope we can get this done," said Loria, "but it's not easy in a town where Rocket means Richard, not Clemens." In 2001, he chose not to renew his land lease. Wrote a columnist: "Hope has never seemed so far away."

Strange, but true: The Twins were baseball's last small-market buckeroo. Minnesota won two Series in five years (1987–'91). It outdrew the Yankees from '87 to '94. "They [now] remain on life-support," Bob Nightengale wrote in February 2000. "They continue to play in the sterile environment of the Metrodome. They will struggle again to draw a million fans." They also coveted a lulu of a park to wake the upper Midwest. "All we need," said President Jerry Bell, "is to get it built."

Their Ellerbe Becket–designed park was unveiled January 31, 1997. It would have four tiers, hold 42,000, and brandish baseball's fifth convertible roof. "Ours is different," said Bell. "The others [Milwaukee, Arizona, Houston, and Seattle] are in view when open. Ours moves completely off the park [in less than 15 minutes]" to canopy an outdoor plaza. Concourses would be wide, gentle, and open to the city. Seats would be green; steel framework, red; exterior light brown brick and Minnesota-native tan Kasota stone. Lengths would stroke a hitter: left to right, 330, 376, 405, 360, and 320 feet (too, wall height: 8). Angles were to ape the Yard's, pens grace right field, and 1,500-seat left-field area (The Porch) overhang the wall 20 feet above the field (v. Tiger Stadium's 34).

In 1999, St. Paul mayor Norm Coleman and the Twins announced a half-percent sales tax increase to build a $325 million park. The city, team, and state would each pay a third. Governor Jesse Ventura quickly body-slammed the plan. "I cannot support public funding," he said, donating $1,000. Owner Carl Pohlad vowed to keep on trucking. Life-support remained.

On October 26, 1960, the Senators decamped for Minnesota. "Why not send 'em [the Twins] back?" a Washingtonian said four decades later. Some would likely keep their bents and biases: Chanel, Nicole Miller, networking and trading cards, debating who's up and down. Others would greet the bigs with more than gingerly enthusiasm. In February 1999, Uncle Sam, business, and local government announced the latest try to retrieve D.C. baseball. Public cash would cover land, infrastructure, roads, and utilities. The city and Washington Baseball Club LLC would build the park.

"All this is part of the Intermodal Transporation Center [a federally owned downtown hub]. Our owners have the money [$3 billion personal wealth]," boasted Mayor Anthony A. Williams. "All we need is the promise [of a team]." The HNTB Architecture–designed park would seat 40–45,000, cost $297–330 million, and lie east of Mt. Vernon Square. Eighteen acres bound Third, Fifth, and K Streets and Massachusetts Avenue. Public, on- and off-street parking would add 12–15,000 spaces. Metro-rail might explore new borders of reminiscence. "If not the Twins," wrote the *Post*, "maybe the Marlins. We'll just keep looking"—like Miami.

The Marlins' 2000 payroll flunked $20 million. "Can't spend any more," said new owner John Henry. "A new ballpark is imperative to everything we're trying to do." Henry chose six sites for a retractable-roof stadium. "Whichever place gives us the most *public* money, we'll go." Ultimately, he spurned Ft. Lauderdale, Pompano Beach, and near Pro Player Stadium for downtown Miami's Bicentennial Park. Finding cash was dicier.

Private cash could only build a 25,000-seat, $100 million park. Said Henry: "That won't allow us to be competitive." Florida governor Jeb Bush squelched a tax on cruise-ship passengers, then formed a nine-member authority to plan how to pay for a park. "It's difficult without political support," Henry said. "And elected officials point to attendance [15,043 per 2000 game] as a reason not to support the stadium. It's Catch-22. We're in a survival mode." (Not surviving: the '00 All-Star Game, scheduled for Pro Player. "We lost it [to Atlanta]," said Henry, "because we haven't moved on our park.")

On December 15, 2000, a Christmas card moved southeast Florida: Henry and Miami-Dade County and city officials backed a $385 million park. Stocking stuffers: 40,000 seats, including 60 luxury suites, 3,000 club seats, 1,500 parking spaces, 2004 debut, and $100 million–plus surplus from a county hotel bed tax. A 4 percent ticket surcharge would help Henry raise another $240 million—except that the Florida legislature adjourned in '01 without OKing a cent.

"If we get this done, we will change our name to Miami [Marlins]," Henry said. "It is our duty to create a new and vibrant Miami." Veterans Stadium was neither. By 2000, state funding made a move inevitable, but not imminent. The Phils and Pirates got money the same day to build new parks. PNC opened in 2001. "We hope," Phillies chairman Bill Giles said by contrast, "to open sometime around 2004." The site was shadowy: by the Vet or at 30th Street Station, a mile from the central business district. In 2000, Mayor John Street urged a park at 12th and Vine Streets: Protestors said it would hurt Philly's Chinatown. Unclear, too: size, cost, architect, and date.

"It'll be grass and intimate," said Giles. "That's what we know." (Ultimately, the city chose to build near the Vet.) What the New York National League Baseball Club knew was the song "Wishin' and Hopin'."

The Metsies' wish: a 45,000-seat natural grass retractable field in Shea Stadium's parking lot, built of brick, limestone, and exposed steel trusses. President Fred Wilpon grew up in Brooklyn. The design aped Ebbets Field's rotunda and irregular outfield. Cantilevered stands would overhang right field. Twelve thousand spots would park the Mets faithful. More marvelous than Marv: a 425-foot-wide platform that carted sod outside the park. "That way we can have non-baseball functions inside," said Wilpon. Hope: a commercial rent or other tax to raise $500 million. "We'll just wait," he added. That thought leapt across the Triborough Bridge.

In April 1998, a 500-pound steel joint fell from Yankee Stadium's upper deck. "We either have to renovate here," said George Steinbrenner, "or we have to move." Flee The House That Ruth Built? Better Boss George buy the Red Sox. Mayor Giuliani urged the pinstripes to stay (estimated cost: $770 million). A city, state, and team study pitched a closed, multisport stadium on Manhattan's West Side, between West 30th and 34th Streets, over the Long Island railroad yards (cost: over $1 billion, estimated HOK). The Stadium lease was due to expire in 2002. New Jersey even floated a baseball-only 50,000-seat park.

"We'll do what's best for the Yankees," said Steinbrenner. The Apple would surely do what's best for them. The Yanks were too New York to ponder losing—or were the Cardinals too Middle American? It was difficult to tell. In April 2000, the Redbirds backed a 49,032–seat palace rising on Busch Stadium's south parking lot. "We need it to keep up with Camden Yards and Enron Field [and doubtless Yankee Stadium]," said general partner Bill DeWitt. On June 19th, 2001, St. Louis announced a $646 million downtown redevelopment plan. Its hub: a park, replacing Busch, by 2005. The Cardinals would surely sell out the entire year. Let Montreal compete then.

"Why can't we build an angular, idiosyncratic park?" Giamatti mused. Virtually every team has, or will.

23

POSTLOGUE

A quarter-century later, former Red Sox broadcaster Ned Martin mused how the 1975 postseason regained baseball's hold on the American sensibility. "The country watched the fanatic fans, the depth of their knowledge, the bandbox of a park. In other words, baseball at Fenway Park like Ebbets or Sportsman's Park. Baseball like it was *meant* to be."

The Red Sox lost that World Series to Cincinnati: More than 6 in 10 Americans saw all or part of its seven-game panache. Strangely, I recall AL playoff Game Two. Carl Yastrzemski launched a net-detector toward the Monster—an out anywhere but Boston. Later, the Wall also helped Rico Petrocelli go deep. Fenway was scene and actor. It *mattered* where the game was played.

When Frank Sinatra sang, "There used to be a ballpark," he bespoke shrines—it may off-put; no other word will do—passing from parent to child the joy of rooting for the home towne team. The last decade has swelled interest in classic parks, spurning boredom and passivity. Enron Field. Pacific Bell Park. Safeco Field, a cathedral in dark green. Each fled an interregnum of inferiority and yawn.

"The early '90s were like the '60s and early '70s," mused Peter Gammons. "There was an ennui to the game." Baseball wished Three Rivers, say, to amount to something, and did; but not quite in the way it had expected, or hoped. "The cookie cutters soured a generation," added George Will. Dueling miracles: A wall crumbles in Berlin; the scales fall from baseball's eyes.

"The Polo Grounds had its short foul lines and vast center field, Ebbets Field its indented right-field fence," Ron Fimrite wrote of park as personality. "The old Yankee Stadium, its death valley in left and center; Crosley Field, its outfield hillock; Baker Bowl, its towering tin wall in right." Today daubs going back to the future—stadium postmodernism, if you will: high and low walls, long and short distances, a berm, a train, a new Monster, a McCovey's Cove.

As children, friends and I compared batting averages, watched the churnings of the American and National Leagues, and traded ten Ted Lepcio playing cards for a dog-eared Mickey Mantle. Baseball ferried past us; we thought of little else.

"So we beat on," F. Scott Fitzgerald wrote in *The Great Gatsby*, "boats against the current, born back ceaselessly into the past." Perhaps parks of springtime memory can row the current named tomorrow.

ABOUT THE AUTHOR

Curt Smith is an author, radio/television commentator, teacher, and former presidential speechwriter. NBC broadcaster Bob Costas says: "Curt Smith stands up for the beauty of words."

Storied Stadiums is his ninth book. Others include *Voices of the Game, Windows on the White House, Long Time Gone, America's Dizzy Dean, A Fine Sense of the Ridiculous, The Storytellers, Of Mikes and Men,* and *Our House: A Tribute to Fenway Park.*

Mr. Smith hosts two series on Rochester, New York, CBS Television affiliate WROC: a weekly political public affairs program, "Perfectly Clear," and the twice-weekly "Talking Point." He also hosts a weekly broadcast series for Fox TV's Empire Sports Network and is senior lecturer in English at the University of Rochester.

Mr. Smith's commentary for Rochester NPR affiliate WXXI has been voted best in New York State by Associated Press and the New York State Broadcasters Association. He has written and coproduced prime-time ESPN documentaries based on his book *Voices of the Game*—and helped write and research ABC/ESPN's *SportsCentury* documentary series.

Formerly a Gannett reporter and *Saturday Evening Post* senior editor, Mr. Smith wrote more speeches than anyone for President George Bush. Among them were the "Just War" Persian Gulf address; Nixon and Reagan Library Dedication speeches; and December 7, 1991, speech aboard the *USS Missouri* on the 50th anniversary of Pearl Harbor.

Leaving the White House in 1993, Mr. Smith then hosted a smash series at the Smithsonian Institution, based on *Voices*, before turning to radio and TV. Raised in Caledonia, New York, the 1973 SUNY at Geneseo graduate has been named among the "100 Outstanding Alumni" of

New York's State University System, is a member of the Judson Welliver Society of former White House speechwriters, and lives with his wife, Sarah, and children, Olivia and Travis, in Rochester.

ABOUT THE ART

Even the Cubs grasp the Cardinal rule of business: Know, then sell, the core of your appeal. Baseball's is memory. Bill Goff is a Philadelphia native, high school classmate of Reggie Jackson's, and graduate of Washington College. As the lithographs in *Storied Stadiums* show, he has merged baseball memory and fine art.

In 1977, Goff opened the world's first sports art gallery on Manhattan's 57th Street Gallery Row. Today the Bill Goff Inc. collection includes more than 150 color likenesses—lithographs—of baseball parks, players, and events. He also produces posters and calendars—"baseball," Goff said, "of the heart, not just mind."

Goff was the first fine art guest curator at the Baseball Hall of Fame and Museum in Cooperstown. He has guest curated three exhibits. Bill and wife Betsy, a sports television attorney, have a 16-year-old son, Kenny, who plays baseball.

Heywood Broun wrote of radio, "Graham McNamee took a medium of expression, and [gave] it a sense of movement and of feeling. Of such is the kingdom of art." Goff's lithographs define the current age of stadia fine art.

To order renderings of baseball parks, write or call: Bill Goff Inc./ Good Sports, 5 Bridge Street (P.O. Box 977), Kent, Connecticut 06757. Phone: 1-800 321-GOFF or 1-860 927-1411. Fax: 1-860 927-1987.

SOURCES

Grateful acknowledgment is made for permission to reprint excerpts from the following:

Beyond the Sixth Game, by Peter Gammons, reprinted by permission of Houghton Mifflin Company, 1985.

FDR: A Centenary Remembrance," by Joseph Alsop, copyright the Viking Press, 1982. Reprinted by permission of Thames and Hudson Limited.

"Hit the Monster," reprinted by permission of *ESPN Magazine,* August 27, 1998.

North Toward Home, by Willie Morris, reprinted by permission of Houghton Mifflin, 1967.

Rhubarb in the Catbird Seat, by Red Barber with Robert Creamer, reprinted by permission of Doubleday and Company, 1968.

Seasons to Remember, by Curt Gowdy with John Powers. Reprinted by permission of Harper Collins, 1993.

Sports Illustrated, reprinted by permission the issues of April 15, 1957; April 13, 1959; April 11, 1960; and April 10, 1961.

The *Baltimore Sun, Boston Globe,* and *Washington Post,* reprinted by their permission.

The *Gas House Gang,* by J. Roy Stockton, reprinted by permission of A. S. Barnes and Company, 1945.

The *Great American Baseball Card Flipping, Trading and Bubble Gum Book,* by Brendan C. Boyd and Fred C. Harris. Reprinted by permission of Little, Brown and Company, 1973.

When It Was a Game, reprinted by permission of Home Box Office, 1991.

Play-by-play commentaries in *Storied Stadiums* are reprinted with the expressed permission of ABC Television, ESPN Television, CBS Radio, and CBS Television.

BIBLIOGRAPHY

Alsop, Joseph. *FDR: A Centenary Remembrance*. New York: The Viking Press, 1982.

Angell, Roger. *Five Seasons*. New York: Simon and Schuster, 1978.

———. *Late Innings*. New York: Ballantine Books, 1982.

———. *The Summer Game*. New York: Popular Library, 1978.

Armbruster, Frank. *The Forgotten Americans*. New Rochelle, New York: Arlington House, 1972.

Baldassaro, Lawrence (ed.). *The Ted Williams Reader*. New York: Putnam, 1991.

Barber, Walter (Red), *Rhubarb in the Catbird Seat,* with Robert Creamer. Garden City, New York: Doubleday, 1968.

The Baseball Hall of Fame 50th Anniversary Book. New York: Prentice-Hall, 1988.

Berry, Henry. *Boston Red Sox*. New York: Rutledge Books, 1975.

Broeg, Bob. *Super Stars of Baseball*. St. Louis: The Sporting News Publishing Company, 1971.

Creamer, Robert. *Babe*. New York: Simon and Schuster, 1974.

Durso, Joseph. *Yankee Stadium*. Boston: Houghton Mifflin, 1972.

Enright, Jim. *Chicago Cubs*. New York: Rutledge Books, 1975.

Falls, Joe. *Detroit Tigers*. New York: Rutledge Books, 1975.

Gammons, Peter. *Beyond the Sixth Game*. Boston: Houghton Mifflin, 1985.

Gowdy, Curt, with Al Hirshberg, *Cowboy at the Mike*. Garden City, New York: Doubleday, 1966.

———. with John Powers. *Seasons to Remember*. New York: Harper Collins, 1993.

Halberstam, David. *Summer of '49*. New York: William Morrow, 1989.

Hirshberg, Al. *What's the Matter with the Red Sox?* New York: Dodd, Mead, 1973.

Holmes, Tommy. *The Dodgers*. New York: Rutledge Books, 1975.

Honig, Donald. *Baseball's 10 Greatest Teams*. New York: Macmillan, 1982.

———. *The American League*. New York: Crown, 1983.

Hutchens, John K., and George Oppenheimer. (eds.). *The Best in the World*. New York: The Viking Press, 1973.

Kahn, Roger. *The Boys of Summer*. New York: Harper and Row, 1971.

Kalinsky, George, and Bill Shannon. *The Ballparks*. New York: Hawthorn Books, 1975.

Leuchtenburg, William E. *The LIFE History of the United States*. New York: Time-Life Books, 1976.

Lewine, Harris, and Daniel Okrent. *The Ultimate Baseball Book*. Boston: Houghton Mifflin, 1979.

Lipstye, Robert. *SportsWorld*. New York: Guadrangle, 1975.

Major League Baseball Promotion Corporation. *Baseball: The First 100 Years*. New York: Poretz-Ross Publishers, 1969.

———. *The Game and the Glory*. Englewood Cliffs, New Jersey: Prentice-Hall, 1976.

———. *The World Series: A 75th Anniversary*. New York: Simon and Schuster, 1978.

———. *This Great Game*. New York: Rutledge Books, 1971.

Manchester, William. *One Brief Shining Moment*. Boston: Little, Brown and Company, 1983.

Michener, James A. *Sports in America*. New York: Random House, 1976.

Morris, Willie. *North Toward Home*. Boston: Houghton Mifflin, 1967.

National League. *A Baseball Century*. New York: Rutledge Books, 1976.

Reichler, Joseph. *Baseball's Great Moments*. New York: Bonanza Books, 1983.

Reidenbaugh, Lowell. *Take Me Out to the Ball Park*. St. Louis: The Sporting News Publishing Company, 1983.

Rosenthal, Harold. *The 10 Best Years of Baseball*. New York: Van Nostrand Reinhold Company, 1980.

Seidel, Michael. *Ted Williams—A Baseball Life*. Chicago: Contemporary Books, 1991.

Shaughnessy, Dan. *The Curse of the Bambino*. New York: Penguin Books, 1991.

Smelser, Marshall. *The Life That Ruth Built*. New York: Quadrangle/New York Times Books, 1975.

Smith, Robert. *Illustrated History of Baseball*. New York: Grosset and Dunlap, 1973.

Smithsonian Exposition Books. *Every Four Years*. New York: W. W. Norton and Company, 1980.

Stockton, J. Roy. *The Gas House Gang*. New York: A. S. Barnes and Company, 1945.

Vecsey, George (ed.). *The Way It Was*. Mobil Oil and McGraw-Hill Book Company, 1974.

White, Theodore H. *In Search of History*. New York: Harper and Row, 1978.

Wood, Bob. *Dodger Dogs to Fenway Franks*. New York: McGraw-Hill Publishing Company, 1988.

APPENDIX

ACTIVE FRANCHISE GENEALOGY

Below are the genesis and evolution of today's thirty major-league baseball franchises. The following abbreviations are used: AA (American Association); AL (American League); NL (National League).

NATIONAL LEAGUE

Arizona Diamondbacks, NL Arizona Diamondbacks, 1998–present.

Atlanta Braves, NL Boston Red Stockings, Reds, or Red Caps, 1876–'82; Beaneaters, 1883–1906; Doves, 1907–'10; Rustlers, 1911; Braves, 1912–'35; Bees, 1936–'40; Braves, 1941–'52; Milwaukee Braves, 1953–'65; Atlanta Braves, 1966–present.

Chicago Cubs, NL Chicago White Stockings, 1876–'93; Colts, 1894–'97; Orphans, 1898; various names, 1899–1904; Cubs, 1905–present.

Cincinnati Reds, NL Cincinnati Red Stockings, 1876–'80 (NL); Reds (merged with Washington Senators AA 1889), 1882–'89; Reds, 1890–'43 (NL); Redlegs, 1944–'45; Reds, 1946–present.

Colorado Rockies, NL Colorado Rockies, 1993–present.

Florida Marlins, NL Florida Marlins, 1993–present.

Houston Astros, NL Houston Colt .45s, 1962–'64; Houston Astros, 1965–present.

Los Angeles Dodgers, NL Brooklyns, 1884–'88 (AA); Brooklyn Bridegrooms, 1889; Bridegrooms, 1890–'98 (NL); Superbas, 1899–1910; Infants, 1911–'13; Robins, 1914–'31; Dodgers, 1932–'57; Los Angeles Dodgers, 1958–present.

Milwaukee Brewers, NL Seattle Pilots, AL 1969; Milwaukee Brewers, AL 1970–'97; Brewers, NL 1998–present.

Montreal Expos, NL Montreal Expos, 1969–present.

New York Mets, NL New York Mets, 1962–present.

Philadelphia Phillies, NL Worcester, MA., Brown Stockings or Nationals, 1880–'82; Philadelphia Phillies, 1883–1942; Blue Jays, 1943–'44; Phillies, 1945–present.

Pittsburgh Pirates, NL Pittsburgh Alleghenies, 1887–'89; Innocents, 1890; Pirates (merged with Louisville Colonels 1900), 1891–present.

St. Louis Cardinals, NL St. Louis Browns, 1892–'97; Cardinals, 1898–present.

San Diego Padres, NL San Diego Padres, 1969–present.

San Francisco Giants, NL Troy Trojans, 1879–'82; New York Gothams, 1883–'85; Giants, 1886–1957; San Francisco Giants, 1958–present.

AMERICAN LEAGUE

Anaheim Angels, AL Los Angeles Angels, 1961–'65; California Angels, 1966–'96; Anaheim Angels, 1997–present.

Baltimore Orioles, AL Milwaukee Brewers, 1901; St. Louis Browns, 1902–'53; Baltimore Orioles, 1954–present.

Boston Red Sox, AL Boston Americans a.k.a. Somersets, Pilgrims, Plymouth Rocks, or Puritans 1901–'06; Red Sox, 1907–present.

Chicago White Sox, AL Chicago White Sox, 1901–present.

Cleveland Indians, AL Cleveland Broncos, 1901; Blues, 1902–'04; Naps, 1905–'11; Molly McGuires, 1912–'14; Indians, 1915–present.

Detroit Tigers, AL Detroit Tigers, 1901–present.

Kansas City Royals, AL Kansas City Royals, 1969–present.

Minnesota Twins, AL Washington Senators, 1901–'60; Minnesota Twins, 1961–present.

New York Yankees, AL Baltimore Orioles, 1901–'02; New York Highlanders, 1903–'12; Yankees, 1913–present.

Oakland Athletics, AL Philadelphia Athletics, 1901–'54; Kansas City Athletics, 1955–'67; Oakland Athletics, 1968–present.

Seattle Mariners, AL Seattle Mariners, 1977–present.

Tampa Bay Devil Rays, AL Tampa Bay Devil Rays, 1998–present.

Texas Rangers, AL Washington Senators, 1961–'71; Texas Rangers, 1972–present.

Toronto Blue Jays, AL Toronto Blue Jays, 1977–present.

ACTIVE FRANCHISE BALLPARKS

Below are the ballparks in which baseball's current thirty major-league franchises have played. Included, respectively: each park's name and league, duration as team home, first and, if applicable, last regular-season big-league game, and opponent and final score.

NATIONAL LEAGUE

*Arizona. **Bank One Ballpark*** (Phoenix, Arizona, NL, 1998–present). First game: March 31, 1998: Colorado 9, Arizona 2.

*Atlanta. **South End Grounds*** (Boston, NL, 1876–1915). First game: April 29, 1876. Hartford 3, Boston 2, 10 innings. Last game: June 3, 1915. New York 10, Boston 3. *Braves Field* (Boston, NL, 1915–'52). August 18, 1915: Boston 3, St. Louis 1. September 21, 1952: Brooklyn 8, Boston 2. *Milwaukee County Stadium* (Milwaukee,

NL, 1953–65). April 14, 1953: Milwaukee 3, St. Louis 2, 10 innings. September 22, 1965 (night): Los Angeles 7, Milwaukee 6, 11 innings. *Atlanta-Fulton County Stadium* (Atlanta, NL, 1966–'96). April 12, 1966 (N): Pittsburgh 3, Atlanta 2, 13 innings. October 24, 1996 (N): New York 1, Atlanta 0. *Turner Field* (Atlanta, NL, 1997–present). April 4, 1997: Atlanta 5, Chicago 4.

Chicago. State Street Grounds (NL, 1876–'77). May 10, 1876: Chicago 6, Cincinnati 0. October 5, 1877: Louisville 4, Chicago 0. *Lakefront Park I* (NL, 1878–'82). May 14, 1878: Indianapolis 5, Chicago 3. May 10, 1882: Chicago 4, Cleveland 3. *Lakefront Park II* (NL, 1883–'84). May 5, 1883: Detroit 3, Chicago 2. October 11, 1884: Chicago 12, Philadelphia 3. *West Side Park* (NL, 1885–'92). June 6, 1885: Chicago 9, St. Louis 2. October 6, 1892: Chicago 5, Louisville 3, 7 innings, darkness. *West Side Grounds* (NL, 1893–1915). May 14, 1893: Cincinnati 13, Chicago 12. October 3, 1915: Chicago 7, St. Louis 2. *Wrigley Field* (NL, 1916–present). April 20, 1916: Chicago 7, St. Louis 6, 11 innings.

Cincinnati. Avenue Grounds (NL, 1876–'77). April 25, 1876: Cincinnati 2, St. Louis. September 29, 1877: Cincinnati 11, Chicago 10. *Bank Street Grounds* (NL, 1880). May 1, 1880: Chicago 4, Cincinnati 3. September 30, 1880: Cincinnati 2, Cleveland 0. (AA, 1882–'83). May 21, 1882: Pittsburgh 10, Cincinnati 9. September 29, 1883: New York 4, Cincinnati 1. *League Park* (AA, 1884–'89). May 1, 1884: Columbus 10, Cincinnati 9. October 15, 1889, double-header: Cincinnati 8, St. Louis 3; St. Louis 2, Cincinnati 1. *League Park* (NL, 1890–1901). April 19, 1890: Chicago 5, Cincinnati 4. October 2, 1901, double-header: Philadelphia 3, Cincinnati 2; Philadelphia 5, Cincinnati 2. *Redland Field* (a.k.a. Palace of the Fans. NL, 1902–'11). April 17, 1902: Chicago 6, Cincinnati 2. October 2, 1911, double-header: Cincinnati 6, St. Louis 2; St. Louis 6, Cincinnati 2. *Crosley Field* (NL, 1912–'70). April 11, 1912: Cincinnati 10, Chicago 6. June 24, 1970 (N): Cincinnati 5, San Francisco 4. *Cinergy Field* (NL, 1970–present. a.k.a. Riverfront Stadium, 1970–'96). June 30, 1970 (N): Atlanta 8, Cincinnati 2.

Colorado. Mile High Stadium (Denver, NL, 1993–'94). April 9, 1993: Colorado 11, Montreal 4. August 11, 1994: Atlanta 13, Colorado 0. *Coors Field* (Denver, NL, 1995–present). April 26; 1995: Colorado 11, New York 9.

Florida. Pro Player Stadium (Miami, NL, 1993–present. a.k.a. Joe Robbie Stadium, 1993–'96). April 5, 1993: Florida 6, Los Angeles 3.

Houston. Colt Stadium (NL, 1962–'64). April 10, 1962: Houston 11, Chicago 2. September 27, 1964 (N): Houston 1, Los Angeles 0, 12 innings. *Astrodome* (NL, 1965–'99). April 12, 1965 (N): Philadelphia 2, Houston 0. October 9, 1999: Atlanta 7, Houston 5. *Enron Field* (NL, 2000–present). April 7, 2000 (N): Philadelphia 4, Houston 1.

Los Angeles. Washington Park (Brooklyn, AA, 1884–'89). May 5, 1884: Brooklyn 11, Washington 3. October 5, 1989: Philadelphia 10, Brooklyn 2, 8 innings, darkness. (NL, 1890). April 28, 1890: Brooklyn 10, Philadelphia 0. September 6, 1890: New York 5, Brooklyn 1. *Eastern Park* (Brooklyn, NL, 1891–'97). April 27, 1891: New York 6, Brooklyn 5. October 2, 1897: Brooklyn 15, Boston 6. *Washington Park* (Brooklyn, NL, 1898–1912). April 30, 1898: Philadelphia 6, Brooklyn 4. October 5, 1912: New York 1, Brooklyn 0. *Ebbets Field* (Brooklyn, NL, 1913–'57). April 9, 1913: Philadelphia 1, Brooklyn 0. September 24, 1957 (N): Brooklyn 3, Pittsburgh 0.

Roosevelt Stadium (Jersey City, N.J., N.L, 1956–'57). April 19, 1956 (N): Brooklyn 5, Philadelphia 4. September 3, 1957 (N): Philadelphia 3, Brooklyn 2. *Memorial Coliseum* (Los Angeles, NL, 1958–'61). April 18, 1958: Los Angeles 6, San Francisco 5. September 20, 1961 (N): Los Angeles 3, Chicago 3, 13 innings, game suspended. *Dodger Stadium* (NL, 1962–present). April 10, 1962: Cincinnati 6, Los Angeles 3.

Milwaukee. *Sick's Stadium* (Seattle, AL, 1969). April 11, 1969: Seattle 7, Chicago 0. October 2, 1969: Oakland 3, Seattle 1. *Milwaukee County Stadium* (Milwaukee, AL, 1970–'97 and NL, 1998–2000). April 7, 1970: California 12, Milwaukee 0. September 28, 2000: Cincinnati 8, Milwaukee 1. *Miller Park* (Milwaukee, NL 2001–present). April 6, 2001: Milwaukee 5, Cincinnati 4.

Montreal. *Jarry Park* (NL, 1969–'76). April 14, 1969: Montreal 8, St. Louis 7. September 29, 1976: Philadelphia 2, Montreal 1. *Olympic Stadium* (NL, 1977–present). April 15, 1977: Philadelphia 7, Montreal 2.

New York. *Polo Grounds* (NL, 1962–'63). April 13, 1962: Pittsburgh 4, New York 3. September 18, 1963: Philadelphia 5, New York 1. *Shea Stadium* (NL, 1964–present). April 17, 1964: Pittsburgh 4, New York 3.

Philadelphia. *Jefferson Street Grounds* (Philadelphia, NL, 1876). April 22, 1876: Boston 6, Philadelphia 5. September 16, 1876: Louisville 7, Philadelphia 6. *Agricultural County Fair Grounds* (Worcester, MA., Massachusetts, NL, 1880–'82). May 1, 1880: Worcester 13, Troys 1. September 29, 1882: Troys 10, Worcester 7. *Recreation Park* (Philadelphia, NL, 1883–'86). May 1, 1883: Providence 4, Philadelphia 3. October 9, 1886, double-header: Philadelphia, Detroit 1; Philadelphia 6, Detroit 1, 6 innings, darkness. *Baker Bowl* (Philadelphia, NL, 1887–1938). April 30, 1887: Philadelphia 15, New York 9. June 30, 1938: New York 14, Philadelphia 1. *Shibe Park* (NL, 1938–'70. a.k.a. Connie Mack Stadium). July 4, 1938, double-header: Boston 10, Philadelphia 5; Philadelphia 10, Boston 2. October 1, 1970 (N): Philadelphia 2, Montreal 1, 10 innings. *Veterans Memorial Stadium* (NL, 1971–present). April 10, 1971 (N): Philadelphia 4, Montreal 1.

Pittsburgh. *Exposition Park* (AA, 1882–'84). May 10, 1882: Pittsburgh 9, St. Louis 5. October 15, 1884: Louisville 9, Pittsburgh 4. *Recreation Park* (NL, 1887–'90). April 30, 1887: Pittsburgh 6, Chicago 2. September 30, 1890: Pittsburgh 10, Philadelphia 1. *Exposition Park* (NL, 1891–1909). April 22, 1891: Chicago 7, Pittsburgh 6, 10 innings. June 29, 1909: Pittsburgh 8, Chicago 1. *Forbes Field* (NL, 1909–'70). June 30, 1909: Chicago 3, Pittsburgh 2. June 28, 1970, double-header: Pittsburgh 3, Chicago 2; Pittsburgh 4, Chicago 1. *Three Rivers Stadium* (NL, 1970–2000). July 16, 1970 (N): Cincinnati 3, Pittsburgh 2. October 1, 2000: Chicago 10, Pittsburgh 9. *PNC Park* (NL, 2001–). April 9, 2001: Cincinnati 8, Pittsburgh 2.

St. Louis. *Sportsman's Park* (NL, 1876–'77). May 5, 1876: St. Louis 1, Chicago 0. October 6, 1877: St. Louis 7, Cincinnati 3. *Union Park* (NL, 1885–'86). April 30, 1885: St. Louis 3, Chicago 2. September 23, 1886: Kansas City, St. Louis 2. *Robison Field* (NL, 1892–1920). April 15, 1892: St. Louis 9, Pittsburgh 3. June 6, 1920: St. Louis 5, Chicago 2. *Sportsman's Park* (NL, 1920–'66. a.k.a. Busch Stadium, 1954–'66). July 1, 1920: Pittsburgh 6, St. Louis 2, 10 innings. May 8, 1966: San Francisco 10, St. Louis 5. *Busch Stadium* (NL, 1966–present). May 12, 1966: St. Louis 4, Atlanta 3, 12 innings.

San Diego. *Qualcomm Stadium* (NL, 1969–present. a.k.a. San Diego Stadium 1969–'80 and Jack Murphy Stadium 1981–'96). April 8, 1969 (N): San Diego 2, Houston 1.

San Francisco. Putnam Grounds (Troy, N.Y., NL, 1879). May 28, 1879: Troy 20, Cincinnati 6. September 20, 1879: Troy 6, Chicago 4. *Haymakers' Grounds* (Troy, NL, 1880–'81). May 18, 1880: Troy 10, Worcester 1. September 30, 1881: Detroit 7, Troy 0. *Polo Grounds* (New York, 110th Street, NL, 1883–'88). May 1, 1883: New York, Boston 5. October 13, 1888: Indianapolis 6, New York 4. *Polo Grounds* (New York, 155th Street, NL, 1889–'90). July 8, 1889: New York 7, Pittsburgh 5. September 10, 1890: Boston 8, New York 5. *Polo Grounds* (New York, 157th Street, N.L, 1891–'57). April 22, 1891: Boston 4, New York 3. September 29, 1957: Pittsburgh 9, New York 1. *Seals Stadium* (San Francisco, N.L, 1958–'59). April 15, 1958: San Francisco 8, Los Angeles 0. September 20, 1959: Los Angeles 8, San Francisco 2. *3Com Park* (San Francisco, NL, 1960–'99. a.k.a. Candlestick Park, 1960–'96). April 12, 1960: San Francisco 3, St. Louis 1. September 30, 1999: Los Angeles 9, San Francisco 4. *Pacific Bell Park* (San Francisco, NL, 2000-present). April 11, 2000: Los Angeles 6, San Francisco 5.

AMERICAN LEAGUE

Anaheim. Wrigley Field (Los Angeles, AL, 1961. Team known as Los Angeles Angels). First game: April 27, 1961. Minnesota 4, Los Angeles 2. Last game: September 20, 1961 (N). Cleveland 8, Los Angeles 5. *Chavez Ravine* (Los Angeles, AL, 1962–'65. a.k.a. Dodger Stadium). April 17, 1962: Kansas City, Los Angeles 3. September 22, 1965: Los Angeles 2, Boston 0. *Edison International Field of Anaheim* (Anaheim, AL, 1966-present. a.k.a. Anaheim Stadium, 1966–'97. Team known as California Angels, 1966–'96, and Anaheim Angels, 1997-present). First game: April 19, 1966 (N). Chicago 3, California 1.

Baltimore. Lloyd Street Grounds (Milwaukee, AL, 1901). May 3, 1901: Chicago 11, Milwaukee 3. September 12, 1901: Chicago 4, Milwaukee 0. *Sportsman's Park* (St. Louis, AL, 1902–'53). April 23, 1902: St. Louis 5, Cleveland 2. September 27, 1953: Chicago 2, St. Louis 1, 11 innings. *Memorial Stadium* (Baltimore, AL, 1954–'91). April 15, 1954: Baltimore 3, Chicago 1. October 6, 1991: Detroit 7, Baltimore 1. *Oriole Park at Camden Yards* (Baltimore, AL, 1992-present). April 6, 1992: Baltimore 2, Cleveland 0.

Boston. Huntington Avenue Grounds (AL, 1901–'11). May 8, 1901: Boston 12, Philadelphia 4. October 7, 1911: Boston 8, Washington 1. *Fenway Park* (AL, 1912-present). April 20, 1912: Boston 7, New York 6.

Chicago. South Side Park (AL, 1901–'10). April 21, 1901: Milwaukee 5, Chicago 4, 10 innings. June 26, 1019: Cleveland 5, Chicago 4. *Comiskey Park* (AL, 1910–'90). July 1, 1910: St. Louis 2, Chicago 0. September 30, 1990: Chicago 2, Seattle 1. *Comiskey Park II* (AL, 1991-present). April 18, 1991: Detroit 16, Chicago 0.

Cleveland. League Park (AL, 1901–'09). April 26, 1900: Cleveland 5, Indianapolis 4. September 6, 1909, double-header: Cleveland 5, Chicago 2; Chicago 5, Cleveland 3. *League Park II* (AL, 1910–'46). April 21, 1910: Detroit 5, Cleveland 0. September 21, 1946: Detroit 5, Cleveland 3. *Municipal Stadium* (AL, 1932–'93. a.k.a. Cleveland Stadium). July 31, 1932: Philadelphia 1, Cleveland 0. October 3, 1993: Chicago 4, Cleveland 0. *Jacobs Field* (AL, 1994-present). April 4, 1994: Cleveland 4, Seattle 3.

Detroit. Bennett Park (AL, 1900–'11). April 19, 1900: Buffalo 8, Detroit 9. September 10, 1911: Detroit, Cleveland 1, 13 innings. *Tiger Stadium* (AL, 1912–'99. a.k.a. Navin Field, 1912–'37, and Briggs Stadium, 1938–'60). April 20, 1912: Detroit 6, Cleveland 5, 11 innings. September 27, 1999: Detroit 8, Kansas City 2. *Comerica Park* (AL, 2000-present). April 11, 2000: Detroit 5, Seattle 2.

Kansas City. Municipal Stadium (AL, 1969–'72). April 8, 1969: Kansas City, Minnesota 3, 12 innings. October 4, 1972: Kansas City 4, Texas 0. *Kauffman Stadium* (AL, 1973-present. a.k.a. Royals Stadium, 1973–'93). April 10, 1973 (N): Kansas City 12, Texas 1.

Minnesota. American League Park (Washington, D.C., AL, 1901–'02). April 29, 1901: Washington 2, Baltimore 2. September 27, 1902: Washington 9, Philadelphia 4. *National Park* (Washington, D.C., AL, 1903–'10). April 22, 1903: Washington 3, New York 1. October 6, 1910, double-header: Boston 5, Washington 2; Washington 6, Boston 5. *Griffith Stadium* (Washington, D.C., AL, 1911–'60). April 12, 1911: Washington 8, Boston 5. October 2, 1960: Baltimore 2, Washington 1. *Metropolitan Stadium* (Bloomington, MN., AL, 1961–'81). April 21, 1961: Washington 5, Minnesota 3. September 30, 1981: Kansas City 5, Minnesota 2. *Hubert H. Humphrey Metrodome* (Minneapolis, AL, 1982-present). April 6, 1982 (N): Seattle 11, Minnesota 7.

New York. Oriole Park (Baltimore, AL, 1901–'02). April 26, 1901: Baltimore 10, Boston 6. September 28, 1902: Boston 9, Baltimore 5. *Hilltop Park* (New York, AL, 1903–'12). April 30, 1903: New York 6, Washington 2. October 5, 1912: New York 8, Washington 6. *Polo Grounds* (New York, AL, 1913–'22). April 17, 1913: Washington 9, New York 3. September 10, 1922, double-header: New York 10, Philadelphia 3; New York 2, Philadelphia 1. *Yankee Stadium* (Bronx, N.Y., AL, 1923–'73). April 18, 1923: New York 4, Boston 1. September 30, 1973: Detroit 8, New York 5. *Shea Stadium* (New York, AL, 1974–'75). April 6, 1974: New York 6, Cleveland 1. September 28, 1975: New York 3, Baltimore 2. *Yankee Stadium* (Bronx, AL, 1976-present). April 15, 1976: New York 11, Minnesota 4.

Oakland. Columbia Park (Philadelphia, AL, 1901–'08). April 26, 1901: Washington 5, Philadelphia 1. October 3, 1908, double-header: Philadelphia 8, Boston 7; Boston 5, Philadelphia 0. *Shibe Park* (Philadelphia, AL, 1909–'54. a.k.a. Connie Mack Stadium, 1953–'54). April 12, 1909: Philadelphia 8, Boston 1. September 19, 1954: New York 4, Philadelphia 2. *Municipal Stadium* (Kansas City, AL, 1955–'67). April 12, 1955: Kansas City 6, Detroit 2. September 27, 1967 (N): Kansas City 5, Chicago 2. *Network Associates Coliseum* (Oakland, AL, 1968 present. a.k.a. Oakland-Alameda County Coliseum, 1968–'98). April 17, 1968 (N): Baltimore 4, Oakland 1.

Seattle. Kingdome (AL, 1977–'99). April 6, 1977 (N): California 7, Seattle 0. June 27, 1999: Seattle 5, Texas 2. *Safeco Field* (AL, 1999-present). July 15, 1999: San Diego 3, Seattle 2.

Tampa Bay. Tropicana Field (AL, 1998-present). March 31, 1998: Detroit 11, Tampa Bay 6.

Texas. Griffith Stadium (Washington, D.C., AL, 1961). April 10, 1961: Chicago 3, Washington 3. September 21, 1961: Minnesota 6, Washington 3. *Robert F. Kennedy Stadium* (Washington, D.C., AL, 1962–'71. a.k.a. D.C. Stadium, 1962–'68). April 9, 1962: Washington 4, Detroit 1. September 30, 1971 (N): New York 9, Washington 0, forfeit. *Arlington Stadium* (Arlington, TX., AL, 1972–'93). April 21, 1972 (N): Texas 7, California 6. October 3, 1993: Kansas City 4, Texas 1. *The Ballpark in Arlington* (Arlington, AL, 1994-present). April 11, 1994: Milwaukee 4, Texas 3.

Toronto. *Exhibition Stadium* (AL, 1977–'89). April 7, 1977: Toronto 9, Chicago 5. May 28, 1989: Toronto 7, Chicago 5. *SkyDome* (AL, 1989-present). June 5, 1989 (N): Milwaukee 5, Toronto 3.

ATTENDANCE

Below are attendance marks for the past and current parks of today's big-league franchises. The following abbreviations are used throughout the text: day game (D); double-header (DH); night game (N); twi-night double-header (TN); opening game (O); best season (B); and worst season (W). Select records are unavailable. All cited are contemporary into 2001.

Arizona. *Bank One Ballpark* (Phoenix, 1998-present). D: 48,682, Los Angeles, May 24, 1998. N: 48,527, Colorado, July 18, 1998. O: 47,465, Colorado, March 31, 1998. B: 3,600,412, 1998. W: 2,942,516, 2000.

Atlanta. *South End Grounds* (Boston, 1876–1915). B: 382,913, 1914. W: 34,000, 1880. *Braves Field* (Boston, 1915–'52). D: 41,527, Chicago, August 8, 1948. DH: 47,123, Philadelphia, May 22, 1932. N: 39,549, Brooklyn, August 5, 1946. O: 25,000, New York, April 16, 1935. B: 1,455,439, 1948. W: 84,938, 1918. *Milwaukee County Stadium* (Milwaukee, 1953–'65). D: 48,642, Philadelphia, September 27, 1959. DH: 47,604, Cincinnati, September 3, 1956. N: 46,944, New York, August 27, 1954. TN: 36,241, St. Louis, August 12, 1953. O: 43,640, Cincinnati, April 12, 1955. B: 2,215,404, 1957. W: 555,584, 1965. *Atlanta-Fulton County Stadium* (Atlanta, 1966–'96). D: 51,275, Los Angeles, June 26, 1966. DH: 46,389, San Francisco, July 18, 1971. N: 53,775, Los Angeles, April 8, 1974. TN: 50,597, Chicago, July 4, 1972. O: 53,775, Los Angeles, April 8, 1974. B: 3,884,720, 1993. W: 534,672, 1975. *Turner Field* (Atlanta, 1997-present). D: 47,522, Philadelphia, April 5, 1999. N: 50,662, St. Louis, July 31, 1998. O: 47,522 Philadelphia, April 5, 1999. B: 3,464,488, 1997. W: 3,234,301, 2000.

Chicago. *State Street Grounds* (1876–'77). B: 65,441, 1876. W: 1877, 46,454. *Lakefront Park* (1878–'84). B: 146,777, 1884. W: 34,343, 1881. *West Side Park* (1885–'92). B: 228,906, 1888. W: 102,536, 1890. *West Side Grounds* (1893–1915). *Wrigley Field* (1916–present). D: 51,556, Brooklyn, June 27, 1930. DH: 46,965, Pittsburgh, May 31, 1948. N: 40,425, St. Louis, May 30, 1999. O: 45,777, Pittsburgh, April 14, 1978. B: 2,813,854, 1999. W: 337,256, 1918.

Cincinnati. *Avenue Grounds* (1876–'77). B: 28,000, 1876. W: 24,000 1877. *Bank Street Grounds* (1880). B/W: 21,000, 1880. *League Park* (1884–'89). *Redland Field,* a.k.a. Palace of the Fans (1902–'11). B: 424,643, 1909. W: 217,300, 1902. *Crosley Field* (1912–'70). D: 35,747, Pittsburgh, April 15, 1924. DH: 36,691, Pittsburgh, April 27,

1947. N: 32,916, Chicago, June 29, 1936. TN: 32,552, San Francisco, August 8, 1966. O: 35,747, Pittsburgh, April 15, 1924. B: 1,125,928, 1956. W: 100,791, 1914. *Cinergy Field* a.k.a. Riverfront Stadium (1970–present). D: 55,596, Milwaukee, April 3, 2000. DH: 52,147, Atlanta, June 23, 1974. N: 54,621, New York, October 4, 1999. TN: 53,328, Pittsburgh, July 9, 1976. O: 55,596, Milwaukee, April 3, 2000. B: 2,629,708, 1976. W: 1,093,730, 1981.

Colorado. *Mile High Stadium* (Denver, 1993–'94). D: 80,227, Montreal, April 9, 1993. DH: 60,613, New York, August 21, 1993. N: 73,957, San Francisco, June 24, 1994. O: 80,227, Montreal, April 9, 1993. B: 4,483,350, 1993. W: 3,281,511, 1994. *Coors Field* (Denver, 1995–present). D: 48,876, Chicago, June 24, 1999. N: 50,400, San Diego, July 3, 1999. O: 48,084, Cincinnati, April 10, 2000. B: 3,891,014, 1996. W: 3,285,710, 2000.

Florida. *Pro Player Stadium* a.k.a. Joe Robbie Stadium (Miami, 1993–present). D: 45,900, New York, October 3, 1993. DH: 35,019, San Francisco, August 1, 1993. N: 46,796, San Francisco, August 27, 1993. TN: 37,007, Philadelphia, September 27, 1998. O: 43,290, Houston, April 12, 1994. B: 3,064,847, 1993. W: 1,218,326, 2000.

Houston. *Colt Stadium* (1962–'64). D: 26,697, Milwaukee, April 16, 1964. DH: 30,027, Los Angeles, June 10, 1962. N: 28,669, Los Angeles, September 12, 1962. O: 26,697, Milwaukee, April 16, 1964. B: 924,456, 1962. W: 719,502. *Astrodome* (1965–'99). D: 52,493, St. Louis, September 12, 1998. DH: 45,115, Atlanta, August 4, 1979. N: 54,037, Cincinnati, September 28, 1999. O: 51,668, Chicago, April 6, 1999. B: 2,706,017, 1999. W: 858,002, 1975. *Enron Field* (2000–present). D: 42,777, Atlanta, May 28, 2000. N: 43,189, Atlanta, September 2, 2000. O: 41,583, Philadelphia, April 7, 2000. W/B: 3,056,139, 2000.

Los Angeles. *Washington Park* (Brooklyn, 1884–'89 and 1898–1912). B: 312,500, 1907. W: 122,514, 1898. *Eastern Park* (Brooklyn, 1891–'97). B: 235,000, 1893. W: 181,477, 1891. *Ebbets Field* (Brooklyn, 1913–'57). D: 37,512, New York, August 30, 1947. DH: 41,209, New York, May 30, 1934. N: 35,583, Philadelphia, September 24, 1949. O: 34,530, New York, April 18, 1949. B: 1,807,526, 1947. W: 83,831, 1918. *Roosevelt Stadium* (Jersey City, N.J., 1956–'57). D: 26,385, New York, August 15, 1956. B: 148,371, 1956. W: 123,389, 1957. *Memorial Coliseum* (Los Angeles, 1958–'61). D: 78,672, San Francisco, April 18, 1958. DH: 39,432, Chicago, September 6, 1959. N: 67,550, Chicago, April 12, 1960. TN: 72,140, Cincinnati, August 16, 1961. O: 78,672, San Francisco, April 18, 1958. B: 2,253,887, 1960. W: 1,804,250, 1961. *Dodger Stadium* (Los Angeles, 1962–present). D: 54,769, San Francisco, September 5, 1966. DH: 53,856, Cincinnati, July 7, 1963. N: 55,185, San Francisco, July 28, 1973. TN: 52,831, Cincinnati, June 23, 1973. O: 53,757, Florida, April 5, 1994. B: 3,608,881, 1982. W: 1,581,093, 1968.

Milwaukee. *Sick's Stadium* (Seattle, 1969). D: 21,900, New York, August 3, 1969. DH: no record. N: 20,490, Baltimore, May 28, 1969. TN: 18,147, Kansas City, June 20, 1969. O: 14,993, Chicago, April 11, 1969. B/W: 677,944, 1969. *Milwaukee County Stadium* (Milwaukee, 1970–2000). D: 54,354, Cincinnati, September 29, 2000. DH: 49,054, Boston, August 1, 1982. N: 55,716, Boston, August 1, 1982. TN: 54,630, Detroit, July 6, 1979. O: 55,887, New York, April 15, 1988. B: 2,397,131, 1983. W: 600,440, 1972. *Miller Park* (Milwaukee, 2001–). O: 42,024, Cincinnati, April 6, 2001.

Montreal. Jarry Park (1969–'76). D: 34,331, Philadelphia, September 15, 1973. DH: 30,416, Los Angeles, July 7, 1974. N: 28,702, Pittsburgh, May 23, 1970: TN: 28,819, St. Louis, June 25, 1969. O: 29,184, St. Louis, April 14, 1969. B: 1,424,683, 1970. W: 646,704, 1976. *Olympic Stadium* (1977–present). D: 57,694, Philadelphia, August 15, 1982. DH: 59,282, St. Louis, September 16, 1979. N: 57,121, Philadelphia, October 3, 1980. TN: 59,260, Pittsburgh, July 27, 1979. O: 57,592, Philadelphia, April 15, 1977. B: 2,318,292, 1982. W: 773,277, 1999.

New York. Polo Grounds (1962–'63). D: 35,624, Los Angeles, July 14, 1962. DH: 54,360, Los Angeles, May 30, 1962. N: 49,431, San Francisco, May 3, 1963. TN: 16,540, Pittsburgh, August 19, 1962. O: 25,251, St. Louis, April 9, 1963. B: 1,080,108, 1963. W: 922,530, 1962. *Shea Stadium* (1964–present). D: 56,738, Los Angeles, June 23, 1968. DH: 57,175, Los Angeles, June 13, 1965. N: 56,658, San Francisco, May 13, 1966. TN: 52,320, St. Louis, August 21, 1998. O: 53,134, Colorado, April 5, 1993. B: 3,047,724, 1988. W: 701,910, 1981.

Philadelphia. Agricultural County Fair Grounds (Worcester, MA., 1880–'82). *Recreation Park* (Philadelphia, 1883–'86). B: 175,623, 1886. W: 55,992, 1883. *Baker Bowl* (Philadelphia, 1887–1938). D: 37,534, New York, May 16, 1938. DH: 38,800, Washington, July 13, 1931. B: 515,365, 1916. W: 112,066, 1902. *Shibe Park* a.k.a. Connie Mack Stadium (Philadelphia, 1938–'70). D: 36,765, Brooklyn, October 2, 1949. DH: 40,720, Brooklyn, May 11, 1947. N: 40,007, Cincinnati, September 19, 1946. TN: 39,705, Brooklyn, August 11, 1952. O: 37,667, Brooklyn, April 16, 1957. B: 1,425,891, 1964. W: 207,177, 1940. *Veterans Memorial Stadium* (Philadelphia, 1971–present). D: 60,985, Chicago, April 9, 1993. N: 63,816, Cincinnati, July 3, 1984. TN: 63,346, Pittsburgh, August 10, 1979. O: 60,985, Chicago, April 9, 1993. B: 3,137,674, 1993. W: 1,343,329, 1972.

Pittsburgh. Exposition Park (1882–'86 and 1891–1909). B: 394,877, 1906. W: 128,000, 1891. *Recreation Park* (1887–'90). B: 140,000, 1887. W: 16,064, 1890. *Forbes Field* (1909–'70). D: 44,932, Brooklyn, September 23, 1956. DH: 43,586, New York, August 31, 1938. N: 42,254, Cincinnati, August 12, 1940. TN: 34,673, Philadelphia, August 16, 1960. O: 38,546, Chicago, April 20, 1948. B: 1,705,828, 1960. W: 139,620, 1914. *Three Rivers Stadium* (1970–2000). D: 55,351, Chicago, October 1, 2000. DH: 49,341, Houston, July 16, 1972. N: 51,292, San Diego, June 8, 1991. TN: 49,886, New York, July 27, 1972. O: 54,274, Montreal, April 8, 1991. B: 2,065,302, 1991. W: 541,789, 1981. *PNC Park* (2001–). O: 36,954, Cincinnati, April 9, 2001.

St. Louis. Sportsman's Park (1876–'77). B: 36,000, 1876. W: 29,000, 1877. *Union Park* (1885–'86). B: 99,000, 1886. W: 62,000, 1885. *Robison Field* (1892–1920). B: 447,768, 1911. W: 110,599, 1918. *Sportsman's Park* a.k.a. Busch Stadium (1920–'66). D: 41,284, New York, September 15, 1935. DH: 45,770, Chicago, July 12, 1931. N: 33,323, Brooklyn, August 25, 1942. O: 26,246, Chicago, April 15, 1962. B: 1,430,676, 1949. W: 256,171, 1933. *Busch Stadium* (1966–present). D: 52,916, Cincinnati, September 28, 1996. D: 49,743, Atlanta, June 23, 1968. N: 53,415, Chicago, July 30, 1994. TN: 52,657, Atlanta, July 22, 1994. O: 52,841, Montreal, April 8, 1996. B: 3,336,493, 2000. W: 1,010,247, 1981.

San Diego. Qualcomm Stadium a.k.a. San Diego Stadium or Jack Murphy Stadium (1969–present). D: 61,247, Colorado, April 4, 1999. DH: 43,473, Philadelphia, June

13, 1976. N: 61,674, Arizona, April 24, 1999. O: 61,247, April 6, 1999. B: 2,555,901, 1998. W: 512,970, 1969.

San Francisco. Putnam Grounds (Troy, N.N., 1879). B/W: 12,000, 1879. *Haymakers Grounds* (Troy, 1880–'81). B: 18,500, 1880. W: 18,000, 1881. *Polo Grounds I* (New York, 110th Street, 1883–'88). B: 305,455, 1888. W: 75,000, 1883. *Polo Grounds II* (New York, 155th Street, 1888–'90). B: 305,455, 1888. W: 60,667, 1890. *Polo Grounds III* (New York, 157th Street, 1891–1957). D: 54,992, St. Louis, April 30, 1941. DH: 60,747, Brooklyn, May 31, 1937. N: 51,790, Brooklyn, May 27, 1957. TN: no record. O: 54,393, Brooklyn, April 14, 1936. B: 1,600,793, 1947. W: 258,618, 1918. *Seals Stadium* (San Francisco, 1958–'59). D: 23,192, Los Angeles, April 15, 1958. DH: 22,721, Pittsburgh, May 4, 1958. N: 23,115, St. Louis, April 22, 1958. O: 23,192, Los Angeles, April 15, 1958. B: 1,422,130, 1959. W: 1,272,625, 1958. *3Com Park* a.k.a. Candlestick Park (San Francisco, 1960–'99). D: 61,389, Los Angeles, September 30, 1999. DH: 53,178, Los Angeles, July 31, 1983. N: 55,920, Cincinnati, June 20, 1978. O: 42,269, St. Louis, April 12, 1960. B: 2,606,254, 1993. W: 519,987, 1974. *Pacific Bell Park* (San Francisco, 2000–present). D, N, and O: 40,930, each 2000 game. B/W: 3,315,330, 2000.

AMERICAN LEAGUE

Anaheim. Wrigley Field (Los Angeles, 1961). D: 19,722, New York, May 7, 1961. DH: 16,297, Kansas City, April 30, 1961. N: 19,930, New York, August 22, 1961. TN: 9,574, Chicago, May 19, 1961. O: 11,931, Minnesota, April 27, 1961. B/W: 603,510, 1961. *Chavez Ravine* a.k.a. Dodger Stadium (Los Angeles, 1962–'65). D: 44,912, New York, June 3, 1962. DH: 12,873, Kansas City, June 10, 1962. N: 53,591, New York, July 13, 1962. TN: 18,902, Minnesota, May 19, 1965. O: 21,864, Chicago, April 11, 1963. B: 1,144,063, 1962. W: 566,727, 1965. *Edison International Field of Anaheim* a.k.a. Anaheim Stadium (Anaheim, 1966–present). D: 63,132, Kansas City, July 4, 1983. DH: 43,461, Chicago, August 5, 1988. N: 63,406, Baltimore, April 23, 1983. O: 51,145, Detroit, April 26, 1995. B: 2,807,360, 1982. W: 744,190, 1972.

Baltimore. Lloyd Street Grounds (Milwaukee, 1901). D: 10,000, Philadelphia, May 26, 1901. O: 3,000, Chicago, May 4, 1901. B/W: 139,034, 1901. *Sportsman's Park* (St. Louis, 1902–'53). D: 34,625, New York, October 1, 1944. DH: 31,932, New York, June 17,1928. N: 22,847, Cleveland, May 24,1940. O: 19,561, Detroit, April 18, 1923. B: 712,918. W: 80,922, 1935. *Memorial Stadium* (Baltimore, Maryland, 1954–'91). D: 52,395, Milwaukee, April 4, 1988. DH: 51,883, Milwaukee, October 1, 1982. N: 51,649, New York, August 16, 1980. O: 46,354, Chicago, April 15, 1954. B: 2,552,753, 1991. W: 774,343, 1963. *Oriole Park at Camden Yards* (Baltimore, Maryland, 1992–present). D: 48,544, Anaheim, July 24, 1999. N: 48,531, Philadelphia, June 5, 1999. O: 44,568, Cleveland, April 6, 1992. B: 3,711,132, 1997. W: 2,535,359, 1994.

Boston. Huntington Avenue Grounds (1901–'11). B: 668,965, 1909. W: 289,448, 1901. *Fenway Park* (1912–present). D: 36,388, Cleveland, April 22, 1978. DH: 47,627, New York, September 22, 1935. N: 36,228, New York, June 28, 1949. O: 35,343, Baltimore, April 14, 1969. B: 2,586,032, 2000. W: 229,688, 1923.

Chicago. South Side Park (1900–'10). B: 687,419, 1905. W: 286,183, 1903. *Comiskey*

Park (1910–'90). D: 54,215, New York, July 19, 1953. DH: 55,555, Minnesota, May 20, 1973. N: 53,067, New York, July 27, 1954. TN: 53,940, New York, June 8, 1951. O: 51,560, Milwaukee, April 14, 1981. B: 2,136,988, 1984. W: 195,081, 1918. *Comiskey Park II* (1991–present). D: 44,008, Chicago Cubs, July 10, 1999. N: 44,249, Chicago Cubs, June 17, 1997. O: 42,890, Boston, April 8, 1994. B: 2,934,154, 1991. W: 1,338,851, 1999.

Cleveland. League Park (1900–'10). B: 422,262, 1908. W: 131,380, 1901. *League Park* (1910–'46). B: 912,832, 1920. W: 159,285, 1915. *Municipal Stadium* a.k.a. Cleveland Stadium (1932–'93). D: 74,420, Detroit, April 7, 1973. DH: 84,587, New York, September 12, 1954. N: 78,382, Chicago, August 20, 1948. TN: 65,934, New York, August 1, 1986. O: 74,420, Detroit, April 7, 1973. B: 2,620,627, 1948. W: 387,936, 1933. *Jacobs Field* (1994–present). DH: 42,673, Detroit, August 13, 1997. O: 42,830, Kansas City, April 12, 1999. B: 3,468,456, 1999. W: 1,995,174, 1994.

Detroit. Bennett Park (1900–'11). B: 490,490, 1909. W: 174,043, 1906. *Tiger Stadium* a.k.a. Navin Field and Briggs Stadium (1912–'99). D: 57,888, Cleveland, September 26, 1948. DH: 58,369, New York, July 20, 1947. N: 56,586, Cleveland, August 9, 1948. TN: 57,271, Chicago, June 21, 1961. O: 54,089, Cleveland, April 6, 1971. B: 2,704,794, 1984. W: 203,719, 1918. *Comerica Park* (2000–present). D: 40,637, Cincinnati, July 16, 2000. DH: 36,917, Kansas City, July 22, 2000. N: 39,745, Minnesota, August 4, 2000. O: 39,168, Seattle, April 11, 2000. B/W: 2,533,752, 2000.

Kansas City. Municipal Stadium (1969–'72). D: 30,035, Milwaukee, May 24, 1970. DH: 31,872, Oakland, April 20, 1969. N: 16,406, New York, June 13, 1970. TN: 18,248, Oakland, June 18, 1969. O: 32,728, Minnesota, April 12, 1971. B: 910,784, 1971. W: 693,647, 1970. *Kauffman Stadium* a.k.a. Royals Stadium (1973–present). D: 41,329, Oakland, September 21, 1980. DH: 35,295, California, June 20, 1971. N: 41,860, New York, July 26, 1980. TN: 42,039, Milwaukee, August 8, 1983. O: 41,086, Toronto, April 8, 1985. B: 2,477,700, 1989. W: 1,151,836.

Minnesota. American League Park (Washington, D.C., 1901–'02). B: 188,158, 1902. W: 161,661, 1901. *National Park* (Washington, D.C., 1903–'10). B: 264,252, 1908. W: 128,878, 1903. *Griffith Stadium* (Washington, D.C., 1911–'60). D: 31,728, New York, April 19, 1948. DH: 35,563, New York, July 4, 1936. N: 30,701, Cleveland, June 17, 1947. O: 31,728, New York, April 19, 1948. B: 1,027,216, 1946. W: 89,682, 1917. *Metropolitan Stadium* (Bloomington, MN., 1961–'81). D: 46,463, Chicago, June 26, 1977. DH: 43,419, California, July 16, 1967. N: 45,890, Kansas City, July 4, 1973. TN: 38,441, Detroit, July 29, 1969. O: 37,529, California, April 17, 1979. B: 1,483,547, 1967. W: 662,401, 1974. *Hubert H. Humphrey Metrodome* (Minneapolis, 1982–present). D: 53,106, Kansas City, September 27, 1987. DH: 51,017, Oakland, July 28, 1990. N: 52,704, Kansas City, September 25, 1987. TN: 51,017, Oakland, July 28, 1980. O: 53,067, Toronto, April 8, 1988. B: 3,030,672, 1988. W: 858,939, 1983.

New York. Oriole Park (Baltimore, 1901–'02). B: 174,606, 1902. W: 141,952, 1901. *Hilltop Park* (New York, 1903–'12). B: 1,289,422, 1920. W: 256,035, 1915. *Polo Grounds* (New York, 1913–'22). B: 1,289,422. W: 256,035, 1915. *Yankee Stadium* (Bronx, N.Y., 1923–'73). D: 69,755, Boston, September 26, 1948. DH: 81,841, Boston, May 30, 1938. N: 74,747, Boston, May 26, 1947. TN: 40,314, Boston, August 29, 1967. O: 54,826, Washington, April 19, 1946. B: 2,373,901, 1948. W: 645,006, 1943. *Shea Stadium* (New York, 1974–'75). D: 53,562, Chicago, June 17,

1975. DH: 53,631, Boston, July 27, 1975. N: 40,165, Boston, July 25, 1975. O: 26,212, Detroit, April 11, 1975. B: 1,288,048, 1975. W: 1,273,075, 1974. *Yankee Stadium* (Bronx, N.Y., 1976–present). D: 56,717, Oakland, April 10, 1998. DH: 55,410, Detroit, October 4, 1980. N: 56,294, New York Mets, June 6, 1999. TN: 55,605, Baltimore, September 10, 1983. O: 56,717, Oakland, April 10, 1998. B: 3,292,736, 1999. W: 1,614,533, 1981.

Oakland. **Columbia Park** (Philadelphia, 1901–'08). B: 625,581, 1907. W: 206,329, 1901. *Shibe Park* a.k.a. Connie Mack Stadium (Philadelphia, 1909–'54). D: 37,534, New York, May 16, 1937. DH: 38,800, Washington, July 13, 1931. N: 37,383, New York, June 27, 1947. TN: 37,684, Cleveland, July 15, 1948. O: 32,825, New York, April 20, 1927. B: 945,076, 1948. W: 146,223, 1915. *Municipal Stadium* (Kansas City, 1955–'67). D: 34,065, New York, August 27, 1961. DH: 34,865, New York, July 15, 1962. N: 33,471, New York, April 29, 1955. TN: 35,147, New York, August 8, 1962. O: 31,895, Detroit, April 12, 1955. B: 1,393,054, 1955. W: 528,344, 1965. *Network Associates Coliseum* a.k.a. Oakland-Alameda County Coliseum (Oakland, 1968–present). D: 51,263, San Francisco, July 17, 1999. DH: 48,562, New York, May 3, 1981. N: 54,268, Arizona, July 8, 2000. TN: 47,768, New York, June 13, 1980. O: 53,498, Detroit, April 3, 2000. B: 2,900,217, 1990. W: 306,736, 1979.

Seattle. **Kingdome** (1977–'99). D: 57,822, Cleveland, March 31, 1998. DH: 32,697, California, August 12, 1985. N: 57,806, Minnesota, April 11, 1994. O: 57,816, Cleveland, March 31, 1998. B: 3,192,237, 1997. W: 636,276, 1981. *Safeco Field* (1999–present). D: 45,194, Chicago, August 11, 1999. N: 45,552, Boston, April 4, 2000. O: 45,552, Boston, April 4, 2000. B: 3,148,317, 2000. W: 2,916,346, 1999.

Tampa Bay. **Tropicana Field** (1998–present). D: 43,373, New York, July 12, 1998. N: 45,369, Detroit, March 31, 1998. O: 45,369, Detroit, March 3, 31, 1998. B: 2,506,023, 1998. W: 1,549,052, 2000.

Texas. **Griffith Stadium** (Washington, D.C., 1961). D: 18,882, Minnesota, May 28, 1961. DH: 27,368, New York, August 13, 1961. N: 22,601, New York, August 11, 1961. TN: 27,126, New York, July 19, 1961. O: 26,725, Chicago, April 10, 1961. B/W: 597,287, 1961. *Robert F. Kennedy Stadium* a.k.a. District of Columbia Stadium (Washington, D.C., 1962–'71). D: 45,125, New York, April 7, 1996. DH: 40,359, Minnesota, June 14, 1964. N: 30,421, New York, July 31, 1962. TN: 48,147, New York, August 1, 1962. O: 45,125, New York, April 7, 1969. B: 918,106, 1969. W: 535,604, 1963. *Arlington Stadium* (Arlington, TX., 1972–'93). D: 41,074, Kansas City, October 2, 1993. DH: 42,163, Detroit, July 10, 1982. N: 43,705, Toronto, July 23, 1983. O: 42,415, Milwaukee, April 10, 1987. B: 2,297,720, 1991. W: 662,974, 1972. *The Ballpark in Arlington* (Arlington, 1994–present). D: 49,332, Chicago, April 3, 2000. DH: 40,852, Detroit, July 1, 1994. N: 47,187, Oakland, July 4, 2000. O: 49,332, Chicago, April 3, 2000. B: 2,945,244, 1997. W: 1,985,910, 1995.

Toronto. **Exhibition Stadium** (1977–'89). D: 47,828, New York, July 1, 1987. DH: 45,102, New York, August 2, 1983. N: 47,686, New York, October 4, 1985. O: 46,028, Kansas City, April 14, 1989. B: 2,778,429, 1987. W: 755,083, 1981. *Sky-Dome* (1989–present). D: 50,533, Cleveland, April 9, 1993. DH: 48,641, California, July 17, 1989. N: 50,532, Boston, September 22, 1993. O: 50,533, Cleveland, April 9, 1993. B: 4,957,947, 1993. W: 1,819,886, 2000.

BALLPARKS: BY CAPACITY

NATIONAL LEAGUE

1.	66,307	Qualcomm Stadium, San Diego
2.	62,418	Veterans Memorial Stadium, Philadelphia
3.	56,516	Shea Stadium, New York
4.	56,000	Dodger Stadium, Los Angeles
5.	50,445	Coors Field, Denver
6.	50,091	Turner Field, Atlanta
7.	49,779	Busch Stadium, St. Louis
8.	49,033	Bank One Ballpark, Phoenix
9.	46,500	Olympic Stadium, Montreal
10.	42,885	Miller Park, Milwaukee
11.	40,950	Enron Field, Houston
12.	40,800	Pacific Bell Park, San Francisco
13.	39,059	Wrigley Field, Chicago
14.	39,000	Cinergy Field, Cincinnati
15.	38,365	PNC Park, Pittsburgh
16.	36,331	Pro Player Stadium, Miami

AMERICAN LEAGUE

1.	57,530	Yankee Stadium, New York
2.	49,200	The Ballpark in Arlington, Arlington
3.	48,876	Oriole Park at Camden Yards, Baltimroe
4.	48,678	Hubert H. Humphrey Metrodome, Minneapolis
5.	47,116	Safeco Field, Seattle
6.	45,887	Comiskey Park, Chicago
7.	45,100	SkyDome, Toronto
8.	45,050	Edison International Field, Anaheim
9.	43,863	Jacobs Field, Cleveland
10.	43,662	Network Associates Coliseum, Oakland
11.	43,370	Tropicana Field, St. Petersburg
12.	40,529	Kauffman Stadium, Kansas City
13.	40,120	Comerica Park, Detroit
14.	33,991	Fenway Park, Boston

BALLPARKS: RANK BY AGE

NATIONAL LEAGUE

1. 1914*   Wrigley Field, Chicago
2. 1962   Dodger Stadium, Los Angeles
3. 1964   Shea Stadium, New York
4. 1966   Busch Stadium, St. Louis
5. 1969+   Qualcomm Stadium, San Diego
6. 1970++   Cinergy Field, Cincinnati
7. 1971   Veterans Memorial Stadium, Philadelphia
8. 1977   Olympic Stadium, Montreal
9. 1993+++   Pro Player Stadium, Miami
10. 1995   Coors Field, Denver
11. 1997   Turner Field, Atlanta
12. 1998   Bank One Ballpark, Phoenix
13. 2000   Enron Field, Houston
14. 2000   Pacific Bell Park, San Francisco
15. 2001   Miller Park, Milwaukee
16. 2001   PNC Park, Pittsburgh

AMERICAN LEAGUE

1. 1912   Fenway Park, Boston
2. 1923   Yankee Stadium, New York
3. 1966++++   Edison International Field, Anaheim
4. 1968+++++   Network Associates Coliseum, Oakland
5. 1973+++++   Kauffman Stadium, Kansas City
6. 1982   Hubert H. Humphrey Metrodome, Minneapolis
7. 1989   SkyDome, Toronto
8. 1991   Comiskey Park, Chicago
9. 1992   Oriole Park at Camden Yards, Baltimore
10. 1994   The Ballpark in Arlington, Arlington
11. 1994   Jacobs Field, Cleveland
12. 1998   Tropicana Field, St. Petersburg
13. 1999   Safeco Field, Seattle
14. 2000   Comerica Park, Detroit

* Indicates the year the original ballpark was built and available for use. Later name changes, alterations, expansions, and occupancy by the present club are disregarded.
+ Known as San Diego Stadium, 1969–'80 and Jack Murphy Stadium 1981–'96
++ Known as Riverfront Stadium, 1970–'96

+++   Known as Joe Robbie Stadium, 1993–'96
++++   Known as Anaheim Stadium 1966–'97
+++++   Known as Oakland-Alameda County Coliseum, 1968–'98
++++++   Known as Royals Stadium, 1973–'93

FACTS AND FILLIPS

CURRENT PARKS

Below are the parks of baseball's present current major-league franchises, listed alphabetically, without regard to league.

BANK ONE BALLPARK. 401 East Jefferson Street, Phoenix, Arizona 85004. (602) 462-6500. Opened: March 31, 1998, with a 9–2 loss to Colorado. Dimensions: left-field line—330 feet. Left-cenetr—374. Deepest left-center—413. Center—407. Right-center—374. Deepest right-center—413. Right-field line—334. Turf: grass. Record crowds: game—48,277, May 24, 1998. Season—3,600,412, 1998. Seating capacity: 49,033. Ticket information: (602) 514-8400. Prices—$43–70 (lower-level premium seats); $29 and $36 (Infiniti Diamond level); $11-26 (lower level); $1–17 (upper level). Official website: www.azdiamondbacks.com

BUSCH STADIUM. 250 Stadium Plaza, St. Louis, Missouri 63102. (314) 421-3060. Opened: May 12, 1966, with a 4–3 victory over Atlanta. Dimensions: Left-field line—330 feet. Left-center—372. Center—402. Right-center—375. Right-field line—330. Turf: grass. Seating capacity: 49,779. Record crowds: game—53,415, July 30, 1994. Season—3,336,493, 2000. Ticket information: (314) 421-2400. Prices—$36 (infield field foxes); $33 (infield loge boxes); $31 (outfield field boxes); $27 (outfield loge boxes); $22 (infield terrace boxes and loge reserved); $20 (outfield terrace boxes and loge reserved); $17 (adult terrace reserved); $10 (bleachers); $9 (adult outfield upper terrace); $8 (children terrace reserved). Official website: www.stlcardinals.com

CINERGY FIELD. 100 Cinergy Field, Cincinnati, Ohio 45202. (513) 421-4510. Opened: June 30, 1970, with an 8–2 loss to Atlanta. Dimensions: Left-field line—325. Left-center—371. Center—393. Right-center—371. Right-field line—325. Turf: grass. Seating capacity: 39,000. Record crowds: game—54,621, October 4, 1999. Season—2,629,708, 1976. Ticket information: (513) 421-7337 or 1-800-829-5353. Prices—$28 and $21 (blue-level box seats); $21 and $16 (green-level boxes); $15 (yellow-level boxes); $14 (red-level boxes); $9 (red-level reserved); $5 ("top six" reserved: sold only sold day of the game unless all other tickets are sold in advance). Official website: www.cincinnatireds.com

COMERICA PARK. 2100 Woodward Avenue, Detroit, Michigan 48201. (313) 962-4000. Opened: April 11, 2002, with a 5–2 victory over Seattle. Dimensions: Left-field line—345. Left-center—398. Center—420. Right-center—380. Right-field line—330. Turf: grass. Seating capacity: 40,120. Record crowds: game—40,637, July 16, 2000. Season—2,533,752, 2000. Ticket information: (313) 471-BALL. Prices: $60 (Tiger Den); $35 (terrace, club); $30 (infield box); $25 and $15 (outfield box); $20 (upper box); $15 (mezzanine); $14 (pavilion); $12 (upper reserved); $8 (bleachers). Official website: www.detroittigers.com

COMISKEY PARK. 333 West 35th Street, Chicago, Illinois 60616. (312) 924-1000. Opened: April 18, 1991, with a 16–0 loss to Detroit. Dimensions: left-field line—330 feet. Left-center—377. Center—400. Right-center—372. Right-field line—335. Turf: bluegrass sod with eight types of grass. Seating capacity: 45,887. Record crowds: game—44,249, June 17, 1997. Season—2,934,154, 1991. Ticket information: (312) 674-1000. Prices—$26 (lower deck box, club level); $20 (lower-deck reserved); $18 (upper-deck box), bleacher reserved); $12 (upper-deck reserved). Official website: www.whitesox.com

COORS FIELD. 2001 Blake Street, Denver, Colorado 80205-2000. (303) 292-0200. Opened: April 26, 1995, with an 11–9 victory over New York. Dimensions: left-field line—347 feet. Left-center—390. Deepest left-center—420. Center—415. Deepest right-center—424. Right-center—375. Right-field corner—358. Right-field line—350. Turf: grass. Seating capacity: 50,445. Record crowds: game—50,400, July 3, 1999. Season—3,891,014, 1996. Ticket information: 1-800-388-7625. Prices—$32 (infield club level); $30 (outfield club level); $27 (infield box); $21.50 (outfield box); $16/13 (lower reserved, infield/outfield); $12 (upper reserved infield, right-field box); $11 (lower reserved corner); $10 (right-field mezzanine); $9 (upper reserved, outfield; lower pavilion); $8 (lower pavilion); $7 (upper reserved corner); $6/5 (lower-upper right-field reserved); $4/1 (Rockpile). Official website: www.coloradorockies.com

DODGER STADIUM. 1000 Elysian Park Avenue, Los Angeles, California 90012. (323) 224-1500. Opened: April 10, 1962, with a 6–3 loss to Cincinnati. Dimensions: left-field line—330 feet. Left-center—385. Center—395. Right-center—385. Right-field line—330. Turf: prescription Athletic Turf (PAT). Seating capacity: 56,000. Record crowds: game—55,185, July 28, 1973. Season—3,608,881, 1982. Ticket information: (323) 224-1448. Prices—$17 (field box); $15 (inner reserved); $13 (loge box); $10 (outer reserve); $6 (top deck, left and right pavilion). Official website: www.dodgers.com

EDISON INTERNATIONAL FIELD OF ANAHEIM. 2000 Gene Autry Way, Anaheim, California 92806. (714) 940-2000. Opened: April 19, 1966, with a 3–1 loss to Chicago. Dimensions: left-field line—333 feet. Left-center—370. Center—404. Right-center—370. Right-field line—333. Turf: Bluegrass. Seating capacity: 45,050. Record crowds: game—63,132, July 4, 1983. Season—2,807,360, 1982. Ticket information: (714) 634-2000. Prices—$24 (terrace MVP); $22 (club loge, field box); $20 (terrace box); $15 (lower view MVP); $12 (lower view box); $10 (view); $8 (right field pavilion, adult); $7 (left field pavilion, adult); $6 (right field pavilion, child); $4 (left field pavilion, child). Official website: www.angelsbaseball.com

ENRON FIELD. P.O. Box 288, Houston, Texas 77001-0288. (713) 799-9500. Opened: April 7, 2000, with a 4–1 loss to Philadelphia. Dimensions: left-field line—315 feet. Left-center—362. Center—435. Right-field—373. Right-field line—326. Turf: grass. Seating capacity: 42,000. Record crowds: game—43,189, September 2, 2000. Season—3,056,139, 2000. Ticket information: (713) 799-9567 or 1-800-Astros-2. Prices: $29 (dugout seats); $28 (club); $25 (field box); $24 (club); $17 (Crawford box): $15 (bullpen box): $12 (mezzanine, terrace deck): $10 (upper deck): $5–1 (outfield deck). Official website: www.astros.com

FENWAY PARK. 4 Yawkey Way, Boston, Massachusetts 02215. (617) 267-9440. Opened: April 20, 1912, with a 7–6 victory over New York. Dimensions: left-field line—310 feet. Left-center—379. Center—390. Deep center—420. Right-center—380. Right-field line—302. Turf: grass. Seating capacity: 33,455. Record crowds: game—36,388, April 22, 1978. Season—2,586,032, 2000. Ticket information: (617) 267-1700 or 617-482-4769. Prices—$55 (field box, loge box, and infield roof); $40 (reserved grandstand); $30 (right-field box and right-field roof); $25 (outfield grandstand); $20 (lower bleachers); $18 (upper bleachers). Official website: www.redsox.com

JACOBS FIELD. 2401 Ontario Street, Cleveland, Ohio 44115. (216) 420-4200. Opened: April 4, 1994, with a 4–3 victory over Seattle. Dimensions: left-field line—325 feet. Left-center—368. Center—405. Right-center—375. Right-field line—325. Turf: grass. Seating capacity: 43,863. Record crowds: game—43,399, September 1, 1999. Season—3,468,456, 1999. Ticket information: (216) 420-4200. Prices—$40 (field box): $27 (baselines box, infield lower box, and view box); $25 (lower box); $21 (infield upper box); $20 (lower reserved, upper box and mezzanine); $19 (field bleachers); $17 (bleachers); $12 (upper reserved); $7 (upper reserved general admission); $6 (standing room only). Official website: www.indians.com

HUBERT H. HUMPHREY METRODOME. 34 Kirby Puckett Place, Minneapolis, Minnesota 55415. (612) 375-1366. Opened: April 6, 1982, with an 11–7 loss to Seattle. Dimensions: left-field line—343 feet. Left-center—385. Center—408. Right-center—367. Right-field line—327. Turf: AstroTurf. Seating capacity: 48,678. Record crowds: game—53,106, September 27, 1987. Season—3,030,672, 1988. Ticket information: 1-800-33-Twins. Prices—$25 (lower-deck club level); $23 (Diamond View level); $15 (lower-deck reserved); $10 (upper-deck club level, general admission lower left field); $5 (general admission upper deck). Official website: www.twinsbaseball.com

KAUFFMAN STADIUM. P.O. Box 419969, Kansas City, Missouri 64141-6969. (816) 921-8000. Opened: April 10, 1973, with a 12–1 victory over Texas. Dimensions: left-field line—330 feet. Left-center—375. Center—400. Right-center—375. Right-field line—330. Turf: grass. Seating capacity: 40,529. Record crowds: game—42,039. August 8, 1983. Season—2,477,700, 1989. Ticket information: (816) 921-8000. Prices—$19 (club box) $17 (field box); $15 (plaza reserved); $12 (view upper box); $11 (view upper reserved); $7 (general admission); $5.50 (Royals nights). Official website: www.kcroyals.com

MILLER PARK. One Brewers Way, Milwaukee, Wisconsin 53214-3652. (414) 902-4400. Opened: April 6, 2001, with a 5–4 victory over Cincinnati. Dimensions: left-field line—344 feet. Left-center—371. Center—400. Right-center—374. Right-field line—345. Turf: grass. Seating capacity: 42,885. Ticket information: 414-902-4000 or 1-800-993-7890. Prices—$50 (field diamond box); $32 (field infield box, club infield box); $27 (field outfield box, loge diamond box); $24 (club outfield box); $23 (loge infield box); $20 (loge outfield box); $16 (terrace infield box); $14 (terrace outfield box); $10 (terrace reserved, field bleachers); $6 (loge bleachers, club bleachers); $5 (terrace bleachers). Official website: www.milwaukeebrewers.com

NETWORK ASSOCIATES COLISEUM. Oakland Athletics, 7677 Oakport Street, Suite 200, Oakland, California 94621. (510) 638-4900. Opened: April 17, 1968, with a 4–1 loss to Baltimore. Dimensions: left-field line—330. Left-center—367. Center—400. Right-center—367. Right field—375. Turf: bluegrass. Seating capacity: 43,662. Record crowds: game—54,268, July 8, 2000. Season—2,900,217, 1990. Ticket information: (510) 638-4627. Prices—$30 (plaza club); $25 (MVP infield); $19 (infield field level); $18 (field level, plaza-infield); $16 (plaza); $8 (upper reserved); $6 (bleachers). Official website: www.oaklandathletics.com

OLYMPIC STADIUM. P.O. Box 500, Station M, Montreal, Quebec H1V 3P2. (514) 253-3434. Opened: April 15, 1977, with a 7–2 loss to Philadelphia. Dimensions: left-field line—325 feet. Left-center—375. Center—404. Right-center—375. Right-field line—325. Turf: AstroTurf. Seating capacity: 46,500. Record crowds: game—59,282, September 16, 1979. Season—2,318,292, 1982. Ticket information: 1-800-GO-EXPOS. Prices—$36 (VIP box seats); $26 (box); $16 (terrace); $8 (general admission). Official website: www.montrealexpos.com

ORIOLE PARK AT CAMDEN YARDS. 333 West Camden Street, Baltimore, Maryland 21201. (410) 685-9800. Opened: April 6, 1992, with a 2–0 victory over Cleveland. Dimensions: left-field line—340 feet. Left-center—417. Center—407. Right-center—393. Right-field line—325 feet. Turf: grass. Seating capacity: 48,876. Record crowds: game—48,544, July 24, 1999. Season—3,711,132, 1997. Ticket information: (410) 481-SEAT. Prices—$35 (club box); $30 (field box sections 20–54); $27 (field box sections 14–18, 56–58); $23 (terrace box sections 19–53); $22 (left-field club sections 272–288, lower box sections 6–12, 60–64); $20 (terrace box sections 1–17, 55–65); $18 (left-field lower box sections 66–86, upper box sections 306–372); $16 (left-field upper box sections 374–388, lower reserve sections 19–53); $13 (upper reserve sections 306–372, lower reserve sections 4, 7–17, 55–87); $11 (left-field upper reserve sections 374–388); $9 (bleachers sections 90–98); $7 (standing room). Official website: www.theorioles.com

PACIFIC BELL PARK. 24 Willie Mays Plaza, San Francisco, California 94107. (415) 972-2000. Opened: April 11, 2000, with a 6–5 loss to Los Angeles. Dimensions: left-field line, 335 feet. Left-center—362. Center—404. Right-center—420. Right-field line—307. Turf: grass. Seating capacity: 40,800. Record crowds: game—40,930, each 2000 game. Season—3,315,330, 2000. Ticket information: (415) 972-2000. Prices—$26 (lower box); $20 (view box, arcade); $16 (view reserved); $10 (bleachers). Official website: www.sfgiants.com

PNC PARK. PNC Park at North Shore, 115 Federal Street, Pittsburgh, Pennsylvania 15212. (412) 323-5000. Opened: April 9, 2001, with an 8–2 loss to Cincinnati. Dimensions: left-field line—325. Left-center—389. Deep left-center—410. Center—399. Right-center—375. Right-field 320. Turf: grass. Seating capacity: 38,365. Ticket information: (800)-BUY-BUCS. Prices—$35 (dugout boxes); $25 (baseline and infield boxes; club-level group seating); $23 (left field and right field boxes); $16 (outfield reserved, deck seating, and grandstand); $12 (bleachers); $9 (left field and right field grandstand). Official website: www.pittsburghpirates.com

PRO PLAYER STADIUM. 2267 N.W. 199th Street, Miami, Florida 33056. (305) 626-7400. Opened: April 5, 1993, with a 6–3 victory over Los Angeles. Dimensions: left-field line—330 feet. Left-center—385. Center—434. Right-center—385. Right-field line—345. Turf: grass. Seating capacity: 36,331. Record crowds: game—45,000, October 3, 1993. Season—3,064,847. Ticket information: (305) 350-5050. Prices— $55 (founders, club); $32 (club level section A); $25 (infield box); $18 (power alley section C); $15 (terrace box, mezzanine box); $12 (club level sections B & C—senior citizens); $10 (outfield reserved, adult); $9 (mezzanine reserved, adult); $5 (outfield reserved, children); $4 (fish tank—last three rows, adult); $3 mezzanine reserved, children); $2 (fish tank—last three rows, children). Official website: www.floridamarlins.com

QUALCOMM STADIUM. P.O. Box 2000, San Diego, California 92112–2000. (619) 881-6500. Opened: April 8, 1969, with a 2–1 victory over Houston. Dimensions: left-field line—327 feet. Left-center—370. Center—405. Right-center—370. Right-field line—330. Turf: Santa Ana Bermuda Grass. Seating capacity: 66,307. Record crowds: game—61,672, April 24, 1999. Season—2,555,901, 1998. Ticket information: (888) 697-2373. Prices—$26 (field level, infield); $24 (club level, infield); $22 (field level, outfield; plaza level, infield; and club level, outfield); $20 (plaza level, outfield); $18 (loge level, infield); $16 (loge level, outfield); $14 (press level); $9 (grandstand/plaza level, view level, and lower infield); $8 (grandstand/club level and view level, infield); $7 (view level, outfield); $5 (outfield bleachers). Official website: www.padres.com

SAFECO FIELD. First Avenue South and Atlantic, Seattle, Washington, 98104. (206) 346-4000. Opened: July 15, 1999, with a 3–2 loss to San Diego. Dimensions: left-field line, 331. Left-center: 390. Center—405. Right-center: 387. Right-field line— 326. Turf: grass. Seating capacity: 47,116. Record crowds: game—45,554, April 4, 2000. Season—3,148,317, 2000. Ticket information: (206) 346-4001. Prices—$37 (terrace-club infield); $32 (lower box); $29 (terrace-club outfield); $27 (field); $18 (view box, lower-outfield reserved); $14 (view reserved); $9 (left-field bleachers); $5 (center-field bleachers).

SHEA STADIUM. 123–01 Roosevelt Avenue, Flushing, New York 11368. (718) 507-METS. Opened: April 17, 1964, with a 4–3 loss to Pittsburgh. Dimensions: left-field line—338. Left-center—378. Center—410. Right-center—378. Right-field line—338. Turf: grass. Seating capacity: 56,521. Record crowds: game—56,738, June 23, 1968. Season—3,047,724, 1988. Ticket information: (718) 507-TIXX. Prices—$64 (Metropolitan Club gold, inner baseline box); $60 (Metropolitan Club); $43 (inner field box, inner loge box); $38 (middle field box); $33 (outer field box, outer loge box, and mezzanine); $29 (loge reserved); $23 (mezzanine reserved, upper box); $12 (upper reserved, back rows loge and mezzanine). Official website: www.mets.com

SKYDOME. One Blue Jays Way, Suite 3200, Toronto, Ontario M5V 1J1 Canada. (416) 341-1000. Opened: Opened June 5, 1989, with a 5–3 loss to Milwaukee. Dimensions: left-field line—328 feet. Left-center—375. Center—400. Right-center—375. Right-field line—328. Turf: AstroTurf 8. Seating capacity: 45,100. Record crowds: game—50,533, April 9, 1993. Season—4,057,947, 1993. Ticket information: (416) 341-1234 and (888) OK GO JAYS. Prices—$44 (premium dugout level); $41 (field level infield); $35 (field level bases); $29 (field level baselines); $23 (100 and 200 level outfield; Skydeck infield); $16 (Skydeck bases); $7 (Skydeck baselines). Official website: www.bluejays.com

TURNER FIELD. P.O. Box 4064, Atlanta, Georgia 30302. (404) 522-7630. Opened: April 4, 1997, with a 5–4 victory over Chicago. Dimensions: left-field line—335 feet. Left-center—380. Center—401. Right-center—385. Right-field line—330. Turf: Prescription Athletic Turf (PAT grass). Seating capacity: 50,091. Record crowds: game—50,662. July 31, 1998. Season—3,464,488, 1997. Ticket information: (404) 249-6400 or 1-800-326-4000. Prices—$40 (dugout level); $32 (club level); $27 (field and terrace level); $18 (field and terrace pavilion); $12 (upper level); $5 (upper pavilion); $1 (skyline). Official website: www.atlantabraves.com

THE BALLPARK IN ARLINGTON. 100 Ballpark Way, Arlington, Texas 76011. (817) 273-5222. Opened: April 11, 1994, with a 4–3 loss to Milwaukee. Dimensions: left-field line—332. Left-center—390. Center—400. Deepest right-center—407. Right-center—381. Right-field line—325. Turf: grass. Seating capacity: 49,200. Record crowds: game—49,332, April 3, 2000. Season—2,945,244, 1997. Ticket information: (817) 273-5100. Prices—$40 (lower box, club box); $32.50 (club reserved); $28 (corner box); $22 (terrace club box); $20 (left-field, lower home run porch); $16 (upper box); $13 (upper home run porch); $12 (upper reserved, bleachers); $6 (grandstand reserved); $5 (grandstand). Official website:www.texasrangers.com

TROPICANA FIELD. One Tropicana Drive, St. Petersburg, Florida 33607. (727) 825-3137. Opened: March 31, 1998, with an 11–6 loss to Detroit. Dimensions: left-field line—315. Left-center—370 and 410. Center—404. Right-center—404 and 370. Right-field line—322. Turf: AstroTurf. Seating capacity: 43,819. Record crowds: game—45,369, March 31, 1998. Season—2,506,023, 1998. Ticket information: (727) 825-3250. Prices: $195 (home plate box); $75 (field box); $40 (lower club box); $35 (diamond club box, diamond club restaurant); $30 (lower box); $23 (lower reserved and terrace box); $19 (upper box); $14 (terrace reserved, outfield); $10 (the beach, upper reserved); $8 (upper general admission). Official website: www.devilray.com

VETERANS MEMORIAL STADIUM. P.O. Box 7575, Philadelphia, Pennsylvania 19101. (215) 463-6000. Opened: April 10, 1971, with a 4–1 victory over Montreal. Dimensions: left-field line—330. Left-center—371. Center—408. Right-center—371. Right-field line—330. Turf: AstroTurf. Seating capacity: 62,418. Record crowds: game—63,186, July 3, 1984. Season—3,137,674, 1993. Ticket information: (215) 463-1000. Prices—$24 (field box); $20 (sections 258-201, terrace box); $18 (loge box); $14 (reserved, 600 level); $8 (reserved, 700 level, adult general admission); $5 (children's general admission). Official website: www.phillies.com

WRIGLEY FIELD. 1060 West Addison Street, Chicago, Illinois 60613-4397. (773) 404-2827. Opened: April 20, 1916, with a 7–6 victory over Cincinnati. Dimensions: left-field line—355 feet. Left-center—368. Center—400. Right-center—368. Right-field line—353. Turf: grass. Seating capacity: 39,059. Record crowds: game—51,556, June 27, 1930. Season—2,813,854, 1999. Ticket information: (773) 404-2827. Prices—$30 (club box); $28 (field box); $23 (terrace box, upper-deck box, family section); $20 (bleachers); $18 (terrace reserved). Official website: www.cubs.com

YANKEE STADIUM (New). East 161st Street and River Avenue, The Bronx, New York 10451. (718) 293-4300. Opened: April 15, 1976, with an 11–4 victory over Minnesota.

Dimensions: left-field line—318 feet. Left-center—379. Deepest right-center—399. Center—408. Deepest right-center—385. Right-center—353. Right-field line—314. Turf: merion blue-grass. Seating capacity: 57,530. Record crowds: game—56,717, April 10, 1998. Season—3,292,736, 1999. Ticket information: (212) 307-1212 or (718) 293-6013. Prices—$65 (Championship Seat, loge); $55 (Championship Seat, main box); $47 (main box MVP); $42 (field box and loge box MVP); $37 (main reserved MVP, main and loge box); $33 (tier box and main reserved); $17 (tier reserved); $15 (tier reserved value); $8 (bleachers). Official website: www.yankees.com

PAST PARKS

Below are prominent past major-league ballparks, listed alphabetically, without regard to league. Unless otherwise indicated, records refer to final year of play.

ARLINGTON STADIUM. Office address: 1700 Copeland Road, Arlington, Texas 76011. (817-273-5000). Opened: April 21, 1972, with a 7–6 victory over California. Closed: October 3, 1993, with a 4–1 loss to Kansas City. Dimensions: left-field line— 330 feet. Left-center—380. Center—400. Right-center—380. Right-field line—330. Turf: grass. Seating capacity: 43,521. Record crowds: game—43,705, July 23, 1983. Season—2,297,720. Ticket information: (817) 273-5100. Prices: $14 (infield box); $13 (reserved box); $9 (plaza); $7 (grandstand reserved); $4 (general admission); $2 (children's general admission).

ASTRODOME. 8400 Kirby Drive, Houston, Texas 77054. (713) 799–9500. Opened: April 12, 1965, with a 2–0 loss to Philadelphia. Closed: October 9, 1999, with a 7–5 loss to Atlanta. Dimensions: left-field line—325 feet. Left-center—375. Center—400. Right-center—375. Right-field line—325. Turf: Artificial turf (Magic Carpet). Seating capacity: 54,370. Record crowds: game—54,037, September 28, 1999. Season— 2,706,017, 1999. Ticket information: (713) 799-9555. Prices—$19 (Stardeck); $16 (field); $14 (mezzanine); $11 (loge); $7 (upper deck); $5 (upper reserved); $4 (pavilion: $1 for children 14 and under).

ATLANTA-FULTON COUNTY STADIUM. P.O. Box 4064, Atlanta, Georgia 30302-4064. (404) 577-9100. Opened: April 12, 1966, with a 3–2 loss to Pittsburgh. Closed: October 24, 1996, with a 1–0 loss to New York. Dimensions: left-field line— 330 feet. Left-center—385. Center—402. Right-center—385. Right-field line—330. Turf: grass. Seating capacity: 52,769. Record crowds: game—53,775, April 8, 1974. Season—3,884,720, 1993. Ticket information: (404) 577-9100. Prices—$25 (dugout); $20 (club); $17 (field and family); $12 (lower pavilion); $10 (upper level); $5 (upper pavilion).

BAKER BOWL. 921-922 Packard Building, Philadelphia, Pennsylvania. (RIttenhouse 9177-78). Opened: April 30, 1887, with a 15–9 victory over New York. Closed: June 30, 1938, with a 14–1 loss to New York. Dimensions: left-field line—341. Center—

408. Right-center—300. Right-field line—280. Turf: grass. Seating capacity: 19,000. Record crowds: game—38,800, July 13, 1931. Season: 515,365, 1916. Ticket information: write 921–922 Packard Building, Philadelphia, Pennsylvania.

BENNETT PARK. Opened: April 19, 1900, with an 8–0 loss to Buffalo. Closed: September 10, 1911, with a 6–5 victory over Cleveland. Dimensions: left-field line—341. Left-center—362. Center—467. Right-center—349. Right-field line—371. Turf: grass. Seating capacity: 14,000. Record crowd: season—490,490, 1909.

BRAVES FIELD. 34 Gaffney Street, Boston, Massachusetts. (STadium 2-9600) Opened: August 18, 1915, with a 3–1 victory over St. Louis. Closed: September 21, 1952, with a 8–2 loss to Brooklyn. Dimensions: left-field line—337 feet. Left-center—355. Center—370. Right-center—355. Right-field line—319. Turf: grass. Seating capacity: 37,106. Record crowds: game—47,123, May 22, 1932. Season—1,455,439, 1948. Ticket information: write to Braves Field, Boston 15, Massachusetts. Prices: $3.50 (skyview); $2.40 (box); $1.80 (grandstand reserved); $1.20 (general admission); $1.00 (pavilion); $0.60 (bleachers).

COLT STADIUM. P.O. Box 1691, Houston 1, Texas. (RI 8-4500). Opened: April 10, 1962, with an 11–2 victory over Chicago. Closed: September 27, 1964, with a 1–0 victory over Los Angeles. Dimensions: left-field line—360 feet. Left-center—395. Deepest center—427. Center—420. Right-center—395. Right-field line—360. Turf: grass. Seating capacity: 33,010. Record crowds: game—30,027, June 10, 1962. Season—924,456, 1962. Ticket information (RI 8-4500). Prices: $3.50 (lower and promenade box); $2.50 (reserved); $1.50 (general admission); $0.50 (children).

COLUMBIA PARK. Opened: April 26, 1901, with a 5–1 loss to Washington. Closed: October 3, 1908, with an 8–7 victory over and 5–0 loss to Boston. Turf: grass. Seating capacity: 13,600. Record crowds: game—25,187, September 30, 1905. Season—625,581, 1907.

COMISKEY PARK. 324 West 35th Street, Chicago, Illinois 60616. (312) 924–1000. Opened: July 1, 1019, with 2–0 loss to St. Louis. Closed: September 30, 1990, with 2–1 victory over Seattle. Dimensions: left-field line—347 feet. Left-center—382. Center—409. Right-center—382. Right-field line—347. Turf: grass. Seating capacity: 43,931. Record crowds: game—55,555, May 20, 1973. Season—2,136,988, 1984. Ticket information: (312) 924-1000. Prices: $11.50 (golden box); $10.50 (loge seat); $9.50 (field box); $7.50 (mezzanine/terrace); $6.50 (reserved grandstand); $5.00 (general admission).

CROSLEY FIELD. 415 Central Trust Tower, Cincinnati, Ohio 45202. (513) 421–4510. Opened: April 11, 1912, with a 10–6 victory over Chicago. Closed: June 24, 1970, with a 5–4 victory over San Francisco. Dimensions: left-field line—328 feet. Left-center—380. Center—387. Right-center—383. Deep right-center—387. Right-field line—366. Turf: grass. Seating capacity: 29,488. Record crowds: game—36,691, April 29, 1947. Season: 1,125,928, 1956. Ticket information: (513) 421-4510. Prices: $3.50 (box); $2.50 (reserved); $1.50 (general admission).

EBBETS FIELD. 215 Montague Street, Brooklyn 2, New York. (Main 4-5091) Opened: April 9, 1913, with a 1–0 loss to Philadelphia. Closed: September 24, 1957, with a 3–0 victory over Pittsburgh. Dimensions: left-field line—348. Left-center—351. Center—393. Deepest right-center—403. Right-center—352. Right-field scoreboard—318. Right-field line—297. Turf: grass. Seating capacity: 32,111. Record crowds: game—

41,209, May 30, 1934. Season: 1,807,526, 1947. Ticket information: Main 4-7030. Prices: $3 and $2.50 (box); $2 (reserved); $1.25 (general admission); $0.75 (bleachers).

EXHIBITION STADIUM. Box 7777, Adelaide Street P.O., Toronto, Ontario M5C 2K7. (416) 595-0077. Opened: April 7, 1977, with a 9–5 victory over Chicago. Closed: May 28, 1989, with a 7–5 victory over Chicago. Dimensions: left-field line—330. Left-center—375. Center—400. Right-center—375. Right-field line—330. Turf: artificial. Seating capacity: 43,737. Record crowds: game—47,828, July 1, 1987. Season—2,778,429, 1987. Ticket information: (416) 595-0077. Prices—$15 (field level, chair); $13 (upper level, chair); $10 (first base reserved, bench); $7 (right field reserved, bench); $4 (general admission).

EXPOSITION PARK. Opened: April 22, 1891, with a 7–6 loss to Chicago. Closed: June 29, 1909, with an 8–1 victory over Chicago. Dimensions: left-field line—400. Left-center—413. Center—450. Right-center—413. Right-field line—400. Turf: grass. Seating capacity: 16,000. Record crowd: season—394,877, 1906.

FORBES FIELD. 3940 Sennott Street, Pittsburgh 13, Pennsylvania. (412) 682-5300. Opened: June 30, 1090, with a 3–2 loss to Chicago. Closed: June 28, 1970, with a 3–2 and 4–1 double-header victory over Chicago. Dimensions: left-field line—365. Left-center—376. Center—467. Right-center—408. Right-field line—300. Turf: grass. Seating capacity: 35,000. Record crowds: game—44,932, September 23, 1956. Season—1, 705,828, 1960. Ticket information: (412) 682-5300. Prices: $4 (box seat); $3 (reserved); $1.75 (general admission); $1 (bleacher).

GRIFFITH STADIUM. Seventh and Florida Avenue, N.W., Washington 1, D.C. (DUpont 7-6333) Opened: April 12, 1911, with an 8–5 victory over Boston. Closed: September 21, 1961, with a 6–3 loss to Minnesota. Dimensions: Left-field line—350. Left-center—380. Center—426. Right-center—379. Right-field line—320. Turf: grass. Seating capacity: 27,550. Record crowds: game—35,563, July 4, 1936. Season—1,027,216, 1946. Ticket information: DUpont 7-4936. Prices—$3 (box seat); $2.50 (reserved grandstand); $1.50 (unreserved grandstand); $0.75 (bleacher).

HILLTOP PARK. 320 Fifth Avenue, New York, New York. Opened: April 30, 1903, with a 6–2 victory over Washington. Closed: October 5, 1912, with an 8–6 victory over Washington. Dimensions: left-field line—365. Left-center—402. Center—542. Right-center—425. Right-field line—400. Turf: grass. Seating capacity: 15,000. Record crowds: game—28,584, October 10, 1904. Season—501,700, 1909.

HUNTINGTON AVENUE GROUNDS. 246 Washington Street, Boston, Massachusetts. Opened: May 8, 1901, with a 12–4 victory over Philadelphia. Closed: October 7, 191, with an 8–1 victory over Washington. Dimensions: left-field line—350. Left-center—440. Center—530. Right-center—424. Right-field line—280. Turf: grass. Seating capacity: 11,500. Record crowd: season—668,965, 1909.

JARRY PARK. P.O. Station, Station R, Montreal, Quebec, H2S 3G7 Canada. (A.C. 514): 273-0433. Opened: April 14, 1969, with an 8–7 victory over St. Louis. Closed: September 29, 1976, with a 2–1 loss to Philadelphia. Dimensions: left-field line—340 feet. Left-center—368. Center—420. Right-center—365. Right-field line—340. Turf: grass. Seating capacity: 28,456. Record crowds: game—34,311, September 15, 1973. Season—1,424,683, 1970. Ticket information: (A.C. 514): 273–0433. Prices—$5.75 (box); $5 and $4 (reserved); $2.75 (grandstand and reserved); $1.50 (bleacher, adult); $1. (bleacher, child); $0.50 (groups of 30 or more).

KINGDOME. 201 South King Street, Seattle, Washington 09104. (206) 628-3555. Opened: April 6, 1977, with a 7–0 loss to California. Closed: June 27, 1999, with a 5–2 victory over Texas. Dimensions: left-field line—331 feet. Left-center—376. Deepest left-center—389. Center—405. Deepest right-center—380. Right-center—352. Right-field line—312. Turf: AstroTurf. Seating capacity: 59,084. Record crowds: 57,816, March 31, 1998. Season—3,192,237. Ticket information: (206) 628-3555. Prices—$20 (box seat); $18 (field level); $15 (club level); $10 (view: $8 for children under 14); $7 (general admission); $5 (Southwest Airlines section).

LEAGUE PARK. Opened: April 29, 1901, with a 5–4 victory over Indianapolis. Closed: September 6, 1909, with a 5–2 victory over and 5–2 loss to Chicago. Dimensions: left-field line—385. Left-center—420. Center—505. Right-center—420. Right—317. Right-field line—290. Turf: grass. Seating capacity: 9,000. Record crowd: season— 422,262, 1908.

LEAGUE PARK II. 6601 Lexington Avenue, Cleveland, Ohio. Opened: April 21, 1910, with a 5–0 loss to Detroit. Closed: September 21, 1946, with a 5–3 loss to Detroit. Dimensions: left-field—375. Left-center—415. Deepest center—460. Center—420. Right-center—400. Right-field line—290. Turf: grass. Seating capacity: 22,500. Record crowds: game—33,628, June 15, 1930. Season—912,832, 1920.

LOS ANGELES MEMORIAL COLISEUM. 930 Wilshire Boulevard, Los Angeles 17, California. (MAdison 3–1261) Opened: April 18, 1958, with a 6–5 victory over San Francisco. Closed: September 20, 1961, with a 3–3 suspended tie with Chicago. Dimensions: left-field line—251. Left-center—320. Deepest left-center—417. Center—420. Right-center—380. Right-field fence—300. Turf: grass. Seating capacity: 94,600. Record crowds: game—93,193 (exhibition), May 7, 1959. Season— 2,253,887, 1960. Ticket information: write to P.O. Box 100, Los Angeles 51, California. Prices—$3.50 (box); $2.50 (reserved); $1.50 (general admission); $0.90 (bleachers); $0.75 (children).

MEMORIAL STADIUM. East 33rd Street, Baltimore, Maryland 21218. (301) 243-9800. Opened: April 14, 1954, with a 3–1 victory over Chicago. Closed: October 6, 1991, with a 7–1 loss to Detroit. Dimensions: left-field line—309. Left-center—360. Deepest left-center—385. Center—405. Deepest right-center—385. Right-center— 360. Right-field line—309. Turf: grass. Seating capacity: 53,371. Record crowds: game—52,395, April 4, 1988. Season—2,552,753, 1991. Ticket information: (301) 338-1300. Prices—$11 (lower box); $10 (terrace box/lower deck and mezzanine box); $8.59 (upper box); $7.50 (lower/upper reserved); $6.50 (lower reserved grandstand); $4.75 (upper reserved general admission and lower general admission adult; $1.50 (children and senior citizens).

METROPOLITAN STADIUM. 8001 Cedar Avenue South, Bloomington, Minnesota 55420. (612) 854-4040. Opened: April 21, 1961, with a 5–3 loss to Washington. Closed: September 30, 1981, with a 5–2 loss to Kansas City. Dimensions: left-field line—343. Left—360. Left-center—406. Center—402. Right-center—410. Right—370. Right-field line—330. Turf: grass. Seating capacity: 45,919. Record crowds: game— 46,463, June 26, 1977. Season—1,483,547, 1967. Ticket information: (612) 854-4040. Prices—$7 (box); $6 (reserved and unserved grandstand); $3 (general admission).

MILWAUKEE COUNTY STADIUM. County Stadium, P.O. Box 3099, Milwaukee, Wisconsin 53201–3099. (414) 933-4114. Opened: April 6, 1953, with a Braves' 3–2 victory over St. Louis. The Brewers' first game was April 7, 1970, a 12–0 loss to California. Closed: September 28, 2000, with an 8–2 loss to Cincinnati. Dimensions: left-field line—315 feet. Left-center—362. Deepest left-center—392. Center—402. Right-center—362. Deepest right-center—392. Right-field line—315. Turf: grass. Seating capacity: 53,192. Record crowds: game—55,887, April 15, 1988. Season—2,397,131, 1983. Ticket information: (414) 933-9000 or 1-800-933-7890. Prices—$28 (diamond box); $20 (lower box); $16 (lower grandstand); $14 (upper box); $8 (upper grandstand); $7 (general admission); $5 (bleacher).

MILE HIGH STADIUM. 1700 Broadway—Suite 2100, Denver, Colorado 80290. (303) 292-0200. Opened: April 9, 1993, with an 11–4 victory over Montreal. Closed: August 11, 1994, with a 13–0 loss to Atlanta. Dimensions: left-field line—335. Left-center—375. Center—423. Right-center—400. Right-field line—370. Turf: grass. Seating capacity: 76,037. Record crowds: game—80,227, April 9, 1993. Season—4,483,350, 1993. Ticket information: (303) R-O-C-K-I-E-S. Prices—$16 (VIP field box sections 102–123); $14 (VIP field box sections 101–102 and infield plaza box); $12 (outfield plaza box sections 103–105 and 120–123 and infield mezzanine); $10 (outfield plaza box sections 101–102, outfield mezzanine, and infield terrace); $8 (outfield terrace and infield view); $5 (outfield view and reserved pavilion); $4 (reserved general admission); $1 (Rockpile, reserved, day of game only).

MUNICIPAL STADIUM. Boudreau Boulevard, Cleveland, Ohio 44114. (216) 861-1200. Opened: July 31, 1932, with a 1–0 loss to Philadelphia. Closed: October 3, 1993, with a 4–0 loss to Chicago. Dimensions: left-field line—320. Left—364. Left-center—375. Center—404. Right-center—370. Right—360. Right-field line—320. Turf: grass. Seating capacity: 74,483. Record crowds: game—86,563 (84,587 paid), September 12, 1954. Season—2,620,627, 1948. Ticket information: (216) 861-1200 or (216) 241-5555. Prices—$12 (box seat); $9.50 (reserved); $6 (general admission); $5 (bleacher).

MUNICIPAL STADIUM. P.O. Box 1969, Kansas City, Missouri 64141. (816) 241-4101. Opened: April 12, 1955, with a 6–2 victory over Detroit. Closed: October 4, 1972, with a 4–0 victory over Texas. Dimensions: left-field line—369. Left-center—408. Center—421. Right-center—382. Right-field line—338. Turf: grass. Seating capacity: 35,057. Record crowds: game—35,147, August 8, 1962. Season—1,393,054, 1955. Ticket information: (816) 241-4101. Prices—$3.50 (box seat); $2.50 (reserved grandstand); $1.50 (general admission).

NATIONAL PARK. Opened: April 22, 1903, with a 3–1 victory over New York. Closed October 6, 1910, with a 5–2 loss to and 6–5 victory over Boston. Turf: grass. Record crowd: season—264,252, 1908.

POLO GROUNDS. 155th Street and 8th Avenue, New York 39, New York. (AUdubon 6-6400) Opened: April 22, 1891, with a 4–3 loss to Boston. Closed: September 18, 1963, with a 5–1 loss to Philadelphia. Dimensions: left-field line—279. Deepest left-center—455. Center—483. Deepest right-center—449. Right-field line—258. Turf: grass. Seating capacity: 56,000. Record crowds: game—60,747, May 31, 1937. Season—1,600,793, 1947. Ticket information: AUdubon 6-1010. Prices—$3.50 (Box); $2.50 (reserved).

REDLAND FIELD. 23 Wiggins Block, Cincinnati, Ohio. Opened: April 17, 1902, with 6–2 loss to Chicago. Closed: October 2, 1911, with a 6–2 victory over and 6–1 loss to

St. Louis. Dimensions: left-field line—360 feet. Left-center—380. Center—420. Right-center—380. Right-field line—360. Turf: grass. Seating capacity: 25,000. Record crowd: season—424,643, 1909.

ROBERT F. KENNEDY STADIUM. Twenty-second and East Capitol Streets, Washington 3, D.C. 20003. (202) 544-2880. Opened: April 9, 1962, with a 4–1 victory over Detroit. Closed: September 30, 1971, with a 9–0 loss to New York. Dimensions: left-field line—335. Left-center—381. Center—410. Right-center—378. Right-field line— 335. Turf: grass. Seating capacity: 45,016. Record crowds: game—48,127, August 1, 1962. Season—918,106, 1969. Ticket information: (202) 544-2800. Prices—$6 (mezzanine box); $5 (field box); $4.50 (upper, low box); $3.50 (reserved grandstand); $2.25 (unreserved grandstand).

ROBISON FIELD. Opened: April 15, 1892, with a 9–3 victory over Pittsburgh. Closed: June 6, 1920, with a 5–2 victory over Chicago. Dimensions (1898): Left-field line—350. Left-center—470. Left-center—520. Center—500. Right-center—330. Right-field line— 290. Turf: grass. Seating capacity: 14,500. Record crowd: season—447,768, 1911.

ROOSEVELT STADIUM. 215 Montague Street, Brooklyn 2, New York. (Main 4-5091) Opened: April 19, 1956, with a 5–4 victory over Philadelphia. Closed: September 3, 1957, with a 3–2 loss to Philadelphia. Dimensions: left-field line—330. Left-center— 397. Center—411. Right-center—397. Right-field line—330. Turf: grass. Seating capacity: 24,500. Record crowds: game—26,385, August 15, 1956. Season— 148,371, 1956. Ticket information: (1957 number). Prices—$3 (box and loge); $2 (reserved); $1.25 (pavilion).

SEALS STADIUM. 16th and Bryant Streets, San Francisco 3, California. (UNderhill 3-7000). Opened: April 15, 1958, with an 8–0 victory over Los Angeles. Closed: September 20, 1959, with an 8–2 loss to Los Angeles. Dimensions: left-field line—361. Left-center—364. Center—400. Deepest right-center—415. Right-center—397. Right-field line—350. Turf: grass. Seating capacity: 22,900. Record crowds: game— 23,192, April 25, 1958. Season—1,422,130, 1959. Ticket information: UNderhill 3-7000. Prices—$3.50 (box); $2.50 (reserved).

SHIBE PARK. Twenty-first Street and Lehigh Avenue, Philadelphia, Pennsylvania 19132. (BA 9-9200). Opened: July 4, 1938 with a 10–5 loss to and 10–2 victory over Boston. Closed: October 1, 1970, with a 2–1 victory over Montreal. Dimensions: left-field line—334 feet. Center—410. Right-center—390. Right-center line—329. Turf: grass. Seating capacity: 33,509. Record crowds: game—40,720, May 11, 1947. Season— 1,425,891, 1964. Ticket information (BA 9-9200). Prices—$3.25 (box seat); $2.25 (reserved); $1.50 (grandstand); $1 (bleacher).

SICK'S STADIUM. 2700 Rainier Avenue South, Seattle, Washington 98144. (206) 725-8500. Opened: April 11, 1969, with a 7–0 victory over Chicago. Closed: October 2, 1969, with a 3–1 loss to Oakland. Dimensions: left-field line—305. Left-center—345. Center—405. Right-center—345. Right-field line—320. Record crowds: game— 21,900, August 3, 1969. Season—677,944, 1969. Ticket information: (206) 725-8500. Prices—$5 (field box); $4.50 (loge box); $3.50 (reserved); $2.50 (general admission); $2 (home run seat, adults); $1 (home run seat, children).

SOUTH END GROUNDS. 101 Tremont Street, Boston, Massachusetts. Opened: April 29, 1876, with a 3–2 loss to Hartford. Closed: June 3, 1915, with a 10–3 loss to New

York. Dimensions: left-field line, 250 feet. Left-center—445. Center—500. Right-center—440. Right-field line—255. Turf: grass. Seating capacity: 5,800. Record crowd: season—382,913, 1914.

SOUTH SIDE PARK. Opened: April 21, 1900, with a 5–4 loss to Milwaukee. Closed: June 26, 1910, with a 5–4 loss to Cleveland. Turf: grass. Seating capacity: 15,000. Record crowd: season—687,419, 1905.

SPORTSMAN'S PARK. 3625 Dodier Street, St. Louis, Missouri 63107. (314) JE5-7400. Opened: July 1, 1920, with a 6–2 loss to Pittsburgh. Closed: May 8, 1966, with a 10–5 loss to San Francisco. Dimensions: Left-field line—351 feet. Deepest left-center—424 feet. Center—422. Right-center—354. Right-field line—310. Turf: grass. Seating capacity: 30,500. Record crowds: game—41,284, September 15, 1935. Season—1,430,676, 1949. Ticket information: (314) JE5-7400. Prices—$3.50 (box field, loge, and terrace); $2.50 (reserved loge and upper terrace); $1.50 (general admission); $1 (bleachers).

3COM PARK. San Francisco, California 94124. (415) 468-3700. Opened: April 12, 1960, with a 3–1 victory over St. Louis. Closed: September 30, 1999, with a 9–4 loss to Los Angeles. Dimensions: left-field line—335 feet. Left-center—365. Center—400. Right-center—365. Right-field line—328. Turf: bluegrass. Seating capacity: 62,000. Record crowds: game—62,084, October 9, 1989. Season—2,606,254, 1993. Ticket information: (415) 467-8000. Prices—$21 (MVP); $16 (upper box infield and lower box); $13.50 (lower reserved); $13 (upper box outfield); $8.50 (upper reserved infield); $7.50 (upper reserved outfield); $7 (pavilion); $5.50 (bleacher).

THREE RIVERS STADIUM. 600 Stadium Circle, Pittsburgh, Pennsylvania 15212. (412) 323-5000. Opened: July 16, 1970, with a 3–2 loss to Cincinnati. Closed: October 1, 2000, with a 10–9 loss to Chicago. Dimensions: left-field line—335 feet. Left-center—375. Center—400. Right-center—375. Right-field line—335. Turf: AstroTurf. Seating capacity: 47,972. Record crowds: game—55,351, October 1, 2000. Season—2,065,302, 1991. Ticket information: 1-800-BUY-BUCS. Prices—$20 (field box infield); $19 (field box outfield); $18 (club box infield); $17 (club box outfield); $13 (terrace box, family box); $10 (reserved seat); $3 (general admission, children 14 and under).

TIGER STADIUM. 2121 Trumbull Avenue, Detroit, Michigan 48216. (313) 962-4000. Opened: April 20, 1912, with a 6–5 victory over Cleveland. Closed: September 27, 1999, with an 8–2 victory over Kansas City. Dimensions: left-field line—340 feet. Left-center—365. Center—440. Right-center—370. Left-field line—325. Turf: grass. Seating capacity: 52,416. Record crowds: game—58,369, July 20, 1947. Season—2,704,794, 1984. Ticket information: (313) 963-2050. Prices—$20 (Tigers' Den); $15 (box seat); $12 (reserved); $8 (grandstand reserved); $2.50 (bleacher).

WASHINGTON PARK. Opened: April 30, 1989, with a 6–4 loss to Philadelphia. Closed: October 5, 1912, with a 1–0 loss to New York. Dimensions (1908): left-field line—376. Left-center—444. Center—425. Right-center—300. Right-field line—302. Turf: grass. Seating capacity: 18,800 (1914). Record crowd: season—312,500, 1907.

WEST SIDE GROUNDS. Room 1003, 134 South La Salle Street, Chicago, Illinois. Opened: May 14, 1893, with a 13–3 loss to Cincinnati. Closed: October 3, 1915, with a 7–2 victory over Cincinnati. Dimensions: left-field line—340 feet. Left center—441. Center—560 feet. Right-center—435. Right-field line—316. Turf: grass. Seating capacity: 16,000. Record crowd: season—665,325. 1908.

WRIGLEY FIELD. 435 East 42nd Place, Los Angeles 11, California. (ADams 2-4761) Opened: April 27, 1961, with a 4–2 loss to Minnesota. Closed: September 20, 1961, with an 8–5 loss to Cleveland. Dimensions: Left-field line—340 feet. Left-center— 345. Center—412. Right-center—345. Right-field line—340. Turf: grass. Seating capacity: 20,457. Record crowds: game—19,930, August 22, 1961. Season— 606,510, 1961. Ticket information: ADams 2-4761. Prices—$3.50 (box seat); $2.50 (reserved); $1.50 (general admission).

YANKEE STADIUM (OLD). East 161st Street and River Avenue, The Bronx, New York 10451. (CYpress 3-4300) Opened: April 22, 1923, with a 4–1 victory over Boston. Closed: September 30, 1973, with an 8–5 victory over Detroit. Dimensions: left-field line—301 feet. Left-center—402. Deepest left-center—457. Center—463. Deepest right-center—407. Right-center—344. Right-field line—296. Turf: grass. Seating capacity: 65,010. Record crowds: game—81,841, May 30, 1938. Season— 2,373,901, 1948. Ticket information: CYpress 3-6000. Prices—$4 (box); $3 (reserved); $1.50 (general admission); $1 (bleachers).

CHAMPIONSHIP TEAMS

On May 4, 1871, at Hamilton Field in Fort Wayne, Indiana, the Kekiongas blanked Forest City of Cleveland, 2–0, in the first major-league game. Below, the championship teams of the big leagues in baseball, with home parks, 1871–1999.

National Association. 1871—Philadelphia, Jefferson Street Grounds. 1872–'73–'74— Boston, South End Grounds.

Union Association. 1884—St. Louis, Union Grounds.

Players League. 1890—Boston, Congress Street Grounds.

American Association. 1882—Cincinnati, Bank Street Grounds. 1883—Philadelphia, Jefferson Street Grounds. 1884—New York. 1885–'86–'87–'88—St. Louis, Sportsman's Park. 1889—Brooklyn, Washington Park. 1890—Louisville, Eclipse Park (I). 1891—Boston, Congress Street Grounds.

Federal League. 1913–'14 Indianapolis, Federal League Park. 1915—Chicago, Wrigley Field.

National League. 1876—Chicago, State Street Grounds. 1877–'78—Boston, South End Grounds. 1879—Providence, Messer Street Grounds. 1880–'81–'82—Chicago, Lakefront Park. 1883—Boston, South End Grounds. 1884—Providence, Messer Street Grounds. 1885–'86—Chicago, West Side Grounds. 1887—Detroit, Recreation Park. 1888—New York, Polo Grounds (110th Street). 1889—New York, Polo Grounds (155th Street). 1890—Brooklyn, Washington Park. 1891–'92–'93—Boston, South End Grounds II. 1894–'95–'96—Baltimore, Union Park Grounds II. 1897–'98—Boston, South End Grounds II. 1899–1900—Brooklyn, Washington Park. 1901–'02–'03— Pittsburgh, Exposition Park. 1904–'05—New York, Polo Grounds. 1906–'07–'08—

Chicago, West Side Grounds. 1909—Pittsburgh, Exposition Park/Forbes Field. 1910—Chicago, West Side Grounds. 1911-'12-'13—New York, Polo Grounds. 1914—Boston, South End Grounds. 1915—Philadelphia, Baker Bowl. 1916—Brooklyn, Ebbets Field. 1917—New York, Polo Grounds. 1918—Chicago, Wrigley Field. 1919—Cincinnati, Crosley Field. 1920—Brooklyn, Ebbets Field. 1921-'22-'23-'24—New York, Polo Grounds. 1925—Pittsburgh, Forbes Field. 1926—St. Louis, Sportsman's Park. 1927—Pittsburgh, Forbes Field. 1928—St. Louis, Sportsman's Park. 1929—Chicago, Wrigley Field. 1930-'31—St. Louis, Sportsman's Park. 1932—Chicago, Wrifley Field. 1933—New York, Polo Grounds. 1934—St. Louis, Sportsman's Park. 1935—Chicago, Wrigley Field. 1936-'37—New York, Polo Grounds. 1938—Chicago, Wrigley Field. 1939-'40—Cincinnati, Crosley Field. 1941—Brooklyn, Ebbets Field. 1942-'43-'44—St. Louis, Sportsman's Park. 1945—Chicago, Wrigley Field. 1946—St. Louis, Sportsman's Park. 1947—Brooklyn, Ebbets Field. 1948—Boston, Braves Field. 1949—Brooklyn, Ebbets Field. 1950—Philadelphia, Shibe Park. 1951—New York, Polo Grounds. 1952-'53—Brooklyn, Ebbets Field. 1954—New York. Polo Grounds. 1955—Brooklyn, Ebbets Field. 1956—Brooklyn, Ebbets Field/Roosevelt Stadium. 1957-'58—Milwaukee, Milwaukee County Stadium. 1959—Los Angeles, Memorial Coliseum. 1960—Pittsburgh, Forbes Field. 1961—Cincinnati, Crosley Field. 1962—San Francisco, Candlestick Park. 1963—Los Angeles, Dodger Stadium. 1964—St. Louis, Busch Stadium. 1965-'66—Los Angeles, Dodger Stadium. 1967-'68—St. Louis, Busch Stadium. 1969—New York, Shea Stadium. 1970—Cincinnati, Crosley Field/Riverfront Stadium. 1971—Pittsburgh, Three Rivers Stadium. 1972—Cincinnati, Riverfront Stadium. 1973—New York, Shea Stadium. 1974—Los Angeles, Dodger Stadium. 1975-'76—Cincinnati, Riverfront Stadium. 1977-'78—Los Angeles, Dodger Stadium. 1980—Philadelphia, Veterans Memorial Stadium. 1981—Los Angeles, Dodger Stadium. 1982—St. Louis, Busch Stadium. 1983—Philadelphia—Veterans Memorial Stadium. 1984—San Diego, San Diego Jack Murphy Stadium. 1985—St. Louis, Busch Stadium. 1986—New York, Shea Stadium. 1987—St. Louis, Busch Stadium. 1988—Los Angeles, Dodger Stadium. 1989—San Francisco, Candlestick Park. 1990—Cincinnati, Riverfront Stadium. 1991-'92—Atlanta, Atlanta-Fulton County Stadium. 1993—Philadelphia, Veterans Memorial Stadium. 1994—No champion. 1995-'96—Atlanta, Atlanta-Fulton County Stadium. 1997—Florida, Pro Player Stadium. 1998—San Diego, Qualcomm Stadium. 1999—Atlanta, Turner Field. 2000—New York, Shea Stadium.

American League. 1900-'01—Chicago, South Side Park. 1902—Philadelphia, Columbia Park. 1903-'04—Boston, Huntington Avenue Grounds. 1905—Philadelphia, Columbia Park. 1906—Chicago, South Side Park. 1907-'08-'09—Detroit, Bennett Park. 1910-'11—Philadelphia, Shibe Park. 1912—Boston, Fenway Park. 1913-'14—Philadelphia, Shibe Park. 1915-'16—Boston, Fenway Park. 1917—Chicago, Comiskey Park. 1918—Boston, Fenway Park. 1919—Chicago, Comiskey Park. 1920—Cleveland, League Park. 1921-'22—New York, Polo Grounds. 1923—New York, Yankee Stadium. 1924-'25—Washington, Griffith Stadium. 1926-'27-'28—New York, Yankee Stadium. 1929-'30-'31—Philadelphia, Shibe Park. 1932—New York, Yankee Stadium. 1933—Washington, Griffith Stadium. 1934-'35—Detroit, Navin Field. 1936-'37-'38-'39—New York, Yankee Stadium. 1940—Detroit, Briggs Stadium. 1941-'42-'43—New

York, Yankee Stadium. 1944—St. Louis, Sportsman's Park. 1945—Detroit, Briggs Stadium. 1946—Boston, Fenway Park. 1947—New York, Yankee Stadium. 1948—Cleveland, Municipal Stadium. 1949-'50-'51-'52-'53—New York, Yankee Stadium. 1954—Cleveland, Municipal Stadium. 1955-'56-'57-'58—New York, Yankee Stadium. 1959—Chicago, Comiskey Park. 1960-'61-'62-'63-'64—New York, Yankee Stadium. 1965—Minnesota, Metropolitan Stadium. 1966—Baltimore, Memorial Stadium. 1967—Boston, Fenway Park. 1968—Detroit, Tiger Stadium. 1969-'70-'71—Baltimore, Memorial Stadium. 1972-'73-'74—Oakland, Oakland-Alameda County Coliseum. 1975—Boston, Fenway Park. 1976-'77-'78—New York, Yankee Stadium. 1979—Baltimore, Memorial Stadium. 1980—Kansas City, Royals Stadium. 1981—New York, Yankee Stadium. 1982—Milwaukee, Milwaukee County Stadium. 1983—Baltimore, Memorial Stadium. 1984—Detroit, Tiger Stadium. 1985—Kansas City, Royals Stadium. 1986—Boston, Fenway Park. 1987—Minnesota, Hubert H. Humphrey Metrodome. 1988-'89-'90—Oakland, Oakland-Alameda County Coliseum. 1991—Minnesota, Hubert H. Humphrey Metrodome. 1992-'93—Toronto, SkyDome. 1994—No champion. 1995—Cleveland, Jacobs Field. 1996—New York, Yankee Stadium. 1997—Cleveland, Jacobs Field. 1998-'99-'2000—New York, Yankee Stadium.

ATTENDANCE LEADERS

Below are teams, with home park, that led their major league in home attendance each year of that league's duration.

Union Association. 1884—St. Louis, Union Park, 116,000.

Players League. 1890—Boston, Congress Street Grounds, 197,346.

American Association. 1882—St. Louis, Sportsman's Park, 135,000. 1883—Philadelphia, Jefferson Street Grounds, 305,000. 1884—St. Louis, Sportsman's Park, 212,000. 1885—Philadelphia, Jefferson Street Grounds, 169,000. 1886—St. Louis, Sportsman's Park, 205,000. 1887—Brooklyn, Washington Park, 273,000. 1888—Brooklyn, Washington Park, 245,000. 1889—Brooklyn, Washington Park, 353,000. 1890—Louisville, Eclipse Park, 206,000. 1891—St. Louis, Sportsman's Park, 220,000.

National League. 1876—Chicago, State Street Grounds, 65,441. 1877—Boston, South End Grounds, 55,240. 1878—Chicago, Lakefront Park, 58,691. 1879—Chicago, Lakefront Park, 67,687. 1880—Chicago, Lakefront Park, 66,708. 1881—Chicago, Lakefront Park, 82,000. 1882—Chicago, Lakefront Park, 125,452. 1883—Boston, South End Grounds, 128,968. 1884—Boston, South End Grounds, 146,777. 1885—New York, Polo Grounds, 185,000. 1886—New York, Polo Grounds, 189,000. 1887—New York Polo Grounds, 270,945. 1888—New York, Polo Grounds, 305,455. 1889—Boston, South End Grounds, 283,257. 1890—Philadelphia, Baker Bowl, 148,366. 1891—Philadelphia, Baker Bowl, 217,282. 1892—Cincinnati, League Park, 196,473. 1893—Philadelphia, Baker Bowl, 293,019. 1894—New York, Polo Grounds, 387,000.

1895—Philadelphia, Baker Bowl, 474,971. 1896—Cincinnati, League Park, 373,000. 1897—New York, Polo Grounds, 390,340. 1898—Chicago, West Side Grounds, 424,352. 1899—Philadelphia, Baker Bowl, 388,933. 1900—Philadelphia, Baker Bowl, 301,913. 1901—St. Louis, Robison Field, 379,988. 1902—New York, Polo Grounds, 302,875. 1903—New York, Polo Grounds, 579,530. 1904—New York, Polo Grounds, 609,826. 1905—New York, Polo Grounds, 552,700. 1906—Chicago, West Side Grounds, 654,300. 1907—New York, Polo Grounds, 538,350. 1908—New York, Polo Grounds, 910,000. 1909—New York, Polo Grounds, 783,700. 1910—Chicago, West Side Grounds, 526,153. 1911—New York, Polo Grounds, 675,000. 1912—New York, Polo Grounds, 638,000. 1913—New York, Polo Grounds, 630,000. 1914—New York, Polo Grounds, 364,313. 1915—Philadelphia, Baker Bowl, 449,898. 1916—New York, Polo Grounds, 552,056. 1917—New York, Polo Grounds, 500,264. 1918—Chicago, Wrigley Field, 337,256. 1919—New York, Polo Grounds, 708,857. 1920—New York, Polo Grounds, 929,609. 1921—New York, Polo Grounds, 973,477. 1922—New York, Polo Grounds, 945,809. 1923—New York, Polo Grounds, 820,780. 1924—New York, Polo Grounds, 844,068. 1925—Pittsburgh, Forbes Field, 804,354. 1926—Chicago, Wrigley Field, 885,063, 1927—Chicago, Wrigley Field, 1,159,168. 1928—Chicago, Wrigley Field, 1,143,740. 1929—Chicago, Wrigley Field, 1,485,166. 1930—Chicago, Wrigley Field, 1,463,624. 1931—Chicago, Wrigley Field, 1,086,422. 1932—Chicago, Wrigley Field, 974,688. 1933—New York, Polo Grounds, 604,471. 1934—New York, Polo Grounds, 730,851. 1935—New York, Polo Grounds, 748,748. 1936—New York, Polo Grounds, 837,952. 1937—New York, Polo Grounds, 926,887. 1938—Chicago, Wrigley Field, 951,640. 1939—Cincinnati, Crosley Field, 981,443. 1940—Brooklyn, Ebbets field, 975,978. 1941—Brooklyn, Ebbets Field, 1,214,910. 1942—Brooklyn, Ebbets Field, 1,037,765. 1943—Brooklyn, Ebbets Field, 661,739. 1944—New York, Polo Grounds, 677,483. 1945—Brooklyn, Ebbets Field, 1,059,220. 1946—Brooklyn, Ebbets Field, 1,796,824. 1947—Brooklyn, Ebbets Field, 1,807,526. 1948—Pittsburgh, Forbes Field, 1,517,021. 1949—Brooklyn, Ebbets Field, 1,633,747. 1950—Philadelphia, Shibe Park, 1,217,080. 1951—Brooklyn, Ebbets Field, 1,282,628. 1952—Brooklyn, Ebbets Field, 1,088,704. 1953—Milwaukee, Milwaukee County Stadium, 1,826,397. 1954—Milwaukee, Milwaukee County Stadium, 2,131,388. 1955—Milwaukee, Milwaukee County Stadium, 2,005,836. 1956—Milwaukee, Milwaukee County Stadium, 2,046,331. 1957—Milwaukee, Milwaukee County Stadium, 2,215,404. 1958—Milwaukee, Milwaukee County Stadium, 1,971,101. 1959—Los Angeles, Memorial Coliseum, 2,071,045. 1960—Los Angeles, Memorial Coliseum, 2,253,887. 1961—Los Angeles, Memorial Coliseum, 1,804,250. 1962—Los Angeles, Dodger Stadium, 2,755,184. 1963—Los Angeles, Dodger Stadium, 2,538,602. 1964—Los Angeles, Dodger Stadium, 2,228,751. 1965—Los Angeles, Dodger Stadium, 2,553,577. 1966—Los Angeles, Dodger Stadium, 2,617,029. 1967—St. Louis, Busch Stadium, 2,090,145. 1968—St. Louis, Busch Stadium, 2,011,167. 1969—New York, Shea Stadium, 2,175,373. 1970—New York, Shea Stadium, 2,697,479. 1971—New York, Shea Stadium, 2,266,680. 1972—New York, Shea Stadium, 2,134,185. 1973—Los Angeles, Dodger Stadium, 2,136,192. 1974—Los Angeles, Dodger Stadium, 2,632,754. 1975—Los Angeles, Dodger Stadium, 2,539,349. 1976—Cincinnati, Riverfront Stadium, 2,629,708. 1977—Los Angeles, Dodger Stadium, 2,955,087. 1978—Los Angeles, Dodger Stadium, 3,347,845. 1979—Los Angeles, Dodger Stadium, 2,860,954.

1980—Los Angeles, Dodger Stadium 3,249,287. 1981—Los Angeles, Dodger Stadium, 2,381,292. 1982—Los Angeles, Dodger Stadium, 3,608,881. 1983—Los Angeles, Dodger Stadium, 3,510,313. 1984—Los Angeles, Dodger Stadium, 3,134,824. 1985—Los Angeles, Dodger Stadium, 3,264,593. 1986—Los Angeles, Dodger Stadium, 3,023,208. 1987—New York, Shea Stadium, 3,034,129. 1988—New York, Shea Stadium, 3,055,445. 1989—Los Angeles, Dodger Stadium, 2,944,653. 1990—Los Angeles, Dodger Stadium, 3,002,396. 1991—Los Angeles, Dodger Stadium, 3,348,170. 1992—Atlanta, Atlanta-Fulton County Stadium, 3,077,400. 1993—Colorado, Mile High Stadium, 4,483,350. 1994—Colorado, Mile High Stadium, 3,218,511. 1995—Colorado, Coors Field, 3,390,037. 1996—Colorado, Coors Field, 3,891,014. 1997—Colorado, Coors Field, 3,888,453. 1998—Colorado, Coors Field, 3,789,347. 1999—Colorado, Coors Field, 3,316,152. 2000—St. Louis, Busch Stadium, 3,336,493.

American League. 1901—Chicago, South Side Park, 354,350. 1902—Philadelphia, Columbia Park, 420,078. 1903—Philadelphia, Columbia Park, 422,473. 1904—Boston, Huntington Avenue Grounds, 623,295. 1905—Chicago, South Side Park, 687,419. 1906—Chicago, South Side Park, 585,202. 1907—Chicago, South Side Park, 666,307. 1908—Chicago, South Side Park, 636,096. 1909—Philadelphia, Shibe Park, 674,915. 1910—Philadelphia, Shibe Park, 588,905. 1911—Philadelphia, Shibe Park, 605,749. 1912—Chicago, Comiskey Park, 602,241. 1913—Chicago, Comiskey Park, 644,501. 1914—Boston, Fenway Park, 481,359. 1915—Boston, Fenway Park, 539,885. 1916—Chicago, Comiskey Park, 679,923. 1917—Chicago, Comiskey Park, 684,521. 1918—Cleveland, League Park, 295,515. 1919—Detroit, Navin Field, 643,805. 1920—New York, Polo Grounds, 1,289,422. 1921—New York, Polo Grounds, 1,230,696. 1922—New York, Polo Grounds, 1,026,134. 1923—New York, Yankee Stadium, 1,007,066. 1924—New York, Yankee Stadium, 1,053,533. 1925—Philadelphia, Shibe Park, 869,703. 1926—New York, Yankee Stadium, 1,027,675. 1927—New York, Yankee Stadium, 1,164,015. 1928—New York, Yankee Stadium, 1,072,132. 1929—New York, Yankee Stadium, 960,148. 1930—New York, Yankee Stadium, 1,169,230. 1931—New York, Yankee Stadium, 912,437. 1932—New York, Yankee Stadium, 962,320. 1933—New York, Yankee Stadium, 728,014. 1934—Detroit, Navin Field, 919,161. 1935—Detroit, Navin Field, 1,034,929. 1936—New York, Yankee Stadium, 976,913. 1937—Detroit, Navin Field, 1,072,276. 1938—New York, Yankee Stadium, 970,916. 1939—New York, Yankee Stadium, 859,785. 1940—Detroit, Briggs Stadium, 1,112,693. 1941—Yankee Stadium, New York, 964,722. 1942—New York, Yankee Stadium, 922,011. 1943—New York, Yankee Stadium, 618,330. 1944—Detroit, Briggs Stadium, 923,176. 1945—Detroit, Briggs Stadium, 1,280,341. 1946—New York, Yankee Stadium, 2,265,512. 1947—New York, Yankee Stadium, 2,178,512. 1948—Cleveland, Municipal Stadium, 2,620,627. 1949—New York, Yankee Stadium, 2,281,676. 1950—New York, Yankee Stadium, 2,081,676. 1951—New York, Yankee Stadium, 1,950,107. 1952—New York, Yankee Stadium, 1,629,655. 1953—New York, Yankee Stadium, 1,537,811. 1954—New York, Yankee Stadium, 1,475,171. 1955—New York, Yankee Stadium, 1,490,138. 1956—New York, Yankee Stadium, 1,491,784. 1957—New York, Yankee Stadium, 1,497,134. 1958—New York, Yankee Stadium, 1,428,438. 1959—New York, Yankee Stadium, 1,552,030. 1960—Chicago, Comiskey Park, 1,644,460. 1961—New York, Yankee

Stadium, 1,747,725. 1962—New York, Yankee Stadium, 1,493,574. 1963—Minnesota, Metropolitan Stadium, 1,406,652. 1964—New York, Yankee Stadium, 1,305,638. 1965—Minnesota, Metropolitan Stadium, 1,463,258. 1966—California, Anaheim Stadium, 1,400,321. 1967—Boston, Fenway Park, 1,727,832. 1968—Detroit, Tiger Stadium, 2,031,847. 1969—Boston, Fenway Park, 1,833,246. 1970—Boston, Fenway Park, 1,595,278. 1971—Boston, Fenway Park, 1,678,732. 1972—Detroit, Tiger Stadium, 1,892,386. 1973—Detroit, Tiger Stadium, 1,724,136. 1974—Boston, Fenway Park, 1,563,307. 1975—Boston, Fenway Park, 1,748,587. 1976—New York, Yankee Stadium, 2,012,434. 1977—New York, Yankee Stadium, 2,103,092. 1978—New York, Yankee Stadium, 2,335,871. 1979—New York, Yankee Stadium, 2,537,765. 1980—New York, Yankee Stadium, 2,627,417. 1981—New York, Yankee Stadium, 1,614,353. 1982—California, Anaheim Stadium, 2,807,360. 1983—California, Anaheim Stadium, 2,555,016. 1984—Detroit, Tiger Stadium, 2,704,794. 1985—California, Anaheim Stadium, 2,567,427. 1986—California, Anaheim Stadium, 2,655,872. 1987—Toronto, Exhibition Stadium, 2,778,429. 1988—Minnesota, Humphrey Metrodome, 3,030,672. 1989—Toronto, Exhibition Stadium and SkyDome, 3,375,883. 1990—Toronto, SkyDome, 3,885,284. 1991—Toronto, SkyDome, 4,001,527. 1992—Toronto, SkyDome, 4,028,318. 1993—Toronto, SkyDome, 4,057,947. 1994—Toronto, SkyDome, 2,907,993. 1995—Baltimore, Oriole Park at Camden Yards, 3,098,475. 1996—Baltimore, Oriole Park at Camden Yards, 3,646,950. 1997—Baltimore, Oriole Park at Camden Yards, 3,711,132. 1998—Baltimore, Oriole Park at Camden Yards, 3,685,194. 1999—Cleveland, Jacobs Field, 3,384,788. 2000—Cleveland, Jacobs Field, 3,456,278.

INDEX

A. L. Park II, 41–42
Aaron, Hank, 178, 236–239, 249, 255, 263, 278, 289, 292, 319, 322–323, 356–357, 368–369, 375, 414, 438–439, 502–503
active franchise ballparks, 546–551
active franchise geneaology, 545–546
Adair, Jerry, 340
Adams, Babe, 73
Adcock, Joe, 178, 213, 221, 235–236, 238, 272, 289
Ade, George, 51
Agee, Tommie, 308–309, 325
Alameda County Coliseum, 327–331
Aldridge, Vic, 76
Alexander, Grover Cleveland, 36, 128, 133, 147
Allbright, Nat, 221
Allen, Dick, 83, 348
Allen, Fred, 88
Allen, Lee, 4–5, 15, 17, 19, 26–28, 32, 37, 67–69, 77, 84–89, 101–103, 107–109, 111, 115, 135, 139, 142–143, 146, 176, 179, 224, 234, 387
Allen, Mel, 120, 193, 197–198, 200, 217–218, 262, 265–266, 402, 427, 429
Allen, Michael, 456–457
Allen, Richie, 247, 313–314
Allison, Bob, 284, 341
Allyn, Arthur, 346–347
Alomar, Roberto, 469, 476
Alomar, Sandy, 368, 475
Alou, Felipe, 239, 273–274, 318, 322, 386, 408
Alou, Jesus, 332, 335–336, 443
Alou, Matty, 279, 339
Alou, Moises, 386, 478
Alston, Walter, 227, 273, 297–298
Anaheim Stadium, 323–326
Anderson, Brady, 469–470
Anderson, Sherwood, 76
Anderson, Sparky, 355–357, 375, 377, 392–393, 447, 449, 487
Andrews, Mike, 330
Angelos, Peter, 5
Anson, Cap, 24, 355
Antonelli, Johnny, 214

Aparicio, Luis, 60, 80, 231–232, 242, 272, 370, 375, 427
Appling, Luke, 82, 149, 305, 461
Arlin, Harold, 75
Arlington Stadium, 362–364, 451–452, 470–473
Armas, Tony, 83, 416
Ash, Gord, 459
Ashburn, Richie, 42, 184–186, 248, 256, 289–290, 359, 361, 450
Ashford, Emmett, 304
Asquith, Herbert, 143
Association Park, 52
Astor, William Waldorf, 137
Astrodome, 301, 311–316, 422–425, 467, 515
Athletic Park, 40
Atlee, Clement, 341
attendance statistics, 551–556, 574–577
Austin, Jimmie, 122, 132
Autry, Gene, 281, 295, 324, 419
Avenue Grounds, 5, 27
Averill, Earl, 94, 145–146, 154, 282, 337
Avery, Steve, 412
Axthelm, Pete, 396

Bacon, Francis, 130
Bagby, Jim, 92, 146
Bagwell, Jeff, 424, 516
Baker Bowl, 35–37, 60, 65–66
Baker, Del, 146, 163
Baker, Dusty, 403, 409
Baker, Frank (Home Run), 67–68, 108, 362
Bakker, Jim, 339
Balfour, Arch, 167
Ball, Lucille, 8
Ball, Neal, 93
Ball, Phil, 132
Ballparks
    attendance figures and, 551–556, 574–577
    capacity of, 557
    facts and fillips, 559–565
    facts of past ballparks, 565–572
    rank by age, 558–559, 558
Bando, Sal, 244, 392

Bank One Ballpark, 505–507
Bank Street Grounds, 5
Banks, Ernie, 57, 127, 168–169, 177, 232, 258, 263, 434, 469, 480, 485
Barber, Red, 20, 60, 86–87, 117, 153, 155, 179–181, 193, 196, 200, 218
Barber, Steve, 338
Barker, Len, 61
Barnard, Ernest, 92
Barnes, Roscoe, 23
Barnhart, Clue, 74
Barnhart, Clyde, 76
Barrow, Ed, 116, 140–142, 191, 194
Barry, Jack, 66, 115
Bartell, Dick, 145
Bauer, Hank, 244, 371
Bavasi, Buzzie, 332
Baylor, Don, 381, 396, 420, 499–502
Beall, Johnny, 128
Bealle, Morris A., 95
Beardon, Gene, 172, 226
Beck, Walter, 37
Beckert, Glenn, 258, 322
Beckett, Samuel, 219
Belinski, Bo, 292
Belinsky, Bo, 295–296
Bell, Buddy, 364, 445
Bell, Gary, 338
Bell, George, 83
Bell, Gus, 252, 445
Bell, Les, 124
Belle, Albert, 325, 453, 470, 475, 481
Bench, Johnny, 255, 330, 355–356, 358, 371, 375, 392, 447, 449, 473, 529
Bender, Chief, 36, 66–68, 122
Bendix, William, 28
Bennett, Charlie, 49
Bennett, James Gordon, 14
Bennett Park, 48–49, 119
Benny, Jack, 88, 180
Benswanger, Bill, 78
Berger, Wally, 125
Berra, Dale, 445
Berra, Yogi, 100, 199–200, 202–203, 233, 251, 259, 264–265, 268, 310–311, 373, 400, 402, 445, 496–498
Bess, Philip, 485–487
Bevens, Floyd, 217
Bicentennial Park, 533
Bickford, Vern, 178–179
Biederman, Les, 73–74, 78, 190, 259
Bieleski, Lennie, 121
Bierbauer, Louis, 38
Big Ballpark, 10
Biggio, Craig, 424–425
Billingham, Jack, 323, 357
Black, Don, 147
Black, Joe, 220
Blackburne, Lena, 79
Blackwell, Ewell, 90, 217
Blair, Paul, 370, 488

Blanchard, Doc, 195
Blanchard, John, 265, 267
Blass, Steve, 353
Blattner, Bud, 160–161
Blefary, Curt, 328
Blomberg, Ron, 268
Blue, Vida, 329–330, 415
Bluege, Ossie, 150
Blyleven, Bert, 430
Boggess, Dusty, 42
Boggs, Wade, 396, 495, 509–510
Bonds, Barry, 435, 406, 408–409, 445–446, 478
Bonds, Bobby, 520
Bonilla, Bobby, 445, 469, 478
Bonura, Zeke, 83
Boone, Bob, 360, 362, 461
Bossard, Emil, 349
Bottomley, Jim, 74, 132–133, 135
Boucher, Joseph A., 171
Boudreau, Lou, 146, 171–172, 226, 228, 243
Boundary Park, 41
Bouton, Jim, 251, 292, 337, 339
Bowa, Larry, 360
Boyd, Oil Can, 397, 453
Boyer, Clete, 233, 265, 268
Boyer, Ken, 249, 251, 267, 425
Brainard, Asa, 26
Branca, Ralph, 212, 215, 220
Brandon, Darrell, 339
Braves Field, 2, 4, 10, 115, 121–125, 176, 178, 243
Breadon, Sam, 46, 132, 161
Brecheen, Harry (The Cat), 157–158
Brennaman, Marty, 529
Bresnahan, Roger, 17
Brett, George, 365–367, 400, 402, 435–436, 490, 510
Brett, Ken, 348, 360
Brewer, Tom, 29
Brickhouse, Jack, 24–25, 83, 166–169, 255–258
Bridges, Tommy, 136, 162
Bridwell, Al, 18
Briggs Stadium, 49, 56, 61, 117–121, 162–165
Briggs, Walter, 117, 162
Bright, Harry, 296
Britt, Jim, 123–125
Brock, Lou, 118, 251–252, 258, 288, 291, 318–319, 346, 416, 417, 425
Broder, David, 129, 481
Broeg, Bob, 6, 27, 45–46, 57, 131–133, 154–156, 159, 162, 249–251, 317–319, 425, 427, 483
Brooks, Arthur, 48
Brosnan, Jim, 253
Brotherhood Park, 16
Broun, Heywood, 63
Brouthers, Dennis (Big Dan), 48
Brown, Gates, 344
Brown, Joe, 187
Brown, Joe L., 352, 354
Brown, Kevin, 478
Brown, Mace, 166
Brown, Mordecai, 25
Brown, Tommy, 182

Brown, Warren, 129, 164
Brunet, George, 292
Brusch, John, 19
Brush, John T., 106
Bruton, Billy, 236, 235
Buck, Jack, 319
Buckeye, Garland, 111
Buckner, Bill, 331, 392, 396–397, 402
Buddin, Don, 29
Buhner, Jay, 382
Bunning, Jim, 186, 247–248, 307, 359–360, 364
Burdette, Lew, 178, 236, 264, 337
Burdock, Jack, 15
Burke, Edmund, 115, 355
Burke, Kitty, 87
Burkett, Jess, 43
Burnes, Bob, 131, 156
Burnett, A. J., 479
Burnett, Johnny, 145
Burns, George, 139
Burns Park, 48
Busch, Gussie, 161
Busch Stadium, 249–252, 534
Busch Stadium, 301, 316–319, 425–427, 481–484
Bush, "Bull Joe", 116
Bush, George H. W., 28, 159, 448–449, 467
Bush, George W., 452, 471, 473, 528
Bush, Guy, 78
Bush, Jeb, 533
Bush, Joe, 110
Butler, Frank, 49
Byrne, Charles, 21–22, 47

Cadore, Leon, 124
Cahill, George, 87
Cain, Bob, 160, 226
Caldwell, Ray, 92
Camden Yards, 1, 5, 61, 92, 409, 455, 459–461,
    466–471, 475, 484, 495, 503, 505, 510, 512–513,
    524, 530, 534
Camilli, Dolph, 179, 181–182
Campanella, Roy, 215, 218, 220–221, 263, 271–272,
    298, 335
Campaneris, Bert, 244, 246, 328, 330, 382
Candelaria, John, 354
Candlestick Park, 62, 275–280, 406–410
Cane, Helen, 77
Canmeyer, William, 6
Cannon, Jimmy, 109, 346
Canseco, Jose, 416, 435, 438, 457, 472, 509
Cantillon, Joe, 97
Capitol Grounds, 40
Capitoline Grounds, 20
Caray, Harry, 127, 159, 169, 249–250, 329, 347,
    350, 379, 448, 533
Caray, Skip, 321, 410–411, 503
Carbo, Bernie, 357, 393
Carew, Rod, 285–286, 326, 334, 419, 431
Carey, Max, 76
Carlton, Steve, 309–310, 360–361, 450
Carney, Art, 7

Carrasquel, Chico, 231
Carrigan, Bill, 115, 119–120
Carroll, Fred, 38
Carson, Johnny, 43, 169
Carter, Gary, 385–386, 397–398
Carter, Jimmy, 326, 401
Carter, Joe, 452–453, 457–458
Cartwright, Alexander, 6, 8, 55, 331
Carty, Rico, 322
Case, George, 150
Casey, Hugh, 179, 181
Cash, Dave, 360, 384
Cash, Norm, 233, 342, 375, 490
Cashman Field, 417
Castilla, Vinny, 502, 506
Cavaretta, Phil, 167–168
Caves, Floyd, 104
Cepeda, Orlando, 274, 276–278, 280, 318, 322, 519
Cerv, Bob, 243
Cey, Ron, 298, 403–404
Chambliss, Chris, 399–400
Champion, Aaron, 26
championship teams, listings of, 572–574
Chance, Dean, 285, 295, 431
Chance, Frank, 25, 166
Chandler, Happy, 210, 216
Chandler, Spud, 181, 196
Chapman, Ben, 143, 193
Chapman, Ray, 93
Chase, Alexander, 63
Chesboro, Jack, 19, 39
Chester, Hilda, 37, 58
Chesterton, G. K., 180
Churchill, Winston, 179, 195, 203, 214, 339, 473
Chylak, Nestor, 373
Cicotte, Eddie, 80–82
Cinergy Field, 5, 449, 529
Cisco, Galen, 30
Clark, Jack, 355, 404, 407, 426, 436
Clark, Will, 408
Clarke, Fred, 39
Clarkson, John, 24
Clemens, Roger, 396–397, 432, 459, 492, 495–498,
    517, 531
Clemente,, 177, 278, 375
Clemente, Roberto, 169, 177, 256, 259–261, 278,
    339, 353, 357, 375, 445–446, 509, 525
Clements, Jack, 34
Clendenon, Donn, 309
Clinton, Bill, 339, 459, 496
Clyde, David, 364
Coakley, Andy, 36
Cobb, Ty, 49–50, 68, 118–121, 124,
    131, 170, 235, 251, 286, 323, 345, 362,
    369, 414, 425, 442, 447, 450, 480, 490, 503, 509,
    513–514
Cochrane, Mickey, 69–71, 121, 136, 162–163,
    345, 362, 473
Colangelo, Jerry, 505–506
Colavito, Rocky, 164, 228–229, 241, 342, 474
Colbert, Nate, 161, 333

Coleman, Jerry, 133, 199–200, 228–229, 332–334, 377, 442, 443, 530
Coleman, Ken, 33, 115
Collins, Bud, 342
Collins, Eddie, 36, 66–68, 80–82, 117, 376
Collins, Jimmy, 30
Collins, Joe, 199
Collins, Ray, 115
Collins, Rip, 135–136
Colt Stadium, 290–293, 301, 313
Columbia Park, 36–37, 66
Combs, Earl, 77, 132, 140
Comercia Park, 490, 513–515
Comiskey, Charles, 9, 25, 78, 84, 231, 462
Comiskey Park, 2, 4, 26, 60, 78–84, 94, 127–128, 141, 146–147, 173, 230–234, 255, 272, 346–350, 379, 454–455, 466, 468, 515
Comiskey Park II, 459–462, 508
Concepcion, Dave, 357, 393
Condon, David, 23–24, 26, 130, 231
Condon, Ed, 79–83
Cone, David, 440, 495–497
Conigliaro, Tony, 340
Conlan, Jocko, 184
Connally, John, 78, 312
Connie Mack Stadium, 186, 247–249, 358
Connolly, Joe, 122
Connor, Roger, 15
Coogan, James J., 106
Cook, Sam, 93
Cooke, Jack Kent, 387
Coolidge, Calvin, 97–99, 141
Coombs, Jack, 37, 66–68, 115
Cooney, Jimmy, 74, 129
Cooper, Cecil, 368–369
Cooper, James Fenimore, 56, 71, 439
Cooper, Mort, 157
Coors Field, 491, 500–503, 525
Cosell, Howard, 401
Costas, Bob, 56, 179–180, 182, 260–261, 266, 318–319, 400, 404–405, 426, 437, 460, 470, 479, 484, 488, 496
County Stadium, 61
Coveleski, Harry, 120
Coveleski, Stan, 92
Cox, Billy, 215–216
Cox, Bobby, 412–413
Craft, Harry, 89
Cravath, Gavvy, 37, 103
Crawford, Sam, 49, 92, 118–119
Crawford, Shag, 309
Creamer, Robert, 193, 231, 252–253
Criger, Lou, 19
Cronin, Joe, 113, 146, 148–149, 151, 158, 183, 198, 396, 434, 491
Crosetti, Frank, 130, 143, 167
Crosley Field, 1, 4–5, 10, 28, 56, 60, 84–91, 163, 252–255, 356, 516, 530, 536
Crosley, Powel, 86
Crowder, Alvin, 148

Cruise, Walt, 124
Crystal, Billy, 266, 506
Cubs Park, 128
Cuellar, Mike, 315, 371–372
Culberson, Leon, 158
Cummings, Candy, 21
Cutshaw, George, 103
Cuyler, Kiki, 74, 76, 129–130

Daley, Pete, 209
Daniel, Dan M., 91, 149
Daniels, Dan, 303
Dark, Alvin, 177, 210–213, 256, 354
Daubert, Jack, 103
Dauss, Hooks, 120
Davalillo, Vic, 361
Davis, Glenn, 195
Davis, Tommy, 295–297, 338
Davis, Willie, 297–298
Davis, Zachary Taylor, 78, 127
Dawson, Andre, 385, 410, 424, 448, 480
Day, John, 14
Dean, Daffy (Paul), 87, 105, 152, 329
Dean, Dizzy, 17, 58, 105, 134–137, 145, 152–156, 165–167, 249, 319, 345, 362, 505
DeBerry, Hank, 104
Decker, Reuben, 20
Delahanty, Ed, 35
Delock, Ike, 115
Demaree, Frank, 130
Demeter, Don, 187
Dempsey, Jack, 68, 76, 141
Dent, Bucky, 14, 172, 395, 399
Denver, John, 373
Derringer, Paul, 88
Devery, Bill, 19
Dickey, Bill, 69, 140, 143, 151, 181, 194, 200, 400, 473
Dickson, Murray, 157
Dierker, Larry, 292, 316
DiMaggio, Dom, 30, 170
DiMaggio, Joe, 57, 89, 146, 153, 172, 181, 185, 190, 192–194, 196, 198–200, 273, 305, 395, 400, 438, 478, 496
DiMaggio, Vince, 331
Disraeli, Benjamin, 68
District of Columbia Stadium, 303
Dobson, Joe, 158
Doby, Larry, 147, 227
Dodger Stadium, 293–298, 402–406
Doerr, Bobby, 83, 129, 170, 172, 331, 491
Doggett, Jerry, 269–270
Donovan, Bill, 37
Donovan, Dick, 209
Donovan, Patsy, 122
Doubleday, Abner, 6
Dovey, John, 123
Dow, Jim, 65
Downing, Al, 298, 323
Doyle, Larry, 107
Drabek, Doug, 445

Drabowsky, Moe, 169
Dressen, Charlie, 197, 205, 211, 220
Dreyfuss, Barney, 38–39, 71–74, 76, 78
Driessen, Dan, 358
Drysdale, Don,
   71, 115, 225, 253, 275, 284–287, 295, 297, 335,
   344, 370, 442
Dudley, Jimmy, 97, 126, 151, 166, 172, 225–229
Duffy, Hugh, 30, 493
Dugan, Joe, 175–176
Duncan Park, 248
Dunn, James, 93
Dunn Park, 92
Dunphy, Don, 191
Durham, Leon, 379–380, 442
Durocher, Leo, 63, 70, 105, 136, 177, 179–182, 190,
   197, 210–212, 214, 216, 218, 236, 258, 308
Durso, Joseph, 106, 137, 139, 191, 339
Dyer, Bill, 34–37
Dyer, Eddie, 158, 171
Dykes, Jimmy, 164, 228

Early, Arnold, 115
Easter, Luke, 226, 331
Eastern Park, 22
Eastman, George, 5
Ebbets, Charles, 21, 101–102
Ebbets Field, 2, 4, 10, 23, 28, 56, 58, 60, 62–63,
   68, 93, 101–105, 159, 179–182, 211–212,
   215–225, 263–264, 269–271,
   282, 290, 308, 311, 468–471, 508, 526,
   533–536
Eckersley, Dennis, 380, 405, 416, 482
Edgar Bergen, 59
Edison International Field, 418–421
Egan, Dave, 122
Egan, Leo, 31
Ehmke, Howard, 69–70, 221
Einhorn, Eddie, 349, 460, 462
Eisenhower, Dwight, 205, 208, 222, 302
Eliot, T. S., 182
Elliott, Bob, 176
Ellis, Doc, 333, 352, 375
Elson, Bob, 167
Elston, Gene, 313
Elysian Fields, 13
Emerson, Ralph Waldo, 49, 527
Engel, Joe, 91
Engle, Clyde, 114
Ennis, Del, 185
Enright, James, 130, 167
Enron Field, 515–518, 525, 534–535
Ernshaw, George, 69
Erskine, Carl, 189, 201–202, 215, 220–221, 335
Evans, Billy, 73
Evans, Darrell, 322, 355, 473
Evans, Dwight, 392, 393
Evers, Johnny, 18, 72, 166
Ewing, Buck, 15
Exhibition Stadium, 387–390
Exposition Park, 38, 74

Exposition Park II, 38

Faber, Red, 80
Face, Elroy, 17, 232, 259
Fairgrounds Park, 44
Falls, Joe, 48, 61, 118, 164, 343, 376
Farley, James, 190
Farrell, Frank, 19
Farrell Park, 19
Faulkner, William, 185
Faust, Nancy, 347
Feeney, Chub, 311, 410
Feller, Bob, 69, 83, 91, 135, 146–147, 150, 164, 171,
   177, 226–227, 316, 474
Felsch, Happy, 80
Felton, Happy, 224
Fenway Park, 31, 33, 56, 59, 67–68, 94, 112–117,
   144, 156, 169–174, 334, 338–342, 381, 392–398,
   419–420, 468, 487, 491–495, 504, 516, 523–525,
   535
Ferdenzi, Til, 51, 59
Ferrell, Rick, 150
Ferrell, Wes, 94, 146
Ferris, Boo, 158
Ferriss, Dave, 171
Fewster, Chick, 104, 139
Fidrych, Mark 'The Bird', 163, 376
Fielder, Cecil, 438, 461, 488
Fields, W. C., 33
Fimrite, Ron, 65, 138, 459, 536
Fingers, Rollie, 330–331, 368–369,
   415, 432, 438–439
Finley, Charles, 62, 179, 244–246, 244, 327,
   329–330, 365, 399, 407, 415
Fisher, Jack, 174
Fisher, William, 23
Fisk, Carlton, 151, 393, 454, 461, 508
Fitzgerald, F. Scott, 536
Fitzsimmons, Fred, 112, 153
Flagshead, Ura, 116
Flanders Field, 118
Flethcher, Al, 37
Flick, Elmer, 35
Flood, Curt, 8, 305, 318, 346
Fonda, Jane, 339
Fonseca, Lew, 94
Forbes Field, 2, 4, 9, 19, 38–39, 56, 60, 71–79,
   84, 187–190, 259–261, 338, 351–352, 446
Ford, Gerald, 361, 376
Ford, Russell, 19
Ford, Tennessee Ernie, 156
Ford, Whitey, 200, 222, 231, 251, 253, 259, 264–268,
   279, 400, 496
Forepaugh Park, 34
Fosse, Ray, 357, 418
Foster, George, 357–358, 393, 447
Foster, Phil, 63
Fox, Nellie, 231–232, 292, 305, 313
Foxx, Jimmie, 65, 69–71, 83, 132, 134, 151, 170,
   183, 280, 482
Franco, John, 56

Franklin, Benjamin, 358
Frazee, Harry, 116
Frederick, Johnny, 105
Freehan, Bill, 118, 343–345, 488
Freeman, Buck, 41
Fregosi, Jim, 325
French, Larry, 162
Frey, Lonnie, 182
Frick, Ford, 153, 177, 180, 242, 249, 265, 270, 276
Friend, Bob, 254
Frisch, Frank, 70, 109–111, 134–137, 155, 307
Froemming, Bruce, 361, 378
Frost, Robert, 302, 384
Fuchs, Emil, 175–176
Fulton County Stadium, 301, 319–323, 410–414, 503
Furillo, Carl, 200, 215, 218, 221, 335, 468

Gaedel, Eddie, 58, 160
Gaffney, James, 123
Galan, Augie, 182
Galarraga, Andres, 500–502, 504
Galehouse, Denny, 157, 172
Galvin, Jim (Pud), 51
Gamble, Oscar, 248
Gammons, Peter, 317, 392, 461, 495, 518–520, 536
Gandil, Chick, 81
Garagiola, Joe, 100, 157–158, 189, 268
Garciaparra, Nomar, 473, 492, 494
Gardella, Danny, 91
Gardiner, John Lion, 106, 137
Gardner, Larry, 114
Garfield, John, 105
Garner, Phil, 355
Garver, Ned, 58
Garvey, Steve, 298, 380, 403, 442
Gaston, Cito, 457–458
Gaston, Milt, 94
Gatling, Richard, 6
Gavin, Jerry, 390
Gehrig, Lou, 70, 140–143, 148, 151, 154, 163, 183, 190, 192–194, 201, 268, 342, 399, 419, 469, 498
Gehringer, Charlie, 70, 121, 162–163, 489, 514
Gershman, Michael, 56, 91
Giamatti, A. Bartlett, 1, 59, 112, 116, 408, 448, 452, 523, 534
Gibson, Bob, 17, 251, 318–319, 341–342, 344, 346, 352, 425, 495
Gibson, Josh, 78, 143, 151
Gibson, Kirk, 20, 377, 404–405, 416, 491
Giebell, Floyd, 146
Giles, Bill, 312–315, 359–360, 451
Giles, Brian, 446
Giles, Don, 112
Giles, Warren, 87, 271, 335
Gillespie, Earl, 236, 439
Gillespie, Ray, 45
Gilliam, Jim, 221, 225, 270, 297, 335
Gingrich, Newt, 339
Gionfriddo, Al, 196, 218
Glasgow, Ellen, 2
Glavine, Tom, 412–413, 495, 497, 504

Gleason, Jackie, 20, 113
Glenn, John, 287
Goetz, Larry, 181
Goldman, Eric, 8
Gomez, Lefty, 69, 130, 142–143, 151, 153, 190, 192, 194–195
Gomez, Preston, 332
Gonzalez, Juan, 435, 452, 472–473, 514
Goodding, Gladys, 63
Gooden, Dwight, 440, 481, 495
Goodman, Billy, 172
Goodman, Ival, 87
Gordon, Joe, 19, 164, 181, 191, 226, 228
Gorman, Tom, 314
Goslin, Goose, 98–99, 132, 162
Goss, Bailey, 47
Gossage, Goose, 118, 377, 395, 442
Gould, Elliot, 348
Gowdy, Curt, 117, 125, 170, 198, 267–268
Gowdy, Hank, 68, 98, 122
Grace, Mark, 480, 506
Graham, Billy, 339
Graham, Frank, 156
Grand Avenue Grounds, 44
Graney, Jack, 92
Grant, Edward Leslie, 107
Grant, M. Donald, 310–311
Grant, Mudcat, 284–285, 335
Grant, Ulysses S., 15
Gravath, Gavvy, 115
Gray, Pete, 156, 191
Green, Pumpsie, 29
Greenberg, Hank, 83, 121, 151, 162–164, 188, 344, 489, 513–514
Greer, Rusty, 472
Gregg, Hal, 196
Grey, Sir Edward, 101
Grich, Bobby, 419–420
Griffey, Ken, 358, 394, 516
Griffey, Ken, Jr., 69, 433–434, 449, 468, 511–512
Griffith, Calvin, 207
Griffith, Clark, 95, 149
Griffith Stadium, 4, 10, 42, 57, 94–100, 147–151, 204, 206, 208–209, 241, 303
Grimes, Burleigh, 103–104
Grimm, Charlie, 103, 130, 165–169, 178, 234, 256
Grissom, Lee, 87
Groat, Dick, 259
Groh, Heinie, 85, 98
Grove, Lefty, 69, 132, 145, 170, 240
Gruley, Bryan, 117
Guerrero, Vladimir, 386
Guidry, Ron, 367, 395, 401
Gullett, Don, 357, 393
Gunther, John, 85–86
Gwynn, Tony, 286, 333, 442, 444, 483, 494

Haas, Mule, 70
Hack, Stan, 162, 168
Haddix, Harvey, 208
Haefner, Mickey, 158

Hafey, Chick, 134–135
Haines, Jesse, 133
Hale, Odell, 146
Hall, Donald, 127
Hall, George, 34
Hall, Halsey, 282–283
Hallahan, Wild Bill, 83
Hamilton Field, 5
Hamilton, Jack, 340
Hamilton, Milo, 161
Hampton, Mike, 424
Haney, Fred, 236, 238
Hanlon, Ned, 47
Hanna, Jay, 154
Hannegan, Bob, 161
Hansen, Ron, 93
Harder, Mel, 145
Harding, Warren, 97
Hardy, Joe, 57
Harmon, Merle, 244–245, 368–369, 439, 452
Harper, Tommy, 338
Harrah, Toby, 364
Harrelson, Bud, 308, 311
Harrelson, Ken, 229, 341
Harridge, Will, 94, 160
Harris, Bucky, 98, 196
Harrison, Benjamin, 41
Harrison Park, 52
Hartman, Harry, 86
Hartnett, Gabby, 111, 130, 151, 165–167
Harvey, Bryan, 477–478
Harvey, Doug, 354
Harwell, Ernie,
    39, 49, 101, 118, 164, 212, 216, 240, 277, 319, 34
    2–344, 376, 513–514
Hatcher, Mickey, 430, 428
Hatton, Grady, 91
Hayes, Rutherford B., 7
Hayne's Park, 362
Hebner, Richie, 301, 352
Hedges, Robert Lee, 131
Hegan, Mike, 338
Heilmann, Harry, 120, 164
Heimlich, Henry, 88
Helms, Tommy, 255
Hemingway, Ernest, 172
Henderson, Dave, 381, 397, 420
Henderson, Rickey, 369, 415–417,
    432, 444, 452, 458
Hendricks, Jack, 86
Hendrix, Claude, 128
Henrgen, Pat, 458–459
Henrich, Tommy, 170, 181, 191–192, 198–199, 226
Henry, John, 478–479, 532–533
Henry, William A. III, 94
Herman, Babe, 21, 87, 104–105, 182, 337
Herman, Billy, 29, 165
Hermann, August, 84–85, 87
Hernandez, Keith, 355, 398, 425
Hernandez, Orlando, 497
Herrmann, Gerry, 28

Hershiser, Orel, 111, 404, 442
Herzog, Whitey, 425–427
Higbee, Kirby, 181
Higgins, Pinky, 29
Hiller, John, 345
Hilltop Park, 19, 106
Hirshberg, Al, 116
Hoak, Don, 259
Hobson, Butch, 33
Hodapp, Johnny, 94
Hodges, Gil, 202, 215, 219–220, 225,
    264, 272, 287, 304, 309–310
Hodges, Russ, 212–213, 276, 279–280, 409
Hodgson, Claire, 142
Hoffer, Bill, 47
Hofheinz, H. Roy, 291–293, 312–313
Hogan, Frank, 111
Hogsett, Chief, 121
Holloman, Bobo, 161
Holmes, Tommy, 176–178
Holtzman, Jerome, 78
Holtzman, Ken, 329–330
Hong Kong Stadium, 525
Hooper, Harry, 114
Hooton, Burt, 378, 401
Hoover, Herbert, 99–100, 102, 141, 148, 167
Horlen, Joe, 346–347
Hornsby, Rogers, 37, 70, 74, 111, 129, 133, 319
Horton, Willie, 344, 382, 514
Hough, Charlie, 401, 451, 477–478
Houk, Ralph, 265, 267–268, 279
Howard, Elston, 202, 236, 265, 267
Howard, Frank, 257, 268, 304, 364, 488
Howe, Art, 417–418
Howsam, Bob, 356
Hoyt, Waite, 21, 27, 77, 116, 139, 253, 255
Hrabosky, Al, 361, 425
Hubbell, Carl, 63, 111–112, 125, 148, 151–154, 407
Hubbs, Ken, 257
Hudson, Sid, 150
Huggins, Miller, 77, 108, 139–143, 192, 399, 497
Hughes, Roy, 146, 164
Huizenga, H. Wayne, 476–478
Hulbert, William, 23
Humphrey, Hubert, 305
Hunt, Ron, 308, 337
Hunter, Catfish, 244, 269, 285, 329–331, 415
Hurst, Bruce, 396–397
Huston, John, 156
Huston, Till, 137
Huston, Tillinghast, 108
Hutchinson, Fred, 146, 249, 253–254, 449

Ilitch, Mike, 489–490
Irvin, Monte, 210
Island Grounds, 52

Jack Murphy Stadium, 331–334, 441–444
Jackson, Bo, 461
Jackson, Joe, 81, 92
Jackson, Reggie, 163, 244, 329–331, 345, 375, 392,

395, 399, 401, 403, 415, 419, 488
Jackson, Travis, 111
Jacobs Field, 409, 454, 473–476, 510, 525
Jacobson, Steve, 22, 216
Jailhouse Flats, 5
James, Bill, 250
James, "Seattle Jim", 122
Jamieson, Charlie, 93
Jarry Park, 334–337, 384
Javier, Julian, 342
Jefferson Street Grounds, 5
Jefferson, Thomas, 167
Jenkins, Fergie, 257–258, 364
Jennings, Hughie, 49
Jensen, Jackie, 29–30, 174
Jeter, Derek, 473, 495, 497–498
Jethroe, Sam, 335
Johnson, Alex, 83, 325, 368
Johnson, Andrew, 40–41
Johnson, Arnold, 186
Johnson, Ban, 7, 25–26, 31, 47–48, 65, 84, 95
Johnson, Cy, 220
Johnson, Dave, 322, 370, 423, 440
Johnson, Ernie, 125, 177–179, 220, 235, 238,
    411, 504
Johnson, Lyndon, 225, 316
Johnson, Randy, 433–434, 461, 507, 512
Johnson, Walter, 76, 96–99, 114, 116,
    134, 150, 195, 209, 297, 423, 494
Jones, Chipper, 502–503, 505
Jones, Cleon, 309, 311
Jones, Dalton, 340
Jones, Randy, 333, 443–444
Jones, "Sad Sam", 116
Jordan, Michael, 461
Jorgensen, Spider, 218
Joss, Addie, 44
Joyce, James, 420
Jurges, Billy, 29, 130, 153, 165
Justice, David, 413, 498
Justice, Richard, 466

Kaat, Jim, 284–285, 348
Kahn, Roger, 20, 101
Kalas, Harry, 296, 361
Kaline, Al, 62, 164, 262, 340, 342–346, 375–376,
    487–490, 513–514
Karger, Ed, 33
Kasko, Eddie, 293
Katt, Ray, 214
Kauffman Stadium, 364–367, 435–437, 526
Kavanagh, Marty, 92
Kaye, Danny, 59
Keefe, Tim, 17
Keeler, Wee Willie, 47
Kell, George, 150, 164, 197
Keller, Charlie, 89, 181, 191
Kelley, Joe, 47
Kellum, Bill, 47
Kelly, George "High Pockets", 109
Keltner, Ken, 146

Kemner, Dutch, 129
Kendall, Jason, 526
Kennedy, Bob, 328
Kennedy, John F., 167, 201, 205, 208–209,
    281, 285, 302, 306
Kennedy, Robert F., 343
Kennedy, Ted, 401
Kent, Jeff, 520
Keough, Marty, 209
Kerr, Dickie, 81
Kessler, Bill, 183
Kessler, Eddie, 183
Kettle, Ma, 156
Key, Jimmy, 456–458, 496
Kezar Stadium, 406
Kilduff, Pete, 93
Killebrew, Harmon, 2, 207–208, 283–286, 341, 375,
    428, 431, 488
Killefer, Bill, 132
Killefer, Red, 128
Kinder, Ellis, 172, 199
Kiner, Ralph, 188–189, 277, 287, 360, 440, 445
King, Larry, 2, 101, 219
King, Martin Luther, 304, 343
Kingdome, 380–383, 432–435, 511–513
Kingman, Dave, 378, 382, 429–430, 483
Klein, Chuck, 37, 78, 129, 170
Klem, Bill, 73, 103, 136
Kluszewski, Ted, 232, 234, 252, 449
Knight, Ray, 397–398, 491
Knoblauch, Chuck, 412, 431–432, 494–495, 497
Koenig, Bill, 163
Koenig, Fred, 383
Koenig, Mark, 130, 140
Konstanty, Jim, 185
Koosman, Jerry, 308–309
Koppett, Leonard, 215
Koufax, Sandy, 115, 267, 272–273, 280, 285,
    295–298, 315, 318–319, 405
Koy, Ernie, 38, 179
Kralick, Jack, 228–229
Kramer, Jack, 157
Krausse, Lew, 328
Krichell, Paul, 140
Kroc, Ray, 333–334
Kubeck, Tony, 72, 259, 262–265, 437
Kuenn, Harvey, 91, 164, 228, 232, 241
Kuhel, Joe, 151
Kuhn, Bowie, 55, 114, 345, 353, 356–357, 388,
    391–392
Kurowski, Whitey, 155–158, 195

La Russa, Tony, 416–417, 454, 482–483
Labine, Clem, 212, 221–223
Laboy, Coco, 336
Lajoie, Napoleon, 36, 44, 92
Lake, Joe, 19
Lakefront II, 28
Lakefront Park, 24
Landis, Kenesaw Mountain, 70–71, 82, 165, 181
Lane, F.C., 138

Lane Field, 331
Lane, Frank, 83–84, 162, 228
Lanier, Max, 157
Lanier, Sidney, 86
Lardner, Ring, 93, 131
Larkin, Barry, 449, 527–528
Larsen, Don, 244, 263–266, 292, 496, 498
Lary, Frank, 163–164, 342
Lasorda, Tommy, 298, 403–405
Latham, Arnie, 45
Lavagetto, Cookie, 42–43, 218
Law, vernon, 168, 259
Lazarus, Emile, 126
Lazzeri, Tony, 133, 140, 183, 190–191
League Park, 2, 4–5, 10, 28, 45, 61, 91–94, 145
League Park II, 28, 44
Leavitt, Charles, 72
Lee, Bill, 165–167
Lemon, Bob, 172, 177, 226–227, 401
Leonard, Andy, 27
Leonard, Dennis, 366–367
Leonard, Dutch, 115, 150
Levsen, Emil, 93
Lewis, Allen, 34–35, 37–38, 65, 68
Lewis, Duffy, 113
Lewis, Lloyd, 107, 134, 154
Leyland, Jim, 446, 478
Leyritz, Jim, 20, 495
Liddle, Don, 214
Lillis, Bob, 313
Lincoln, Abraham, 39, 105, 265
Lincoln Park Grounds, 26
Lindberg, Richard, 81
Lindbergh, Charles, 99
Lindell, Johnny, 195
Lindstrom, Fred, 98, 111–112
Linn, Ed, 59
Lloyd Street Grounds, 5
Lloyd, Vince, 209, 255–256
Lobert, Hans, 37
Lofton, Kenny, 467, 504
Lolich, Mickey, 319, 345–346
Lombardi, Ernie, 60, 87, 89–90, 327
Lombardo, Carmen, 108
Lonborg, Jim, 33, 339, 341–342
London, Jack, 32
Long, Dale, 168, 189, 209
Longworth, Alice Roosevelt, 42
Lopes, Davey, 298, 403–404
Lopez, Al, 105, 125, 231, 234
Loria, Jeffrey, 386–387
Louis, Joe, 191
Lowe, Bobby, 31
Lowell, Robert, 22
Lucchesi, Frank, 186, 360
Lucchino, Larry, 443, 460, 466, 530
Luzinski, Greg, 360–361
Lyle, Sparky, 401
Lynn, Fred, 163, 392, 419, 454
Lyons, Ted, 83

Mack, Connie, 36, 49, 65–71,
    83, 242, 359, 364, 372, 403, 415
MacPhail, Larry, 179, 195–196, 200
MacPhail, Leland Stanford, 86–88, 402
Maddox, Garry, 360, 422–423, 450
Maddux, Greg, 413, 481, 497, 504–505
Madlock, Bill, 378, 445
Magerkurth, George, 59, 153, 180
Maglie, Sal, 211, 214, 223
Malzone, Frank, 30
Mamaux, Al, 74
Maney, Joe, 125
Manhattan Field, 16
Manning, Jack, 24
Mantilla, Felix, 29
Mantle, Mickey, 42, 77, 135, 164, 200, 202,
    205, 241, 259, 262–268, 313, 342, 345, 400, 419,
    484, 536
Manusch, Heinie, 99, 132
Maranville, Rabbit, 122, 125
Marichal, Juan, 71, 276, 278, 280
Marion, Marty, 137, 155, 157, 167, 231
Maris, Roger, 242, 244, 253, 265, 279,
    282, 342, 400, 409, 433, 461
Marquard, Rube, 67, 93, 107
Marshall, Jim, 378
Marshall, Mike, 286, 331, 337, 403
Martin, Billy, 200–202, 285, 364, 375, 389, 399–402,
    416, 428–429, 436
Martin, Ned, 185, 248, 341, 394, 535
Martin, Pepper, 70–71, 134–136
Martin, Red, 248
Martinez, Edgar, 433–434
Martinez, Pedro, 17, 386, 492, 494–495, 497–498
Masi, Phil, 177
Mathews, Eddie, 178, 235–239, 292, 322, 503
Mathewson, Christy, 17, 36, 46, 67, 73, 86, 107,
    238, 273, 333
Matlack, Jon, 310, 353
Mattingly, Don, 402
Mauch, Gene, 90, 247–248, 337, 419
Maxwell, Charlie, 164
May, Lee, 255, 371
Mayberry, John, 246, 365, 390
Mayer, Erskine, 37
Mays, Carl, 93, 115, 119
Mays, Willie, 62, 187, 190, 194, 211, 213–214, 223,
    227, 238, 249, 255, 266, 273–280, 307, 310–311,
    315–316, 337, 406, 408, 410, 419, 473, 484, 494
Mazeroski, Bill, 76, 259–261, 279, 391, 445
McAdoo, William Gibbs, 97
McAllister, "Screech Owl", 77
McAuliffe, Dick, 341, 343–345
McBride, Bake, 361
McCarthy, Joe, 70, 129, 143, 171–173, 191–193,
    195, 199–200, 264–265, 497
McCarthy, Tommy, 31
McCarver, Tim, 248, 251, 267, 318–319,
    360, 408, 440
McClatchy, Kevin, 525–526
McCormick Field, 225

McCormick, Frank, 87–89
McCormick, Harry, 18
McCormick, Jim, 43
McCormick, Mike, 280
McCovey, Willie, 71, 255, 274, 277–280, 287, 289, 406–407, 410, 536
McDonald, Arch, 41, 149
McDonald, John, 87
McDougald, Gil, 200, 202, 228, 264, 496
McDowell, Jack, 461
McDowell, Sam, 228
McFadden, George, 66
McGee, Willie, 426–427, 479
McGinnis, Stuffy, 67
McGinnity, Iron Man, 47
McGinnity, Joe, 17
McGraw, John, 16, 19, 33, 47–49, 63, 67, 83, 98, 107–114, 152, 198, 403
McGraw, Tug, 308, 310, 362, 410
McGriff, Fred, 390, 413, 456–457, 509
McGwire, Mark, 56, 69, 138, 416–417, 478, 481–484, 488, 494, 502, 507
McHale, John, 164, 337, 384, 489
McHale, Willie, 45
McInnis, Stuffy, 33, 37
McKechnie, Bill, 76, 88–89, 134, 176
McKeever, Ed, 102, 104
McKeever, Steve, 102
McKinley, William, 7, 28
McLain, Denny, 62, 305, 319, 343–346, 495
McMahon, Ed, 43
McMillan, Norm, 129
McMorris, Jerry, 499–502
McMullin, Fred, 81
McNally, Dave, 370–372
McNally, Mike, 116
McNamara, John, 396–398, 420
McNamee, Graham, 110
McNeely, Earl, 98
McQuade, Francis X., 108
McRae, Hal, 366–367, 402, 435
McVey, Cal, 27
Meany, Tom, 122, 182
Medwick, Joe, 136–137, 154
Mejias, Roman, 112
Melton, Bill, 348
Melton, Cliff, 153
Memorial Stadium, 5, 239–242, 269–273, 370–375, 455–456, 465, 469
Mencken, H. L., 75
Menke, Dennis, 330
Merkle, Fred, 18, 114–115, 487
Merman, Ethel, 151
Merullo, Lennie, 167
Messer Street Grounds, 51
Metrodome, 427–432
Metropolitan Park, 14
Metropolitan Stadium, 282–286, 428
Meusel, Bob, 77
Meusel, Irish, 110
Meyer, Dick, 162

Michaels, Al, 218, 355, 357–358, 406–408, 420
Michner, Don, 285
Midway Stadium, 282
Mile High Stadium, 499–500
Millan, Felix, 356
Miller, Bing, 70
Miller, Bob, 185
Miller, Dots, 73
Miller, Jon, 328, 374, 469, 510
Miller, Marvin, 8
Miller, Otto, 93
Miller Park, 527–529
Miller, Ray, 470
Miller, Stu, 62, 278, 371
Miller, Victor, 134
Milwaukee County Stadium, 234–239, 367–370, 437–439
Mincher, Don, 338
Minoso, Minnie, 231, 233, 331, 349
Mitchell, Clarence, 93
Mitchell, Kevin, 397–398, 408
Mix, Tom, 82
Mize, Johnny, 154–155, 200, 210, 226
Moeller, Doug, 114
Molitor, Paul, 369, 431, 438, 456, 458
Monbouquette, Bill, 209, 234
Monday, Rick, 244, 329, 378, 385, 403
Money, Don, 359
Monroe, Marilyn, 194
Moon, Wally, 62
Moore, Jimmy, 132
Moore, Terry, 155
Moore, Wilcy, 140
Moose, Bob, 357
Moran, Pat, 36, 86
Morgan, Cy, 67
Morgan, Joe, 315–316, 407, 422
Morgan, Joe, 355, 357–358, 392–393, 447–450
Moriarity, George, 165
Moriarty, George, 94, 119, 165
Morris, Jack, 377, 413, 430–431, 454, 457, 487
Morris, Wright, 88
Mota, Manny, 335, 361
Mueller, Don, 211, 213
Mueller, Emmett, 38
Mullin, George, 49, 118
Mullin, Willard, 105, 135
Mungo, Van Lingle, 59
Municipal Stadium, 61–62, 93, 144–146, 225–229, 365, 453–454, 476
Municipal Stadium (Kansas City), 242–246
Munson, Thurmon, 395, 400–401
Murcer, Bobby, 268
Murphy, Bob, 287, 309, 439
Murphy, Dale, 411, 503
Murray, Bill, 27
Murray, Eddie, 374, 431, 469–470, 475
Murray, Jim, 269, 271, 281, 294, 297
Murtaugh, Danny, 189, 353–354, 445

Musial, Stan, 77, 136, 157, 159, 161–162, 168, 177, 221, 236, 249–251, 256, 258, 263, 302, 319, 323, 425, 450, 502, 526
Mussina, Mike, 469
Mutrie, Jim, 105
Myers, Billy, 89
Myers, Chief, 114

N. W. Olympic Grounds, 40
Naimoli, Vince, 508–509
National League Park II, 43
Navin Field, 4, 10, 49, 61, 119
Navin, Frank, 118, 120, 162
Neis, Bernie, 124
Nelson, Lindsey, 14, 141, 210, 287–288, 308–310, 314, 439
Nelson, Rocky, 190
Nen, Dick, 250
Nettles, Craig, 396, 400–401, 442
Neun, Johnny, 120
Nevers, Ernie, 132
Nevins, Allen, 9
Newcombe, Don, 215, 220, 264, 335
Newhouser, Hal, 146, 163–164, 514
Newhouser, Hank, 489
Newsom, Bobo, 89, 163
Newsom, Louis Norman, 150
Nichols, Charles (Kid), 31
Nicholson, Bill, 167, 169
Nickerson Field, 125
Nicollet Park, 282
Niehaus, Dave, 380–383, 432, 435, 511–512
Niekro, Joe, 410–411, 414, 423
Niekro, Phil, 322, 503
Nixon, Richard, 6, 56, 127, 197, 204, 207, 225, 276, 281, 287, 305, 326, 339, 402, 459
Nolan, Gary, 357
Nomo, Hideo, 502
North, Billy, 330
North Side Ball Park, 127
Norworth, Jack, 55
Novello, Don, 519
Novikoff, Lou, 168

Oakdale Park, 34
Oakland Coliseum, 415–418
Obata, Helmuth, 64
O'Brien, Buck, 113
O'Day, Hank, 18
Odom, John (Blue Moon), 244, 329, 331, 375, 416
O'Doul, Frank, 37
O'Doul, Lefty, 105, 273
Oeschger, Joe, 124
O'Leary, Charlie, 49, 132
Olerud, John, 441, 458, 507, 514
Oliva, Tony, 284–285, 340, 431
Olmo, Luis, 182
Olympic Stadium, 383–387
O'Malley, Peter, 399, 403
O'Malley, Walter, 21, 182, 215, 219, 223–224, 269–273, 277, 281, 293–295, 298, 403

O'Neil, Steve, 145
O'Neill, Paul, 402, 413
O'Neill, Tip, 32, 113, 116, 123, 397
Oriole Park, 467
Oriole Park I, 46–47
Oriole Park IV, 47–48
Orlando, Johnny, 183
Orsmby, Red, 64
Orth, Al, 19
Osteen, Claude, 297
Otis, Amos, 366
O'Toole, Patsy, 163
Ott, Mary, 156
Ott, Mel, 111–112, 148, 152, 154, 210, 280
Owen, Marv, 136
Owen, Mickey, 181
Owens, Jesse, 179
Ozark, Danny, 34, 360

Paar, Jack, 75
Pacific Bell Park, 409, 491, 518–520, 535
Paciorek, Tom, 383
Pafko, Andy, 167
Page, Joe, 196
Paige, Satchel, 83, 160, 226, 232, 244–246
Palmer, Jim, 370, 372, 455, 470
Pancus, Hancus, 191
Pappas, Milt, 241, 254, 378
Parish, Larry, 451–452
Parker, Dave, 374, 411, 417, 447
Parker, Wes, 297
Parnell, Mel, 172–173, 198
Parrish, Larry, 489
Parrott, Harold, 180
Pascual, Camilo, 208
Passeau, Claude, 168
Patek, Fred, 366
Patterson, Red, 205
Paul, Gabe, 44, 144, 282
Paula, Carlos, 207
Peckinpaugh, Roger, 76
Pelty, Barney, 79
Pendleton, Terry, 412–413
Pennock, Herb, 68, 116, 133, 140
Pepitone, Joe, 292, 297
Perez, Tony, 325, 352, 355–358, 393–394, 447–450, 529
Perini, Lou, 125, 237
Perranoski, Ron, 296
Perry, Gaylord, 280, 333, 364, 383, 406, 432, 453
Perry, Jim, 285
Perry Park, 50
Pesky, Johnny, 158, 170–172
Petrocelli, Rico, 341–342, 393, 535
Pfeffer, Jeff, 103
Philadelphia Baseball Grounds, 34
Phillips, E. Lawrence, 41
Piazza, MIke, 405, 441
Piersall, Jim, 29, 174, 205, 289
Pilot Field, 466
Pinella, Lou, 246, 395, 424, 434, 448, 511

Pinson, Vada, 252–254
Pinza, Ezio, 122
Pipgras, George, 116
Pipp, Wally, 140
Pittinger, Charles, 176
Plank, Eddie, 36, 66–68, 122
Plew, Herbie, 205
Podres, Johnny, 202, 215, 222, 293, 296–297
Pollett, Howie, 157
Polo Grounds, 2, 4, 9, 14–16, 18, 28, 48, 56, 63,
    80, 98, 105–112, 114, 118, 148, 151–154,
    210–215, 218, 221, 227, 280–282, 286–290,
    301, 306–308, 536
Post, Wally, 252, 293
Potter, Nels, 157
Povich, Shirley, 40–41, 150–151, 303–305
Powell, Boog, 328, 370, 456
Power, Vic, 61, 243, 284
Powers, David, 208
Powers, Jimmy, 217
Price, Frank, 163
Prince, Bob, 63, 71, 187–189,
    260, 332, 352, 367, 527
Pro Player Stadium, 476–479, 533
Puckett, Kirby, 412, 428–431
Pulliam, Harry, 18

Quigley, Ernie, 162
Quinn, Bob, 117

Race, Elroy, 190
Radbourn, Charlie "Old Hoss", 15, 51
Rader, Doug, 316, 364, 424
Radke, Brad, 431
Raines, Tim, 385
Ramirez, Manny, 476
Ramos, Pedro, 208
Rand, Sally, 92
Rariden, Bill, 80, 123
Raschi, Vic, 185
Rawlings, Johnny, 123
Ray, Edgar, 313
Reach, Albert J., 34
Reagan, Ronald, 28, 129, 165,
    169, 221, 230, 328, 380, 447, 471
Recreation Park, 5, 34, 48
Redding, Jack, 14, 17, 31, 34, 36, 47–48,
    67, 123–124, 223, 246, 272, 332, 381, 529
Redford, Robert, 122
Redland Field, 5, 77, 84, 86
Reese, Andy, 111
Reese, Jimmie, 58, 138, 142–143, 179, 181, 185, 196,
    202, 211–212, 215–217, 219–222, 225, 264, 270,
    272
Reese, Rich, 329
Reichler, Joe, 197
Reidenbaugh, Lowell, 50–51
Reilly, Rick, 271, 496
Reinhart, Art, 124
Reinsdorf, Jerry, 349–350, 454, 460–462
Reiser, Pete, 179, 181, 196

Renko, Steve, 337
Rennie, Rud, 146–147
Rettenmund, Merv, 372
Reyburn, John E., 66
Reyes, Nat, 91
Reynolds, Allie, 196, 198–200, 217
Rhem, Flint, 133
Rhodes, Dusty, 214
Rice, Grantland, 32, 109, 131, 139, 162
Rice, Harry, 142
Rice, Jim, 392, 395, 397, 493
Rice, Sam, 99
Richard, J. R., 316, 422
Richards, Paul, 291–292
Richardson, Bobby, 259, 263, 266, 279, 496
Rickard, Tex, 220
Rickey, Branch, 46, 58, 132, 155, 182, 188–189,
    219, 247, 287, 311
Ridgewood Park, 21–22
Rigler, Cy, 99
Rigney, Bill, 285, 324, 326
Rijo, Jose, 448
Ripken, Cal, 374, 431, 433, 455, 469–470, 482
Ripple, Jimmy, 89
Risberg, Charles (Swede), 81
Rivera, Jim, 209
Rivera, Mariano, 497
Riverfront Stadium, 5, 355–358, 365, 447–449,
    467, 473
Rivers, Mickey, 451
Riverside Park, 52
Rixey, Eppa, 86
Rizzuto, Phil, 194, 196–197, 199, 265, 399–401, 496,
    498
Robert F. Kennedy, Jr. Stadium, 305
Roberts, Robin, 185, 199, 274, 292, 450, 494
Robertson, Bob, 353
Robertson, Dave, 80
Robinson, Brooks, 241–242, 309, 370–373, 455–456,
    468, 470, 526
Robinson, Eddie, 230
Robinson, Frank, 252–254, 325, 370–372, 375, 449,
    453, 455, 470, 488
Robinson, Jackie, 147, 177, 182, 191, 212, 215, 217,
    219–220, 223, 225, 264, 298,
    335, 386, 405, 441, 449, 487, 526
Robinson, Wilbert, 47, 103–105, 108, 354
Robison Field, 10, 45, 46, 131, 132
Robison, Frank D., 43, 46, 93
Rocker, John, 505
Rockne, Knute, 141
Rockwell, Norman, 88, 95
Rocky Point Park, 52
Rodriguez, Alex, 434–435, 473, 511–512
Rodriguez, Ivan, 473
Roe, Preacher, 157, 162–163, 199, 215, 220
Rogel, Billy, 136
Rogers, Steve, 337
Rogers, Will, 70, 153
Rohr, Billy, 113
Rojas, Cookie, 187, 248, 366

Rolen, Scott, 451
Rolfe, Red, 143
Rollins, Rich, 338, 341
Roosevelt, Franlin Delano, 87, 147–148, 150, 181, 190, 195, 201, 203
Roosevelt, Theodore, 32, 42, 105, 346
Root, Charlie, 129
Rosar, Buddy, 66
Rose, Pete, 177, 254–255, 310–311, 323, 339, 355–357, 361, 393–394, 410, 442, 447–448, 450–451, 480, 529
Roseboro, John, 71, 273, 295, 297
Rosen, Al, 226–227, 331, 474
Rosen, Goody, 182
Rosenthal, Harold, 16, 19, 22–23, 108–109, 140–141, 153, 182, 191, 193, 195, 225, 264, 268, 306–307
Rossetti, Dante Gabriel, 28, 476
Rothstein, Arnold, 81
Rousch, Edd, 81, 86
Rowe, Lynwood, 121
Rowell, Carvel, 182
Rowland, Clarence (Pants), 108
Rowswell, Rosey, 187–188
Rucker, Nat, 102
Rudi, Joe, 329–331, 381, 392, 415
Rudolph, Dick, 122
Ruell, Muddy, 98, 159
Ruffing, Red, 130, 156, 181, 192, 181
Rugo, Guido, 125
Runnels, Pete, 292
Runyon, Damon, 110, 131
Ruppert, Jacob, 108, 137, 192
Ruppert Stadium, 243
Rusie, Amos, 17
Russell, Bertrand, 450
Russell, Bill, 298
Russell, William Hepburn, 123
Ruth, Babe, 56, 68, 75, 78, 83, 87, 105, 109–111, 113, 115–116, 120–121, 125, 130, 132–134, 138–143, 148, 151, 174, 195–198, 201, 242, 245, 262, 268–270, 305, 323, 342, 354–355, 381, 387, 393, 396, 399, 433, 468, 483, 487, 493, 498
Ryan, Nolan, 325, 376, 417, 419, 423–424, 438, 453, 471, 473

Saam, Byrum, 65–68, 183, 247–248, 335, 425
Saberhagen, Bret, 435–436
Sabin, Albert, 88
Safeco Field, 434, 510–513, 527, 535
Safire, William, 6
Saigh, Fred, 161
Sain, Johnny, 91, 177
Sale, I. Kirk, 40
Sallee, Slim, 46
Sandberg, Ryne, 379, 479
Sanguillen, Manny, 372
Santiago, Jose, 33, 341–342
Santo, Ron, 258
Saucier, Frank, 160

Sauer, Hank, 168
Sawyer, Eddie, 185–186
Scanlon, Michael, 40
Schaeffer, Germany, 49
Schalk, Ray, 81
Schang, Wally, 116, 139
Scheffing, Bob, 168
Schenley Park, 60, 73, 189, 261
Schieffer, Tom, 471–472
Schilling, Curt, 494, 523
Schiraldi, Calvin, 397–398, 419
Schmeling, Max, 145, 191
Schmidt, Mike, 84, 248, 302, 314, 360–362, 378, 450, 494
Schneider, Russell, 43–44, 91–93, 227
Schoendienst, Red, 157, 161, 236, 249, 318–319, 361
Schott, Marge, 447, 449, 529
Schulte, Fred, 148, 167
Schultz, Joe, 338–339
Schwab, Matty, 211
Score, Herb, 93, 228–229, 440, 453
Scott, Everett, 110, 116, 140,
Scott, Mike, 423, 440
Scott, Ray, 283
Scully, Vin, 117, 179, 270–271, 278, 294–295, 398, 403, 502, 519
Seals Stadium, 273–275, 338
Seaver, Tom, 197, 308–311, 330, 333, 402, 439, 447
Segui, Diego, 338, 381
Selig, Bud, 75, 184, 235–236, 286, 305, 367–368, 438, 527
Selkirk, George, 143
Selma, Dick, 332
Seventh Street Parks I, 50
Seventh Street Parks II, 50
Sewell, Joe, 92
Sewell, Luke, 156
Sewell, Rip, 78, 171
Seybold, Socks, 42
Shaner, Skinny, 116
Shannon, Mike, 251, 318
Shantz, Bobby, 183, 186, 291–292
Sharkey, Jack, 141
Shawkey, Bob, 67–68, 139, 143, 400
Shea Stadium, 6, 289, 301, 306–311, 439–441, 533
Shea, William, 306
Sheehan, Tom, 142
Shepard, Bert, 204
Sherdel, Willie, 134
Shibe, Ben, 65, 71
Shibe Park, 2, 4–5, 10, 37, 55, 60, 64–71, 78, 183–187, 248, 365
Shocker, Urban, 131
Shore, Ernie, 115
Shors, Toots, 210
Short, Chris, 247–248, 313
Short, Robert, 363–364
Shotton, Burt, 37
Showalter, Buck, 506–507
Sick's Stadium, 337–339, 381
Siegel, Morrie, 304–305

Siegel, Morris, 40–41, 95–96, 149, 209
Sievers, Roy, 233–234
Simmons, Al, 69–71, 82, 132, 151
Simmons, Curt, 183, 185
Simmons, Joe, 51
Simmons, Lon, 274–278, 406–407
Simon, Paul, 305
Singleton, Ken, 336–337, 373–374
Sirko, Irk, 351
Sisler, Dick, 65, 185, 219
Sisler, George, 119, 131
Sisti, Sibby, 90, 177
Skowron, Bill, 265
SkyDome, 456–459, 515
Slaughter, Enos (Country), 91, 155, 157–158,
    226, 235, 244, 263, 319
Smith, Al, 139
Smith, Earl, 99
Smith, Ed, 194
Smith, Elmer, 93
Smith, Hal, 259
Smith, John, 182
Smith, Ken, 20–21, 70, 106, 139, 152, 195
Smith, Mayo, 341, 344, 346
Smith, Ozzie, 122, 426–427
Smith, Reggie, 340, 342, 403
Smith, Stu, 274
Smoltz, John, 412–413
Snead, Sam, 169
Snider, Duke, 215, 219, 221–224, 263, 275, 335, 405
Snodgrass, Fred, 67, 114
Snyder, Gerry, 335–336
Soden, Arthur, 30
Solari, Augustus, 44
Sosa, Sammy, 259, 481–483
South End Grounds, 30–31
South End Grounds II, 31
South End Grounds III, 31, 123
South Side Park, 25
Southside Park II, 25
Southworth, Billy, 134, 157, 177–178
Spahn, Warren, 177–178, 235–238, 253, 262, 280,
    305, 439, 503
Speaker, Tris, 33, 92–93, 113–114, 197, 362, 392
Spear, Joseph, 64–65, 302, 366, 466, 529
Spencer, Ted, 17
Spender, Stephen, 145
Spezio, Ed, 332
Spink, J. G. Taylor, 132
Sportsman's Park, 45–46, 57, 251, 317, 526, 535
Sportsman's Park, 4–5, 131–137, 154–162
St. George Grounds, 15–16
Stallings, George, 34, 49, 68, 122
Stanky, Eddie, 177, 182, 212
Stanley, Bob, 19
Stanley, Mickey, 345–346, 375
Stargell, Willie, 78, 260, 298, 307, 321, 352–355,
    374, 385, 425, 445–446, 526–527
Stark, Abe, 59
Staub, Rusty, 292, 311, 336
Steadman, John, 46–48, 240, 370, 374, 467, 469

Steffens, Lincoln, 182
Stein, Gertrude, 327
Steinbeck, John, 287
Steinbrenner, George, 268, 399, 402, 424, 495–496,
    534
Stengel, Casey, 21, 43, 49, 59, 102–104, 109–111,
    122, 176, 198–200, 202, 205, 227–228,
    237, 262–265, 287–291, 301, 306, 308, 314, 318,
    327, 329, 358, 376–377, 400, 405, 440, 497
Stennett, Rennie, 75, 354
Stephens, Vern, 157, 170, 172
Stephenson, Riggs, 129
Stevens, Bob, 277–278, 328
Stevens, Harry M., 17, 152
Stevens, Wallace, 176
Stewart, Bill, 177, 180
Stewart, Dave, 390, 405, 416, 457
Stobbs, Chuck, 205
Stone, Ron, 248
Stoneham, Charles A., 108, 111–112
Stoneham, Horace, 153, 274–276, 406–407
Stovey, Harry, 51
Stratton, Monte, 83
Strawberry, Daryl, 385, 440
Street, Gabby, 134
Stribling, Young, 145
Stuart, Dick, 29, 65, 112, 190, 259, 396
Sullivan, Frank, 29
Sunday, Billy, 76
Sutcliffe, Rick, 379, 404, 467
Sutter, Bruce, 479
Sutton, Don, 298, 403, 419
Suzuki, Ichiro, 512
Swanson, Evar, 129
Swanson, Gloria, 110
Sweasy, Charlie, 27
Swoboda, Ron, 308–309

Taft, William Howard, 4, 95
Tanner, Chuck, 355, 526–527
Tatis, Fernando, 405, 482
Taylor, Charles, 33
Taylor, Zach, 160–161
Tebbetts, Birdie, 146, 198–199, 228, 242, 252
Tekulve, Kent, 355
Tenace, Gene, 329
Terry, Bill, 71, 111–112, 135, 151–154, 307
Terry, Ralph, 244, 260, 266
Terwilliger, Wayne, 336
Thayer, Ernest, 269, 477
Thomas, Frank, 82, 461–462, 472, 514
Thome, Jim, 475–476
Thompson, Chuck, 204, 242, 295, 338, 370–372,
    455
Thompson, Henry, 210–211
Thomson, Bobby, 18, 63, 210–213, 295, 391
Thove, Harry, 90
Three Rivers Stadium, 38, 51, 351–356, 364,
    446, 466, 473, 523–527, 536
Throneberry, Marv, 42–43, 244, 289, 304, 435, 440
Tiant, Luis, 229, 285, 370, 392, 395

Tiger Stadium, 49, 56, 61, 62, 117–121, 342–346, 375–378, 479, 487–491, 513–514, 516
Tinker, Joe, 166
Tobin, Jim, 176
Tobin, John, 116
Tolan, Bobby, 356
Toney, Fred, 85
Topping, Dan, 195, 243
Torre, Joe, 239, 311, 319, 321, 408, 484, 495–498
Totten, Hal, 128
Tovar, Cesar, 285–286
Trachsel, Steve, 482–483, 485
Tracy, David, 160
Trammell, Alan, 376–377, 376, 461, 489
Travers, Aloysius, 68
Travis, Cecil, 150
Traynor, Pie, 76–77, 445
Tropicana Field, 507–510
Trotsky, Hal, 146
Trout, Dizzy, 163
Troy, John, 15
Trucks, Virgil, 164
Truman, Harry, 40, 203, 242, 359, 497
Turley, Bob, 223, 241, 263–264
Turner Field, 503–505, 510
Turner, Ted, 410–414, 504
Turnpike Stadium, 363
Tyler, George "Lefty", 122

Uecker, Bob, 35, 248–251, 339, 369, 437
Union Grounds, 6, 20, 23, 26–27
Union Grounds Park, 45
Union Park, 5, 38
Union Street Park, 51
Updike, John, 2, 174

Valentine, Bobby, 364, 441
Valentino, Rudolph, 76
Valenzuela, Fernando, 403–405, 443
Valli, Violet Popovich, 130
Van Horne, Dave, 336–337, 385
Vance, Dazzy, 104–105
Vander Meer, Johnny, 60, 88–90, 179, 200, 254
Vander Waal, John, 502
Vaughn, Arky, 77, 149
Vaughn, Hippo, 128
Vaughn, Jim, 85
Vaughn, Mo, 420, 492
Veach, Bobby, 119
Vecsey, George, 171
Veeck, Bill, 8, 24–26, 58, 61, 79, 81–82, 94, 128–130, 144, 147, 160–161, 165, 168, 226, 228, 232–234, 240, 315, 347–350, 379, 460–461, 480–481
Ventura, Jesse, 532
Vernon, Mickey, 204, 206–207
Vescey, George, 56
Veterans Stadium, 358–362, 364, 450–451
Veto Park, 44
Vincent, Fay, 408
Viola, Frank, 259, 422–423, 429–430
Vitt, Ossie, 146

Vizquel, Omar, 476
Von der Ahe, Chris, 44–46
Von Der Horst, Harry, 46
von der Rohe, Ludwig, 302
Vosmik, Joe, 94

Waddell, Rube, 36
Wagner, Billy, 424
Wagner, Honus, 9, 32, 37, 39, 76, 103, 122, 189, 205, 286, 434, 444, 445
Wagner, Leon, 282, 295
Wagner, Robert, 286–287
Walker, Curt, 86
Walker, Dixie, 182
Walker, Harry, 158, 316
Walker, Larry, 494, 501–502
Walker, Rube, 304
Wallop, Douglass, 202
Wallopp, Douglas, 187
Walpole Street Grounds, 30
Walsh, Ed, 26, 44, 79
Walters, Bucky, 88–89
Wambsganss, Bill, 93
Wambsoans, Bill, 104
Waner, Lloyd, 77
Waner, Paul, 39, 74, 77–78
War Memorial Stadium, 248
Ward, Arch, 83
Ward, John Montgomery, 15
Warhop, Jack, 109
Warneke, Lon, 130
Washington, George, 85
Washington Park, 21
Washington Park II, 21–23
Waterman, Fred, 27
Wayne, John, 169, 183, 315
Weaver, Buck, 81
Weaver, Earl, 309, 371, 373–374, 390, 470
Webb, Del, 195, 243, 324
Webb, Jack, 56
Webb, Skeeter, 164
Wedge, Will, 140
Weed, Hamilton, 20
Weegham Park, 127
Weeghman, Charles, 127–128
Weil, Sid, 86
Weis, Al, 309, 315
Welch, Mickey, 15, 51
Welk, Lawrence, 174
Wells, David, 459, 496
Wertz, Vic, 164, 174, 214, 227
West End Park, 48
West, Max, 176
West Side Grounds, 25–26, 128
West Side Park, 9
Westgate Park, 331
Westinghouse, George, 23
Westrum, Wes, 91
Wheat, Zack, 103, 109, 307
Whitaker, Lou, 376, 489
White, Bill, 251, 276

White, Dick, 485
White, Doc, 26
White, Frank, 362
White, Theodore H., 294
Whitehill, Earl, 148
Whitman, Walt, 193
Wilhelm, Hoyt, 213–214, 241, 322, 347
Wilhelm, Kaiser, 37
Will, Frederic, 57
Will, George, 57, 109, 468, 485, 536
Williams, Bernie, 56, 497, 495
Williams, Billy, 127, 258, 322, 480
Williams, Cy, 37
Williams, Dick, 241, 330–331, 340–341,
    380, 385, 432–433, 442
Williams, Edward Bennett, 466
Williams, Jack, 128, 505–507
Williams, Jimy, 24, 122, 525
Williams, Ken, 131
Williams, Lefty, 81
Williams, Matt, 409, 507
Williams, Ted, 29–30, 59, 77, 83, 112–114, 158–159,
    163, 170–174, 178, 183, 192, 198, 200,
    228, 305, 331, 363, 381, 487, 491, 493–494, 524
Williamson, Ned, 24
Willis, Vic, 39
Wills, Maury, 287, 295, 335, 337, 383, 425
Wilpon, Fred, 533–534
Wilson, Bert, 129
Wilson, Chief, 74
Wilson, Don, 292, 315–316
Wilson, Hack, 37, 70, 129
Wilson, Jimmy, 37
Wilson, Mookie, 19, 398, 423
Wilson, Willie, 362, 367, 435
Wilson, Woodrow, 37, 96, 181
Wine, Bobby, 187
Winfield, Dave, 333, 424, 431, 444, 457–458
Winthrop, John, 88
Wise, Rick, 357
Witt, Whitey, 132
Wolf, Warner, 376
Wolfe, Thomas, 157, 263
Wolff, Bob, 160, 204–208, 263
Wood, Joe, 114–115
Wood, Kerry, 481, 485, 492
Wood, Smoky Joe, 30

Wood, Wilbur, 348
Woodling, Gene, 199, 209
Woods, Jim, 188–189
Wright, Clyde, 325
Wright, George, 27, 66
Wright, Glenn, 74, 76
Wright, Harry, 26, 30
Wrigley Field, 2, 4, 6, 57, 75, 81, 83, 94, 126–130,
    147, 164–169, 232, 249, 255–259,
    334, 338, 378–380, 392, 437, 449, 454, 469–471,
    479–487, 510
Wrigley Field (Los Angeles), 280–282, 280
Wrigley, Philip, 167
Wrigley, William, 128–130
Wyatt, Whitlow, 181
Wynn, Early, 31, 80, 151, 177, 226–227,
    229, 231–234, 388, 423
Wynn, Jimmy, 292, 315, 424

Yamauchi, Hiroshi, 433
Yankee Stadium, 2, 4, 6, 19, 56, 63, 100, 108, 110,
    133, 137–143, 153, 190–202,
    214, 218, 245, 263–269, 308, 392, 398–402,
    470, 495–498, 534, 536
Yastrzemski, Carl, 2, 77, 112–113, 323, 339–344,
    375, 392, 395–396, 453–454, 491, 493, 535
Yawkey, Thomas A., 30, 59, 113, 116–117,
    149, 339, 392, 394, 493
Yeats, W. B., 110
Yerkes, Steve, 114
York, Rudy, 114
Yost, Eddie, 207
Young, Cy, 32, 43, 51, 92
Young, Dick, 13, 19, 102, 154, 182, 196, 201, 210,
    214, 218, 221, 223,265, 286, 306, 308, 398,
    440
Young, Robert, 153
Youngs, Ross, 110
Yount, Robin, 368–370, 438–439
Yvars, Sal, 213

Zachary, Tom, 98
Zarilla, Al, 86
Zimmer, Don, 364, 393, 394, 453
Zimmerman, Heinie, 80
Zinn, Guy, 113
Zisk, Richie, 83, 310